Create Dynamic Charts in Microsoft® Office Excel® 2007 and Beyond

Reinhold Scheck

PUBLISHED BY
Microsoft Press
A Division of Microsoft Corporation
One Microsoft Way
Redmond, Washington 98052-6399

Library of Congress Control Number: 2008938214

Printed and bound in the United States of America.

1 2 3 4 5 6 7 8 9   QWT   3 2 1 0 9 8

Distributed in Canada by H.B. Fenn and Company Ltd.

A CIP catalogue record for this book is available from the British Library.

Microsoft Press books are available through booksellers and distributors worldwide. For further information about international editions, contact your local Microsoft Corporation office or contact Microsoft Press International directly at fax (425) 936-7329. Visit our Web site at www.microsoft.com/mspress. Send comments to mspinput@microsoft.com.

Microsoft, Microsoft Press, Access, ActiveX, Excel, PivotChart, PivotTable, PowerPoint, SmartArt, Visual Basic, Windows, and Windows Vista are either registered trademarks or trademarks of the Microsoft group of companies. Other product and company names mentioned herein may be the trademarks of their respective owners.

The example companies, organizations, products, domain names, e-mail addresses, logos, people, places, and events depicted herein are fictitious. No association with any real company, organization, product, domain name, e-mail address, logo, person, place, or event is intended or should be inferred.

Acquisitions Editor: Juliana Aldous Atkinson
Developmental Editor: Sandra Haynes
Project Editors: Valerie Woolley and Thomas Pohlmann
Editorial Production: Media Service Gerhard Alfes
Translation: Lemoine International Inc., Salt Lake City, UT
Cover: Turnstyle Design

Body Part No. X14-95102

Contents at a Glance

Table of Contents

What do you think of this book? We want to hear from you!

Microsoft is interested in hearing your feedback so we can continually improve our books and learning resources for you. To participate in a brief online survey, please visit:

www.microsoft.com/learning/booksurvey/

What do you think of this book? We want to hear from you!

Microsoft is interested in hearing your feedback so we can continually improve our books and learning resources for you. To participate in a brief online survey, please visit:

www.microsoft.com/learning/booksurvey/

How to Use this Book

Why Would Anyone Need This Book in the First Place?

A few hundred pages solely dedicated to Excel charts? Using a program in which it has always been so easy to present numbers in a spreadsheet? Is it not simply a case of selecting a range and starting the Chart Wizard, which will then guide you through a few key steps to ensure that you make the right decisions in the right places? Furthermore, the new features available in Microsoft Excel 2007 enable you to create better, more aesthetically pleasing charts in less time. Or do they?

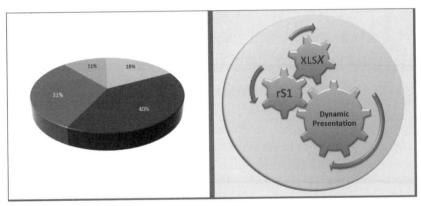

FIGURE I-1 Creating objects like those requires very little time and effort in Excel 2007

In reality, Microsoft Excel 2007 is better, faster, and more aesthetically pleasing, especially in terms of its design capabilities where enormous progress has been made. There is much greater user support and, in many respects, it has been made easier. With a little practice, it will take you just a few minutes to create aesthetically pleasing images like those shown in Figure I-1. In other words, what has always been relatively easy to do has now been made even easier. Furthermore, many things that were previously beyond the scope of the user's design options are now easily available to everyone. How is this possible? What are the necessary working techniques? In this book, you will find detailed information as well as notes and instructions. However, they alone would not have been enough to justify writing a book because the Excel help, which traditionally has been a source of information to users (albeit not a particularly popular source, and only used reluctantly by many), provides perfectly adequate and competent support when switching over or introducing yourself to the new version, if your primary concern is to create high-quality charts, that is.

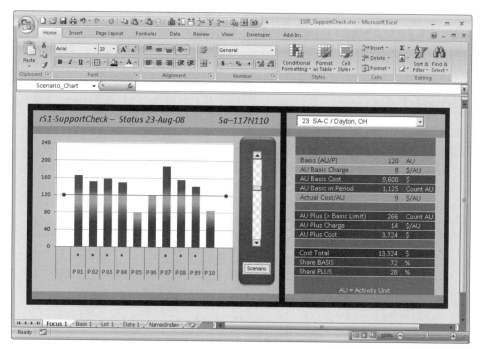

FIGURE I-2 You too can create such complex, scenario-based costing models

Of course, you will not want to or have to content yourself with "normality" in this book. The example shown in Figure I-2, which also plays a key, exemplary role in Chapter 11 "Fulfilling Special Requirements", demands, in terms of content, considerably more than can be achieved by simply applying the general information provided in the Excel help.

Note Figure I-2 shows the focus sheet for a combined costing, report, and analysis model. Different customers have availed of support activities assigned to different activity classes. In each case, a customer's most recent activity periods are imported, at a mouse click, into a chart where they are differentiated according to agreed activity types. In this view, it is possible to immediately envisage a different scenario and alternative costing/valuation by continuously changing a limit (indicated by the horizontal bar in the chart). The purpose of this chart is to use the horizontal bar to determine what may have been a more cost-effective solution for the customer while bearing in mind the conditions agreed and the activities actually performed during this period. This solution may then also serve as a standard for future agreements. Of course, none of the above requires an ounce of programming.

You can look forward to taking an excellent journey through the world of Microsoft Office Excel 2007 and all it has to offer. Any brick walls you may encounter as a result of the program's restrictions or your own limitations will only be due to the fact that we will occasionally push against the spreadsheet's boundaries. You will be amazed by the many possibilities. And how easily they can be achieved if you systematically use structured methods in a targeted manner.

This book will enable you to create complex and highly dynamic numbers presentations as well as impressive graphics that will win over your audience. Excel 2007 at its very best, and it doesn't require a single line of programming. This will be proven in the coming pages.

Version Restriction: Excel 2007 and beyond

It is certainly not easy to immediately warm to the redesigned Microsoft Office 2007 user interfaces for Word, PowerPoint or Excel. They may well appeal to first-time users, but anyone who is an experienced, long-time user of Microsoft Office programs will certainly need a few days, if not longer, to gain an overview of these new user interfaces, and to adjust to the idiosyncrasies associated with the new version. During this period of adjustment, repeated attempts to work with these programs may well frustrate and bewilder users, and possibly even provoke an outburst of fury! However, once this phase passes, both the innovations and benefits associated with Office 2007 will shine through and come into their own.

> **Note** According to the information available at the time of going to press, the procedures and techniques described in this book should also remain valid for any post-2007 versions of Excel. However, in the absence of such future versions, it is not possible to put the above statement to the test.

This book wishes to convey that Excel is particularly successful in this regard, which will be to the benefit and, better still, the delight of the reader.

It's Not All New, but Much of It Is Significantly Different

For all of the explanations and figures in this book, I have used Microsoft Excel 2007 on Microsoft Vista Ultimate. Only in Chapter 1, "Basic Information—Basic Techniques", have I compared this latest version of Excel with earlier versions by providing a partial comparison of Versions 2003 and 2007, partial in the sense that it is limited to the basic creation and use of charts.

> **Note** All of the figures have been created using an English version of Microsoft Office, whose custom language settings support several foreign languages and input locales, including two Asian fonts. Consequently, some of the dialog boxes shown in the figures may contain additional tabs and/or additional entries that are not available in the standard installation.

This book addresses the highly specialized topic of charts. This is a broad subject area whose contents and restrictions are defined in Chapter 1. The term "specialization" simultaneously implies "restriction" since here you can only expect to receive a fraction of the information that will make it easier for you to switch over to Excel 2007. I therefore beseech you not to expect to receive high-level support from this book, as this essentially goes beyond the subject of charts and their dynamic use.

The technical and design conditions of Excel 2007 differ greatly from earlier versions of Excel, to the point that backward compatibility is subject to considerable restrictions. The new features prevent universal, in other words, version-independent use. Therefore, a model that you create using the resources available in Excel 2007 (in accordance with the instructions provided here) can only be used in Version 2003 or older with restrictions.

In Excel 2007, you will find numerous save options that were previously unknown to you as well as some options you may recognize from earlier versions of Excel, for example, the option to save a workbook as a backward-compatible file. If, when creating an Excel 2007 file, you use resources that did not exist in earlier versions, and you then explicitly try to save this file as an Excel 97-2003 workbook, your attention will be drawn to a dialog box containing the possible incompatibilities. Let's take a look at the example provided in Figure I-3 where the user applied conditional formatting to a numbers column. However, this type of conditional formatting (data bars) is not available in earlier versions of the spreadsheet. Therefore, when he tries to save such a file as an Excel 97-2003 workbook, the program issues a warning message indicating that there may be a "significant" loss of functionality.

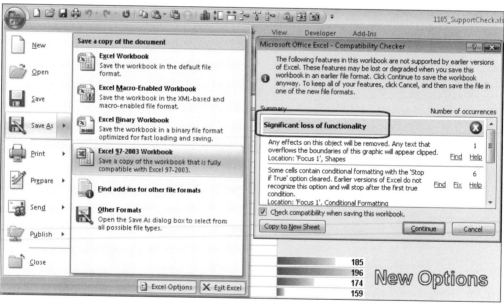

FIGURE I-3 The result of the compatibility check advises the user of a possible loss of functionality

Another problem occurs when you save a file in the new default file format *.xlsx* available in Excel 2007 and then try to open such a file in an earlier version of Excel, for example, 2003. The target program converts the file and creates a document that you can use and edit, but may be missing certain, possibly essential, parts of the source file created in Excel 2007.

Therefore, this book is ultimately dedicated to Excel 2007 and later versions of this program whose contents and results you should, in all likelihood, use in only these modern versions of the program. To clarify, everything that you will read in the coming pages is specific to those possibilities and idiosyncrasies associated with Excel 2007 (and beyond), some of which *cannot* be used in earlier versions of Excel, or at least *not in this way*. (Even though much of what will be shown here can be performed in older versions of the program, it is achieved there in another, occasionally considerably more cumbersome manner). Consequently, the information conveyed in this book can be applied to earlier versions of Excel, but more in theory than in praxis.

Objectives—Approaches—Possibilities

What Realistic Goals Can I Set Myself?

This is an exercise book. You can also use it as a reference book if you are already a highly proficient user of Excel 2007. However, to get the most from this book, I recommend that you work through each chapter in succession. By doing so, you can achieve the following:

- By applying competent procedures, you can create meaningful, effective, and dynamic Excel models as well as presentations based on Excel resources without considerable effort, and without having to acquire any programming knowledge.

- With very little effort, you can reproduce your tables and charts at any time and convert them to other display and/or application formats.

- You can show other users how to create modern, future-proof Excel solutions and justify the procedures used.

How Successful Can I Hope to Be?

Anyone who makes clever use of the possibilities outlined in this book and consistently applies its content to tasks can hope to achieve the following:

- Users who initially have a low to average knowledge of Excel will quickly achieve professional results (variable solutions that take account of various special requirements).

- Conventional users of Excel will be able to produce impressive, dynamic number and text presentations without having to dispense with known static presentations (PowerPoint, for example).

- Inexperienced users of Excel will also be able to use their own solutions independently, without any problems, and in a user-secure manner.

- You can still impress those among your audience who have been overloaded with presentations in the past.

What Prior Knowledge Do I Require?

You do not require any expert knowledge or extensive user knowledge in order to understand the examples provided in this book and to develop your own solutions. If you follow my advice and work through each chapter in succession, you should not experience any major difficulties in terms of comprehension and use. However, this publication, which is geared towards a special topic, cannot and does not wish to be an "all-inclusive" Excel user guide. Consequently, readers of this book need to have some basic knowledge of Excel, including Version 2007. In other words, my formulations and instructions assume that you have sufficient basic knowledge of the tasks outlined below or that you have obtained or can obtain such information from other sources:

- Creating, saving, and managing files (in Windows Explorer)

- Organizing and managing Excel workbooks (for example, insert, copy, move, delete, and rename worksheets)

- Organizing the structure of Excel worksheets (for example, fill, copy, insert, move, and delete cells, rows, and columns)

- Creating, formatting, and revising simple lists and data tables

- Writing and editing (changing, modifying, duplicating) simple non-nested formulas of different reference styles (relative, absolute, mixed)

- Working simultaneously with several active programs and windows in Microsoft Windows

- Using program helps

Use of the rS1.Method

As is the case with all of my books on Excel, the "rS1.Method" is once again the main basis for all solutions and models in this book. The "rS1.Method" is a detailed set of rules that comprises table functions, the use of certain functions or formulas, and the use of controls. I developed this standard and have used it in numerous solutions for many years. At its core is an absolute, yet varied structure, coupled with the consistent use of range names of a certain type and syntax.

Many of the examples provided in this book use the rS1.Method. Therefore, the user must accept the following: if you wish to reproduce these solutions, you must understand the procedure. Consequently, there is no way of avoiding the theory behind the method. However, the relevant information does not form part of this book, but is stored separately on the CD-ROM.

 On the Companion CD The relevant file is stored under \Materials\rS1_Method_2007.pdf.

I recommend that you print out the document and preferably read it before you study Chapter 2 where you will be introduced to the solutions and models used here. While reading this book, keep your printout to hand, so that you can understand the examples and their structure at all times.

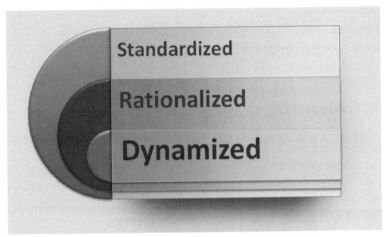

FIGURE I-4 The rS1.Method defines a standard, rationalizes your solutions, and makes them dynamic

Note The text element shown in Figure I.4 has been created using *SmartArt*. You'll find information about this feature in Chapter 12.

Design and Materials

This section primarily focuses on notations, materials, and indexes.

Notations

The terminology used in this book, at least where Excel functions are concerned, corresponds to those terms used in the English version of Microsoft Excel 2007.

The following notations are used for functions and formulas:

- A function's syntax display is used for an abstract description or explanation of the function, for example:

  `=OFFSET(reference,rows,cols,height,width)`

- Its actual notation is then used to correctly display a formula applied to a worksheet, for example, `=IFERROR(C4/D4,"")` or `=INDEX(rD1.Actual07,$G6,F$7)`.

Note The function =IFERROR(value,value_if_error) belongs to one of those efficient new formulas available with Excel 2007. The value argument represents a specific arithmetic operation. If this produces the error value #N/A, #VALUE!, #REF!, #DIV/0!, #NUM!, #NAME? or #NULL!, your custom specification for the value_if_error argument is shown in the cell. If the arithmetic operation is successful, the result of this operation is shown in the cell. Therefore, in comparison with earlier versions of the program, it is now considerably easy to trap possible error values that are displayed.

A practical example is provided in Chapter 11.

Examples and Materials

The CD-ROM accompanying this book contains numerous sample files and materials.

- *Samples files* are half-finished or completely finished Excel workbooks that support the descriptions provided in each chapter. Such files are stored in a main Samples folder for each chapter. The notes associated with these files use the path together with the file name, for example, \Samples\1006_RadarComparison.xlsx.

Note Most of the sample files have a presentation worksheet (or several such sheets) with the sheet name *Focus 1* (*Focus 2*, and so on). These worksheets are designed for a screen resolution of 1024 x 768 pixels, mainly because most modern projectors can handle such a screen resolution without any difficulty, but cannot cope with a higher resolution or at least not well enough to produce an acceptable quality.

Incidentally, this screen resolution is also the minimum resolution for correctly displaying the new Ribbon in Excel 2007. You'll find more information about this topic in Chapter 1, "Basic Information–Basic Techniques."

A directory of sample files that provide information about making charts dynamic through **F9** (simulating the import of new values) and through controls (actually importing new values) as well as information about using conditional formatting is available on the CD-ROM under \Materials\CD_Samples_Index.xlsx.

Note The author's main residence is Berlin, Germany and he took most of the examples provided in this book from his own practical experience. As a result, most of the examples have their origins in Europe and apply the units of measurement and specifications that are customary there. Furthermore, many of the examples deal with special questions from the areas of Controlling, Medicine or Science. Consequently, at first glance, some readers may find some of the examples somewhat unusual. On the other hand, however, these examples, in this form, reflect the author's vast and varied experience and are therefore very authentic. Above all, they represent the wide range of areas in which Microsoft Excel can be applied. For this reason, the publisher decided to retain the majority of the examples in their authentic form in the translation of this book.

- *Materials* are files of different types that support your work and help you to retain an overview. Such files are stored in a main folder called *Materials*. Once again, the notes associated with these files use the path together with the file name, for example, *\Materials\rS1_Method_2007.pdf.*

- *Bonus Material* includes Chapter 22, "Analyzing Data with PivotTable Reports" from the book "Microsoft Office Excel 2007 Inside Out."

Hardware and Software Requirements

You'll need the following hardware and software to work with the companion content included with this book:

- **Microsoft Windows XP, Windows Vista or later.**

- **Microsoft Office Excel 2007 or later.**

- **1.6 GHz Pentium III+ processor, or faster.**

- **1 GB of available, physical RAM.**

- **Video (1024 x 768 or higher resolution) monitor with a color setting of at least medium (16 bit).**

- **CD-ROM or DVD-ROM drive.**

- **Microsoft mouse or compatible pointing device**

> **Digital Content for Digital Book Readers:** If you bought a digital-only edition of this book, you can enjoy select content from the print edition's companion CD.
> Visit **http://go.microsoft.com/fwlink/?LinkId=130866** to get your downloadable content. This content is always up-to-date and available to all readers.

Indexes

If you want to use this book as a reference book, two different indexes will prove helpful:

- The (Subject) Index lists keywords, technical terms, and functions.

- The Index of Procedures contains page references to descriptions for specific procedures or step-by-step instructions.

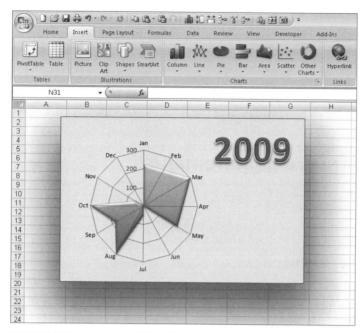

FIGURE I-5 Very soon you will be able to create charts like the one shown above

Support for This Book

Every effort has been made to ensure the accuracy of this book and the contents of the companion CD. As corrections or changes are collected, they will be added to a Microsoft Knowledge Base article.

Microsoft Press provides support for books and companion CDs at the following Web site:

http://www.microsoft.com/learning/support/books/.

Questions and Comments

If you have comments, questions, or ideas regarding the book or the companion CD, or questions that are not answered by visiting the sites above, please send them to Microsoft Press via e-mail to *mspinput@microsoft.com.*

Or via postal mail to

Microsoft Press, Attn: Create Dynamic Charts in Microsoft Office Excel Editor
One Microsoft Way
Redmond, WA 98052-6399

Please note that Microsoft software product support is not offered through the preceding addresses.

Chapter 1
Basic Information—Basic Techniques

Excel 2007: New Look—New Structures

Excel 2007 is much different from the version you've been used to. To explain all of these differences in detail would require the equivalent of software training and would clearly go beyond the scope of this book. In this first chapter, I will therefore stick to explaining basic principles that will help you to easily follow the descriptions aligned to the main topic and theme of the book.

Design of the Access Options

If you haven't already seen the images in the new version, you'll be surprised by the dramatically changed appearance of the program when you install the new version of Microsoft Excel and open it for the first time. Particularly noticeable is the Ribbon, which takes up a good 20% of the displayable area in the upper area of the application window. It replaces the menus and task-specific toolbars, which have disappeared and won't be reintroduced. So, there's no way around it: you'll have to familiarize yourself with the program's new command structures.

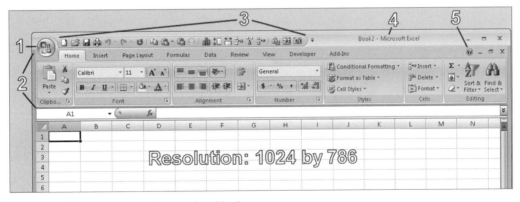

FIGURE 1-1 Changed access options and positioning

In relation to Figure 1-1, we'll first look at an overview of the most important elements of the command area (details about this are provided further on):

1. You select the *Office Button* to open a menu, which you can use to open new or saved workbooks, save, print, or close workbooks, or manage Excel options. More information is provided later.

1

2. The Ribbon, which is split into tabs, contains different task groups that are displayed with command buttons that correspond to the toolbars used in the previous version.

3. You can set up a custom *Quick Access Toolbar* on the upper corner of the screen. Those of you with experience of using earlier Excel versions will want to place the most important command buttons here, so you can avoid using the function toolbar and also avoid access options that (initially at any rate) appear complicated, or that you won't be able to remember quickly enough.

4. When you extend the *Quick Access Toolbar*, the title of the workbook is positioned farther to the right of the screen.

5. The command button for the Excel help function will now appear as a question- mark icon on the outer right of the Ribbon.

You will learn more about defining the *Quick Access Toolbar* and using the Ribbon later in this chapter.

I'd recommend from now on you consistently use Excel in full-screen mode and therefore set a screen resolution no lower than 1024 by 768 pixels on Windows Vista, because this setting will ensure that all command buttons on the Ribbon's tabs will be displayed fully. If you minimize the Excel window, or set a lower screen resolution, only a reduced set of commands will appear in the Ribbon and you'll be forced to click an arrow icon to access the command buttons that aren't displayed. This would rapidly negate the advantages of being able to access different commands more quickly.

FIGURE 1-2 Note screen resolution and color quality

Much more importance is also attached to the color quality in Microsoft Office 2007 than in previous versions. The graphical resources of programs have been considerably enhanced and improved. If you want to use the new options fully, you will have to work with the highest possible color quality (32-bit color depth).

> **Note** You can access the dialog box shown in Figure 1-2 for setting the screen resolution and color quality on Windows Vista. Select the *Start* button, then click *Control Panel* and choose the *Display and Change* option, followed by *Change Screen Resolution*, or right-click an empty space on the desktop and then choose the *Change/Display* command.

Formula Bar

Two new features in the redesigned formula bar are quite useful. These are shown in Figure 1-3:

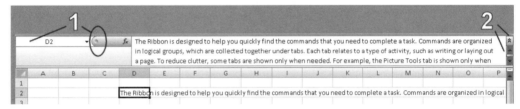

FIGURE 1-3 Improved work options in formula bar

1. The name box on the left of the formula bar was previously too narrow for those users who consistently worked with range names and could not display longer names fully when drop-down name lists were expanded. This interfered with various control steps. The problem is now solved by the fact that you can use a "slide" (elliptic mark in Figure 1-3) to increase and decrease the name box. This provides a significant advantage for users in particular of the rS1.Method recommended in this book, which requires having to deal very intensively with range names.

2. In Excel 2007, a cell can now contain a maximum of 32,767 characters and a formula can be 8,192 characters long. To ensure that you can display these amounts of text clearly in the formula bar, you can now extend the single-row item to several rows and, if this still isn't sufficient, you can use a scrollbar to move in the area extended in this way.

> **Note** You will learn more about the specifications and limitations of Excel 2007 in the "Overviews and Materials" section further on.

Worksheets

Those of you who found the space provided in the worksheets of previous Excel versions too small, can now cut loose: the last cell of the worksheet is now in row 1,048,576 and in column XFD, which corresponds to column number 16,384.

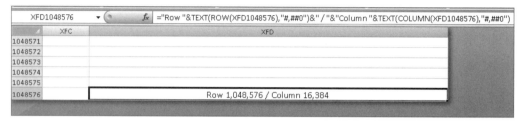

FIGURE 1-4 Space sufficient in worksheet? Space provided should be sufficient for the majority of all cases

Sheet Tabs and Status Bar

A lot has also been done to the lower area of the application window. See Figure 1-5 for more information:

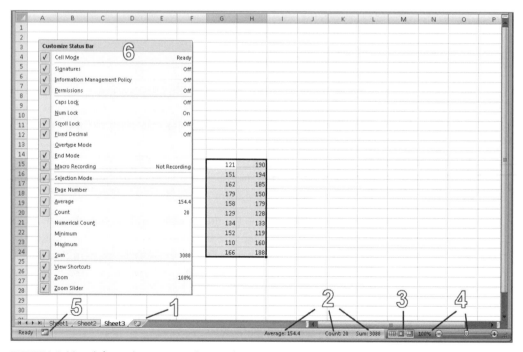

FIGURE 1-5 More information, more settings options

1. On the sheet selector, you can add a new worksheet by clicking a small command button.

2. Many users like to use the costing results display in the status bar to check accuracy or consistency when constructing formulas, for example. This overview was extended: in addition to the *Average, Count* and *Sum* default values, you can still also (see Number 6) display other calculation results of the selected area simultaneously.

3. Three small command buttons enable you to switch quickly between the *Normal, Page Layout*, and *Page Break Preview* worksheet views.

4. The newly formulated elements for controlling the zoom option are very helpful for many purposes, in particular for design work and checking design work. You can change the view continuously, quickly, and effortlessly between zooming in and out from 10 % to 400 %.

Options

The settings you had to implement in previous versions using the complex *Extras/Options* dialog box can now be achieved in a completely different way:

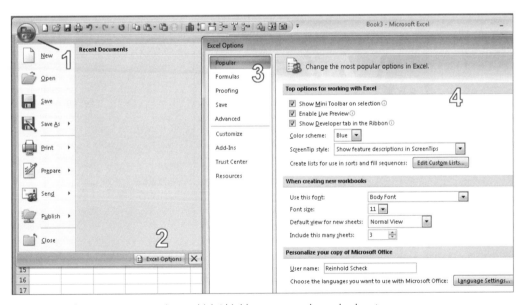

FIGURE 1-6 The new route to options, which I highly recommend you check out

1. Click the *Office Button.*

2. Click the *Excel Options* button at the bottom of the menu now open.

3. Select a category from the *Excel Options* dialog box.

4. Decide on the settings you require under the specifications of the relevant selected category.

Below is an overview of those settings that I recommend you use when working with this book (and, incidentally, for other work with Excel 2007).

> **Note** Note that I don't mention all available Excel options in the following list of settings. I only discuss the ones that are closely related to the themes and contents of the book. However, I won't mention all of these settings for the time being because some only apply in relation to specific solutions, so it will be more useful to describe them in the context of such examples.

Popular Category

Show Mini Toolbar on selection Enable this option. Not only will you then be able to access a cell after you right-click, but with selected text you can also immediately access a toolbar containing the most important formatting tools. This appears in conjunction with the context menu or by itself.

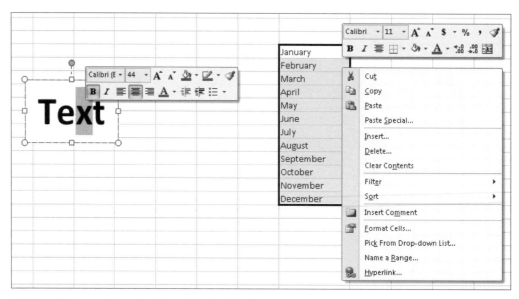

FIGURE 1-7 The most important formatting tools in direct access

Enable Live Preview Enable this option, which is particularly important for designing your models and which lightens your workload considerably compared to earlier versions of Excel. By simply pointing to a selection option, you can see the effect of your selection in a preview even before you choose a setting. This is particularly useful for formatting work. Once you're satisfied with the preview results, you can make your decision by clicking the mouse button. This naturally saves you many unnecessary steps.

Show Developer tab in the Ribbon   Enable this option. The display of the *Developer tools* tab in the Ribbon, which you achieve using this setting, is essential for your work with this book. This is of particular importance with regard to using control elements, which you could not access without the *Developer tools* tab.

ScreenTip Style   Select *Show feature descriptions in ScreenTips* to display information that describes these buttons when you point to a command button. You'll certainly find this very useful when acquainting yourself with the considerably changed program.

When creating new workbooks   Here, you determine the default values relating to font, font size, worksheet views, and number of new sheets that you want to use when you open new workbooks.

> **Note** The new *Calibri* font available in Office 2007 is very suitable for many display purposes and therefore recommended.

Formulas Category

Calculation Options   If possible, the workbook calculations should always occur *automatically* when you use the solutions described in this book. This is because very complex solutions involve large parts of the functionality and dynamics being implemented using table formulas. These must achieve their adjustment performance for each custom change to a view; for example, using a control element.

Working with Formulas   Enable *Formula AutoComplete*. When you use this option, after you enter the equals sign and some letters, a list of proposals matching your entries appears, containing functions from which you can choose in order to make it easier to write your formula correctly. You transfer the selected formula by double-clicking it or pressing the **Tab** key in the formula bar.

Error Checking   I still find the *Enable background error checking* option quite impractical and more of an annoyance than a help, in particular because error bars can also be displayed if Excel does not correctly interpret a correct, but complex, formula.

If the error checking remains disabled, you can ignore the selection under *Error checking rules*.

Proofing Category

AutoCorrect and Spelling Correction have been consistently designed features of Microsoft Office for a long time now. This is now reflected in similar access and settings options.

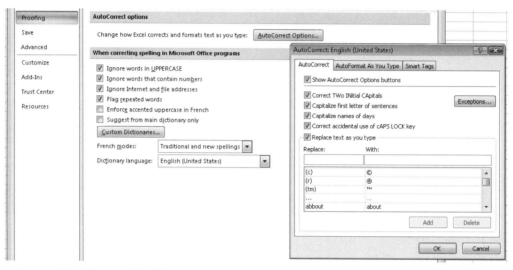

FIGURE 1-8 AutoCorrect and Spelling Correction

Here, and also in Word, you specify which of your entries are to be changed or customized automatically and which spelling rules are to be used.

Save Category

You will naturally save the majority of your Excel 2007 files in the new default *.xlsx* file format. However, a look at the corresponding drop-down list is certainly of interest. You'll find a list of all file formats here that are available when you choose the *Save As* command in the new Excel version.

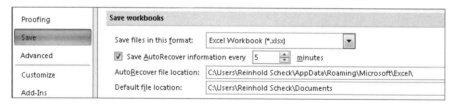

FIGURE 1-9 Important settings and information on the *Save* topic

Set a relatively short time (five minutes) for the *Save AutoRecover information every* option. Especially when you're processing some of the complex examples in this book, it will be important not to lose any significant parts of your work if Excel or Windows crashes.

Advanced Category

> **Note** The following suggestions may seem strange to those of you used to working differently. They are based on my own personal experience and habits (or, you might say, "quirks") in dealing with Excel. The bottom line is not to accept anything that may be obstructive, disruptive, or irritating.

Editing Options   You should deactivate the *After pressing Enter, move selection* setting. When writing, checking, and correcting complex formulas, it doesn't make sense for you to leave the active cell after you press the **Enter** key. You save yourself unnecessary steps if the cell you're currently using remains selected.

You should also *not* select the *Allow editing directly in cells* setting. Editing directly in the cell and writing long formulas often displays the data unsatisfactorily, specifically whenever the formula is longer than the width of the active cell and its display overlaps adjacent table areas, which may be important for controlling or editing the formula. If you suppress editing directly in the cell, you can still only write and edit formulas in the *formula bar.* This is the desirable situation.

Cut, Copy and, Paste   I still find the appearance of option buttons in the worksheet disruptive in my work and therefore recommend that you disable the top two options in this group.

However, the *Cut, copy, and sort inserted objects with their parent cells* option is really useful. When objects are changed, this option ensures that they retain their reference to the cells where they were originally created.

Display   Under the *Formulas/Working with Formulas Category* above, I suggested that you enable the *Formula AutoComplete* option. If you've done this, it's now also useful to select *Show function ScreenTips* here. Selecting this option means that, in addition to the picklist, a brief explanation will be displayed when you select one of the list entries (see Figure 1-10).

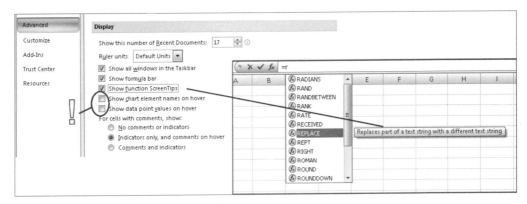

FIGURE 1-10 Both chart-specific settings in this group are particularly important.

Several examples in this book are templates or recommendations for developing presentation charts. In a public presentation, it's extremely annoying when texts or values are displayed when you point to a chart element or data point in ScreenTips. Therefore, disable both corresponding options, viz. *Show chart element names on hover* and *Show data point values on hover.*

Display Options for Selected Workbooks and Worksheets   The very welcome new features in Excel 2007 mean that, with the support of dialogs, you can now individually set the display options for the workbooks that are currently open, and for the individual worksheets of these workbooks (see Figure 1-11).

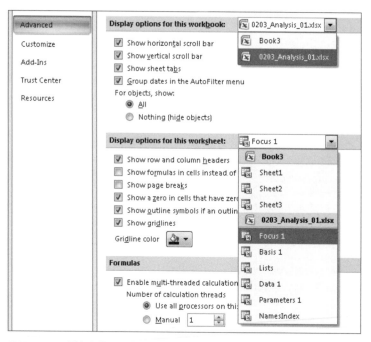

FIGURE 1-11 This is how you control the appearance of workbooks or worksheets and the processing power.

Formulas   Naturally, you should make the optimum capabilities of your computer available for Excel. This will apply in particular whenever you need Excel to make comprehensive calculations that are also to be performed very quickly. You should therefore enable the *multi-threaded calculation* and Excel should of course *use all processors on this computer.* See also Figure 1-11.

Calculation Options and General Information   As you can see in Figure 1-12, you can now also set the calculation options individually for the workbooks that are currently open.

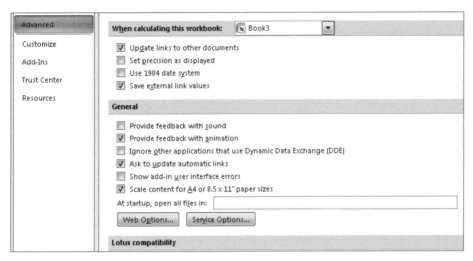

FIGURE 1-12 The calculation options can also be calculated based on specific workbooks.

No recommendations can or will be discussed here for the options in the *General* area.

Customize Category

The *Quick Access Toolbar* is a custom combination of frequently required command buttons that are not to be accessed via the Ribbon, but rather directly by the user. In terms of the purpose and type of design, this corresponds to a *custom toolbar* from early versions of Microsoft Excel. However, you can no longer move and place the modern type where you wish on the application window, as you used to do. Instead, it's linked to two positions: you'll either find this toolbar above or below the Ribbon. More information is provided later in this chapter.

It's relatively easy to create and change the toolbar in the *Customize* dialog box of the *Excel options*. Above all, it's foolproof, which means that you now no longer need to fear the earlier errors that could easily occur, such as accidentally destroying the default toolbar.

I recommend that you perform the following steps shown in Figure 1-13 when creating the toolbar for the first time:

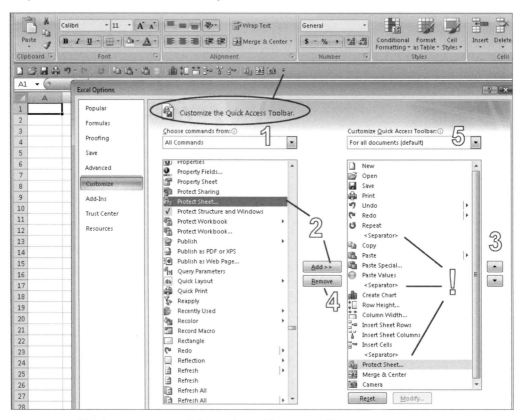

FIGURE 1-13 This is how you create and change the *Quick Access Toolbar*.

1. Click the *Office Button*, followed by *Customize*.

2. In the *Choose commands from* dialog box, select the *All Commands* option to obtain a complete, alphabetically arranged overview of each command button, which you can transfer to the toolbar.

   Alphabetically choose a command that you want to be a component of the toolbar and then click the *Add* button. This transfers the command to the picklist on the right. You don't have to worry about a logical or an ergonomic layout yet because you'll be able to change the positions as you wish later. Keep doing this until you have compiled your required set of commands. Also remember to add some *separators* so that you'll be able to create clearly arranged groupings in the toolbar at a later stage. (Separators are vertical lines. The *<Separator>* entry is located at the very top of the alphabetical list.)

3. Now select the transferred *command buttons* or *separators* one by one and move them to the required position using the two *arrow buttons*.

4. If you want to remove a *command button* or *separator*, select it from the dialog box list on the right and click the *Remove* button.

5. In the dialog box on the upper right of the screen, you see that you can also set up a *Quick Access Toolbar* as a default Excel 2007 document and also assign certain workbooks to your own specific toolbars in this way.

Add-Ins Category

Here you'll find a list of add-ins that are currently installed and available. The *AddIn Manager* was previously used to manage (for example, add or remove) add-ins. You can access the familiar dialog box by selecting the *Excel Add-ins* option from under *Manage:* and then clicking the *Go* button. You don't require specific Excel add-ins when working with this book because some of the formulas only made available by add-in in early versions are now contained in the default formula option.

Trust Center Category

In the Trust Center, you can access all security information provided under Microsoft Office Online. With the touch of a button, you can branch to different settings that will help you determine the security level of your application.

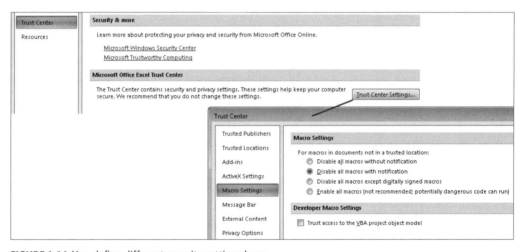

FIGURE 1-14 You define different security settings here.

Resources Category

When using this group, always keep your application up-to-date and remain informed. In the *Resources* category, you also have access to the *Microsoft Office Diagnostics*, which you can use to determine whether your installation may need repair. If this is the case, an attempt will be made to solve the problem using the built-in utilities provided in Windows.

For all kinds of queries and checks, it's important to know specifically which software version is currently installed. You'll find corresponding detailed information when you click the *About* button.

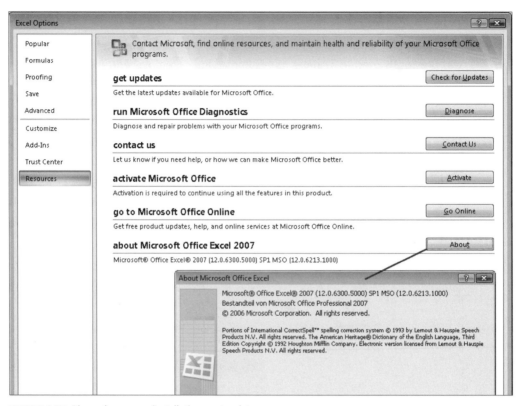

FIGURE 1-15 Always keep your installation up-to-date

The Ribbon

Experienced users will naturally miss the menu structures and toolbars from earlier program versions. Many users also have gotten used to using "task panes," but even these are still only sparsely available.

Because there is no possibiltiy to return to earlier designs of the user interface in Excel 2007, it's important that you get used to the new specifications quickly. This is also essential when dealing with this book, where I will use the terms introduced in the following paragraphs in other chapters for all explanations and instructions.

First, let's look at the structure of the *Ribbon* as displayed in Figure 1-16:

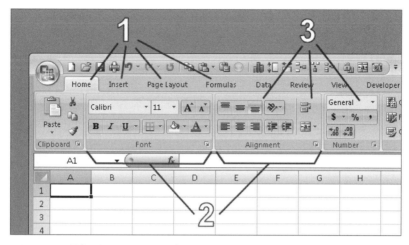

FIGURE 1-16 Tabs (1), groups (2) and command buttons (3)

1. Like the menu titles in earlier versions, the titles of task-oriented *tabs* appear at the top of the screen. When you click one of these titles, a list of *command buttons* appears classified by *group*.

2. The *groups* are visually separate from each other and have a text description at the bottom that attempts to describe the task complex represented by the group.

3. Some of you switching to the new version will be familiar with several of the *command buttons*, while others will first need to familiarize yourselves with them. Allow yourself time to do this and check out what will and won't work.

Dealing with this structure requires familiarization because quite a few assignments do not necessarily appear logical and a sequence of commands that functions in accordance with ergonomic rules is only partly possible. This is mainly because, in particular with the design tasks frequently addressed in this book, you have to search for several commands in different parts of a tab that are relatively far removed from each other or are on different tabs. After the first few months working with Excel 2007, I still don't know why it would be better or easier to process wide and horizontal structures and graphically designed structures instead of compact, vertically-oriented lists with text entries.

Those of you, who do not use command buttons for certain task complexes, but instead consistently work with the complex dialog boxes, may be glad that at least some of these dialog boxes still exist. In terms of type and content, they also don't differ greatly from the previous familiar structures and will therefore be a pleasant "transitional aid" for many Excel 2007 users.

An example of how you access these "conservative" dialog boxes is shown in Figure 1-17:

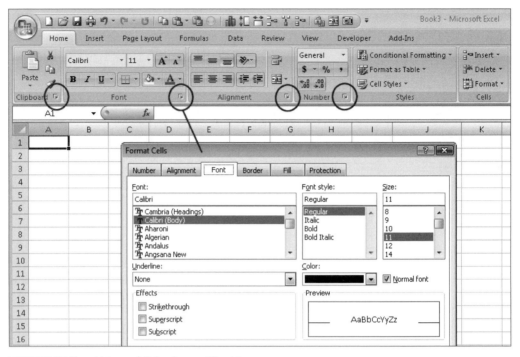

FIGURE 1-17 The old type of dialog boxes still exist.

Some of the *groups* displayed in the *Ribbon* have small arrows in the lower right-hand corners. This represents a "launcher" for a specific dialog box. For example, if you click the *Launcher* in the *Font, Alignment,* or *Number* group, the *Format Cells* dialog box opens containing each task-specific activated tab.

The *context-related tools* are displayed in Figure 1-18. These are special *tabs* that open when you enable a specific object (a chart, for example).

To edit the Chart object, the *Chart Tools* with the three tabs *Design, Layout,* and *Format* were added to the Ribbon.

These tools in turn contain several *groups*, some of which include *command buttons* and others a variably large number of graphical elements, that you can use to assign one of the format or layout versions stored in the program to the selected object. You can scroll vertically in some of these groups using arrow command buttons (see selection in Figure 1-18) or sometimes display them completely on half the screen.

In the example in Figure 1-18, the chart is selected and the special *Design* tab, from which the *Chart Layouts* group is currently selected, has been enabled in the Ribbon. This could help you to provide the chart with a specific overall layout. This is a procedure that I don't recommend, or only recommend very cautiously, for reasons which I will explain in later chapters.

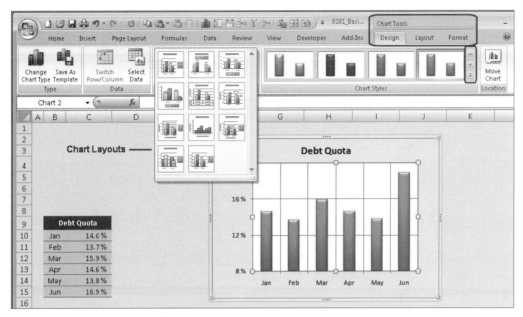

FIGURE 1-18 *Context-related tools* enable you to access design templates programmed in Excel.

Another version of the command structure shown in the *Ribbon* appears as *program tabs* in place of the standard tabs when you switch to a mode that is not a standard editing mode. Figure 1-19 shows the status of the *Ribbon* after you call *Print Preview*.

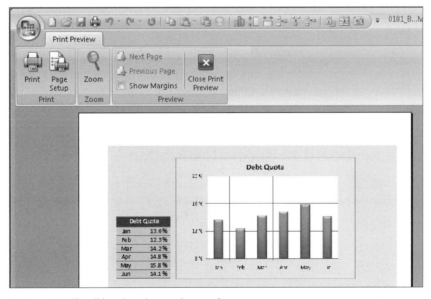

FIGURE 1-19 The ribbon in print preview mode

Quick Access Toolbar

I've already explained how to arrange the *Quick Access Toolbar* set of commands. In addition, Figure 1-20 displays a menu that opens after you click the small command button on the right of this toolbar. In my opinion, the selectable specifications in the upper part of the menu aren't relevant because you can arrange or change the toolbar according to your own ideas, wishes, and requirements. You can also access this customization mode by clicking the *More Commands* entry in the displayed menu.

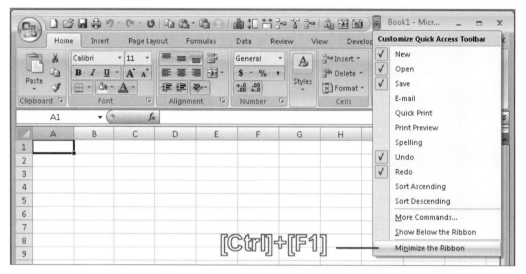

FIGURE 1-20 The menu for customizing the *Quick Access Toolbar*

You can use the second to last menu entry to decide alternatively whether the *Quick Access Toolbar* is shown above or below the *Ribbon*. Finally, you can also use the last menu entry here to minimize the Ribbon display on the tab titles. You can do this more quickly using the **Ctrl+F1** shortcut.

Using the Keyboard to Access the Ribbon

Those of you used to executing commands in Excel mainly with the **Alt** key will miss the underlining of correspondingly useful characters in Excel 2007. The following is an alternative method:

FIGURE 1-21 This is what the command structure looks like when you use the keyboard.

1. Briefly press the **Alt** key and release it again. The primary access key information is now displayed.

2. Now press the key(s) assigned to the required command. In the example in Figure 1-21, if you wanted to create a chart, you would now have to press the key sequence **0 7** in accordance with the information in the *Quick Access Toolbar*. If the *Formulas* tab was your objective, you would have to press the **M** key. In the last case mentioned, the selected tab would be displayed, and you would also now be able to see each of the command buttons contained there with access key information.

3. You exit the mode by using the **Alt** key once again or pressing the **Esc** key or by clicking in the worksheet with the mouse.

The Office Button

In Excel 2007, the Office Button that we already discussed, opens a menu where the most important administrative tasks for working with workbooks and worksheets are grouped.

It's very worthwhile to check all the options offered here. This applies especially to several new technical features that make Excel even much more interesting for business use than the program has already been.

For the purposes of this book, these technical aspects are only of secondary interest. I'll discuss some of them in later chapters if they apply to the topic that I'm dealing with there.

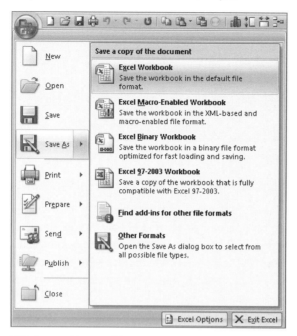

FIGURE 1-22 You use this menu to manage your work with Excel 2007.

Overviews and Materials

Those of you who want to achieve success quickly in using Excel 2007 need to be patient when switching over or introducing yourself to the new version. A lot of things will be easier for you later if you take the trouble beforehand to refer to the Excel help options to find out which new features are provided in the program and how you can deal with the many changes.

To ensure that your daily work with the program will then be somewhat easier, some files that will give you a better overview are stored in the materials list on the book's CD. The basic information is contained in some important files, which I'll describe briefly here:

- You'll find a directory of sample files with information about dynamization under \Materials\CD_Samples_Index.xlsx.

- The Functions.xlsx file is a filterable Excel table, in which 114 functions are listed. They have been allocated grouping assignments to enable you to easily create your own groupings organized by topic using sorting processes and/or filters. The ID 1 column is used for the same purpose. You can insert and store any type of entries that will facilitate filtering oriented towards your own purposes.

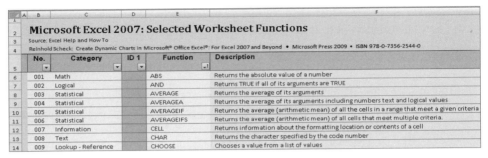

No.	Category	ID 1	Function	Description
001	Math		ABS	Returns the absolute value of a number
002	Logical		AND	Returns TRUE if all of its arguments are TRUE
003	Statistical		AVERAGE	Returns the average of its arguments
004	Statistical		AVERAGEA	Returns the average of its arguments including numbers text and logical values
005	Statistical		AVERAGEIF	Returns the average (arithmetic mean) of all the cells in a range that meet a given criteria
006	Statistical		AVERAGEIFS	Returns the average (arithmetic mean) of all cells that meet multiple criteria.
007	Information		CELL	Returns information about the formatting location or contents of a cell
008	Text		CHAR	Returns the character specified by the code number
009	Lookup - Reference		CHOOSE	Chooses a value from a list of values

FIGURE 1-23 You can extend the list of functions available on the CD.

- You use the *Shortcuts.xlsx* file, which is also structured as a filter list, to obtain information about numerous shortcuts that you can use in Excel 2007.

- Finally, the *Specifications.xlsx* file will show you the considerable extent to which the limitations of Excel have been addressed. I've already mentioned the huge number of cells per worksheet. Added to that are several other redesigns, which represent an enormous increase in performance options and reserves. Here are two examples:

  - Although you could create all colors in earlier versions of Excel, you could only use 56 per workbook. This limitation has been removed, so that all 16.7 million PC colors are now available for direct access.

  - The memory management of Excel 2007 has now been designed with 2 GB memory, double the amount in Excel 2003.

- The *NumberFormat.xlsx* file contains a list of custom number formats that you can extend to suit your own requirements and from which you can transfer special number formats into other worksheets.

Basic Concepts and Structures

> **Caution** To some extent, the terms and procedures used in Excel 2007 for charts and their processing differ greatly from what you know from early versions of the program. I therefore highly recommend that you read this section before implementing practical examples.

Let's start with the most important basic concept. What is actually a "chart"? You'll come across several versions when you search for definitions of the word in different sources. For example, the chart might be a patient documentation to a nurse, a table of accounts to a banker or a fingering manual to a musician. The term "chart" (which in Latin-Greek origins roughly meant "leaf of paper, tablet") is generally interpreted as a "graphical representation of numeric values in a form that is easy to understand." However, that obviously doesn't mean that numbers are converted into pictures (not even in Excel) because graphical representations of texts and contexts such as those images that play a role in the *SmartArt* topic in Chapter 12 , "More Than Numbers," (flow charts, organization charts, process descriptions, "Chevron lists," and similar objects) are also charts. Therefore, the term needs to be broadened a little to mean "graphical representation of numeric values and/or contexts in a form that is easy to understand." That's how we'll define it here.

However, the main focus is entirely on the more classic type of chart: an object for visualizing mathematical/statistical contents that converts a numerical basis into a comprehensible graphical display. This exists in numerous versions and also in facets of versions. The primary objective of this book is to design something like this perfectly with Excel.

Before you can enjoy the pleasure of being creative, however, you have to conquer a small mountain. The theoretical phase will continue. I can't and mustn't spare you from this because you'll understand instructions and descriptions of examples considerably better if you're familiar with the vocabulary used in Excel and therefore also in this book, even if it's accompanied by the occasional gnashing of teeth on my part.

> **On the Companion CD** The figures in this section were created using a file named
> *\Samples\0101_BasicSamples.xlsx,* which you will find on the book's CD. Opening this file before
> reading on will help you to understand the following descriptions.

Let's move on to the definitions. I'll just discuss the most important terms here for introductory purposes only. You'll find additional information and explanations (for example, with the support of the index) elsewhere in the book. The sequence of topics below is based on work contexts and mainly uses groupings and arrangements that correspond to the structure of Excel 2007.

Chart Types and Data Sources

You can quickly create a simple chart with all its default elements using the following steps. You probably won't particularly miss the multilevel Chart Wizards of earlier versions.

1. Select the data range that contains the chart's source data. Ideally, this is a rectangular area filled with numbers that contains row labels on the left and column labels on the top. You will see that this base form of the data source is not essential at all, but that there are also many options you can use to create charts from complex data ranges.

2. Enable the *Insert* tab in the *Ribbon* and in the *Charts* group click a button that displays the type of required chart, or click the *Launcher* on the lower right of the group for the *Insert Chart* dialog box.

3. Graphical list ranges with subtypes are now displayed. When you point to one of these subtypes, a brief label text is displayed. When you click one of the figures, the corresponding chart is displayed based on the selected data and with a selection frame. The object is created as an *embedded chart* in the standard version; therefore, it appears on a table worksheet. This is also how it will be in all models described here.

 Note The type you select is not definitive. You can change the type of a complete chart at any time or also use different chart types within a single chart.

Chart Type

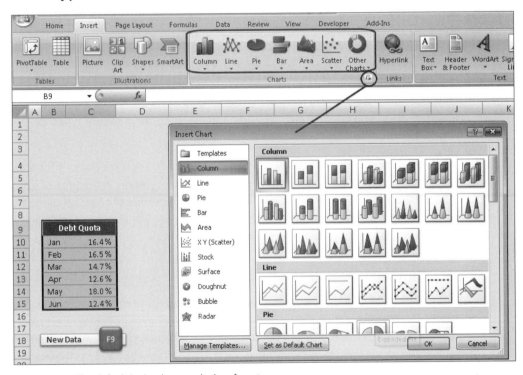

FIGURE 1-24 The default is simple—results in a few steps

The following chart types are available in Excel 2007 with different numbers of subtypes in each case. This is the sequence in which they appear in the *Insert Chart* dialog box:

- Column charts
- Line charts
- Pie charts
- Bar charts

- Area charts

- XY (scatter) charts

- Stock charts

- Surface charts

- Doughnut charts

- Bubble charts

- Radar charts

> **Note** The simple column chart ("clustered column" subtype) is the default chart type in the basic setting. You use the default chart type when you choose a data range and then create a chart using the **Alt+F1** shortcut without selecting a type.
>
> If you want to change the default chart type, open the *Insert Chart* dialog box shown in Figure 1-24, select a chart (sub)type, and then click the *Set as Default Chart* button.

All types mentioned will play roles in this book. In Chapter 3, "Perceiving, Interpreting, Understanding," you will find recommendations for using the different types for different purposes.

Experienced Excel users will quickly realize that, unfortunately, expectations for a wider choice of chart types have not been met. The few enhancements in the area of subtypes are so impractical they can't be considered innovations. Therefore, the familiar range that has been available for years basically remains in use. However, we'll show in later chapters that this in no way prevents you from using the charts in a huge number of ways.

Data Sources

As already indicated, a chart does not have to be based on a related data range, but can instead contain information jointly displayed from different sources that don't have much in common with each other. You can set and edit the particular references to source areas individually and also if the entire data source is a complete table block, as in the worksheets of the *0101_BasicSamples.xlsx* sample file. See Figure 1-25:

> **Note** You will learn how to deal with the individual features (for example, how to go to the *Select Data Source* dialog box displayed in Figure 1-25) in the Basic Techniques section.

Chart Data Range   The *Chart Data Range* is the reference to all chart data, not just to the numbers but also to the data from which the *Axis Labels*, *Legend*, and possibly *Chart Title* are created.

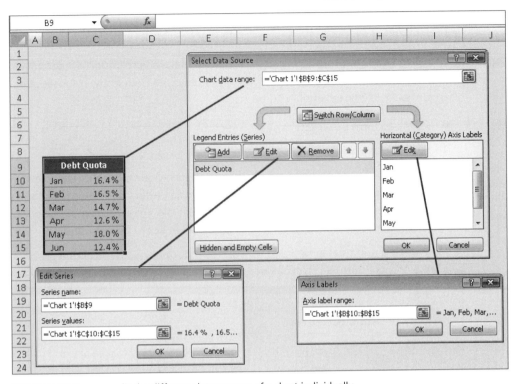

FIGURE 1-25 You can edit the different data sources of a chart individually.

Legend Entries   Legend entries contain the data (generally, texts) that can be used to interpret the chart's data series. If there is only one data series, as is the case in the *Chart 1* worksheet of the sample file, Excel automatically creates the text for the legend and for a chart title from the legend entry reference. If there are several data series, the reference is used for labeling the legend only.

Axis Labels   The reference for the axis labels refers to those source ranges (and also to text entries in the majority of cases) that are used to label the chart's categories.

Note The terms *Value Axis* and *Category Axis* are no longer instantaneously used in Excel 2007. In terms of prompting, we mainly refer to a horizontal axis and a vertical axis.

Formattable Elements

You can format all the chart elements listed below in many ways. There are some enormous differences here compared to previous versions of Excel. This applies both to the available options and to ways of dealing with the program in technical terms. Not everything that has been added will appear useful or helpful at first glance, and some not even at second or third glance.

Overall, however, the abundance and "designability" of visualization effects make them very important and beneficial in many ways for this book's discussion of presentation charts.

In relation to the chart formatting topic, I'd like to make a very important comment in advance, because this formatting will be implemented quite frequently in subsequent chapters. Each formattable chart element can be:

- Removed from the chart;

- Hidden using a specific coloring (element color = ambient color);

- Made transparent partially or fully by setting a color transparency between 0% and 100%. This new feature in Excel 2007 in particular, offers the chart designer many new and interesting approaches that not only affect the "lovely appearance," but also help to considerably improve the value of information about visualization.

A chart created using default editing operations is normally composed of a *chart area*, *plot area*, one or more *data series*, *axis*, various *labels*, and (optionally) different analysis elements.

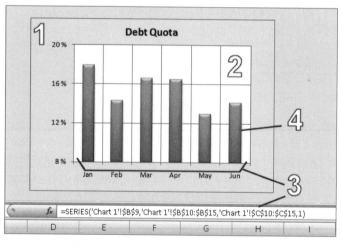

FIGURE 1-26 Chart area (1), plot area (2), data series, (3) and data point (4)

Chart Area

The *chart area* (identified by the number 1 in Figure 1-26) is the graphical base element of the *chart*, effectively the "container" of all elements that exist in the chart.

You select the *chart area* by clicking an empty space of this element with the mouse. In the selected status, the *chart area* displays an object frame with small selection points on its corners and edges known as *selection handles*. When you click one of these points with the mouse, the mouse pointer becomes a double-headed arrow and you can scale—that is, reduce or increase—the object continuously while holding down the mouse button.

When you point in a selected *chart area* with the mouse, the mouse pointer becomes a four-headed arrow and you can move the chart on the screen to a different position while holding down the mouse button.

When you press and hold the **Ctrl** key and then click the *chart area*, the chart is selected as a graphics object. It doesn't subsequently show a frame, but only four corner markings. In this situation, you can move the chart on the screen in small steps using the **left arrow**, **right arrow**, **top arrow** and **bottom arrow** keys, an ideal method for positioning charts precisely.

Plot Area

The *data series* and *gridlines* are plotted on the *plot area* (identified in Figure 1-26 by the number 2).

You select the *plot area* by clicking an empty space of this element with the mouse. The selected *plot area* also has *selection handles*, which you can use to scale the area. When the mouse pointer appears as a four-headed arrow, move the *plot area* within the *chart range*. Make sure that the axis labels are linked to the *plot area*; their position will therefore also follow an increase or reduction of the *plot area*.

> **Tip** Always make sure to design the space generously between axis labels and the border of the chart range. This has more than optical benefits, as you'll see in later chapters.

Data Series

Data series (identified in Figure 1-26 by the number 3) are those chart elements that you use to display values and/or relations of figures. You determine which graphical elements you'll use for displaying a data series primarily by selecting the *chart type* and *chart subtype*.

You select a complete *data series* by clicking one of its *data points* (in other words, one of the columns). All individual elements of the *data series* are then selected, and the data series formula with the formula reference of the data series (see Figure 1-26) is displayed in the *formula bar*. It can be edited there, which is often the easier way for the proficient user to adapt the reference of one or more data series of a changed display requirement.

Data Point

A *data point* (identified in Figure 1-26 by the number 4) is the single element of a *data series*. It therefore normally displays a single value of this *data series*. A *data series* usually consists of several *data points*. However, you might also have a situation where—although a chart has a complex *data series*—only a single one of its *data points* is displayed (you'll come across quite a number of these types of examples in this book).

There are two procedures available for selecting a *data point* quickly:

- The "delayed double-click," which involves clicking a *data point* and thereby first selecting the whole *data series*. After a short queue time, you click this *data point* again to select it individually. Practice makes perfect here also; if you click too quickly in succession, you enable the *Design* tab of the *Chart Tools* with a normal double-click.

- Any chart element is selected. You then select the required *data series* by pressing the **top arrow** or **bottom arrow** keys (repeatedly, if necessary) and moving to the required *data point* by pressing the **right arrow** or **left arrow** keys.

Labels

To head off any criticism, I'd just like to say from the outset that the layout of the object displayed in Figure 1-27 (which is a modification of the chart that you'll find in the *Chart 2* worksheet of the *0101_BasicSamples.xlsx* sample files) does not in any way correspond to what I'd like to present to you in this book as a successful design. The form shown in the image was only selected in order to concisely introduce the elements described in the following section.

> **Note** Note that the numbering from Figure 1-26 is continued in Figure 1-27.

With the exception of the *Legend*, and occasionally *Data Labels*, I recommend that you only use the labels presented here rarely. If something like this is necessary, I much rather prefer to use *text boxes*, as you'll see in later examples. This is mainly because you can format these objects in a better-designed way, edit them better, and position them more easily.

Chart Title   The *chart title* (identified by the number 5 in Figure 1-27) should provide clear information about what's illustrated in the chart. The formatting should clearly identify the text as the heading, but not make it stand out too much. A new option in Excel 2007 is to use an *overlay title*, which doesn't cause any displacement when it's added, meaning that it won't change the size and positioning of other chart elements, and therefore more or less has the properties of a text box.

Axis Title   You can set up the *axis title* (identified by the number 6 in Figure 1-27) both for horizontal as well as vertical axes of the chart. Only the vertical axis was filled accordingly for the figure. These texts should indicate what's illustrated in the *axis labels* (more about that later). In the majority of cases, however, this type of display is unnecessary, particularly if your chart has logical and clearly formatted axis labels.

Legend   The *legend* (identified by the number 7 in Figure 1-27) is one of the main design elements of a chart. This applies whenever the chart contains several *data series* that can usually only be identified uniquely if the legend text, along with the legend symbols, allow the viewer corresponding assignment options.

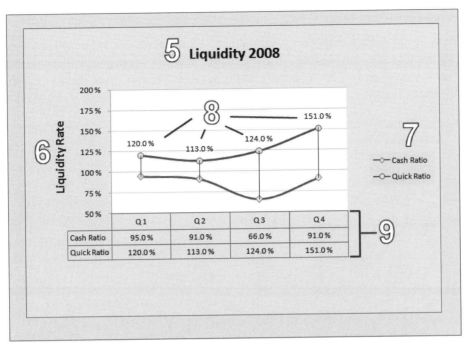

FIGURE 1-27 Chart title (5), axis title (6), legend (7), data label (8) and data table (9)

Note that you can place a *legend* anywhere you wish on the chart, and you not only can format the overall legend but format specific text elements of it.

Data Labels   The *data labels* (identified by the number 8 in Figure 1-27) provide additional information about individual data points. They must always be used if it's important to provide specific information in the chart that can't be conveyed in any other way. Nevertheless, I generally wouldn't recommend overloading a visual presentation with too much accompanying information. Therefore, only use *data labels* if you specifically need to highlight or clarify certain details. Therefore, you should generally only apply *data labels* to particularly important *data points*.

In Figure 1-27, the values of the *data points* are shown in the *data labels*. The use of *data series names* or *category names* (as substitutes or in any combination) is also possible.

Data Table   The *data table* (identified by the number 9 in Figure 1-27) is an adoption of the tabular data basis of the chart into the chart itself and is linked to the chart axis where the categories are illustrated. The width and distribution of the *data table* and its cells will depend on the size of the *plot area* and complexity of the *grid*.

Only use the *data table* if you want to display a few values with it. As a construct with multiple lines, it's usually more confusing than helpful.

Axes

Many users handle a chart's *axes* and their immediate labels in a rather careless way. This is a pity because axes are a key design element. Not only can they significantly impact the informational value and validity of a chart, but they can change and even distort this information. Therefore, I recommend that you pay close attention to the setting up and editing of axes.

> **Note** Note that the numbering from Figure 1-27 is continued in Figure 1-28.

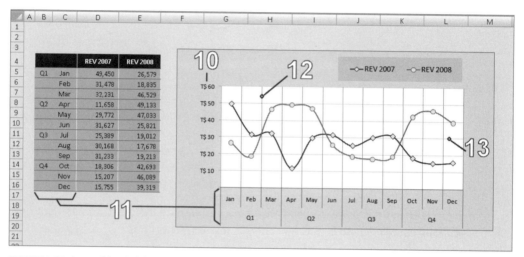

FIGURE 1-28 Axes with axis labels (10, 11) and gridlines (12, 13)

Vertical and Horizontal Primary Axis   In most cases, the *vertical primary axis* (identified by the number 10 in Figure 1-28) is the "value axis." The values of data series are displayed in automatic or custom tiling (scaling) in this axis's label. The value display is determined by the data material itself. It's a completely different story with the *horizontal primary axis* (identified by the number 11 in Figure 1-28). Its label values (in the majority of cases, these are texts) are transferred from the *chart data range*. As you can see in Figure 1-28, the source of the *axis labels* must in no case be single-column or single-line only. The *horizontal primary axis* is usually the "category axis," whose tiling (if no custom settings have been defined) is based on the number of *data points* included in the chart.

As you'll see later in several examples, both axes can be changed and formatted in very varied ways and are therefore (I'll gladly repeat myself where this subject's concerned) particularly important for the appearance and impact of your chart.

Each of the two *primary axes* can also be on the opposite position. Based on Figure 1-28, the *horizontal primary axis* could therefore be on the upper edge of the *plot area* and the *vertical primary axis* on the right beside the *plot area*. You can also set up *secondary axes* so that two horizontal and/or vertical axes will appear opposite each other. You will also find uses in this book.

Gridlines   The *gridlines* are handled in conjunction with the *axes* here because they are immediately structurally assigned to them. They continue the tilings of the *axes* in the chart's *plot area*: The *primary vertical gridlines* (identified by the number 12 in Figure 1-28) are plotted from the *horizontal primary axis*, and the *primary horizontal gridlines* (identified by the number 13 in Figure 1-28) are plotted from the *vertical primary axis*.

I have two basic recommendations for using and designing *gridlines*:

- Before you use *gridlines*, specifically check whether a vertical or horizontal tiling is actually required in the *plot area*. You often don't need these types of lines to understand the chart. Therefore, only use these elements if a partitioning optical tiling of the plot area is absolutely necessary. This is always the case if gridlines can emphasize the chart's informational value or help the viewer to differentiate the values or categories more closely.

- In most cases, *gridlines* are plotted too vividly by default in Excel and subsequently often dominate the overall impression unduly. Therefore, use corresponding formatting to make sure that the effect of the *grid* does not become the dominant factor.

Analysis Elements

Displaying relationships and precisely specifying details are just some of the things you can do with Excel's analysis elements. All these elements are enhancements to *data series* that already exist in the chart and are set up as options.

> **Note** Note that the numbering from Figure 1-28 is continued in Figure 1-29 and Figure 1-30.

High-Low Lines, Drop Lines, Trendlines   *High-low lines* (identified by the number 14 in Figure 1-29) are vertical connections of *data points* on *2D line charts*. They give the display a more two-dimensional effect and are therefore particularly well suited to clarifying the absolute distance between the values of two lines. For the evaluation, it's not especially important here whether the distance value visualized in this way is positive or negative.

Drop lines (identified by the number 15 in Figure 1-29) are vertical connections between *data points* and *category axes*. They are used in *line charts* or *area charts* to clarify the size of relevant values (their distances from zero or from the smallest value of the *value axis*) and emphasize its effect. This will usually only make sense, from an optical perspective, if the chart displays a single *data series*.

Several *trendline* versions (one of which is identified by the number 16 in Figure 1-30) are suitable for displaying the development trend of a data series.

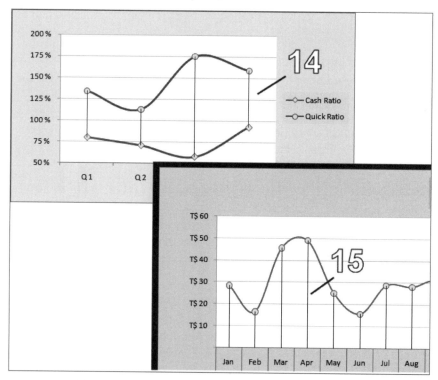

FIGURE 1-29 High-low lines (14) and drop lines (15)

Error Bars   Error bars (identified by the number 17 in Figure 1-30) indicate possible error amounts of individual or all *data points* of a *data series*. You can display error bars in the following chart types: two-dimensional bar, column, line, area, XY (scatter), and bubble charts.

Up/Down Bars   Using *up/down bars* (identified by the number 18 in Figure 1-30) correspond to the *high-low lines* already mentioned above and must also be limited to *line charts* with two *data series*. Unlike *high-low lines*, these two-dimensional elements don't express any absolute relation between *data points*, but instead indicate "greater than" or "less than" in an evaluated formatting: First as a state, and also to the extent of its scale.

Note   Illustrate the effect of *up/down bars* on the active *Chart 3* worksheet of the *0101_ BasicSamples.xlsx* sample file by pressing the **F9** key several times in succession to generate new figures for the two data series of the chart.

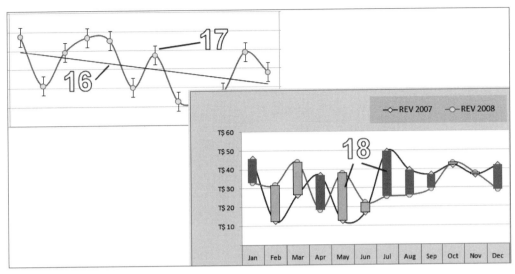

FIGURE 1-30 Trendline (16), error bars (17) and up/down bars (18)

Basic Approach

Having explained the most important basic concepts and elements in conjunction with charts, we can now deal with access and procedural methods. Naturally, the entire range of options will only come to light when complex examples appear in later chapters and, in particular, when you've achieved a comfortable routine as a result of your own exercises. Especially for those of you switching over from older versions of Excel, this will not be particularly easy because the routine you already have will be more of a hindrance than a help in getting used to using new functions easily (the longer you've practiced it, the harder it will be to change it).

Below, you'll find a selection of the Excel 2007 command set, insofar as it has a bearing on creating and editing charts.

Ribbon Commands

You've already become familiar with some chart-specific command buttons on the Ribbon in relation to Figure 1-24.

In the following paragraphs, you'll see something similar again in another illustration (see Figure 1-31). Here's the step-by-step description of what previously occurred:

1. The user created and selected a tabular basis for a chart data range (E13:014).

2. He or she then enabled the *Insert* tab in the *Ribbon* and clicked the *Line* command button in the *Charts* group there.

3. In the selection resulting from step 2, the user opted for a default setting, the *Line with Markers*. You'll get a brief description of the relevant chart subtype, together with explanations about its use, when you point the mouse to one of the preview images.

4. Clicking the corresponding image was sufficient to create the chart in a basic form capable of being developed. The user now selected the automatically created *chart title* in the chart by clicking it and deleted it by pressing the **Delete** key. Finally, the user used the selection handles within the framework of the selected *chart area* to form the object into a shape as shown in Figure 1-31, and as corresponds to the status in the *Data 1* worksheet of the *0102_PracticeData01.xlsx* file.

> **On the Companion CD** Open the *\Samples\0102_PracticeData01.xlsx* file on the CD-ROM.

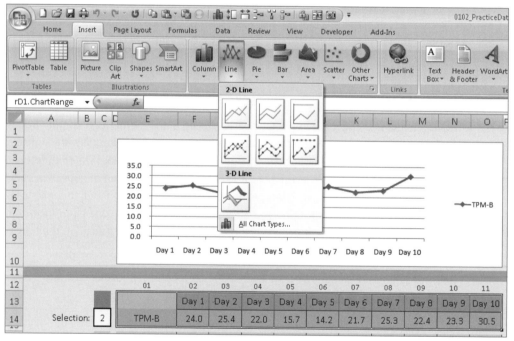

FIGURE 1-31 A simple line chart developed from a two-line chart data range

Use this file for some exercises now and for the rest of the chapter.

- When you click the chart or one of its elements, you simultaneously open the *chart tools* that are inserted in the *Ribbon* with the three *Design, Layout,* and *Format* tabs that can now be enabled there. If you've double-clicked, the *Design* will already be enabled.

> **Note** Those of you, who for years were used to double-clicking to open the relevant for-matting dialog boxes for individual elements of a chart, will now find it a little difficult to learn that this double-click action no longer works in this way.

- A single click will always be sufficient to activate chart tools for further access to data, unless you've executed other actions beforehand in the table area of the worksheet.

Give one or the other method a try and feel free to carry out very different experiments. If something fails completely or you can no longer find your way back to an earlier state, all you need to do is close the file and open it again. These are only initial attempts at learning the new command structures in Excel 2007. You're in no way required to produce successful results or designs here; detailed explanations or also critical remarks about some of the new program features are only to be expected in later chapters. But first let me say this: Many things are possible, a great many things, and many of them you haven't yet seen, at least not in Microsoft Excel. In my opinion, however, this simply means that—although you should know very well everything that *can* be done lately in the area of chart design—under no circumstances should you feel that you're also being asked to use or apply everything that's possible in your exercises.

Before you begin with some small experiments, I just have a couple of comments about the structure of the example. You'll see before you a functional worksheet, split into three parts. Although it in no way satisfies the expectations of the rS1.Method already discussed in the introductory chapter, it can nevertheless already present some of its basic principles. From the bottom up:

- Measurements are stored in the E16:021 source data range, which were collected on 10 different days and five different measuring points (*TPM-A* to *TPM-E*). Day-specific averages are calculated in the last and sixth lines of this range. It doesn't matter what type of values these are for the time being; assume, for example, that they might be outdoor temperatures in degree Celsius.

- The higher-level E13:014 range contains the chart basis. It only takes over one of the data times of the source data range in each case. You decide which one by entering a number between one and six in the C14 cell highlighted in yellow with the *rD1.DataSel* range name. The formulas in the chart basis ensure that the required line appears to-gether with the correct legend label in the chart, in accordance with the details in the C14 cell (explanations about this are provided in the next chapter).

But now, in relation to Figure 1-32, we'll move on to the set of commands of the three *Chart Tools* tabs. The requirement for all descriptions is that a chart is the active, that is, currently selected, object:

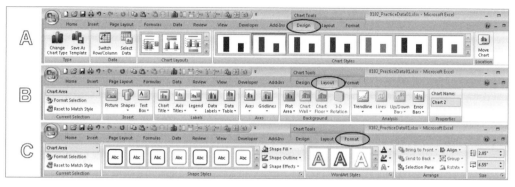

FIGURE 1-32 A vast number of options—there's quite a lot to learn and observe there

- **A—*Design* tab:**

  - You can use the command buttons in the *Type* group to select a different *chart type* than the one currently available, or save the properties of a completely formatted and filled chart as a template for later uses of the same kind.

  - In the *Data* group, you optionally switch back and forth between rows and columns when navigating the chart data reference. You use the *Select Data* button to open the *Select Data Source* dialog box that was already introduced in Figure 1-25 and where you can edit chart element references.

  - The *Chart Layouts* group provides different, complex design suggestions that you could use on your chart with a mouse click.

  - The *Chart Styles* group offers a comprehensive range of design suggestions for the *data series*. You can assign this formatting with just one click.

  - The *Move Chart* command button enables you to position the chart in a separate chart worksheet (something I only expressly recommend in a few exceptional cases) or move it as an integrated chart to another worksheet of the active workbook.

- **B—*Layout* tab:**

  - In the *Current Selection* group, you can open a list where the elements of the currently selected chart are listed and can be selected (see also Figure 1-33, Section A). There is also a command available there that you can use to open the formatting dialog box for the previously selected element. The third command in the group enables you to remove custom formatting and return to the default Excel formatting.

  - The three command buttons in the *Insert* group enable you to add different graphical objects to the chart. In this book, you'll see that using these commands will accommodate a broad range of designs.

❑ With the resources of the *Labels* group, you have different types of access to those elements that were already introduced further above under the *Labels* sub-heading, namely, *chart title, axis title, legend, data labels,* and *data table.*

❑ You use the commands in the *Axes* group to set the basic settings for axes and gridlines.

❑ The *command buttons* in the *Background* group affect the plot area and, if they exist, the elements of 3D charts.

❑ The *Analysis* group supports you when you want to work with *trendlines, drop lines, high-low lines, up/down bars,* and *error bars.*

❑ Finally, you can use the *Properties* command to name the chart. This is generally only interesting if you want to access the chart within programming.

■ **C—*Format* tab:**

❑ The *Current Selection* group that I already described above in relation to the *Layout* tab is also available on the very left.

❑ The *Shape Styles* group commands enable you to select numerous options including outlines, fills, coloring, and effects. First select a specific chart element and then point with the mouse to the different selection options to see, in the preview, what the formatting of the chart or current element would look like after you actually set it.

❑ The specifications in the *WordArt Styles* group enable you to apply the complex WordArt design options to texts and labels of every type within your chart.

❑ You can use the command options in the *Arrange* group in an interesting way if there are other graphical objects beside the chart in your worksheet. This will often be relevant for the examples presented in this book. You can group or layer the objects and, in a task pane (which opens on the right-hand corner of the screen after you select the *Selection Pane* command) specify which of the objects listed there are to be selected or removed from the view.

❑ In the *Size* group, you can determine the chart's dimensions using metric specifications. When you click the *Launcher* on the lower right in this group, the assigned *Size and Properties* dialog box (which is probably already missed by experienced users) opens and includes the commands of its *Properties* tab. These commands are very often important for making a chart's development work much easier.

Calling Formatting Dialog Boxes

Even if you appreciate all the new improvements and interesting automatic features in Excel 2007, those of you who want to develop and design professional-looking visualizations that comply with your individual requirements will have to go even further than the specifications in the previously described tabs (*Chart Tools*) allow you to go. As the range of "servic-es" continues to grow, you should be able to handle the specific formatting dialog boxes of the program. A repair or "fine-tuning" would simply not succeed with automatic templates to be used if there are many tasks. In the following chapters of the book, I'll discuss in detail the consequences of this, both generally and specifically. Initially, the goal is to develop a func-tion that you can use, or in line with the method you're used to using, to access these dialog boxes as easily as possible.

The dialog boxes for formatting chart elements have been completely revised. This not only applies to their appearance, but also to enhanced design options unknown by you up to now. In other words, everything that can be assigned automatically or semi-automatically using the *Chart Tools* (that is, the *Design, Layout,* and *Format* tabs) described in the previous section can also be created in each of its parts and in each facet through user actions. Consequently, there's huge potential here for individual design and a need to deal with all new features and unfa-miliar functions. As a precautionary note, I should mention that this will require considerable effort to learn and you can also expect to feel frustrated occasionally. But don't let yourself be too impressed by the abundance of what's being offered, and please don't apply the brakes. It's all about making discoveries, so explore what the 2007 version has to offer. If impressively designed, dynamic figures presentations are important for you, then this is *the* program for you (and where you're currently reading about it, *the* book for you).

So, how do you access the formatting dialog boxes that are so important? There are several options available, and it's very likely that you'll like one of them so much that it'll become your standard procedure.

Access Using the Ribbon Tabs

You've surely already discovered, when checking out the *Chart Tools,* that the *More Options for* … command appears at the end of quite a few menus. You can select this command to open the specifically-assigned formatting dialog box.

I've also already discussed the command combination available in the *Layout* and *Format* tabs of the *Chart Tools.* Once again, as shown in Figure 1-33, Section A, in the *Selection* group, use the *Chart Area* command to open a list and click the element there that you want to edit. The element is selected. Then, use the *Format Selection* command to open the rel-evant formatting dialog box.

> **Tip** You can also use the *Chart Area* command specifically to select elements that exist in the chart, but that are formatted invisibly. You'll also receive help here if you specifically have to select elements that are very close together and therefore can't be selected using the mouse pointer or can only be selected with great difficulty. This might occur when, for convenience sake, you initially include a large number of data series in the chart when you generate the object, then immediately delete quite a few of them again because they're not necessary for the display you want.

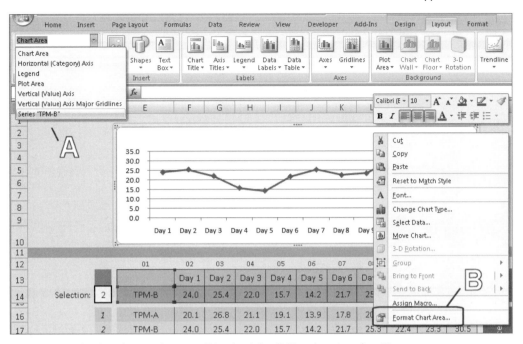

FIGURE 1-33 Selecting elements by menu (A) or by right-clicking the mouse key (B)

Access Using the Context Menu

In Figure 1-33, letter B, when you right-click a chart element, a context menu appears whose lowest entry in each case opens the way to the formatting dialog box.

> **Note** I think it's a little more difficult in Office 2007 to click small chart elements with the mouse than it was in previous versions. If this remains the general impression, it would be a minor drawback for users preferring mouse operations.

Access Using Keys

In the context of Figure 1-34, you have already selected an arbitrary chart element using an arbitrary method. You can now use the **top arrow** or **bottom arrow** keys to "scroll" to the next respective element to select it. If the selected element has subelements like *data series* with *data points*, *legends* with several *legend entries*, and so on, you can also use the **left arrow** or **right arrow** keys to switch between these subelements.

However, if you've now selected an element, open its formatting dialog box using the **Ctrl+1** shortcut.

> **Note** The **Ctrl+1** shortcut applies universally for all access to objects with the objective of formatting.

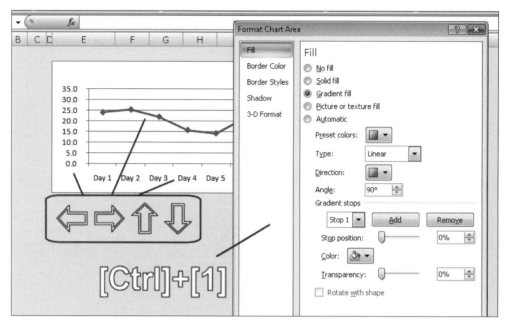

FIGURE 1-34 Changing selections using arrow keys and opening dialog boxes using shortcuts

> **Tip** You can also use the arrow keys specifically to select elements that exist in the chart, but are formatted invisibly.

I've saved the best till last, as is only right. Whichever method you'll ultimately use to select an element and open a formatting dialog box, an extremely nice improvement will be available: You'll no longer need to close the dialog box after you complete a formatting task. Instead, you'll immediately be able to select and edit the next chart element because the dialog box will adjust its content accordingly. This is truly a blessing for those of you who love compact operations, what I refer to as "formatting your way through a chart."

And it gets even a little better: Despite such a fluid "run," Excel 2007 treats each formatting specification as an individual operation, which enables you to use the *Undo* function to partially reverse any of your decisions, selected individually.

Chapter 2
New Approaches—Getting Started

Now that we've covered the most important basic principles of using Excel 2007 in Chapter 1, we can start to get our hands dirty. However, we'll continue to work with an example for the time being, in order to clarify rules and lay a solid foundation for future work.

I'll start by describing the working and structural model that provides a basis for many of the examples in this book. Next, I'll explain the key formulas that play dynamic roles in such models, and which are of particular importance in this book. I'll then introduce an example based on these, which I'll first outline and then guide you through with step-by-step instructions that will let you reproduce it for yourself. You'll get the most of out this book if you adopt this hands-on approach from the start because the structure and design of this model are used again and again in many other solutions presented later on.

See, do, understand, and transfer the knowledge: This is the path to successful, independent learning, and you can get started on that path right now. However, it you're not quite ready, you can skip all but the first two sections of this chapter, and return to it again once you've read some more theoretical information in Chapters 3 through 6.

Charts Are Presentation Objects

The structure, design, and intuitiveness of almost all the examples used in this book are intended to meet two rigorous demands and unite them in an integrated fashion. These are: first, suitability for your own objectives (what do I want to achieve?) and, second, suitability for the existing or future requirements of your target audience (what do they want to see and experience, or what do you want them to see and experience?). Visualizations fall into one of the following two main categories, depending on how much they are tailored to suit the target audience: *charts for presentation* and *charts for publication*.

A chart for presentation, or **presentation chart**, is selected and designed according to the known or expected needs of a certain audience. We can distinguish between the following types of presentation format:

- A *live* presentation is held before a live audience, which views the chart on a monitor or projector screen. The speaker explains and, if necessary, supplements the information presented on the chart in a manner appropriate to the audience. The chart is usually dynamic (i.e., can be changed with a mouse click), and usually has a sophisticated graphical design.

- With an *anonymous* presentation, on the other hand, there's no direct contact between the presenter and the public. The chart must stand on its own merits, and can't rely on help from a speaker to enhance its effect. As a result, its design must fulfill more rigorous requirements. In this case, the presentation medium plays a key role in addition to the content. Media used for anonymous presentations include visual display units at trade fairs and similar events, and the Internet.

At this point, I'd like to clear up an unfortunately very popular misconception that has brought many unhappy memories to many equally unhappy presenters (and their audiences). Never forget:

Countless experiments have shown that an audience attending a presentation wants:

- to be impressed
- to be entertained
- to be stimulated
- and to be informed

...in that order! In other words, don't allow yourself to be fooled into thinking that the information value of your data and charts alone is enough to ensure a successful presentation, or even that it should play an important part in determining the design.

The term **chart for publication** is predominantly used here to refer to charts that are printed in a predefined format or in a format of your own choosing, for a non-specific readership or a readership defined by the type of publication, which is usually a limited readership. This audience frequently possesses in-depth specialized subject knowledge. The printing process and print medium also play key roles in the selection and design process. This type of chart often appears in scientific publications of all kinds. These, too, must be "presentable" enough that readers will see what the author wants them to see or wants to illustrate. It's usually easier to develop and complete this type of chart than to create a chart for a live presentation.

Almost all of the solutions provided in this book, be they simple, basic models or complex, dynamic chart models, are therefore aimed either directly or indirectly at an audience, and should be tailored to the requirements of that audience. Much more is involved here than if you were simply visually presenting information for your own purposes on your own workstation. Analyzing your own data using your own methods for your own use naturally requires much less time and effort. You can employ strategies and techniques that would be inappropriate in a live presentation, or that would be unacceptable were you to hand over your solution to another person, whose expertise as a user is almost certainly unknown to you. Therefore, tools such as *PivotTable reports* and *PivotChart reports*, which are extremely useful when used for your own information and to prepare presentations, only play a minor role in this book.

Excel allows you to create static charts that are simple yet effective and elegant, and which produce impressive and very flexible results. Some of these can be described as "multivariable." You'll be introduced to examples of these and have a chance to create your own in later chapters. However, once you hand over your solution (for example, to a presenter or customer), all of this potential is routed through a very narrow channel. You can never assume that a user, whose expertise is unknown to you or whom you are unable to directly assist in using your solution, will be capable of using techniques beyond the simple click of a mouse or the touch of a button. This statement doesn't betray any prejudice towards Excel novices on my part. On the contrary, I simply want to underline the basic rule of incorporating intuitiveness into all dynamic solutions, to ensure that they are as simple and reliable as possible. Users should never be able to use a command incorrectly and generate a screen view or data combination that they don't understand and don't want to see, and then be unable to undo this step on their own. This chapter highlights the fact that the "simplest" solution, which is usually also the most effective, is often the most difficult to develop.

The Basic Model

 On the Companion CD In order to better understand the key concepts in this chapter, you should have referred to the rS1.Method information on the CD-ROM, as recommended in the Introduction. Do this now if you haven't done so already, and read the relevant document, which you'll find under *Materials\rS1_Method_2007.pdf*.

In the following discussion, we'll formulate requirements that can't be met by any conventional, static chart solution. In later chapters, you'll come across many examples that don't have this kind of multiform structure, and which you can use to fulfill your target-oriented objectives without having to think much about methodology. Even in my own customer solutions, I only use my rS1.Method fully and with all of its implications in order to solve particularly challenging problems or to create models that customers can then refine according to their own requirements and take ownership of. In such cases, the inner workings of the models must remain clear and comprehensible after months or even years.

So, why then am I already introducing you to a structural model that isn't essential for relatively simple visualization purposes? Because I want to make the point from the outset that planning your approach and sticking to the rules won't automatically guarantee success, but it will make your job much easier or at least more manageable. Once you accept this principle and begin to put it into practice, you may soon find that major problems with Excel— uncontrolled growth being chief among them—become minor ones, while existing minor problems may even disappear. So, I'll start with quite a tough challenge and hope, with good reason, that going "one size smaller" will come naturally to you later on.

Structures of the Excel Workbook

Before we start, you need to understand the structural model that is used throughout this book to provide a theoretical and practical basis for your work. You are going to approach the task of preparing a presentation chart solution (of any type) from two different directions: Thinking from finish to start, and doing from start to finish. To explain what I mean by this, we'll break the process down into five steps from A to E, which are shown in Figure 2-1.

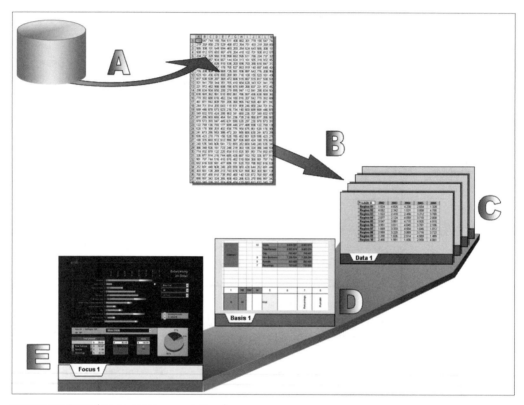

FIGURE 2-1 From data source to presentation focus

According to the rS1.Method, the development of a presentation solution can be simplified by breaking it down into a five-step model. In the beginning, it doesn't matter whether all of the steps are required for each and every solution or whether additional steps are required to handle more complex requirements.

The steps outlined below are to be viewed as workflows. They may be completed with just a few smooth, swift strokes, or may involve complex processes comprising many steps.

Note This book doesn't include any recommendations or instructions relating to the transfer or copying of data from source systems into Excel. Many different tasks, options, and processes are involved in doing so, and these can be organized in many different ways. As a result, I would be very unlikely to come anywhere close to providing sufficient information to satisfy all readers (i.e., users of all conceivable types and combinations of systems). This discussion will therefore be limited to the organization and handling of data that is already *in* Excel, regardless of its origin. Based on a considerable amount of personal experience, I assume that any system that stores or manages data in any form is capable of transferring all or part of this data to Excel, or of making it available (i.e., accessible) to Excel. This doesn't have to involve a download or a query. ASCII, CSV, or similar file formats still have their uses today.

Of course, you'll still hear some system providers claim that this isn't the case, at least when it comes to promoting their system. They may well have their reasons for saying so, and it's not my place to dispute those here, but I can tell you that this simply don't apply in the case of Excel.

Step A The required data is located in a source system of any kind. In a large corporation, this could be an SAP system, for example. In a small or medium-sized enterprise, it could be a data warehouse, industry-specific database, or Microsoft Access. A process-support software application (such as Microsoft Project) is yet another potential data source. In any case, the system contains data (of any kind) that can be transferred to Excel. A query, download, or other form of transfer results in a more or less bulky Excel table, which serves as *master data*, and will be referred to as such here.

In a scientific context, *master data* refers to an initial version of data that has been collected or measured. It's complete but not sorted into any specific order. For example, if you conduct a survey (Excel is an excellent tool for designing and evaluating questionnaires), the result will be a collection of all answers, usually in the order in which they were entered. This is your master data.

In the next step, you transform your initial master data (*Master data A*) into a structured set (*Master data B*). In doing so, you impose a specific order on it. For example, the results of your survey may be grouped together and indexed by region, based on the ages of the respondents, listed alphanumerically, etc. The result is an organized set of master data. An intentional structuring for the purpose of analysis is already at work here.

In subsequent steps, the master data is checked, supplemented if necessary, and then organized, (for example, according to frequency), and divided into *classes*. The results, in turn, provide a basis for a graphical representation and are then processed in additional evaluation and presentation formats.

These procedures are very similar to the methods described in this book.

Step B   In many cases, the collection of data resulting from step A has a number of deficiencies as a data source for a chart or the basis for a presentation:

- It often contains much more data that is needed.

- It often does not contain all of the data needed.

- It often contains data in a form that can't be used directly.

The available data that can be used is transferred selectively and in an ordered manner into an Excel workbook. This is done using formulas or, if there's no alternative, by copying and pasting.

Step C   The transferred data is formatted as required for the purpose of visualization. This produces the model's "data sheets." In almost all cases, these are the data sources that can be directly used to create a chart or chart presentation.

> **Note** It's a myth perpetuated by many tool providers that it's possible or even easy to generate sufficiently versatile presentations that can be designed to suit the requirements of your audience from a source system (step A) directly and without any detours. This myth is dispelled indirectly in this book.

Step C usually comprises several different sub-steps:

- The data is defined in several worksheets with identical structures. Depending on your purpose, a single worksheet may also suffice.

- The data is cleansed as necessary (adjusted, corrected, and completed). This may be a quick process or a laborious task. You can expect the latter if, for example, forecasts are required and you have clearly structured actual data but no equivalent planning data, or if complex aggregation is required, which occurs frequently in practice.

- The data is calculated and indexed as required. The parameters used for this purpose depend on the nature and objective of the task in hand, and aren't generally taken from the source system.

Step D   The data sheets created in step C provide a chart basis. Creating this basis is usually the most creative but also the most challenging step. This basis consists largely (or sometimes even wholly) of formulas that compile the chart data. In a dynamic model, these formulas must also respond when a user (presenter) clicks the mouse in *focus* (see step E) using controls. These formulas produce user-defined configurations of the data from the data sheets (i.e. from step C). These comprise:

- Subsets of data and/or

- Results of calculations based on subsets and/or

- Structural transformations of data subsets (e.g. automatic sorting)

Note The term "subset" is used here because it almost never happens that all data on the data sheets is shown at once in a chart.

Step E   What is referred to as the *focus* (one or more worksheets) is a model's façade, and in the final version this is often all that is still visible of the workbook. In other words, it's what is ultimately displayed. To ensure a target-oriented design, you must carefully consider the preparation of this vital yet essentially passive element; passive in that it only displays what was generated in its basis. The greatest challenge to be met in this regard is to remove the obvious while adding the meaningful; i.e., mastering the art of simplicity.

Conceptualizing from E to A—Implementing from A to E

Earlier, I recommended approaching the solution from two opposing directions. Exactly what is meant by this is illustrated in Figure 2-2:

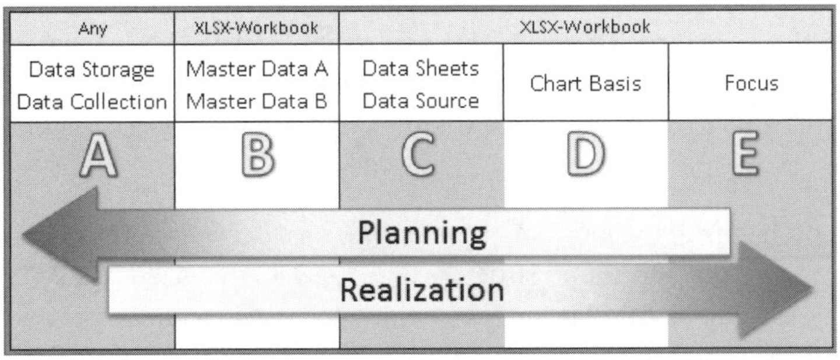

Any	XLSX-Workbook	XLSX-Workbook		
Data Storage Data Collection	Master Data A Master Data B	Data Sheets Data Source	Chart Basis	Focus
A	B	C	D	E

Planning
Realization

FIGURE 2-2 Working towards a solution from two directions within your model

To *conceptualize* your model, you must start with your objective and work backwards; i.e., proceed from step E to step A. Ask yourself the following questions as you do so:

1. Focus—what do I want to present?

2. Chart basis—which tools and methods can I use?

3. How do I need to organize and structure my data source(s) so that these methods can be applied? Which data is required and in what format?

4. How can I bring the required data together, if necessary, in the form of master data?

5. Is the data stored in a source system and how can I transfer it to master data?

To *implement* the model, you must proceed from step A and work towards step E. Specifically, you can plot the individual steps along this path as follows:

1. You obtain or receive data from a source system.

2. If necessary, you use this data to compile your master data. This takes the form of an Excel workbook or, as in many real-life scenarios, a pivot table.

3. You transfer all or part of the data, manually or using formulas, into worksheets in another Excel workbook, where it's given an organizational structure and revised and supplemented if necessary. The result is a presentation-specific data source.

4. You make variable use of this data source to create a chart basis (which can be controlled with controls if necessary).

5. You display the data from the chart basis in the focus of the model.

However, the process is rarely as simple as this in practice. Up to this point, I've tended to focus on straightforward variants. In reality, all manner of problems may occur along the way, and you may need to make detours, loops, or even deliberate steps backward.

Problems and Their Solutions

The structure model shown in Figure 2-1 represents an ideal. In many cases, it simply can't be implemented in this pure form. Often, this is because the primary data source (source systems) can't provide the data in the form needed to create a complex, versatile presentation. This is only rarely due to a weakness in the software. In most cases, a structural or task-specific problem or an organizational deficiency is at play.

So far, so bad! But problems of the kind listed earlier may also occur in data-processing systems that have an efficient and sound structure and are well organized. The following problems are frequently encountered by anyone hoping to create multi-variable or scenario-specific charts when checking the data in the source systems:

- Much more data exists than you require, or the data is differentiated to a much greater degree than you need.

- Not all of the data required is available. Or, the data is available but in various locations, in various versions and forms, and at different times (intervals).

- The data exists in a form that can't be used directly. It requires modification.

The reality is, as ever, more complicated than the theory.

Step A: You may need to look for the data in several source systems. Possible reasons for this include the following:

- Planning data is organized and stored in a different manner than actual data.

- Similar calculation parameters (such as HR statistics relating to budgetary data) need to be grouped together for organizational purposes.

- To calculate a forecast or to create a long-term key-figure report, you require combinations of data that is currently operational and older data that has already been archived.

In this case, you may create two or more sets of master data from various sources. But that's not always enough. Some of the primary source data may need to be edited or supplemented manually. Possible reasons for this include the following:

- Planning data does not exist or is incomplete. Or, it does exist but its degree of aggregation differs from the actual data.

- The actual data you require isn't available at the specific time you need to report on it.

- The data required isn't available in a database that can be queried because it hasn't been managed and maintained in this way, or because of (actual or alleged) technical problems.

- The data you require is stored in various locations in different Excel lists or Word tables or, even worse, is only available in hard copy (printed lists), or, worst of all, isn't available at all because it has been promised but hasn't been calculated or supplied.

- Calculation parameters of all kinds aren't available in the system (more about this later) and can't be made available.

You're therefore confronted with the task of manually editing the master data or source data in the presentation file (i.e., the worksheets in step C). In no way should you consider yourself to be at an automatic disadvantage or view this as an organizational deficiency. In many cases, the exact opposite is true. Here are two examples that illustrate this point:

- Many top-quality Excel presentations are as impressive as they are because they're tailored exactly to the needs and expectations of a specific target group or decision maker: a management team, a bank, etc. These presentations very often make use of supplementary data, control parameters, and scenario-specific specifications, none of which *can* be contained in a source system because they belong to the individual configuration of this one, key presentation and are developed and used exclusively for this purpose.

- In many instances, it isn't useful, appropriate, or even possible to use the master data in a presentation directly. Consider, for example, a typical scenario in which the results of data collection or of a survey are to be presented in a presentation chart. In this case, all kinds of groupings, aggregations, refinements, and calculations are required before the data collected can be "showcased" to ensure that the results can be even be represented or understood.

So don't worry if your source data appears to be lacking or insufficient in certain respects. Excel is such a powerful program that allows you to create such impressive, aesthetically pleasing, and effective charts and presentations that it's definitely worth the effort of having to iron out some difficulties in the preparation phase. You may not encounter these difficulties at all in your scenario, as they often don't arise. In other words, everything may run like clockwork and your path from step A to step E may be smooth, straight, and wonderfully simple.

Digression: Important Functions and Formulas

In the previous section, I referred to the fact that the formation of a chart basis—i.e., the route taken by the data in steps C through D—is usually organized using formulas. These create a definable *extract* of the data sources, which can be modified using controls. I therefore will refer to some of the relevant functions, which are called *lookup and reference functions* in Excel, as *extracting* functions. We'll be using the three most important of these soon, so I'll briefly digress in order to explain this subject. Other functions from the same group will come into play in later chapters.

On the Companion CD Open the *\Samples\0201_Extract.xlsx* file on the CD-ROM.

The *0201_Extract.xlsx* file contains the structure model described above in condensed form. Elements A and B aren't included, while elements C, D, and E are summarized on a single worksheet. Note the following points with reference to Figure 2-3:

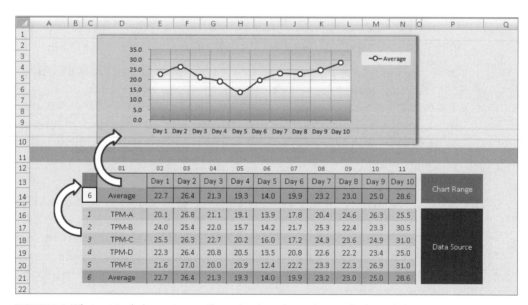

FIGURE 2-3 What *not* to do in most cases: three structure elements on a single worksheet

1. The source data (which you'll recognize from Chapter 1) is in cells D16:N21, and it simulates structure element *C* described in the last section, which would normally have one or more worksheets of its own.

2. Extracting formulas (the subject we'll get to next) are used to create a chart basis from this source data, which is represented here by structure element *D* in cells D13:N14.

3. The chart basis is, in turn, the basis for the chart, shown here in rows 1:10, which represent structure element *E*.

The file has three worksheets of the same type. However, the creation of the chart basis is organized differently on each of these. The chart is dynamic. In other words, it can show any of the six data series from the data source as the user wishes. I'll now explain exactly how this is done.

The INDEX Function

Open the *Function 1 INDEX* worksheet in the sample file. As you know from Chapter 1, entering a number between *1* and *6* in cell C14 inserts corresponding source data series inserted into the chart basis and incorporates them into the chart.

> **Note** on the terminology used in this book: An Excel *function* is an instruction to the program to perform a calculation. All functions comprise the function name, followed by *arguments* in parentheses, each with a separating comma. *Syntax* refers to the correct format and sequence of the function name and the corresponding arguments.
>
> If you want to insert the complete syntax of a formula into the formula bar (you'll see later what a convenient and efficient way this is to develop formulas), press after typing the function name and the opening parenthesis the shortcut **Ctrl+Shift+A**.
>
> In this book, the term *formula* refers to a function with arguments that have assigned references or variables, and which is therefore capable of executing an arithmetic operation and returning its result.

The INDEX function has two different syntax variants, but we'll only use the first of these in this book: =INDEX(array,row_num,column_num). This calculates a value from a defined array (from a two-dimensional cell range). The value to be calculated is located within the array by specifying the row_num and column_num.

The formula =INDEX($D$16:$N$21,$C$14,E$12) in cell E14 (which serves as an example for all formulas in cell range D14:N14, shown in green) acts as an instruction to Excel to do the following: "Find a certain value in the array in cell range $D$16:$N$21." The relevant value is in the row of the array whose position is defined in cell $C$14, and in the column whose position is defined by the value in cell E$12. In the example shown here (Figure 2-4), the value in cell E21 is read. This is the sixth row in the second column of the array in cell range $D$16:$N$21.

| E14 | | | | f_x | =INDEX($D$16:$N$21,$C$14,E$12) | | | | | | | | |

	A	B	C	D	E	F	G	H	I	J	K	L	M	N
11				=INDEX(array,row_num,column_num)										
12					01	02	03	04	05	06	07	08	09	10	11
13					Day 1	Day 2	Day 3	Day 4	Day 5	Day 6	Day 7	Day 8	Day 9	Day 10
14			6	Average	22.7	26.4	21.3	19.3	14.0	19.9	23.2	23.0	25.0	28.6
16			1	TPM-A	20.1	26.8	21.1	19.1	13.9	17.8	20.4	24.6	26.3	25.5
17			2	TPM-B	24.0	25.4	22.0	15.7	14.2	21.7	25.3	22.4	23.3	30.5
18			3	TPM-C	25.5	26.3	22.7	20.2	16.0	17.2	24.3	23.6	24.9	31.0
19			4	TPM-D	22.3	26.4	20.8	20.5	13.5	20.8	22.6	22.2	23.4	25.0
20			5	TPM-E	21.6	27.0	20.0	20.9	12.4	22.2	23.3	22.3	26.9	31.0
21			6	Average	22.7	26.4	21.3	19.3	14.0	19.9	23.2	23.0	25.0	28.6

FIGURE 2-4 The *INDEX* function requires details of the array, row, and column.

The INDEX function is always particularly useful if the array is known and is constant; in other words, if the location of the values to be determined isn't constantly changing.

The VLOOKUP Function

Open the *Function 2 VLOOKUP* worksheet in the sample file.

The =VLOOKUP(lookup_value,table_array,col_index_num,range_lookup) function searches for the lookup_value in the column on the extreme left in the table_array. Based on where (i.e. in which row) it finds this value, it then determines the column of the array specified by the col_index_num, and returns the value it finds there.

The range_lookup argument is the logical value TRUE or FALSE, which determines whether VLOOKUP is to search for an exact or approximate match for the lookup_value. The *V* in VLOOKUP stands for *vertical* (in reference to the vertical processing of the first column in the array).

Important I almost always use the logical value FALSE for range_lookup. This has the following two benefits:

❑ It means that only *exact* matches for lookup_value are found, which is exactly what we want to happen. This means that the formula is only used if the first column of the table_array (i.e., the column that is searched) contains bijective matches, such as account numbers, HR numbers, or customer numbers. If the search item isn't found, the corresponding formula returns the error value #N/A. As you'll see later, this is actually the result you want in certain use cases; for example, if the target range is expected to contain data that does not (yet) exist in the source range.

❑ In this case, the range to be searched does *not* need to be sorted alphanumerically. Note, however, that this range *must* always be the first column in the table_array.

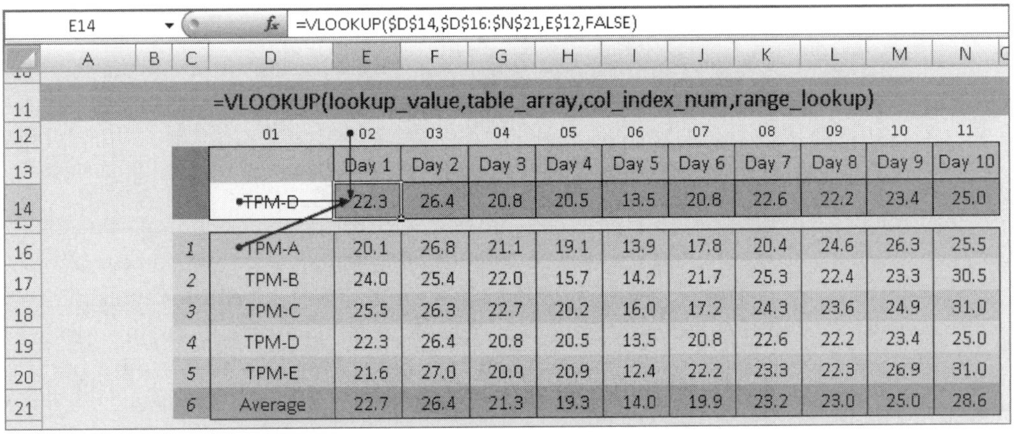

E14				*fx*	=VLOOKUP($D$14,$D$16:$N$21,E$12,FALSE)								
	A	B	C	D	E	F	G	H	I	J	K	L	M	N

			=VLOOKUP(lookup_value,table_array,col_index_num,range_lookup)										
11														
12				01	02	03	04	05	06	07	08	09	10	11
13					Day 1	Day 2	Day 3	Day 4	Day 5	Day 6	Day 7	Day 8	Day 9	Day 10
14				TPM-D	22.3	26.4	20.8	20.5	13.5	20.8	22.6	22.2	23.4	25.0
16		1		TPM-A	20.1	26.8	21.1	19.1	13.9	17.8	20.4	24.6	26.3	25.5
17		2		TPM-B	24.0	25.4	22.0	15.7	14.2	21.7	25.3	22.4	23.3	30.5
18		3		TPM-C	25.5	26.3	22.7	20.2	16.0	17.2	24.3	23.6	24.9	31.0
19		4		TPM-D	22.3	26.4	20.8	20.5	13.5	20.8	22.6	22.2	23.4	25.0
20		5		TPM-E	21.6	27.0	20.0	20.9	12.4	22.2	23.3	22.3	26.9	31.0
21		6		Average	22.7	26.4	21.3	19.3	14.0	19.9	23.2	23.0	25.0	28.6

FIGURE 2-5 The *VLOOKUP* function uses a search criterion.

In the *Function 2 VLOOKUP* worksheet, you can enter a search criterion (the lookup_value; in this case, a text string) in cell D14, which has a yellow background. This search criterion must be found in the D16:D21 source data range.

Cell E14 contains the formula =VLOOKUP($D$14,$D$16:$N$21,E$12,FALSE), which serves as an example for all formulas in the green cell range E14:N14 . The instruction to Excel is therefore as follows: "Find the the lookup_value defined in cell D14 in the first column of the array located in cell range $D$16:$N$21. This will determine the correct row in the array. Then find the column in the array whose position is defined by the value entered in cell E$12." In the example shown here (Figure 2-5), the value in cell E19 is read as a result. This is the point at which the row that has the entry *TPM-D* in the first column in the array intersects with the second column in the array.

The VLOOKUP function is always particularly useful if the array is known, but the values to be determined are always located in different row positions (for example, if arrays are sorted randomly).

Note The VLOOKUP function has an equivalent function with a similar syntax. This is the HLOOKUP function, in which the *H* stands for *horizontal*. Rather than searching for the search criterion in the first column in an array, it searches the first row, and uses a col_index_num rather than a row_index_num.

The OFFSET Function

Open the *Function 3 OFFSET* worksheet in the sample file.

I consider the OFFSET function to be the *star performer* among the extracting functions. It returns a reference to a range that is offset a certain distance from an initial starting point.

The OFFSET(reference,rows,cols,height,width) function returns a value (cell content), which is offset from the specified reference argument by a certain number of rows and columns. The reference argument thus defines the starting point for accessing another cell or cell range. From a single cell, you can therefore access any other cell in any other direction, as well as cell ranges of any height (=number of rows) and width (=number of columns) with this function. In other words, you can create arrays from the formula itself! You therefore have a very user-friendly option at your disposal for completing very difficult tasks based on very simple structures. This will be illustrated later on.

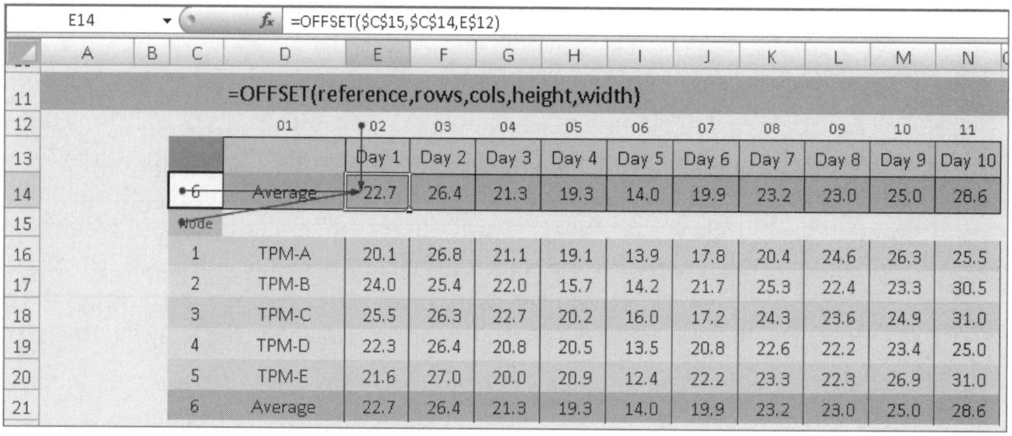

	E14			*fx*	=OFFSET($C$15,$C$14,E$12)									
	A	B	C	D	E	F	G	H	I	J	K	L	M	N
11				=OFFSET(reference,rows,cols,height,width)										
12				01	02	03	04	05	06	07	08	09	10	11
13					Day 1	Day 2	Day 3	Day 4	Day 5	Day 6	Day 7	Day 8	Day 9	Day 10
14			6	Average	22.7	26.4	21.3	19.3	14.0	19.9	23.2	23.0	25.0	28.6
15			Node											
16			1	TPM-A	20.1	26.8	21.1	19.1	13.9	17.8	20.4	24.6	26.3	25.5
17			2	TPM-B	24.0	25.4	22.0	15.7	14.2	21.7	25.3	22.4	23.3	30.5
18			3	TPM-C	25.5	26.3	22.7	20.2	16.0	17.2	24.3	23.6	24.9	31.0
19			4	TPM-D	22.3	26.4	20.8	20.5	13.5	20.8	22.6	22.2	23.4	25.0
20			5	TPM-E	21.6	27.0	20.0	20.9	12.4	22.2	23.3	22.3	26.9	31.0
21			6	Average	22.7	26.4	21.3	19.3	14.0	19.9	23.2	23.0	25.0	28.6

FIGURE 2-6 The *OFFSET* function is very versatile.

On the *Function 3 OFFSET* worksheet, you can enter a value between *1* and *6* in cell C14, which has a yellow background. When you do so, the corresponding source data series is inserted into the chart basis and incorporated into the chart itself.

Cell E14 contains the formula =OFFSET($C$15,$C$14,E$12) (which serves as an example for all formulas in cell range D14:N14, shown with a green background). Here, you use just three of the five possible arguments in this formula. The arguments width and height are optional, and aren't required here. The formula serves as an instruction to Excel to do the following: "Find a certain value based on cell C15. Starting at cell C15, go down the number of rows specified in cell C14 (which you entered) and across the number of columns (to the right) defined in cell E12." In the example shown here (Figure 2-6), cell E21 is read, which is six rows down and two rows to the right of C15.

Note As stated above, this formula can create an offset in any direction you wish. For example, if you want to climb upwards from `reference`, you must enter the row argument with a minus sign. If you want to access rows to the left of your reference, you must enter the column argument with a minus sign.

In the sample file and in the figure above, you'll notice that cell C15 (the reference cell for our formula) is assigned the text *Node*. This refers to a very important convention from the rS1. Method. In many cases, the *node* (which will be called *rD1.Node*, *rD3.Node02*, or *rP2.Node*, etc. according to the method's naming conventions) is the starting point or reference point for all access to a source data worksheet for the purpose of extraction and/or calculation. Very often in my solutions, I only need to define this single reference point for each source data sheet in order to obtain complex and variable results.

The OFFSET function is particularly useful if you don't want to use a defined array or are unable to do so. You can therefore use the function independently of the actual current size of the range to be queried.

Suggestions for Improvement

The formulas demonstrated in the three examples above have a number of deficiencies that make using them problematic, although not completely unsuitable, for our purpose of creating an elegant presentation. They are particularly problematic if their capabilities aren't deployed on a single worksheet, but instead must work in a system that requires diverse and changing access options to a range of sources within a workbook, as is very often the case with presentation models. In short, these formulas must become much easier to read and interpret. This is very simple to achieve if you use range names in these formulas instead of cell references wherever possible; ideally range names that obey defined rules and therefore very quickly lend a "meaningful" character to the solution from the point of view of the user or designer. You'll find several examples of this in the sample model introduced further on.

Naturally, the source data, chart basis, and chart are only combined on a single worksheet in this example in order to provide a sufficiently panoramic view for my explanation of the three key functions. In a "real-life" model, it would be unlikely for everything to be combined on one sheet like this. According to the rules of the methods applied in this book, the source data ranges must at a minimum be kept on separate worksheets to the presentation of results.

Model Structures—A Practical Example

In this section, we'll bring together the explanations provided in this chapter and explore them more deeply. The focus here is on structural components and the use of specific formulas. First, though, I'll provide some background information and some pointers on using the sample file.

On the Companion CD Open the *0203_Analysis_01.xlsx* file on the CD ROM.

The similarly named file *0202_Analysis_00.xlsx* is provided for the exercises described later and largely consists of master data and source data.

Scenario

A large retail business with 100 branches has historically experienced problems with sales over the summer months, partly due to the product range, but also to a drop in customer numbers during the vacation season. The company therefore launched a five-week promotional campaign to attract more customers into its branches and compensate for the expected usual dip in sales. The campaign was intended as an initial test run. The success of the campaign was therefore scrutinized in detail. Specifically, analysis focused on whether the branches did actually win more customers and whether this contributed to a significant jump in sales.

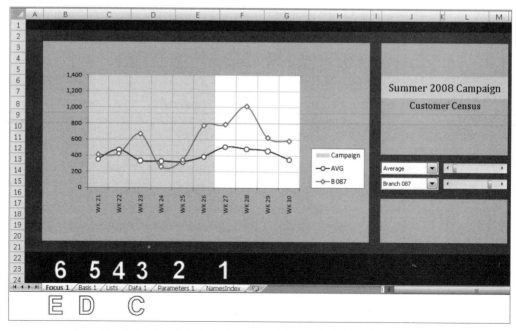

FIGURE 2-7 This workbook structure is typical of many models used in this book.

The Excel solution presented here focuses exclusively on the aspect of customer numbers; i.e., it shows the results of a customer census taken on 10 consecutive Saturdays in May, June, and July in all 100 branches within a specified time period. Since there are known to be clear differences in the levels of customer acceptance at the company's various branches, the company wanted to be able to compare each branch with all of the others, as well as to examine the average results for all branches. This can be done using a "focus," whereby controls allow you to display the results of each individual branch, as well as the maximum, minimum, and average values for all branches.

The first six columns (light green background) in the chart show the key figures that were measured during the promotional campaign, while the remaining four columns (white background) effectively represent what was called the "reverberation" of the campaign.

Four controls are shown on the right of the screen, each of which allows you to compare two data series in any combination. You can use the two *Combo-Box controls* to select a branch or aggregated value (*average, maximum, minimum, none*). The *scroll bars* next to these are linked with the list items, and therefore allow you to browse quickly through them (for example, moving click by click to detect any distinctive features in the line curves), while the drop-down controls allow you to make a carefully considered selection based on individual branches.

Note This data is based on a real-life scenario, which has been adapted and rendered anonymous for the purpose of this book. Structurally, however, the data remains very close to the actual results of the survey. See if you can estimate whether the campaign was successful in raising customer numbers. Note that significant differences were found between the individual branches. In an example used later in the book, you'll find out exactly how the campaign influenced sales figures and gauge its success.

Structure of the Workbook

The file *0203_Analysis_01.xlsx* has five worksheets, which are described below. I prefer to present the structure from right to left or, in a three-dimensional sense, from back to front, in accordance with the sheet selector and the recommended design process. The reason is that, in a finished model of this type, you very often only see or show the worksheet that is located the furthest to the left (the "focus") in the foreground of a presentation, while all other worksheets in the file are invisible or, in a sense, disappear into the *back*ground.

The workbook and its worksheets are usually structured according to the rules of the rS1.Method. Note the following points with reference to Figure 2-7:

1. On the *NamesIndex* worksheet, a small table is defined, listing the range names that are currently valid in the workbook. This is intended only as an informational tool (important during development and, in particular, afterwards), but has no effect on the functionality of the solution.

2. The *Parameters 1* worksheet contains the master data of the individual branches (which are anonymous here), which specifies the name of the branch, branch code, region (North, South, East or West), and an indication of the city size for each of the branches.

3. The *Data 1* worksheet is the data source for the model, and contains the results of the customer census. The constants and calculations used to generate the data series represented in the chart are defined here. If you refer to Figure 2-1, you'll see that this worksheet corresponds to step C in the standard model described earlier.

4. The data and structures shown on worksheet *Lists 1* relate to the focus controls. This is where you'll find the definition ranges of these elements and where each of the "action values" are added that appear when the user activates the controls.

5. The *Basis 1* worksheet corresponds to step B in the standard model. It contains the chart basis, which is generated in part with formulas and in part with constants.

6. Finally, the *Focus 1* worksheet is the solution's "public face," and allows users to make a whole range of comparisons between the data from specific branches. All they need to know is how to use their mouse. This worksheet corresponds to step E in the standard model.

Structural Components in Detail

Later on, you'll have an opportunity to replicate this example yourself, step by step. Before you do, I want to draw your attention to a number of important details relating to the individual worksheets. I won't enter into the nitty-gritty details of each. Instead, I'll focus on key informational and methodological aspects. These will help you keep your objective constantly in view when creating a solution, and will mean that you won't have any problems understanding its components and design in the future.

NamesIndex Worksheet

As stated above, the names index (*NamesIndex* worksheet) is only provided to allow you to check certain information. Step-by-step instructions for doing so are provided below. But first I want to look at the optimization of column width (which is important not just in the context of this list) and the relevant options in Excel 2007. Perform the following steps:

- Place the mouse pointer on the line between the column you want to adjust and the column to its right in the column header. Double-click when the mouse pointer changes to a double-headed arrow. You'll be familiar with this function from earlier versions of Excel.

- Select an entire column or the relevant cell range within this column. Select the *Home* tab in the *Ribbon*. In the *Cells* group, click the *Format* button and select the *AutoFit Column Width* option.

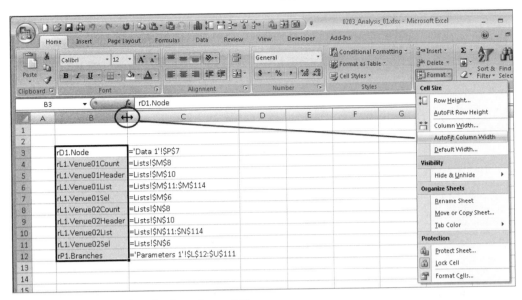

FIGURE 2-8 Two options for adjusting column width

Parameters 1 **Worksheet**

There are two points to note in relation to this worksheet. Row 3 and column G contain two examples of an important auxiliary construction that is typically used in the rS1.Method. These are numerical series, which indicate how many rows and columns are contained in an array, or indicate which row or column in an array belongs to a particular item of content.

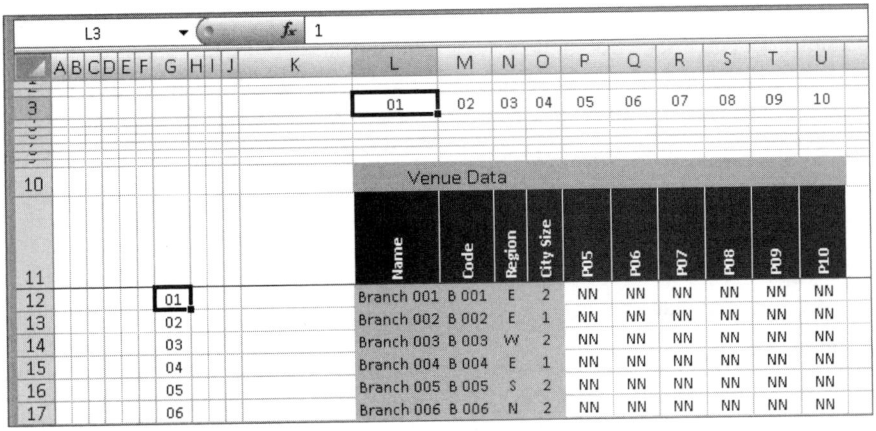

FIGURE 2-9 Numbering is added to the parameter data array

In order to distinguish such elements from other data, I usually assign specific formats to them. I mostly use a slightly smaller font size, a font color (usually blue) that isn't used else-where in the worksheet, and a number format that differs from the standard. In the example shown here (see Figure 2-9), I have used the user-defined number format 00, as I do in almost all similar cases. You'll learn more about this later in the practical exercises.

Columns P through U are filled with the placeholders "NN." Additional data relating to the individual branches can be added here later.

Data 1 Worksheet

We need to look at this worksheet in a little more detail.

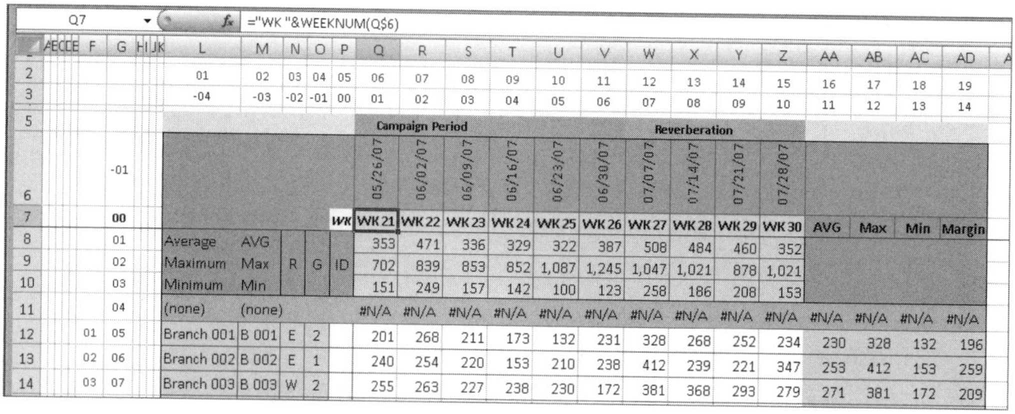

Q7 =“WK “&WEEKNUM(Q$6)

	F	G	L	M	N	O	P	Q	R	S	T	U	V	W	X	Y	Z	AA	AB	AC	AD
2			01	02	03	04	05	06	07	08	09	10	11	12	13	14	15	16	17	18	19
3			-04	-03	-02	-01	00	01	02	03	04	05	06	07	08	09	10	11	12	13	14
5								Campaign Period						Reverberation							
6		-01						05/26/07	06/02/07	06/09/07	06/16/07	06/23/07	06/30/07	07/07/07	07/14/07	07/21/07	07/28/07				
7		00					WK	WK 21	WK 22	WK 23	WK 24	WK 25	WK 26	WK 27	WK 28	WK 29	WK 30	AVG	Max	Min	Margin
8		01	Average	AVG				353	471	336	329	322	387	508	484	460	352				
9		02	Maximum	Max	R	G	ID	702	839	853	852	1,087	1,245	1,047	1,021	878	1,021				
10		03	Minimum	Min				151	249	157	142	100	123	258	186	208	153				
11		04	(none)	(none)				#N/A	#N/A	#N/A	#N/A	#N/A	#N/A	#N/A	#N/A	#N/A	#N/A	#N/A	#N/A	#N/A	#N/A
12	01	05	Branch 001	B 001	E	2		201	268	211	173	132	231	328	268	252	234	230	328	132	196
13	02	06	Branch 002	B 002	E	1		240	254	220	153	210	238	412	239	221	347	253	412	153	259
14	03	07	Branch 003	B 003	W	2		255	263	227	238	230	172	381	368	293	279	271	381	172	209

FIGURE 2-10 Clear formatting differences—but no coincidences

- In rows 2 and 3, and columns F and G, you'll see once again the numerical series mentioned above used as an auxiliary construct. The numerical series don't increase in parallel, and you'll notice that the numbers highlighted in blue also include some negative values. As you'll see yourself later when developing your own model, both of these features have to do with the positioning of the "node," which I employ as a reference for the OFFSET function that I like to use so often. The figures in red are intended to make the parameter data easier to read. This is why, for example, the red 01 is placed in row 12, the row containing the data from the first of the company's branches. The formulas created on the basis of this data are introduced later in this chapter.
- I almost always give the "node" a nice strong yellow background, so that its position can be detected at a glance.
- All cells containing formulas have a light gray blue background to visually distinguish them from other cells in the worksheet. This distinction is particularly important and useful during the design phase of your solution. Partial locking of cells while the solution is in development isn't really possible and would be of little use, but the color coding of cells should ensure that formulas aren't accidentally overwritten. It's also important, for various practical reasons, to be able to identify as quickly as possible which worksheet data is calculated and which is constant.

- The L11:AD11 cell range has been assigned a particularly striking color because it contains a special construct that isn't used very often. The step-by-step instructions provided later explain in more detail how this construct is used to give the user the option of completely hiding the data series on which the chart is based by selecting the option *none*. This option is provided in the most prominent position of the selection list in the user's focus (i.e., at the very top of the drop-down list).

- The column with the header *ID* and a light green background is also a special construct, designed to help with individual filtering of a list.

- Finally, the two colors used in row 5 in conjunction with the labels *Campaign* and *Reverberation* help to identify which data belongs to which evaluation segments without reference to a chart during the development phase.

On the whole, then, this is a pretty colorful worksheet! But it's important to note that careful consideration was given to the use of each of these colors, and that they are all provided to make the sheet easier to use. Naturally, in a worksheet intended for presentation or publishing, different, much less colorful and, in some cases, more subtle color schemes would be used.

Lists 1 **Worksheet**

The two column-specific data ranges on the *Lists 1* worksheet relate to the focus controls. Two similar ranges are required in order to allow the user to create two data series in any combination, both of which are based on the same background data.

Once again, you should by now recognize some of the methods used here. Numbers are employed as auxiliary elements in row 3 and column D, and the cells containing formulas have a specific color coding.

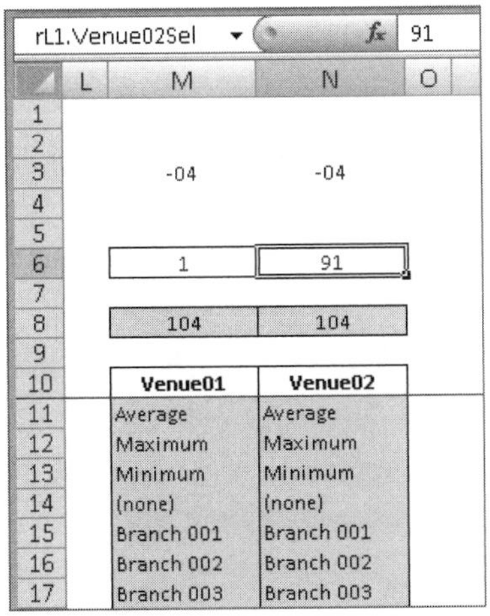

FIGURE 2-11 Structures relating to controls

Note Remember to always use the same colors to provide the same type of information. This is the only way to ensure that this approach remains useful in the long term.

Texts are defined in rows 11 through 114, which will be visible to the user when a branch is to be selected in the user's focus selection lists. The value determined when the user clicks to make a selection or alternatively uses one of the scroll bars appears in one of the frame cells in row 6. More details are provided about this later in the step-by-step instructions on how to set up controls.

Basis 1 Worksheet

It will hardly come as a surprise to learn that the *Basis 1* worksheet also contains blue numbers in its own rows and columns as auxiliary elements. Once again, the cells containing formulas have a light gray blue background.

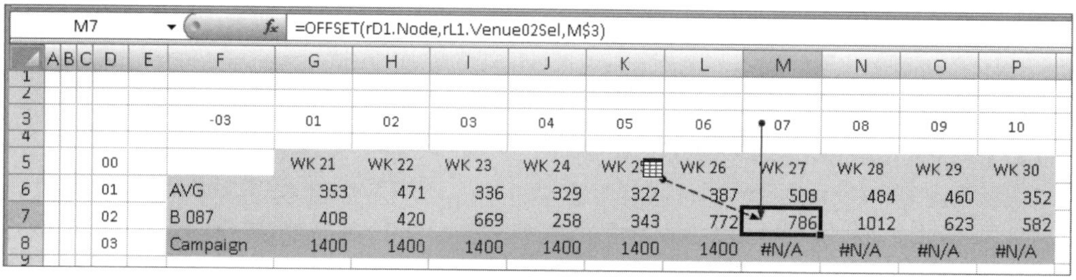

M7			*fx*	=OFFSET(rD1.Node,rL1.Venue02Sel,M$3)								
ABC D	E	F	G	H	I	J	K	L	M	N	O	P
3		-03	01	02	03	04	05	06	07	08	09	10
5 00			WK 21	WK 22	WK 23	WK 24	WK 2	WK 26	WK 27	WK 28	WK 29	WK 30
6 01		AVG	353	471	336	329	322	387	508	484	460	352
7 02		B 087	408	420	669	258	343	772	786	1012	623	582
8 03		Campaign	1400	1400	1400	1400	1400	1400	#N/A	#N/A	#N/A	#N/A

FIGURE 2-12 Color coding to distinguish between formulas and constants

Since this chart basis also contains constants defined by the developer, the corresponding cells have a different background color to the formula cells.

Focus 1 Worksheet

The *Focus 1* worksheet was introduced earlier in Figure 2-7. Not much can be said to explain it because this type of worksheet tends to have a very individual design, which depends completely on the purpose of the visualization and on the requirements of the target audience.

A Solution Emerges

Excel 2007, like Word 2007 and PowerPoint 2007, is ideally suited in every respect to the creation of effective and visually attractive documents and presentations. The range of colors, fonts, and effects available has been significantly enhanced, and anyone who previously had cause to complain about this or that design deficiency in these programs may be astonished by what is now possible. That's the upside.

Naturally, there also is a downside. In reality, Microsoft Excel has always been a program whose full functional capabilities have never been fully exploited by most users. Many users soon became content to use only those functions that they have managed to figure out for themselves. The program did pretty well what they wanted and needed it to do. Anything that repeatedly resulted in frustration, errors, or problems (be it a due to a lack of experience or a deficiency in the software) tended to be simply forgotten. Users also didn't miss features that they didn't know about. They often just settled for doing the obviously workable and developed their own routines around that. However, the new version of the program requires a major attitude shift. The higher level of intuitiveness in the new version makes it much easier to access a whole range of features and, above all, makes these more obvious, which was the intention. However, this also means that the program needs to be played with a lot more, at least when you're first getting used to it. This is associated with a new, relatively significant problem. If you tinker with the program enough, you'll also make lots of mistakes. If you try out a lot of new things without plotting out a precise route to the results you want to achieve, you may make mistakes you won't be able to correct. If you have to put up with many errors (or believe that you have to), you may very soon lose interest in using the new or improved program resources to best effect. I have little doubt that the problem of untapped resources, which has always been a definite drawback of Excel's huge capabilities, will only continue to grow. I'll follow up this prediction with an appeal to readers: Please work through the examples in this book slowly and carefully, and, if possible, only experiment with the features described or suggested in the various instructions provided.

Layout and design naturally play a particularly important role in the charts and presentation variants described here. This is demonstrated in detail in later chapters. Excel offers new features that were never available in its older spreadsheets, which now seem more rigid by comparison. Rigidity hasn't actually been a feature of Excel for a many years now, but the program was previously used by many people as though it was. This may soon change, and this book may well support progress in that direction.

Now it's time for a practical example to illustrate what we've learned, before we can finally get to the practical instructions. In Excel 2007, *styles* have a much more important role to play than in older spreadsheet versions. These can be used in very interesting ways and some have a high aesthetic value. However, the wide range of alternatives available puts them almost outside the grasp of many users who previously only wanted Excel to be able to manage figures and calculations. This becomes readily apparent when we realize that all of the details of almost all formatting assigned to a style can be adjusted to suit user-specific requirements.

To avoid confusion in this regard, I'll use the same standard in almost all of the examples in this book, namely the integrated theme called *Office*. A later chapter provides information about using various themes but, with this exception, I'll refer only to the *Office* theme in this book. This brings us to a very important basic requirement for creating any solution, namely the definition of a theme (i.e., a design) at as early a stage as possible. The main point here is that, if you subsequently make a global change to a theme, you may unwittingly cause colors, fonts, and formatting effects to change in many parts of your model, and may then be unable to undo these changes without excessive effort, unless you make a global change back to your original theme.

Choosing a Theme

You're now going to start working with a file whose standard theme has already been defined, and which you don't need to change. However, if creating your own, new solution, proceed as follows before you do anything else:

1. Open a new, blank worksheet, and select the *Page Layout* tab in the *Ribbon*. In the *Themes* group, click the *Themes* button.

2. In the overview displayed, click the theme you want to assign to your workbook as the default theme, together with its colors, fonts, and effects.

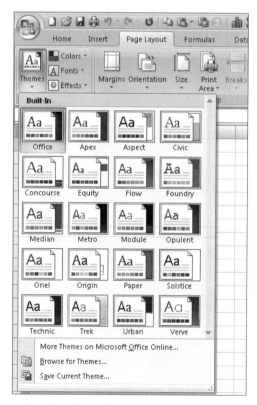

FIGURE 2-13 The *Office* theme is used here.

3. Independently of this (and this is critical, in my view), you can also create distinctions and make selections in the *Themes* group for *colors*, *fonts*, and *effects*, in each case deviating from the integrated specifications of the set theme. Figure 2-14 shows, for example, that you can choose the combination color theme = *Opulent*, font theme = *Equity* and effects theme = *Origin*. However, I would explicitly advise against such an approach, as there would be little sense to it.

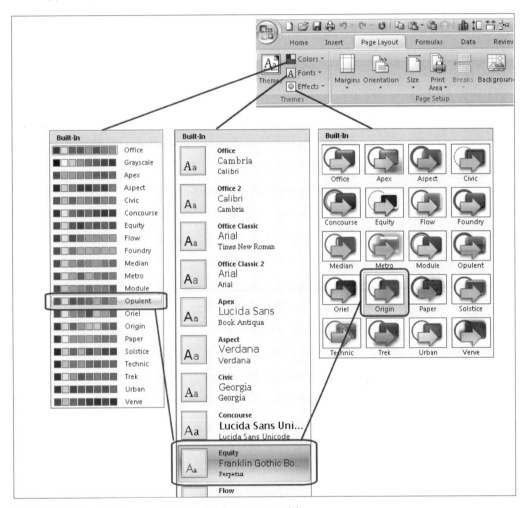

FIGURE 2-14 Mixed designs are also possible but not essential!

These initial settings don't prevent you from making other decisions in regards to other details of color, font, or form as you go along. However, you'll only be able to select options (for example, the specific styles of the *chart tools*) that match your chosen theme.

This book places a strong emphasis on the effects that can be achieved with a well-directed use of color. Before we get started on the practical side of things, I'd therefore like to introduce you to some new terminology used in Office 2007 in reference to colors and color groups.

The *theme colors*, which you select as the default colors for your workbook as described above, comprise four *text* and *background colors*, six *accent colors*, and two *hyperlink colors*. The options for selecting colors independently of a theme are described in other chapters. The only important points to note about the terminology shown in Figure 2-15 are as follows:

In the color palettes that appear in various connections with user actions, the main colors available (depending on the selected theme) are arranged according to a certain pattern. This pattern is of no particular significance when it comes to individual color selections be-cause all colors, regardless of what they are called and of their position in the palette, can be used for any purpose. However, it's both interesting and useful to observe that the Excel de-velopers have obviously gone to considerable lengths (and rather successfully) to coordinate the various color effects. As a result, when you use a combination of colors belonging to a predefined theme, you can often produce a very pleasing overall effect.

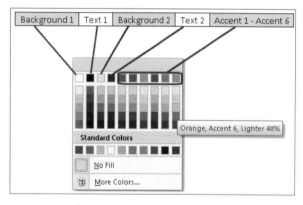

FIGURE 2-15 The standard palette in the various color dialogs

The top row of the palette contains the colors belonging to a theme, organized into back-ground, text, and accent colors. Below this row, five variants of each of the colors are pro-vided, in varying shades from light to dark.

Important To recap: These palette colors are linked to a specific, integrated theme, which you can select using the methods described above. If you want to link these colors to individual elements of your model and then decide at a much later stage that you want to use a differ-ent theme (with different colors), the original links you created are replaced with the new color combinations. The only way to reverse this effect is to change back to the theme you originally selected, or to change all of the colors yourself, which would usually be extremely laborious.

An additional row in the palette provides 10 standard colors and a *More Colors* option, which brings you to a dialog box in which all 16.7 million colors can be defined and assigned to an element in your model. This topic is discussed in detail in Chapter 4, "Colors, Areas, and Outlines."

The dialog box extract shown in Figure 2-15 may appear slightly different in connection with many functions. Additional options may be possible, depending on the action and on the element selected.

What's This About—And How Do I Do It?

This section is all about creating a model solution. It contains many, but far from all, of the components that are of central importance in this book. However, if you want to join in and get your hands dirty, you'll have plenty of work for the remainder of this chapter. Based on a workbook I've already prepared, you'll have an opportunity to put together a complete, dynamic presentation solution, identical to the one we encountered earlier in the section en-titled *Model Structures—A Practical Example*.

There will be many different things to see, do, and learn in this section, namely:

- Set up and take account of the structure components of a model developed in accor-dance with the rS1.Method

- Create and add elements of the model in a logical sequence

- Generate number series and numbers, and implement user-defined cell formatting

- Apply various methods to develop and replicate formulas

- Define range names and use these in formulas

- Generate and use simple controls

- Create a line chart and format its elements

The purpose of all of this is to provide you with a comprehensive overview of methods and procedures that will help you deal with the examples used later in this book, based on the very thorough grounding you'll receive here. There's no reason to fear that the essential basic information you require is only provided here in this chapter and won't be repeated later. However, the information is presented in its clearest and most detailed form here in order to fully prepare you for your "first flight."

Open the following files on the CD-ROM:

❏   \Samples\0202_Analysis_00.xlsx and

❏   \Samples\0203_Analysis_01.xlsx.

The first is a "raw" version, in which only a few structures have been prepared. You can use this file to follow the instructions provided next.

The second is the finished model; i.e., the product of the steps described here.

You can use one of the following three approaches to developing the sample solution, or indeed a combination of these:

- Do you feel that you are still relatively inexperienced in using Excel, including earlier versions of the program?

  If so, set aside a couple of hours, either all at once or over the course of several sessions, to go through the instructions below step by step, and perhaps also conduct a few experiments of your own based on the additional information provided. Save the \Samples\0202_Analysis_00.xlsx file from the CD-ROM to your hard disk under a different name, and then begin the exercises. It will be useful to keep the "finished product" (i.e., the \Samples\0203_Analysis_01.xlsx file) open as you work through the exercises, so that you can compare your efforts with the results expected.

- Do you have a sound basic knowledge of Excel, and feel relatively at home with the topics listed at the start of this section (things to see, do, and learn)?

  If so, compare the finished model in 0203_Analysis_01.xlsx with the instructions provided for the purpose of comparison, and try to understand exactly what was done in what context (and why it was done this way and not that).

- Are you a very experienced Excel user and have already used the rS1.Method to create dynamic presentation models?

  If so, use the finished model in 0203_Analysis_01.xlsx to check what is new and what has changed in Excel 2007 in relation to the development of complex solutions. In other words, assess at this point what value your previous Excel experience and practices have retained in the new version. You are likely to be pleased at some things and disappointed at others.

Of course, regardless of your level of experience, you will get the most out of this book by taking a hands-on approach. It's therefore advisable that you follow these instructions with some practical exercises on your own initiative, even if you've already advanced beyond the novice stage.

Is All the Groundwork Done?

Before we can get started with the practical work, the various program options must be defined. However, if you've already read and implemented the relevant information from Chapter 1, you can proceed without further delay.

If, on the other hand, you haven't yet set up the options as described there, you'll experience some difficulties implementing the steps described below because some of the features or resources mentioned won't be available to you.

There's one more point I'd like to make about choosing the best way to do things. The various Microsoft Office programs have always allowed you to do the same thing several different ways. This hasn't changed in Excel 2007. On the contrary, you won't be surprised to learn that you now have more ways than ever to achieve the same objective. Naturally, I don't want to bore you to tears by listing out all possible alternatives in each case. Instead, I'll suggest the approaches that I believe will produce the desired results relatively quickly and reliably. Of course, as any experienced Excel user will know, you tend to develop your own very specific and "personal" techniques and "knacks" for doing things after many years of using the program, and these will sometimes be very unfamiliar to other users. This of course may be the case here too. Therefore, I'll ask you to bear with me here and for the rest of the book if you find that the methods I describe differ from those that you find effective or useful. If you want to and are able to use a different approach to achieve the same objective, please feel free to do so. What ultimately counts is the result.

Even at this relatively early stage of describing techniques, there will be some opportunity to enter into a little more detail regarding some of the options in the new version of the program, certain methods, or specific formula constructions. In other words, we'll be taking a few short excursions into other terrain while on the way to our scheduled destination.

Initially, we'll have to do so in a relatively detailed and what may seem, at times, a relatively roundabout manner. However, as we advance through the exercise, and possible initial uncertainties about Excel 2007 diminish, I'll cut these descriptions increasingly short by referring to ground that we've already covered.

Defining the *Parameters 1* Worksheet

On the *Parameters 1* worksheet, you're going to set up the auxiliary constructs that have already been set up in row 3 and column G in Figure 2-9. You're then going to assign a range name to the range that contains the data of the individual branches as constants (and can be edited).

Setting Up Auxiliary Rows and Columns

1. Select cell L3, enter the number *1* and press **Enter** to complete your entry.

2. Click the fill handle, which is the tiny square in the bottom right corner of the cell border. Press and hold down the **Ctrl** key. Holding down the left mouse key, drag the fill handle to the right until you reach column U and have written a number series from 1 to 10.

> **Note** If you keep the **Ctrl** key pressed while doing so, the number series is progressed linearly. Otherwise, the content from the first selected cell is copied to all of the others. Note that a small text box appears during this operation, which provides a preview of how you are filling the cells in the series.

3. Next, select row 3 in its entirety. Select the *Home* tab in the *Ribbon*. In the *Font* group, click the small arrow next to the *Font Color* button to open the color palette. Click *More Colors* and, in the dialog box that appears (with the title *Colors*), select the *Standard* tab. Select a bright blue color (suggestion: second row from the top, third color from the right; see Figure 2-16).

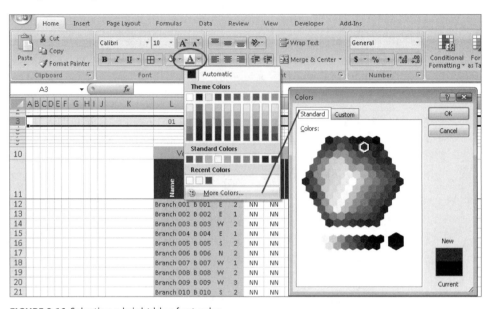

FIGURE 2-16 Selecting a bright blue font color

4. Now, use the command buttons in the *Alignment* group to center the numbers horizontally and vertically.

5. Keep the selection and click the launcher to open the *Format Cells* dialog box in the *Number* group. On the *Number* tab, select the *Custom* entry in the category list. You can then enter a custom format under *Type*. You want the single-digit numbers to be written with a leading zero. Therefore, enter two zeroes to assign the number format 00 (see Figure 2-17).

> **Note** We'll be returning to custom number formats in later chapters, where they play an important role. Note the difference between the characters # and 0 when defining a number format.
>
> In a custom format, the number sign # stands for a digit that *may* be written. This is used, for example, in the thousands format with a separator, which has the code #,##0 (see the format list in Figure 2-17).
>
> In a custom format, a zero stands for a digit that *must* be written. If, for example, a number has just one digit, you can select the 00 number format to ensure that a leading zero is automatically inserted.

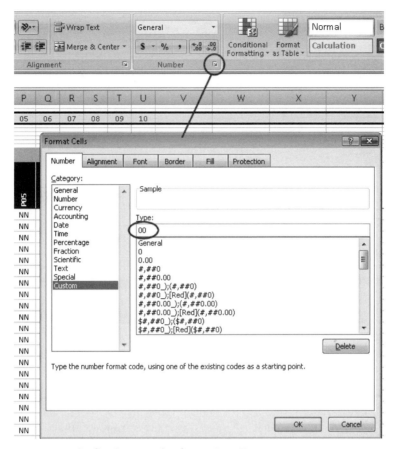

FIGURE 2-17 Configuring a number format (step 5)

6. Next, select cell L3 and copy it to the clipboard. Then select all of column G.

7. In the *Clipboard* group in the *Ribbon*, click the down arrow on the *Paste* button.

> **Caution** In this case, you want to access the *Paste Special* option. Therefore, do *not* click the clipboard icon (which corresponds to the *Paste* command) or use **Ctrl+V**, for example, in order to avoid more than a million digits being written to column G. The only way to access the menu shown in Figure 2-18 is to click the small arrow pointing downwards. In the menu displayed, click *Paste Special* to open the relevant dialog box.

8. In the *Paste Special* dialog box, select the *Formats* option, and choose *OK* to close. You've now copied the alignment, font color, and customer number format from row 3 to column G.

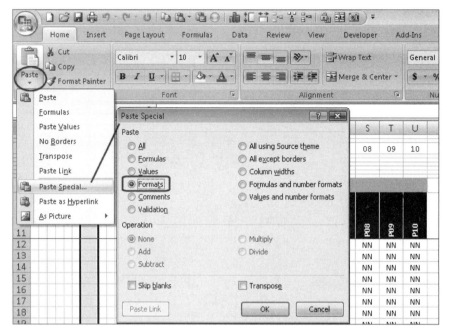

FIGURE 2-18 Make sure to select the correct paste option in step 8

9. Now enter the figure 1 in cell L12, press and hold down the **Ctrl** key, and drag the handle (see step 2) from L12 to L111 to create a number series up to 100.

This step is required in several sheets in your workbook and is to be repeated there. Therefore, select the method that seems best or most convenient to you (the same applies to the copying methods).

Assigning a Range Name

Next, you need to define the branch data as a constant array on the *Parameters 1* worksheet. You therefore need to assign a range name to this data.

1. Select the cell range L12:U111. Shortcut: Select cell L12 and press and hold down the **Ctrl+Shift** keys. Then press first the **down arrow** key, and then the **right arrow** key.

2. Next, use the key combination **Ctrl+F3** to open the *Name Manager* dialog box, and click the *New* button. In the small text box, enter the name **rP1.Branches**, which is a typical rS1-name. Its prefix indicates that it's a name that appears on a "P" sheet, most likely a parameter sheet.

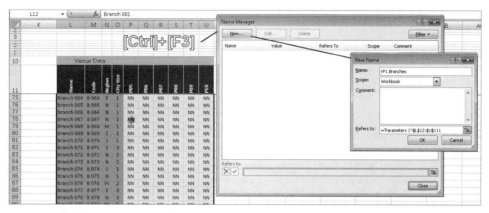

FIGURE 2-19 One of the methods for defining a name

Note If you're used to working with an older version of Excel, you'll have already noticed, after this first encounter with name management, that there are several new features in Excel. More information will be provided about these in other contexts in this book.

There are also other ways to create a range name:

❏ Select the range you want to name, and enter the name text in the *Name box* at the left end of the *formula bar*. I don't recommend that you use this method as a rule, because it's more beneficial for you to become accustomed to using the *Name Manager* from the out-set. It proves an indispensable tool when developing complex models with many names that may have to be modified, changed, or deleted.

❏ Open the *Name Manager* from the *Ribbon*, rather than with the keyboard shortcut speci-fied above. The *Formulas* tab contains the *Defined Names* group. Here you'll find the *Name Manager* button and the *Define Name* button, which you can use to call the *New Name* dialog box directly.

❏ Select the cell range you want to name, and use any method to open the *New Name* dia-log box. Enter a name of your choice, and click in the *Refers To* text box at the bottom of the dialog box. If this already contains a reference, select this in full. Then select the range you want to name in the worksheet behind the dialog box.

3. Check immediately whether the name has been correctly assigned. There are several ways to do this:

❏ Click the tiny down arrow to the right of the *Name* box in the formula bar. This opens a list of assigned names (for the moment, this will be sparsely populated with just a single entry). You can click the name to select the corresponding range. Check whether this action marks all of the cells to which you want to assign the range name.

> **Important** This kind of nitpicking check may appear unnecessary to some readers. But please don't skip over it! Even if you're not already a fan of Excel range names, you'll soon come to value them as extremely useful tools. But one thing that's certain to perplex and bewilder you is the formula errors or procedural errors that arise when a name is incorrectly assigned. This happens, for example, if a name is accidentally assigned to the wrong cell, or does not cover the correct cell range and excludes rows and/or columns, or includes certain cells by mistake.

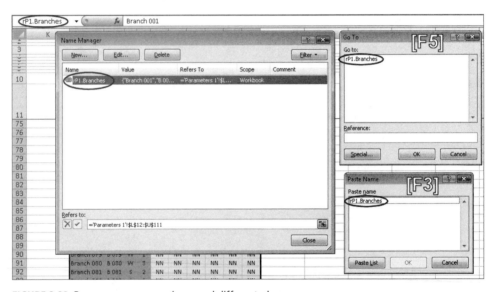

FIGURE 2-20 Range names appear in several different places

❏ The *Name Manager* dialog box also contains a *Refers To* text box, in which you can enter the name's cell reference. You can also make any necessary corrections here.

❏ You'll also find the list of assigned range names in the *Go To* dialog box (shortcut: **F5**). From there, simply double-click a name to locate and select the corresponding range.

❏ Finally, you can also use the *Paste Name* dialog box (shortcut: **F3**). However, you can't check the assignment of names here. As you'll see later, this dialog box is useful as a very efficient way to determine the use of range names in formulas.

Defining the *Data 1* Worksheet

On the *Data 1* worksheet, the necessary auxiliary columns and rows have already been set up for you. The numbers shown in various positions and colors in rows 2 and 3, and columns F and G serve various purposes when it comes to creating formulas, as you're about to find out.

This and subsequent worksheets are concerned largely with the use of formulas. For this reason, I've inserted a brief discussion below on the subject of *reference styles*. I frequently find when giving seminars that this feature is more likely to cause confusion than to ease the operation of the program.

In Excel formulas, a distinction is made between relative and absolute cell references. It's particularly important to be aware of this fact and to bear it in mind when creating formulas. If you want to replicate a formula or cut and paste it into a different location, the cell reference is modified in different ways depending on the reference style used in the formula. Several options are available. Note the following points regarding Figure 2-21, which shows four simple formulas, all referring to cell B2:

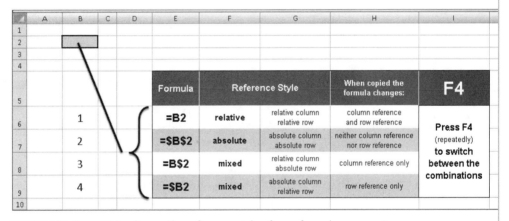

FIGURE 2-21 Press **F4** to change the reference style of your formula arguments

1. The reference style of the formula in cell E6 is *relative*. If the formula is copied to another cell, the reference to the column and to the row will change. For example, =B2 may change to =C3 or =AD255 , etc., depending on the new position.

2. The user has changed the reference style to *absolute*. If the formula is copied to another cell, neither the row reference nor the column reference changes, and the cell reference remains =$B$2. This is because the dollar signs have been placed before the row and column references. You can use your keyboard to enter these characters, but this isn't the preferred method. A much easier and, above all, more reliable method is to press **F4** after you enter or generate the reference (and the cursor is blinking after the reference or the reference is selected).

> By repeatedly pressing this key, you can change the reference style as often as required; in other words, select any of the references styles 1 to 4 described here.
>
> 3. The user has used the **F4** button to change the reference style to *mixed* (in this case, relative column and absolute row). If the formula is copied to another cell, the reference to the column changes but the reference to the row does not. For example, =B$2 changes to =C$2 or =AD$2, etc.
>
> 4. The user has used the **F4** button to change the reference style to *mixed* (this time, absolute column and relative row). If the formula is copied to another cell, the reference to the row changes but the reference to the column does not. For example, =$B2 changes to =$B3 or =$B255, etc.
>
> In this context, it is important that you know how to replicate a formula *before* you enter that formula, wherever possible.

Freezing Panes

First, you should ensure that the pane stays in view by locking or freezing the worksheet horizontally between rows 7 and 8. You can then use the scroll bar to move the data in rows 8 to 111 independently of the frozen block of cells in rows 1 to 7.

1. Select the cell on the far left of the first row *below* the pane you want to freeze; i.e., the first row that you don't want to freeze, which is cell A8 in our example.

2. Select the *View* tab in the *Ribbon*, click the *Freeze Pane* button in the *Window* group, and select the *Freeze Pane* menu option.

The horizontal line now visible between rows 7 and 8 indicates the freezing level. Rows 1 to 7 are now frozen, while you can scroll through the remaining rows on the worksheet. The black dividing line is for display purposes only, and won't be printed.

Entering Formulas

First, you need to enter the formulas that are to calculate the average, maximum, and minimum values of the customer census results in the range Q8:Z10.

I suggest using an approach whereby all formulas are first written as average formulas in a single step, before they all are gradually assigned the "correct" functionality using a very simple procedure. The row labels used in rows 8 to 10 ultimately determine which calculation type will appear in which row.

1. If necessary, use the vertical scroll bar in the frozen pane to make row 8 visible. Select the cell range Q8:Z10. The active cell is Q8.

2. Begin by entering the AVERAGE function. As soon as you enter the equals sign and the first letter, a list of all functions that start with this letter appears below the formula bar. You can use the **down arrow** and **up arrow** keys to make your selection in this list, and then insert it into the formula bar using the **Tab** key. Alternatively, double-click the function of your choice.

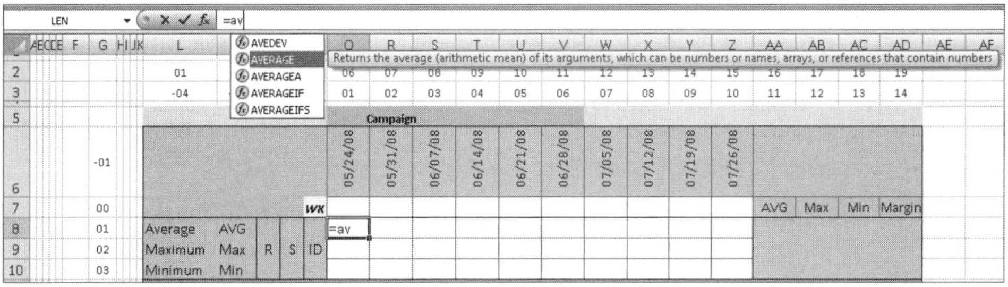

FIGURE 2-22 You can simply select the formula from the list provided, rather than entering it yourself.

3. Enter an opening parenthesis. The formula is the aforementioned =AVERAGE(, which should now be assigned its reference. The insertion point (blinking cursor) appears after the opening parenthesis. Select cell Q12, press **Ctrl+Shift** and then the **down arrow**. The relevant column range (Q12:Q111) is then selected and used as a reference in the formula.

4. Next, press **F4** repeatedly until the reference becomes a mixed reference (relative column, absolute row), so that our formula now reads =AVERAGE(Q$12:Q$111.

5. Now enter a closing parenthesis. It isn't absolutely essential in this case, but it's good to get into the habit of doing so as it will be required in more complex formulas. The formula bar is still active, with a blinking cursor after the formula. If that's not the case, click after the formula to activate the formula bar. The formula should now be entered simultaneously into all selected cells in the range Q8:Z10. You can do this with the multiple entry function by pressing **Ctrl+Enter**.

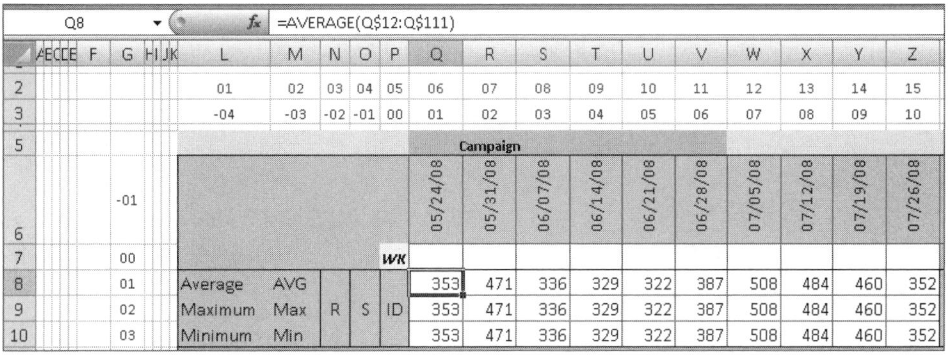

FIGURE 2-23 The references are correct, but only the formulas in row 8 are doing what they should.

Your unfinished worksheet should now appear as shown in Figure 2-23: Rows 8, 9, and 10 now contain formulas for calculating an average value. If the reference style has been selected correctly as mixed (relative column, absolute row), these formulas will all refer to rows 12 through 111, and identical results will therefore appear in each of the three rows. The references are now correct but the functions in rows 9 and 10 are not. This is easy to change:

6. Select the range Q9:Z9. We want the text *Average* to be replaced with *Max*. Press **Ctrl+H** to open the *Find and Replace* dialog box (see Figure 2-24).

Alternatively: In the *Ribbon*, select the *Home* tab and the *Edit* group, click the *Find and Replace* button, and select the *Replace* option.

In the *Find what* box, enter **Average**, and enter **Max** in the *Replace with* box. Then click the *Replace All* button. DON'T close the dialog box at this point.

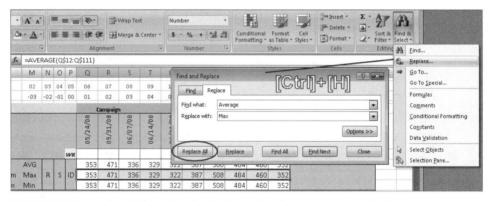

FIGURE 2-24 The *Find and Replace* function is also very useful when working with formulas.

7. Keeping the dialog box open, select the range Q10:Z10. Here, you want to replace the text *Average* with *Min*. In the *Replace with* text box in the dialog box, overwrite **Max** with **Min**, click the *Replace All* button, and then choose *Close*.

The result is that the average values of the customer census is now calculated in row 8, the maximum values in row 9, and the minimum values in row 10.

Points to Note in Relation to Functions in the *Data 1* Worksheet

The =AVERAGE(reference) function returns the arithmetic mean of the numbers in reference by adding them together and dividing the total by the count of those numbers.

The =MAX(reference) function returns the largest of the numbers in reference.

The =MIN(reference) function returns the smallest of the numbers in reference.

The =INDEX(array,row_num,column_num) function was explained earlier in a separate section.

The =WEEKNUM(serial_number,return_type) function calculates the number of calendar weeks that fall within the serial_number to which the formula refers. return_type is a value used to define the day on which a week starts. The default setting is *1*, and assumes that a week starts on Sunday. If the return_type argument is assigned the number *2*, Excel assumes that a week starts on Monday.

Incidentally, the WEEKNUM Excel function is of limited use in a European context. This function is essentially used to indicate the week in which January 1 falls each year (i.e., week 1). However, this is standardized in Europe, where week 1 is always the first week to include four days that fall in the new year. The WEEKNUM function therefore returns results that don't match the standard European calendar week numbers in some years.

In Excel, a date is a serial number. Counting begins (in Microsoft Windows) on January 1, 1900. What you see as a date in a cell is normally just the specific formatting of a serial number (which can be changed in many different ways). Excel is only capable of calculating calendar dates (for example, to calculate periods) if it "knows" that December 24, 2007 is equal to the serial number 39,440, for example).

In the next step, we're going to apply the method used above to create formulas for the branch data. In other words, we're going to calculate the average, maximum, and minimum values for specific rows. Three examples from row 12 are shown in Figure 2-25.

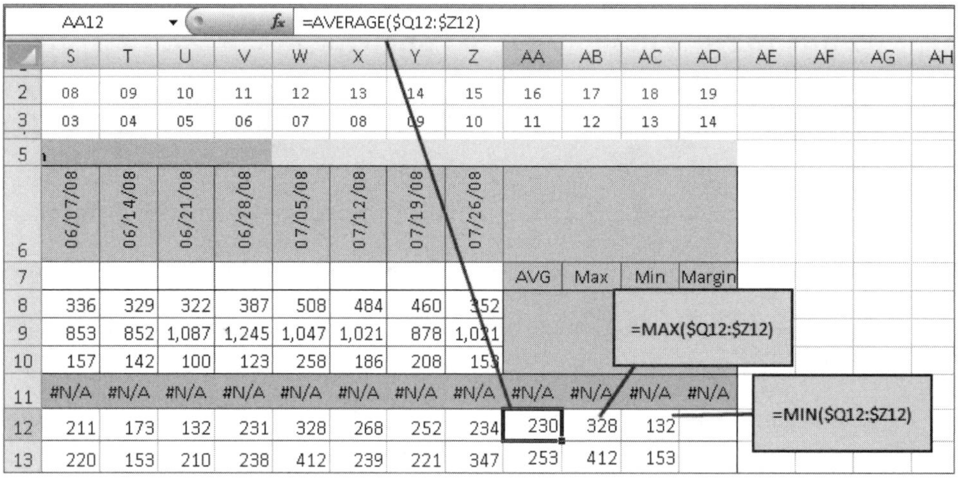

| AA12 | | | | ▾ | | f_x | =AVERAGE($Q12:$Z12) | | | | | | | | |

	S	T	U	V	W	X	Y	Z	AA	AB	AC	AD	AE	AF	AG	AH
2	08	09	10	11	12	13	14	15	16	17	18	19				
3	03	04	05	06	07	08	09	10	11	12	13	14				
5																
6	06/07/08	06/14/08	06/21/08	06/28/08	07/05/08	07/12/08	07/19/08	07/26/08								
7									AVG	Max	Min	Margin				
8	336	329	322	387	508	484	460	352								
9	853	852	1,087	1,245	1,047	1,021	878	1,011	=MAX($Q12:$Z12)							
10	157	142	100	123	258	186	208	15								
11	#N/A	#N/A	#N/A	#N/A	#N/A	#N/A	#N/A	#N/A	#N/A	#N/A	#N/A	#N/A				
12	211	173	132	231	328	268	252	234	230	328	132	=MIN($Q12:$Z12)				
13	220	153	210	238	412	239	221	347	253	412	153					

FIGURE 2-25 Row-specific average, maximum, and minimum values are also required.

1. Select the range AA12:AC111 and use the method described above to enter a formula in the active cell AA12 to calculate an average based on columns Q to Z.

2. When you've generated the reference, press **F4** repeatedly until the reference as a mixed style (absolute column, relative row), so that our formula now reads =AVERAGE($Q12:$Z12.

3. Enter a closing parenthesis and then press **Ctrl+Enter** to enter the formula in the entire range selected.

4. Select the generated formula in column AB and replace the text *Average* with *Max* as described above. Then replace *Average* with *Min* in column AC the same way.

Now all that's left to do in this range is enter simple formulas to calculate the difference between the maximum and minimum values for a branch. Let's use a conventional approach for a change:

1. Select cell AD12 and enter the formula =AB12-AC12. Press **Enter**.

2. Click the fill handle, which is the tiny square in the bottom right corner of the cell border, and replicate the formula by dragging it downwards until you reach cell AD111.

You've now created a range of formulas for cells whose formatting is identical to the constants provided in the worksheet. To help you keep track of everything, you could assign a different color to all cells containing formulas, as follows:

1. Select the entire worksheet or just a single cell, so that the following command applies to all of the worksheet.

2. Open the *Go To* dialog box (see Figure 2-20) using the shortcut **F5** or **Ctrl+G**.

3. Click the *Special* button in the dialog box and select the *Formulas* option in the *Go To Special* dialog box that opens. When you choose *OK*, all cells containing formulas are selected.

4. Next, right-click in the selected range to open the context menu. The *mini toolbar* also appears, showing the main *formatting tools* (see Figure 2-26). Click the *Fill Color* button and, when the color palette appears, assign a specific color to the selected cells. Remember that you should be consistent in your choice of color so that you can tell at a glance which cells contain which kind of content during the design phase.

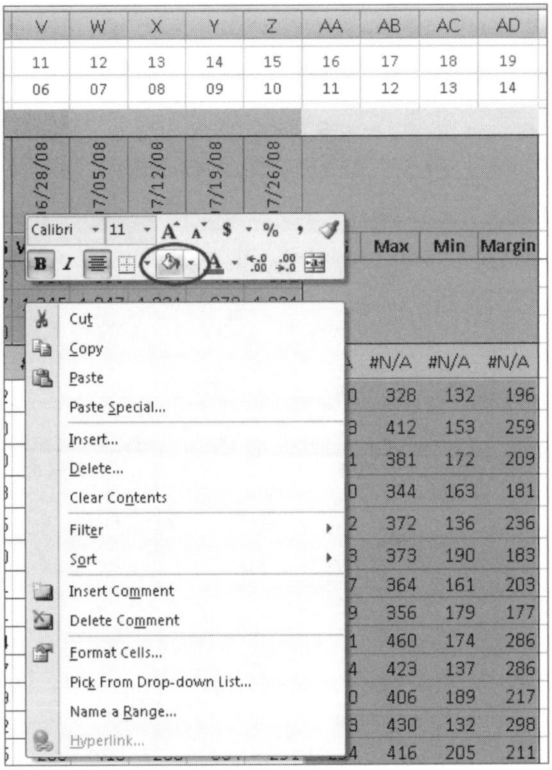

FIGURE 2-26 Assign a unique color to the cells that contain formulas.

The next step is to assign formulas to the L12:0111 cell range. This will produce row labels stretching across four columns, indicating the names and characteristics of the individual branches. This data is then copied directly into the parameters worksheet. The method described here is very useful in this case, but in general it has a number of potential drawbacks.

- Benefit: In many models, you can centrally define the parameters (usually master data) that are required in several locations and then readout these wherever they are needed. It's then very easy to maintain the parameters in a single location in your workbook, no matter how complex a structure it may have.

- Drawback: This reading of parameters using the formulas described below is only a useful and low-maintenance method if the structure of the model is constant. By constant, I mean that it's not necessary during the data analysis to sort the data-specific elements (names, accounts, cost centers, etc.) in a manner that differs from what was originally defined (although I can only think of a few cases in which this is would be necessary). In this case, you could take a different approach to creating formulas, one which still permits central parameter maintenance but—whenever this isn't viable—allows you to use redundant parameter management instead, even if you do so with gritted teeth!

I'm referring to a method that has previously only been described as a theoretical possibility: the use of range names in formulas. This has many advantages, the most welcome of which is the fact that, unless you specify otherwise, names apply everywhere in the workbook as a whole. This means that you can access ranges you've named from any location in any worksheet.

> **Note** One of the new features in Excel 2007 is the power to decide, when assigning a name, whether the name is to be valid in a certain worksheet only, or (the only option used here) in the workbook as a whole.

The method described below for filling a large table range with formulas is based on the procedures described above, but differs from these in several respects. This is because a different formula structure is used here and also in order to present you with other alternatives in this area.

1. The formulas are to be entered in the range L12:O111. However, you need to select cell L12 first.

2. Enter =index(, including the opening parenthesis, and press **Ctrl+Shift+A**. A small dialog box opens, in which you can select one of two different syntax variants. This happens with this particular function but as an exception, which rarely occurs in Excel. Almost all functions have a single syntax. Select the first version. The syntax =INDEX(array,row_num,column_num) is then inserted into the formula bar, and the first of the arguments is selected and can be immediately overwritten.

> **Tip** I almost always use this method when entering formulas and find it really cool. Of course, I also do so when I know the syntax of a function and could enter the formula without this aid. The advantage is that I can see the formula arguments in the correct sequence and—with the correct separators in the right places—double-click the individual arguments to select them and simply overwrite them. This streamlines the process of creating a formula and, above all, make it much more reliable as part of the overall process.

3. The array we require, namely the branch master data, is located in the *Parameters 1* worksheet and has already been assigned the range name *rP1.Branches*. We now want the formulas to access this array. Press **F3** to display the small *Paste Name* dialog box, which you'll recognize from Figure 2-20. Double-click the required name, which is then used as the first argument in the formula.

4. Next, double-click the second argument (row_num) in the formula so that it can be overwritten. Then click in cell F12 (which contains the number 1) to use it as a reference and press **F4** repeatedly until this reference has a mixed reference style (absolute column, relative row).

5. Next, double-click the third argument (column_num) in the formula so that it can be overwritten. Then click in cell L2 (which contains the number 1) to use it as a reference and press **F4** repeatedly until this reference has a mixed reference style (relative column, absolute row).

6. Press **Enter** to finish entering the formula. The finished formula =INDEX(rP1. Branches,$F12,L$2) (see Figure 2-27) serves as an instruction to Excel to do the following: "Find the content of a cell located in an array named *rP1.Branches*. In this array, go down the number of rows specified in cell F12 and across the number of columns (to the right) specified in cell L2."

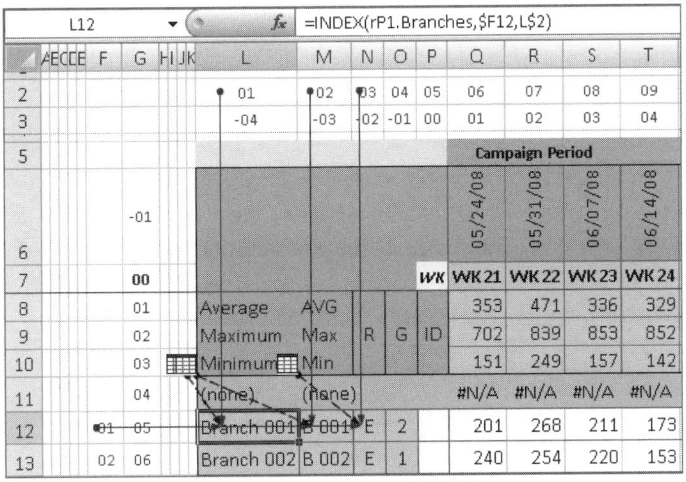

L12					f_x	=INDEX(rP1.Branches,$F12,L$2)					
	A E C C E	F	G	H I J K	L	M	N O P	Q	R	S	T
2					• 01	?02	?3 04 05	06	07	08	09
3					-04	?-03	?02 -01 00	01	02	03	04
5								**Campaign Period**			
6					-01			05/24/08	05/31/08	06/07/08	06/14/08
7					00			WK WK 21	WK 22	WK 23	WK 24
8					01	Average	AVG	353	471	336	329
9					02	Maximum	Max R G ID	702	839	853	852
10					03	Minimum	Min	151	249	157	142
11					04	(none)	(none)	#N/A	#N/A	#N/A	#N/A
12		01	05		Branch 001	B 001 E	2	201	268	211	173
13		02	06		Branch 002	B 002 E	1	240	254	220	153

FIGURE 2-27 The index formulas access the auxiliary constructs (shown in red).

Because the correct references styles have been selected and the variables for the row and column arguments are in the correct sequence in column G and row 2, the formula can now be applied to the entire range L12:O111 in a single step. To do this, we'll switch methods once again and select a large range using the *Go To* dialog box:

7. Again select cell L12, which contains the formula to be copied. Then press **F5** to open the *Go To* dialog box, and enter the cell reference O111 in the *Reference* box. Press and

hold down the **Shift** key. Then choose *OK* in the *Go To* dialog box. The entire range L12:O111 is then selected.

> **Tip** This method is the same as manually selecting a "From-To" range by clicking the cell in the top left corner of the range, pressing and holding down the **Shift** key, and then clicking the cell in the bottom right corner of the range. If the range is very large and can't be viewed on-screen in its entirety, and if you know the reference of the cell in its bottom right corner, you can also use the *Go To* box as described in step 7 to jump to the "To" cell in the range.

8. Click in the formula bar after the formula to activate it. Then enter the formula for the entire range using **Ctrl+Enter**, just as you've done several times already. The formula is adjusted to the correct rows and columns, incorporates the variables from column G and row 2, and uses these to generate a list with four columns (copied from the *Parameters 1* worksheet), which provides the table with its row labels.

The formulas in the range Q7:Z7 are still missing. Here, the numbers of the relevant calendar weeks are to be calculated on the basis of the calendar data for the customer census. These will be used later as labels for the *primary horizontal axis* in the chart. A combination of text characters and formula results is used in the following description.

1. Select the cell range Q7:Z7. In the active cell (Q7), enter an equals sign to start your formula, followed by quotation marks, and then the character string *WK*, followed by a blank space and, finally, more quotation marks (see Figure 2-28).

2. Next, enter the character & (ampersand), which is Excel's text operator, followed by the WEEKNUM(function, and click cell Q6, which contains the date whose calendar week we want to determine. Press **F4** to select a mixed reference style (relative column, absolute row), enter a closing parenthesis, and press **Ctrl+Enter** to apply the formula to the entire range selected. As a result, the text *WK* is linked, cell for cell, with the column-specific calculation result of WEEKNUM.

| Q7 | fx | ="WK "&WEEKNUM(Q$6) |

	AECDE F	G HIJK	L	M	N O P	Q	R	S	T	U	V	W	X	Y	Z
2			01	02	03 04 05	06	07	08	09	10	11	12	13	14	15
3			-04	-03	-02 -01 00	01	02	03	04	05	06	07	08	09	10
5							Campaign Period					Reverberation			
6		-01				05/24/08	05/31/08	06/07/08	06/14/08	06/21/08	06/28/08	07/05/08	07/12/08	07/19/08	07/26/08
7		00			WK	WK 21	WK 22	WK 23	WK 24	WK 25	WK 26	WK 27	WK 28	WK 29	WK 30
8		01	Average	AVG		353	471	336	329	322	387	508	484	460	352
9		02	Maximum	Max	R G ID	702	839	853	852	1,087	1,245	1,047	1,021	878	1,021
10		03	Minimum	Min		151	249	157	142	100	123	258	186	208	153

FIGURE 2-28 Text characters and calculation results are linked with the text operator &.

Note Three points to note on the method described above:

❑ As you'll see, there are many scenarios in which texts need to be linked to calculation results, or text characters are required in order to determine the correct calculation result. The same basic rule applies in all cases: Text characters in a formula must always be placed within quotation marks.

❑ Strictly speaking, my instruction to use **F4** to select a mixed reference style (relative column, absolute row) wasn't necessary because the formulas are located in a single row and aren't to be copied to another row. In this case, a mixed reference is used out of habit rather than necessity. However, the more this becomes a habit for you, the less likely you are to make mistakes when creating references.

❑ Information about the noteworthy features of the WEEKNUM function in the box above entitled "Points to Note in Relation to Functions in the *Data 1* Worksheet."

This brings our creation of formulas in this worksheet to a close. As a final step, use the method described earlier to select all of the cells that contain formulas and assign the same color to all of these.

Defining the Node

All that's left to do now in the *Data 1* worksheet is to define the *node*, which is so important for the rS1.Method. Select cell P7 (highlighted in bright yellow), press **Ctrl+F3** to open the *Name Manager*, click the *New* button, and enter the name *rD1.Node* for the cell.

The key role played by the node is in relation to the OFFSET function. The ideal (but not mandatory) position for the node is one row above and one column to the left of the top left corner of the array that is to be read (see Figure 2-29).

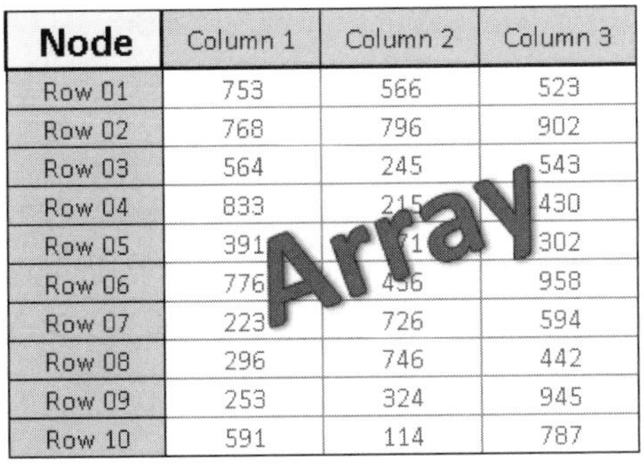

Node	Column 1	Column 2	Column 3
Row 01	753	566	523
Row 02	768	796	902
Row 03	564	245	543
Row 04	833	215	430
Row 05	391	71	302
Row 06	776	456	958
Row 07	223	726	594
Row 08	296	746	442
Row 09	253	324	945
Row 10	591	114	787

FIGURE 2-29 The ideal position for the *node*.

Note Incidentally, it doesn't matter whether the cell defined as the *node* is empty or e.g. contains a text.

In auxiliary row 3 and auxiliary column G, you'll see numbers in blue font, which indicate the distance of the column or row from the node. This information will be required when developing other formulas in other worksheets.

The *Data 1* Worksheet: A Summary

This worksheet now has all the elements that the model requires. It also contains several elements that are completely superfluous to the purpose specified here by way of an example. It thus displays a very typical redundancy, which is characteristic of the rS1.Method.

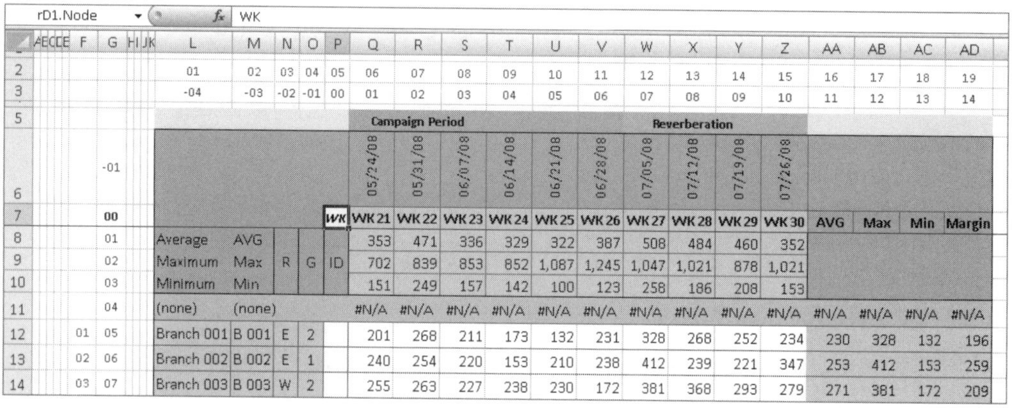

rD1.Node | WK

	F	G	L	M	N	O	P	Q	R	S	T	U	V	W	X	Y	Z	AA	AB	AC	AD
2			01	02	03	04	05	06	07	08	09	10	11	12	13	14	15	16	17	18	19
3			-04	-03	-02	-01	00	01	02	03	04	05	06	07	08	09	10	11	12	13	14
5								Campaign Period						Reverberation							
6		-01						05/24/08	05/31/08	06/07/08	06/14/08	06/21/08	06/28/08	07/05/08	07/12/08	07/19/08	07/26/08				
7		00					WK	WK 21	WK 22	WK 23	WK 24	WK 25	WK 26	WK 27	WK 28	WK 29	WK 30	AVG	Max	Min	Margin
8		01	Average	AVG				353	471	336	329	322	387	508	484	460	352				
9		02	Maximum	Max	R	G	ID	702	839	853	852	1,087	1,245	1,047	1,021	878	1,021				
10		03	Minimum	Min				151	249	157	142	100	123	258	186	208	153				
11		04	(none)	(none)				#N/A	#N/A	#N/A	#N/A	#N/A	#N/A	#N/A	#N/A	#N/A	#N/A	#N/A	#N/A	#N/A	#N/A
12	01	05	Branch 001	B 001	E	2		201	268	211	173	132	231	328	268	252	234	230	328	132	196
13	02	06	Branch 002	B 002	E	1		240	254	220	153	210	238	412	239	221	347	253	412	153	259
14	03	07	Branch 003	B 003	W	2		255	263	227	238	230	172	381	368	293	279	271	381	172	209

FIGURE 2-30 This version of the worksheet can be used for various purposes.

The two most important reasons for this are as follows:

- The data sheet is intended not only as a source for a comparative line chart, but also to be used in other contexts to enable different analytical analyses using filter techniques.
- Elements have been used that allow the model designer to satisfy more than the standard requirements.

Specifically, these are as follows:

- The text labels from column L are used by the controls that the user finds in the *Focus 1* worksheet to select a branch and thus the display of a data series. This configuration can be used when presenting the chart to management or in a public forum. However, the model may also be used by other individuals, such as a financial controller who prefers to makes selections using the short labels found in column M, which can easily be copied into the selection lists.
- The same applies to the entries in rows 6 and 7. The calendar week numbers are currently used as a label for the primary horizontal axis. However, since the corresponding calendar dates are also available, these can easily be added to the axis label instead of or alongside the calendar week numbers.

- The information in columns N and O isn't displayed in the chart. However, it will be used later in a filter analysis of the composition of the groups based on region, city size or both.

- Similarly, the row-specific calculated data in columns AA to AD can be used for various analyses in conjunction with the filtering of the list.

Finally, note the following point in relation to the sequence of entries in column L. These texts appear, as stated above, in the list controls, where they are used to select the data series that are to be displayed in the line chart. When a drop-down list is opened, it's important that the element that is used most frequently (according to the developer's expectations or the user's requirements) appears first in the list of possible entries. In the data structure presented here, it's likely that a comparative analysis between aggregated values (average, maximum, and minimum values) in relation to the individual branches will be used relatively frequently. The aggregate values have therefore been placed at the top of the worksheet. However, the user may just as frequently want to view a single data series only in the chart. For this reason, a series with #N/A data was inserted into row 11 with the label *(none)*, which when selected causes the data series to disappear in the line chart.

Defining and Preparing the *Lists 1* Worksheet

In the *Lists 1* worksheet, we'll finally be making use of the OFFSET function, which I've mentioned several times. In accordance with the rS1.Method, the list contents of controls aren't normally taken directly from the corresponding data sources (which, in this case, would be the *Parameters 1* or *Data 1* worksheet). Instead, these are compiled in a separate worksheet (*Lists 1*) and assigned range names there. The main advantage of this approach is that the user can be provided with selection lists containing several variants (i.e., modifications of the primary data sources) when using controls, such as shorter or longer texts, sorting options that deviate from the source range, and many more.

Two types of control are used in the example provided here, namely *drop-down lists* and *scroll bars*. Both have to do with the cell structures in the *Lists 1* worksheet.

> **Note** Chapter 7, "Colors, Areas, and Outlines," explains in a nutshell controls, their various types and applications, and their uses. Here I'll limit myself to providing the most important information about the two simple controls used in the sample model, and only at the level of detail you need in order to replicate this model for yourself.

Earlier, in the section entitled "Model Structures—A Practical Example," I explained what you can do with the four controls located on the right of the *Focus 1* worksheet. Note the following points in relation to how these elements apply to the cell ranges in the *Lists 1* worksheet (see Figure 2-31 and Figure 2-32):

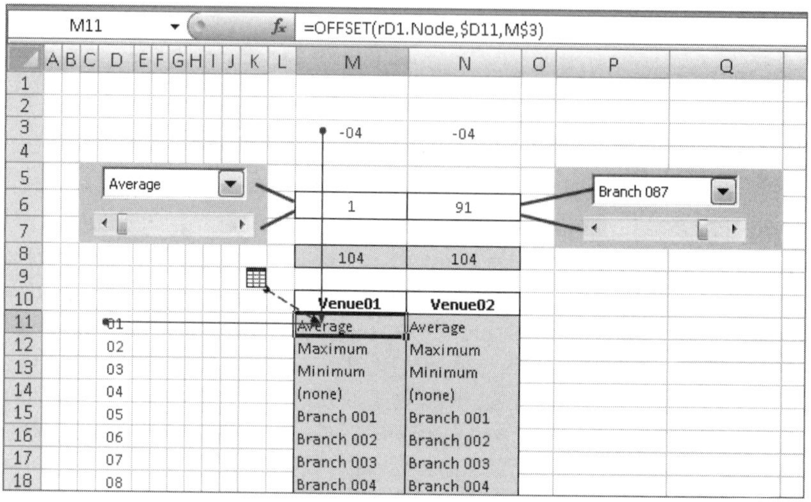

FIGURE 2-31 Each pair of controls is connected with a separate cell range.

The first *drop-down list* should take its list contents from cell range M11:M114, which is assigned the name *rL1.Venue01List* . The list's output value (the number that appears when the user clicks on a list content) should point to cell M6, which is assigned the name *rL1.Venue01Sel*. Note the use of the figure *01* in the range names.

In the same way, the first *scroll bar* should take its output value (the number that appears when the user uses a function element of this scroll bar) from cell M6, which has the name *rL1.Venue01Sel*. This creates a coupling between the two controls.

The second *drop-down list* and the second *scroll bar* are to be linked the same way with the cell range with the relevant name in column N. The range names differ in a single, crucial respect: the use of the figure *02*.

Defining Names

Select the relevant cells or cell ranges, press **Ctrl+F3**, and use the method described above to define the eight range names, which are shown in Figure 2-32, with arrows indicating their assignment to the corresponding cells. The two range names ending in *List* apply to cell ranges M11:M114 and N11:N114, which aren't shown in full here.

The range names ending in *Count* and *Header* are optional, and aren't required in most solutions. However, because they are occasionally used in complex models and are often used in programmed solutions, I've made a habit of assigning them to the relevant positions.

Another element that wasn't essential and could have been omitted here is the use of the count formula =COUNTA(rL1.Venue01List) in cell M8 (which has the name *rL1.Venue01Count* in the finished model) and the corresponding formula in cell N8.

The =COUNTA(reference) function calculates how many cells in reference contain data of any kind.

The =COUNT(reference) function calculates how many cells in reference contain numbers (cells containing other data types aren't counted).

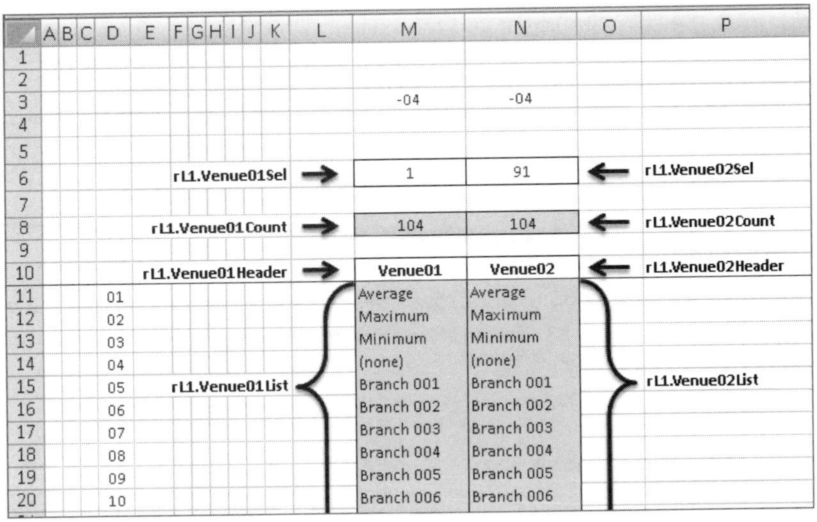

FIGURE 2-32 Range names in the *Lists 1* worksheet

All of the range names in this model are now complete, and you can now generate a list of these range names (see Figure 2-8) as follows in order to check them:

1. Open the *NamesIndex* worksheet and select the cell that is to contain the first list entry.

2. Press **F3** and then click the *Paste List* button in the *Paste Name* dialog box that opens.

3. Change the font size if necessary and assign the optimal column width to both columns (name texts and assigned references).

Entering Formulas

In a single step, you can enter all of the formulas with which the lists are generated for both ranges.

1. Select the cell range M11:N114. In the active cell (M11), start entering the formula as shown in Figure 2-31. Stop after the opening parenthesis, i.e.: =OFFSET(

2. Press **Ctrl+Shift+A** to insert the formula syntax. Remove the arguments from the syntax that aren't required here; i.e., height and width, so that all that remains in the formula bar is =OFFSET(reference,rows,cols).

3. Double-click to select the argument reference and then press **F3**. The list of available range names appears. Double-click *rD1.Node* to add this name to the formula as the reference.

4. Double-click the rows argument and then click cell D11. Press **F4** repeatedly until a mixed reference style (absolute column, relative row) is selected (i.e., $D11).

5. Double-click the cols argument and then click cell M3. Press **F4** repeatedly until a mixed reference style (relative column, absolute row) is selected (i.e., M$3).

6. Press **Ctrl+Enter** to enter the formula in all selected cells. The formula is adjusted automatically, and the texts from range L8:L111 in the *Data 1* worksheet are returned, with both the selected column ranges now displaying identical contents.

The =OFFSET(rD1.Node,$D11,M$3) formula used as an example here acts as an instruction to Excel to do the following: "Find the value of a cell by starting at the cell with the name *rD1.Node* and going down the number of rows specified in cell D11 and across the number of rows to the left specified in cell M3 (the direction is *left* rather than right because the value in M3 is preceded by a minus sign)."

Tip You can now test for yourself how versatile these structures can be once you've completed all of the necessary preparation. The variables in cells M3 and N3 control the column offset of the formulas. Enter a *-3* instead of a *-4* in one or both of these cells. The dependent list contents are then adjusted, and the full texts are replaced with the abbreviated versions from the M8:M111 range of the *Data 1* sheet.

Then switch back to *-4* because you want to use the full texts in this model to help the user make a well-directed selection.

Constructing formulas this way gives you a great deal of flexibility and, in many cases, frees you from having to construct and manage arrays. In such cases, it no longer matters where something is located in the source data range because you can easily extract any type of content from any location using offset formulas, which have the ability to move all over the worksheet like a spider in a web.

Make sure that you are absolutely clear about how this formula works in connection with the auxiliary structures that have been created for this purpose. The variables defined (which can easily be changed) for the column offset and row offset determine which cells are read in the source data range. All you need as your starting or reference point is the *node*.

Go to the *Data 1* worksheet. The figures in blue font in column G and row 3 indicate the distance of the columns or rows from the *rD1.Node* (shown with a yellow background), which you defined earlier in cell P7. These figures are provided for information purposes only and have a temporary use; i.e., they provide a panoramic view to help the developer of the model construct offset formulas.

Generating and Using Controls

Go back to the *Lists 1* worksheet. There's now nothing to stop you implementing the necessary controls. First, you'll generate and test these in this worksheet, then copy them to the *Basis 1* worksheet and test them again, Finally, you'll use them for their intended purpose in the *Focus 1* worksheet of the model.

> **Note** Two different types of control have been available in Excel for years, namely *form controls* and *ActiveX controls*. Detailed information about both is provided in Chapter 7, "Elements of Dynamization." In our example, we only need to use two objects belonging to the *form controls* category, which are very easy to generate and to use.

1. Select the *Developer* tab in the *Ribbon*, and click the *Insert* button in the *Controls* group.

2. Note the following points with reference to Figure 2-33: In the top half of the list, click the second object from the left below the title *Form Controls*; i.e., the *Combo Box* (which I refer to as a *drop-down list* in this book in accordance with its function). Release the mouse button and move the cursor to a free cell in the top left of the worksheet. Excel is now ready to draw an object, and the cursor changes from an arrow to a plus sign.

3. Hold down the mouse button and drag to draw a small rectangle with proportions based on the examples shown in Figure 2-31 and Figure 2-33.

4. Right-click the control to select it, and select the *Format Control* option in the context menu. If necessary, open the *Control* tab in the dialog box that appears. Here you define the properties that the control will have in this model.

   As you can see, you need to define an *input range* and a *cell link* in this dialog box. The input range refers to the list definition range (i.e., the cell range) that contains the texts that are to appear in the drop-down list. You know that you've already given this area a name: *rL1.Venue01List*. Unfortunately, you can't insert this name using the **F3** button in this case. Instead, you must enter it in the box next to *Input range* or paste it in from the clipboard (with **Ctrl+V**) if you've already copied it there.

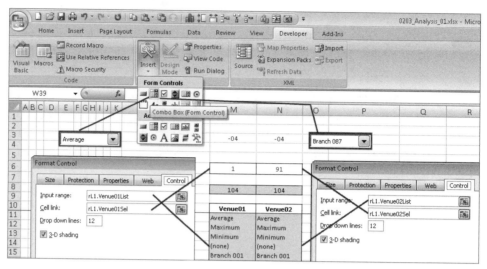

FIGURE 2-33 Assignments are required for the controls to work.

5. If you follow the rules of the rS1.Method to the letter, the *cell link*, which is the cell to which the user's "click result" will be directed, will be none other than *rL1.Venue01Sel*. This simplifies subsequent steps for you. Select the name you've just defined as your *input range*, and press **Ctrl+C** to copy it to the clipboard. Next, click in the *Cell link* box, press **Ctrl+V** to paste the name from the clipboard, and then replace the *List* element of this name with *Sel*.

   Let's sum up what we've done so far. The control takes the texts that are to appear as a drop-down list from a range with the name *rL1. Venue01List*. When the user clicks to make a selection, it then inserts a number into a cell with the name *rL1. Venue01Sel*.

6. The setting you make here for the *dropdown lines* determines how many list entries are visible when the user clicks on the element's drop-down arrow to display the list. The list has 104 entries, and so it makes little sense to display all at once. I recommend that you select *12*, which will provide a relatively comprehensive selection in most cases without taking up too much screen space.

7. Enable the *3-D shading* option (you should always do this for similar objects, to make them look better on a color background), and press *OK* to finish defining the properties of this control.

8. It's essential that you now test the control before proceeding any further. Click in a different area in the worksheet to deselect the element. Click the list's drop-down arrow to open it, and click the first entry shown. The figure *1* should now appear in the linked cell, M6, which has the name *rL1.Venue01Sel*. Select the final entry in the control, and check that the figure *104* appears in the linked cell.

> **Note** If you want to select the control object to resize or move it, click the object while holding down the **Ctrl** key. The object now appears inside a dotted selection border, which you can click and move with the mouse. Point *in* the selected object to move it. When the pointer changes to a cross pointer, click and hold down the mouse button and drag the object to the position you want. For more precise positioning, select the object and use the **left arrow**, **right arrow, up arrow**, and **down arrow** keys.

You've now positioned the first control on the left of the screen to indicate that this object is associated with the definition range on the left. You can now create the second control as a copy of the first in just a few moves.

9. Select the control object you've just created (with the **Ctrl** key pressed) and copy it to the clipboard. Select a cell to the right of the list (near to column P, see Figure 2-33) and paste the content from the clipboard here.

10. If you now right-click the duplicate control, you can sit back for a moment and enjoy the benefits of using the naming conventions of the rS1.Method for the first time. All that's left for you to do is replace the figure 01 with 02 to adjust the name references on the *Control* tab.

The next steps are illustrated in Figure 2-34. You now need to add two *scroll bars*, which are to be functionally linked with the drop-down lists that I've mentioned before.

1. Select the *Developer* tab/*Controls* group in the *Ribbon* and click the *Insert* button again.

2. Under *Form Controls*, click the *Scroll Bar* object (third from the left in the second row). Point in an area in the left of the worksheet near to the first *drop-down list* and, holding down the left mouse key, drag to draw a small rectangle. This should be the same size as or slightly larger than the *drop-down list*.

3. Right-click the control and choose the *Format Control* option in the context menu. If necessary, open the *Control* tab. Now define the properties shown in the upper part of the screen in Figure 2-34:

   ❏ *Minimum value* = 1 (the minimum value corresponds to the extreme left position of the *scroll box*; i.e., the slider on the scroll bar)

   ❏ *Maximum value* = 104 (the list to be controlled has 104 entries. The maximum value corresponds to the extreme right position of the *scroll box* on the scroll bar)

   ❏ *Incremental change* = 1 (each time one of the two *arrows* on the scroll bar is clicked, the output value increases by 1)

   ❏ Page change = 10 (each time the user clicks in the area to the left or right of the *scroll box*, the output value of the control increases by 10)

   ❏ Cell link = *rL1.Venue01Sel*: the same link you assigned to the first drop-down list. If two controls have the same cell link, they are functionally connected, which means that they have a mutual influence on one another.

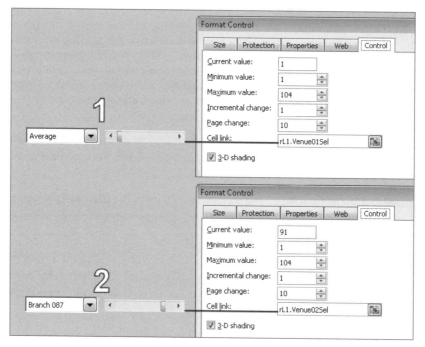

FIGURE 2-34 The scroll bars use the same links as the drop-down lists.

4. Now create a copy in the same way you did for the drop-down lists above, position this next to the second drop-down list, and change the cell link to *rL1.Venue02Sel*.

5. Check that all four controls are working correctly and pay particular attention to their cell links. The objects positioned on the left can only change the value in the *rL1. Venue01Sel* cell (in mutual synchronization), while those on the right can only change the value in the *rL1. Venue02Sel* cell.

6. The controls are created and tested in the *Lists 1* worksheet, but they aren't needed there. Hold down the **Ctrl** key and select all four controls. Then press **Ctrl+X** to cut them out of the worksheet. Open the *Basis 1* worksheet and paste the objects there. You should now position the controls clearly as shown in Figure 2-35. If you would find it helpful, assign a number to each, to help you know which control influences which number series when you start creating and checking formulas in the next step.

Defining and Preparing the *Basis 1* Worksheet

The formulas and constants in the *Basis 1* worksheet serve as a basis for the chart that the user sees in the focus of the model and can adjust using the controls.

Before we start to generate the few formulas required here (a very easy exercise for you after all the preparation you've already done), I want to briefly explain the row-specific component of this worksheet. Note the following points with reference to Figure 2-35:

- Row range G5:P5: The calendar week specifications are used to label the chart's primary horizontal axis.

- Row range F6:P6: The data configured using the two controls from group 1, and which generates the blue line in the chart, is inserted into this range.

- Row range F7:P7: The data configured using the two controls from group 2, and which generates the orange line in the chart, is inserted into this range.

- Row range F8:P8: Here you define as constants the data that generates the area with the light green background in the chart to show how long the campaign lasted in the customer project that is represented.

Formulas of the Variable Chart Basis

You're already familiar from the previous section with the OFFSET function and how efficiently it can be used. Because this is the only function we'll be using here, all you need is the following brief set of instructions:

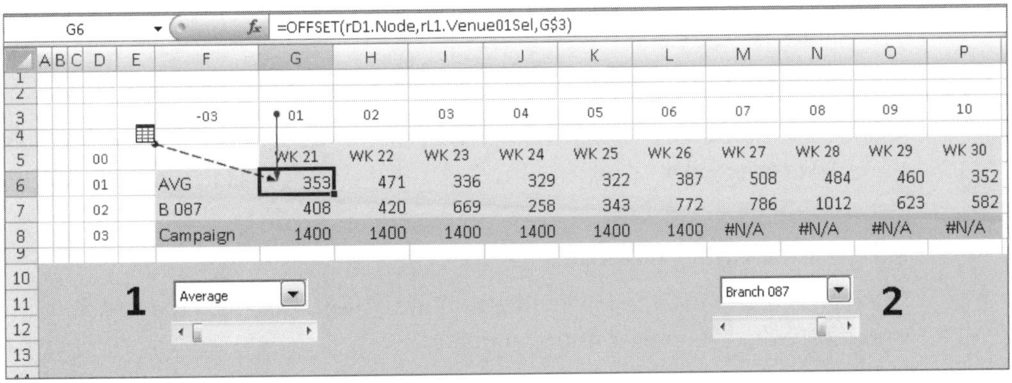

FIGURE 2-35 Test the interaction between the formulas and controls in the *Basis 1* worksheet.

1. Select the range F6:P7 and enter the formula below in the active cell (F6) as described earlier. Press **Ctrl+Enter** to assign the formula to the entire range selected.

   The formula =OFFSET(rD1.Node,rL1.Venue01Sel,G$3) finds a value that is the same number of rows away from the *rD1.Node* cell as the value specified in cell with the name *rL1.Venue01Sel*, and the same number of columns away from the node as the value in cell F3. In other words, you use the control to generate a number that is output in cell *rL1.Venue01Sel*. This number is, in turn, the row argument of the OFFSET formulas used here. The column argument, meanwhile, is defined in auxiliary row 3 and can be changed if necessary (for example, if you need the source data to be inserted in the reverse sequence, which happens more often that you might imagine). Note that the flexibility of the method comes into play here once again, and the labels in column F are extracted from the data source in abbreviated form rather than in full text format.

2. The two formula rows don't currently respond to the various controls. However, this is easily changed. Simply select the range F7 : P7, change the name *rL1.Venue01Sel* in the active cell to *rL1.Venue02Sel*, and press **Ctrl+Enter** to apply it to all cells in the selected range.

At this point, you should perform a careful check to ensure that using the controls produces the right results in the right cells. You should also use the controls to insert various number series, and then check the source data to ensure that the correct values were delivered. Make the same selections for both data rows during these checks to see whether the numbers are identical. I hope you won't consider these checks super-fluous. Experience shows (and you'll see for yourself) that it's exactly those errors that you imagine at the outset will never happen that are the most difficult to pin down and correct when they do.

3. Select the G5 : P5 range, enter the formula =OFFSET(rD1.Node,$D5,G$3) in the active cell, and press **Ctrl+Enter** to confirm the entry. These formulas take the texts specifying the calendar week numbers from the *Data 1* worksheet and use these to label the chart's primary horizontal axis. Cell F5 remains blank.

4. Next, enter the label *Campaign*, the figure *1400*, and the error values *#N/A* in row 8 as shown in Figure 2-35.

5. Apply a color to all cells containing formula as described on page 80/81.

You've now completed all the preparations needed to develop the dynamic chart shown in the focus of the model.

A Dynamic Chart Emerges

The chart is created and tested in the *Basis 1* worksheet. Only then is it copied to the *Focus 1* worksheet, where it receives its final format.

Note the following points with reference to Figure 2-36:

1. Ensure that you have enough space on the screen to afford you a panoramic view of the table data, controls, and chart while completing the steps outlined below. For this reason, I've clicked on the two controls in group 2 while holding down the **Ctrl** key, and moved these to the bottom left of my screen.

2. To help you keep the lines completely separate from one another while editing the chart, it's advisable to use the controls to read two clearly distinct data series. For example, you could use group 1 to read the *maximum* and group 2 to read the *minimum*, or use the settings *Average* and *Branch 087*, as shown in Figure 2-36.

3. Select the range F5 : P8, which provides a basis for the chart as a whole. Select the *Insert* tab in the *Ribbon*, and click the *Line* button in the *Charts* group. From the list of options displayed, select the default *Line with Markers*. This selection is the most suitable for most display purposes where a line chart is required.

4. After you click to make this selection, the chart is generated, and is shown with the standard Excel 2007 border. Use the *selection handles* on this border to give the chart a manageable size, keeping in mind that the most important thing for now is that it can be edited. As you can see, all essential chart elements already exist and all you need to worry about is formatting. You may, for example, wonder why the finished model contains a green area on the left for WK 21 to WK 26, while the basic model you've just generated only shows a horizontal line with the value 1,400 for this period. However, this line will soon be transformed into an area and must simply be ignored for now.

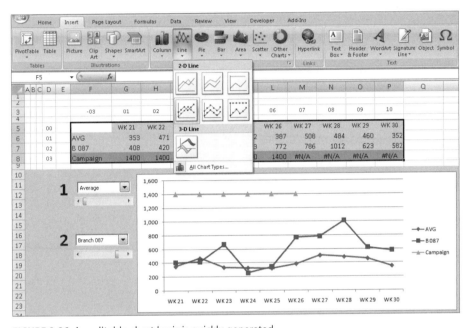

FIGURE 2-36 An editable chart basis is quickly generated.

5. Now it's time to set the two variable data rows free, using your controls to read the data in any combination of your choice. The legend will naturally be adjusted to suit your selection.

Tip In the next step, you'll remove the chart and controls from this worksheet and add them to the focus of the model. This step is optional, and there are many situations in which it makes sense to leave these objects in their basic form in the *Basis 1* worksheet so that they can be changed or enhanced for testing purposes, even in the finished solution.

6. Select the chart and press **Ctrl+X** to cut it to the clipboard. Open the *Focus 1* worksheet, select cell B3, and press **Ctrl+V** to paste the chart from the clipboard. Repeat this process for the controls, and position these in the cell range provided, i.e. J13:M16. The worksheet should now appear as shown in the *0203_Analysis_01.xlsx* sample file and in Figure 2-7.

Defining the *Focus 1* Worksheet

In the remaining steps, each element in the chart is formatted. The procedures described next and the screen shots provided only explain what you need to know to produce a more or less identical copy of the Focus 1 worksheet in the *0203_Analysis_01.xlsx* sample file. In later chapters, you'll come across several models in which the formatting and design of chart elements is described and explained in great detail. Here, however, we simply want to complete the solution and ensure that the model has a well-ordered appearance to match its dynamic functions.

> **Important** To implement the step-by-step instructions below, you'll need to use some techniques and options that differ considerably from those familiar to you from former versions of Excel. The relevant procedures have already been described in Chapter 1 under *Basic Functions*. Therefore, I'll simply refer to these here. You might want to reread Chapter 1 to remind yourself of the main points. Note in particular the new options that make formatting objects much easier in Excel 2007: You can keep the formatting dialog box open at all times as you work through the various chart elements.

The sequence of steps I've chosen here isn't yet based on a structured concept, but it does take account of didactical principles and is intended to help the beginner become gradually familiar with the multiform formatting dialog system of Excel 2007.

Formatting the Chart Area and Plot Area

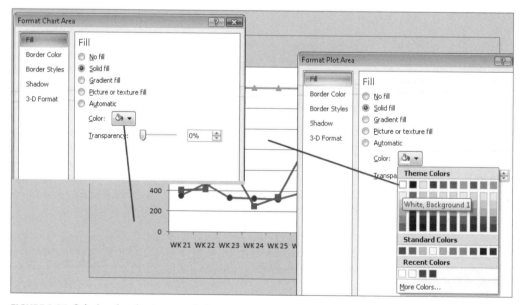

FIGURE 2-37 Coloring the *chart area* and *plot area*

1. Select the *chart area* and use the *selection handles* to drag it to a size and shape of your choice. Do the same with the *plot area*.

2. Select the *chart area* and open the formatting dialog box; for example, by right-clicking in the chart area and selecting the *Format Chart Area* option in the context menu, or by pressing **Ctrl+1** on your keyboard.

3. Select *Fill* and then the *Solid fill* option, click the *Color* button, and assign a light blue color to the *chart area*, which matches or is identical to the surrounding fill color of the table.

4. Keeping the dialog box open, select the *plot area,* and assign a white fill color to it the same way.

Formatting the Variable Data Series

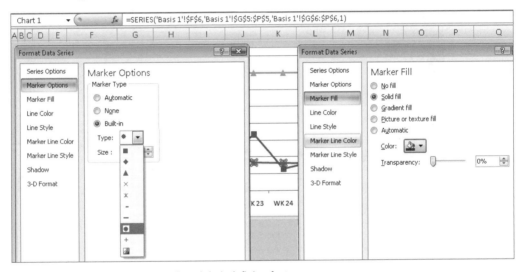

FIGURE 2-38 The data series are assigned their defining features.

Select the first of the variable data series (i.e., one of the two series that can be changed using the controls) and make the following settings in the formatting dialog box, where the title has now changed to *Format Data Series*:

1. Select *Marker Options*, select the *Built-in* option, click the *Type* button, and select the circle icon in the lower part of the list, to which you should assign the size 7.

2. Select *Marker Fill*, select the *Solid fill* option, and choose white as your fill color.

3. Select *Marker Line Color*, select the *Solid line* option, and choose a bright blue line color.

4. Select *Marker Line Style*, select a *width* of 1.5 pt, and, at the bottom of the dialog box, select the *Smoothed line* option, which will give your data series a smooth and elegant shape.

5. Select *Line Style* and choose a width of 1.5 pt. here also.

6. Select *Line Color*, select the *Solid line* option, and choose the same color you chose in step 3 for the *marker line.*

Now select the other variable data row and repeat steps 1 to 6 described above. However, select a diamond shape as the *type* in step 1, and select a bright orange color as your marker line color.

Formatting the Primary Vertical Axis

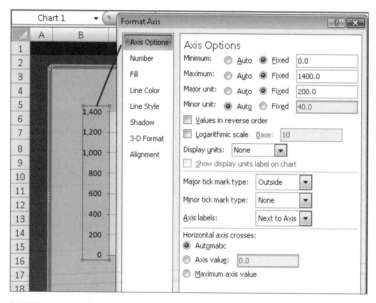

FIGURE 2-39 Assigning a user-defined fixed scale to the *primary vertical axis*

1. Select the *primary vertical axis* and, under *Axis Options*, select a fixed scale range, starting at *0* and ending at *1,400*, with a major unit of *200*. Among other things, this enables a precise comparison between the data rows because the axes can't now be re-scaled automatically, and so each data series will assume the correct position in the chart.

2. Select *Number,* and choose a thousands format with a separator.

3. Under *Line Color* and *Line Style*, you can select various options, which have already been explained in the previous step.

Formatting the Static Data Series and Gridlines

You've now assigned a fixed maximum value of 1,400 to the primary vertical axis. As a result, the static data series for which you defined this same value on the *Basis 1* worksheet now appears at the top of the plot area. You now want to turn this line into an area that fills the part of the plot area that corresponds to the campaign period of the project (i.e., calendar weeks 21 to 26) with a specific color.

Because the marking of this data series is a little more complex than in other cases, I'll describe the procedure in detail here:

1. Select the *Chart Tools/Layout* tab in the *Ribbon*, click the drop-down arrow in the *Current Selection* group, and select the *Series "Campaign"* entry. This data series is then selected.

2. Now open the *Chart Tools/Design* tab, and click the *Change Chart Type* button in the *Type* group.

3. In the dialog box that opens, (see Figure 2-40), select *Column* as the chart type and select the first chart sub-type shown—*Clustered Column*—as the chart type of the series. Click *OK* to convert the line into columns.

4. Select the columns generated, and open the *Format Data Series* dialog box again. Select *Series Options*, and move the slider for the *Gap Width* setting all the way to the *No Gap* position on the far left. This corresponds to a gap width of 0 percent, which you also could have entered in the field provided. This brings all the columns together in one area.

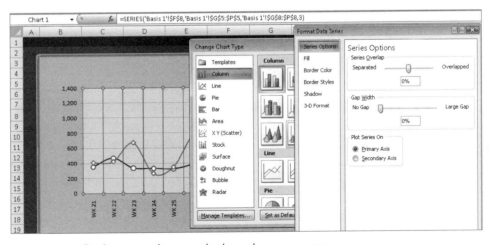

FIGURE 2-40 A line becomes columns, and columns become an area

5. Next, select the *Fill* command, and then select the *Solid fill* option. Choose a green color and set its *transparency* with the slider or by entering the value 66 percent. As a

result, the area you created in the previous step becomes partially transparent, so that the *horizontal gridlines* underneath can be seen.

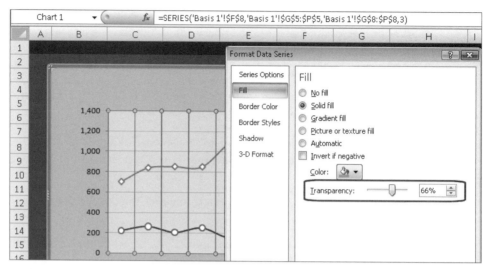

FIGURE 2-41 A transparent area allows the gridlines to be seen

6. Open the *Chart Tools/Layout* tab in the *Ribbon*, and select Gridlines/*Primary Vertical Gridlines/Major Gridlines* in the *Axes* group to add the vertical gridlines to the plot area.

7. Select the *gridlines* (you must select the horizontal and vertical gridlines separately), and enter a subtle line color and weight.

Formatting the Primary Horizontal Axis

Finally, select the primary horizontal axis and make the appropriate formatting settings. I won't prompt you with any hints or suggestions this time!

You've now been introduced to a range of possible settings, which will have an even more important role to play in later chapters. At this stage, you should try to get your bearings by becoming familiar with all of the possible options, with what's familiar to you from your experience of earlier Excel versions, and what may be completely new to you.

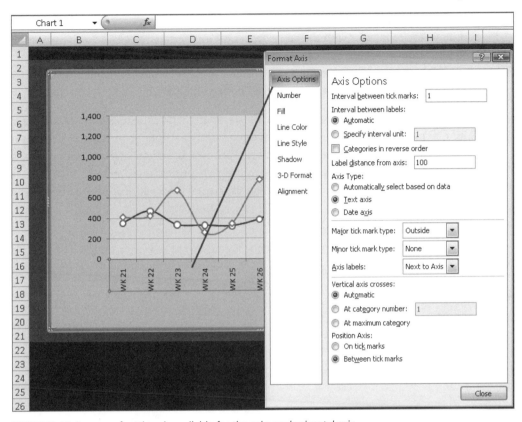

FIGURE 2-42 A range of settings is available for the *primary horizontal axis*

Summary

Of course, we're not finished yet—not by a long shot! Apart from the fact that a number of small details are yet to be clarified (for example, how to format legends, insert logos, and enter labels), there's still a lot for you to learn about the options for editing, changing, and improving the appearance of the example introduced here. However, now that you've completed this guided tour of the structures of the rS1.Method and the basic functions in Excel 2007 (which you've no doubt found strenuous), we'll leave these for later chapters.

You've seen how using the new program version is, in some respects, more complex and therefore more difficult than before. The main reason is undoubtedly the vast number of enhancements that have been made in terms of design options. I've already pointed out that the focus of this book isn't on the many predefined styles available with Excel. Instead, it examines the options for user-defined and dynamic chart designs of all types. If you want to rise to the challenge and put in the effort required to achieve demonstrable results that *don't* just look like one-size-fits-all solutions, you'll need to really immerse yourself in the program, and keep raising the bar for yourself along the way. You've already begun this process here.

But this was just the start. You now know how to construct a basic model for a dynamic solution. You're familiar with the key extracting functions, have seen a real-life example of a basic model in action, and can assess its various structural components. Finally, you've walked through all of the steps necessary to produce a useful and attractive model, which, with some modifications, could be used even by the uninitiated.

We've now mapped out the route to our destination. Of course, it won't always be a complex or complicated as this. Many of the examples and descriptions to come will have less relevance for you, and some will have more. However, once you've made your way to the end of the book, you'll know how to develop impressive, professional, and effective chart solutions. When you look back on the example in this chapter, it will appear useful but rather simple by comparison.

Chapter 3
Perceiving, Interpreting, Understanding

In the summary of the last chapter, the following statement was of particular importance: "We've now mapped out the route to our destination." In other words, you've taken a look at the main topics covered in this book and, after staking out the route for a highway that will lead us to our destination, you've acquired some hands-on experience using Excel 2007. However, before we can continue along this route, we must discuss the basics in further detail. This is because each time you design an Excel chart (whatever its purpose), you should be able to not only explain *how* you created the chart, but *why* you chose this *particular* chart type above all others. Such self-imposed responsibility for explaining your decision must be grounded in theory. One such theory, known as "the theory of perception and understanding" is a major concern. The phrase "perception and understanding" speaks to a phenomenon that permeates our daily lives, helps us make the right decisions, and yet leads to our worst mistakes: we do not understand everything we perceive as it actually is. Therefore, much of what we want to understand ourselves and make understandable to others breaks down under the natural limitations of human perception or suffers from deficiencies in our interpreting skills. Furthermore, that which we can perceive with our limited senses but which is beyond our ability to understand has no chance whatever of being translated into beneficial action. This is a vast topic because it affects the future of humanity. However, in a book devoted to Excel charts, I can only highlight this issue. Therefore, let's now take a closer look at the topic of perception and the consequences associated with the charts that we choose to design.

Perception and the Laws of Perception

What we see or understand to see in certain circumstances is the result of a very complex brain activity. This, like each of our physiological potentialities, is subject to certain universal laws and limitations that must be considered and observed when designing charts and other visual images.

Determining Our Limitations

Let me begin with a clearly unreasonable demand:

 On the Companion CD Open the file *\Samples\0301_MallCupola.xlsx* on the CD-ROM.

In the context of Figure 3-1:

You are visiting a posh shopping mall and you are looking up at its cupola. Above you float four partially transparent spheres, each a different color and size. Each of the spheres can change its volume and move "three-dimensionally" within the curve of the dome; that is, up and down and side to side. From your standpoint, the spheres become smaller when they float upwards and larger when they gravitate downwards. This is a typical Excel chart. If you press **F9** to generate new data, the spheres will change their position and size.

> **Note** All of the visual illustrations and photos used in this book, partially available in *Materials*\ *Pictures*, were provided by *Nina Schiller*, a communications designer.

The chart illustrates the weekly revenue of four of the most exclusive shops in this shopping mall. The following rules will help you interpret the chart:

- Each color is assigned to one of the shops.

- The volume of the sphere represents the revenue in dollars.

- The sphere's height within the dome indicates the number of business transactions made to generate the revenue. If some of the spheres fully or partially overlap each other, the relationship of revenue to the number of business transactions is the same or similar. However, those spheres that are positioned higher in the dome and whose color effect is weaker are more important.

- The orientation of each sphere's center to the structure of the dome, moving clockwise from the 12 o'clock position, shows the extent to which current revenue deviates from revenue for the previous year.

- If one of the spheres floats into the dead center of the dome, this signals the highest revenue for all comparable weeks unless...

FIGURE 3-1 Easy to understand

Let's stop there. Naturally, all of this is contrived nonsense and the caption for the figure is a tongue-in-cheek. We simply *can't* understand it. We might understand it if a well thought-out and well illustrated interpretative text accompanied the figure, along with all kinds of supporting additional displays. However, we would then immediately ask for: a) the reason for such data in the first place, and b) the presentation of this data in a complex chart that also would necessitate an explanation.

Given all this, I can't help wondering why various publications or live presentations use charts that, although in a less spectacular way, place a similarly high and purely unnecessary demand on the ability of their beloved target audience to interpret these charts. Those people who think that they have removed themselves from the ordinary limitations of basic human abilities should—as far as I'm concerned—reexamine how well they actually use these abilities.

The basic rules to be deduced from the above example are as follows:

- "If you can't find an easy way to use simple means to convey the information that you *want* to impart, then it is better not to show it at all!"

- "If you expect someone to find an easy way to use simple means to explain something that you do not understand at the first attempt, then you know that others will also expect the same from you."

I now wish to take a few examples from the file *0302_Limits.xlsx* to explain what we mean by "an easy way" and also where we already fail when using "simple means."

The sample files belonging to this chapter contain many charts that have relatively simple structures and formats. Some show formats that were previously impossible to achieve in Excel or were only possible with considerable effort. This can and should also be an incentive for you to experiment with different formats.

Most of the charts provided here are less than challenging and relatively well suited to testing the different format assignments and format combination assignments integrated into Excel 2007. This is a procedure that I recommend with reservation because, even though it is yet to be substantiated, it nevertheless belongs to the extensive new features of Excel and therefore requires practice. One of the goals of this book is for you to also be able to set up, by your own efforts, most of the formats that were recently semi-automated in Excel. It will save you time and effort to initially assign integrated format combinations of varying complexity to charts and then partially modify this combination in detail.

Therefore, if you wish to use the sample files for this chapter to test the format combinations, I recommend that you proceed as follows:

1. Rename the relevant file and save it to your hard disk.

2. If necessary, unprotect the sheet (*Review* tab/*Changes* group/*Unprotect Sheet* command button). Then click the chart that you want to use for the formatting tests. By doing so, you insert the *Chart Tools* and their three tabs (*Design, Layout,* and *Format*) into the *ribbon*.

3. Determine the options available:

   ❑ On the *Design* tab page, use the *Chart Styles* or the *Chart Layouts*.

   ❑ Use the *Layout* tab to experiment with different chart labels, grids, and lines.

   ❑ Use the commands of the *Format* tab/*Shape Styles* group to determine which of the many display variants your overall chart and its individual elements can accept.

Naturally, you are not expected to tackle all of these many options yourself. Later in this book, you will receive detailed information and step-by-step instructions. Nevertheless, most readers will gradually experiment with the program's new features and will benefit from this hands-on approach.

On the Companion CD Open the file \Samples\0302_Limits.xlsx on the CD-ROM. You can press **F9** to change the data in all seven worksheets. By doing so, you obtain numerous displays of varying complexity, ranging from difficult to understand to completely unintelligible.

- *Perception 1* worksheet: In one quick glance, try to determine how many columns are displayed each time you press **F9**. Several factors can make this difficult, namely the total number of columns present, the groups formed in each case, and the length of time you require to familiarize yourself with the entire display. Even if you know that no more than 10 columns are permitted, it is sometimes extremely difficult to spontaneously determine whether there are currently six or seven columns, for example. After some time, your confidence in estimating the number of columns grows even if the number of columns exceeds five.

- *Perception 2* worksheet: It becomes even more difficult if you have to process additional information. Each column now has a different height and an unsightly color or pattern. Even if the formatting remains exactly the same in each chart, it takes you longer to recognize this before you can estimate the number of columns as easily as you did in the previous example.

- *Perception 3* worksheet: If you have become familiar with the layout in the *Perception 1* worksheet, you will not have serious trouble determining the number of elements here. However, this success is short-lived because the color combination used here is particularly unfavorable for our optical system. Therefore, your eyes become strained very quickly and you need to look away (for more information, see Chapter 4 , "Colors, Areas, and Outlines").

- *Perception 4* worksheet: To frighten you even more, this worksheet uses not only the headache-inducing red/blue combination, but drastically impairs your ability to identify the individual columns by presenting all kinds of unwanted additional information.

- *Perception 5* worksheet: To help you relax, we return to a more harmonious and friendly image (at least in terms of the colors used). However, because the elements are no longer displayed in linear form, the potential learning curve achieved earlier with the columns is weakened considerably. Furthermore, for various combinations (not only for overlapping elements), it is extremely difficult to quickly determine the correct number of points without actually counting them.

- *Perception 6* worksheet: It is even more problematic if the points are inflated to form hollow circles that sometimes overlap with each other, making it difficult for you to differentiate between them, and thus considerably damaging your perception.

- *Perception 7* worksheet: In some cases, it may help to draw a line that connects the circles to each other, so that it is easier for you to count them. This is helpful if the line creates an easy-to-follow "route" that leads you from one circle to another. However, if the line takes confusing twists and turns and has random "hooks," it is hardly a "good design." In fact, the recognition process is hindered rather than helped. This is espe-cially true because our perception of a complex image initially places the line over the circles. Therefore, to identify the circles themselves, you require a type of "filter pro-cess" that once again weakens your perception of the line.

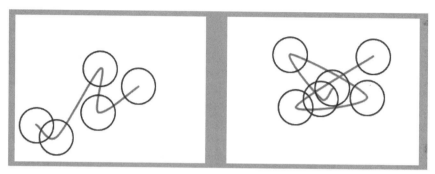

FIGURE 3-2 The line can help or considerably hinder your perception.

It becomes quickly apparent that even a simple request to count 10 or fewer columns can be problematic under certain circumstances and can expose specific limitations in our brain ac-tivity. This section is entitled "Determining Our Limitations." These limitations exist wherever the biological evolution of humanity has been at work.

100 Million Years

In March 2007, the highly regarded natural scientific journal *Nature* published a report that presented an almost complete bloodline of all of today's mammal types. During a four-year research project, scientists established that our previous assumption that the "higher mam-mals" first came into being after the dinosaurs became extinct approximately 65 million years ago was completely wrong. We can now assume that all orders of today's higher mammals came into being approximately 100 to 85 million years ago. This period of time, regardless of whether it spanned 65 or 100 million years, is enormous, and even though we can acknowl-edge it, calculate it, and chart it, we can't fully "comprehend" it. Nor do we need to: at least not in this book. However, it is important to note that the evolutionary development of any sensory systems that help us to more or less find our way in this world took much longer than we can possibly comprehend.

Fossils, which are the remains of the *Homo sapiens* (the mammal also known as "modern man"), date back to approximately 150,000 years ago, which is nothing when compared with the period of 100 million years quoted above (just try creating a comparative representa-tion of both figures in one chart). However, let's pretend that we can comprehend a period of time spanning 150,000 years. Then let's consider the extremely minuscule percentage that represents this period of 150,000 years in which the perceptive capabilities of this *Homo sapi-ens* had to process something other than natural phenomena under natural conditions. How would the presence of tools, textiles, buildings, coaches, factories, artificial light, vehicles, air-planes, televisions, computers, or multifunctional cell phones have influenced the physiology of our perception? They wouldn't have in the slightest. Our fives senses (sight, hearing, smell, taste, and touch) are all that was and could be developed during this incredibly long period of time. They combine in a system that can help a highly adaptable life form exist in his natural environment, feed himself, procreate, and resist or flee various threats to his being. A survival system whose entire prehistory, history, and behavior span much more than 100 million years does not and can't differ greatly from the survival system that was possible or necessary 1,000, 10,000, or even 100,000 years ago. It is this system that we must continue to use to live, survive, cross roads, cope with multifunctional cell phones, and interpret charts and dialog boxes in Excel 2007. What gives us the edge over our mammal cousins, however, is something known as "cultural evolution"; namely, our extremely distinctive learning aptitude (supported by language) and our talent to quickly and effectively adapt to changing conditions by acquiring and transferring knowledge. However, the "perception system" discussed here, especially visual perception, is the primary result of a very long development history and is the current intermediate result of our "biological evolution."

In a nutshell, the earlier characteristics of our eyes and the process of interpreting impressions transmitted through them belong to a life form that had to prevail in a completely natural environment over a period of time that is simply too long for us to fully comprehend. Every non-natural phenomenon that has produced impressions and requirements within the extremely short period of only a few thousand years—however dramatic and fast-growing it may be—must still be processed using this "conservative" system.

I used the phrase "A survival system ... does not and can't differ greatly ... ." My apologies if this sounds somewhat negative. Anyone who researches perception repeatedly stumbles across something surprising, impressive, and wonderful, even after many years of research and thousands of other staggering findings. However, these also come up against very specific, very "natural" universal laws and—most important to this chapter—clear limitations.

How Does Visual Perception Work?

Whether we see something or actually perceive something (that is, accept it to be "true") is conditioned by all kinds of external and internal influences that can't be discussed here. *What* we then perceive or understand via optical input is the result of a very complex brain activity for interpreting what we see.

See, assess, and respond, all done as quickly as possible. What is it? What does it mean to me? What do I do now? Such very short-linked "decision chains" have always been associated and continue to be associated with survival. We are continuously exposed to such aptitude tests, and the primary skill of those who pass them is the ability to quickly arrange images into categories in order to compare them more easily. Only after an assessment—even if this happens wholly or partially subliminally—is sufficient "classified material" available to support a response.

What we know as "visual perception" is an extremely complex, sometimes puzzling process. It comprises numerous components that, in turn, are subject to various determinants (for example, physiological, psychological, social, and cultural determinants). In the case of our subject—the image perception of charts—the following is true of a rough basic paradigm of a stimulus-response model:

1. There is electromagnetic radiation (light rays).

2. The radiation is received as a light stimulus from an optical system (eye).

3. The stimulus received is converted (chemically or electrically) and transmitted along pathways to different parts of the brain.

4. The stimulus received in the brain is decoded and then interpreted. This requires a highly dendritic system that is capable of spontaneous interpretation, but that must also access both legacy and ancillary information.

5. If procedures 1 – 4 take place, the brain triggers a response to the stimulus. Whether this is "measured and correct" in today's sense can only be verified once the response has been triggered. The response *can* be deliberate, but only occasionally. The majority of responses to visual stimuli happen involuntarily and are based on the basic evolutionary principles addressed above.

In general, the main objective of a procedure designed in this way is the ability to survive, whether you have to perceive something that appears to be appetizing from a distance, whether a ravenous scowling tiger appears two meters away from you in the jungle, or whether someone says "as you can see here" and then proceeds to show you a completely unintelligible chart.

To summarize:

- The way in which perception works has a great deal to do with the development history of humanity (biological evolution). An individual's history, personal situation, time, appearance, and equipment (aspects of cultural evolution) are secondary.

- To ensure a response to a sensation within the shortest timeframe possible, there must be systems that can decode stimuli or stimulus combinations unknown to us. If such systems exist, they must (for "safety reasons") work with very stable regularity, that is, with a foolproof universal law.

Such guidelines are the basis for understanding the "laws of perception." I will present some of these to you in the next section, primarily through the use of sample charts. These will lightly touch on something that you most likely know from many examples as an "optical illusion."

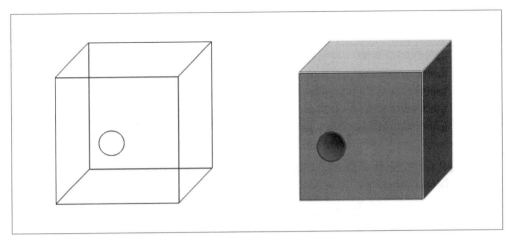

FIGURE 3-3 They are not cubes—but only the one on the left can cause confusion.

Each one of us has conducted our own "perception experiments" at least once and busied ourselves with images that convey all kinds of illusions. These frustrated us because, for example, our brain is unable to choose between one or more possible perceptions. The "Necker Cube" (shown on the left in Figure 3-3), and named after the Swiss mathematician Louis Albert Necker, is one of many well-known optical illusions. What is left, what is right, what is top, what is bottom, what is the front, and what is the back? Try to figure it out. What purpose does this serve? The next time you look at the cube, it may be different. Biological and cultural perception problems rub shoulders with each other here. To assess the space, depth, and distance, we require differences in color, brightness, size, and comparable size. We also need experience in recognizing and assessing unnatural shapes.

The Most Important Laws of Perception

Let me use the file *0303_Perception.xlsx* to illustrate some of the laws that influence our perception and their major importance when designing visualizations.

On the Companion CD Open the file \Samples\0303_Perception.xlsx on the CD-ROM.

It may be interesting to work through the examples with another person in order to establish which perceptions are common to you both and which are not.

The "laws" (an often disputed term) described here do not have a uniform naming convention nor a universally valid classification or structure. I am merely using the following definitions because they have been used widely in modern publications.

Here's something a little wicked to get us started: Take a look at Figure 3-4:

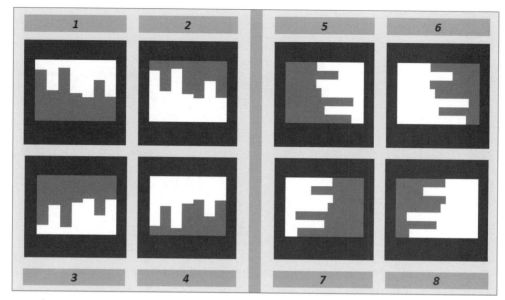

FIGURE 3-4 What is the foreground? What is the background? Which chart is correct?

I'd like to answer this immediately: Even the caption for Figure 3-4 is one of those little evil tricks that you will encounter in the sample file. It isn't that I want to trick or provoke you, but such examples are a good way of proving which perception phenomena take place in our brains.

Now let me answer the third question in the caption: All eight charts are "correct," as each of them is based on the same data series. Sometimes the bright area is the background and sometimes the dark area is the background. However, the more important question for us is: Which of the objects *seem* to be correct?

The Law of Figure and Background

Our perception tries to determine whether something in our field of vision is a "figure." For this purpose, it must be possible to distinguish between proximity and background. The better the figure fits into a meaningful pattern or comparison pattern, the more definite (and faster) the perception. Figure and background are directly related to each other and influence each other. We can't perceive anything unless there is a background. Even what seems to be a void is interpreted as a background.

The significant keywords from an evolutionary viewpoint are: "Is there something there? What is it? How far away is it? Is it moving? Is it moving towards me? Is it moving away from me?"

Examples Press **F9** several times to create new charts in the *Shape 1*, *Shape 2*, and *Shape 3* worksheets.

In the *Shape 1* sheet, it is extremely difficult to identify what is the foreground and what is the background, which *figure* actually visualizes the numbers, or what is the area in front of this figure. Sometimes, the only way to identify the data series and the plot area is to actually click the chart.

Note The worksheets in this file are protected without a password. If you want to examine the data background or formatting in detail, unprotect the sheet.

Can you identify the foreground and background of the charts in the *Shape 2* worksheet? This question is slightly crueler. There is no visible background in the *plot area*. Instead, you see two reciprocating series of columns that always fully complement each other.

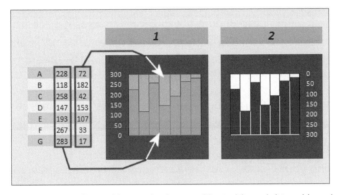

FIGURE 3-5 A chart without a background but with upright and hanging columns.

Figure 3-5 indicates what you can't immediately see in the worksheet because of the special formatting (this requires the reader to have some basic knowledge of designing charts).

- Each chart has two *data series* in column form, each with its own *vertical axis*.

- The data in the left numbers column comprises random numbers between 100 and 300. The data in the right numbers column is the difference between the left column and 300.

- The scale of both vertical axes is fixed at 300.

- The *secondary vertical axis*, which belongs to the data series from the right numbers column, is defined with *values in reverse order* and, as a result, the columns *hang* in the plot area (this is not generally a feature of columns, but results in the entire background area being covered here).

- The *Gap Width* option for both series of columns is set to *No Gap* (0 percent). As a result, both series of columns become areas and the *plot area* itself is no longer visible.

> **Note** Was there an easier way to represent this information? Perhaps using a stacked column chart and formatting it accordingly would have been easier. Would you now like to represent this information in exactly the way described above? If not now, maybe later. That would be a rather challenging exercise. However, you would learn considerably more than you would by using a stacked column chart.

Press **F9** several times. The charts remain the same; that is, increasingly harder from charts 1 to 4 even though you already know the trick for interpreting these charts. Note how your brain really tries to dispense with the virtually invisible background.

View the *Shape 3* worksheet: At long last, charts that make sense. Finally, we have clear relationships and recognizable figures against identifiable backgrounds. Each chart looks strangely different even though the same data is plotted each time. This is at least a starting point. Among other things, it allows us to deduce the following important piece of information: Because these charts have such varied effects, you can never remain indifferent to the display objectives that can be achieved with each chart type. These will be covered in greater detail in the section entitled "Which Diagram for Which Purpose."

Let's begin with a little game: Press **F9** until you see a shape in chart 7 that looks something like a kite, the hull of a boat or, at the very least, a hand axe or something that you recognize. Note how your brain is pleased to discover such a "figure."

Consequences of Designing your Charts   Clear relationships increase acceptance among observers. They can:

- Provide clearly identifiable backgrounds
- Use formatting to clearly separate a "figure" (the data series) from its background
- Create "figures" using easy-to-understand shapes
- Create depth effects using gradual brightness: a dark background, a somewhat brighter midground (optional), and finally a bright foreground

The Law of Simplicity or "Good Figure"

This law, also known as the "law of precision," is frequently regarded in Gestalt psychology as a central higher-level principle that comprises other laws. It states that, from the options available, people will always find the simplest, clearest way of combining individual parts so that they form a whole. This takes place under an uncompromising pressure to identify what they see. The meaning that stands out as being the present "best"—i.e., the "correct" meaning—is assigned to the sensation. This is almost always the meaning that can be assigned most quickly to a clear figure.

In this context, please understand the word *figure* in abstract terms, in the sense of a reference pattern. In our consciousness, each sensation, whatever it is, can only have one present meaning. This is also the case with highly complex "figures" that comprise multiple combinations of several simultaneous sensations. As a result, people occasionally respond incorrectly in critical situations that require fast response, with fatal consequences.

Significant questions from an evolutionary viewpoint are: "What do I see there? Is it a lurking predator or simply the tree's shadow?" This ambiguity needs to be resolved immediately. Otherwise, the response will be inadequate. Even if several interpretations are possible, the consciousness must and can deduce just one meaning.

If you doubt that statement, think back to the "Necker Cube," which you have already seen in Figure 3-3, and which is also shown in the *Cube* worksheet in the sample file. Of course, this is not a cube, but rather a two-dimensional line drawing that resembles a cube. However, if your brain wants it to be a cube, then it *is* a cube because we have learned what a cube is and how it looks. But *how* do you see it? From the top or from the bottom? Are you looking at its left or right outer surface? Is the hole in the front or back wall of the cube? After a few brief attempts, you can see everything without any difficulty. However, your consciousness only permits one interpretation at a time. Even if you know all the different possibilities, you can't perceive everything *simultaneously*.

Examples   In simple terms, we are crazy about figures and patterns. We like to commit ourselves to them immediately. In the *Shape 1* sheet, most observers will decide that the upright columns are the "best" figures.

Furthermore, if you zoom into one of the charts, stare at it, and change it by pressing **F9** several times, note how the movement and/or the new figure influences your perception and even changes it.

With regard to the charts in the *Shape 2* sheet, most unbiased observers (that is, those who do not know about the trick concerning the absent background) will decide that chart 1 or 2 is *good* and *correct* even if they think both look a little odd.

What about the *Shape 3* sheet? Take a minute to look at it. Forget why you are looking at this sheet. It does not matter *why* these charts were created. Press **F9** to move between the current characteristics of the different figures. Each figure represents the same data series. However, which figure best represents this data series?

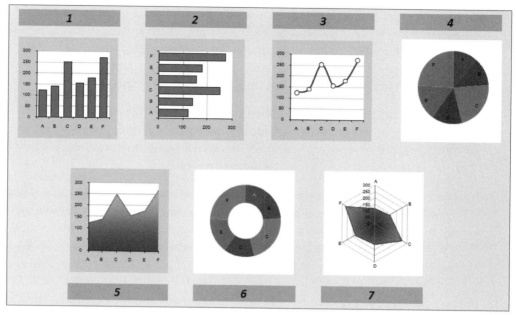

FIGURE 3-6 Which figure best represents the data series?

This is not just a matter of taste. Most observers will state a preference for charts 1 to 3, and maybe even 4, if nothing is said about the informational content. These four charts show clear, easy-to-understand images that we trust to a certain extent.

Consequences of Designing your Charts   Clear, trustworthy figures ease understanding and increase acceptance among observers, so observe the following guidelines.

- Simple and regular shapes help the observer to reduce his perception effort. Support your figure with a definite background and an intelligent color selection.

- Do not leave any room for doubt among observers. Avoid decision conflicts among observers. If, while looking at your chart, just one person begins to shake his or her head in confusion, you have already lost. It is not even necessary for that person to say, "Huh?"

- If the purpose of the presentation or the data material does not prohibit it, always choose the easiest display option from the numerous display options available. This is particularly true of mixed chart types.

The Law of Proximity

Things that are near to each other form an entity, group, or figure, and things that are apart do not belong together.

What sounds like a key phrase in sociology is also a basic rule for questions concerning layout. It would be nice if it were that simple. If this law was routinely observed, there would not be millions of careless (to the point of being abysmally) designed web sites, user interfaces, dialog boxes, tab pages, advertising brochures, pages in books, dissertations, scientific posters, or charts.

Examples   The *Proximity 1* and *Proximity 2* worksheets present charts that at first appear to be perfectly harmless, but—after you press **F9** several times—demonstrate just how the *law of proximity* works.

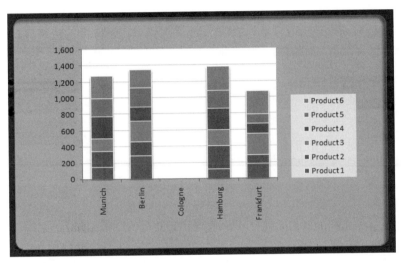

FIGURE 3-7 Groups that are not groups

Each time you press **F9** to create the chart in the *Proximity 1* worksheet (see Figure 3-7), there is always a gap that affects one of the cities. If it affects one of the three middle cities (*Berlin, Cologne,* or *Hamburg*), two apparent groups remain in the result: either two groups of two or one group of three with one "outsider."

This impression can be supported further if each member in an "apparent group" has formal similarities, which you can see in Figure 3-7 (for example, the absolute and relative height of all of the columns).

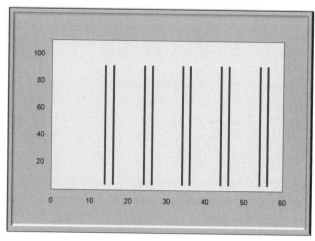

FIGURE 3-8 Columns that are not columns

In terms of our perception, the chart in the *Proximity 2* worksheet (see Figure 3-8) is even more sophisticated. First of all, you see columns that do not actually exist in this figure. Two lines in close proximity to each other form the *figure* of a column (this may have something to do with the fact that you *expect* to see columns in this chart). If you now press **F9** several times, the following happens:

- Sometimes, the "apparent columns" separate horizontally and form two groups, each with a different height (and therefore a different *significance*).

- In the image, the apparent columns move to the left or right or they move upwards and downwards. Sometimes, if they rely heavily on the margin or the "ground," they have a completely different effect than they would have if they were uniformly distributed and "stood" or floated harmoniously in the plot area.

- Occasionally, the middle column disappears, leaving two groups of two (one on the left and one on the right).

> **Note** If I were to explain the relatively complex construction of this chart and its data background, it would lead us too far away from the discussion at hand. I'll just share two brief pieces of information that may be of interest to advanced users:
>
> ❏ This is a *scatter chart (XY)* whose points have been hidden. What you see as lines are merely the *Y error bars* assigned to the points, minus and plus, whose random lengths are determined by the data in the table.
>
> ❏ Make the formula structure of the data range clear to yourself (for example, by using **Ctrl**+'). Here, several coincidences resulted in a structured relationship that produced the desired effects.
>
> Use the **Ctrl**+' key combination to toggle between the results view and formula view of a worksheet.

Consequences of Designing Your Charts Clearly defined areas and groups increase acceptance among observers.

- When arranging all of the layout elements, pay attention to interdependencies in content and to the necessary separations. Then, in accordance with these guidelines, create "correct" (that is, sufficiently large or sufficiently small) horizontal and/or vertical gaps between elements, between groups of elements, and between elements and their labels.

- Distribute the elements harmoniously and uniformly. If possible, avoid large gaps if you do not want to produce "apparent groups."

- Do not understand empty areas as unsightly "holes" in your chart, but rather as excellent, deployable layout tools.

The Law of Closure

In our perception, completely closed outlines produce figures. However, we even perceive incomplete figures as whole entities. We ignore the gaps and interpret these figures as whole. Elements that are framed by lines become groups, and elements that are separated by lines do not belong together.

Example The *Closure* worksheet contains a line chart whose data series are incomplete. Press **F9** to create several different lines and note the way in which your brain "closes" the gaps. In the case of the upper line, in Figure 3-9 for example, it is incredibly difficult to imagine that the gap would be closed by a *downward* curve. For these types of two-line models, our perception also establishes a relationship with the other line in each case. Our hasty interpretation leads us to perceive a synchronous wave or a wave in the opposite direction. The possibility that the line could *not* oscillate within the gap seems most improbable in the example shown in the figure.

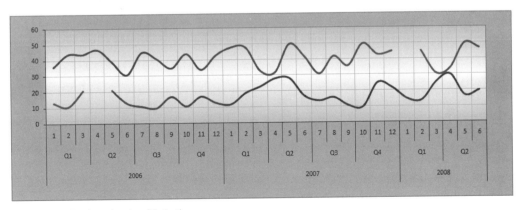

FIGURE 3-9 Our imagination fills in the gaps

> **Note** The chart formatting contains innovative formatting that could be also implemented in earlier versions of Excel (with limits on quality and with great difficulty), but can now be achieved much more easily in Excel 2007 with just a few mouse clicks:
>
> ❏ A gradual color gradient with more than two color components (this *plot area* contains three colors, namely blue, yellow, and green from top to bottom)
>
> ❏ A gradual color gradient in a chart line (Here, the upper and lower lines, when viewed from left to right, gradually change from blue to red and from red to blue respectively)
>
> Of course, proposed uses, technical descriptions, and instructions are also added elsewhere.

The chart represents an imaginary history of monthly data accumulated over a period of two and a half years. The label on the *primary horizontal axis* is divided into a series of months, quarters, and years. Simple vertical separators automatically created in Excel have been used to visually illustrate the corresponding segments. The instructions are provided elsewhere.

Consequences of Designing Your Charts   Definite shapes and structures increase acceptance among observers.

- Do not leave anything open to free interpretation.

- Use borders or distinct colors to create groups and do not use lines to separate objects that belong together if you want the observer to quickly identify a group.

The Law of Continuity

The harmonious continuity of an arrangement of objects or the harmonious movement or apparent movement of objects produces a "mental continuation" of what you actually see beyond a "critical point" or beyond the end shown in an image.

Examples   The *Continuity* worksheet contains two charts whose line gradients are very similar (see Figure 3-10).

In the model on the left, you can hypothesize about the path that the upper line will continue to follow after the first intersection, but you can't *know* this. Most observers spontaneously opt for a downward trend as it is most probable. Therefore, they form an assumption here to help interpret the chart.

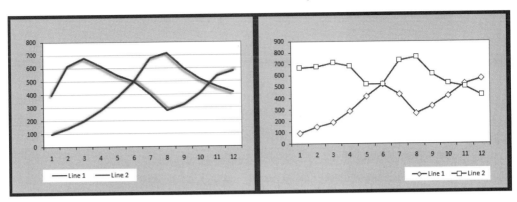

FIGURE 3-10 Crystal clear? Of course not—It just seems to be!

Furthermore, the use of only weak differentiating marker points in the model on the right does not help much. It is still hard to identify the correct path. At first glance, you will only correctly interpret very few of the combinations that you can generate here by pressing **F9**.

Consequences of Designing Your Charts   Distinct differences in formatting increase acceptance among observers.

- Never leave it to the observer to guess interdependencies and paths. In particular, bear this in mind if color-formatted charts are to be printed in monochrome. Because this often happens, it is important to remember this point.

- If necessary, indicate in your presentations and in any other data material that a continuous path *will not* necessarily continue in the same wave in the next unseen step; that is, either upwards or downwards. A rapidly increasing line at the end of a year can also sink dramatically again in January. In fact, this is the norm in some companies that are heavily dependent on the Christmas holiday trade.

Summary

I could cite other laws of perception here, but because these have only secondary importance for the purposes of this book I'll leave them out of our discussion. Now I will summarize the content of this chapter.

Anyone who observes your chart, be it in a publication or as part of a presentation, is physiologically conditioned to recognize and interpret as quickly as possible the information being presented in the chart and its significance. If this does not happen reasonably quickly, both the observer's readiness to perceive and his or her acceptance of the information being presented diminish; that is, the person may quickly lose interest in your work or presentation. Anyone who wants to avoid this is well advised to consistently observe the central universal laws of human perception. In so doing, you should:

- Lay the foundations for clear relationships by making a clear distinction between the foreground and the background (and the midground if you wish).

- Make a point of using simple and trusted "figures." There are numerous data types and data constellations whose information is best visualized using a simple universally recognized column chart. In other words, the column chart is not only a good choice, but often the best possible choice. Columns do not have to be jazzed up as three-dimensional elements with color gradients.

- When designing charts, use areas and groupings liberally. Give yourself and your observers free spaces and leave gaps if you require visual separation. You are not obliged to cram a screen or chart area with as much information as possible. Nothing is more unsightly than a rectangle crammed full of different types of visual information.

- Do not leave anything to chance or to random, involuntary, incorrect, or free interpretation. Do not be afraid of "patronizing" your target audience. Show what you want to show (or should show) and not what you assume everyone could somehow already see if he or she wanted to see it or made the effort to see it.

- Use distinct differences in formatting to represent what belongs where as well as the proportions and significance of the chart elements. Use symbols or symbolic elements to position and highlight information.

This brings us back to the idea of "cultural evolution." We are capable of interpreting abstract symbols (characters, numbers, pictograms, and so on), deriving information from these symbols and relating them to our experiences. Such associative connections expand our potential for understanding and explaining data, both of which naturally concern charts.

Which Charts for Which Purpose

Note the following points in relation to the configurations provided in this section:

- Most of the charts displayed and described here are also available on the CD-ROM as files that you can examine. If you want to experiment, change, or test anything in the worksheets (which I encourage you to do), first rename the file, save it to your hard disk, and then use the following command sequence to unprotect the sheet: *Review* tab/*Changes* group/*Unprotect Sheet* button.

- The main purpose of this section is to present the most important chart types. Therefore, I will not show you any completely finished or extensively formatted sample solutions. Nevertheless, I'm sure that you will discover one or more special constructions or formats that interest you and that you want to examine and reproduce before reading the later chapters in this book that contain the technical information.

- I will not present all types and subtypes. Here, we will work through only the main uses of those types that are important for your daily work. Types and subtypes that are used rarely or have a special purpose are not discussed here, but will be introduced later in connection with a real-life example.

■ The charts shown here do not attempt to correctly meet the requirements of a specialist area nor do they show any real data, only imaginary values.

■ You may still not know some display types or you may want to learn how to create such charts. I must ask you to be patient for a little while longer until we reach the technical instructions provided in Chapter 7, "Elements of Dynamization."

■ Some of the figures show questionable or unsuitable charts. These are highlighted with appropriate markers (for example, crossed out using continuous or dotted lines) and/or mentioned in the text.

For my recommendations and instructions, I have divided the chart types integrated into Excel 2007 into three main groups according to their usability, based wholly on subjective assumptions and all kinds of positive and negative experiences. In the context of Figure 3-11:

Note Even though the overview provided in Figure 3-11 was taken from the relevant Excel dialog box, we had to compress it due to lack of space. However, because we have retained the group headers, a 1:1 assignment should work when comparing it to the original overview.

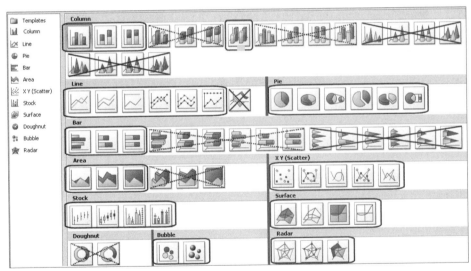

FIGURE 3-11 Some types are questionable; other types you can do without.

■ I have drawn borders around those charts that I recommend because they are effective and problem-free. This book contains examples and suggested uses for most of these types.

- There are also charts whose use is questionable in my opinion. These include almost all 3-D charts, whose weaknesses and problems I will address in a separate section later. Such types, which I would not recommend and would only use in exceptional cases, have been crossed out using a dotted line in the previous figure.

- A third and rather large group, which I regard as being completely unsuitable, have been crossed out using a continuous line in the previous figure. I will discuss this group in greater detail below. Unfortunately, all of the chart subtypes that have been added to Excel 2007 (compared with earlier versions of Excel) belong to this group.

Drawbacks of 3-D Charts, Cones, and Pyramids

Most 3-D charts are not independent types, but only graphically modified 2-D charts. From the functionally oriented perspective of a well arranged information layout, only 3-D charts whose type actually delivers and requires real three-dimensionality such as the 3-D surface chart or the three-axis column chart with rows (see Figure 3-12, left) are of interest. Keep in mind that you should only use the latter type if the data is sufficiently clear when displayed in this way; that is, if none of the markers obscure each other.

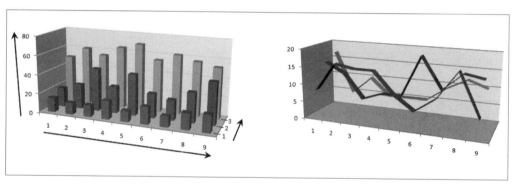

FIGURE 3-12 The version on the left can be used. The version on the right is nonsense.

Sometimes, a 3-D pie chart can convey information more quickly to observers than its comparable two-dimensional variant.

Whether 3-D charts really "look better" than their 2-D variants is a matter of individual taste. You will find only a few 3-D charts in this book. This is mainly because I can find only a few "pros" along with the arguments listed above. However, there are numerous "cons" also listed in this chapter. It is not necessary for me to provide different figures here. Take some time to test them yourself with some examples and with different data sources. Consider the following:

- 3-D charts follow the aforementioned law of figure and background only poorly, occasionally or perhaps never. Nor do they correspond to the principle of precision; that is, the law of simplicity and the good figure. That is why anyone who is interested in such charts or finds them appealing can't justify them. Furthermore, anyone who thought that the 2-D charts in earlier Excel versions were too "flat" may now use many formatting options that can convert two-dimensional images into attractive vividly and sculpted looking objects. However, the importance of these should not be exaggerated.

- A three-dimensional display of a two-dimensional area always requires greater effort by observers to interpret the chart. This can degenerate into laborious "sorting efforts" if paths are to be assigned and understood. In this sense, the 3-D line chart (see Figure 3-12, right) is an imposition rather than a sensible display option. In fact, it is almost nonsensical because it flouts the laws of perception described earlier.

- Some 3-D charts (columns, bars, pies) have to use an additional color for each marker in order to produce their apparent depth effect. This can be very confusing for the observer, especially if there are a many elements, some of which overlap with each others and are therefore painstaking to differentiate.

The conical, cylindrical, and pyramid charts, even those that have been newly added, are nothing more than display variants of 3-D columns or 3-D bars. I refuse to use them. The round columns are acceptable. However, the conical and pyramid shapes do not fulfill any requirement known to me, nor do they satisfy any particular presentation purpose. A steadily tapering shape undoubtedly signals, at first glance, that the base contains more than the vertex and that the quantity displayed steadily decreases. Corresponding data structures do exist, but they should be visualized in a completely different way, for example using scatter (XY) charts.

In general, do not use 3-D charts, especially conical or pyramid charts, unless you have good reason to disbelieve the arguments presented here.

Essential Types, Their Symbolism and Applications

I will begin this section on essential types by providing a brief description of the symbolic value of the basic elements: How one or more such elements affect our system of perception, which continuously seeks to interpret what we see. I will then formulate an abstract goal, derive a concrete goal, and finally show you a suitable chart that fulfills both goals.

Columns

> **On the Companion CD** Open the file *\Samples\0304_Columns.xlsx* on the CD-ROM.

Its Symbolism The two-dimensional column (even if it is not filled) is an area and therefore has content. The two-dimensional column also already works as an object: It has weight, volume, and sometimes mass. It stands firm on a base and represents something. A column can't be attached to something. It can "float," but only if a color has been assigned to define its lightness. The wider and/or darker a column, the heavier it seems. A column that is wider than its height has a "chunky" appearance.

The more columns are displayed next to each other, the less meaningful each individual column becomes. The smaller the gap between columns, the less significant the space between each column. The narrower the column, the more vulnerable it seems and the more weight it loses. Columns soar from the base and aspire. The distance covered we do not perceive to be a distance, but rather an extent. Its highest point does not define its perceived value; that is, the column is primarily regarded and evaluated as a whole.

Clustered Columns This example is provided in the *Columns 1* worksheet and in Figure 3-13:

- **Abstract goal** You want to compare different values against each other.

- **Concrete goal** You want to show the differences in total revenues, comprising different revenue elements (REV-01 to REV-06) recorded within a fiscal year.

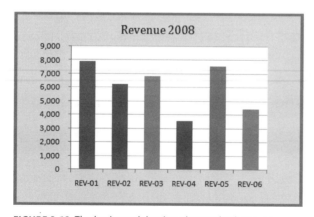

FIGURE 3-13 The basic model: using *clustered columns* to compare values

Below are some ways you can define and understand relationships and references between data table and chart:

- Check whether the sheet is protected and unprotect it, if necessary.

- Left-click an empty space in the chart. The data table displays color markings that are used to visually identify the table ranges to be used in the chart.

- Right-click an empty space in the chart and choose the *Select Data* command from the context menu. In the *Select Data Source* dialog box displayed, enter and select the reference to the entire *chart data range*. At the same time, the table range in question receives a marquee.

- Left-click one of the data series (a column, a segment in a stacked column, a line, an area, a slice of "pie," and so on). The data table displays color markings that visually identify the table ranges that belong to the data series currently selected.

The *chart data range* is the range of cells D4:E10. The revenue elements (REV-01 to REV-06) form the categories in the *primary horizontal axis* (other frequently used, although not always valid, terms are *category axis* or *X axis*) and their labels. The numeric values determine the height of the columns and the scale used to subdivide the *primary vertical axis* (also referred, sometimes inaccurately, as *value axis* or *Y axis*). The *major gridlines* of the *primary vertical axis* are horizontal lines drawn on the *plot area* to make it easier to determine the height of a column.

Stacked Columns   This example is provided in the *Columns 2* worksheet and in Figure 3-14:

- **Abstract goal**   You want to compare absolute values against each other and, at the same time, show the absolute proportion occupied by each category element in relation to the category as a whole.

- **Concrete goal**   You want to visualize the overall significance of four revenue elements (EA-01 to EA-04) in three fiscal years as well as the absolute proportion that pertains to each fiscal year.

The ideal solution for this task is to display specific subvalues by placing them on top of each other to represent one overall value. In the sample chart that follows, the *data series* are formed from the *columns* in the data table.

Important   You can easily change the data series' orientation from columns to rows or vice versa. Naturally, this does not require you to change the table structure of the source data. Right-click an empty space in the chart and choose the *Select Data* command from the context menu. In the *Select Data Source* dialog box displayed, click the *Switch Row/Column* button.

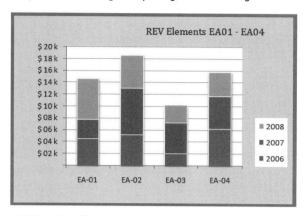

FIGURE 3-14 Differentiated comparison of absolute quantities in a *stacked column chart*

The *stacked column chart* places absolute values on top of each other, thus visually presenting comparative subsets that are also combined to form comparative total quantities. We first perceive the composition of the segments, and not the total value, because our view follows the colors rather than the shapes. This is generally the case.

Stacked Columns (100 percent)   This example is provided in the *Columns 3* worksheet and in Figure 3-15:

- **Abstract goal**   You want to compare the relative values against each other and, at the same time, show the relative proportion occupied by each category element in relation to the category as a whole.

- **Concrete goal**   You want to visually present the significance of four revenue elements (EA-01 to EA-04) in three fiscal years as well as the relative proportion that accounts for each revenue element.

Use *stacked columns (100 percent)* for such tasks. In the sample chart that follows, the *data series* are formed from the *rows* in the data table.

This chart type is an extremely useful and popular variant. This is because we trust the use of the number 100 and easily comprehend that values are estimated as subsets of this number. This also strengthens any associated visual displays and gives them their power of persuasion, as shown here and in examples provided in other chapters in this book. The *stacked column chart (100 percent)* shows the relative proportion of individual elements in relation to the whole and is therefore particularly helpful in highlighting the significance of individual elements over a period of time. Examples of such use include proportion of product sales revenues in relation to total sales, proportion of cost types in relation to total costs, and proportion of population groups in relation to the total population etc.

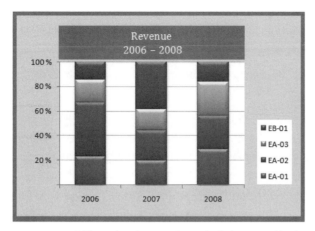

FIGURE 3-15 Differentiated comparison of relative quantities in a *stacked column chart (100 percent)*

Variants   *Columns 4* worksheet, Figure 3-16:

When you use column charts, you can choose from numerous variants. As a result, you can use this chart type for numerous display tasks. Do not be deterred by the opinions of some who declare that this form of visualization is "too simple." Yes, it's true that it is simple and easy, but this is exactly why it is a perfect choice as it obeys the aforementioned law of *simplicity or "good figure."*

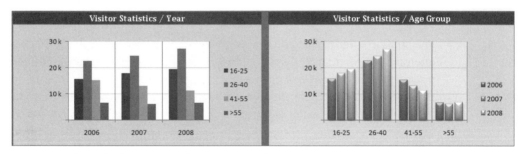

FIGURE 3-16 Several column chart variants can be used

Two Examples   In Figure 3-16, you see visitor statistics for an information center. The consultants complete questionnaires in which they are asked to specify their age, among other things. The findings in these questionnaires provide excellent overviews of the trends seen over the years and also may reveal new requirements.

Both charts are based on the same figures, but they differ greatly in the statements they make. This is particularly true for the extremely important "first glance" at visualizations.

- On the left-hand side: The *Visitor Statistics / Year* chart shows that, irrespective of any changes to the total figures, the *relative distribution* across the four age groups in the three years examined clearly remained pretty constant; that is, the largest remained the largest, the smallest remained the smallest, and so on. On closer inspection, however, a downward trend is clearly visible in the "41 to 55 years of age" group. The *data series* in the chart are based on the *rows* in the table.

Such a distribution chart (a value frequency distribution based on classes or groups) is also known as a "histogram."

- On the right-hand side: The *Visitor Statistics / Age Group* chart, which uses the same data table, gives a completely different impression at first glance. Here, the group-specific trends are immediately visible: The first and second groups demonstrate an upward trend, the third group demonstrates a downward trend (discussed above), and the fourth group does not change significantly.

The *data series* in the chart are based on the *columns* in the table.

Both of these visualizations clearly show how charts transcend tables. The base table is very small and clear. It contains just 12 figures. However, its informational value is boosted and improved enormously when displayed in graphical form. It is considerably more difficult, and takes much longer, to glean the same information from the table alone. This in not an issue of intelligence, but rather of perception. Our evolution is not yet so far advanced that we can comprehend abstract characters (numbers), distributed into boxes, as an image that can be quickly interpreted. However, if we transform abstract information into graphical information, that is, into simple figures—the simpler the better—it suddenly becomes pretty easy.

In this context, I'd like to make two further appeals to you:

- In a public presentation made using a beamer, the audience's ability to perceive and interpret the information being imparted is considerably lower than if the same information was printed out or if each audience member could view this information on his or her own monitor. There are several physiological and psychological reasons for this, all of which are beyond the scope of this book. Therefore, it is excessive—and even unkind and disrespectful—to expect participants to draw conclusions from a tiny numbers table or text table, whether or not this table is aided and assisted by a presenter.

- When designing a chart, always note the key phrase that should govern your choice of chart type and formatting: "What do I want to show and what do I want it to say?" Of course, the verb "to say" not only applies to charts in presentations, but to charts in publications, perhaps even more so because you *can't* say anything more once the chart is published.

In the context of the last two samples discussed above, use grouped elements only if you want to make group-specific statements.

> **Note** In the charts shown in both Figure 3-16 and the *Columns 4* worksheet, note the fact that they also obey two additional laws of perception mentioned earlier in this chapter, namely the laws of *closure* and *proximity*.
>
> The following is a reminder of the technical information that already played a role in Chapter 2, "New Approaches—Getting Started": If you want to connect columns to an area, set its *Gap Width* to *No Gap* or *0 percent*. If you want to visually separate grouped columns from each other, increase their *Gap Width* accordingly.
>
> Sample approach: Right-click a chartcolumn and choose *Format Data Series* from the context menu. The dialog box of the same name contains the various *Gap Width* options on the *Series Options* tab page.

Bars

> **On the Companion CD** Open the file \Samples\0305_Bars.xlsx on the CD-ROM.

Its symbolism A bar is long and robust. It can support and connect. It is horizontal, not vertical. The length of a bar is a range rather than a value. Therefore, you can use a bar to beautifully represent something that you can only poorly represent with a column, namely a "time interval." For this purpose, the bar is much more suitable than a line because our perception of a line is a length that lacks volume and that therefore can't contain any visible "quantity" such as time.

A small bar is short, not low, and a large bar is long, not high. Long bars are primarily not "larger," but rather more significant (or more important or better) than shorter bars.

A bar can be attached to something and, like a column, it can "float" easily.

> **Note** From a technical perspective, both column charts and bar charts are handled, for the most part, in exactly the same way. Therefore, my earlier orientation of rows and columns in the data series as well my guidelines on creating gaps between bars apply to both column charts and bar charts.
>
> All of the bar charts presented here are non-standard charts because the *primary horizontal axis* is across the top of the chart rather than across the bottom of the chart. To make this setting, proceed as follows:
>
> 1. In a standard bar chart, select the *primary horizontal axis* and press **Ctrl+1** to open the *Format Axis* dialog box.
>
> 2. Activate the *Axis Options* tab and then the *Categories in reverse order* option.

Clustered Bars   This example is provided in the *Bars 1* worksheet and in Figure 3-17:

- **Abstract goal**   You want to compare different values against each other and display them in ranking order.

- **Concrete goal**   You want to show the 10 countries/regions in the European Union (EU) with the largest surface area and show how these scales relate to each other.

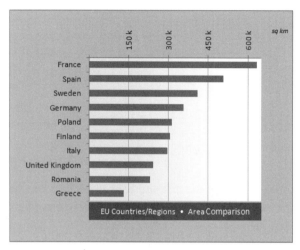

FIGURE 3-17 The basic model: using *clustered bars* to compare values and ranking

A bar list sorted in descending order is ideal for comparing values. It shows not only the ranking order but its comb-shaped structure and the immediately discernible difference between each of the "teeth" of the comb also clearly shows the relations being examined. For example, you immediately notice the clear, disharmonious "leap" between Romania and Greece at the lower end of the scale. This is not significant here, but it could be important for other data types if they concern harmonious and/or accurately defined increases or decreases (for example, for certain drug effects).

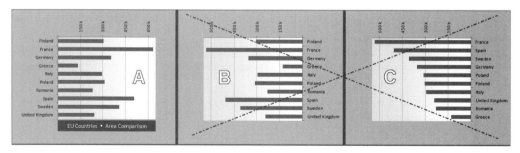

FIGURE 3-18 Such bar charts are unsuitable here.

For the subject matter to be visualized here, the charts types shown in Figure 3-18 are questionable if not completely unsuitable. An alphabetical arrangement (variant A) can only be described as moderately successful. The observer immediately (almost automatically) looks for a comparative orientation and feels impelled to create his or her own interesting arrangement. This can succeed to some extent (if perhaps also an imposition), but it soon becomes impossible if there are more comparison values.

> **Note** An alphabetical arrangement or another non-value oriented arrangement of categories only makes sense if *this* is exactly the order in which the observer should be guided or if this will facilitate the observer's understanding of the data.

I have shown the completely unsuccessful variants B and C above in order to illustrate another law of perception and its effect. In our culture, we read (and observe) from left to right and from top to bottom. Therefore, we also initially scan the "image" chart in this way. Consequently, for us, bars tend to run from left to right. Our brain finds it less acceptable if bars run "in reverse," that is, from right to left.

Stacked Bars   This example is provided in the *Bars 2* worksheet and in Figure 3-19:

- **Abstract goal**   You want to produce a value- and proportion-oriented overview of absolute periods of time that comprise as subsets units of time that have already been totaled.

- **Concrete goal**   In project planning for specific processes, you want to visualize how many days were devoted to process preparation and execution.

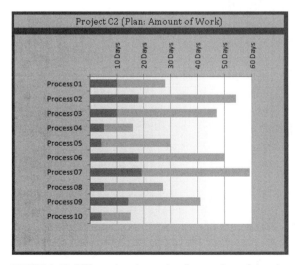

FIGURE 3-19 Differentiated overview for number of days in a *stacked bar chart*

A stacked bar chart was chosen for this purpose. This examination is based on *processes*; that is, on those parts of a total effective volume that can be described. Because the total time for each process largely depends on the nature and scope of the work involved, it does not make sense to display this information in a ranking order. In this example, however, it is especially important that the proportional quantity devoted to the preparation time be accepted before a process is executed. Because we scan such "images" from left to right, a dominant color was chosen for the important *preparation time* subset, which is not only eye-catching in the individual bars, but also assumes an almost two-dimensional characteristic (which could be even further strengthened by reducing the gap width) when you naturally view the chart as a whole. Such effects are also achievable with column charts, which we also examine from left to right, but to a much lesser extent.

Stacked Bars (100 percent)   This example is provided in the *Bars 3* worksheet and in Figure 3-20.

- **Abstract goal**   You want to produce a relative and comparative overview of periods of time that comprise as subsets several units of time that have already been totaled.

- **Concrete goal**   You want to show how much of the costly working time in the operating rooms in a hospital is productive in a revenue sense; that is, used for work that can be invoiced. Both an average yearly-based synopsis and an overview of the different disciplines are required.

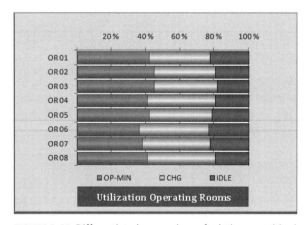

FIGURE 3-20 Differentiated comparison of relative quantities in a *stacked bar chart (100 percent)*

A *stacked bar chart (100 percent)* is particularly successful at fulfilling this requirement. Here, the 2-dimensional effect achieved in the previous example, and already discussed, is further strengthened by having a very low gap width (15 percent). Nevertheless, the bar differentiation remains for the purpose of detailed analyses. This is achieved by the seemingly 3-dimensional color formatting in the bar segments.

Note You will learn more about colors, color effects, and color formatting in Chapter 4.

Also note the position and horizontal extension of the legend. As a result, observers imme-diately make a visual assignment between the data series and the information they contain. You can move a legend to anywhere in the chart area and scale its two dimensions.

Lines

 On the Companion CD Open the file *\Samples\0306_Lines.xlsx* on the CD-ROM.

Its symbolism   A line can be many things: a dash, row, rope, cord, lace, border, marking, connection, link, or sequence. The line can be straight and rigid or it can twist and turn. It can run, follow a path, rise, fall, plummet, oscillate, and float. The line moves from one location to another. It therefore covers a route and can change its course anywhere along this route. This change is "trend-setting."

In many word compositions, the line is a paradigm, prescription, arrangement, and regulation (*to stand in line, guideline, linear, to toe the line, line of credit, borderline, line of demarcation, front line*). In other meanings, it defines orientating, largely symmetrical systems (*gridlines, lined paper, linear distribution*).

The richness of this term is also reflected in the use of "line" as a chart element. In terms of its symbolic power, I must also refer to another very significant "perception effect." A closed line forms a shape: from an empty space, it creates an image with content. Therefore, the line in a chart is frequently interpreted as a graphical simulation of an area (namely its upper edge) and is sometimes used as such.

Line charts are suitable for expressing different kinds of data in an easy-to-understand man-ner. This has made them extremely popular for a long time now as a means of visualizing numbers. There are, for example, thousands of cartoons that illustrate the line chart as *the* chart prototype (for economic charts, in particular).

The subtypes recommended for use here are the same as the three subtypes recommended for column charts and bar charts; namely, the simple type, the stacked type, and the stacked type (100 percent). Each has two variants, *without Markers* and *with Markers* (see Figure 3-22), resulting in six subtypes in total. However, this differentiation between charts with and without markers only affects your initial selection because you can always easily add or re-move markers for each line.

The alternative use of lines instead of areas was favorable in earlier versions of Excel because it enabled users to successfully compare several two-dimensional phenomena (with specific quantities) against each other without problems.

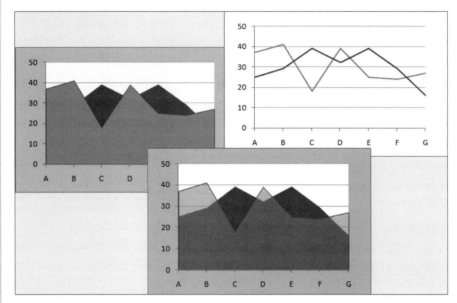

FIGURE 3-21 Line charts can also be used to display areas.

However, enormous strides have been made recently in this area and elegant solutions are now available for many of the design problems experienced in the past: In Office 2007, you can make each color-fill transparent and you can also determine the degree of transparency as a percentage (for more information, see Chapter 4). Therefore, it has also become very easy to work with overlapping areas and various alternative constructions—for example, lines instead of areas. In the *AreasLines* worksheet in the sample file *0306_Lines.xlsx*, press **F9** several times to test how the the different variants, all of which are based on the same data, compared directly with each other.

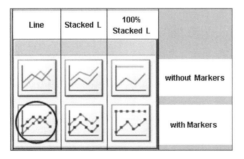

FIGURE 3-22 The simple line with markers can cope with most tasks.

The simple line chart is sufficient for most line display tasks. The stacked variants are only suitable in exceptional cases and, generally, are much more difficult to understand than their equivalent stacked column charts or stacked bar charts. This is because a line drawn above another line does not stay still (you've already heard this been said of the "stack"). Instead, it "floats." Therefore, according to our initial perception, the lower of the two lines can't be the "ground" for the upper line; instead, both lines have the same "ground," namely the primary horizontal axis. As a result, the stacked effect is lost when we interpret such charts.

Now let's take a look at some examples that use only the simple line chart (either with or without markers):

Example 1   This example is provided in the *Lines 1* worksheet and in Figure 3-22:

- **Abstract goal**   You want to compare two data series that run continuously in regular intervals and concern different data types. Furthermore, you want to evaluate the waveforms produced.

- **Concrete goal**   You want to show whether the development of costs and revenues within a fiscal year oscillate harmoniously with each other or whether there are—intentionally or unintentionally—movements in opposite directions or even critical dissonances.

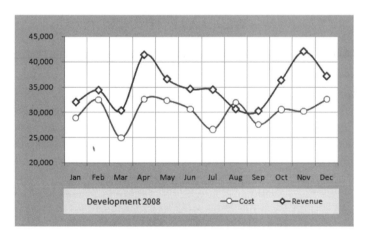

FIGURE 3-23 The line chart is particularly easy to understand if it shows continuous comparisons

You are already familiar with this display type from the complex example provided in Chapter 2.

The line chart's unique strength is its ability to describe movement and direction (it moves upwards, downwards, or remains the same). If you really want to emphasize categories and intervals, it is helpful to use different types of markers. In the sample chart provided, markers are primarily used to show whether there are any parallel waveforms, when they exist, and when they do not. The actual monthly values are of secondary importance here. As a result, the axis gridlines have been faded in terms of their formatting, so that observers give their undivided attention to the lines and their relationships.

Example 2   This example is provided in the *Lines 2* worksheet and in Figure 3-24:

- **Abstract goal**   You want to compare two data series that run continuously in regular intervals and concern the same data type. Furthermore, you also want to evaluate the intervals.

- **Concrete goal**   You want to represent a location's temperature curve (in degrees Celsius) in monthly intervals over a period of seven months and highlight the high-low ranges between the maximum and minimum temperatures.

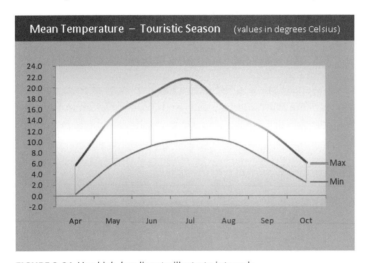

FIGURE 3-24 Use *high-low lines* to illustrate intervals

For this purpose, you draw two data series as horizontal lines and then use vertical high-low lines to connect their markers, which will be hidden later. Sample approach:

1. Double-click one of the two data series lines to add the *Chart Tools* tab to the *ribbon*.

2. Activate the *Layout* tab. In the *Analysis* group, choose the *Lines* command and then the *High-Low Lines* command.

High-low lines are good at supporting you in quickly detecting typical changes in intervals. In the example shown, it is clear that the intervals between the maximum and minimum temperatures in spring and summer are considerably greater than the intervals in late summer and fall. That would happen if you were to repeat a run of this type several times to identify it as a representative run.

Note Note that the information contained in this example is also supported by gradient color fills: this is the case for both the plot area (which ranges from cool blue to moderate yellow to warm red) and the upper temperature line whose colors are considerably more vivid. Because this example concerns Scandinavia, a mean temperature in excess of 20 degrees Celsius is considered to be "warm."

Example 3   This example is provided in the *Lines 3* worksheet and in Figure 3-25:

- **Abstract goal**   You want to achieve a space-saving representation of numerous measurement values as a chain.

- **Concrete goal**   You want to show how the characteristics and waveform of 100 values that have been measured consecutively behave in relation to a mean axis value of zero (0).

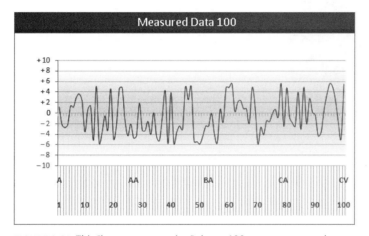

FIGURE 3-25 This "long concatenation" shows 100 measurement values.

This "long concatenation" is the simultaneous visual presentation of a large number of markers. This type of line chart (occasionally also known as an "oscillogram") is particularly suitable if you want to examine typical and/or cyclical oscillations over a long period of time.

Pie (Circle)

On the Companion CD Open the file \Samples\0307_Pie.xlsx on the CD-ROM.

Its Symbolism   The circle is the ideal two-dimensional shape. In our perception, it is a complete area and each point on its circumference is equidistant from the imaginary center. The circle is a wheel that can be easily turned (along with its contents). It is easy to divide the circle (therefore a pie or a gateau) "fairly." Halves, quarters, or smaller slices of the circle are not "new" parts, but rather segments of the whole (in our experience, half a moon is a half-moon but half a wheel is nonsense).

Let's take a look at four examples of different pie charts:

Examples 1 and 2   This example is provided in the *Pie 1* worksheet and in Figure 3-26:

- **Abstract goal**   You want to represent the proportions of an individual element in relation to the element as a whole.

- **Concrete goal**   As part of your analysis of a survey, you want to show the relative proportions of the age groups who participated in the survey.

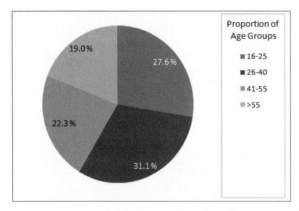

FIGURE 3-26 Very suitable for a small number of segments and different values

A pie chart is particularly effective and immediately meaningful if you want to visualize a small number of data points that have considerably different values.

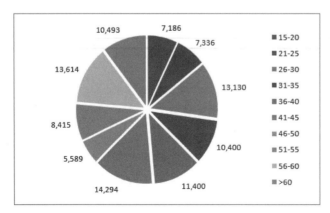

FIGURE 3-27 Unsuitable for a large number of segments and minor differences in value

In particular, you should make sure that your pie charts do not contain too many segments (see Figure 3-27). Otherwise, an observer's perception system quickly becomes overburdened and is unable to differentiate between each segment. A pie that has lots of narrow multicolored "slices of pie" to indicate minor differences in value is very confusing and totally unsuitable as a means of demonstrating compositions or differences, unless you want to visualize "uniformity."

However, if your data is suitable for pie charts and it meets the objective of your design (that is, to merge small segments into larger segments), then the pie chart is once again effective.

The *Pie 2* worksheet contains this variant of pie chart, which is also shown in Figure 3-28:

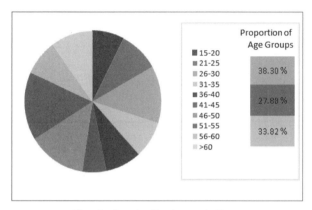

FIGURE 3-28 The pie chart is effective again if you can group together smaller segments.

Here, our perception successfully differentiates between the colors in the pie chart; that is, it identifies a green group, a blue group, and an orange group of segments. Their relative total values are provided in a three-line table accompanying the legend. This table's coloring further strengthens the observer's impression that there are three groups. Once the observer makes this rough differentiation, it is generally relatively easy for him to understand and identify differences between the smaller segments in the pie chart.

Example 3   This example is provided in the *Pie 3* worksheet and in Figure 3-29:

- **Abstract goal**   You want to represent the importance of individual elements in relation to their whole and to compare these elements under different aspects and/or conditions.

- **Concrete goal**   Using the example of the Benelux countries/regions, you want to show the relationships between the number of inhabitants and the surface area, both for each individual country/region and compared against the other two countries/regions.

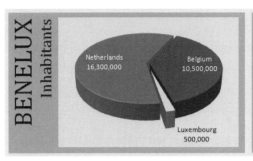
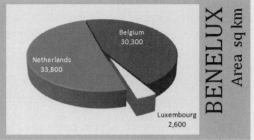

FIGURE 3-29 Rarely used but very effective: comparative pie charts

During a presentation, such a display (as an indirect interpretation) can quickly illustrate the fact that the *Netherlands* has the highest population *density* and that *Luxembourg* has the lowest. To ensure that the relatively small segment *Luxembourg* is sufficiently discernible, especially in relation to the number of inhabitants, a *3-D pie* is chosen, which is then further strengthened by something known as a *pie explosion*.

> **Note** Quite a few of the sample charts in this chapter will reappear in later chapters where their technical development will be explained in greater detail. For example, in Chapter 8 "Chart Types—Conventional and Exceptional," you will learn how both of the *Benelux charts* shown here were created. You will also learn some tips and tricks in relation to creating a pie explosion.
>
> Example 4 will also reappear in Chapter 8.

Example 4   This example is provided in the *Pie 4* worksheet and in Figure 3-30:

- **Abstract goal**   You want to achieve a clear comparative representation of your data whereby a larger number of smaller segments are pitted against some large segments.

- **Concrete goal**   You want to visualize the revenue of 12 products. Four of these products generate a lot of revenue and are of relatively equal ranking while the other eight products combined do not generate much more revenue than one of the "big four."

The *Bar of Pie* type is particularly suitable for this purpose. Some of the segments of the pie are connected to one individual segment within the pie. Their original breakdown is then transferred to a neighboring stacked column.

> **Note** Unfortunately, the incorrect type description *Bar of Pie* has not been corrected in the new Excel version. The rectangular summary of subsegments within a "slice of the pie" is not a stacked *bar*, but rather a stacked *column*; that is, the relative segment value is not indicated by its width, but by its height.

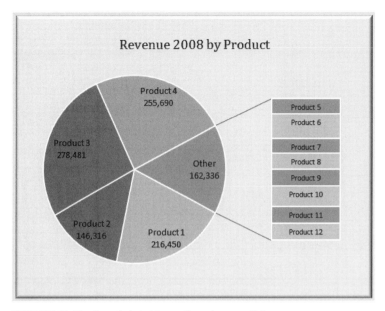

FIGURE 3-30 The *bar of pie* subtype allows for a partial summary.

XY (Scatter)

On the Companion CD Open the file *\Samples\0308_Scatter.xlsx* on the CD-ROM.

Its Symbolism The basic element of a XY (Scatter) plot is the point, whether it is a single one or a whole cloud of points. The point is inconspicuous, but assertive. It can terminate, clarify, emphasize, and subdivide. We come to the point, have a point to make, and some-times speak pointedly. We can get right to the point, state that something is a moot point, and sometimes even say "I don't see the point," which sometimes brings us to the point of no return!

On its own, the point can be extremely important, but when there are lots of points (for ex-ample, as pixels or dots), it becomes an inconspicuous or invisible part of the whole. A line or an area can also be a collection of points.

The XY (Scatter) chart, available in Excel, and its subtypes are used predominantly in science. I will introduce them as such in Chapter 11 , "Fulfilling Special Requirements." For the moment, I will only describe what some users regard as a seemingly strange application of this display type and show some sample uses. Its main feature: The chart does not have any *primary horizontal* and *vertical axes*, but rather two uniform *value axes* of equal status. In terms of the language used in earlier versions of Excel, this means that no distinction is made between the *value axis* and the *category axis*. Instead, two *value axes* are used.

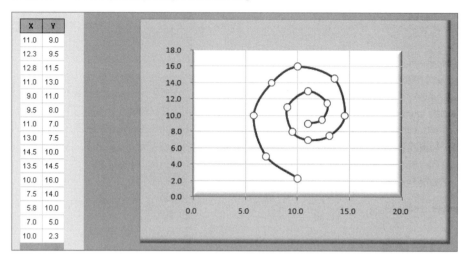

X	Y
11.0	9.0
12.3	9.5
12.8	11.5
11.0	13.0
9.0	11.0
9.5	8.0
11.0	7.0
13.0	7.5
14.5	10.0
13.5	14.5
10.0	16.0
7.5	14.0
5.8	10.0
7.0	5.0
10.0	2.3

FIGURE 3-31 Two values determine the position of each data point.

Therefore, unlike the other chart types, each data point can adopt any position in a two-dimensional area. This is the only way to comprehend how a data series drawn as a line can also become a spiral. We will show this, for example, in the *Axes* worksheet in the sample file or in Figure 3-31.

In the following paragraphs, I have chosen to show just three of its many possible uses:

Example 1   This example is provided in the *Scatter 1* worksheet and in Figure 3-32:

- **Abstract goal**   You want to represent whether and, if necessary, how two different measurements relate to each other.

- **Concrete goal**   You want to visualize the findings of a study that examined, among other things, the weight of people who were a certain height. You want your chart to show how the weight/height relationships for all people examined were distributed as a whole.

Figure 3-32 shows the XY (Scatter) chart chart type as an accumulation of *data points*; occasionally also known as a "point cloud." Each element in the cloud—that is, each point—also denotes one weight/height relationship. The cloud, visually strengthened by the trendline that was inserted, has the expected form. As a whole, there is a clear relationship between weight and height.

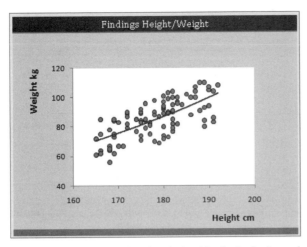

FIGURE 3-32 The weight/height relationships in the findings of a study

 Note The *scatter diagram* or *scatter plot* visualizes XY coordinates as isolated points. Therefore, each point denotes the coordinates of two values. In other words, each *data point* in the XY (Scatter) chart does not require one individual value, but rather a pair of values in order for it to be displayed in the chart.

Example 2 This example is provided in the *Scatter 2* worksheet and in Figure 3-33:

- **Abstract goal** You want to represent how frequently defined group values appear in a certain number of measurements.

- **Concrete goal** You want to show the distribution of specific grades as a curve in order to detect regularities or specific irregularities and to examine whether these concern an expected "normal distribution."

What you see here is not a line chart, even if this seems at first to be a likely assumption and a possible solution. The curve is drawn by an interpolated line (see the box) to which the *data points* are connected. The grades in the first table column and the number of times each grade was awarded in the second table column are the basis for the positions occupied by these points. The additional calculations in the table are used to calculate and display the average grade.

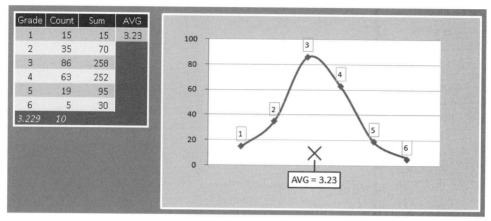

FIGURE 3-33 Distribution of grades in a scatter chart

In simple terms, this *interpolation* is achieved by calculating additional values between two known points. These values can, in turn, be used to show how the unknown (unmeasured points) could be positioned. In the example (similarly when drawing a straight line in an Excel line chart), it is assumed that there is a uniform, oscillating, harmonious distribution of the intermediate values; namely, the hidden values between known or measured data points. As a result, the entire line becomes "smooth" and does not run in a "zigzag" manner that would be the result of straight connections between known points.

There are several different interpolation procedures as well as some associated mathematical problems and application difficulties. However, these do not play any role in our context.

Example 3   This example is provided in the *Scatter 3* worksheet and in Figure 3-34:

- **Abstract goal**   You want to represent how two measurement values that have scales of equal length and equal importance relate to each other.

- **Concrete goal**   You want to visualize the findings of a study where quality and quantity are of equal importance and therefore have been normalized in a two-axis scale ranging from 0 to 100. It would therefore make sense to achieve a maximum of 100 quality points and 100 quantity points for each measurement.

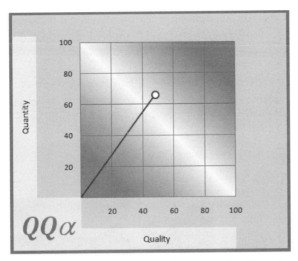

FIGURE 3-34 Each position in the *plot area* can be affected by a "QQ point."

In the example shown, there is one very noticeable "QQ point." Because this point is a coordinate of quality and quantity, it can occupy any position in the scales' square. To reinforce its effect, a line is drawn to connect this QQ point to the scales' zero point. As a result, it becomes a pointer and is assigned a meaningful length. The further the point moves away in *both* directions from the zero point, the closer it gets to the "green area" of the color segment being evaluated. Therefore, high quality or quantity alone is not enough to achieve a good two-dimensional high-ranking result. As an aside, this addresses a problem associated with many one-dimensional studies that parade themselves as "benchmarking" or something similar. Those making such studies often forget that many aspects of our everyday lives, even those that you can measure and scale, are multifaceted and each attribute is worthy of equal ranking and simultaneous consideration.

Other Chart Types

This next section comprises those chart types that are generally less important and therefore used less often than the chart types described above and, as a result, play less important roles in this book.

 On the Companion CD   Open the file *\Samples\0309_VariousTypes.xlsx* on the CD-ROM.

Area   The *area chart* is a modified (enhanced) *line chart*. You already saw an example of an area chart in Figure 3-21.

Most of the column chart's symbolism (described earlier) also applies to area charts. Furthermore, you can also connect columns to areas by not having gaps between columns as shown in the histogram in Figure 3-16 and also in Chapter 2.

In the chart, the area *stands*. As a result, it either becomes a wall or, if it shows summits and valleys, a mountain range. This latter feature makes the area chart particularly suitable if you want to represent changes to "aggregated" values across time intervals.

Because we perceive an area as being a background rather than a foreground, considerable care must be taken when choosing colors for such a chart (soft, delicate, and pale colors). In the case of mixed chart types, you can easily place other objects *in front of* an area.

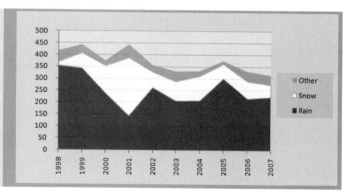

Amount of Precipitation			
Year	Rain	Snow	Other
1998	355	16	46
1999	344	66	34
2000	239	116	21
2001	144	245	55
2002	263	67	28
2003	208	82	41
2004	209	104	20
2005	302	62	12
2006	218	74	40
2007	225	52	39

FIGURE 3-35 In principle, you should use the area chart in stacked form.

> **Tip** Before using an area chart, always test how the same data would be represented in a column chart. The effect can differ greatly, but your objective will primarily determine which chart is best.

The example provided in the *Area* worksheet (see Figure 3-35) shows the differences between total amounts of precipitation (cumulated values) in a particular location over a period of 10 consecutive years, broken down into absolute proportions for rain, snow, and other forms of precipitation. Its main focus is the change in these values over the years.

The relative (and often unavoidable) disadvantage associated with stacked area charts is their visually appealing yet sometimes incorrect "mountain effect" background. Primarily, the image does not give the impression that there are stacked layers or changing and different strengths (thickness), but rather that there are three areas *one behind the other*, each of them touching the base of the primary axis.

Doughnut The *doughnut chart* is a variant of the *pie chart*. Its apparent advantage over the pie is that it can represent more than one data series. However, its main disadvantages are as follows:

- If you want to represent only *one* data series, the doughnut chart is superfluous because the pie chart can represent one data series as well, if not better.

- If you want to represent more than one data series, it is difficult to understand and defeats the purpose of using a chart in the first place, because you then have to explain it in detail (see Figure 3-36, Figure C). The most important reason for not using this chart is simple: There is no "natural" paradigm for embedded rings, each of which comprises different segments.

I only use the doughnut chart for purposes that do not actually correspond to its original purpose:

- As a half doughnut to visualize the allocation of seats in parliaments, and

- As a half doughnut for creating scales. This will be discussed in greater detail in Chapter 8. The following is just some brief additional information in relation to Figure 3-36 and the *Doughnut* worksheet in the sample file:

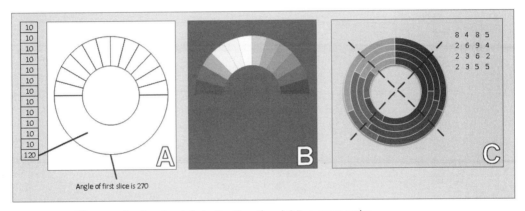

FIGURE 3-36 What can the doughnut do better than the pie? Represent scales.

Figure *A*: The doughnut chart shown is based on 13 values whereby the 13th value is the sum of the other 12 values. This produces a chart that comprises two half doughnuts, one that contains 12 segments and one that contains just one segment. This half doughnut is turned downwards through 270 degrees.

Figure *B*: The large downward-turned half doughnut is hidden by removing its filling and its border color. The remaining, visible 12 segments are assigned different colors, chosen user-defined fulfilling the basic prerequisites for displaying a scale.

Radar   The primary appearance of a radar chart is a spider's net, more or less filled with different elements. In terms of its symbolic effect, the *net* must not be fully considered and evaluated as a *net* because only its *gridlines* form the net, not its *data series*. In most applications, these are either:

- Lines closed to form shapes (with our without *data point markers*) or

- Filled shapes, therefore areas, or

■ Combinations of both

Therefore, the radar chart is a *line chart*, an *area chart* or a mixture of both. In particular, you can deploy its greatest strength if you want your chart to represent profile comparisons. It is unbeatable in this regard, as you will see in Chapter 10 , "Presentation Solutions That Pack a Punch."

Despite its excellent display qualities, the radar chart is still rarely used in Europe, so anyone who uses it there probably will have to explain this chart type to many of the people in his or her target audience. However, once it is understood and accepted, it frequently and quickly becomes an indispensable favorite for any comparative inspection.

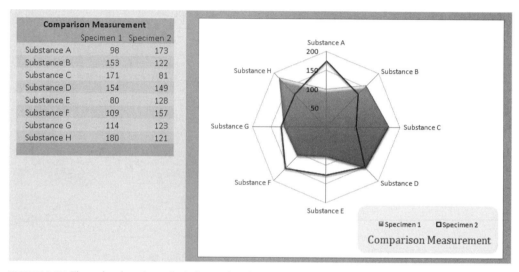

Comparison Measurement		
	Specimen 1	Specimen 2
Substance A	98	173
Substance B	153	122
Substance C	171	81
Substance D	154	149
Substance E	80	128
Substance F	109	157
Substance G	114	123
Substance H	180	121

FIGURE 3-37 The radar chart is particularly good at showing similarities and differences in profiles.

The profile comparison shown in Figure 3-37 is also provided in the *Radar* worksheet in the sample file where you can vary its appearance by pressing **F9**.

A radar chart does not have a *primary horizontal axis*. Instead, all categories are constructed outwards from a central point. However, in return, each category has its own *vertical axis*. The *data series* line is formed by "spinning a thread" from axis to axis until returning to the first axis, thus creating a shape that our perception understands as a profile. This is particularly effective if you format a base profile (reference profile) as an area (as shown in the sample file and in the figure above) and then place the comparison profile over the base profile as a "hollow form."

Bubble   The customer analysis shown in Figure 3-38 is also provided in the *Bubble* work-sheet in the sample file.

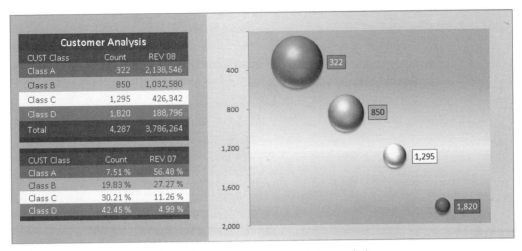

Customer Analysis		
CUST Class	Count	REV 08
Class A	322	2,138,546
Class B	850	1,032,580
Class C	1,295	426,342
Class D	1,820	188,796
Total	4,287	3,786,264
CUST Class	Count	REV 07
Class A	7.51 %	56.48 %
Class B	19.83 %	27.27 %
Class C	30.21 %	11.26 %
Class D	42.45 %	4.99 %

FIGURE 3-38 Significant and critical major differences in this customer analysis

Similarly, the *bubble chart* is not an independent type, but rather a variant of the XY (Scatter) chart. In addition to determining a horizontal and vertical position, you can also process a third value that determines the size of the bubble. In other words, the point is inflated (with an optional 3-D effect) to denote volume.

In the chart shown in Figure 3-38, it immediately becomes apparent how disharmonious and problematic it is that the company's revenues are distributed across four customer catego-ries. If something pierces the large bubble (where approximately 7.5 percent of the custom-ers generate 56 percent of the company's revenue), not only will the bubble burst, but the entire business might be deflated. Similarly, the small bubble representing customer group D is also critical: Approximately 42.5 percent of the customers (1,820 customers) generate only 5 percent of the revenue.

In the display, note the differences between the sizes of the bubbles and their labels: The vol-ume represents the revenue while the label (and the position of each bubble along the verti-cal scale) represents the number of customers who generate this revenue.

Surface   Once again, the surface chart is not an independent type with its own descriptive symbolism. It is mainly used in two variants:

- The 3-D variant works as follows: It is a view, from different changing angles, of an area created by placing a "cloth" over a 3-D chart that comprises a series of columns but whose columns remain hidden (see Figure 3-39, left). As a result, the area shows bev-eled edges, hills, and valleys. The same colors belong to the same height (value groups). In this sense, a topographic map is a good reference pattern (for example, green = low, yellow = high, brown = mountains—the darker the color, the higher the mountain—all of which are capped by the white peaks of the eternal snow zones).

- The 2-D color variant works as follows: Columns that have different heights have different colors. All of the columns are arranged close to each other, without any gaps, and you have a bird's eye view of the chart as a whole. Therefore, you do not see any height differences, but rather color differences and their progressions. This special variant is shown in the image on the right-hand side of Figure 3-39.

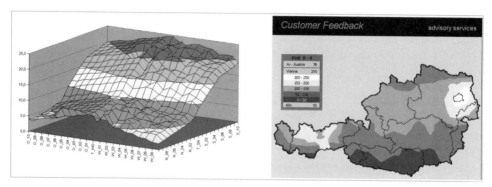

FIGURE 3-39 The perspective 3-D variant and a special use of the 2-D variant

Note In Excel, you can construct a 2-D surface chart that can be adapted to a country's/region's boundaries and therefore show regional distributions in a very clear and impressive manner. However, it is relatively complicated and would require a lengthy description of the procedure involved. Because its implementation is only of interest to a relatively small group of readers, such a detailed description is beyond the scope of this book.

Stock Chart and Mixed Chart Types   The standard stock chart and its subtypes are not only used to display exchange rate data but are also suitable for visually presenting some types of scientific data collections. However, such special uses are also beyond the scope of this book.

Many presentations and publications only become highly impressive and persuasive when you mix not only subtypes but also main chart types. Bountiful evidence supporting this statement will be provided in the chapters to follow.

Chapter 4
Colors, Areas, and Outlines

At the start of Chapter 3, "Perceiving, Interpreting, Understanding," I set you the impossible challenge of trying to understand the bizarre "Mall Cupola chart," which you were not meant to take seriously. I must warn you that I'm going to take a similar approach in some parts of this chapter. Not because I enjoy annoying my readers a little every so often (nothing could be further from the truth). The real reason is that Excel 2007 also sets its users some challenges (serious ones this time), and you'll need to spend time pondering—and occasionally—puzzling over these before you can overcome them.

From a visual point of view, the Microsoft Office Suite offers an impressive new range of complex, multifaceted features. Great! However, if you want to do more than simply use predefined styles (and I assume you do, given that you're reading this book), it will take time for you to learn exactly what you can do with all these shiny new design effects. And you'll need more time on top of that to get used to the options, dialogs, and Help texts that sometimes are confusing and not very user-friendly. Finally, you'll need even more time to read this and other chapters so that you'll understand all of the possibilities open to you when designing a professional chart. But don't lose heart: it will be worth it in the end! Excel 2007 is a program that can produce results that are particularly satisfying for users who never understood the aesthetic possibilities of spreadsheets or assumed that these options were too complicated to use. If you've taken little notice of these or believed that they weren't worth getting to know, the new program and this book may help you realize that—when it comes to presenting figures and results—the packaging is at least as important as the content, just as in real life.

Colors and Color Systems

"Window dressing" is a colorful expression that has relevance for chart design. Originally, "window dressing" simply meant displaying goods in a decorative and attractive manner in a shop window. These days, it's more often used to refer to dishonesty and deception; what a shame.

It's not my intention to show you how to dress things up to make them appear better or more attractive than they are. But one of the main purposes of this book is to explain how you can make clever use of color to aid perception, to send certain signals to your audience, and to draw more attention to your charts. And, if one side benefit is that you also inject some color into what may be an otherwise drab story (in terms of content), who could hold that against you?

You can make just as many mistakes when it comes to using colors as you can by ignoring the laws of perception. However, I'll have to cut my discussion of this important and almost limitless subject relatively short. Some theory is required, though, primarily when it comes to anatomical, physiological, and physical reality.

How We See

Our "seeing" amounts to a multifaceted perceived impression that our light receptors generate by processing electromagnetic waves. For these waves to be absorbed, we first require an optical receiver system. The eye is often compared with a camera, and the comparison works well. However, in an age of digital photography that is largely automated (at least in everyday use), that comparison may not be so clear.

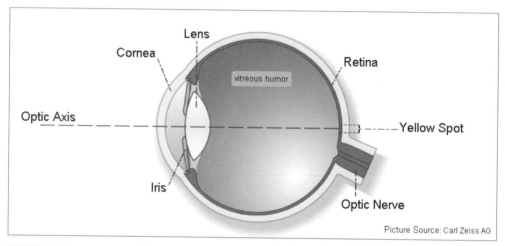

FIGURE 4-1 The eye—one of the many small and great wonders of human perception

Put in very simple terms, this is how we see:

- Rays of light (in the form of electromagnetic waves) enter our eyes and penetrate the cornea, lens, and vitreous humor (a jelly-like, transparent mass) to reach the retina (which lines most of the eyeball), where it generates a chemical reaction, resulting in the transmission of a signal along the bundled fiber pathways of the optic nerve to the brain.

- Light is refracted (diverted) several times on its way to the retina. The main element responsible for accurate refraction is the flexible lens. In a normal, healthy eye, a sharp, minimized, and reversed image is received by the retina, just as in a conventional camera.

- An imaginary optic axis through the exact mid-point of the lens leads to the yellowish anatomical structure of the retina. This "yellow spot" is where our vision is the sharpest.

Our main impressions of color also originate here at the yellow spot and its immediate surroundings. To see something "properly," we use our eye muscles to point this optic axis at what we want our brains to interpret.

■ The intensity of the light is key to the quality of our vision. The pupil is a round opening in the iris, which allows light to penetrate the eye. Just like a camera's aperture, the pupil expands and contracts to regulate how much light is received.

Given the busy lives most of us lead these days, our eyes rarely have an opportunity to relax (for example, by gazing lazily at a green field or blue sky), even when we're on vacation. Our optical system works very hard when we're at work and at play, often harder than it is designed to do (from an evolutionary perspective). We spend most of our time in intense, stimulating environments that put constant pressure on our powers of perception. As a result, our optical system has to constantly adjust to new challenges, which is difficult and tiring if it never gets a rest. For example, you may need to focus on something that's outside your field of vision, moving too fast, too far away, too bright or too dark, or that has a blurred outline. Your eyeballs have to turn, lenses have to narrow or thicken, and pupils contract or expand. Other auxiliary systems often lend a hand. For example, you can move your head in the right direction, use the muscles around your eyes to help reduce the amount of light received, pop your eyes wide open, or squint to focus on something close up.

The eyes are also given unnecessary and bothersome extra work to do if the laws of perception discussed in the last chapter are ignored. If a person can't understand something at a glance, they have to focus on it again, and view it a different way (you can sometimes tell that people are doing this because their heads are tilted to one side).

So, if you want to do your audience a favor, save their eyes as much work as possible. A harmonious, well-balanced selection and combination of colors will go a long way towards achieving this.

Spectrum and Color Receptors

We only interpret a very small range of the electromagnetic spectrum as light. We perceive waves with lengths of approximately 440 nm to 800 nm as different colors (*nm* stands for nanometer, or one billionth of a meter: 0.000000001 m). The retina has three different kinds of receptors that allow the perception of color. These are called cones (or cone cells). We have blue, green, and red color receptors, which may work alone (green receptors only) or—as is usually the case—work together in combinations of varying proportions. For example, spectrally pure (unmixed) light with a wavelength of 400 nm only activates the blue receptors. However, if light with a wavelength of 500 nm hits the retina, all three types of cone are activated, but at varying levels of intensity.

Based on what we've learned so far, we can see that one important principle is that all of our impressions of color are based on a perceived mixture of blue, green, and red.

On the Companion CD Open the *\Samples\0401_ColorMix.xlsx* file, which will help you understand the explanations below. Open the *Color Spectrum* worksheet.

The *Color Spectrum* worksheet in the *0401_ColorMix.xlsx* file shows screen shots of the dialog boxes that I'll be discussing a little later in this chapter. It also shows a color spectrum with some details about wavelengths in nanometers.

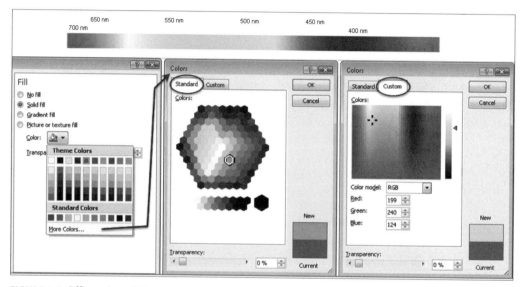

FIGURE 4-2 Office color palettes and color spectrum on the *Color Spectrum* worksheet

You'll understand the following general statements better by looking at the spectrum and hexagonal color palette in the center of the worksheet.

- The wavelengths of blue light are very different from those of red light.

- Light containing a high proportion of red is perceived as warm, while light containing a lot of blue is perceived as cold.

- Our blue receptors are the most sensitive. This is most obvious in diffused lighting conditions, in which blue tones appear brighter.

- Colors in the range of 550 nm are considered to be "average colors" that are pleasing to the eye. These include mixtures of green, blue, and yellow that are not overly intense (pastel colors).

- If our color receptors are barely stimulated or not stimulated at all, we perceive this as the color black.

- If all receptors are stimulated to the same and high degree, we perceive this as the color white (if you mix all the colors in the spectrum, you get white).

Now it's time to put your color receptors to the test. Use the *0401_ColorMix.xlsx* file and perform some heroic experiments for yourself; but please stop before the optical effects in the worksheets (not all of which are entirely pleasant) give you a headache or make you dizzy!

- The *Red Blue* worksheet shows two spectrally "pure" colors with very different wavelengths. Only one of your cone types will be stimulated at a time. Your powers of perception will therefore have a very hard time distinguishing between these two colors. You'll really notice this if you let your eyes wander over the screen without moving your head. Test the effect again, if you like, using the \Samples\0302_Limits.xlsx file introduced in Chapter 3 (*Perception 3* and *Perception 4* worksheets).

- The combinations of other intense colors in the other worksheets aren't so hard on the eyes. To test this, switch quickly between the various sheets, for example using **Ctrl+Page Up** and **Ctrl+Page Down**. The closer the wavelengths of different spectrally pure colors, the easier it is to perceive and interpret them in combination.

- In the *Red Green Blue Yellow* worksheet, you can make your eyes work even harder if you use the **F9** key. The faster you make the busy color mosaic change, the sooner the intense color combination will become hard on your eyes. And, just to be really mean, I've hidden a rather nasty blue and red "surprise" for your eyes in the workbook, which will appear at random (sometimes it appears very quickly; sometime it takes some time. If you keep experimenting long enough, you're sure to come across it).

- The *R & R* worksheet is called that because the colors it contains all have wavelengths in the pleasant range of 550 nm and will provide your eyes with some well-earned rest and relaxation. But, even here, changing the small pattern very quickly puts a strain on your eyes as they make fast adjustments, and can have an unpleasant effect.

Calibrating Your Screen

You may be unable to fully reproduce some of the effects listed above. There may be technical and other reasons. One of these spells bad news in terms of this chapter's topic: you may not see the colors exactly as I saw them when preparing the sample file. Unfortunately, no two monitors will display colors in exactly the same way, even if they're two identical models from the same production line. In addition, the colors change as the screen ages, as will our perception of these colors as we ourselves grow older. There's not a lot anyone can do about that, and these kinds of problems don't get in the way of technology.

All you can do is calibrate your monitor, which will have the effect of fine-tuning it to the standard. You require appropriate software to do this, although software provided with the monitor usually only appears to do so. But even if you have the right calibration software (which doesn't come cheap) and use it every couple of weeks as you should, what benefit is it to you in this context? Well, if you adorn your elegant presentation chart with a soft, light, pleasant, and freshly calibrated shade of brown, and this then appears on the customer's monitor or on a projector screen as a dirty yellow, then you'll have gained nothing by calibrating your screen because the calibration only affects *your* PC. If you work in or collaborate with professional publishing environments (such as graphics and typesetting studios, print shops, etc.), then calibration is a useful step (provided that everyone involved does it, and does it the same way), but it has few benefits for personal use or if used in an uncoordinated manner.

This isn't much consolation. The best advice I can offer you is to test any colors that are going to be "made public" on other monitors, ideally on the end-device on which the planned presentation is to be made.

This is bad enough. But, there's no point hiding it from you: there's worse news to come in relation to another color-related topic. Unfortunately, the colors that you see on your screen rarely match up with those that are printed. This is particularly difficult or annoying to deal with if you need to have someone else do the printing for you and can't ask for a sample to evaluate and approve.

> **Note** If you use Windows Vista or Windows XP, you won't be able to avoid these issues but you'll certainly be able to take some action to help things run more smoothly. For relevant information and instructions, open Windows *Help and Support* and search for *color management*.

Color Models and Their Use in Excel 2007

> **Note** As we discussed in Chapter 2, "New Approaches—Getting Started," the *Office* theme is the only integrated Excel theme used as an example in this book. The theme naturally plays a key role in determining a chart's color scheme. If necessary, go back to Chapter 2 (specifically, the sections entitled *A Solution Emerges* and *Choosing Themes*) and remind yourself how integrated themes are used. You'll also find some information there about *theme colors*, which we'll discuss again in this chapter.

Two color models or color systems based on very different approaches have roles to play in creating a color scheme on your PC and then bringing it to life in the printed version.

- **Additive colors** are produced when rays of light with different wavelengths fall on the same part of a white surface at the same time. The rays are effectively mixed or "added" together. Various combinations of this kind from light sources of the primary colors (red, green, and blue) are used, for example, to display colors on your PC monitor. You can use the RGB or HSL color model (more about these later) in Microsoft Office (including Excel) to produce any additive color. You can choose from approximately 16.7 million different color combinations.

- **Subtractive colors** are produced when one or more colors of the spectrum are lost through absorption from the light falling on a surface. If all of the light waves are absorbed, the resulting color is perceived as black. If none of the light waves are absorbed, the color is perceived as white. The CMYK system used for printing (refer to the information in the box below) is based on a subtractive color model.

If your Windows operating system has optimized color quality (32-bit; see Figure 1-2 in Chapter 1, "Basic Information—Basic Techniques"), you can generate 16,777,216 different colors with Microsoft Office. Excel has been greatly enhanced and improved in this regard. In earlier versions, you could also generate all PC colors, but you were limited to using just 56 of these per workbook. This restriction is now gone, and you can use all colors at any time for any element to which color can be applied. However, I question whether this is always a good thing. Excel workbooks can become much more colorful, but will that necessarily make them more attractive? After all, the two don't always go hand-in-hand.

Our practical discussion of color begins with a short step-by-step guide for applying a solid fill to a *chart area*:

First, enter some numbers in a couple of cells and use these to generate a chart of your choice.

1. Right-click an empty space in the *chart area*. The *mini toolbar* and context menu appear (see Figure 4-3, left). The *mini toolbar* contains the most important formatting tools. Click the arrow to the right of the *Fill Color* button to display a selection view (see Figure 4-3, right). The primary palette with the *Theme Colors* is shown, with some additional *Standard Colors* below this, as well as a number of menu options, which we don't need to discuss right now.

   A different way to achieve the same result is to click the *Format Chart Area* option in the context menu. This opens a complex dialog box (see Figure 4-2, left), where you must first click *Fill*, then select the *Solid fill* option, and finally click the fill icon in *Colors*. Detailed information is provided later in this chapter about the completely new design of the formatting dialog boxes.

   You can now click one of the palette colors shown in order to assign it. However, since we're discussing the subject of "color models," we want to elaborate on this initial selection.

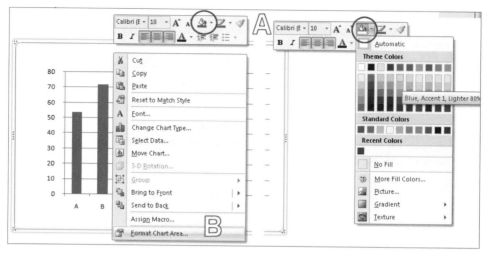

FIGURE 4-3 How to open the initial color selection (A = Directly, B = Indirectly)

2. Click the *More Colors...* option in the color palette to open the *Colors* dialog box, with the *Standard* and *Custom* tabs (see Figure 4-4). The options available on the *Standard* tab alone are sufficient to satisfy many additional requirements. The hexagonal color palette offers 127 different colors, including a range of 15 gray tones, also known as achromatic colors. Click a color to select it and then click *OK* to complete the step.

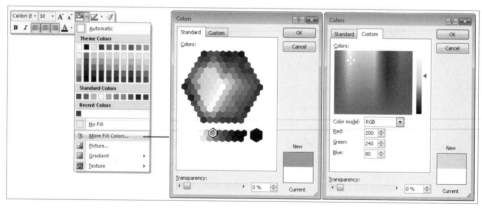

FIGURE 4-4 You now have all the colors you could possibly need

3. However, if you require greater accuracy or more variety, open the *Custom* tab, and define a color yourself (you'll be spoiled by having so much choice). There are two ways to do this:

❑ Option 1—flexible and judged "by eye": use the mouse to move the white cross around the color spectrum shown in the rectangle. When you release the mouse button, countless variations of the basic color selected are shown in a color column on the right. You can use a sliding arrow to choose a color variant of your choice.

❑   Option 2—determined by default settings (models) and color values entered: choose between *RGB* and *HSL* as your *color model* (I'll come back to these in a moment), and then enter a number between 0 and 255 in each of the three fields below, which together define your desired color.

The result of the Excel formula =256^3 (corresponds to 256³) is 16,777,216, which is the total number of colors that can be generated on Windows using the RGB or HSL models. In optimal conditions, the human eye can distinguish between approximately 6 million different colors. So why offer 10 million more? This extravagance isn't simply due to the programmers getting carried away. Rather, it has to do with the technical components of the two color models themselves.

1. Select *RGB* (short for *red, green,* and *blue*) as the *Color Model.* You can now select or enter a number between 0 and 255 in each of the assigned fields. In other words, you define how many of the 256 potential units of red, green, and blue you need to make up your combined color.

2. Define a color that's easy on the eye: R100 – G200 – B50. Now change the *Color Model* setting to *HSL.* Some initial confusion may be caused by the completely different selection options that suddenly appear, namely *Hue, Saturation (Sat),* and *Luminosity (Lum).* In addition, the values now shown (71 – 153 – 125) are entirely different from those you just selected for your green color in the *RGB* model.

Let me explain what these refer to in case you're confused. First, *HSL* stands for *hue, saturation,* and *lightness.* In the dialog box, *lightness* is represented by the "*Lum*" (luminosity) setting. The HSL color model has 256 different hues or shades of color (from 0 to 255), all of which can have different degrees of saturation and lightness. This gives us a total of 256³ possible colors that can be defined, which is the same as in the RGB model.

As you've seen, the values and value combinations of the two models are completely different. If you need to generate colors this way on a regular basis, it therefore makes sense to choose one system and stick with it.

> **Note** The RGB model is quicker to pick up in everyday use because it involves "mixing" colors, which is something we've all learned to do. As children, most of us will have been amazed by the colors we can create by mixing watercolors together.
>
> However, you may prefer the HSL model if you're primarily concerned with creating a certain effect. For example, *saturation*, which lends intensity to a color, plays an important part in how that color is perceived. If these concerns are foremost in your mind when selecting a color, you're sure to find that HSL has more to offer.
>
> The *achromatic* colors are the gray colors of the spectrum between white and black. In the HSL color model, these are all hues that have different intensities but the same saturation value (0, zero).

No matter which model you choose, you may still need to know and use the exact RGB value or HSL value of a color. Should this need arise, it's best if you can refer to lists, templates, or reference files.

If a company adopts a *corporate design*, it will specify, as a minimum, which RGB and HSL values the "company colors" are to have. Many enterprises have very far-reaching specifications and rules governing the strategic use of various colors, described in detail, and indicating the correct color values to use in each case.

If you want to accurately measure a screen color (i.e., define its values), most graphics programs have a pipette tool that you can use to point to colors and display their RGB values or HSL values. These programs include very extensive systems for defining and modifying colors. This is important because you'll naturally want to be able to copy any object you create or edit with a Windows-executable graphics program to Excel and use it there for visual impact.

Some graphics software may also allow you to use the *CMYK* subtractive color model. This is useful to the designer at the print or pre-print stage, if not earlier. Some confusion may arise and several adjustments may need to be made in switching between RGB and CMYK/HSL and CMYK when working with the copy shop or print shop at this stage. Some essential basic information about CMYK is provided below:

This system mixes the colors (often referred to as "process colors") C = cyan, M = magenta, and Y = yellow, and, if necessary, adds K = (key, or black) to the mixture. The optional inclusion of the "key color" black creates the contrast or "depth" of the printed color.

Various printing systems require the conversion of colors from the RGB or HSL color system to the CMYK color system. This process is known as CMYK separation. The resulting CMYK colors are similar to the RGB or HSL colors originally defined but are rarely identical to these. A direct conversion of RGB colors into CMYK colors isn't possible. As a result, there are always differences, big or small, between the colors displayed on a monitor and those on the printed page. This is one of the main problems still associated with digital printing: you can't expect the colors you see on-screen to be replicated exactly on paper. It's therefore essential that you insist on getting a proof copy when you place an order for printing, and remember too that the printer and paper used significantly affect how the printed color will appear.

Coloring Elements

Designing objects and their elements can be a pleasure with Office 2007. The relevant options have been vastly enhanced over earlier versions. These options include the formatting of charts and the application of color to chart elements, which is the central topic discussed in this section. But before we start on the technical details, there are a few brief points to note in relation to the "power" of color effects.

The Power of Color Effects

If you want to design the color effect of certain objects or areas so that they stand out and appear more important or interesting than others (or less so), you need to follow some basic rules. The most important of these is: never choose colors without giving some thought to your choice or based your choice solely on how they appear in the palette. Choose carefully and don't be too conventional or obvious in your choices (green for hope, and so on). The most important points to consider are as follows:

- The law of figure and background, which I explained in relation to perception in the last chapter, applies equally to color. The brighter a color is (in relation to other colors), the more it will appear to be "in the foreground" or "close" to you. You should therefore use varying grades of brightness to give your worksheet an impression of "depth."

- Colors that have a hue (i.e., chromatic colors) have a more powerful effect than those that don't (achromatic or grayscale colors). Consider the possibility that, in certain cases (for example, if your work is to be both presented *and* published), you may need two versions: one color version for the screen and another for the monochromatic printout.

I use the term "monochromatic" because, these days, even a conventional printer that's referred to as a "black-and-white printer" won't be limited to printing just black (white can't be printed in this case!). Instead, it will be able to print a single color (mostly black) in many different shades; i.e., as a grayscale version of a colored template.

Note that chromatic colors that are unique and clearly identifiable on-screen will appear identical in a monochrome grayscale printed version. In the case of colored line charts in particular, it's essential that you check the monochrome hard copy. This is because lines that make an equally "strong" impression and therefore appear as having an equal weighting in the color version may appear to have varying degrees of importance in the monochrome printout. That's because one line color may be printed as black and another as gray.

- A "pure" color (for example, a pure red, green, or blue that isn't mixed with other colors) has a much more powerful effect than a mixed color. This effect is related to the physiology of the receptors in our retina, as explained above.

- A highly saturated color (saturation is best defined using the HSL model) has more visual impact than a color with slight saturation only.

- Multicolored is more effective than monochrome.

- Warm colors (> 600 nm in the spectrum) have more impact than cold ones (< 500 nm in the spectrum).

You should primarily use colors that are "powerful" according to the list above for elements of the chart that you want to strike your audience immediately at first glance (for example, for the data series). Use less powerful colors primarily as fills for different areas of the workbook (plot area, chart area, worksheet, legends, text fields, etc.). If you want to emphasize certain elements in particular, use several different color effects at once; for example, choose a color that is pure *and* warm and *highly* saturated.

General Information About the Approach

 On the Companion CD Open the \Samples\0402_PracticeTemplates.xlsx file on the CD-ROM.

You can use the worksheets in the *0402_PracticeTemplates.xlsx* file for the exercises described below, or use models of your own that are of the same or a similar type. The practice file contains some worksheets with simple basic configurations and content:

- The *Text* worksheet for coloring text characters and filling cell ranges.

- The *Columns, Bars, Line, Area, Pie, Scatter, Radar* worksheets for practicing how to apply color to a whole range of chart elements.

- The *Shapes* and *Pictures* worksheets, in which you can experiment with various background colors to see how these change the effect of graphical objects. These pictures will become relevant again later in this chapter, when we move from talking about color to discussing other ways to manipulate objects.

The "Live Preview" feature mentioned in Chapter 1 will play an important role in the methods described here. Please check again that this new option is enabled in Excel 2007 (*Office button/Excel Options/Popular/Enable Live Preview*).

To recap: Microsoft Office always allows you to do the same thing in several different ways. This applies to certain techniques and menu options and to the ways in which program users can most easily find the application information they need and then put this into practice. In Excel 2007, it's not very easy to pin down procedures that are effective in meeting our sometimes very complex requirements, while also clearly illustrating the range of options available. I've decided to suggest an approach that will allow you to make good use of the predefined, integrated settings and templates, but also to change the results produced by these at any stage from the outset. I believe that this is essential to the creation of a personalized design ("personalized" from the perspectives of both the designer and the target audience). After all, you wouldn't do justice to the often excellent options available with the new version if you were to keep churning out the same designs month after month, year after year. Anyone can immediately identify the usual generic designs ("here we go, another typical Excel style") and no one will be fooled if you just keep dressing up the same old thing in slightly different clothing.

For this reason, I'm going to show you, from the very start, not just what's *easy* to do, but rather how easy it is to create the design you want in accordance with your specific requirements.

Coloring Table Structures

Open the *Text* worksheet in the *0402_PracticeTemplates.xlsx* file, or use a worksheet of your own containing text.

Character Font

You'll find all of the key tools for designing and changing selected fonts in the *Font* and *Alignment* groups of the *Home* tab in the Ribbon. Alternatively, right-click and use the tools in the *mini toolbar*, or select the *Format Cells* option in the context menu and then open the *Font* tab in the dialog box that appears. This *Format Cells* dialog box is, as mentioned in Chapter 1, one of the relics from earlier days of Excel that you'll still come across in the 2007 version. It may help you feel more comfortable in your surroundings while you're still getting used to them.

To define a font color, first select the relevant cells. Then click the *Font Color* button in the *Font* group of the *Home* tab in the *Ribbon*, and point (don't click) at the color you want to preview in the selected cells. Only click to define a color when you've made your final choice (see Figure 4-5, left).

The very useful preview doesn't work if you click the *More Colors* option in the palette and use the dialog box that opens or the RGB or HSL color model to define a color. You still can't assess the success of your settings until you click *OK* to confirm your selection.

Tip You can also use the options in the *Font* group of the *Home* tab to define font formats in charts (axis labels, legends, etc.). Simply click to select the element you want to format and then click the relevant button in the Ribbon. You can choose from an extensive range of tools and access these quickly. Only commands that aren't available for the relevant element (for example, vertical alignment, indents, etc.) are hidden.

Cell Ranges

It's just as easy to define fill colors for a selected cell range as it is to choose a font color. The *Fill Color* tool in the *Font* group in the Ribbon provides a preview function, and you can also select *More Colors* to open the *Colors* dialog box (see Figure 4-5, right).

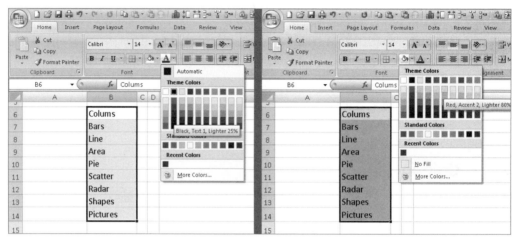

FIGURE 4-5 It's now much easier to define font colors and fill colors for cell ranges.

You can also take a very different approach and right-click in the selected cell range, select *Format Cells* in the context menu, and then open the *Fill* tab (see Figure 4-6). This dialog box looks a lot like the one from Excel 2003 (or earlier versions) and it works the same way. You'll notice this clearly if you click the *Fill Effects* button, which opens another dialog box that may be very familiar to you.

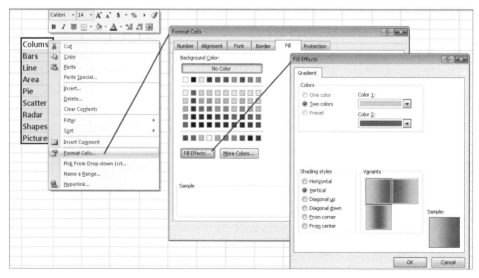

FIGURE 4-6 Now you can also apply a gradual gradient fill to cell ranges.

What's new here is that it's now also possible to assign a gradual progression of various shades of colors (i.e., a gradient fill) to table cells or ranges of table cells:

1. Choose the colors you want to use in the fill effect in the *Color 1* and *Color 2* boxes.

2. Under *Shading styles*, select the basic direction of the gradient. The *Variants* box then displays all available options.

3. In the *Variants* box, click the option you want to select, which is then displayed as a preview in the *Sample* box.

4. Click *OK* twice to assign the defined gradient to the selected cell range.

> **Note** Naturally, you can continue editing the filled cell range as you normally would. In later chapters, you'll see how the new table range fill options can produce very useful effects in transparent charts.

What's the same is the way the dialog box is used: pretty much as in earlier Excel versions. I've held this dialog box up as a paragon of Excel's virtues in other books through the years. This is because it's easy to understand, the workflow follows a logical sequence, and it abides by the laws of perception described in Chapter 3. The big fat fly in the ointment is the fact that this type of dialog box wasn't very common in previous Office versions, and I'm afraid it's the only one of its kind to survive in Excel 2007. As you're about to see, the new, updated tools are not nearly as well equipped to meet the need for clarity, simplicity, and well-structured intuitiveness at every step.

To complete this section, I must briefly mention the option of filling cell ranges with *conditional formatting*, meaning—in the broadest sense—a variable definition of cell colors based on table values. A huge range of new options have been added here also, and these will come into focus later in the book.

Coloring Chart Elements

You can use any of the *Columns, Bars, Line, Area, Pie, Scatter,* and *Radar* worksheets provided in the practice file for the exercises in coloring of chart areas as chart elements. Of course, it's advisable to try out different techniques or try to produce different effects on different worksheets.

Coloring Areas

Here, I use the term "area" to refer to the *chart area, plot area,* and two-dimensional *data series,* or to *data points* such as columns, bars, and similar elements that have an area that can be filled. We must also include the *data point markers* of a *line chart* or *XY (Scatter) chart* in the category of "area" (although I find this rather odd) because their formatting is subject to the same basic rules (including those for complex gradients) as the areas listed above.

Using and Changing Integrated Styles   We'll begin with a step-by-step guide to assigning several different formats to different elements at the same time. This will allow you to define the basic look of your chart, including its colors.

> **Important** But first things first: it's very important to bear in mind that the formatting style described below will affect several elements of your chart simultaneously. If you then change the format of some of the individual elements, and later go back and change the overall formatting style of the chart, your individual changes will be "overwritten."

Follow the following steps with reference to Figure 4-7:

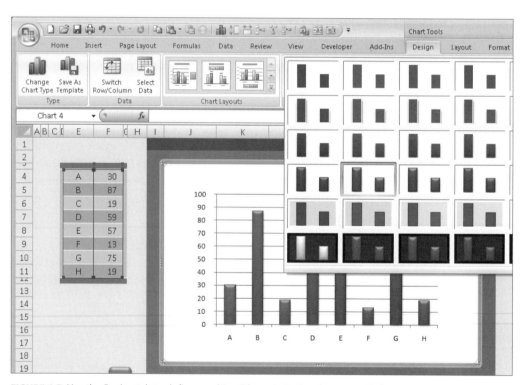

FIGURE 4-7 Use the *Design* tab to define combined formats to the chart as a whole

1. Select the chart to add the *Chart Tools* tabs to the Ribbon.

2. Select the *Design* tab and open the *Chart Styles*. Various chart styles are proposed here, which correspond to the current chart type, and also contain format combinations belonging to the selected theme (in the sample file, this is the *Office* theme, as mentioned earlier).

3. Click one of the proposed styles to assign the format combination to your chart (a preview of what this will look like in reality isn't available here). As you'll notice in the final

result, if not earlier, these formatting combinations not only specify fill colors but also define the outlines and shapes of the markers.

4. You can now select some of the elements you've just formatted and adjust them to suit your own requirements, but make sure you've read and understood the earlier cautionary note before you do so.

You can also change the individual elements using the integrated styles provided by the *Chart Tools*. Follow the steps below with reference to Figure 4-8:

1. The *Chart Tools* tabs are still visible in the Ribbon, or can be shown again by selecting the chart. Next, open the *Format* tab.

2. Select a two-dimensional element in your sample chart (for example, the *chart area,* *plot area,* or the columns of the *data series* in the column chart).

3. In the *Shape Styles* group, open the palette of currently available examples (framed in blue in Figure 4-8), and point with the mouse (don't click) to the proposed shape styles to preview how these would look when applied to the selected chart element.

4. Then click the format combination of your choice to format the selected element accordingly.

Once again, this applies not only fill colors but also outlines (borders) and shapes to selected elements.

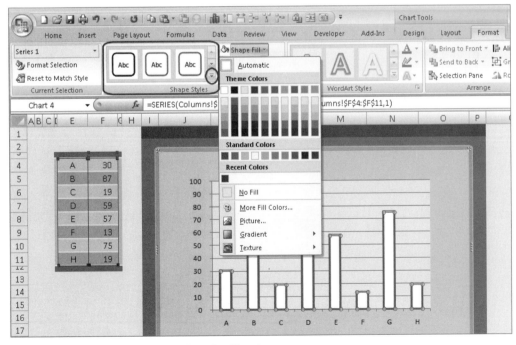

FIGURE 4-8 The *Format* tab also includes color fill options.

If you only want to change the color of a selected area of your chart, click the *Shape Fill* button in the *Shape Styles* group (see Figure 4-8), and select a color from the palette, using the helpful preview function as an aid. Once more, note that if you select the *More Fill Colors* option to open another selection from the palette, the preview no longer works, and you'll only be able to judge the results when you choose *OK* to apply the selection in the *Colors* dialog box.

When formatting a table range in a worksheet containing embedded charts, you may find that, when you change the fill color of a large cell range or of the entire worksheet, your choice of color may not blend in harmoniously with the colors you've assigned to a chart in the same worksheet. If you want to change the color of individual elements of the chart, you don't need to go right back to the *Chart Tools* again. The color options on the *Home* tab remain active even after you exit the table range in the worksheet and continue working in the chart. This means you can save yourself a detour through the *Chart Tools* when you want to make small or even large changes to your color choices, including the preview (see Figure 4-9).

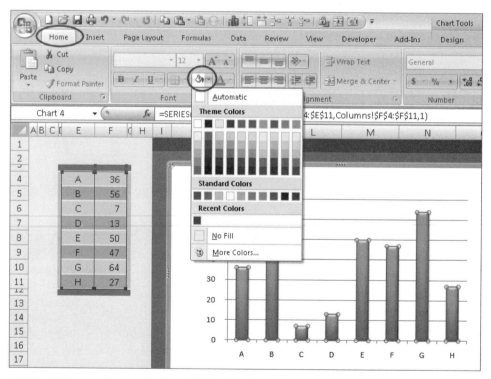

FIGURE 4-9 You can also use the *Home* tab to color chart elements.

Dialog Box for Coloring Areas with Solid Fills   I've already mentioned one of the greatest benefits offered by the revamped formatting dialog boxes in Excel 2007: the fact that you can make all the necessary settings for various objects and their elements, and then switch worksheets and so forth without having to exit the dialog box. Note, however, that your settings are applied immediately; in other words, before you close the dialog box. Therefore, if they haven't worked properly or you're unhappy with them in any way, you should choose the *Undo* option to get rid of them as soon as possible.

You'll have to learn to live with the drawbacks of the new program design, at least if you want to be able to use the multiform formatting options in a professional manner to suit your own requirements. Unfortunately, the dialog box I praised earlier as an ideal specimen (see Figure 4-6) is the only one of its kind. I imagine that it will take most users a little time to develop fluency in using the differentiated formatting options while also keeping errors to a minimum. The information and suggestions provided below may help you in this endeavor, but they certainly won't apply to every possible scenario.

> **Note** I can't agree with the argument that an extensive enhancement of options and resources inevitably makes the associated application techniques much more complicated. On the contrary, there are examples (not too many, admittedly) that provide convincing evidence that even highly complex systems can very simply and systematically be made easy to grasp and to use. And I'm not just thinking of software.

It's still a relatively simple procedure to color a two-dimensional chart element with a solid fill. Follow the steps below with reference to Figure 4-10 (on the left):

1. Right-click the chart element you want to format, and select the *Format (name of element)* option in the context menu.

2. In the dialog box shown on the left, select the *Fill* option, followed by the *Solid fill* option on the right.

3. Click the fill symbol next to the *Color* box, and proceed as already described several times.

   Because a direct preview isn't available with this method (you click a color to select it and the palette then closes), you should use the Ribbon options specified above in the case of solid fills. However, this isn't the case if you also want to assign a transparency to your color fill.

4. To set *Transparency*, use the slider provided or enter a value between 0 percent and 100 percent as the degree of transparency of your color fill. Here, once again, a "virtual preview" is available because you can see the effect of each change immediately while still keeping the controls in view. It's therefore best to use the slider to define an approximate transparency and then, if necessary, enter a percentage value for a more precise definition.

Caution Transparency is an extremely useful and versatile design tool. However, it does take some practice to achieve the desired effects, and you should give yourself sufficient time to do this. It will be a while before you feel ready to configure the infinitely variable degrees of transparency available. These also change the color selected, sometimes significantly, depending on the effect and the intensity of the background fill color, which will now be visible through the transparent area to a greater or lesser degree. As with many other tasks, it makes sense to plan your strategy here, rather than taking a "trial-and- error" approach. First, make a choice (if possible, a final choice) as regards your background color before you make any areas on this background transparent. This can be applied as a general rule; i.e. not just for chart elements, but also for the many shape objects that you can use to design and decorate your worksheets (Ribbon/*Insert* tab/*Illustrations* group/*Shapes* button). I'll discuss these in detail in Chapter 5, "Graphical Objects."

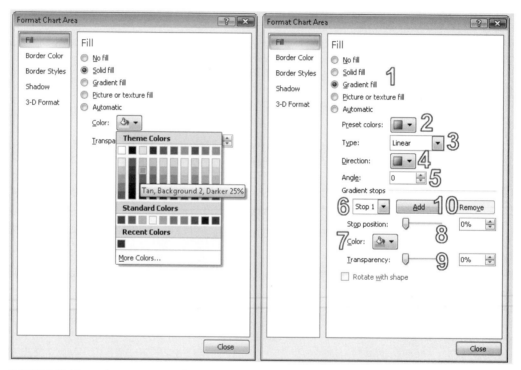

FIGURE 4-10 The options are outstanding, but the dialog box layout is less than perfect.

Using the Dialog Box for Coloring Areas with Gradient Fills Using multicolored fills (known as "gradient fills") to color chart areas can prove useful, informative, and visually effective. However, I've also seen many cases where designers have used gradient fills just because they could; in which case this feature is merely used as an unnecessary gimmick, and this is how it usually comes across.

In Office 2007, the *Gradient fill* option (as it's now called) offers a vast range of configuration and grading options, which will by far outstrip any options you may be familiar with from standard software applications. I can't discuss all the relevant details and variants within the confines of this book. Over the course of several examples, you'll be introduced to relevant solutions and suggestions, some of which I've supplemented with detailed comments and explanations. However, I strongly advise you to conduct your own extensive experiments in order to tap into the rich design potential that's available.

I'll start with an introduction to the formatting dialog box and the terminology used there. The explanations below correspond to the numbers shown on the right in Figure 4-10. It's very important to note that I'm *not* suggesting you follow these steps in sequence. A step-by-step guide is provided later in this chapter, with some practical examples by way of illustration.

You choose the *Fill* option on the left of the formatting dialog box.

1. If you then select *Gradient fill* on the right of the dialog box, additional controls relating to this option are displayed.

2. The *Preset colors* setting allows you to open a list of proposed templates, a feature which I find largely superfluous. I've only used it when first becoming accustomed to Excel 2007, and only then to find out how these sometimes kaleidoscopic gradient color schemes are technically realized. If you click one of the preset color schemes, it is applied to the selected element in the worksheet.

3. The *Type* setting allows you to configure the basic direction of the gradient. (This more or less corresponds with the options in the *Shading styles* area in the traditional dialog box shown in Figure 4-6.)

4. Once you've selected a *type*, a list of available options is displayed in the *Direction* box. These indicate which gradient directions are available based on the selected *type* (this corresponds to the options in the *Variants* area of the traditional dialog box).

5. If you select *linear* as your type, you can then enter a number between 0 and 360 (degrees) in the *Angle* box to rotate the entire color fill at any angle you like.

   The final decision you need to make relates to the *gradient stops*. *Gradient stops* is a complex setting that allows you to define all of the following, either directly or indirectly:

   ❑ Color used

   ❑ Position in the gradient where this color is located

   ❑ Area (from – to) occupied by this color within the gradient

   ❑ Transparency of the color

   The various properties that can be configured only apply to each individual *gradient stop* (or, to put it more simply: to each color in the gradient), rather than to the fill as a whole. The new program version gives you relative freedom in deciding how many different colors to use in a gradient (you can add and delete *gradient stops*). This means that you have countless possibilities at your disposal, including the number of colors multiplied by the combined number of gradient types, directions, rotations, color saturation within the gradient, and transparencies.

6. Select a *gradient stop* from the *stop list* to edit or delete it. After you make your selection, the properties that currently apply to this stop are shown in the assigned controls.

7. Here you decide which *Color* is to be granted "membership" of the gradient fill area.

8. The *Stop position* setting allows you to determine the location and the saturation of this color relative to the others used in the gradient, either using the slider provided or by entering a percentage value (I'll provide more details about this in a bit when we come to the practical examples).

9. The *Transparency* setting allows you to determine the degree of transparency of each color either using the slider provided or by entering a percentage value.

10. The two *Add* and *Remove* buttons allow you to configure the number of *gradient stops* that can be used in the current fill. Click *Add* to add another *gradient stop*, and then enter this color's values for *Color, Stop position,* and *Transparency*. In the *stop list* (see step 6), click a *gradient stop* and then click *Remove* to delete this *gradient stop*.

This is where the technical details come to an end. Now it's time to put what you've learned into practice. There are several different logical ways to proceed with this dialog box, depending on what you want to do. I'll explain to you (in theory, followed by some practical examples) the procedures I've become accustomed to using, and you can then try these out yourself. The following recommendations are based on the assumption that the chart element to be formatted has not yet been filled with any color.

1. Justification and planning: you should only use a color fill if you have good reason to do so. If you can't think of one, then don't bother. An indiscriminate use of formatting often has the same effect as makeup that's been too heavily applied. It can look really unappealing and over-the-top, as though you were trying to plaster over something you wanted to hide. You should be able to answer "Yes" to at least one of the following questions before you decide to use a color fill:

   ❏ Does the color fill convey or support information?

   ❏ Does the color fill help the point being made in the chart to be understood more readily or more clearly?

   ❏ Does the color fill make your chart more attractive? Not to you, but to your target audience! Does the formatting support a particular interest or strongly held feeling among your target audience?

   If you decide, after pondering these questions, that there is good reason to use a color fill, then you need to know how you want the chart as a whole to appear before you get started. This was useful, but not essential, when using earlier versions of the program, where the choice of options was relatively limited. Now, though, in Excel 2007, the number of available design options has virtually exploded, and this isn't always an entirely positive development. Unplanned, random tinkering with an almost endless number of variants may have many undesirable effects for the designer, the first of which is invariably tedium, and the worst is an attitude that can be summed up as follows: "I'm still not entirely happy with it. But I really can't be bothered spending any more time on it, even if I had any time to spare. Oh, well, I guess I'll just leave it as it is." This is one of the biggest mistakes you can make as a chart designer. After all, it's a pretty bad sign if even *you* don't even like your design.

To sum up: before you start, be clear about how you want the end result to appear. Moving on, follow the steps below with reference to Figure 4-11:

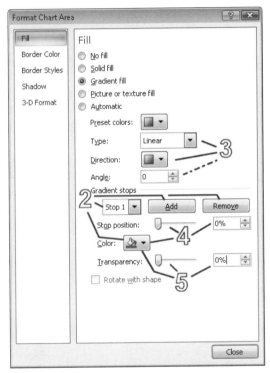

FIGURE 4-11 Basic workflow sequence (Step 2 onwards) when starting with "a blank canvas"

2. First, you need to make a basic setting when you open Excel. If you're confused by the settings displayed—i.e., if the last settings you made have been automatically adopted—you'll need to first close and then re-open Excel. Three *gradient stops* are proposed, with *stop positions* set at *0%, 50%,* and *100%.* This means that three colors will be blended evenly along the gradient. You should therefore decide in advance whether you want to use three, more than three, or just two colors in the gradient. Based on your decision, you can then add or remove stop positions here.

Next, select each of the remaining stops in turn and assign a color to each.

3. In the drop-down list for *Type*, select the basic direction of the gradient and, in the *Direction* box, select one of the gradient variants displayed (you also have the option of rotating a linear gradient at an angle). The advantage of making these settings now rather than when you start working on the chart formatting is that the preview templates you can display for the *Direction* option allow you to view and make a rough appraisal of the colors you actually want to use.

4. Select each individual stop in sequence from the drop-down list, and use the slider or enter a percentage value to define the *stop position* of each. It would make little sense to describe the details of all the possible factors you could take into account when making these selections. You should therefore practice making different selections with different objectives in mind, and in this way develop your own basic routine. You can also refer to the practical examples in the following section for assistance.

5. If you decide from the outset that you want to assign transparencies to some or all of the *gradient stops*, you can do this as described in step 4. In many cases, it's more efficient (provided you can put up with a number of detours and additional intermediate steps), to wait to configure the transparencies until you're satisfied with the preliminary results of your gradient in terms of color, gradient direction, and the positioning and relative saturation of the individual colors (as defined by the *stop positions*).

    Select each individual stop in turn from the drop-down list, and use the slider or enter a percentage value to define its transparency.

Alternative approaches and workflow sequences may be appropriate if your intention is to correct, remove, or replace existing color fills. To practice doing this, use the file provided for the next section or create your own file containing several charts and, if necessary, several different chart types.

Putting Color Fills into Practice

 On the Companion CD Open the \Samples\0403_Ireland.xlsx file on the CD-ROM.

I've never missed an opportunity yet in any of my books to take a short trip to Ireland, my "second home." The *0403_Ireland.xlsx* file has four worksheets containing line diagrams that are to be used to simulate any data connected to Ireland and its national colors. After a brief introduction, I'll make some suggestions for putting this into practice.

■ The chart in the *Ireland 1* worksheet has solid fills in its *chart area* and *plot area*, and is therefore ideally suited to the configuration of new gradients.

- In the *Ireland 2* worksheet, the *plot area* has a solid fill, while the *chart area* has six different *gradient stops* corresponding to six different shades of green, which seemed appropriate since we're talking about "the Emerald Isle."

- The *plot area* in the *Ireland 3* worksheet is a monochrome white. Behind this, the *chart area* has a gradient fill comprising three *gradient stops* (with the default Excel settings of 0%, 50%, 100%), representing the Irish national colors (green, white, and orange). This example clearly illustrates that this setting sometimes produces unsatisfactory results when there is an abrupt transition between three colors. Here, the white isn't "strong" enough to have a weighting equal to that of the other two colors, and therefore is hidden behind these in the image as we perceive it.

- This problem is corrected in the *Ireland 4* worksheet. Here, the *chart area* now has four *gradient stops*, two of which (those in the middle) are white. The positioning of the gradient stops also ensures that the colors are more clearly separated from one another. The plot area has a solid yellow fill, and, with a transparency of 50 percent, allows the colors of the *chart area* to show through. I've also added a map of the island for a decorating effect, and positioned this in front of the chart with slight shading (a similar use of objects is discussed in Chapter 5, and is also applied in several of the practical examples in the book).

> **Note** Experienced users may note that, in the last worksheet described, I could have used a picture, such as an image of the Irish flag, in the chart area. This is true in principle, not just in this case but in general, and applies to any kind of colored background. In fact, the next section explains exactly how it's done. However, the use of a gradient fill is much more versatile, at least in Excel 2007. It allows you to easily meet a wide range of design requirements, such as "softening" the transitions between the colors, rotating the flag, altering the proportion of the total area occupied by an individual color, highly differentiated fine-tuning of each individual color, and much more. All of this would be more time-consuming if you were to use a picture instead.

As your first exercise, I suggest you create a gradient fill based largely on the default settings. The chart's plot area should have a vertical fill consisting of two colors, changing from a dark to a light green from the bottom up. Follow the steps below with reference to Figure 4-12:

1. Open the *Ireland 1* worksheet and right-click in the chart's *plot area*. Select the *Format Plot Area* option in the context menu and then select the *Gradient fill* option in the dialog box that opens.

2. In the drop-down list for the *Gradient stops* setting, select Stop 3, and press the *Remove* button. The drop-down list may contain only two stops or more than three stops, depending on the settings you previously made elsewhere. Only gradient Stops 1 and 2 should remain.

3. In the drop-down list for the *Gradient stops* setting, select Stop 1, and define a relatively dark shade of green in the *Color* box for this stop. Follow the same steps to define a much lighter shade of green for Stop 2.

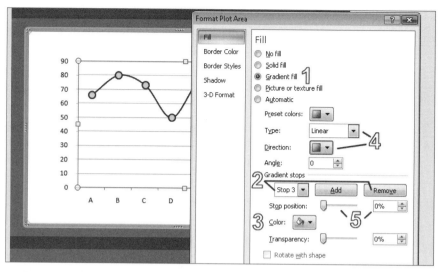

FIGURE 4-12 How to create a relatively simple, conventional gradient fill

4. In the drop-down list for the *Type* setting, select *linear*, and for *Direction* select the color template where the darker color is on the bottom and the lighter color is on top.

5. In the drop-down list for the *Gradient stops* setting, select Stop 1, then define the value 0 percent (move the slider all the way to the left) as the *Stop position*. Then define a *Stop position* of 100 percent for Stop 2. This means that the gradient will comprise equal portions of the two colors, and that each will run into the other to an equal degree.

> **Tip** Of course, you should also play around a little with the settings before you close the dialog box; for example, change the colors, then the type, the associated direction variants, and the transparencies. However, the most important experiment to conduct is the following, because it's a relatively difficult one to understand. Change the stop positions of the colors to see how this changes their portions in the gradient and how this also affects the differentiation between the colors; in other words, the "flow" of the transition from one color to the other. The best way to learn this is by experimenting; it's difficult to formulate clear rules regarding the percentage portions of colors in a gradient fill and the mutual dependencies and influences of these.

For the next exercise, go to the *Ireland 2* worksheet. Here you'll check and, if you like, change an existing gradient fill. Follow the next steps with reference to Figure 4-13:

If you open the dialog box for formatting the *chart area* and examine its gradient fill, you'll see that six different stops have been defined for this gradient, each representing a different shade of green. As you can also see in the figure above, the various stop positions have been defined with very different distances between them. As a result, the distribution of color is not an equal one.

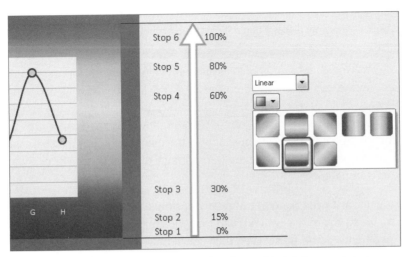

FIGURE 4-13 Not quite the famous "40 shades of green" but six is a good start

As exercises, I recommend checking how the chart's appearance and impact changes when you:

- Select different variants for *Type* and *Direction*
- Change the value of the *Stop position* for individual *gradient stops*
- Change the colors and/or transparencies of various *gradient stops*
- Add or remove *gradient stops*
- Change the existing model so that, for example, the entire *plot area* is located as far as possible in a light area, while the areas above and below this are darker and identical, with the six colors blending harmoniously into each other

In the *Ireland 3* worksheet, the colors of the Irish flag are used in equal portions in the gradient fill in the *chart area*. I've already referred to the problem of the perceived disappearance of the white color here. Therefore, take this opportunity to try replacing the white color (Stop 2) by another, stronger color (even if the good people of Ireland wouldn't be too happy about it!) and note how the overall effect clearly changes. Of course, you can also conduct additional experiments of your own along the lines of those I've described.

I won't describe the overall appearance of the *Ireland 4* worksheet just yet, as we want to remain focused on fill variants for the moment. By adding a fourth *gradient stop*, I've managed to produce a fairly accurate representation of the Irish tricolor. Take a look at the *stop positions* I've used for this purpose:

- Stop 1 (green) has a *stop position* of 33 percent.
- Stop 2 (the first white) has a *stop position* of 34 percent.
- Stop 3 (the second white) has a *stop position* of 65 percent.
- Stop 4 (orange) has a *stop position* of 66 percent.

| **Note** You can't use decimal places when defining stop positions.

You should use this worksheet primarily to experiment with different transparency settings for the *plot area*. In the version provided on the CD-ROM, a pale yellow fill was defined with a transparency of 50 percent. As a result, the background colors can still be identified relatively clearly (in an Excel chart, the *chart area* rather than the border provides the *background* for the plot area). See for yourself how the overall effect of the chart sometimes changes dramatically when you change the transparency of the *plot area* or change its color (and, in turn, its transparency).

You can already tell, just by looking at this relatively simple practice file, that a huge range of options is available to you in this context, and that you could quite happily spend an entire afternoon experimenting with these. Even then, you'd only come halfway close to finding out all that can be done and what works best visually. All the more reason to proceed with caution here. If your aim is to develop appropriate, coherent designs in a professional context, then you shouldn't ever allow the range of possible options to lead you into indecision, or let excessive tinkering cause you to lose sight of the simplest solution, which is also often the best.

Picture and Texture Fill   Going strictly by the organizational structure of this chapter, the subject of *picture and texture fills* doesn't really belong in a discussion about "coloring" chart elements. However, I want to include it here because the design principles, techniques, and effects are so similar to those that apply to the coloring of two-dimensional elements. A sample/practice file is available for this section also:

 | **On the Companion CD** Open the \Samples\0404_Stadium.xlsx file on the CD-ROM.

The *0404_Stadium.xlsx* file contains visual representations of the attendance figures of a large stadium. Here, the stadium operator is particularly keen to highlight the point that the 75,000-seat capacity was filled to an acceptable level at at least three out of 10 events, even though the attendance figures overall were rather low.

The workbook contains two sample charts, which will immediately strike you as being very different, even though they are based on the same data. The solution in the *Model 1* worksheet consists of a basic column chart, which largely uses simple default settings and has just one distinguishing feature; i.e., a *polynomial trendline*.

This type of chart works well because of its clarity, simplicity, and convincing message, and in no way could be described as "deficient." On the contrary, its design is almost perfectly suited to many different purposes.

Note Classifying different types of trendlines and defining the basis on which they're calculated touches on a very complex area of mathematics, which lies outside the scope of this book, and would certainly be of little interest to most readers. The same will certainly apply to some other topics raised in later chapters. However, so much in-depth information is now available on the Internet, even in relation to specialized subjects like this, that those of you with inquiring minds will have no difficulty finding good, and even very good, articles dealing in general or in detail with different aspects. In relation to the current example, you'll find a large number of detailed, informative sources if you search for "polynomial."

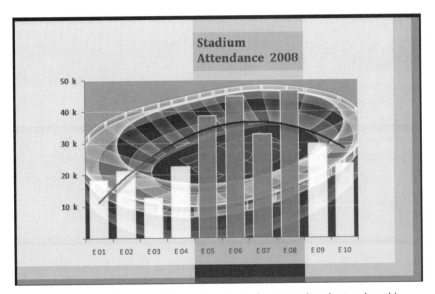

FIGURE 4-14 Some effort goes into creating a typical presentation chart such as this

The version in the *Model 2* (see Figure 4-14) has an entirely different effect. In this case, the design is geared much more towards the interests of the target audience. In a public presentation (in this case, the audience consisted of sponsors and potential event organizers), there should be a clear distinction between the values that will be perceived as "good" and those that are merely satisfactory. Here, the designer also tried to create a lasting good impression by adding some decorative effects. It's not very difficult to reproduce this type of chart in Excel 2007. Planning, preparation, and dedication to the task are more important than techniques in this case. We'll meet this chart again in later chapters. Here, I've focused on describing how to add an image like this to the *plot area*. If you want to try this out for yourself, the relevant description is provided in the following paragraphs, and the *Model 1* worksheet provides a starting point for the exercise. It may be useful to save the file to your hard disk under a different name before you start working on it.

In this case, an image of the stadium to which the chart refers will provide the fill for the plot area. Graphics software was used to generate various templates of varying sizes, layouts, and colors to satisfy different requirements. The version finally used here you'll find on the CD-ROM.

On the Companion CD Sample pictures, which can be used in some of the exercises, are provided under *Materials\Pictures*.

Follow the steps below with reference to Figure 4-15:

1. Select the *Model 1* worksheet, and open the dialog box for formatting the *plot area*.
2. Click the *Picture or texture fill* option to load the relevant settings into the dialog box.
3. Click the *File* button. The *Insert Picture* dialog box opens, where you can search for pictures in the relevant folders and select them as fill elements in your chart.

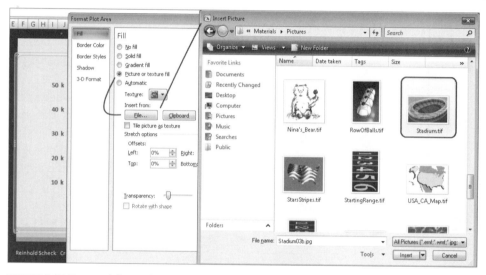

FIGURE 4-15 How to define a picture as a fill element for your chart

4. If you want to follow the example of the *Model 2* worksheet, select the *Stadium.tif* file, which is suitable to be used as a background. Paste the file by pressing the *Insert* button.

5. Experiment a little and discover what changes you can make now using the options in the lower part of the *Format Plot Area* dialog box:

   ❑ The *Stretch options* settings allow you to change the percentage values to determine the degree to which the picture is offset from the individual borders of the plot area.

   ❑ The *Transparency* setting allows you to define whether the picture is to have less of a visual impact by making it partly transparent using the now familiar method described earlier.

   ❑ You can also select *Tile picture as texture* to use the picture as a kind of "tile." If you do this (which I don't recommend, as explained in the box that follows), additional *tiling options* appear in the dialog box. These allow you to scale the tiles and change their offset from the borders of the plot area.

This version of Microsoft Excel also gives users the option of filling charts with *textures* (also referred to as *structures* elsewhere in the program). These add a pattern to surfaces, which in most cases makes them appear as though they are made of material. In the dialog box shown in Figure 4-15, you can click *Texture* to select one of these.

In most cases, filling an area with several individual pictures of the same type (i.e., tiles) is only really useful if these tiles produce a harmonious overall image or result in a surface with a "normal" appearance, which is seldom the case. Textures (of fabric or natural materials, for example), which appear to be completely symmetrical, or whose slight irregularities are repeated regularly throughout the pattern, do not have greater visual impact than floral wallpaper. There are very few good reasons to use photographs or other images that are also highly differentiated as tiles, at least when designing charts.

Therefore, I only recommend using texture fills in very few exceptional cases. In the vast majority of cases, the results are aesthetically unsatisfactory, and usually appear rather unoriginal and artificial. Moreover, because this kind of design has been around and, unfortunately, overused for years, you run the risk of your audience classifying it as old-fashioned, and therefore uninteresting or even boring. The same applies to the use of ClipArt (which you can also access from the dialog box described above), even if it does now contain some new and well-designed templates. But, then, this is a recurrent problem: a well-designed, accessible template is going to be used very frequently and, as a result, will become over-exposed, so that the public will soon tire of it. If I ever make use of such collections (for example, in Office Online), I usually only select photographs. When designing a chart for a customer, particularly if it's for an important presentation, I never use generally accessible templates of any kind. Instead, I use photographs, graphics, patterns, etc. that I've created or ordered myself, or incorporate relevant material available in the customer's own collections (for example, as part of a corporate design) if it fits the bill.

You can use the outstanding design features of Excel 2007 to create presentation charts with a very professional look. If this is what you want to do, I strongly advise that you avoid using another of the fill options available with the program; i.e., using pictures to fill two-dimensional data series (columns, bars etc.). Some people may find columns filled with stacked cars used to illustrate automobile sales figures, or a long chart bar containing a string of 12 company logos very amusing. However, if you're going to take your audience seriously—and have them take you seriously at all times—you're better off not messing around with your design like this. Any presentation provides sufficient opportunity to create a positive, enjoyable (where appropriate), but always serious impression by including interesting visual effects and, more important, by providing interesting explanations of the data presented.

Experiment some more, for example by using other pictures provided on the CD-ROM, changing the position of the picture (in the chart area instead of the plot area), using different transparencies, changing the data series and/or the surrounding colors—whatever you like. The overall effect may change dramatically as a result and it's important for you, as the designer, to understand *why*.

Now for some more details about the properties and features of the design in the *Model 2* worksheet. Some you'll understand easily thanks to the information you've been given so far, and you can play around with making changes to these. Others will be explained later in this chapter or in subsequent chapters, but you can certainly still explore and experiment with these even now.

- *No fill* is defined for the *chart area*, meaning that it's completely transparent. The entire background design extending beyond the *chart area* consists of formatted table cells.

- The chart title is a *text field* without a fixed position, rather than a chart element or the content of a table cell.

- When these color assignments were made, particular attention was given to the need for a target- audience-oriented approach, as described earlier. For the presentation to succeed, it needs to draw the immediate attention of the sponsors and potential event organizers to the important columns of events *E05* to *E08*.

- If you reduce or enlarge the *plot area*, the color fill will automatically adapt to this change. If you use a photograph as a fill, as in this example, be sure to scale the fill proportionately to avoid ugly distortions of the image.

- The columns fall into one of two color categories, which also have slightly different degrees of transparency. The structures of the stadium building show through, but that doesn't interfere with the perception of the columns themselves.

- The trendline also has a gradient fill, and slight shading was added to it. This shading is easier to see in the *Model 1* worksheet.

- The rising trendline lines up nicely with the stadium oval. This is no fortunate coincidence. On the contrary, it was taken into account during the planning and design of the chart and the picture.

Marker Fill   The formatting of data point markers as an area is more of a curiosity than a serious design option. In Excel 2007, this anomaly is primarily due to technical reasons, which have no real consequences for day-to-day use.

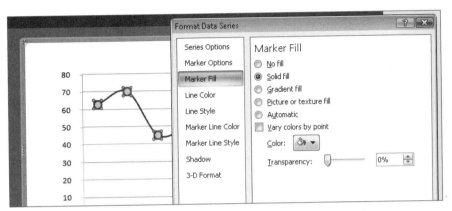

FIGURE 4-16 It's also possible—but not compulsory—to treat data point markers as areas

When formatting a *line chart* or *XY (Scatter) chart*, you can use the same options for the data point markers (referred to primarily as *markers* in the program) that apply to the design of larger areas (chart area, plot area, two-dimensional data series, etc.). There are a few, extremely rare cases in which a designer is likely to actually use these options. As a general rule, however, you should color markers with solid fill; or, if you want the chart gridlines to be visible in the marker, use the *No fill* option.

Coloring Lines and Outlines

No other significant changes have been made to the color-formatting options for areas and lines in Excel 2007. In this context, a line is—technically speaking—a long, narrow area. Therefore, what you've learned and practiced in the previous sections in relation to the technical options for coloring areas applies equally to lines and outlines in most scenarios. However, by "equally," I mean that the same method is applied, not that the effect is "equally good." Once again, just because something can be done doesn't mean that it *has* to be done. You've already seen some examples of a gradient fill being applied to data series lines. In each case, there was a good reason to do so. However, it would be less interesting, and also less useful, to apply all of the various options available to line elements that play a purely structural role and don't provide any information in the current chart.

When formatting charts, the following can be treated as *lines* or *outlines*:

- *Data series lines* (see Figure 4-17)

- *Marker lines* (meaning the borders or other line structures of markers (see Figure 4-17)

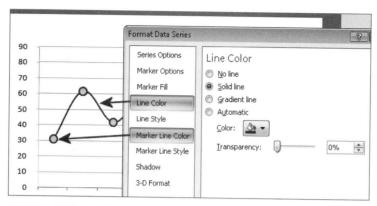

FIGURE 4-17 The border of a marker is called a *marker line* in the dialog box.

- *Axes* and their associated *gridlines*

- *Borders* of two-dimensional elements (*chart area, plot area, columns, bars,* etc.)

- Analytical lines, such as *trendlines, high-low lines, drop lines,* or *error bars*

For all these elements, you can use the color fill options described above, and use the program's dialog boxes accordingly. Other ways to format lines and outlines are discussed in the next section.

Creating and Changing Lines and Outlines

Our eyes are used to identifying the shape and form of a shape based on differences in color, brightness, and the presence of shadows. Sharply defined outlines, brightly colored borders, or dividing lines aren't a common feature of our natural environment, and so it's not part of our biological makeup to be able to perceive these. You therefore need to be prudent in your use of lines and outlines, and exercise restraint when deciding how strong and colorful these should be. In many cases, it's preferable to use shadows (now much easier in Excel 2007) rather than lines.

At the end of this section, I'll provide a list of the elements included in the category of lines and outlines in Excel 2007. For the sake of simplicity, I refer to all of these elements as *lines* in the discussion below. We'll start with the options for creating and/or changing lines.

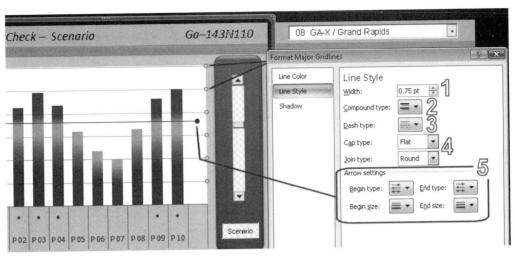

FIGURE 4-18 The configuration settings for *line style* are also very versatile.

Follow the steps below as they apply to Figure 4-18 (left side of the dialog box):

- You can color a line, and you've already learned how to do this in the previous section.

- The instructions below explain how to define the *line style*.

- The settings for *shadows* are then discussed in the next section.

The steps below for defining the *line style* follow the numbered sequence shown in Figure 4-18. Before you start, note once again that you'll need to explore and experiment with the very wide range of options in order to learn which are useful when designing a chart and how you can achieve satisfactory visual results as quickly as possible.

1. Enter or select a value to define the *width* of a line (referred to more accurately elsewhere in Excel as *weight*). Here you can also enter a value with decimal places. The maximum possible width of a line is 1584 pt, although I'm not sure why you'd ever need such a monster.

2. In the *Compound type* box, use the pictured default values to specify whether you want to use a simple line or, if need be, a double or triple line.

3. *Dash type*: The line can appear as a continuous line or as a series of dots or short dashes.

4. The selection options for the *Cap type* and *Join type* settings are rarely relevant when formatting line elements in charts and can simply be disabled here. These features are of more interest to professional graphic designers.

5. The *Arrow settings* allow you to define certain properties for the start and end of a line. These also play a relatively minor role in the design of chart-specific lines because arrows or arrow-like shapes are rarely used as integral components of charts. If they are

used, it's normally as additional graphic objects that are inserted into the chart. In this case, it's also useful to be able to define a *Begin type, End type, Begin size,* and *End size.*

The arrow in Figure 4-18 illustrates one of the rare examples of the use of these options in the formatting of chart elements. Here, a accurate horizontal data series line ends with a round end point. More details about the general settings for arrows are provided in Chapter 5.

Shading Areas and Lines

As mentioned earlier, shapes can be displayed and emphasized much more effectively by using different colors, levels of brightness, and, above all, by adding shadows, than by using lines. Take a look around your current surroundings (where you are right now), and you're likely to find countless examples to illustrate this point.

Shadows can be added to most chart elements in Excel 2007. You can use shadows to highlight certain elements and to lend depth to the overall picture. Here too, it's better to exercise some restraint than to exhaust all possibilities. But above all, make sure that you use shading correctly so as to avoid confusing your audience or provoking a reaction along the lines of "Hmm... that looks odd." We don't normally notice the angle or color of a shading effect, but we can notice very quickly if something is wrong.

Therefore, remember the following:

- Shadows are produced by light falling directly on a surface. In the natural world, the light usually comes from a single source, in which case the directions of the shadows cast by the illuminated objects are all identical. The eye is capable of perceiving the shadows formed when there are two light sources with different strengths coming from different directions. However, you should always use the simplest model. Therefore, if you configure several shadows in a chart, they should all appear as though there was a single light source, and their directions should be the same.

- A shadow always is or appears to be darker than the shape that casts it. Therefore, avoid using shadows that appear lighter than the elements to which they're applied (what is perfectly possible in Excel).

- Only rarely is a shadow pure black. As a rule, a shadow's color is a darker version of the color of the surface(s) on which the shadow falls. It's very easy to imitate this effect in Excel 2007 by selecting black as the color of the shadow and using the transparency of the shadow color to define the desired degree of lightness (or darkness).

The options for manually defining and designing shadows are explained below with reference to Figure 4-19. Select the chart element you want to shade and open its formatting dialog box. When you click *Shadow,* the relevant tools are displayed as follows.

1. Click *Presets* for a preview of the predefined effects. As you'll see from the extensive list, shadows are classified into one of three main types:

   ❑ The shadow is cast entirely by the object itself (for example, by a box), and is therefore *Outer*.

   ❑ You look into the open or opened object (into the box) and see the shadow formations, which are therefore *Inner*.

   ❑ The shadow falls on a surface that's at a different level. As a result, the shadow has *Perspective*.

   To remove a shadow, select *Presets* as before, and click the *No shadow* option.

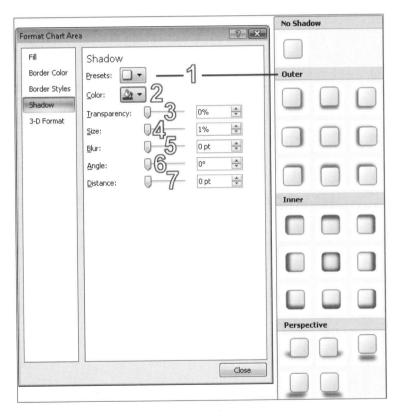

FIGURE 4-19 Configuration options for shadows

2. When it comes to selecting a *color* for the shadow, everything we covered in relation to colors earlier in the chapter applies. Remember, however, that the easiest way to achieve a natural-looking shadow effect is to use a transparent variant of black, as mentioned above. To do this, you must first explicitly fill the area on which you want the shadow to fall, before you create the shadow, including its color, and define its transparency.

3. You should be familiar by now with the two controls (slider and percentage value input field) for defining *transparency*.

4. The *Size* of the shadow expresses, as a percentage, the ratio of its dimensions to those of the object casting it. A shadow may be larger or smaller than the object itself, depending on the light source, the direction from which the light is falling, the background on which the shadow is cast, and its distance from the object. The possible settings you can make here range from 1 percent to 200 percent.

5. The *Blur* setting allows you to enlarge the shadow, while simultaneously making it softer (diffuse). Here you can enter a value between 0 pt and 100pt. Bear in mind that, in natural conditions, shadows very rarely appear with clearly defined outlines.

6. With the *Angle* option (0° to 359.9°), you can play at being the sun. This tool allows you to change the direction from which the light falls on the object, and therefore the position of the shadow in relation to the object. In other words, the *Angle* setting lets you rotate the shadow around the object or, in the case of an inner shadow, inside the object.

7. The effect of changing the angle position as described in step 6 above is particularly clear and striking if you change the *Distance* of the shadow from the object. First, set the distance (between 0 pt and 200 pt) and then use the *Angle* setting to test the various positions of the shadow.

Of course, you'll achieve the best results if you combine all of the settings in a coordinated manner. You won't be surprised when I tell you that the only way to find out which of the thousands of options will help you get the possible best results is either by attending a specific training course or by experimenting diligently until you've reached a sufficient level of experience.

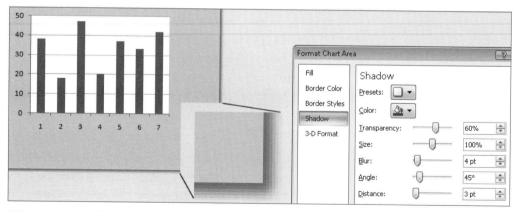

FIGURE 4-20 Typical settings for a standard shadow

However, you may simply want to use the complex shadow options to make a slight change or correction to the predefined program templates. This wouldn't be a bad decision, provided you have the time and interest to undertake detailed "shadow casting."

In any case, if this section has fulfilled its objective, you should now have a detailed understanding of a shadow definition (see Figure 4-20) that's typical of Excel 2007 and can be automatically assigned, and to make systematic changes to it if necessary.

Note The shadow defined in this way is linked to the object that casts it, which is as it should be. If you delete the object, its shadow also disappears. Although this seems obvious, it's worth noting the following background explanation.

Due to the insufficient differentiation options in earlier versions of Microsoft Office, a shadow sometimes had to be drawn as an independent object and then visually linked with that object. Of course, this is still possible in Excel 2007, but is only necessary if you want to represent a shadow falling on a 3D shape. However, this is rarely required when designing charts.

Assigning "Shape Styles"

The final section in this chapter provides a summary and overview of the topics covered so far. However, it doesn't merely repeat what's already been said, but rather describes alternatives for formatting chart elements.

You've now read in some detail about how you can use specific dialog boxes to define or change custom formats. I've already described the ability to do so as a prerequisite for using the program professionally. If you don't have a thorough understanding of what can be configured and changed using custom settings and exactly how these settings work, then the automatic features of a graphically oriented program will almost seem to become your arch-enemy when you try to produce a successful design, never mind a successfully customized design. However, in such an innovative program as Excel 2007, you don't need to follow a complicated manual route to design every little detail. In many cases, it's faster and more effective to assign certain basic formats automatically, and then use the formatting dialog boxes described above to modify these in accordance with your individual requirements. The *chart tools* I've mentioned many times provide valuable assistance if this is the approach you take.

In the descriptions provided below, I assume that you've created a complete chart, both in terms of content and structure, and that you now want to assign various formats to it. Click a chart element to display the *Design, Layout,* and *Format* tabs belonging to the *chart tools* in the *Ribbon*. The instructions provided below refer exclusively to the options provided in the *Format Styles* group of the *Format* tab.

On the Companion CD To practice using these options, it's best to use the *\Samples\0402_PracticeTemplates.xlsx.* file introduced at the start of the chapter.

Combined Basic Formats for Shape, Fill, and Outlines

Follow the steps below with reference to Figure 4-21:

I've already discussed the combined assignment of shapes, fills, and lines (borders) above in connection with Figure 4-8. In the *Shape Styles* group, open the palette of currently available examples and point with the mouse (don't click) to the proposed shape styles to preview how these would look when applied to the selected chart element. Then click the format combination of your choice to format the selected element accordingly.

You can then revise the details of these assignments, i.e.:

- Change or refine the assignments using the features described below
- And/or with very precise, customized actions using formatting dialog boxes

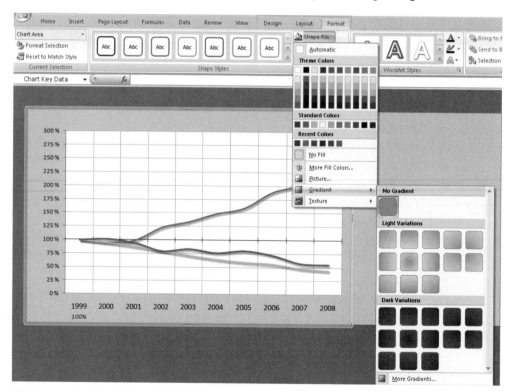

FIGURE 4-21 Defining combined formats and fills using the *chart tools*

Shape Fill

Follow the steps below, again with reference to Figure 4-21:

The following options are shown when you click the *Shape Fill* button:

- *Colors*: use the technique described earlier to assign a *theme color* belonging to a specific theme (the *Office* theme is used almost exclusively in this book) or a *standard color*, or choose *More Fill Colors* to assign a custom color.

- *Picture*: this option opens the *Insert Picture* dialog box, which you normally access by selecting *Fill/Picture or texture fill/File* or from the Ribbon via *Insert/Illustrations/Picture*; i.e., when you use the formatting dialog box described earlier.

- *Gradient*: when you click this option, you get a graphical display of the various gradient directions possible, which you can use to configure a simple gradient, or change the type or direction of an existing one. The *More Gradients* option below the templates brings you to the formatting dialog box.

- *Texture*: when you click this option, you get the same range of proposed uses that appear in the formatting dialog box when you select *Fill/Picture of texture fill/Texture*.

Shape Outline

Select a line or an element that has a border, and then choose the *Shape Outline* option. Follow the steps below with reference to Figure 4-22:

- *Colors*: Assign a *theme color* or a *standard color*, or choose *More Outline Colors* to assign a custom color.

> **Note** You can choose *No Outline* to delete the border around an object or to make a line invisible, for example.

- *Weight:* If you select this option, you get a graphical overview of line weights that can be selected. If this isn't sufficient, you can also select the *More Lines* option to open the formatting dialog box. Here, the line *weight* is referred to as the line *width*.

- *Dashes:* This option opens a selection of dash types and also allows you to access the formatting dialog box by selecting *More Lines*.

- *Arrows:* This option displays several arrow variants with different settings (begin type, end type, etc.), and naturally also allows you to make more differentiated settings in the dialog box.

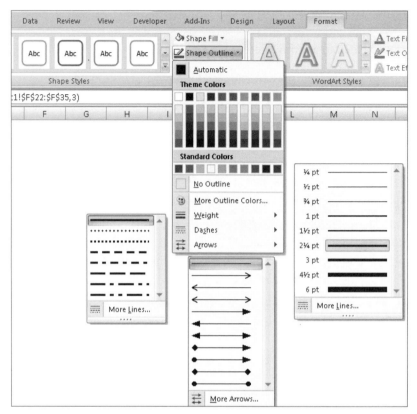

FIGURE 4-22 Line formatting options under *Shape Styles/Shape Outline*

Shape Effects

In this chapter, we've only discussed the selection options available under *Shape Effects* in reference to the use of shadows. However, the possibilities for design creativity and control extend far beyond this. As you can tell from the overview that appears when you click *Shape Effects* (see Figure 4-23), a group of settings with a very complex structure is provided here for visual handling and transformation of graphic objects. These are only of limited interest to the creation of charts and their elements, but play a key role when it comes to adding supplemental visual enhancements to presentation charts to attract the audience's attention.

These also include many adjustment options that fall into the "3D" category. I'm not referring here to the use of 3D to represent data series (an approach I've already criticized), but rather the creation of interesting visual effects for presentation.

Chapter 5 provides an introductory overview of *shape effects*.

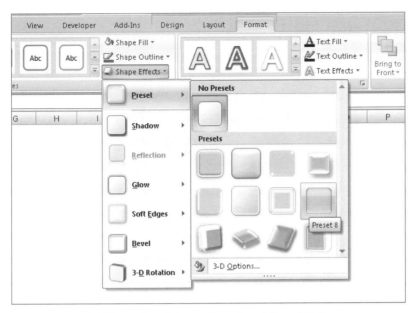

FIGURE 4-23 An initial overview of the configuration of *Shape Effects*

Size and Properties

When designing presentation charts and charts for publication, various requirements will demand that you define precise measurements of a chart area. Often, this also involves specifying that the defined size of the chart or the ratio of its height to its width must not change, even if the table range in which the chart is located undergoes structural transformations. This might happen, for example, if rows and/or columns are added or deleted, or changes are made to the height and width of individual cell ranges.

In earlier program versions, all you had to do was double-click the *chart area* to open the *Format Chart Area* dialog box with its *Patterns*, *Font,* and *Properties* tabs. This access option is no longer available, and has been replaced by the series of options described below.

Follow the steps in the next few paragraphs with reference to Figure 4-24:

You want to define exact dimensions of a chart (chart area) and prevent your settings from being undone by future changes to the table structure. The following instructions assume that the *Chart Tools* are currently displayed in the Ribbon with the *Format* tab open, and that the *chart area* or one of its chart elements is selected.

Caution When you define the exact dimensions of a chart, it's irrelevant which of the chart elements is currently selected. The dimensions you define always and exclusively apply to the *chart area,* even if this isn't the element currently selected.

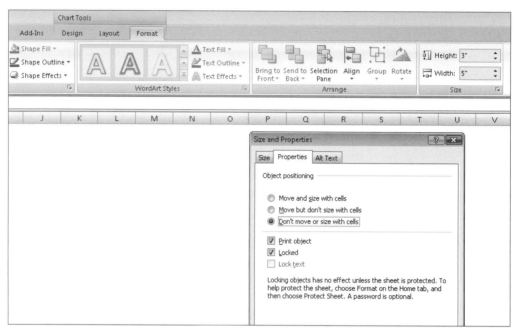

FIGURE 4-24 Well-hidden but important—dialog box for defining positioning properties

1. Change the size displayed in the *Size* group, or click the group's "launcher" to open the assigned *Size and Properties* dialog box.

2. Define the absolute (exact) dimensions of the chart area on the *Size* tab. Alternatively, you can make a relative (percentage) change to the existing dimensions (of a selected chart area) in the *Scaling* section of the dialog box. Note that you can *lock* the *aspect ratio* here, so that the relative scaling will keep the chart in proportion.

3. Go to the *Properties* tab and make the following settings:

   ❑ Select the *Move but don't size with cells* option if you want your chart to change its position on the table background when you add or delete rows or columns, but you don't want its dimensions to change when you change the height of the rows or the width of the columns behind the chart. This setting is usually very useful during the development phase of your solution because you may frequently need to change table structures even if you're already perfectly happy with the chart contained in this table.

   ❑ Select the *Don't move or size with cells* option if you want your chart to almost "float" freely above the table background. In other words, you don't want it to move when you add or delete rows or columns, and you don't want its dimensions to change when you change the height of the rows or the width of the columns behind the chart. This setting is likely to prove useful or even essential if you use transparent charts and you want to use the table structures for background formatting. (You've already seen an example of this in Figure 4-14.)

Chapter 5
Graphical Objects

Do you like to draw? Do you have fun tinkering with stuff? Do you enjoy checking out whether something that already looks good could look even a little bit better? If so, then this will be quite a "risky" chapter for you, because you might rapidly lose yourself in the limitless design options that Word, PowerPoint, and Excel 2007 now offer. If you answered "yes" to the questions just asked (I would have), you should at first either skim through the following pages ("I'll just see if there's anything interesting here that I don't know about yet") or immediately take time to intensively learn the program's comprehensively extended design section. "Intensively" in this case doesn't mean what we frequently refer to as "in-depth," because you only get a slightly more detailed overview. What works? How does it work? Where do I find something? Discussing how you could change things in this or that variation and the reason or reasons for doing things this way or that, or for not doing something, would truly be sufficient material for another book.

You'll therefore only get an overview; in other words, a structured combination of the graphics offered. Nevertheless, this is a quite comprehensive chapter, considering that the *Colors* area related to the "Custom Design" topic already was discussed fully in the previous chapter. You can see that Excel 2007 has much more to offer than before in the area of graphics, perhaps much more than you'll be able, or want, to use for editing and designing charts (including time-consuming presentations).

Object Types and Basic Techniques

You'll receive information about creating, handling, and editing different types of graphical objects. The differences between these will affect the tools and techniques you'll use. I must therefore first clarify which graphical objects I'll refer to and how these are to be classified. This main section will then deal with basic information about the general technical handling of these types of objects.

Object Types

How are graphical objects to be differentiated in terms of this chapter?

Drawing Objects

Drawing objects are all graphical objects that you create yourself using the features and tools available in Excel 2007, and/or they can be the elements and contents of graphical objects that you can change as you wish within clearly defined limits. These include:

- Two-dimensional *shapes*

- *Text boxes* (a specific variation of two-dimensional shapes)

- Lines and curves (which are also included as *shapes*)

- *WordArt* (text as graphics)

You insert a drawing object into an Excel worksheet by creating it using a tool available in Excel or by transferring it as a copy from somewhere else.

Picture Objects

Picture objects are all graphical objects that you *can't* create using the features and tools available in Excel, and their elements and contents you *can't* change. Your design options apply to environmental structures (for example, borders and shadows) or the overall appearance (for example, contrast, brightness, size or shape), but not to the actual content. Typical representatives of this group are digitalized photos or objects that were created using a graphics software and then saved as a picture file in any format (*bmp, tif, jpg, png*, and so on).

You insert a picture object into an Excel worksheet by transferring it as a file or copying it from somewhere else.

Charts   Charts based on numbers are also graphical objects; however, they work differently because they're neither pure drawing objects nor pure picture objects. Although they have structures, elements, and contents that you can create and change using the features and tools available in Excel. In many respects, they elude free, custom design capability.

Controls   In Chapter 2, "New Approaches—Getting Started," you already learned about using controls in conjunction with setting up dynamic charts. This is an extremely important prerequisite for the backgrounds and intentions of this book.

Controls are also graphical objects that are basically handled like drawing objects in the way they're created and can be changed graphically; however, in other respects, they don't have any closer relationship to drawing objects or picture objects. Furthermore, because there are two different types of controls which—even with all their dissimilarities—both play their roles in this book, I don't want to discuss the topic in further detail here. I refer you instead to the detailed description in Chapter 7, "Elements of Dynamization."

Object Combinations   The object combinations compiled in worksheets are design variations that are ideally suited to presentations and are used repeatedly in this book.

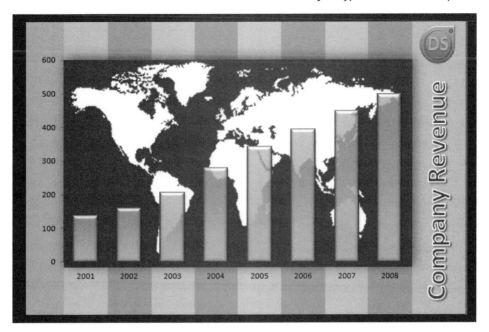

FIGURE 5-1 A collection of different graphical objects

Figure 5-1 shows a presentation chart that you'll find on the CD-ROM as the \Samples\0502_ Graphics02.xlsx file. I'll explain the content and creation of this in the last section of this chapter. This is a combination of different formatting options and graphical objects:

- The color formatting of table areas form the background.

- The *chart area* and *plot area* of the chart are completely transparent and the data series (columns) is filled with a partially transparent, gradual color gradient.

- There is a picture object (the map of the world) behind the chart. The *chart area* or *plot area* is *not* filled here, but rather this picture object is an independent object which is completely independent of the chart in terms of its shape and size.

- The logo is a picture object, but it was created from different drawing objects (shapes and WordArt) and only then made into a picture object (*tif* file) in a graphics software.

- The chart title rotated at 90° is a WordArt object.

Such combinations often use the strengths of their individual components or help to compensate for or conceal the weaknesses of individual components.

The term *object combination* is also applicable if an object becomes an integral part of another object. This is the case, for example, if you use a picture object as fill for a chart element or any other two-dimensional shape.

Using the Practice Material

You will find descriptions here that will help you create, insert, position, and arrange different types of graphical objects, change their shape and content, format them, and combine them with other graphical objects of the same or a different type. For all of these types of operations you need—in addition to an "it's easy when you know how" attitude—a little imagination, a considerable amount of experience, and (last but not least) technical talent. In a nutshell, it's back to the word "practice;" i.e., that which makes perfect.

To acquire basic knowledge and practice the necessary skills, use the Excel files and materials or your own workbooks and collections of objects relating to this chapter, which are stored on the CD-ROM.

Those of you who learn how to use graphical objects in Office 2007 will make a great many discoveries and experience quite a few surprises. Therefore, it's essential to save any intermediate results you've achieved and document particularly interesting results as much as possible within the file. If you're going to use the CD-ROM templates for your exercises, I'd highly recommend that you save them under different names on your hard drive.

> **Note** Open the \Samples\0501_Graphics01.xlsx file on the CD-ROM and insert new worksheets into this workbook, if necessary.
>
> You'll find several prepared worksheets in the file that I'll refer to repeatedly during the course of this chapter and that you'll also recognize to some extent in the figures.
>
> ❏   The first two worksheets contain area objects that are variably complicated to handle.
>
> ❏   In the *Lines* worksheet, you'll find several different types of objects that you can use to learn the basics of working with non two-dimensional drawing objects.
>
> ❏   The next worksheet contains two WordArt objects that, as unassuming as they seem at first, might motivate you for complex design practice.
>
> ❏   A worksheet with picture objects completes the workbook.

In the following description of general techniques, note that the information and pictures essentially relate to drawing objects but that the descriptions also can apply to picture objects and charts.

Creating, Inserting, and Selecting Objects

A worksheet contains a graphical object after you have either inserted it from some other source or have created it within the workbook using the appropriate tools for this purpose. You can access the two activities from the *Insert* Ribbon/tab in the *Illustrations* group.

Figure 5-2 shows an example of *Shapes*.

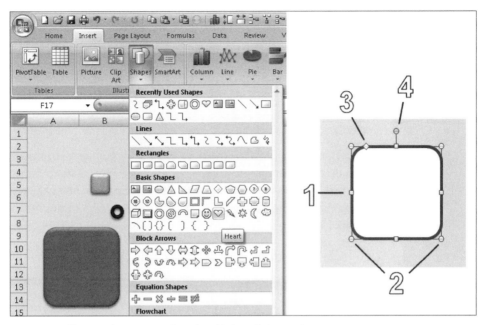

FIGURE 5-2 Shapes: a large reservoir and multiple variation options

Click the *Shapes* command button and then select an icon from the comprehensive range available. Choose one of three creation options:

- Double-click the icon to select it and insert a symmetrical basic variation into your worksheet. "Symmetrical" in this case means that the dimensions of the shape would fill a square or circle, for example.
- Click the icon of your choice once and point with the mouse (the mouse pointer becomes a cross) to the area in the worksheet where you want to draw the object. Then:
  - ❑ Click again to create a symmetrical basic variation in this area, or
  - ❑ Hold and drag diagonally in any direction a shape that you see as a preview. Provided you don't release the mouse key, you can change the shape in any way you wish.

An object created in this way is selected and is typically displayed as such in this case. The description of the numbering in Figure 5-2 is as follows:

1. You use the handles (also often known as "grips") on the object's edges to scale (change the dimensions of) the shape's level (width, height) or direction using the mouse. This is illustrated further in Figure 5-3.

2. You use the handles on the object's corners to scale it in two directions.

3. Some drawing objects also show different numbers of small diamond-shaped, yellow selection points. You use these to transform the object using the mouse. This is illustrated further in Figure 5-8.

4. You use the green handle to rotate the object continuously with the mouse. This is illustrated further in Figure 5-6.

You can use different options if you want to select several objects simultaneously:

- Click the first object to be selected, press and hold the **Ctrl** key (or the **Shift** key or **Ctrl+Shift**) and then click other objects.

- Click the *Find & Select* command button in the Ribbon/*Home* tab of the *Editing* group.

- Choose the *Select Objects* command. Then use the mouse pointer to completely surround all the objects you want to include in the selection. This creates a transparent area that shows you in a preview which objects will be selected when you release the mouse key. If you want to cancel this selection mode—that is, you want the mouse to assume its default functions again—press the **Esc** key or double-click any empty space in the worksheet.

Moving and Scaling Objects

To move an object, you must first select it. Then:

- Point with the mouse in the selected object. When you see a four-headed arrow in the object (see also Figure 5-3), you can hold and drag the object in any direction across the screen.

- When you press and hold the **Shift** key when moving the object, the direction of movement will be restricted to the horizontal or vertical axis.

- When you press and hold the **Alt** key while moving the object, the movement option will be based on the worksheet's gridline. The object will move in a clumsy way and use the gridlines as anchor positions. With this type of positioning, make sure that the program always tries to create the object on the gridline closest to one of the edges. This use of the **Alt** key also works if, as previously described, you simultaneously limit the direction of movement to axes using the **Shift** key.

- For fine positioning, move the selected object using the **left arrow**, **right arrow**, **top arrow** and **bottom arrow** keys.

Note To position a chart precisely using the arrow keys, you must temporarily make it a "quasi drawing object" by clicking it in any area while holding down the **Ctrl** key. Four small selection points subsequently appear on the corners of the *chart area*. In this mode, you can use the arrow keys to move the chart point-to-point. After you click the chart again (this time without pressing the **Ctrl** key), the usual object status for charts in Excel 2007 will be enabled again. Clicking the *chart area* gives it a selection border again, whereas clicking a different chart element creates a specific selection for this element.

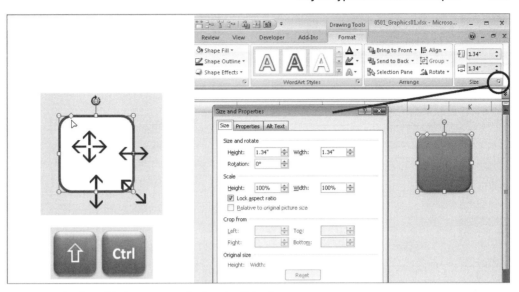

FIGURE 5-3 Scaling with the mouse and using the dialog box

Scaling an object means resizing it proportionally or disproportionally. To scale an object, you must first select it. In the context of Figure 5-3:

- When you point with the mouse to one of the four handles on an edge of the object, the mouse pointer becomes a horizontally or vertically oriented double arrow, and you can continuously increase or decrease the object by moving this edge. This scaling only occurs in one axis direction, meaning it's disproportional. When you press and hold the **Alt** key here, the resizing will adjust to the grid of the table cells.

> **Tip** Adjusting to the table grid is very useful when you design charts, particularly if you use the table structure as the background of a transparent chart and therefore have to ensure an exact match between the positioning of chart elements and the table grid (see also Figure 5-1 and the \Samples\0502_Graphics02.xlsx file).

- When you point with the mouse to one of the four handles on a corner of the object, the mouse pointer becomes a diagonally-oriented double arrow and you can continuously increase or decrease the object in two directions by moving this edge. This scaling is also disproportional, unless you drag it with the mouse to an angle of exactly 45°, which you'd probably do more by accident than by design.

- When you press and hold the **Shift** key when scaling using a corner handle, the scaling becomes proportional and the object is increased or decreased equally in both directions. The resizing occurs in the direction in which you're dragging (the object therefore shifts its midpoint here). The additional use of the **Alt** key adjusts, again, the object to the table grid.

- When you press and hold the **Ctrl** key when scaling using a corner handle, the scaling will also become proportional. In this case, the resizing occurs from the object's midpoint. The midpoint therefore remains in its place and the object expands or shrinks in equal measure.

You can generally only accomplish an exact sizing of a selected object by using the corresponding command structures, which you can access via the Ribbon by double-clicking the object. You will then find the input options for size specifications in the object-specific tools (see the upper right portion of Figure 5-3) or access to a dialog box. Alternatives are as follows.

- The double-clicked graphical object is a drawing object: the *Drawing Tools* tab is inserted into the Ribbon and the input fields for determining the *shape height* and *shape width* are located in the *Size* group. Clicking the Launcher (marked with a circle in Figure 5-3) opens the *Size and Properties* dialog box.

- The double-clicked graphical object is a picture object: the *Picture Tools* tab is inserted into the Ribbon and the input fields to determine the *shape height* and *shape width* are located in the *Size* group. Clicking the Launcher also opens the *Size and Properties* dialog box here.

> **Note** You'll also find the command for calling the *Size and Properties* dialog box in the context menu of an object on which you right-click.

You can use the *Size* tab in the *Size and Properties* dialog box to set an object's dimensions and scaling.

- You'll find input fields for defining the height and width for resizing purposes.

- You can enter percentages for the *Scale* and

  - Relate this to the picture in its current display or to its original size (the dimensions of the original picture file) by disabling or enabling the *Relative to original picture size* setting.

  - If you enable the *Lock aspect ratio* setting, the scale becomes proportional. In this case, all you need to do is change the percentage in one of the two fields before you close the dialog box.

Determining Positioning Properties

In the *Size and Properties* dialog box previously mentioned, you'll also find the *Properties* tab with the *Object positioning* section. You can set the dependency of the object from the table structure there using three different options.

I already discussed this topic at the end of Chapter 4, "Colors, Areas, and Outlines" in connection with positioning charts. Therefore, I'll give just a brief recommendation here for how to proceed.

- Choose the *Move and size with cells* option if you always want the dimensions and positioning of your object to change when you insert rows and/or columns, or when you change the width or height of rows and/or columns that lie behind the chart. Based on my experience, I think there are only very few reasons to proceed accordingly. Therefore, the next two options mentioned are of far more practical significance.

- Choose the *Move but don't size with cells* option during the development phase of a worksheet. The objects will then change their position but not their dimensions when you insert or delete rows or columns or resize them.

- Choose the *Don't move or size with cells* option if you want to ensure that your object will virtually "hover" over the table background; in other words, it'll be totally independent of the table structure. This is always useful if you have completed designing your model as far as possible and perhaps need only a few structural changes relating to the table grid.

Duplicating Objects

You can transfer each object to the clipboard by selecting it and using the copy command, and insert it into any other area again from there.

Apart from that, those duplication methods that are possible within a worksheet and without the detour through the clipboard are interesting and worthwhile, especially in the chart solutions described in this book.

> **Tip** When solutions are developed using the rS1.Method, objects need to be duplicated quite frequently. This applies in particular to using controls, and also to using decoration objects and other different types of graphical design features. It's very important to first completely format an element with the design features (based on its type, content, formatting, and function) to be duplicated before you duplicate it, and to carefully check its properties and effect.
>
> Several duplications can be made based on a single primary object, and this technique is useful for quite a few solutions. Of course, it's particularly annoying if you discover at the end of your work that you've already made mistakes in the primary object, which you now have to correct uniformly little by little and piece by piece in the duplicated objects.

- **Simple Duplication**: Select the object (source object) to be duplicated, press the **Ctrl** key and drag with the mouse as if you wanted to move the object to another area. What you're actually moving in this case is a duplicate.

- **Axis-Specific Duplication**: Select the source object, press the **Ctrl+Shift** shortcut and drag a duplicate in either a horizontal or vertical direction with the mouse.

- **Axis-Specific Duplication Using the Table Grid as Positioning Help**: Select the source object, press the **Ctrl**+**Shift**+**Alt** shortcut, and drag a duplicate in either a horizontal or vertical direction with the mouse.

The three described duplication procedures also work if you have selected several source objects simultaneously.

Arranging Objects

> **Note** The objects in the *Areas 1* worksheet of the *\Samples\0501_Graphics01.xlsx* file are well suited for the methods described in this section.

Arranging objects is a task that you'll encounter very often when designing appealing presentation solutions. On the one hand, this involves effectively "layering" several objects. Layering involves creating an object stack that the viewer looks at from above and in which he can only partially see one or several elements. It also means (often simultaneously) linking different objects to a group that then appears—and can be dealt with if so desired—as a single object.

Foreground and Background

It's pretty easy to "stack" objects. The following actions relate to the content of Figure 5-4.

Double-click or right-click to select the object, whose position you want to change in the stack.

- Double-click: *Drawing Tools* or *Picture Tools* will appear in the Ribbon with its *Format* tab and the *Arrange* group where the *Bring to Front* or *Send to Back* commands are available.

- Right-Click: You'll find the just-mentioned commands in the context menu.

- In both cases, you also have the subsequent option to move the position by one level, send the object to the back completely, or bring it to the front completely.

> **Note** Note that Office 2007 also has considerably more to offer than its previous versions for stacking objects. This is mainly because you can make the color fills of objects completely or partially transparent, and interesting effects can be achieved in this way (see the simple example on the right in Figure 5-4).

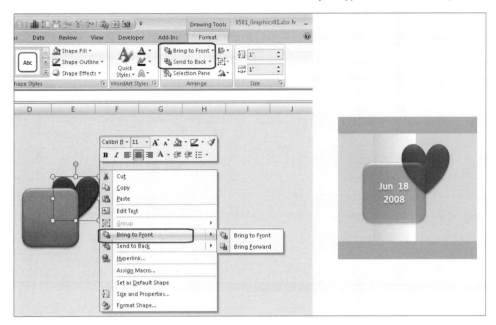

FIGURE 5-4 Two options for creating object stacks

Grouping Objects

The procedure and approach for grouping objects is very similar to stacking objects.

You have selected several objects and want to create a group from this selection, and you want to treat this group as a single object in further processing. In Office 2007 you don't need to ungroup a group created in this way if you want to change some of its parts comprehensively and individually.

The following is a description of the procedure shown in Figure 5-5.

1. Use one of the methods described above to create a multiple selection of different objects. Choose the *Group* command from the context menu or from the *Arrange* group of the *Drawing Tools* or *Picture Tools*.

2. When you click a single member (object) of a group, the whole group is selected. A rectangular border appears, in which all members of the group are placed. In this status, all commands that you subsequently execute on each member of the group will be used in the same way. You can therefore move, position, arrange, and format the whole group.

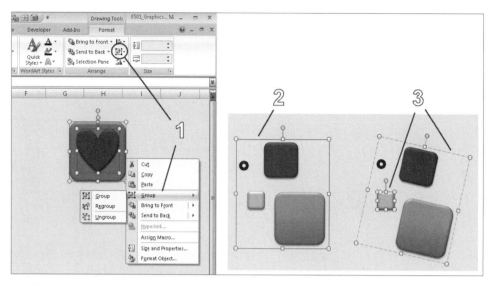

FIGURE 5-5 Members of object groups can also be handled as a single object

3. You want to edit a single member of an object group separately, without expanding the group itself. First click the object in question to select the group, and then click a second time to select the object individually *in* the group. The group's border now appears as a dashed line to indicate that the single group member is the active element, not the entire group. In this status, all commands that you now subsequently execute only apply to the active element.

Note the following.

- ❏ When you now click the dashed border of the group or touch one of its handles, the activity will revert to the group.

- ❏ If you scale or move a single group member in such a way that it no longer fits into the dashed border of the currently existing group, the group area will increase automatically. In other words, even an element that you apparently move out of the group will remain a member of the group; the group size adjusts itself to the new positioning of all members as a whole.

In terms of the status of number 3 shown in Figure 5-5, the group identified by number 2 was duplicated and the copy was then slightly rotated to the right. The small rounded rectangle was then selected as a single group member and its rotation removed again.

As you may expect, there are commands (see the left-hand side in Figure 5-5) that you can use to remove a group or re-establish a temporarily removed group.

Rotating Objects

You'll often want to rotate an object to achieve a particular display effect. You basically have two options for rotating an object. In the context of Figure 5-6:

■ You select the object and point with the mouse to the green rotation handle. In this case, the mouse pointer "wraps" itself as an arrow around this rotation handle. You can now rotate the object as you wish while holding down the mouse key.

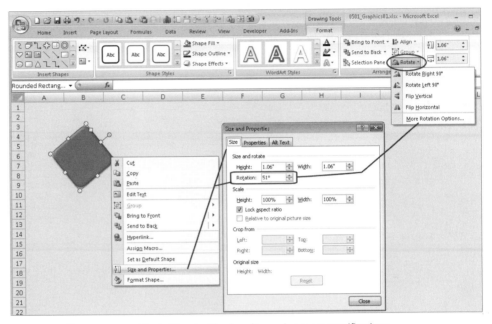

FIGURE 5-6 You rotate an object either by "freehand" or using exact specifications.

■ If you want the rotation to be measured exactly in degrees, use the rotation commands in the *Arrange* group of the *Drawing Tools* or *Picture Tools* or of the *Size and Properties* dialog box. The rotation commands in the Ribbon (see the right-hand side of Figure 5-6) are self-explanatory. You use the *Size* tab of the mapped dialog box mentioned to rotate an object with your choice of exact degree specifications. If you enter or set positive numbers, the object will be rotated to the right, whereas negative numbers will rotate it to the left.

Tip It can be quite difficult to rotate a manually rotated object back to its original position manually again. It's much easier if you call the *Size and Properties* dialog box for the selected object and set the rotation to zero or to a value that may have previously existed.

Using Drawing Tools and Picture Tools

The details already described for charts and their *Chart Tools* also apply for drawing objects or picture objects. In addition to object-specific commands, there's an abundance of formatting variations available that you can access from the Ribbon as specifications. You can, in turn, subsequently change or remove most of these specifications in detail by using specific dialog boxes.

Figure 5-7 provides an initial overview: the Drawing Tools (commands for designing drawing objects) are displayed in the upper half and the Picture Tools (commands for picture objects) are displayed underneath.

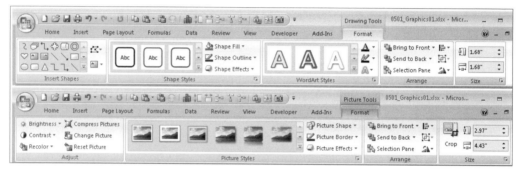

FIGURE 5-7 The complete command sets of the drawing tools and picture tools

You'll see right away that there's a clear difference in command sets. This means that you'll have to deal with and master a very broad spectrum of options.

I'm now going to abandon the generally accepted method of presenting information and describe particular options for dealing directly with specific object types. Therefore, note that—where the following descriptions are concerned—you'll be expected to be familiar with the basic methods mentioned earlier.

Drawing Objects and Drawing Tools

To recap: drawing objects are all graphical objects that you create yourself using the features and tools available in Excel 2007 (or in Word 2007, or in PowerPoint 2007) and/or the elements and contents of those objects that you can, to a certain extent, change as you wish. These include *shapes* (areas and lines), *text boxes* (as a special form of areas), and *WordArt*.

Changing the Design and Content of Integrated Shapes

To insert an integrated shape, you activate the *Insert* tab in the Ribbon and click *Shapes* in the *Illustrations* group. You then select the shape of your choosing in the comprehensive icon list (see also Figure 5-2). In the first main section of this chapter, I already described in detail what you normally need to be aware of here and which non-specific design options are available to you. To summarize, you can:

- Create such a shape as a symmetrical or an asymmetrical variation
- Scale it proportionally or disproportionally
- Move and position it
- Duplicate it
- Arrange it in layered stacks together with other objects
- Link it to a group with other objects
- Rotate it

In the first main section of this chapter, I've already described the techniques required for this purpose. What else can you do with objects, design-wise? A whole lot, as you'll see below.

Design Changes Using the Mouse

In addition to the handles on the corners or in the middle of edges and the green rotation handle, many of the integrated shapes display other "grips" after they're clicked. These appear as yellow-colored, diamond-shaped handles. When you point to one of these handles with the mouse, the mouse pointer turns into a stemless arrow (see the upper left-hand side of Figure 5-8), and you can drag the yellow marker in different directions that are restricted by internal specifications. This is how you can change the design of the whole shape.

This option isn't available for some shapes. Some Shapes only have one of the yellow adjustment handles, while others have two, three, or four of them. The more of these types of handles there are, naturally the more varied the range of adjustment options to be combined from them.

The changes made in this way only affect the figure, in other words, the external shape of the object. Other setups such as those for formatting or implementing text are not affected, or are only indirectly affected, by the changes I've just described.

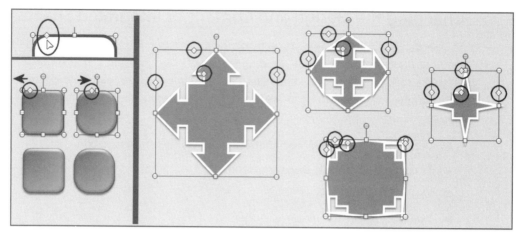

FIGURE 5-8 From 1, you get X amount: there are many adjustment options

Figure 5-8 shows six of the thousands of possible variations.

- On the left of the figure, the rounded rectangle only shows one of the yellow handles on its top edge. If you drag this handle to the right—that is, to the vertical center axis— the corners become much more rounded and the shape becomes softer. If you drag the handle completely to the center, the rectangle will become an oval (or a rounded square will become a circle). Naturally, it also works exactly the same way the other way around: the more you move the handle to the left, the less round the corners of the object become and the harder the shape becomes, until the corners finally become rectangular. This means that it'll be important for you to think about the basic selections you're going to choose: You can't make any other shape from the "rectangle" shape, but you can make several from the "rounded rectangle" shape, including the standard rectangle.

- On the right-hand side of the figure, the *quad arrow callout*, as it's "officially" known, has four of the yellow adjustment handles. You'll probably want to spare yourself (and me, too) a list that describes all the possible shapes. Try a few if you wish. There are four versions displayed in the figure, but you can produce a lot more. And this wealth of designs applies to just one object!

Changing Shapes into Other Shapes

There are various reasons to change an existing shape into another shape: not just in everyday life, but also in Excel. It's an easy decision to make because it's very simple to implement these types of ideas—in Excel at least. Let's take the example of Figure 5-9:

FIGURE 5-9 Making a heart out of a cloud? All it takes is a couple of mouse clicks.

You're working on cloud nine and already have created it as a shape, but now you want to make it a heart shape again. That's pretty easy to do:

1. Double-click the cloud to display the *Drawing Tools* in the Ribbon, and click the *Edit Shape* command button in the *Insert Shapes* group.

2. Choose the *Change Shape* command from the selection that now appears. All the details that you're also offered when you want to insert a new shape are subsequently displayed.

3. All you need to do now is click the heart to change the shape. All the properties set for the original shape are retained. This also applies to size and proportions. If you change a flat rectangle into a star, for example, the result will not exactly be a convincing star shape, but you already know how to correct this easily.

Other Commands of the Edit Shape Category

You can see from the commands shown in Figure 5-9 that you can also *convert* an integrated shape to *freeform*. This means, in effect, that the conversion options are limitless from now on. You can subsequently use the integrated shape as a template, the outline of which you can redesign completely and in any detail you wish. The *Reroute Connectors* command that is also part of the *Edit Shape* options applies to line connections between objects. This topic is one of those discussed in the "Creating and Formatting Connectors" section, which begins on Page 229.

Adding Text to Shapes

The fact that you can add text to almost every two-dimensional shape is exceptionally important for a multitude of design tasks. This also applies to the production of presentation or publication charts.

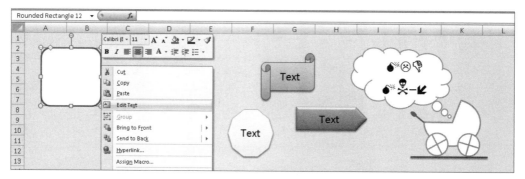

FIGURE 5-10 There are hardly any restrictions on how to label two-dimensional shapes

The corresponding setup is extremely easy. You right-click the object and choose the *Edit Text* command from the context menu. The cursor then blinks in the shape and waits for your input. Those attributes that are part of a *text box* (I'll provide explanations about this in the next section) are consequently added to the two-dimensional shape, in addition to its other properties.

Note Just a note about the detail on the extreme right in Figure 5-10: the baby silently swearing to itself is clearly thinking in the *Wingdings* font, an absolutely amazing achievement at this tender age.

Text Boxes and Their Properties

The *Text Box* is a special variant among integrated two-dimensional shapes. In its simplest form, it's a rectangle you can fill with text and format in a variety of ways and to which you have access using different command paths.

Examples of two of these are shown in Figure 5-11:

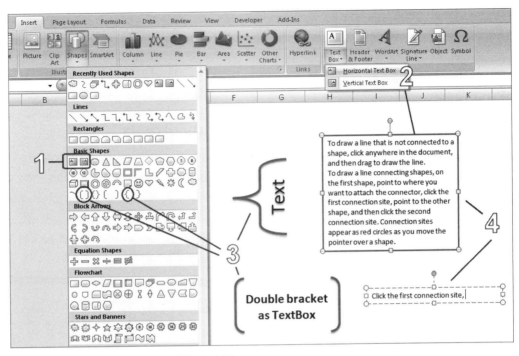

FIGURE 5-11 *Text Box?* This can be all kind of things.

1. You'll find two text boxes in the *Basic Shapes* group for the overall shapes available. The one on the right is referred to as a *Vertical Text Box*. This applies to the basic orientation of the text to be entered, which initially appears rotated by 90°. However, the difference between the left of the two objects, the "normal" text box, with its primarily horizontal text orientation, is largely irrelevant because you can define text orientation in each text box or object with text-box properties in several different ways.

2. The two text box types are also provided in the Ribbon, which you'll find in the *Insert* tab of the *Text* group.

3. As mentioned in the previous section, each two-dimensional shape can also adopt the properties of a text box. In relation to the illustration in Figure 5-11, also note that shapes that not appear as closed shapes can also be areas. Therefore, not only can the double brackets provided contain text, but so can the four single brackets.

4. A text box can include two different modes and be edited differently as a result:

   ❏ In Shapes mode, the marker lines are drawn as a full line and you can edit the object as a two-dimensional shape.

   ❏ In Text mode, individual (or all of the) formatting lines are drawn as dashed lines, and the cursor blinks in the text that you can now edit.

   If a text box or an object with text-box properties already contains text, click the border of the object to activate it as a shape (although in the text) in order to activate text mode.

To set specific properties of a text box, or of a two-dimensional shape set up as a text box, right-click the element and choose the *Format Shape* command from the context menu.

After you click the *Text Box* command button in the dialog box that subsequently appears, you'll have access to several design options.

Formatting Shapes and Changing Formats

I already dealt with the assignment of integrated formatting and their custom changes to some extent in Chapter 4 when we discussed formatting chart elements. Therefore, the following explanations will be less detailed.

> **On the Companion CD** To practice the procedures described here, I recommend that you use the *Areas 1* and *Areas 2* worksheets in the \Samples\0501_Graphics01.xlsx file.

Assigning Formats with Drawing Tools

Before you assign integrated shapes to your drawing objects using *Drawing Tools*, you should have completed your preparatory work by doing the following.

- You've selected and set the basic design for the workbook (keyword "*Office*").

- The objects to be formatted are ready in terms of their basic shape, contents (for example, texts), size, and position.

- You've saved the file you prepared in this way.

The reasons for this preparation is that working with integrated formats can produce numerous results, which you'll be surprised by, find impossible, like (even if they don't correspond to the effect you intended), and which will possibly change your plans, as there's quite a lot more that can occur before we get to the final design. Quite frequently, you'll only accept your decisions after a lot of to-ing and fro-ing, or you may even reject them. Sometimes the best solution if there's total confusion is to return to a basic version where all important basic attributes exist in the originally intended way; you go back to square one, so to speak.

Combined Formats, Theme Fills, Shape Fills, Shape Outlines

There's only a little information in this section that hasn't already been covered in Chapter 4. Open the *Format* tab of the *Drawing Tools* in the Ribbon by double-clicking the drawing object and you subsequently have access to combined format specifications, *Shape Fill* commands, and *Shape Outline* commands in the *Shape Styles* group (see Figure 5-13, *A* and *B*).

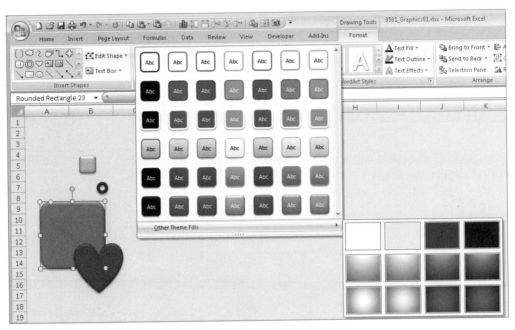

FIGURE 5-12 Other options for setting up shape fills

In the screen shown in Figure 5-12, when you open the list of combined format specifications that's populated with picture icons, you'll find the *Other Theme Fills* command at the bottom. You can use this to branch to other graphically displayed options.

Shape Effects

The *Shape Effects* command button in the *Drawing Tools* represents an extremely broad range of options. There are many different kinds of more or less decorative display variations. We'd need a separate book to discuss them all with the appropriate level of detail and pro-and-con explanation. Such an "in-depth" learning process has no place in a book whose main topic is *charts*.

Many of the things that you can now semi-automatically assign as *shape effects* could also be created in the earlier versions of Excel (using the tools of the *Drawing* and *Picture* toolbars), although this also required considerably greater effort. When corrections and adjustments were required, this was much easier to do than it is in Excel 2007. Certainly, the results were also simpler overall: not worse, simpler. This can be a negative or a positive assessment. Since I've advocated simplicity in design in my previous publications, it should be clear what my position is on this matter. I fear, in any case, that I'm going to come across a deluge of unsuccessful and "jazzed up" designs in the coming years, be it via Word, PowerPoint, or Excel. The reasons for these designs won't have to do with the content to be displayed or the requirements of target groups; they'll only exist because they can and because they more or less come about by accident ("See, that looks quite good too"). The unnecessary bells and whistles that were restricted to countless PowerPoint presentations up to now, will, unfortunately, also populate Excel and Word more frequently.

 Note The sequence below differs slightly from the arrangement of commands in Excel.

Presets In the context of Figure 5-13, letter *C*:

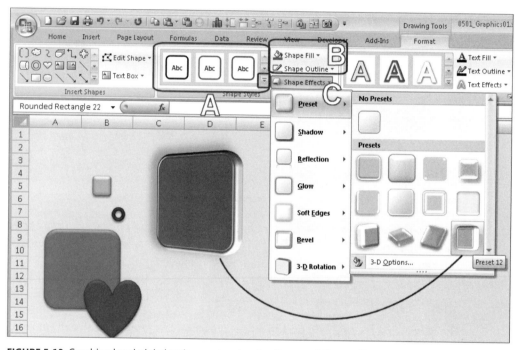

FIGURE 5-13 Combined and global assignments using the *Presets* of *Shape Effects*

1. Select the object that you want to assign specific effects to and choose the *Shape Effects* command.

2. A list containing effect groups is subsequently displayed. Click one of the list entries to obtain the graphical objects provided for the relevant group.

3. In the compilations, click one of the icons to see, and you can judge the implementation of this formatting type in the selected object.

In order to learn by doing, I highly recommend that you work with the *Presets* first. These are combined formats, in which several of the possible shape effects are summarized. Those of you who are interested in their details (which I strongly recommend) can subsequently check the formatting dialog boxes to see which settings were used to achieve these effects and how the appearance changes when corrections are made.

Note You can use the effects mentioned in the following paragraphs individually and in combination.

Shadow, Glow, Soft Edges

- *Shadow* is a very useful effect that I described in Chapter 4 in the discussion of shading chart elements (refer to the descriptions for Figures 4-19 and 4-20).

- *Glow* is an effect that provides a soft-focus color for the immediate environment of a shape. Technically speaking, this is a "shadow" that is somewhat bigger than the shape itself and is directly behind it; therefore, it surrounds the shape completely like a border.

- *Soft Edges* have the effect of blurring the outline of a shape. Depending on the number of points selected, the object will appear as though seen by someone with increasingly defective vision, up to the point where it's almost unrecognizable.

Reflection   Reflection variations can be used for all kinds of impressive decorations (naturally, used extremely sparingly). Incidentally, these effects often look better with text or rectangular pictures than with uneven or round shapes.

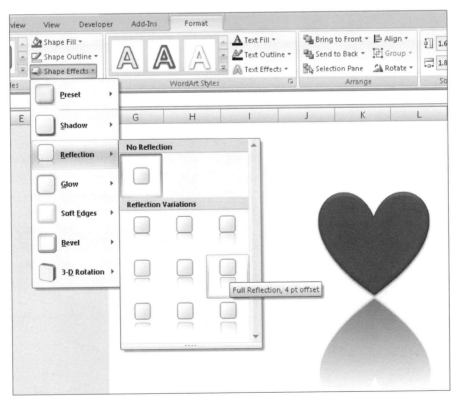

FIGURE 5-14 Note the names of effects that you like

> **Tip** With the abundance of new features, options, variations, and also variations of variations, it'll be useful to create notes on the effects or formatting combinations that you particularly like and think will be suitable for future use. You'll then be able to use these notes to find out what the effect is "officially" called in Excel. You can see these texts (see Figure 5-14) when you point with the mouse to the relevant effect icon.

Bevel   *Bevel* is a really good effect that you can use for several purposes, including designing chart elements. It's an optical change of the upper and lower object edges that's achieved using brightness and shadow effects. You can use it to give a shape "profile." The shape subsequently no longer appears two-dimensionally "flat," but instead looks like a three-dimensional object, only one area of which is facing you. In contrast to three-dimensional *perspectives*, where you see several areas of an object, this representation is more pleasing on the eye and doesn't force the viewer to concentrate on it in order to interpret it. This is a good trait to look for in making an object attractive. This applies in particular for larger, two-dimensional objects used in charts (chart area, plot area, columns, and so on).

3-D Rotation   You can use these effects when you want to simulate three-dimensional perspectives. This is of secondary importance for designing charts; therefore, the following information here will be brief.

To be able to give a two-dimensional area visible three-dimensionality, you must extrude this area (extrusion meaning geometric parallel translation). Handling colors, lighting directions and shadows to achieve as realistic an effect as possible in this case will be extremely demanding. Due in part to its very well-designed specifications, Office 2007 can save you a ton of work here.

Nevertheless, there's a small problem when using the specifications shown in Figure 5-15 for the *3-D Rotation*: when you select a two-dimensional area and then use one of the rotation specifications on it, you often can't judge what the outcome of this effect will be. Although you're now rotating the object, you can't display the three-dimensionality in this case because the object still doesn't have any "physical depth," so the lights and shadows required for 3-D perception are not formed. Consequently, if you want to know what a specific *3-D rotation* of your drawing object will look like, you must first convert the area into a three-dimensional object. The easiest way to do this is (at least, temporarily) to assign the object a *bevel*, explained in the previous section.

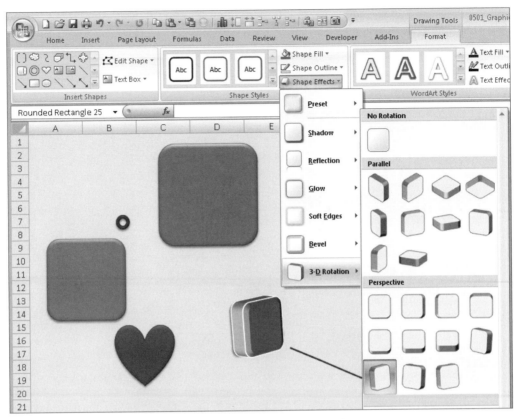

FIGURE 5-15 The object was beveled first and then perspectively rotated.

In relation to the possible rotations—each of which can be corrected later in every detail—the graphical specifications are self-explanatory. However, when making your selection, you should keep in mind that three-dimensionality resulting from the options provided in the *Parallel* category is largely of geometrical interest (engineering drawings, and so on). The extruded area isn't resized in this case, so a realistic-looking tapering off of the simulated body into the "background" does not occur. However, this can be achieved when you select specifications from the *Perspective* category.

When you click the *3-D Rotation Options* command, you'll see the formatting dialog box, where you'll now find a wide choice of fine-adjustment settings and modification options.

Assigning Formats Using Dialog Boxes

To use the new formatting dialog boxes for designing a drawing object, you observe the same prerequisites and conditions as the formatting of two-dimensional chart elements; therefore, I don't need to repeat the corresponding explanations from Chapter 4. I assume that you already know how to define or change *color fills, line colors, line styles* and *shadows* in detail. The following descriptions therefore only apply to formatting that's related to three-dimensional effects.

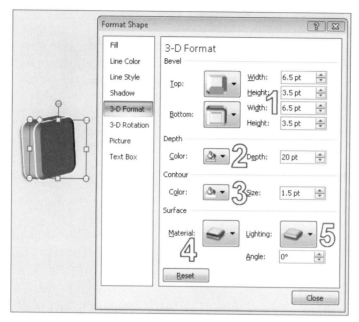

FIGURE 5-16 Detailed assignments and adjustments with the *3-D Format* command group

The following is a description of the settings in the *3-D Format* tab in accordance with the numbering in Figure 5-16.

1. *Bevel* commands: the *Top* and *Bottom* terms relate to the corresponding edges of the object. By clicking one of the two icons, you open a graphical display of the available edge types. Choose an edge type and, if required, change its height and width by entering or setting sizes.

2. In the *Depth* category, you define the color of the side areas that develop from the extruded area and the depth of the shape extending to the "back."

3. Number 3 is the *Contour*, where you can set the color and weight of the contour lines of the three-dimensional body. In the vast majority of cases, however, this option is superfluous.

4. In the *Surface* category, you choose a material type, which simulates a specific composition for the three-dimensional body.

5. You define a *Lighting type* and rotate the lighting to the front of the three-dimensional shape using the *Angle* option. In doing so, you can influence which side of the simulated body gets the best lighting.

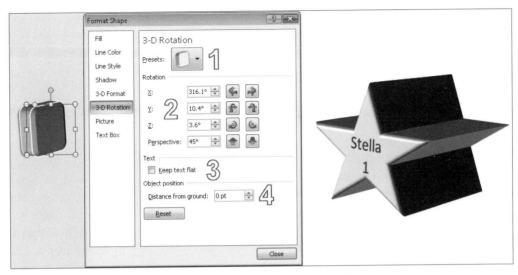

FIGURE 5-17 You can also adjust the font in the object in a 3-D rotation if you wish

The following is a description of the settings in the *3-D Rotation* tab in accordance with the numbering in Figure 5-17.

1. *Presets*: Here, you also go to the selection that you already know from Figure 5-15: different rotation specifications, divided into the *Parallel*, *Perspective* and *Bevel* groups.

2. You define the rotation of the object by gradually changing the three X, Y, and Z axes. It's best to check which of your actions will achieve which result. The editing options are as follows.

   ❏ You can enter the necessary values in degrees (this requires the most experience and consideration).

   ❏ You can change the degree of rotation by clicking the small arrows immediately beside the input fields. While you keep pressing and holding the mouse key, the object will continue to rotate in the corresponding axis.

   ❏ You can also rotate the object further to the right by clicking the larger icon buttons. The rotation occurs in bursts; you can't initiate continuous rotation by pressing the mouse key.

   ❏ You can use the *Perspective* option to define the "degree of truncation" of the three-dimensional shape (the extent to which the body's dimensions taper off into the "background") with values between 0 and 120. Trying things out here will also serve you better than any theoretical description.

3. *Keep text flat*: As you can see on the right-hand side of Figure 5-17, a text in a shape is rotated together with this shape. To prevent this (though there are very few good reasons to do so), you can enable the *Keep text flat* option.

4. *Distance from ground*: This means the distance from the *background*. If you present the table area or another two-dimensional area that is behind the perspective object, such as a wall, by changing the distance values (possible from 0 to 4000), you drag the object to the viewer's position and therefore away from this wall in the background.

Lines, Arrows, and Connectors

In many illustrations in this book, you see lines and arrows that are used to refer to particular relationships or specific elements. Modern human perception is conditioned to pay particular attention to such structures and tracking them with the eye. In this respect, leading lines of every kind are the most suitable option to use for informational support because they affect concentration in a controllable way. However, this advantage may disappear very quickly if the viewer has to deal with too many lines, too many different lines, or lines that are too complicated. Therefore, use lines with caution and avoid using them if there's no clear reason to do so.

On the Companion CD The illustrations and explanations in this section partly relate to the *Lines* worksheet in the *\Samples\0501_Graphics01.xlsx* file.

Differences in Line Types

There are differences you need to bear in mind about using line objects and the options to edit them. The following are descriptions of the details shown in Figure 5-18.

- Type *A* with three selectable shapes, known as a *line,* an *arrow,* and a *double arrow.* Technically, however, these shapes are not regarded as different; they simply have different design shapes at the beginning and/or end of them. These three features in one facilitate quick access, but you can apply any design feature to each of these straight lines, as shown in Figure 5-19.

- Type *B* with six selectable shapes: *connectors* are very special lines in terms of their use and design requirements. They connect graphical objects to each other and also subsequently maintain this connection if the graphical objects in question are moved to other positions. The multiple selections provided simply serve to increase user-friendliness here; you can vary each of the available connectors in any way you wish. I'll provide more information about this in the context of Figure 5-20.

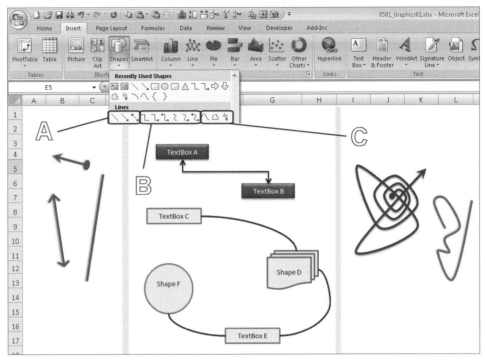

FIGURE 5-18 The three different line types place different demands on the design.

- Type C: *freeform shapes*, which are assigned to lines in Office 2007, amount to a mixture of shapes:

  - An open outline created as a freeform shape (as an apparent line) is actually an *area* that you can fill with colors, textures, or graphics, something you can't do with Types *A* and *B*.

  - Nevertheless, the open outline created as a freeform shape also has technical properties of a Type *A* line. You can apply corresponding design shapes, like the winding arrow in the *Lines* worksheet, to the beginning and/or end of them (see also the upper right-hand side in Figure 5-18).

- Type *D* (not illustrated here): Almost all of the lines (data series lines, gridlines, analytical lines, or axes) that are available in a chart or can be set up there correspond to Type *A*, and you can apply numerous formatting options to them.

Formatting Lines and Arrows

The following details relate to the shape known as Type *A* in Figure 5-18; in other words, they're about the line, the beginning and end of which you can design in a particular way.

The formatting dialog box for this type of shape basically offers the same options that I already introduced in Chapter 4 in relation to the topic of formatting chart lines (see Figure 4.18). For this reason, I'll only provide a description of variances or additional information:

- *Fill*: You can't fill this type of line; therefore, you can't apply a gradual gradient to it.

- In terms of the *line color*, to the using of *shadows* and to the setting up of a *3-D Format* or *3-D Rotation* the options and editing techniques already described apply. You'll quickly be able to identify the few restrictive exceptions by opening the corresponding tabs.

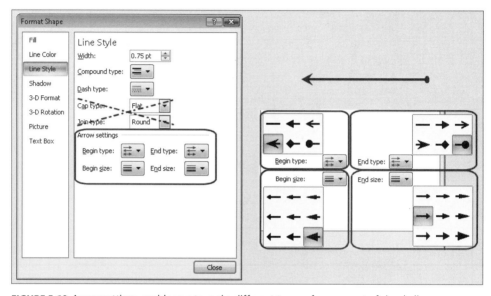

FIGURE 5-19 Arrow settings enable you to make different types of arrows out of simple lines.

- In addition to *Width* (weight), *Compound type*, and *Dash type*, you'll mainly use the *Arrow settings* when you're determining the format of the *line style*. A summary of the possible combinations of *Begin type*, *End type*, *Begin size*, and *End size* is shown in the right half of Figure 5-19.

To determine the line measurements exactly, you can right-click the object and choose the *Size and Properties* command from the context menu. In the *Size* tab of the dialog box that subsequently appears, you'll also be able to indirectly orientate a line vertically or horizontally with precision. This is particularly helpful if this orientation was not completely successful when you created the line or if you're not sure about it, especially where thin, inconspicuous lines are concerned. The measurements for *Height* and *Width* to be set up in the dialog box don't affect the weight (thickness, weigth) of the object, but rather its external dimensions. This means that:

- If you set the *Height* of a Type *A* line to 0 (zero), it will be exactly aligned horizontally.

- If you set the *Width* of a Type *A* line to 0 (zero), it will be exactly aligned vertically.

Creating and Formatting Connectors

The *connector* is a line between two graphical objects and has specific properties:

- It can "dock" onto certain connection points of a graphical object's border and stays firmly attached to this connection point (even if you move the object) until you specifically detach the connection again.

- It can assume different gradient shapes (straight, elbow, curved).

- You can change the gradient shape using the yellow adjustment handles.

- You can use the arrow settings shown in Figure 5-19 on the ends.

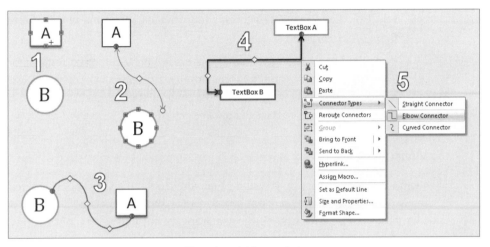

FIGURE 5-20 Connectors—a very specific and useful line variation

Proceed as follows to create a connector. Along the way, I'll describe the details shown in Figure 5-20:

1. Objects A and B already exist and you want to apply a *curved double-arrow connector* to them. Enable the *Insert* tab in the Ribbon and click the *Shapes* command button in the *Illustrations* group. Then choose the above-mentioned tool from the *Lines* category. Point with the mouse to object A. The mouse pointer becomes a cross, and the connection points possible for this object appear as red dots on the edges of the object.

2. Point with the mouse to the dot from which you want to draw the connection and hold and drag a line in the direction of object B. As soon as you've come close enough to the target object, connection points may appear as red dots and you can attach the line directly to one of these points to "dock" it.

   If you release the mouse key before you complete the connection, although the line is drawn its starting point subsequently appears as a red dot and the as-yet unattached end point appears as a light-blue dot. You can select this end point using the mouse and move it toward the target object to create the connection.

3. As soon as a connection is made and you select the series line, its starting and end points appear as red dots. If the line can be shaped, the yellow adjustment handles appear on the corresponding areas. Now you can format the line any way you wish based on the conditions already described.

When carrying out "modification work" in a worksheet, you often need to draw a connector line differently in terms of type and gradient. There are different options for this:

4. You can transform the connector line using the yellow, diamond-shaped handles and select the round, red start and end points with the mouse, remove it from the object, and then dock it onto another of the area of the object.

5. If you want to change the basic shape of the connector line, right-click the line, and select the *Connector Types* command from the context menu to then choose one of the three types provided in the submenu.

If you've shaped a connector multiple times, you might get unsatisfactory results, which are hard if not impossible to undo . In such a situation, it's often easier to reset the connector to an original shape. To do this, choose the *Reroute Connectors* command from the context menu for the selected line.

WordArt

WordArt offers a gallery of text styles that you can handle like shapes. This feature has already been available for years but only in Office 2007 has reached a level of development that satisfies more advanced design requirements without several of the previous absurdities.

When designing presentation charts, I like to use WordArt objects for labels that I want to make particularly noticeable. For example, I use it for general headings or for labeling the central navigation (the first worksheet, containing hyperlinks, of a comprehensive Excel presentation module; see Chapter 12, "More Than Numbers").

From a technical point of view, *WordArt* is a mixture and combination of objects already introduced. It's a container that essentially has the characteristics of a *text box* and contains text characters and other characters that have many of the properties of two-dimensional drawing objects. In many respects, you can therefore set up whole strings and several of their characters in such a way as if they were the integrated shapes described earlier.

Before you work with *WordArt,* it makes sense to get an overview of the properties and design options of text boxes and integrated shapes. This is also relevant because I'm going to describe in detail only those aspects that differ from contents already mentioned. A description of the possible detail changes using formatting dialog boxes won't be provided here either. If you're interested, you can check what design options are available by selecting the *WordArt* container or the string and then using the **Ctrl+1** shortcut.

On the Companion CD The illustrations and explanations in this section relate to the *WordArt* worksheet in the *\Samples\0501_Graphics01.xlsx* file.

Inserting WordArt, Editing, and Formatting Text

Using the basic functions of *WordArt* isn't particularly demanding for users. Enable the *Insert* tab in the Ribbon and click the *WordArt* command button in the *Text* group. The resulting dialog box contains numerous types of formatting. However, so that you can learn by doing and understand how to design individual objects, I recommend that you first choose the simplest of the design features; in other words, the option on the very top left-hand side.

After you click the icon, the container appears with the wording *Your Text Here* in the worksheet. The object is in text mode, as you can tell by the dashed border, and the text there is highlighted and can be overwritten immediately.

The following recommendations apply to editing and general formatting.

- If you want to edit the container as a whole, right-click its border. Not only is the context menu displayed, but a mini toolbar appears that includes the main commands for formatting text. The formats you assign in this mode affect the whole object, including the complete string.

- If you want to format individual characters, first select the character(s) and then point with the mouse to the now shadowy-looking mini toolbar to activate this and then make the corresponding selection.

- As far as possible, the editing of strings conforms to the same rules that you're familiar with from other text-editing processes in Microsoft Office programs.

Assigning Formats with Drawing Tools

A very comprehensive range of integrated formats and diverse design options are naturally also provided again here. You can access them in the way you're already familiar with: you click the *WordArt* object to expand the Ribbon with the *Drawing Tools* and its *Format* tab. The commands or command groups are available in the *WordArt Styles* group and are listed next in accordance with their numbering in Figure 5-21.

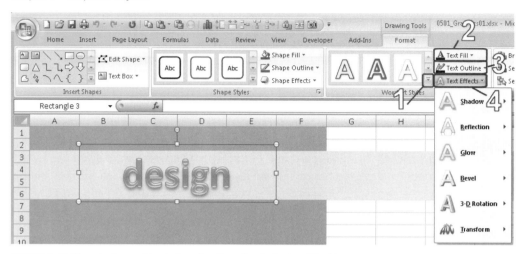

FIGURE 5-21 There's also a wide choice of options for designing *WordArt*

1. Here, you open a palette of different styles. When you assign one, you can specify whether it is to be applied to the whole object or only to the selected text.

2. You can use the *Text Fill* commands to handle the string or several of their characters in the way you're familiar with by now when using drawing objects; that is, you can fill them with colors, gradual gradients, textures, and picture objects.

3. You use the commands associated with the words *Text Outline* to change the external outline of the character.

4. You can also use the effects described earlier for designing shapes for handling *WordArt* objects. The *Transform* command here deserves more explanation, which I'll provide later in the context of Figure 5-23.

Table Cell as Text Source for WordArt

When producing challenging and dynamic presentation models in Excel 2007, an important goal is to incorporate as high a degree of flexibility as possible without actually having to do programming. You'll often achieve such objectives more easily than you thought possible by using a number of tricks.

This also involves being able to link a text container to an Excel table cell to show the string that exists in this "source cell." Mind you, this doesn't just apply to *WordArt*, but to *each* text container. Therefore, it also applies to *text boxes* and any two-dimensional drawing objects to which you add text.

An important and noteworthy restriction is that you can only link the graphical object to a single cell. However, with clever planning and design, this hardly matters because you can use controls to very flexibly manipulate the content of this text source cell with a combination of specific formulas. I'll describe the corresponding designs in detail in later chapters.

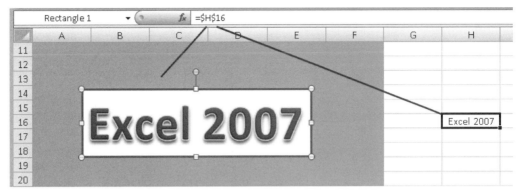

FIGURE 5-22 You can link a *WordArt* object to a table cell.

You can quickly perform the few steps for linking a cell to an object, as shown in Figure 5-22:

1. You have created and formatted a *WordArt* object. Enter a text that you want to appear in the *WordArt* object in any cell (in the example displayed, it's H16). Click the border of the object to select it as a shape (the object frame must appear as a full line).

2. Type an equal sign in the formula bar to begin the formula. Click the cell that you want to be the text source and then press the **Enter** key to create the link. The content of the cell appears in the *WordArt* object.

3. Change the string in the linked cell to see how the new contents are adjusted to the size of the *WordArt* object.

Transforming WordArt

The transformation of *WordArt* text is a type of formatting that's seen quite frequently, though this doesn't mean you should use it casually. In contrast, there are very few good reasons to transform a string in its entirety. Therefore, use the effect with care, remembering that not everything that's different from the "norm" is more appealing or more interesting.

If you want to transform a *WordArt* string, select the container and choose the *Transform* command, as shown in Figure 5-23. Then choose a particular transformation type from the default types pictured.

Note that the string appears to partly leave the area of the container in many of these types of transformations. If a text transformation makes sense, however, it's usually better to hide the container.

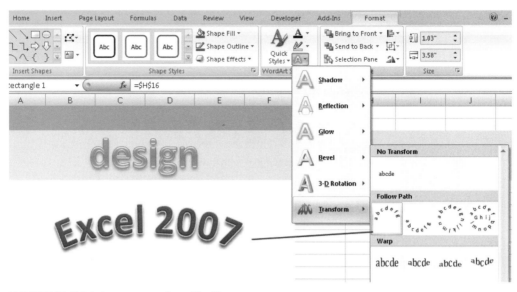

FIGURE 5-23 This is how you transform *WordArt* text.

SmartArt

From an application-specific point of view, Microsoft Office is taking a completely new approach to present texts graphically with the use of *SmartArt*. The visualization objects (powerful shapes with text contents) that can be created easily with this feature are primarily meant to help you understand complex or complicated relationships or sequences. You'll find information about this topic in Chapter 12.

Picture Objects and Picture Tools

I'll just briefly repeat what I mentioned at the beginning of this chapter with regard to the difference between the *Drawing* and *Picture* graphical objects:

- You can create and change a *drawing object* using tools available in Excel 2007. I've already discussed *two-dimensional shapes*, *lines*, and *WordArt* from this group.

- You can't create or edit the content of a *picture object* using the tools available in Excel 2007, but you can change its surrounding structures (for example, borders and shadows) or its overall appearance (for example, contrast, brightness, size, or shape).

Those of you who've followed this chapter up to this point—and even interrupted your reading to practice one or another of your own exercises with drawing objects—will have little difficulty using picture objects. Although there are considerable differences in design capability, the procedures basically required correspond generally (scaling, positioning, duplicating, using picture tools, and so on) and specifically (using formatting dialog boxes) to what you've already read about dealing with drawing objects.

> **On the Companion CD** The illustrations and explanations in this section relate to the *Pictures 1* worksheet in the *\Samples\0501_Graphics01.xlsx* file.
>
> You'll also find some picture objects for your own experimental purposes in the *\Materials\ Pictures* directory on the CD-ROM.

Inserting and Adjusting Pictures

To insert a picture object that's available as a file into an Excel 2007 worksheet, enable the *Insert* tab in the Ribbon and click the *Picture* command button in the *Illustrations* group. In the dialog box that subsequently appears, find and select the file, and paste it into the worksheet. The picture object is then highlighted, and you can position, scale, or duplicate it. However, the range of design options and commands will be completely different if you click the object and then display the *Picture Tools* with its *Format* tab in the Ribbon.

In earlier versions of Microsoft Office, commands for adjusting picture objects were placed in the *Picture* toolbar. If you were familiar with the tools available there, you'll also be able to get good results quickly with the *Picture Tools* of Excel 2007. The next list of tools follows the numbering in Figure 5-24.

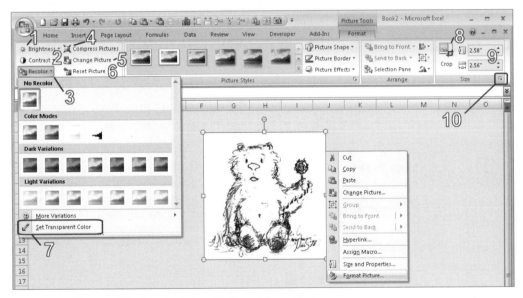

FIGURE 5-24 Here you'll find the tools for adjusting picture objects.

1. *Brightness*: You can change the brightness with an increment of 10 percent to a span from minus 40 percent to plus 40 percent by clicking the icons. If you want to define it in more detail, you can use the *Picture Corrections Options* command to go to a formatting dialog box and continuously change the brightness along a range of minus 100 percent to plus 100 percent.

2. *Contrast*: The options for changing the contrast correspond to the specifications made for the brightness under number 1.

3. *Recolor*: You'll find several options here to color a picture in monochrome. Therefore, not only can you change a color picture into a grayscale picture as you could in earlier versions of Microsoft Office, but you can also apply all other colors accordingly as a "uniform color." In addition to four *color modes*, several *Dark* or *Light Variations* are also available as integrated specifications. However, you can also use the *More Variations* command to use all available colors for this formatting purpose.

   I'll discuss the *Set Transparent Color* command under number 7 later.

> **Note** In presentations, monochrome pictures can sometimes be much more appealing than pictures in original colors. Use the effect if you want to tone down a color effect that's too strong or even "flashy" or if you want to adjust the entire picture of a specific coloring (for example, of a corporate design). The results are often considerably better than they would be if you tried to reduce brightness and/or contrast to achieve similar results.

4. *Compress Pictures*: This command enables you to reduce the space requirements of inserted pictures with the support of dialogs.

5. *Change Picture*: You use the *Insert Graphic* dialog box to replace a selected picture object with another picture object.

6. *Reset Picture*: With a single click of the mouse, you can undo all changes previously made to this picture in Excel. You therefore all but reproduce the original state.

> **Note** The influences on picture objects described here and in the following sections concern formatting, not changes. This means that the object itself doesn't change, just its appearance. This therefore has the same character as the formatting of e.g. the number 12345, which can appear in many different versions and variations in its table cell (different colors and sizes, with or without decimal places and separators, with text supplements, as a date, as text, and so on), but which is never anything other than the number 12345.

7. *Set Transparent Color*: You can access the command if you've already chosen the *Recolor* command (see above under number 3). After selecting the tool in the picture, click the color that you want to remove. It's important to know that you can only remove *a single* color in this way in each case. If you subsequently want to delete another color again, the previously created transparency will be undone. You can use this tool in a variety of very interesting ways in various contexts, examples of which you'll see in later chapters. However, an important basic requirement for creating attractive or effective low transparency is the option to remove large-scale color areas from the picture. This tool is therefore only interesting for those picture objects that contain relatively few colors, or for which there's a completely monochrome background that you can remove by clicking the mouse means and thereby "extract" all other contents of the picture. Nevertheless, this is almost never the case in digitized photographs or scanned pictures. Even a piece of sky that appears completely blue can consist of hundreds of blue tones in a digitalized picture, of which you can only remove a single one with the *Set Transparent Color* command. Therefore, it hardly makes sense to use the tool for photographs or detailed drawings.

8. *Crop*: After choosing this tool, you select with the mouse one of the "grips" that appears on the picture's border and move it inwards to crop the area of the picture, or outwards to expand the display area shown of a previously cropped picture (the size of the picture doesn't change in this case, only its visible area).

9. *Size*: You determine the exact dimensions of the picture here.

10. *Size and Properties* dialog box: When you click the launcher in the designated area, a dialog box—that's been mentioned several times—opens and you can use it to handle the picture under exact controllable conditions in relation to size, rotation, scaling, and cropping. Furthermore, in the *Properties* tab, you'll then have access to the usually recommended *Move but don't size with cells* option that I've already explained.

Charts in Combination with Graphical Objects

At the very beginning of this chapter, I introduced you to a combination of different objects, the handling and redesign of which should be somewhat easier for you to understand from now on.

 On the Companion CD Open the *\Samples\0502_Graphics02.xlsx* file on the CD-ROM.

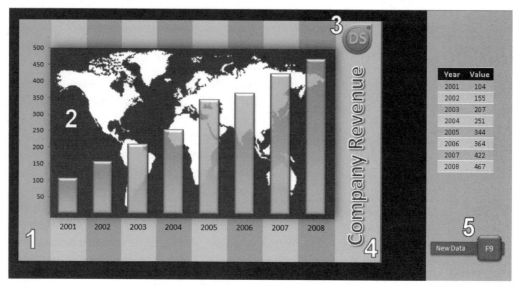

FIGURE 5-25 You often only get the desired effect using a combination of different objects.

Here are some comments I'd like to repeat based on the numbering in Figure 5-25:

1. You see a chart, whose *chart area* and *plot area* are completely transparent. The background structures are generated from table range colorings and from a picture object.

    (Charts based on numbers are not pure drawing objects or pure picture objects. Although they have structures, elements, and contents that you can create and change using the features and tools available in Excel, in many respects they can't be freely custom-designed.)

2. The map of the world behind the chart's plot area is a picture object that you'll find as the *Worldmap.tif* file in the *\Materials\Pictures* folder on the CD-ROM.

3. The logo, which you'll also find in the aforementioned folder, is a picture object that was initially composed of different Office 2007 drawing objects and then saved as a picture file in a graphics program.

4. The chart title rotated by 90° is created as a *WordArt* object and is therefore part of the group of drawing objects.

5. The *"New Data F9"* reference is a grouping of two different drawing objects; namely a text box and a rounded rectangle that text was subsequently added to. Therefore it also received text-box properties as a result.

Chapter 6
What, For Whom, How, and With What?

While the last chapter was very practical, this chapter is more theoretical. However, this does not mean that you should skip it. It deals with very important aspects of planning, technical preparation, and straightforward reproduction of your Excel 2007 products, thus ultimately making your work a lot easier. To ensure that their results not only work well but look good (two completely different things), users need the right façade. That is why first impressions count so much. The design should be pleasing, both to you and others. You'll be glad to know that it is quite easy to create a solid base for your design. All you have to do is observe a few important basic rules.

How Are Results and Approaches Determined?

When preparing a presentation or publication solution in Excel 2007, regard it as a work order that has to be processed according to certain project-management models: someone uses the standard procedure to set you a task, there are specific approaches for handling this task, and ultimately there is a result. It does not matter if the project is large and complex or small and straightforward, the preparation model for successful work is the same:

- An objective is formulated, and it is a clear and distinct objective that does not need to be revised.

- In turn, a plan is formulated from the objective: how will we achieve this objective, which resources will we use, and by when will we complete it?

- Accurate planning is the basis for classifying, checking and, if necessary, procuring resources. Which resources are available? Data, materials, specialist knowledge? What can I do myself? In which areas will I most likely require assistance from others?

Now it's full steam ahead!

No defined objective, no project. You may be thinking: "That goes without saying." However, that's not always the case, at least when it comes to defining an objective. Often the attitude is one of "let's get started and we'll see what happens." Worldwide, there are countless examples of Excel solutions that were created with reckless abandon. Frequently, these are products of questionable quality that are a waste of time and effort for all involved.

From Assigning Tasks to Defining Objectives

It's often much harder than you might think to formulate an accurate working objective. It depends on numerous factors. Sometimes, it is not possible to reconcile all of these factors, even after lengthy consideration. However, such difficulties should not arise here, as I will use the example provided in the file *0601_Indicators01.xlsx* to describe a relatively easy way to assign tasks and define an objective.

> **On the Companion CD** Open the file *\Samples\0601_Indicators01.xlsx* on the CD-ROM.

You should see an almost complete product that was created in accordance with the rS1.Method rules. A beta version is shown. However, only the focus sheet will be seen in the final version.

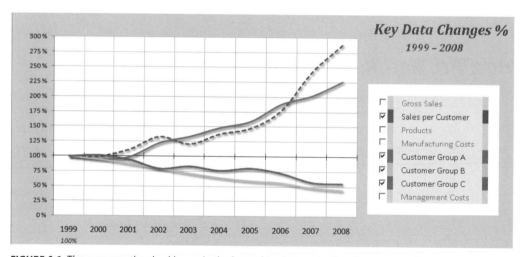

FIGURE 6-1 The user uses the checkboxes in the legend to choose the lines he wants to display.

The model's main attributes are as follows:

- The line chart in the *Focus 1* sheet shows the trend for eight data types over a 10-year period.

- The initial values in 1999 were set to 100 percent. Therefore, the lines show progressive percentage changes or fluctuations from these initial values.

- The accompanying legend not only explains but controls the chart: the user can click one or more of the subtly-colored legend entries to determine how many of the eight data series are to be shown in the plot area. Each assigned line is then displayed, and its color is highlighted in the legend. When you click the legend text, it has a stronger color. If you click it again, it returns to its initial state (line hidden, legend text faded).

Chapter 10, "Presentation Solutions That Pack a Punch," describes the technical aspects involved here. Chapter 6 deals only with the backgrounds and strategies. Read and evaluate the steps that ultimately led to this display variant that (like almost all of the solutions presented in this book) is based on a realistic scenario.

Scenario and Assignment of Tasks

A manufacturing company has implemented a long-term concept over a 10-year period, the results of which can be described in general as follows:

- Both gross sales and sales per customer have risen considerably.

- The total number of products has decreased while the quality of the products has improved. The company has planned for and accepted an associated rise in manufacturing costs.

- The total number of high-revenue A customers has risen while the total number of lower-revenue B and C customers has fallen. The accompanying fall in the total number of customers has also caused considerably reduced management costs.

These and other results of the company's successful corporate policy are to be presented to a bank. It is hoped that a comprehensive presentation will encourage the bank to make positive decisions that will further help the business.

The data available clearly supports the results listed above. However, it is extremely difficult to display this data. One of the many display problems quickly becomes evident in rows 16 to 24 of the *Data 1* sheet: the correlative data comes in very different values (values in millions next to values in tens and hundreds) and, as a result, you are unable to present all of this information in just one chart. However, this is exactly what the management requested, which brings us to our task: "We want to be able to show the success of the corporate policy in such a way that we can convincingly clarify all of the corresponding interdependencies between the eight chosen data categories. We must format and present the data in an easy-to-comprehend, relatively efficient manner. Finally, we also want to be able to display data in response to any questions asked."

Defining Objectives

Of course, the set of tasks formulated above is still not a defined objective; that is, you can't develop a real work order from this set of tasks. To define an objective, you first require something tangible, which is frequently the result of a long and laborious discussion.

Good, useable working objectives fulfill two key requirements. First, they can be implemented in factual, functional plans. Second, they are also verifiable; that is, you can determine whether or not they have been achieved. The way in which a working objective is formulated determines such verifiability. Therefore, it is generally a good idea to differentiate such objectives according to didactic thought patterns; for example, to regard a data presentation as a lesson or lesson plan in terms of its preparation, implementation, and performance measurement. In this context, I'll make the theoretical distinction between three types of objectives and assign a practical formulation to each. The more tangible something is, the easier it is to formulate a practical objective, and the easier it is to fulfill this objective.

> **Note** The data presented here played a very important role in the meeting with the bank, but it was only one of a number of presentations. Therefore it was necessary to develop more objectives than are described below.

Such classroom-style definitions only concern the "learners." That means the people who are mostly known in this book as the "target audience." In our example, they were the decision-makers from the bank who attended the presentation.

Cognitive Objectives   *Formulation based on learning theory:* the members of the target audience get to know and understand something, comprehend something (new), and can then apply this knowledge. They know the components that form a whole, can describe facts, and—if necessary—form opinions based on this newly acquired knowledge.

Formulation in this example: the members of the target audience know the data development of the eight chosen data types in the period between 1999 and 2008. They can describe the interdependencies between developments, the context in which these developments are present, and which measures achieved which trend changes. They can also form questions and draw their own conclusions.

Affective Objectives   *Formulation based on learning theory:* the members of the target audience adopt attitudes towards something. They develop feelings and make judgments. They note certain aspects for the first time or they change their minds about something. They are interested and prepared to do something or they dismiss something.

Formulation in this example: the members of the target audience evaluate the results owing to the corporate decisions made over the last 10 years and deem them to be successful. They also regard them as positive factors for the future. Their positive appraisal of the results concerns the corporate policy as a whole and the strategically desired and achieved long-term changes to the product portfolio, customer structure, and sales figures in particular.

Pragmatic Objectives   (This type of objective is also frequently described as a "psychomotor" objective.)

Formulation based on learning theory: the members of the target audience can take practical action or apply technologies, including some that are new to them.

Formulation in this example: the members of the target audience decide in favor of the different forms of financing requested by the company.

Implementing the Objectives in Our Example

Our example is less concerned with figures and more with trends and interdependencies between these trends. As a result, a line chart based on the value 100 was the perfect choice. In the context of Figure 6-1 and Figure 6-2:

- Displaying all eight data series at the same time is ineffective because it is asking too much of the observer's ability to differentiate and interpret. However, because you can show and hide each individual row as required, it is possible to clearly show every interdependency that exists between the rows. If you wish, you can work this out yourself using Excel and decide how many useful charts are in this worksheet.

- The model's dynamics permit optional configurations and can therefore display trend combinations that the presenter did not intend to show, but can show if they help to answer any questions raised by the target audience.

In a numerical presentation, nothing is more impressive (and therefore more successful) than the presenter's ability to come up with visualizations on the spot that help to answer a question or illuminate a topic under discussion. Even if the data presented is not particularly relevant, just the fact that you are the "numbers wizard" who—with one wave of your magic wand—can show the right information at the right time gives you great powers of persuasion and increases your standing as presenter, thus giving you the upper hand in controversial situations. This is one benefit that I have often witnessed, experienced, and consider essential. For me, it is also one of the most compelling arguments in favor of a numerical presentation with Excel. This is because:

- If you have hundreds of static PowerPoint slides, could you find the right slide at the right time? Even if you created each slide, this wouldn't be possible. At least not in a stressful situation, which presentations frequently create, especially if discussions are permitted or necessary.

- Is it possible to use some controls to produce an optional data combination and store hundreds or even thousands of different charts (and, if required, the associated tables) ad hoc in a single Excel worksheet? This can be easily achieved using the methods and procedures described in this book. And this almost always helps when you, as the presenter, are under pressure.

I'll outline my reasons for sticking to the solutions based on the rS1.Method (or comparable models) and limiting my use of the pivot system when we get to the section entitled "For Your Own Information or for Management?"

I wish to make one final comment in relation to the comparison between PowerPoint and Excel. Note that the presentations described in this book will be shown in full screen mode (to be described later); in other words, without the distracting "Excel padding."

- "Upward" and "downward" movements along the chart can be seen clearly in relation to the horizontal central axis, set at 100 percent. When these are applied to suitable interdependencies (such as view B in Figure 6-2, which represents customer types in relation to sales per customer), the images are easy to comprehend and very persuasive. By having "open-ended" lines that seem to diverge, they automatically give the impression of being "forward-looking," which was one of the requirements when formulating the objective. If you can create a similarly positive outlook towards the future, then you do not have to say much more when you present this image. The sheer power of such images can't be achieved by or replaced with words alone.

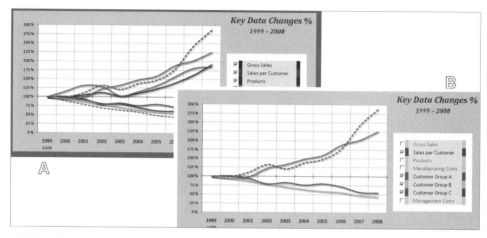

FIGURE 6-2 Version *A* is unmanageable, but dynamic Version *B* is perfectly suited.

- The numbers match up well with the presentation objectives. When accompanied by a compelling speech, they can't help but be *persuasive*. The chart is well formatted, and it's fun to see its dynamic multiplicity. Take full advantage of this, switching frequently between views and returning to the views that you have already shown to strengthen their impact. If some of the members of your target audience have knowledge of Excel, don't neglect the opportunity to inspire professional curiosity: "no programming required." If you can show your audience something similar to what we've shown here at the start of your presentation, you are well on the way to creating a good atmosphere and receiving positive feedback. Second only to the personality of the presenter, the aesthetics of a solution is the most important requirement for achieving affective objectives; that is, feelings, sentiments, and judgments.

The Six Ws and one H

The heading for the main section you've been reading is "How Are Results and Approaches Determined?" The focus is a product—for example, an Excel data presentation—the production of which is a project. One possible approach towards a successful project is to try to accurately formulate its objectives. Another approach is the method of the "six Ws and one H, which you can also easily apply to objective formulations. Here, you must answer the seven W questions in relation to the product: "**W**ho, **W**hom, For **W**hich Purpose, **W**hen, **W**hat, **H**ow, and **W**hy?" You can answer these questions yourself or discuss them in a group. If you can arrive at clear and definite answers for all seven questions, your work will not only be successful, but your methodology will be efficient.

I find the seven questions to be a useful basic principle for systematization, standardization, and planning as well as a basis for consideration and a framework for implementation. Let's take a closer look at each:

- *Who?* The person(s) responsible for the project: you will either assume responsibility yourself or you will entrust someone else with this task. Do you want to or have to do it yourself? Very well, but are you equipped, both in terms of knowledge and ability? Do you have a stake in this project? Can you spare enough time for this project? Will your efforts pay off? Have you done something like this before? Who will help you if your own knowledge and experience are not enough? Which aspects of the project can you or should you delegate to someone else? Is everything OK? Excellent, then let's get started.

- *Whom?* The target group: frequently, this question, which concerns the target audience, is greatly underestimated. For whom is the project intended? What are the wishes, knowledge, and abilities of the target audience? Are they receptive or do they need to be prepped? What are the known, probable, and assumed information requirements of this target group? Who are the members of this group? Will the target group take notice of your product by themselves, voluntarily and possibly with some curiosity, or is it only you who wants them to do this?

- *For **which** purpose?* What should the product "convey"? What content is required here? Information or sentiment? If both are required, in what proportion? What are the reasons for and against making the product?

- *When?* What is the deadline for having everything ready? What do you mean by "having everything ready" (not just your work on the Excel model but everything else)? Is the deadline realistic, and is it suited to the type, content, and purpose of the product?

- *What?* The type of product and content: a broad area. In fact, a very broad area with countless possibilities. Finding the right one, the most suitable one, has a lot to do with the other five Ws and the H. Should you choose a version that may be a little different, better, more intelligent, fresher than your competitors' ideas, or should you stick with a tried and tested formula? Should you use an established standard or even create your own? Have you made your final decision? Are your colleagues happy with your decision? If so, then stick to your decision and dismiss any doubts you may have, because if you do not have faith in the decision you have made, your work will suffer.

- *How?* The implementation: are there models, templates, examples, rules, requirements, specifications, and obligations? Often, it's ideal if there are strict guidelines such as ISO or ANSI, corporate design, or the formulated information requirements of the target audience. These do some of the work for you and even silence possible critics. However, it's not so good if there are clear specifications that stifle your imagination or conflict with your inner beliefs.

- **Why?** The search for meaning can be incredibly difficult to satisfy. What is the real, honest reason for making this product? If you can't or don't wish to give a reason, then it's worth asking why this product should even exist. You should never create a presentation just for the sake of having one.

For Your Own Information or for Management?

This section heading also has a lot to do with the question posed at the start of the main section, namely "How Are Results and Approaches Determined?" The purpose determines not only the resources, but also the content and designs to which you apply these resources.

- If it is your task to examine complex datasets from different perspectives, analyze them in great depth, select and condense them for presentations, and even more, you need to be very proficient in Excel. Here, your own visual information is paramount, and many direct or indirect opportunities to work with Excel await you. Naturally, you can't use most of the solutions described in this book directly without some limitations. However, it is possible to use them indirectly: quite often, they convey information to people who are less proficient in Excel.

- If it is your task to condense those complex sets of figures or to provide data that has already been interpreted and then present this information to management in an efficient, simple, visually appealing, and foolproof manner, then the solutions described in this book are perfect for your work.

In other words (based on the *PivotTable* and *PivotChart* examples), an Excel expert who is a fiscal controller or analyst often finds that the Pivot system provides a lot of what he needs and, in some cases, everything he needs. However, in terms of information to be presented to management (as I mean it in the context of this book), the pivot systems is largely unsuitable (we'll discuss this later).

Useful and efficient management information is always intended for upper management irrespective of the role that higher-level managers assume in the company, so they are ultimately the target audience for an internal presentation. The manager receives the data that he requires to make his own decisions at the right time, in the right volume, and in the right combination. The keywords here are "reporting with the target audience in mind." In an ideal situation, the manager can present and explain the data and its interdependencies himself without having to depend on others. This involves being able to use the simplest tools (for example, the mouse) to see exactly what he needs and wants to see without risking an error. Nothing less is needed, but also nothing more, which is where misunderstandings frequently arise. The intelligence of such a presentation solution generally lies in its "appealing simplicity," which is exactly why it requires considerably more preparation and design work than you might think.

If you are proficient in PivotTables and PivotCharts and work with OLAP systems that may be connected to data warehouses, or if you can use similar resources, then you will occasionally ask the following question when reading this book: "why go to such lengths?" I'll explain why below, but first let me clarify some of these terms as well as justify the use of such systems:

The **data warehouse**, in its ideal form, is an integrated structured collection of company data in one central location. It obtains its data from many different sources, for example, any upstream systems—including heterogeneous systems—which in turn include databases. Data may also be supplied from other sources, including manual input. The structure of such data can vary greatly. As a result, it is harmonized in the data warehouse and cleaned, if necessary. This homogenization process facilitates the system's main task, namely providing a summarized, fast, and variable view of the operational company data (which resulted from different business processes). From a technical perspective, the data warehouse is designed in such a way that it facilitates dynamic queries and analyses at different stages and levels, thus fulfilling the many different information requirements of many different target audiences.

The term **OLAP** (Online Analytical Processing) is a collective term for analytical procedures and methodologies within an information system. It makes sense to apply the procedure if you want to quickly sift through large or very large volumes of analysis data and then compile this data for further consideration. The main feature of the OLAP tools provided by different manufacturers is its multidimensionality. This allows data to be considered from different angles; for example, sales data from a time, account, cost center, sales region, department store, or sales employee perspective, and so on. These systems are very fast and extremely efficient. We, as mere mortals, find it difficult to comprehend its substantial structure because we do not have multidimensional but rather three-dimensional imaginations. OLAP cubes with multiple partitions are frequently used as an alternative way to visually display data. The OLAP tools obtain their data from a data warehouse (described earlier) or access a company's operational data directly. Most of these tools use Microsoft Excel as an analysis client.

The **PivotTable**, an Excel standard, is a special way of displaying complex datasets in a simple transparent manner. The data can originate from a complex Excel list or an external data storage system that you can query directly or indirectly (using Excel resources). The use of the term *pivot* implies that you can freely rotate the area under consideration around the analysis data so that you obtain one of many possible views or systematic arrangements of the data. To enable data to be displayed in PivotTables or PivotCharts without difficulty, the data source must satisfy certain structural requirements; that is, its data records must have a uniform structure.

A *PivotTable* is a customized variable dynamic table while a *PivotChart* is a customized variable dynamic chart. Both are created with a corresponding command on the *Insert* tab of the Ribbon and other subsequent actions.

All of the aforementioned systems offer enormous benefits when it comes to facilitating the multivariable and fast analysis of complex datasets. However, their use as tools for management information or public presentations is very limited. The many benefits of such a system are evident in its versatile data retrieval and the way in it reorganizes and displays results. However, the more options are available, the greater the propensity for error. For example, in the result, you may see data other than the data you want to see, you may see data in an unintentional constellation, or, even worse, you may not see any data at all. This is not a major problem if you are viewing the result in private, but it would be quite annoying in a live presentation, to put it mildly. For this reason, I would discourage inexperienced employees from using these tools. This is why pivot systems are almost always ruled out for management information purposes.

There are many practical uses for *PivotTables* and *PivotCharts*. In Excel 2007, they have numerous additional features. Even a brief description of these in every possible context is beyond the scope of this book. However, if you wish to learn more, please refer to the CD-ROM, which contains additional information about these features.

> **On the Companion CD**   The file *Materials\Excel07InsideOut_Ch22.pdf* provides extensive information about the topic. This file is an extract from the book *Microsoft Office Excel 2007 Inside Out* (ISBN 9780735623217), also published by Microsoft Press. This extract describes how to use *PivotTable tools* and their *Options* and *Design* tabs as well as the *PivotChart tools*. The latter essentially corresponds to the information you will obtain in this book in relation to using *chart tools*.

In conclusion, data warehouses, OLAP tools, and the pivot system, when used in the right working environment, are excellent tools for obtaining information for your own purposes. However, most of the solutions outlined in this book are geared, either directly or indirectly, towards a "target audience," or a public audience in the broadest sense, and should therefore satisfy their information requirements. This task has to fulfill far more than the visual information capabilities you need in your own working environment. In private, you can deploy strategies and technologies that are either unsuitable in a public presentation or not permitted if you wish to pass on your solution to others whose user proficiency is unknown to you.

In the context of Figure 6-3, I'll provide some information about a model that satisfies the requirements formulated in this chapter. Its construction is discussed in Chapter 10. For now, we will simply discuss the resources used to ensure information and user security for management information.

You are already familiar with the basic scenario from Chapter 2, "New Approaches—Getting Started," which examined the number of customers targeted with a "summer campaign" in 100 branches. This time, we are examining the sales generated. Let's assume that the user has not used Excel before, but he can open an Excel file, either from Explorer or after starting the program, and he can use the mouse to open a drop-down list and click a clear text entry. However, that's the extent of his proficiency in Excel, which is perfect in this situation. In the scenario shown below, there are four simple drop-down lists that facilitate the use of multivariable chart displays. The user can use the list entries shown below to produce a specific selection combination.

Branch Type	Region	City Size	Founding Year
All Types	All Regions	All City Sizes	All Founding Years
Retail Shop comb.	North	< 100.000	FY before 2006
Retail Shop sole	East	100.000 – 500.000	FY before 2005
Integrated (Dept. Store)	South	> 500.000	FY before 2004
	West		FY before 2003
			FY before 2002
			FY before 2001
			FY before 2000

Because the worksheet is protected, the user can only use the four controls. He can always "click" within the drop-down lists, but nothing more than that, so he can't display any unwanted or meaningless charts.

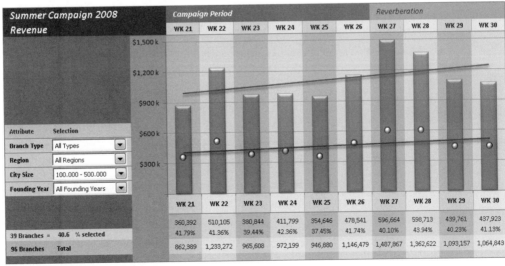

FIGURE 6-3 Anyone wishing to use this chart to convey information only needs to know how to use a mouse

By looking at the series of points in the chart, he can evaluate those results that correspond to the settings that he has made. Furthermore, he can relate these results to all of the branches (the columns). In both cases, a trend line is shown, which makes it easy to comprehend the differences between the "whole" and the custom subsets with regard to the success of the "summer campaign." Below the chart is a table whose colors have been synchronized with the colors in the chart, so you can read which values have been recorded in the display if you need to.

In this case, this is always adequate for management information. Despite the user's poor knowledge of Excel, he can show the data he wants to show, he can analyze it to a certain extent, and he can quickly see only the data that is relevant to this report.

If he, as the manager, wants to know more detailed information, we can hope he has well-informed employees who can provide him with the detailed information he requires and interpret it for him.

Have You Got Something to Say?

Or do you only have something to show? It is important to make this distinction because it should also be key to determining your Excel product type. Both of the models I've introduced can clarify what is meant here.

- The chart for the meeting with the bank (see Figure 6-1) requires a presenter, both in terms of its concept and overall design. At this moment, it is part of the presenter's toolkit, and it helps him to give a lively presentation. It shows results that require a lot more descriptive and background information than are provided with this chart. Its strength lies in the visual evidence of a successful corporate policy. Anyone who has sufficient experience (including extensive supporting knowledge) to eloquently present this information in its many forms will find this flexible chart an excellent aid for delivering a successful speech.

- The chart for direct management information, on the other hand, is based on a completely different conceptual design (see Figure 6-3). It is limited to directly showing collated data and therefore is purely a tool that conveys information. Despite its variability, it is relatively static. For each of its settings, it conveys only the information actually displayed in its respective images. Anyone who knows what this chart represents and who, for good measure, has the relevant supporting information ("insider knowledge") does not require much additional explanation.

Unfortunately, such differences too often are only partly observed or not observed at all when designing a chart. What should be fast, simple, perfectly informative, clear and concise management information is overshadowed by superfluous information and meaningless setting and selection options. What should support a gripping, highly responsive, and vivid public speech is deposited in anemic PowerPoint presentations with attempts to conceal its lifelessness through fidgeting (so-called animations).

Models

A model can have one of two roles: it can be a sample that can be imitated, or it can be a valid model; that is, a template to be used for specific purposes. This template may correspond to a norm, an agreement, or an instruction. Both roles for models apply here.

Sample Templates

I save "sample templates" as normal Excel workbooks. These are tried and tested solutions that have the target audience in mind, have neutral content for several purposes, and are defined as "samples that can be imitated." I recently started to save them twice in Excel 2007: once as an *xls* file, which is fully compatible with earlier versions of Excel, and once as an *xlsx* file for use in Excel 2007 projects. Such workbooks can be real gems if you remember them and if, after several months or years, you still know which data they calculated, how they calculated it, and why they calculated it *in this way.* Hence my recommendation to document everything. By effortlessly reproducing work that you have already successfully implemented, you can then take great pleasure in further "exploiting" your sample template; that is, reverting to finished or half-finished building blocks. Of course, this speeds up new developments considerably and also provides some security. If you use elements that have already been tried and tested in practice, then it doesn't take long to test whether they will fulfill certain tasks and work as you want them to.

The Excel Template

A completely different requirement arises when you want to create something new, but require a standardized basis. The customizable *Excel template* is a specific Excel storage format that corresponds to the *Word template* in terms of its type and use. Note the design freedom that such templates afford you. In using one, define the "basics," but avoid special structural specifications. If you do too much at this stage, you will often restrict your work rather than ease it, unless you create a very special template for a very special, frequently recurring purpose. Otherwise, your *Excel template* should contain only a few functional elements or none at all, yet all of the basic structures that ease a certain type of development. Such a template then represents a version that can be reproduced at any time, without any difficulty, and frees the user from always having to create the same standardized basic framework. The file *rS1_Standard.xlsx* on the CD-ROM contains a typical model. It fulfills the basic requirements for a workbook to be created in accordance with the rS1.Method. I will use this sample file to outline the work steps involved in creating an *Excel template.*

On the Companion CD Open the file *\Materials\rS1_Standard.xlsx* on the CD-ROM.

In the context of Figure 6-4:

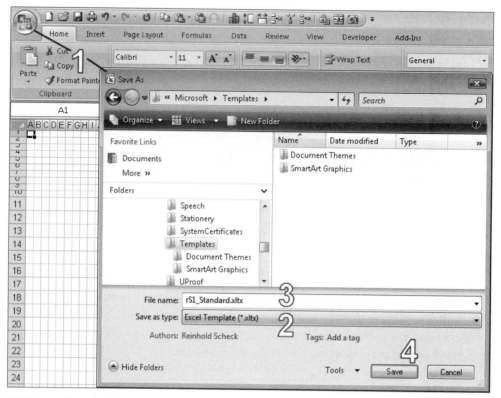

FIGURE 6-4 Note the above when saving templates

1. The file *rS1_Standard.xlsx* is open. Click the *Office Button* and then choose the command *Save As*.

2. In the dialog box, select *Excel template* as the *Save as type*.

3. If necessary, enter another name as the *File name*.

4. After you click *Save*, the file is stored as a template (with *xltx* as its file type) and it can be reproduced.

If you now wish to start a project for which you require this *Excel Template*, described in the context of Figure 6-5, you must proceed as follows:

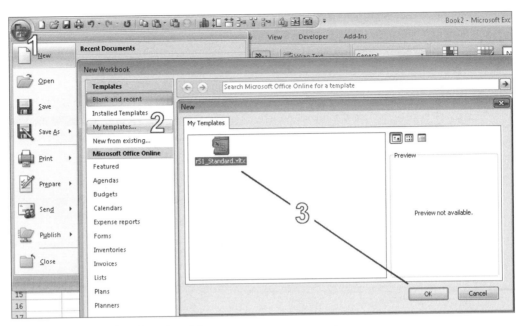

FIGURE 6-5 The steps for using a template

1. Click the *Office Button* and then choose the command *New*.

2. In the *New Workbook* dialog box, choose the command *My templates*.

3. A *New* dialog box is now displayed. Its *My Templates* tab displays the custom Excel templates available. When you have located and selected the template, click OK. Instead of the actual template, a copy of the template now opens.

4. If you want to save this copy of the template, the default specification is automatically set again as the save variant for this type. Therefore, you routinely save the copy of the *xltx* template as a "normal" workbook; in other words, as an *xlsx* file.

This procedure protects the saved template against inadvertent changes and possible damage. Therefore, the use of sample templates is far superior in this regard. However, in order to retain an overview, you should only define such files as *Excel templates* if they fulfill all the requirements for a generalized base variant.

The Chart Template

Excel 2007 also provides its users with numerous integrated layouts and formats for designing charts. These compete with your own design variants. However, I once again suggest that you use your own variants in most cases. Your individuality does not have to conflict with a certain conformity; quite the opposite. You have created a complex chart solution that fulfills all of your requirements and fully satisfies the purpose of creating and displaying this chart. To a certain extent, it bears your "hallmark" and therefore, in my opinion, expresses your primary role. Naturally, it doesn't make sense to want to repeatedly create another detailed "sample" result from scratch for the same purposes. Nor does this have to happen, because you have the option of saving a custom *chart template*. Later on, you can assign its many properties to every other chart.

You use the *chart template* to define formal details that will be copied in full to the "target chart" when you use the template later. If you do not consider and follow a few guidelines beforehand, you may experience unwanted effects that will be hard to correct. Therefore, please note the following:

- Is the design type of the chart from which you want to create a template actually universal in nature? In other words, can you use this exact chart (including its formatting) time and time again for the same purpose?

- Which details are characteristic and important and therefore should be reproduced?

- Which formatting details are important for only the current version, bearing the target audience in mind (and should be removed or made neutral before saving the chart as a template)?

- If the template were used, which other details could cause problems for the target chart? This concerns the axes (custom scaling and number formats) or analytical lines, for example. Such structures should also be removed or standardized before you save the chart as a template.

Therefore, my earlier advice about preparing the *Excel template* also applies here: define the "basics," but avoid any particular specifications. The chart template should contain all of the basic structures that are copied to the same or a similar model. Incidentally, it either contains standards that we know from experience occur in specific designs focused on their target audiences, or it contains nothing but basic formatting.

Once such preparatory work is complete, it is then extremely easy to create the chart template. In the context of Figure 6-6:

1. Select the chart that, according to the above list, is suitable for use as a chart template.

2. In the Ribbon, enable the *Design* tab under *Chart Tools* and click the *Save As Template* command button in the *Type* group. A dialog box is displayed in which you recognize the automatically assigned storage location and the file names of the chart templates that you may have already saved.

3. The chart is saved as an Excel 2007 chart template file (whose file type is *crtx*). Enter a file name that represents the purpose of this template, and that you will still recognize later. Choose *Save* to complete the process.

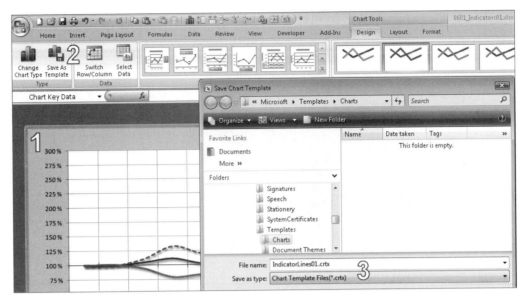

FIGURE 6-6 Note the above when saving chart templates

If you now want to create a chart using the template that you saved earlier, adopt the approach described in the context of Figure 6-7:

1. Select the area that contains the data for the chart to be created.

2. In the Ribbon, enable the *Insert* tab, and click the *Launcher* for the *Charts* group in order to open the *Insert Chart* dialog box.

3. In the dialog box, click the *Templates* command button to open the *My Templates* tab. Choose the template whose properties you wish to use to create the new chart.

4. Choose *OK* to create the chart by using the defined configuration and formatting characteristics.

5. In the dialog box, you can also click *Set as Default Chart* to set this custom type as your preferred standard. The *Manage Templates* command button opens a dialog box in which you manage the files for the defined templates.

Note Of course, you can also use your own chart template if you have already created a chart. For example, choose the command *Change Chart Type* from the context menu for this chart.

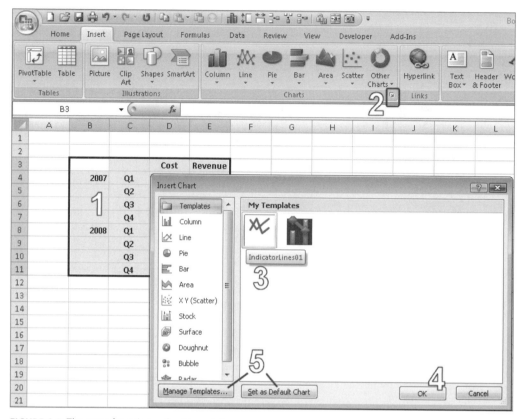

FIGURE 6-7 The steps for using a chart template

The Importance of Looking Good

Yes, it is important to look good. Even if you do not intend to pass on your solution to others, you should still take pride in what you have created and will possibly use on a regular basis.

> **Note** In this book, the term "presentation" is used in different ways. Normally, this is understood to mean "the act of presenting something to the public." However, in my approach to design tasks and my handling of software, I take it a step further: Even in my own non-public information environment, I am entitled to formal quality and therefore try to achieve this in private.

What is regarded as good-looking, and how is this achieved? What is attractive or beautiful? The books that address such basic questions present many good-looking, attractive, and beautiful opinions on the matter. However, I will not reference them here since I am only concerned with "charts."

Only charts? Such a casual attitude would automatically produce poor designs. Why? Because a chart is an image and that alone is a challenge. Our initial perception of an image always regards it as a whole. As a result, first impressions always count, even for charts. At the first-impression stage, its content is secondary. If first impressions prove to be unpleasant, observers might not form any second impressions. Will observers still be interested in the content? Probably not.

Therefore, anyone wishing to use charts to document, influence, sell or bid for something (why else do charts exist?) must, at the very least, endeavor to make the chart look good. It is even better if they can make the chart look attractive or even beautiful. This can be achieved in Excel 2007, which in this regard is far superior to previous versions of Excel.

We've now established that a chart should look good or at least good enough to prevent it from discouraging its observers. A chart should also contain enough information to be understood. This addresses the conflict between aesthetics and function and between purpose and a need to be pleasing to the eye. Such conflicts can cripple your design efforts, especially if you do not have a strategy. You must regard your development of a chart solution as a complete composition. From the outset, all of its aspects (content, functions, layout, forms, colors, design embellishments, and other padding) must be considered as a single entity.

If you have to create a chart image, you should apply the most important graphical composition rules used for paintings, good photos, or attractive page layouts. It would be impossible for me to present all of these in detail here. That is another book or possibly three! However, I'll point out the most important features:

Composing means, among other things, arranging, compiling, and structuring different elements with the aim of creating a product whose main impression is formed by its overall effect.

Here I will outline the general principles that you should observe when preparing to achieve a positive overall effect or one that fulfills an objective, the most important being:

- Screen layout and print page layout

- Type area and layout grid

- Formatting and measurements

- Lines and borders

Note When the term "chart" is used in this chapter, it frequently involves not only the numbers-based object but also the overall image shown on screen or in an expression. In other words, a chart includes the numbers-based object together with additional environmental structures such as the table components, backgrounds, design embellishment, and so on.

Which Layout?

Before we discuss *layouts* in detail, we must first explain the term itself because it can be used in many different contexts. Even in the narrow sense associated with graphical displays, this term can have many interpretations. For example, layout could mean the following:

- A basic outline

- A working template that is furnished with details and therefore can be implemented directly as a set of guidelines

- Part of a whole (such as a specific text print image or a basic image design)

- The overall aesthetic design of a product ("the book has a very modern layout," for example).

Here, I will predominantly discuss the "planning" aspect of this term. Therefore, the layout is a design framework; in other words, a standardized specification that nevertheless permits room for individual flair.

With regard to the topics discussed in this book, one main layout question stands out above all others: "How big must or should my chart be, and where should I position it on the page?" There is no single clear and concise answer because we must consider several aspects.

Chart Layout for Print Publications

For a publication chart that appears in printed matter, the question just posed is less significant, at least in most cases. The chart is usually a pictorial element on a printed page whose overall layout (page setup, margins, fonts, set type, and so on) is either defined as a specification or essentially can't be influenced by you.

Chapter 12, "More Than Numbers," will provide answers to important print-publication questions in relation to your model. Here is just a snippet for the time being:

- If you are unsure about the sizes, colors, and configurations you should use to develop print versions of your work, you should seek advice about such specifications, either by asking the project sponsor or by consulting with the printing service provider.

- If you do not have any useable specifications for size, err on the side of caution and create charts that are too big rather than too small. If a chart has to be scaled down to size, the result is still generally useable and of good quality. However, if a chart has to be blown up to size, the quality of the result usually suffers.

Layout for Presentation Charts

With regard to the layout for a screen or projector-based presentation, the screen resolution is the main determining factor. Only exceed a resolution of 1024 x 768 pixels if you are sure that the video projector you choose can handle a higher resolution and still ensure satisfactory quality.

The screen resolution determines the space available to you, so that you can display your chart in full without having to scroll. Therefore, this available space defines an upper limit that always applies if you actually want to use the entire screen area to display your chart.

The reverse scenario can be similarly problematic: you have a lot of space; too much in fact. The obvious idea is to simply blow up the chart to a size that uses all the space. Generally, however, the result is not aesthetically pleasing. Compare and evaluate both yourself: the file *0602_BigAndSmall.xlsx* contains two charts that have the same configuration but are a different size.

On the Companion CD To observe the comparative effects of both charts in the file *\Samples \0602_BigAndSmall.xlsx*, press **F9** repeatedly to create a new data series, and then press the key combination **Ctrl+Page Up** or **Ctrl+Page Down**, for example, to switch back and forth between the two *Small* and *Big* worksheets.

How much space is actually available to you? This is determined first by the screen resolution (which should now remain at 1024 x 768 pixels) and second by the view that you have set. The difference is apparent in Figure 6-8.

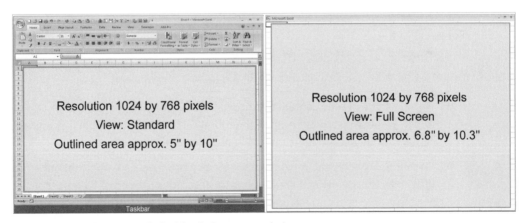

FIGURE 6-8 Nearly a *1:1.5* ratio for identical screen resolutions

The ratio between the standard view in Excel 2007 and the *Full Screen* view in Excel 2007 is nearly 1:1.5, which is a considerable difference. This should prompt you, at a very early stage, to decide how you want to produce your chart. Naturally, the harmonious positioning of the object greatly depends on the dimensions of the total visible area.

Note Below you will learn how to set up the *Full Screen* view.

Considering the example shown in Figure 6-9, you want to position a small presentation chart in the standard view of the Excel screen:

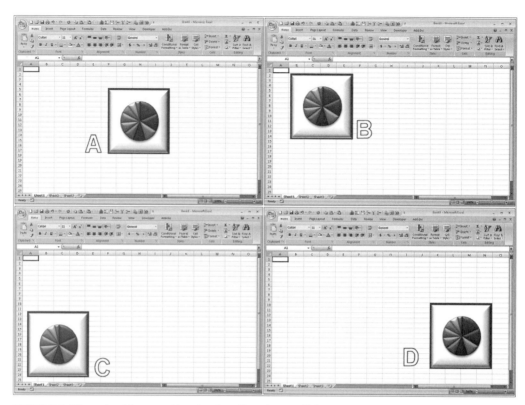

FIGURE 6-9 Where should you position the chart if you have sufficient space?

- *Version A*: the exactly centered horizontal and vertical alignment is often a solution forced by uncertainty rather than the intention to look good. Charts positioned in the center quickly appear to be dull and uninteresting.

- *Version B*: probably the most favorable. If our visual perception is not influenced in any other way (for example, by a foreground structure surrounded by a border, a directional perspective line, or a fixation point that "draws us in"), we tend to "read" the screen from left to right and from top to bottom. Therefore, the object's positioning in Version B is in tune with our senses.

- *Version C*: everything that speaks in favor of Version B speaks against Version C. I disapprove of positioning a chart here in what is otherwise an empty page. It would only be acceptable if the chart object were "held" on the page and stabilized by other elements (text, images, or color areas, among others). Otherwise, it could quickly become unpopular with observers.

■ *Version D*: Its problems are similar to C, but it is slightly better. However, observers would question why there is a "hole" above the image (whereas an equally large "hole" *below* the image, for example in Version B, generally goes unnoticed).

What Does Excel 2007 Offer in Terms of Design Layout?

This is an easy question to answer:

■ It offers a great deal in terms of print design layout

■ It offers very little in terms of screen design layout, or at least nothing that is easy to handle

Almost all of the commands on the *Page Layout* tab of the Ribbon concern the print page setup (see Figure 6-10). The *Page Setup*, *Scale to Fit*, and *Sheet Options* groups are associated with the *Page Setup* dialog box that you may know from earlier versions.

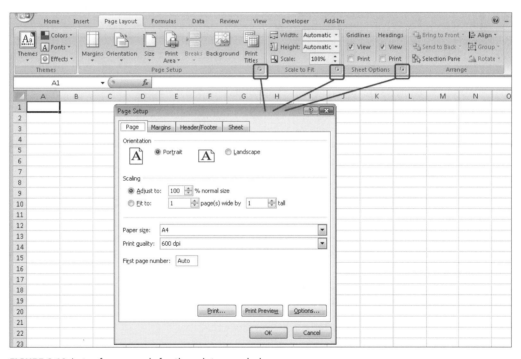

FIGURE 6-10 Lots of commands for the print page design

Rather than print out your chart solution, you want to show it on screen or use a projector (which is more in line with the intentions of this book)? This will be a little harder to handle.

> **Note**   Can we regard Excel as an almost perfect, multivariable, and very aesthetically pleasing program for presenting figures? Unfortunately, this notion has been alien to program developers for years now and it looks like this will continue to be the case. This is a great pity because— apparently without reason—developers have passed up the opportunity to make the program more aesthetically pleasing, which has been a much sought-after trait in Microsoft Office for a long time. Since Excel 2000, however, it is difficult to find a good reason for choosing the static and therefore potentially bland slide-based speech-supporting concept of PowerPoint over the spreadsheet's dynamic capabilities of presenting figures. Chapters 7, "Elements of Dynamization," and 11, "Fulfilling Special Requirements," provide some evidence to support this statement.

If you search the other tabs in the Ribbon for commands that could help you when designing for the screen, you will find just a few. Even those commands that fall under "Layout" mostly serve other purposes. In the context of Figure 6-11:

- *Section A*: the *Design* tab under *Chart Tools* contains a group entitled *Chart Layouts*. Here, you could determine (if you wish) the default elements and combinations that your chart should contain in its initial configuration.

- *Section B*: even though the *Layout* tab under *Chart Tools* contains many commands, they affect the chart design only.

- *Section C*: finally, the *View* tab contains options that you can use to influence the page layout. These can be either temporary or permanent actions and will be discussed in more detail in the next few sections.

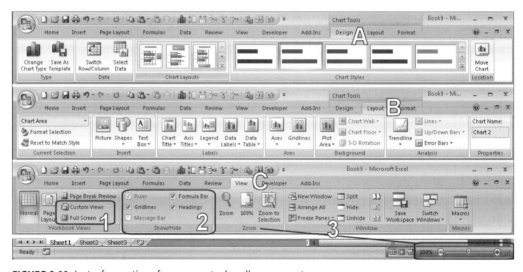

FIGURE 6-11 Just a few options for an easy-to-handle screen setup

Screen Setup Commands

When creating a presentation solution, you must distinguish between the screen settings for the development phase and the screen settings for the view of the finished product. This is certainly true if you want to present the finished solution in full-screen mode. Even though the latter is now more elegant than before, some difficulties remain. You can't switch easily between a design view and presentation view, as you can do for example in PowerPoint. This is a problem because in Excel your available workspace is clearly smaller than the subsequent presentation area (see Figure 6-8). It is generally not a good idea to use the zoom feature to compensate for the lack of space because, for many development steps, you have to zoom in rather than zoom out.

Therefore, you must accept that the bothersome movement back and forth between the work view and the presentation view is sometimes unavoidable. The relevant commands are marked and numbered in Section C of Figure 6-11:

1. You can save and retrieve different combinations of screen-view settings as *Custom Views* by assigning a name to each view. When you click this command, a dialog box opens in which you can name and define the current screen display. To reproduce this view at any time, use the same dialog box to call the name that you assigned to the view.

   The *Full Screen* command produces a view that I call the "presentation view." All elements with the exception of the Excel title bar are removed. Consequently, the maximum available area is displayed, which corresponds to the current screen resolution (for example, 1024 x 768 pixels, as used above). However, for the version to be shown in public, it may be necessary to hide some of the additional work elements discussed in points 3 and 4 below.

   To exit the *Full Screen* view, you must press **Esc**.

2. In the context described here, the options assigned to the *Show/Hide* command concern showing or hiding the following:

   ❑ *Gridlines*,

   ❑ *Formula Bar*

   ❑ *Headings* (in other words, the row and column labels). Unfortunately, it is not possible to access the elements discussed under point 4 here.

3. The *Zoom* settings play a major role during the development phase. Considerable progress has been made, when compared with earlier versions. On the right-hand side of the status bar, there is a slider for gradually increasing/decreasing the zoom settings between 10 percent and 400 percent. The slider's default position is 100 percent. This pleasant tool essentially makes the three command buttons in the *Zoom* group redundant. Their functions are as follows:

❏   The *Zoom* command opens a dialog box in which you can specify the zoom level of the document.

❏   The *100%* command restores the default zoom level of 100 percent.

❏   The *Zoom to Selection* command zooms in the selected area to 400 percent.

The functions associated with the three aforementioned commands are coupled with the zoom slider described earlier.

4.   Without reference to the figure: If you wish to show or hide the *scroll bars* and *sheet tabs*, you must take pains to familiarize yourself with the *Excel Options*. To do this, click the *Office Button*, choose the command *Excel Options* and then the command *Advanced*. Then make the relevant settings in the category entitled *Display options for this workbook*.

This set of commands plays a significant role if your work is associated with the topics discussed in the next few sections.

Tip It almost goes without saying that the *Full Screen* view is set for Excel presentations. However, it is almost impossible to work in this view because you can't access the commands you require. As mentioned earlier, it is generally not a good idea to zoom out. Therefore, in the development phase, you must work and think for an area size that you will only occasionally see in full-screen mode. One tip for alleviating this problem is to assign a special color, in the *Full Screen* view, to the area that will actually be shown later. You can then easily keep an eye on this colored area when you occasionally use the zoom commands. Once you have completed your work in the development phase, you can remove this color or replace it with the final background design.

However, after you apply this temporary color, you must not make any more major changes to the row height or column width.

Another aid, one that I frequently use, is to apply a striking color to the border of a rectangle (a shape), make its area transparent, and define its size to almost the size of the *Full Screen* view. I then place this object elsewhere and use it occasionally as a "gauge" if, during my work, I do not wish to switch to the *Full Screen* view.

Type Area and Layout Grid

A visual composition must accomplish more than just positioning a chart. It involves the layout and the skillful consolidation of individual elements. In this regard, the model shown in Figure 6-3, for example, is already very sophisticated and more difficult to produce than it may seem at first glance. Those basic considerations that also play a very big role when preparing printed matter will help you to successfully complete such tasks. Therefore, consider your screen as a blank sheet of paper (in landscape format) whose layout you have to configure.

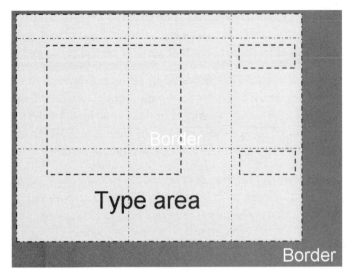

FIGURE 6-12 The layout grid helps you when composing the overall effect.

In terms of layout, you should never use all of the area actually visible. Your presentation area, therefore, has margins on all sides. Only in exceptional cases should a colored outline be used to indicate these margins. Similar to a page of printed matter, the margin is an area that is generally out of bounds (that is, no elements can be added here) and whose dimensions must have a harmonious structure.

> **Tip** Broad margins and other free areas can frequently increase the elegance and "perceived value" of the overall effect.
>
> Ensure a variable margin width for the worksheet as follows:
>
> 1. Keep (at least) Row 1 and Column A completely blank.
> 2. Set the *Move but don't size with cells* property for all objects (numerical charts, drawing objects, screen objects, controls, and so on).
> 3. At the end of your work, use the height of Row 1 and the width of Column A to control the upper and left margin widths. In one easy step, you can move all of the screen contents vertically or horizontally.

The remaining area (indicated by the bold dotted border in Figure 6-12) is known, in the printing industry, as the *type area*. Like an empty page of a book or newspaper, this area accommodates all of the elements that play a role in the layout of your presentation worksheet. In some cases, you may only have to position the numerical chart in this area. However, as the figure illustrates, this area can contain several extremely different elements, such as the chart area, tables, the title and other text, explanatory text fields and comments, controls for the chart's dynamics, and screen objects or drawing objects as design embellishments.

Furthermore, this area may have specific row and column colors, notes in the form of headers or footers, and much more. It can be difficult to give each element a good and, most importantly, a "correct" position in this area. It's a matter that requires careful consideration.

All of the above is even more complex if the sheet not only serves for view but needs to be utilized, for example by a presenter. If this is the case, your product must not only look good, but it must also satisfy ergonomic requirements. For example, how will the user be guided? What should he find easily? Where should he find it? Does it require secure access? The topic of *ergonomics* will be discussed further below, in a separate section.

In addition to the knowledge you'll gain with experience, such tasks are made easier by preparing the layout grid (indicated by the light dotted line in Figure 6-12, for example) in your mind's eye. Before starting, consider the elements required as well as their size and position in the chart. However, the following is even better than simply deliberating:

- Grab a pencil and a sheet of paper and make a rough outline.

- Each time you add an element, ask yourself *why* you are doing so. If you can't give yourself a convincing answer, your decision may be flawed.

Area Design

In terms of formatting, very few words should be used in the orientation of a numbers-based chart. Let's assume that the landscape orientation is used for most chart layouts. Generally, the portrait orientation is used only for bar charts with extensive data series. The two large areas of the chart, *chart area* and the *plot area*, are very important in terms of layout.

Area Relationships

The area relationships between the *chart area* and *plot area* require consideration and frequently experimentation. The most important basic questions are:

- Does it look good? Does it look interesting? Is it, in the best sense of the word, "pleasing?"

- Are the visually distinguishable margins and areas in harmony with each other and "appealing to the eye?"

- Is the arrangement clear? In terms of content, do all of the important individual elements look good, and are they displayed in such a way that reflects their importance?

- Is the size of the *plot area* appropriate to its content (the content density)?

Note In relation to the last point above:

One of the most interesting phenomena associated with human behavior is the pronounced tendency to conserve one's energy (you could also call this "nature's law of convenience").

On a more serious note: if you have a chart that fills the screen or projection screen, you can only expect its observers to move their eyes back and forth without complaint if the chart contains enough information to make this extra effort worthwhile. If observers see very little, despite having made the effort to move their eyes back and forth, they will (generally subconsciously) feel inconvenienced. A word of warning: do not create unnecessarily large *plot areas* for charts.

Several factors should influence your decisions. Compare the list of points below with Figure 6-13, which I have provided as an example. Do not forget that this is just one of many equally acceptable variants.

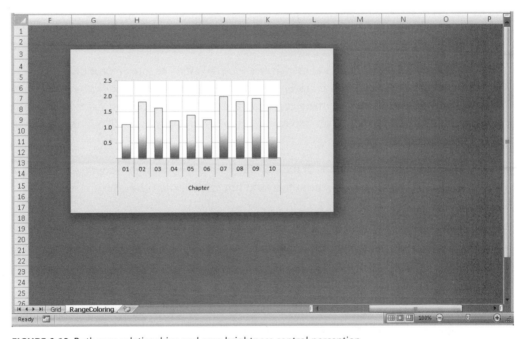

FIGURE 6-13 Both area relationships and area brightness control perception

- The margin between the *chart area* and the row and column headings (hidden during the presentation) is neither too wide nor too narrow. Even wider would be acceptable, but narrower would have a tendency to look "squashed."

- The width/height relationship is different for the *chart area* than for the *plot area*. Such differences help prevent bland uniformity, which quickly becomes the case with completely symmetrical compositions.

- The "suspense" created by asymmetry is further strengthened by moving the *plot area* within the *chart area* down a little and to the left and therefore away from the imaginary center axes.

Observe the following basic rule: symmetrical proportions are stylish, but can quickly appear to be bland, whereas unusual proportions spark interest, but can quickly appear "contrived and artificial" if they are overdone.

Dimensions

You rarely need to worry about half an inch when creating presentations to be shown on screen or using a video projector. However, this does not mean that you can disregard the exact dimensions in the rectangular chart element. The width/height relationship is extremely important for an aesthetically pleasing first impression as well as for dealing with later considerations. The next few sections provide some brief information about two systems that you can use as the basis for "good" proportions.

The "golden section" (also known as the "golden ratio" or "divine proportion") is a mathematical width-to-height division ratio of 1 to 1.618 (rounded off) that has been used and loved since the Renaissance by many European artists as a basis for their harmonious designs. The fact that it also concerns an "ideal proportion" frequently found in nature was proven 800 years ago.

Nowadays, the proportions of the standardized paper sizes for layouts, e.g. letter or A4 (ISO 216), also play a very large role, and not just in print products.

Of course, when determining dimensions or gaps, it is generally OK to disregard the positions after a decimal point for both systems. To observe the golden section as 1.61803398874989 48482045868343656 would be excessive. However, if you adhere to the rounded versions of these systems (5:8 for the golden section and 5:7 for ISO 216), you will always produce harmonious images.

In saying that, however, we should remember that unusual proportions arouse interest. Therefore, do not shy away from other dimensions. Even a dimension whose shape and formation appears to be cumbersome, angular, crooked, or even offputting can, after having attracted attention or even caused irritation, reveal its charms and have the desired effect. Many successful marketing campaigns adopt this idea.

If you want to measure a product or its elements in accordance with exact specifications, such as aspect ratios, you may find the content of the file *Shapes_Measurements.xlsx* helpful.

On the Companion CD The file *Shapes_Measurements.xlsx* is contained in the *\Materials* folder on the CD-ROM.

This file contains numerous objects whose exact dimensions are referenced in the object itself or are discernible in another way. To check this, you can also click the objects and then read the measurement or set up a new measurement in the Ribbon under *Drawing Tools*, *Format* tab, and *Size* group.

> **Note** When you use cm or other metric values, you may notice that you sometimes have to tolerate minor and generally negligible inaccuracies with decimal places. This is because Excel does not support metric measurements in the background and, as a result, there may be minor deviations in your shapes' admeasurements.

Some of the objects have area fills and some are transparent. Copies of these objects can be transferred to your worksheets and used as calibers or "rulers." In terms of your work, these may help you more than the relevant dialog boxes.

Brightness and Colors

In addition to dimensions, the brightness levels of an area are important for that first impression. Once again, we will discuss this in the context of Figure 6-13:

- The entire dark area recedes behind the other elements, and it is immediately clear to observers that this is definitely the entire background. As a result, the brain doesn't have to bother with it any more (less work!).

> **Note** Visual perception requires a clear separation between the foreground and the background as well as an impression of depth, even in two-dimensional objects. For this purpose, the entire background should be darker than any other area on screen (dark implies far away). Never present charts on a screen or with the use of a projector without having an immediately discernible background. If a background has a weak color or is completely colorless, observers first have to realize that this is actually the background. This takes time and effort!

- The brighter *chart area* sets itself apart from the background, but it is not imposing. It nevertheless gives the desired impression of being a supporting element.

- The very bright *plot area* and the "figures" displayed there draw us in. This is what it's all about. The observer does not have to find anything himself. Instead, he is guided to the most important area.

In the first main section of Chapter 4, "Colors, Areas, and Outlines," you learned essential information about colors and color selections. Here are a few notes in relation to assigning colors to areas:

- Generally, dark blue is a good background color for presentations that take place in darkly lit rooms while white is a poor background color for video presentations. Avoid choosing very saturated colors as background colors.

- Warm colors (from the red, yellow, or green palette) leave a pleasant overall impression, but they can be intrusive. Do not choose warm colors for area designs. Instead, choose them when you want to make some details stand out. Alternatively, add warm spots of color to cold area designs (blue, violet, gray) if you want to achieve a friendlier overall effect. Because objects with warm colors appear to be closer than those with cold colors, never use them for background designs.

- Dark colors are "weightier" than bright colors. You can take this meaning literally, especially if you use color fills. If you create vertical color gradients in areas, you should generally ensure that the colors brighten as they rise. If you create horizontal structures in areas, you should ensure that they brighten as they travel from left to right.

- Multi-colored charts look ridiculous, which is fine if you want your chart to have the fun element associated with a country fair or circus. In that case, reach deep into your pot of paint and use a thick brush to apply it with broad strokes! Otherwise, I strongly recommend that you use carefully prepared palettes with caution and consideration.

Lines and Borders

It's still popular to use as many lines, borders, and little boxes as possible, as is the desire to make them as intense and colorful as possible and—better still—to squash or bundle them together. This applies to tables and charts alike. Why is this so? I've no idea. In nature, there are practically no visible borders. Almost all decisions made about surroundings ("this is the object, so that must be its background") are based on the observer's impressions of light and shade. Therefore, borders do not play a significant role in human perception. Maybe we use them so much in presentations simply because the formattable gridlines of Excel and other such programs have encouraged a tendency within us to form "data prisons." How else would you explain the layouts in Figure 6-14?

Naturally, your data and its purpose will ultimately determine how many lines and borders you will use as well as their intensity and color. However, do not neglect to check the different effects they can have. The CD-ROM contains a sample model whose data is identical to Figure 6-14 but whose formatting is completely different:

On the Companion CD Open the file \Samples\0603_BordersLines.xlsx on the CD-ROM.

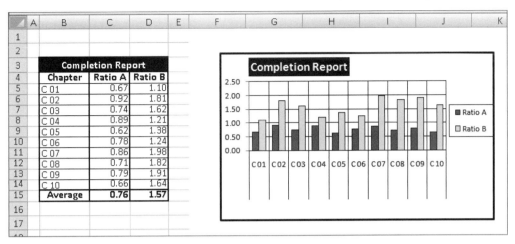

FIGURE 6-14 Better safe than sorry: numbers can never escape such prisons!

The formatting differences between the *Grid* and *RangeColoring* worksheets are considerable. While the first sheet looks as if it fell victim to a "borders fetishist," the second sheet is formatted in a way that reflects both the options available in Excel 2007 and the assertions presented in this book.

One of the new features in Excel 2007 that I particularly like is the design color palettes and their (predominantly) carefully chosen and well-coordinated combinations. When designing tables, these generally make it easy to completely dispense with the use of cell borders, as shown on the left-hand side of the *RangeColoring* worksheet and Figure 6-15.

Furthermore, the associated chart only uses lines where they support a differentiation in value or category. The intensity and color of these lines are very conservative, but nevertheless sufficient for normal-sighted observers to effortlessly distinguish between each line.

Note In the above example, both the column height (in other words, the value) and the different categories were relatively important. Consequently, horizontal and vertical gridlines were used. However, there are numerous scenarios in which you could confidently dispense with the use of either. Therefore, your routine should not always involve the use of such lines.

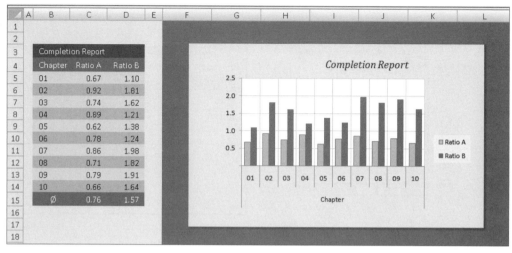

FIGURE 6-15 The table does not need any borderlines, while the chart needs only a few.

The following three comments concern the labels used on the primary horizontal axis in both examples:

- In both sheets, the reference to these two-row axis labels is A5:B14.

- In the *Grid* worksheet, a space was entered in each cell in the area A5:A15. The presence of these spaces (even if you can't see them) next to the primary label texts causes Excel to use lines to separate the axis labels in the chart.

- In the *RangeColoring* worksheet, cell A5 contains the hidden formatted text *Chapter*. The remaining cells in the reference area A5:A15 are empty. This specification causes Excel to use lines to separate the axis labels for the first caption line while the second only obtains an outer box and its content—the text from A5—is centered.

> **Note** You can access the axis label references by right-clicking the chart and choosing *Select Data* from the context menu. On the right-hand side of the dialog box displayed (for ... *Axis Labels* ...), click the *Edit* button.

A Question of Ergonomics

A neutral definition of ergonomics is the adaptation of working conditions to human capabilities. Therefore, an ergonomic chart design is one in which the user has the best possible "working conditions" on his screen. In this section, I will discuss only those models that require action by the user.

A dynamic chart can't be dynamic all by itself. To be dynamic, it needs a user who creates certain displays with certain intentions. Which actions are necessary? How, with what, and where? This is where ergonomic design comes into play. These are extremely important and complex questions because they have a lot to do with the level of acceptance that your solutions receive. However, don't worry. I will keep this section brief and practical. If you wish to obtain more detailed theoretical information about ergonomics, the international ISO 9241 standard, "Ergonomics of Human System Interaction," has hundreds of specifications and guidelines.

The structures of the two solutions shown in Figure 6-16 enable me to make some important comments on ergonomics. You were introduced to Model A in Figure 6-1 and Model B in Figure 6-3. They exhibit one major difference in terms of ergonomics: in Model A, the controls for "click actions" by the user are to the right of the data series, while they are to the left in Model B. Why is this?

Even though the practical use of controls will not be discussed until Chapter 7, their selection and positioning applies to both theoretical and fundamental questions that have far-reaching consequences for composition strategies. As a result, let's take a moment to address some of the relevant design standards.

- The primacy for selecting and positioning controls belongs to the chart's "information logic." What is to be used, where it's to be used, and how it's to be used depend on the type, value structure, content density, and presentation objective. All other points (even the points outlined below) are secondary.

- The user should:
  - ❑ Not adopt unnecessarily long approaches to locating a control
  - ❑ Not be forced to "make long jumps" between elements
  - ❑ Be supported by visual signals, if necessary

- Preferably, various different controls that produce similar or identical effects should be positioned next to each other.

- When selecting and positioning controls, you should also take account of the symbolic nature of their use: is something hanging from it (see the "plumb line" in Figure 6-17 below) or standing on it? Has it been dragged, moved (from where to where), lifted, lowered, inserted (back and forth or on and off)?

- An interdependency between the switch and its effect should be immediately discernible and spatially coordinated if possible. Consider, for example, that there are drivers who, despite having spent several years behind the wheel, can't seem to get used to having a button for controlling an electric window in the central console, and not next to the window itself.

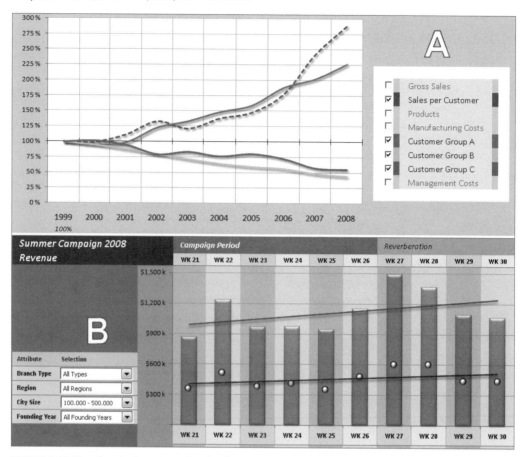

FIGURE 6-16 Use of controls to customize the chart content

Model A   The presenter uses eight *CheckBoxes* to show or hide the chart lines at random. In this chart, the trend lines and their progressive deviation from the 100 percent axis or other base lines are extremely important. The *primary horizontal axis* stretches over a 10-year period and the real-time aspect of the *plot area* is on the right. With a mouse click, the user can quickly generate a new version of the chart on the left. Here, the quickly discernible interdependency (requested above) between the switch and its effect is also supported by the color change in the legend area. A logically effective response occurs immediately next to the switch; namely, colors intensify with "On" and fade with "Off."

Model B   You operate four drop-down lists known as *ComboBoxes* to expand an existing column chart with another data series (points with a trend line) composed according to your chosen criteria. Here, it was not as easy to set up an ergonomically acceptable sheet structure as it was in Model A, mainly because the chart is not "free." As a transparent object that uses the table background for its different formations, the chart has its position tied to those table columns that contain the calendar weeks and their data. These, in turn, can't be arranged on the left of this worksheet—which can also be used for filtering purposes—because the leading data of the data rows must be displayed here. In short the controls cannot be positioned to the right of the chart. They *must* be positioned to the left of the chart (it will be easier to understand in Chapter 10 where you'll take a closer look at the model). This fundamental disadvantage for right-handed people (as they must grasp beyond their reach) is relatively minor here because all of the other conditions addressed in the above box were sufficient. Here, it is particularly interesting to note the following: the user employs his selection combination to create a data series that is almost always a subset of the whole (the column height) and therefore appears in the lower half of the chart. Consequently, the controls and their labels are positioned at the height of the lower third of the chart. This gives rise to a direct spatial interdependency between the user's action and its result.

Completely different design premises played a role in the chart shown in Figure 6-17:

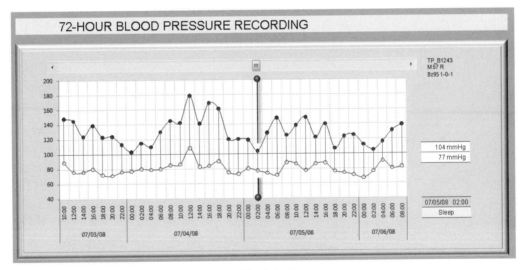

FIGURE 6-17 A control (*Scroll Bar*) as "rails" for a "plumb line"

Here, the function of the *scroll bar* control is comparable with the guide rails for the plumb line of a curtain. To direct the observers' attention, the presenter draws a vertical marker line through the two rows of 36 data points that measure blood pressure over a period of 72 hours. The data associated with the points that the movable marker touches are displayed in a tabular legend (center and lower right) as value, time, and status information (here, status means the sleep-wake state of the patient).

In such constructions, it is completely logical for the scroll bar's "slider" to appear directly above the marker line because it is effectively its "point of suspension." Therefore, whatever setting the user makes will be set *wherever* he made the setting. Here, the scroll bar is purely a technical element that is irrelevant in terms of design. It would not make ergonomic sense to shorten it, place it elsewhere, or replace it with another less space-consuming control.

I'd like to make a final comment on the unusual area design of this object: in terms of content, the chart's data shows an interdependency that is important for the chart's overall evaluation. The values themselves and the gaps between them are important, but also the lines across the time interval are particularly significant. Therefore, for evaluation purposes, it is necessary to represent all 36 value pairs as a long chain and a complete entity. Because the screen design makes it inappropriate to reduce the width of this chart, we simply have to tolerate the elongated landscape format.

Do Your Figures Need More Format?

I can't respond to this question from a content and quality perspective, nor do I wish to. However, it is necessary to comment on their appearance in tables or charts.

Appearances Can Be Deceptive

On the Companion CD Open the file \Samples\0604_DateFormats.xlsx on the CD-ROM.

The following important fact is known by most users, but is frequently overlooked in terms of its effects: what you see in an Excel table cell or in an Excel chart label does not necessarily have to be what this cell actually contains. Failure to recognize this often leads to painstaking troubleshooting. Date values demonstrate this point particularly well. Considering the example in Figure 6-18, the number 39685 is contained in each cell in the area C3:C15. Here, *you* see formatted versions of the number 39685, but Excel only "sees" the value 39685 in each of these cells (and can therefore use it in calculations).

Note The date 25.08.2008 was the 39,685th day after 01.01.1900. However, instead of using a date notation that we can interpret, Excel uses serial numbers (that is, a continuous count), so that it can calculate calendar dates. If you enter a date in the usual way or, for example, write the actual system date using the formula =TODAY() or the key combination **Ctrl+Shift+;**, the serial number that Excel requires is automatically generated and then displayed in such a way that it is "legible for humans."

The same applies to times, which Excel calculates by using the value 1 for 24 hours and a fraction of 1 for a specific time. Therefore, *high noon* is not 12.0, but 0.5.

A	B	C	D	E	F	G
	No.	Value of all cells is 39685		Formats (mostly custom)		
	01	08/25/08		mm/dd/yy		
	02	Mon 25-Aug-2008		ddd dd-mmm-yyyy		
	03	Monday, 08/25/2008		dddd, mm/dd/yyyy		
	04	8/25/2008		m/d/yyyy" "		
	05	2008–08–25		yyyy–mm–dd		
	06	25-Aug-08 was a Monday		dd-mmm-yy" was a "dddd		
	07	Monday		dddd		
	08	payable before ---------------- 8/25/08		" payable before "*-m/d/yy" "		
	09	Year: 2008 • Month: August • Day: 25		"Year: "yyyy" • Month: "mmmm" • Day: "dd		
	10	This is day 39685		" This is day "General		
	11	USD 39,685.00		"USD "#,##0.00" "		
	12	39685		General		
	13	39685		@		

FIGURE 6-18 What you can make from *39685*, and some more.

Let's look at the sequential numbering in Figure 6-18. On the left-hand side of the figure (Column C), you see several different "appearances" of the same number. On the right-hand side of the figure (Column E), you see the custom formats that are responsible for these display formats. The next section will describe how you can create these custom formats.

1. The format mm/dd/yy is the popular standard for calendar dates to be arranged into neatly aligned vertical columns. Each date comprises three sets of two numbers with two separating forward slashes. The mm and dd formats instruct Excel to proceed as follows: "write the month and day as two-digit numbers." In the case of the year, one y would also prompt the two-digit notation.

2. The format ddd   dd-mmm-yyyy writes the weekday (automatically determined by Excel) as abbreviated text followed by two spaces: the day as a two-digit number with a hyphen, the month as "Aug," a hyphen, and a four-digit year.

3. The format dddd,   mm/dd/yyyy writes the weekday in full followed by a comma, two spaces, and the date format that you know from Point 1 above, but with a four-digit year.

4. In principle, the format m/d/yyyy"   " corresponds to Point 1 above without forcing a two-digit display for the month and year. Furthermore, the date is enhanced by three spaces between the quotation marks. This moves the visible cell content away from the cell's right-hand margin. I frequently use variations of this method (a different number of spaces) to prevent the cell content from "sticking" to the gridlines. Because it is so

important, allow me to repeat myself: the spaces generated in this way do not exist in the cell; they are merely displayed.

You can also add spaces without quotation marks to a number format. In this case, however, this would be unfavorable because the spaces would not be recognized as part of the format in the corresponding lists (see Figure 6-19).

> **Note** You can add the following characters without quotation marks to a number format: € $ - + / ( ) : ! ^ & ~ { } = < > and the space. However, if you want to connect such characters with other characters, for example, to display *1,234 k $*, you must once again use the quotation marks in the format code. The next section will provide information about the sample format #,##0.00," k $ ".

5. Similarly, the format yyyy-mm-dd or yy-mm-dd is easy to understand. This notation is also the most advantageous because it is easy to sort.

6. The format dd-mmm-yy" was a "dddd, which comprises independent text, the date, and the text generated by the format, now no longer requires a detailed explanation.

7. The format dddd reduces the display for the number 39685 to the full text of the weekday for this date.

8. The format "   payable before "*-m/d/yy"   " begins with text (that also contains spaces). Then the character that follows the asterisk is repeated as long as the cell has space until the start of the date display. Therefore, in this scenario, the following is true: wide cell = lots of dashes, narrow cell = very few dashes, but always a completely filled cell in either case. The asterisk in the format is an instruction to repeat the character that follows it (even it this character is a space) until the place is full.

9. The format "Year: "yyyy" · Month: "mmmm" · Day: "dd is a variant of Point 5 above. Additional text explicitly mentions the words "year," "month," and "day," each of which is separated by a centered bullet (more information below).

10. The format " This is day "General explains which Excel-specific "day number" this concerns. The text in quotation marks is written in advance and then followed by the actual number. The format General shows the actual cell content.

11. The format "USD "#,##0.00"   " does not make sense here because it converts a date value into a currency amount. However, take a closer look at the formatting used (the thousand separator and two decimal places) as it will play a role later in this chapter.

12. The same as Point 10, but without the introductory text.

13. The formatting mark @ defines the number as text. Therefore, within the cell, it moves to the left if the alignment formatting does not prompt any other changes to the cell.

Note Here is some supplementary information: the one-digit numbers in the cell area B3:B15 in Figure 6-18 display a leading zero. This zero does not exist in the cell, but rather is created by a format. I generally center such numbering. To produce a neat column, one-digit numbers should also be displayed as two-digit numbers. This is achieved with the custom number format 00. If required, a three-digit number format could be achieved with the format 000, and so on.

Creating and Assigning Custom Formats

You can define custom number formats from scratch (using format codes that you have entered yourself) or you can base new number formats on existing formats. These existing formats can be both integrated number formats and your own defined creations.

Note Custom number formats are saved along with the workbook in which they are created. Therefore, if you want to access a number format that you have already created, but you're now working in a new file, you must copy the number format to this new file. The next section provides information on this topic.

Number formats are defined using encoding that must be stored in accordance with specific syntax rules. First, let's look at a simple example (already mentioned above): in a sequential number series, you want a leading zero to precede the one-digit numbers 1 to 9. Using the example in Figure 6-19:

1. Select the area that contains the numbers to be formatted. In the Ribbon, activate the *Home* tab and click the lower right arrow symbol in the *Number* group. The *Format Cells* dialog box is displayed with the active *Number* tab. (Alternative procedure: right-click the selected table area and choose the *Format Cells* command from the context menu. Then activate the *Number* tab in the dialog box.)

2. On the left-hand side of the tab page, choose the *Custom* entry for *Category*.

3. Highlight the content (the current format code) in the *Type* input line, so that you can then overwrite it. Alternatively, simply delete the content.

4. Enter the code 00 and choose *OK* to assign it to the selected table area.

If you want to use the format that you have defined in this way somewhere else in this workbook, open the dialog box (as described above) and choose what you need from the format list on the *Number* tab page. Excel places the custom number formats at the end of this list.

To delete a custom format, select the format, and then click the *Delete* button.

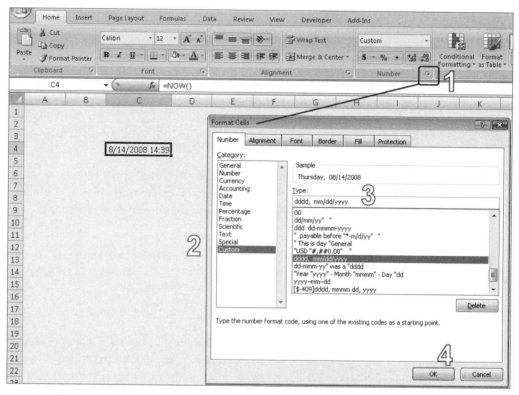

FIGURE 6-19 The custom number formats are placed at the end of the list.

To use the encoding of an existing format as the basis for a new format, proceed as follows. The task: you want to shorten numbers already formatted with the thousand separator and two decimal places to a "thousand," remove the decimal places, and insert the text character k $. The number 123456.78, currently displayed as 123,456.78, should appear as *123.46 k $* and be moved one space away from the cell's right-hand margin.

1. Select the cells whose existing format you wish to change and open the dialog box for number formatting as described above.

2. Click the *Custom* entry for *Category*. If the selected numbers have a uniform format, the current format code is imported into the *Type* input line. Here, the encoding is, for example, #,##0.00 (the differences between the # and 0 format codes will be explained below).

3. Supplement the code as follows: a comma and the character sequence quotation mark, space, k, space, $, space, quotation mark. Therefore, #,##0.00 should become #,##0.00," k $ ".

4. To complete the task, choose *OK*. The number *123456.78* is then shown as *123.46 k $*, and it's all indented one space from the right.

Let me explain the formatting marks 0, # (digit placeholder) and , (comma, thousand format),

To format numbers with decimal places, add a digit placeholder to the format (after the decimal point). If a number has more digits after the decimal point than placeholders in the format code, the number in your display is rounded accordingly.

> **Important** It's important to remember that the number *displayed* is the rounded, not the actual value. If Excel uses the number handled in this way in a calculation, it will continue to use the actual value. Therefore, formatting a number does not influence its saved value. Excel generally calculates with a precision of 15 decimal places, whether or not you see these places in a cell.
>
> However, you can use the *Precision as displayed* option to adjust the precision of calculations in a workbook to the formatted numbers currently displayed. This permanently changes all of the values to the formatted values. Then you cannot revert to the values that existed originally.
>
> How it works: Click the *Office Button*, choose the *Excel Options* command button, and then the *Advanced* category. In the *When calculating this workbook* section, activate the checkbox next to *Set precision as displayed*.

If there are more digits than placeholders *before* the decimal point, these digits are also displayed. If the format only contains octothorpes (the number sign / hash mark # as placeholder) before the decimal point, numbers lower than 1 begin with a decimal point.

The digit placeholder 0 (zero) is a "mandatory" character. The position encoded in the format in this way *must* be displayed, even if the number formatted in this way does not contain a corresponding value. Therefore, for example, a *1* with the format 0.00 becomes *1.00* or—as described earlier—a *1* with the format 00 becomes *01*.

The digit placeholder # is an "optional" character. The position encoded in the format in this way *can* be displayed if the number formatted at this position does contain a corresponding value. The *1* in the format #,##0.0 is displayed as *1.0* and the number *12345.67* in the same format as *12,345.7*.

The formatting mark , (comma) creates the thousand separator *within* the code, but it also shortens the display to "thousands" at the end of any number code. Therefore, two commas at the end shorten to millions. Such examples are given in the discussion of Figure 6-21. There, you will also obtain information about using the digit placeholder ? (question mark).

Documenting and Copying Number Formats

Even if you are proficient in creating custom number formats, there will always be times when you want to quickly assign a specific custom format that you have used before but have now forgotten how to encode because you last used it so long ago.

If you want to avoid these hiccups, you can create documented sample files that not only jog your memory, but also allow the required format to be copied directly to a target file. The *NumberFormat.xlsx* file on the CD-ROM is one such template that you can use.

> **On the Companion CD** Open the file *Materials\NumberFormat.xlsx* on the CD-ROM.
>
> The *Number Formats 1* worksheet corresponds to Figure 6-20, and the *Number Formats 2* worksheet corresponds to Figure 6-21.

Anyone who uses Excel to accomplish operational reporting systems for internal or external purposes (which other program would be better suited to this task?) possibly has good uses for the specifications contained in this file. First, let's take a look at the example in the *Number Formats 1* worksheet.

The task: You want the numbers that appear in periodic reports to automatically be shown with a striking value-dependent color: success values in blue, failure values in red, and zero values in black. Because an excess in sales, for example, is usually favorable, but an excess in costs is usually unfavorable, two different formats are required here: one format that colors positive numbers blue and negative numbers red, and one that colors positive numbers red and negative numbers blue. Such flexibility is achieved through the use of number formats, as shown in Figure 6-20. In Columns C and I, you see a total of four blocks with formatted numbers. The parentheses in Columns D and J reference the format code defined here as documentation text, as it was determined for the corresponding cells in Columns C and I.

Here, I used threepart formats whose sections were subdivided by semicolons. The format code in the first section applies to positive numbers, the second to negative numbers, and the third to zero values.

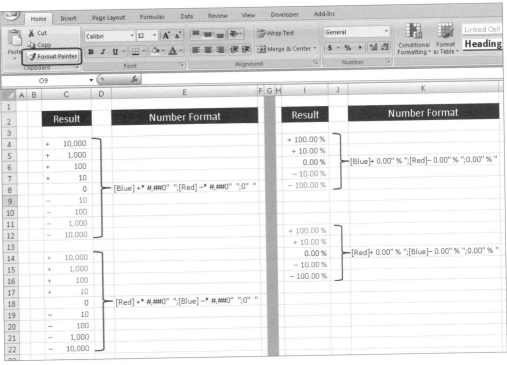

FIGURE 6-20 A template for copying number formats to other files

- Let me describe the formatting [Blue] +* #,##0"   ";[Red] -* #,##0"   ";0"   " for the cells C4:C12 as an informal instruction to Excel:

  - First section: write positive numbers in blue, begin with a space, then write a plus sign, then enter as many spaces (the character after the asterisk) for which the cell has places until the beginning of the number, then write the number with a thousands separator and without decimal places, and close with two spaces.

  - Second section: write negative numbers in red, begin with a space, then write a "wide minus sign" (an *en dash*, ANSI character 150, for which additional information is available in Chapter 12), then write as many spaces as the cell can hold until the beginning of the number, then write the number with a thousands separator and without decimal places, and close with two spaces.

  - Third section: write zero values without defining a color (that is, use the default font color) and close with two spaces.

By inserting an unknown number of spaces (depending on the column width), you create vertical uniformly aligned "leading sign columns" that simplify the overview in printed versions, in particular, and also make a good impression.

> **Note** The color assignments for a format must always be in square brackets and located in the first place in the relevant formatting section. You can use the following text color definitions: [Black], [Blue], [Cyan], [Green], [Magenta], [Red], [White], and [Yellow].
>
> The conditional checks that can be used in format codes are also set in square brackets, as can be seen in an example above. If color assignments and conditional checks are used together, the color encoding is placed before the conditional check. Example: the two-part format [Blue] [>800]#,##0 $;[Red][<300]0 $ ensures that dollar values greater than 800 are colored blue, values lower than 300 are colored red, and every value in between is displayed in the default font color.

The format in cells C14:C22 is identical up to the reversed color values (plus = red, minus = blue).

The formats in the cell areas I4:I8 and I12:I16 use the aforementioned principle, but dispense with using spaces between the leading character and the number. Instead, as a special feature, they show a space between the number and the percentage. In order to comply with some national conventions, I use the latter, which deviates from the Excel standard (what does not provide for a space for integrated percentage formatting).

Therefore, the worksheet contains cells with formatted numbers as well as the corresponding format codes for documentation purposes. However, the worksheet is not for read-only purposes. You can also use it without difficulty.

Do you require one of the formats in a target file?

1. In the source file, select a cell that contains the format of your choice. Then, in the Ribbon, click the *Home* tab and choose the *Format Painter* command button, (indicated by an rectangular shape in Figure 6-20) in the *Clipboard* group.

2. Switch to the target file and use the mouse to indicate the cells to which this format should be assigned.

As an alternative, copy formatted cells in the source files, switch to the target file, mark the target cells, and choose the command *Paste*, *Paste Special*, and the *Formats* option.

You may want to save yourself the hassle of writing relatively complex format code and instead use the format code text that you defined in the source file for documentation purposes in another file as a template for another similar format code. In that case:

1. In the source file, select the cell that contains the code text and then select this text in the formula bar.

2. Use **Ctrl+C** to copy the selected content in the formula bar to the clipboard. Then press **Esc** to cancel editing mode.

3. Switch to the target file. Select the cells for which you want to use a modified version of the format code.

4. Open the *Format Cells* dialog box with the *Number* tab. Click the *Custom* entry for *Category* and delete or select the content in the *Type* input line.

5. Use **Ctrl+V** to paste the content of the clipboard and change it, if necessary. Then choose *OK* to assign the format.

The use of the *Number Formats 2* worksheet, shown in Figure 6-21, is in line with my earlier comments: it is a piece of documentation and, at the same time, a template for copying formats. However, you will find another enhanced documentation structure here. It allows you to test the effects of applying the formatting without losing sight of what you have actually entered and how the formatting alters this input.

The left-hand side of the sheet is described below, while the right-hand side has been left blank for your own purposes.

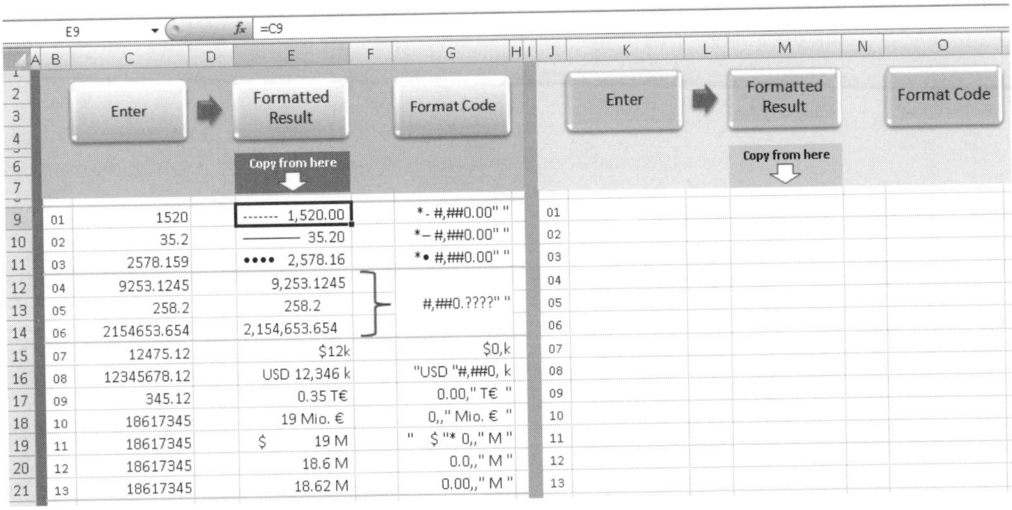

FIGURE 6-21 How to clearly document your custom number formats

- Column C with *Enter* as its header is formatted as *standard*. Here, you enter values whose formatted appearance you wish to view in Column E.

- Column E, which has *Formatted Result* as its header, contains simple reference formulas that copy the input values from Column C, line for line. The individual cells in Column E are configured with different custom number formats that you can easily copy to other files using the procedure described above.

- The number format code that was set up for the cells in Column E is documented in the neighboring cells in Column G.

Here are a few comments in relation to the formats that we have defined:

- Cells E9:E11: Various "fill" characters, the number of which is determined by the column width, are entered in the format code after the asterisk (as introduced above). From top to bottom:

  - The "hyphen," which is the minus sign on the keyboard.

  - The "en dash" (ANSI character 150; additional information available in Chapter 12), which is twice as long as the hyphen and already shown in Figure 6-20. If you enter this character repeatedly, you create a continuous vertically centered line, at least when you use most default fonts.

  - The vertically centered bullet, (ANSI character 149; more information available in Chapter 12).

- Cells E12:E14: use the placeholder ? (question mark) to consistently align numbers to the decimal point in the case of number columns with a different number of decimal places. This placeholder replaces insignificant zeros with spaces.

- Cells E15:E21: several different thousands and millions formats both with and without currency symbols (thousands = a comma after the number formatting. millions = two commas after the number formatting).

Number Formatting in Charts

Naturally, you can also use all number formats (including custom formats) in charts. Here, they are essentially required to set up the axis labels. Occasionally, they are also used to label data points, and you will learn some tricks for doing this.

The procedure differs slightly from what you may already know from earlier versions of Excel. In the context of Figure 6-22:

First select the axis (or the element for whose label you wish to determine a number format) and then open the formatting dialog box. Then click *Number*.

- If you want to use the number formats that exist in the chart's data source, activate the *Linked to source* checkbox on the Number tab page. If you then want to change the number format in the data source, this change is also copied to the chart.

- If you want to use number formats that are independent of the chart's data source, deactivate the *Linked to source* checkbox. Then select a *category* to import the available formats into the *Type* list. Choose from these entries.

- If you want to set up a custom number format in the chart, click the *Custom* entry for *Category*, enter the corresponding code in the *Format Code* input line, and then click *Add* to assign your definition and add it to the *Type* list. If, when entering the code, you make a mistake that prevents Excel from applying the formatting, the program does not notify you. When you click Add, nothing happens and you are simply left to figure out why it won't work.

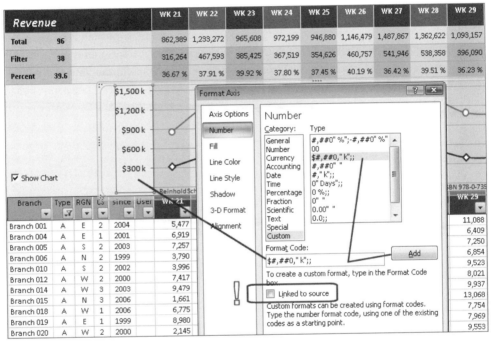

FIGURE 6-22 You can also use custom number formats in charts.

Note In Figure 6-22, you will recognize a custom format that I frequently use in charts but rarely in tables. In its basic form `$#,##0," k";;` (the desired number format followed by two semicolons), it prevents Excel from displaying negative numbers and zero values (a threepart format in which negative numbers and zero values are not defined).

Its main purpose is to suppress the display of zeros, which are not only meaningless or superfluous for some chart designs, but can also be distracting.

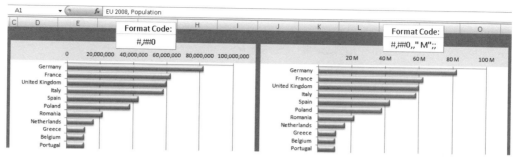

FIGURE 6-23 Dispense with superfluous zeros when formatting numbers in charts

Note that you don't have to use your chart to display numbers. Instead, you may want to show relationships, scenarios, or tendencies. Use the option to format your axis labels irrespective of the tabular source data and dispense with anything that is unnecessary. Therefore, do not use decimal places if they do not serve any immediate informational purpose, and shorten your numbers to "thousands" if you can. In short, keep number formatting in charts as clear and concise as possible and make use of the many formatting options that Excel has to offer.

Chapter 7
Elements of Dynamization

From here on, we're going to slowly but surely pick up steam. I've already mentioned dynamic, multivariable Excel solutions a couple of times, and you've already encountered some (admittedly rather rudimentary) examples of these. By the end of this chapter, you'll be more familiar with the four components that really allow you to make the most of Excel's flexibility and the benefits it offers in terms of visualization. The necessary structural basis is provided by the rS1.Method. In this chapter, we'll combine the use of:

- Standardized range names

- Controls

- Extracting formulas

- Conditional formatting

In order to follow the instructions here without difficulty and to implement these with ease in the exercises I suggest or those of your own design, you'll need to feel at home with some of the content covered earlier. This content includes:

- The 32-page attachment, \Materials\rS1_Method_2007.pdf, on the CD-ROM. The information it provides about naming conventions (Sections 3.2. and 3.3.) and controls (Section 3.4.4) is particularly important for understanding the descriptions below and putting these into practice.

- The section entitled "A Solution Emerges" in Chapter 2, "New Approaches—Getting Started." It explains some of the elements and techniques that will play roles here. Ideally, you'll not only have read the step-by-step instructions in that section, but also have followed these with some exercises of your own.

- Chapter 5, "Graphical Objects," which explains how to deal with graphical objects. In this chapter, we'll also examine the controls that can be created, copied, and changed in essentially the same way as drawing objects.

Theme and Variations

A small analysis of key indicators is used as an example throughout this chapter. Three files are provided on the CD-ROM for this purpose:

- \Samples\0701_Indicators_01.xlsx (variant no. 1, the "green" variant; so named because of the dominant color in the *Focus 1* worksheet), in which you'll use some basic form controls to dynamize the chart display in the *Focus 1* worksheet. This model doesn't contain any conditional formatting.

- *\Samples\0702_Indicators_02.xlsx* (variant no. 2, the "blue" variant), which contains ActiveX controls. This variant is somewhat more extravagant and also user friendly in its appearance, and two of its worksheets contain some conditional formatting.

- *\Samples\0703_Indicators_00.xlsx*, which is a "hollow form" containing only the data and workbook structures you can use to replicate the solution (and I strongly recommend that you do).

Purpose and Structure of the Model

First, open variant 1—that is, the *\Samples\0701_Indicators_01.xlsx* file—and familiarize yourself with its content and functions.

> **Note** The slightly more complex *0702_Indicators_02.xlsx* model is introduced later in the chapter. However, because that section primarily focuses on deviations from the basic variant described here, as well as the elimination of shortcomings and functional enhancements, it would be very useful for you to become familiar with this simpler version at this stage. Remember, too, that when it comes to putting the theory into practice, you won't always need to make use of all the bells and whistles available, no matter how convenient or attractive they are.

Which Analyses Can We Run?

The Management team at a manufacturing company periodically instructs the Controlling department to calculate certain key performance indicators using a dynamic Excel solution for analysis and evaluation. The summarized version provided here contains the monthly indicators for *Cash Ratio, Quick Ratio, Current Ratio, Profit-Turnover Ratio, Outstanding Receivables Quota, Debt Quota, Production Volume, Utilized Capacity, Quantity stored, Labor Time performed, Absence from Work,* and *Employee Turnover.* All figures are expressed as percentages. The figures for January through October 2008 are shown.

You'll notice many similarities to the chart solution introduced in Chapter 2. However, the selection options there were rather one-dimensional (a comparison of two data series of the same type). Here, however, you can control four different kinds of information with just a few mouse clicks:

- The length of a data series (the number of month-specific markers shown)

- The category of data series displayed

- The choice of showing or hiding the company-internal margins defined for the category selected (values may fluctuate within the range from – to)

- The choice of showing or hiding the industry average for the selected category

Management can make different selections in the *Focus 1* worksheet while analyzing the data. Note the following points with reference to Figure 7-1:

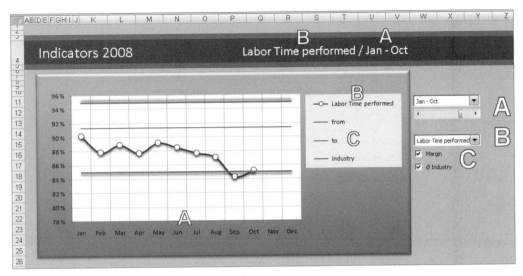

FIGURE 7-1 Five controls determine the content of the dynamic chart.

- Controls *A*, on the right of the chart: The *combo box* control has a drop-down list, in which you can choose between 12 different time intervals: the month of January plus all of the possible intervals ranging from the start of January to the end of any other month in the same year. Clicking on the relevant entry determines how many subsequent months' data is displayed in a blue data series with round markers. If the monthly values for a certain month aren't yet available (as is the case for November and December in the example shown), the data series isn't extended. The period shown is also indicated as a text in the chart header.

  This drop-down list is linked with a *scroll bar* control. You can use this control in the same way to lengthen or shorten the data series to show the data from a certain period of time (from January to ...).

> **Note** To some, this option for changing the length of a data series may appear nothing more than a design frill. However, I consider it to be an interesting and useful option for two reasons. First, it allows you to reveal your data in stages over the course of a presentation (which, in many cases, will help your audience to understand the point you want to convey). Second, it allows you to easily pass on information in a condensed version, while ensuring that your data set is still complete and up-to-date. This could be useful for external reporting.

- Control *B*: Another *combo box* allows you to specify which of the 12 indicator series is shown in the main data series of the chart mentioned in relation to control A above. The indicator category selected is also shown in the chart header.

- Controls C: The two checkboxes allow you to decide whether to show three indicator values, which are then displayed as horizontal lines.

    - If you select the *Margin* checkbox, an olive-green *from* line (bottom) and an orange *to* line appear in the chart. The values represent the company-specific margin within which fluctuations of the indicators aren't classed as critical or even problematic. Since seasonal dependencies are of no significance to this company, the same margin applies for the entire year. The two lines disappear from the chart if you deselect the checkbox. This action also removes the corresponding legend texts.

    - If you select the *Ø Industry* checkbox, a light-blue line appears, which represents the industry-specific average value for the indicator currently selected. The lines disappears from the chart if you deselect the checkbox. This action also removes the corresponding legend text.

The option to display these lines was configured as part of the design of this chart because a wide range of perspectives, requirements, and reporting obligations apply to the data it represents, and a variety of impressions can be derived from it. Play around with these options and you'll see how dramatically the effect changes; for example, a line oscillates freely, an oscillating line moves between or beyond borders, and another entwines itself around a straight line.

Excel only plays a secondary role in making this an effective solution. The most important factor is the company's ability to "own" these figures (in the true sense of the word). This involves a consistent use of indicators (which also allows management to keep track of the day-to-day flood of information) and, in particular, representation of these in the form of actual data that can be compared with specific margins based on planning and analysis and with industry values. The result is that these figures immediately tell you what can be expected, what was planned, and how (or if) both can be aligned with reality. All that's missing is the option of comparing the data with older data from previous years. This feature was indeed part of the real-life solution on which this example was based, and I've only omitted it here for the sake of clarity.

In its simplified version, the model has some small inconsistencies and fallings and, on closer inspection, also reveals a number of information gaps. Some of these are eliminated in variant 2 (discussed later). First, I want to provide some information about the basic structural components of the solution, which are almost identical in both variants.

How Is the Workbook Structured?

The structure of the workbook is based on the precepts of the rS1.Method. The individual worksheets are described below, proceeding from right to left or, technically speaking, from "back to front."

NamesIndex **Worksheet**   The 10 range names assigned in this workbook are listed here, together with their references. This worksheet serves as documentation only. Creating a model like this helps you keep track of the various interdependencies and the arguments of the formulas used. It also helps you detect naming errors or reference errors.

To generate a list like this, select the top left cell in the range in which you want the list to appear, and press **F3**. In the *Paste Name* dialog box that appears, click the *Paste List* button, and then optimize the width of the two list columns so that their values can be clearly read. If a names index already exists, you must delete it before you generate a new list. This becomes necessary when you realize that some of the original names are superfluous and delete these with the *Name Manager*. In this case, the new list would be shorter than the old one, and therefore wouldn't overwrite all of the names listed.

The options for defining a range or object name are described in Section 3.4.6 of the *\Materials\rS1_Method_2007.pdf* attachment. Therefore, I'll merely provide a quick synopsis here.

Select the cell or cell range you want to name, and then use one of the following methods:

- ❑ Enter the name in the *name box* on the left of the *formula bar*, and press **Enter** to confirm.

- ❑ Select the *Formulas* tab in the Ribbon, and click the *Define Name* button in the *Defined Names* group. Then enter the name in the *New Name* dialog box.

- ❑ Select the *Formulas* tab in the Ribbon, and click the *Name Manager* button in the *Defined Names* group. Alternatively, use the **Ctrl+F3** shortcut. In the *Name Manager* dialog box, click the *New* button.

When defining range names, the last two methods described above are recommended, as they are more flexible and fail-safe than the first.

When defining object names (for example, naming controls), select the object, and then use the first method described above. If you use ActiveX controls, you can also enter the name in the *Properties* dialog box (more about that later).

Lists 1 **Worksheet**   The definition ranges of the controls are of key importance to the dynamics of a model. You'll find these in the *Lists 1* worksheet, where they're defined in accordance with the rules of the rS1.Method. For a detailed description of these, refer to Section 3.4.5 in the *\Materials\rS1_Method_2007.pdf* attachment. This is normally a boring and painstaking task. However, it will pay off because you'll accomplish the rest of your work more easily and quickly than you will with conventional methods.

Note the following concluding points on this worksheet in reference to Figure 7-2. Here, I've used the same ABC sequence from Figure 7-1, which was used earlier to describe the controls themselves.

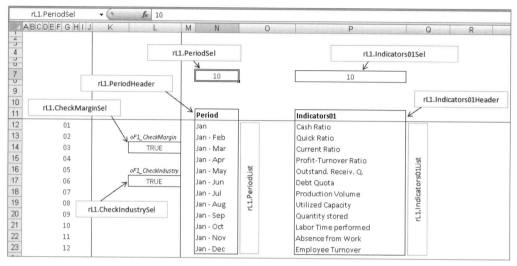

FIGURE 7-2 Of particular importance: range names in the *Lists 1* worksheet

- **Controls *A*:** There are three named ranges for the *combo box* control for selecting time periods (which has *oF1_BoxPeriod* as its object name):

    - The N12:N23 cell range with the name rL1.PeriodList contains 12 periods of time; i.e., it represents the content of the drop-down list. This data is defined in the form of constants.

    - The N11 cell with the list header is called rL1.PeriodHeader.

    - The numeric value (in this case, a number between 1 and 12) that the user generates by clicking on an entry in the drop-down list, and which is subsequently used as an argument variable by formulas, is to appear in cell N7, which has the name rL1.PeriodSel. This cell is also linked with the *scroll bar* control (object name: *oF1_ScrollPeriod*), which similarly outputs numbers between 1 and 12 depending on the action executed by the user. Because both controls share the same cell link, they are also functionally linked with each other. The *combo box* moves the slider along the *scroll bar*, while the *scroll bar*, in turn, determines the list selection in the *combo box*.

> **Note** Use a combination like this if you're using simple form controls and need both a specific, text-oriented selection option and the ability to casually "click through" a step-by-step display.
>
> If you use ActiveX controls, you can use the **up arrow** and **down arrow** keys to scroll through a drop-down list. In this case, the link shown in this example isn't necessary, at least not for this purpose.

- Control *B*: As with the *oF1_BoxPeriod* control described above, three range names have been defined for the second *combo box* (which has the object name *oF1_BoxIndicators01*): `rL1.Indicators01List` for cell range `P12:P23`, `rL1.Indicators01Header` for cell P11, and `rL1.Indicators01Sel` for cell P7. The list contents are similarly defined as constants. The name `rL1.Indicators01Header` is not used in this solution. However, it has been created here because it may well be used in a future enhancement of the solution (this type of redundancy is typical of the rS1.Method).

  You may also have spotted another deliberate redundancy. It is likely that this kind of model may also be used, in the future, to compare key indicators. In this case, you would require two functionally independent selection lists with identical content (we've seen something similar in Chapter 2). Following our naming conventions, the names of these lists would differ only by a number (*Indicators01* and *Indicators02*), which will save you a lot of time and effort later. Therefore, there's no reason not to (and good reason to) allow for that possibility when assigning names here.

Data 1 **Worksheet** All of the information that is to be visualized in the focus worksheet is gathered together here. Note the following points in relation to Figure 7-3 (working from the top down):

- In row 2 and column G, you'll recognize the standard auxiliary structures of the rS1.Method; i.e., number series, which in this case represent the respective distance from the cell named `rD1.Node` (cell J11). OFFSET formulas use this node to determine all of the values that are required by the chart basis (*Basis 1* worksheet). This worksheet contains no other names.

- The values used to represent the margins of individual indicators and their corresponding industry averages are defined in rows 6 through 8. These are calculated and input at the end of a fiscal year.

- The abbreviations denoting the indicator categories in row 9 are for information purposes only.

- The full names of the indicators in row 11 are defined as constants, as are the aforementioned short names.

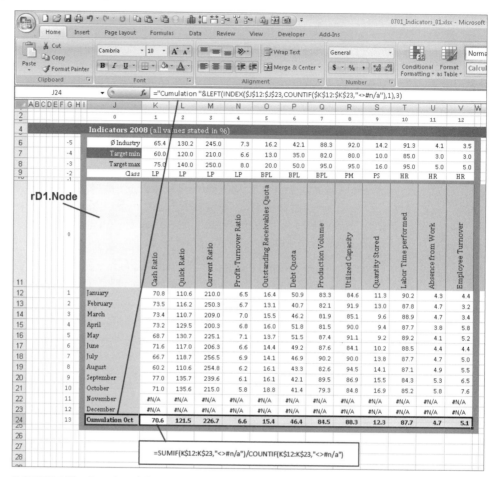

FIGURE 7-3 The *Data 1* worksheet contains all of the information that is to appear in the focus.

- The Controlling department enters the monthly values calculated for the indicators in rows 12 through 23. These are all percentages calculated from various reference values. Their display format with just a single decimal place is sufficient in this case, even for the lower values for *Profit-Turnover Ratio*, *Absence from Work*, and *Employee Turnover*. If, at any point over the year, data is not yet available to fill certain cells in accordance with the structure of this cell range, these cells are filled instead with the error value #N/A. These placeholders can then gradually be overwritten with the monthly values as they are calculated. This means that, at certain times of the month, some indicators will be calculated while others will not be available. However, thanks to the use of #N/A, the data series in the line chart will always be drawn correctly; i.e., it will end at the exact position that represents the last existing data point.

The #N/A error value in a chart basis suppresses the drawing of a data point in the re-sulting chart. This is of particular significance in line charts if some values are missing in the data table of a data series. If these were omitted entirely, gaps would appear in the line. If zero were used, the line would naturally drop to zero. The use of #N/A, however, means that the cell in question can be completely ignored when the chart is drawn, and the line simply joins up with the next available data point. If the data series ends with #N/A values, the line simply stops as instructed. Should all cells in a data series contain the value #N/A, then no data point is drawn, and so there is no line. You'll use this op-tion in our example when using controls to show and hide certain chart lines. This will become clear later in relation to our discussion of formulas in the *Basis 1* worksheet.

- The use of #N/A as a placeholder in calculation row 24 makes it a little more difficult than usual to calculate the average. The AVERAGE function cannot be used here be-cause a formula that recognizes the error value #N/A in its reference itself always has the value #N/A as its result. This is for a very good reason: it prevents incorrect calcula-tions based on incomplete data. However, as you can see in the figure above and in the worksheet, this isn't a difficult problem to overcome. For a more detailed explana-tion of the calculation used here, refer to the "Formulas" section. The same applies to the formula that is used in cell J24 to determine a text that expresses the current cumulation.

  This is the only row in the *Data 1* worksheet to contain formulas. This is different in the variant in the *0702_Indicators_02.xlsx* file, which has a more convenient configuration. More about that later.

Basis 1 **Worksheet**   This worksheet may also be a little puzzling at first to the inexperienced user (but don't worry, this won't last too long). As is usual with the rS1.Method, this work-sheet largely consists of formulas. These respond directly to changes in the values in the *Sel* cells of the *Lists 1* worksheet, and thus indirectly to actions executed by the user with the help of the controls in the *Focus 1* worksheet.

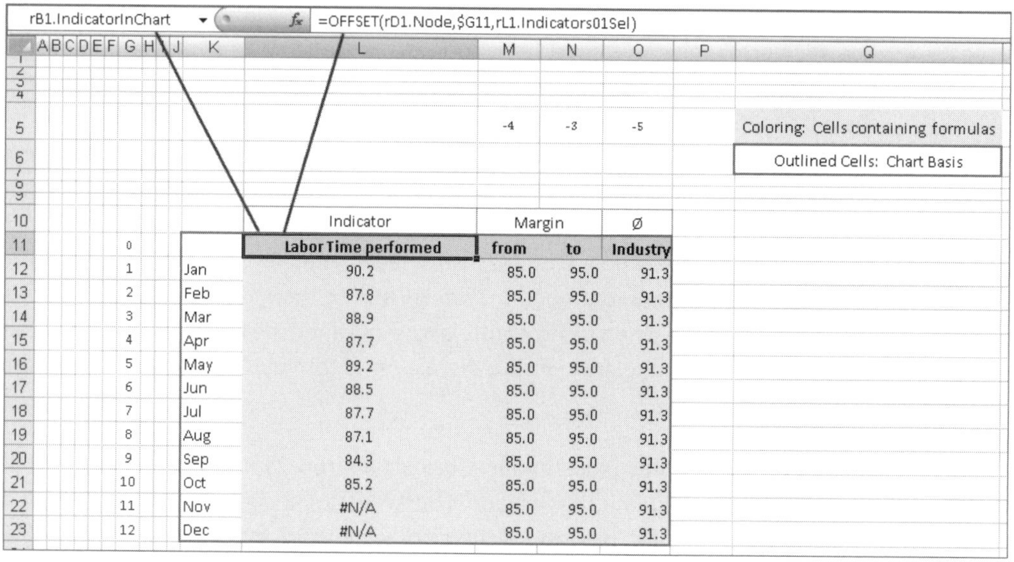

| rB1.IndicatorInChart | ▼ | f_x =OFFSET(rD1.Node,$G11,rL1.Indicators01Sel) |

		K	L	M	N	O	P	Q
5				-4	-3	-5		Coloring: Cells containing formulas
6								Outlined Cells: Chart Basis
10			Indicator	Margin		Ø		
11	0		**Labor Time performed**	**from**	**to**	**Industry**		
12	1	Jan	90.2	85.0	95.0	91.3		
13	2	Feb	87.8	85.0	95.0	91.3		
14	3	Mar	88.9	85.0	95.0	91.3		
15	4	Apr	87.7	85.0	95.0	91.3		
16	5	May	89.2	85.0	95.0	91.3		
17	6	Jun	88.5	85.0	95.0	91.3		
18	7	Jul	87.7	85.0	95.0	91.3		
19	8	Aug	87.1	85.0	95.0	91.3		
20	9	Sep	84.3	85.0	95.0	91.3		
21	10	Oct	85.2	85.0	95.0	91.3		
22	11	Nov	#N/A	85.0	95.0	91.3		
23	12	Dec	#N/A	85.0	95.0	91.3		

FIGURE 7-4 The *Basis 1* worksheet largely consists of formulas.

All of the data columns within the strong outline (range K11:O23) supply the chart content.

The L11 cell is the only cell in this worksheet to have a range name: *rB1.IndicatorInChart*. The text in this cell is also determined using a formula, and also appears as the header in the *Focus 1* worksheet; see Figure 7-5.

Focus 1 **Worksheet**   The external appearance of the solution was described and its functions explained earlier.

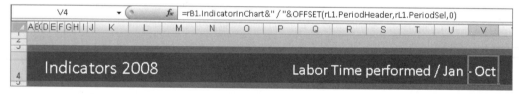

| V4 | ▼ | f_x =rB1.IndicatorInChart&" / "&OFFSET(rL1.PeriodHeader,rL1.PeriodSel,0) |

Indicators 2008   Labor Time performed / Jan - Oct

FIGURE 7-5 The header describing the current content is determined using a formula.

All I need to add at this point is the fact that the indicator category/period combination currently displayed in the chart is also specified in the chart header as a combined text. This character string is determined using a formula, which is also explained later.

So What's New in Variant 2?

So much for the structural components of the *0701_Indicators_01.xlsx* workbook, referred to below as *variant 1* and as the *basic model*. Before we examine this in more detail, there are a few key points to share about the difference between the basic model and the

0702_Indicators_02.xlsx file, whose components are discussed in detail later in the section entitled "Variant 2 (Advanced Model)."

The enhanced model is a little easier to use and, above all, implements the principles of the rS1.Method more consistently. The essential differences between it and the basic model are as follows:

- It contains a *Parameters 1* worksheet and uses formulas to transfer the data defined there to the *Data 1* and *Lists 1* worksheets. In other words, it allows for central data maintenance.

- More range names are used and are processed in formulas.

- The *Data 1* worksheet has conditional formatting, which is used to indicate where the indicators move outside of the desired or anticipated margins. In other words, it acts as an additional visualization aid.

- In the *Focus 1* workflows, the *form controls* are replaced by their equivalent *ActiveX controls*. There are also some structural changes that make the model easier to understand and to use, as well as text tips that appear whenever a period is selected in which no data is available for the final month(s).

Variant 1 (Basic Model)

This section explains the design of the *0701_Indicators_01.xlsx* file, with a particular focus on its dynamic elements. You'll also learn a little about form controls and about the use of typical rS1 range names in formulas.

Form Controls

> **Note** I'd like to remind you that the following discussion assumes that you're already familiar with some of the basic information about controls provided in Section 3.4.4 of the *\Materials\ rS1_Method_2007.pdf* file.

Basics

User-friendly controls of various types can make Excel presentation models dynamic, attractive, and foolproof. This statement—and those that follow in this introductory section—apply to both types of controls; i.e., *form controls* and *ActiveX controls*.

Controls are ready-to-use, pre-programmed tools that can also be customized. Their greatest benefit for any of the solutions described in this book is that they enable multi-variable formula access to source data. This essentially works as follows.

1. You click a control (click a list entry, select an option, click an arrow). In other words, you make a *selection*. This is a very important concept in the examples presented here because it is used when naming features of the models.

2. The control responds to the selection made with the mouse by outputting a value in a certain, user-defined cell, which, in theory, may be located anywhere in the workbook (in rS1 models, however, it is almost always located in the *Lists 1* worksheet). The control's output value is a number or a logical value. If you use *ActiveX controls*, it may also be a text.

3. The output value is the processed result of your selection. You can then use it directly or indirectly as an argument in a formula. The enormous benefit of this is that you can control part of (or, in some cases all of) the solution with your mouse without any need for programming.

The basic commands for configuring and designing controls are in the *Controls* group of the *Developer* tab in the Ribbon. If you click the *Insert* button there, a visual menu of all available objects is displayed, divided into two groups.

> **Note** The *Developer* tab is not automatically displayed after you install Excel 2007. However, you can make it permanently available by clicking the Office button/*Excel Options/Popular* tab/*Show Developer tab*.

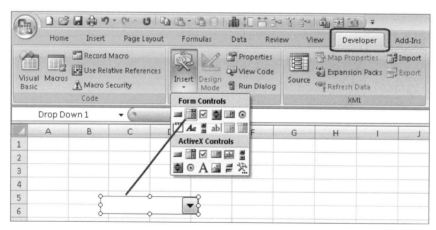

FIGURE 7-6 Controls are part of the *Developer* tab in Excel 2007.

If you want to generate a *form control*, or change the shape or size of an existing one, follow the same instructions provided for drawing objects in Chapter 5. The creation of the control itself is very simple indeed:

Note When using the rS1.Method, you should first create the control in the *Basis 1* worksheet, test it there in terms of both its functionality and its effects on the formula results, and then (and only then) copy it to its final destination in the *Focus 1* worksheet. You've already practiced using this approach in Chapter 2.

1. Click the icon of the control you want to use in the selection menu (see Figure 7-6). If you then move the mouse pointer in the worksheet (*without* holding down the mouse button), the mouse pointer changes to a crosshair.

2. Click the location where you want to position the control and, holding down the left mouse button, drag the handle diagonally until the control is the size you want (a sizing border allows you to preview the size).

Tip If you hold down the **Alt** key at the same time, the table-gridlines serve as a grid to help you size the object.

3. The control is created when you release the mouse button.

4. If you want to change the shape and size of an existing *form control*, first select the object like a graphics object by holding down the **Ctrl** key and clicking it, or by right-clicking the object, which simultaneously opens the context menu. It then appears with sizing handles and can be resized as required, just like any other graphics object. To select several controls at the same time, select each of the controls in turn while keeping the **Ctrl** key held down.

5. If you want to assign an object name to the control, keep the **Ctrl** key held down, click the object to select it, and enter a name in the *name box* in the *formula bar*.

Using Form Controls

If you've never used *form controls* to dynamize calculation models, you'll be amazed at just how much you can do in Excel with relatively simple tools. The objects can handle any requirements, thanks to flexible control. Nevertheless, the options for customizing them (formatting, functional range) are very limited. They are compatible with earlier versions of Excel (Version 5.0 and higher) and are very well suited to the design of simple models or use with electronic questionnaires. However, you should ensure that models created with these tools are rarely used in solutions with graphically complex designs and are not used in solutions that are to be subsequently enhanced with program source code.

An important question to ask yourself initially is the following: What are you hoping to achieve by doing things this way? A functionally well thought-out application will be evaluated negatively by users if it's awkward to use, unnecessarily complicated or illogical. So, when you're designing a model, you should ask yourself what's really needed, what situations are likely to arise, and how users can achieve their objectives without too much trouble. This will determine to a large degree your choice of controls and how you use them. Note the following points in relation to these:

> **Note** The list below is limited to the controls that are used in the rS1.Method, and uses the same sequence used to structure the selection menu on the *Developer* tab (see Figure 7-6), which also corresponds to the numbering used in relation to page 24 of the *Materials\rS1_Method_2007.pdf* attachment.

1. Always use a *combo box* if you want to allow users to select from a list of (in most cases) text items, and you want or need to save space on selection options when your selection list has many entries.

2. Use a *check box* if you want your user to be able to switch between YES/NO-type options (in the chart in our example, you can choose to display data series or not).

3. Use a *spin button* if you want to allow users to move step-by-step, back and forth, through a range of information. This would be the case if, for example, you want to be able to "shimmy" forwards or backwards from one month to the next within a fiscal year.

4. Use a *list box* if you want users to be able to select from a small number of list entries and if there's enough space on the screen for the object (otherwise, you can also use *combo boxes*, which are primarily intended for long lists).

5. Use *option buttons* if you want the user to be able to select from several similar alternatives (for example, one of three different rounding algorithms available for planning figures). Also use them if—this is an important factor in your choice of control—you have enough space on the screen for several option fields (otherwise, you can save space by putting all of the options in a *combo box*).

6. Use a *scroll bar* if you want the user to be able to move through a large range of information in small *or* large steps.

Configuring Form Controls

After you create a control, the next step is to configure it. Only a few simple steps are required in this case (as opposed to *ActiveX controls*). At least, they are simple and easy to follow if you've followed the conventions of the rS1.Method by creating relevant definition ranges in the *Lists 1* worksheet and assigned the "correct" names to these according to the method (see Figure 7-2).

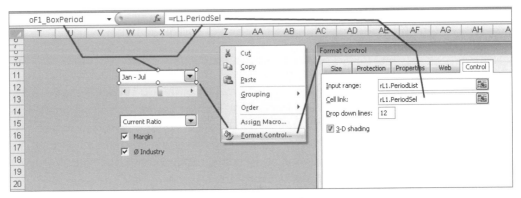

FIGURE 7-7 A simple dialog box helps you configure the control.

Now let's get back to our *0701_Indicators_01.xlsx* file. The following step-by-step instructions are based on the example of the *oF1_BoxPeriod* control (which is a *combo box*), and are illustrated in Figure 7-7. Here I'm assuming that the control is in the *Focus 1* worksheet and that it's a new element (i.e., it hasn't already been configured at this stage).

1. I admit that the rS1 range names aren't exactly convenient for entering as text. You can usually press **F3** to add an existing range name to a cell or formula. This also works in some dialog boxes, but not in all; the one here being a case in point. However, you can make your job easier by copying the correct name texts to the clipboard.

   Click the arrow to the right of the *name box* in the *formula bar*. In the names index that appears, click a name that you require in order to configure the control, for example, *rL1.PeriodSel*. This click selects the range that has this name, and *Lists 1* becomes the active worksheet, if that isn't already the case. Click the name to select it in the *name box*. Press **Ctrl+C** to copy the selected name to the clipboard. Press the **Esc** key to stop using the *name box* (not an essential step, but it's best to be on the safe side).

2. Go to the *Focus 1* worksheet, right-click the *combo box* control to select it, and open the context menu. Select the *Format Control* option. A dialog box consisting of several tabs opens.

3. Next, open the *Control* tab. Here you can define the functional properties of each control. Place the cursor in the *Cell link* box and paste the name *rL1.PeriodSel* from the clipboard (press **Ctrl+V**).

4. Press **Ctrl+V** again in the *Input range* box (this refers to the list content range, and is known as the *ListFillRange* in the case of ActiveX controls). Press **Backspace** to delete the *Sel* character string, and replace it with *List*.

5. Enter the number 12 in the *Drop down lines* box. The list has 12 entries only, so that, when a user clicks the control's drop-down arrow it will open in full, and all entries will be visible at the same time. This makes selection easier.

6. Select the *3D shading* checkbox. You should, in principle, do this for controls of this type (or at least those used on a color background) to provide a more vivid appearance.

7. Press *OK* to close the dialog box. The control has now been fully configured. Its name is displayed in the name box in the formula bar, while its cell link is shown as a formula in the formula bar itself (see Figure 7-7). Press the **Esc** key or click anywhere in the worksheet to deselect the control. Click the control's drop-down arrow to display its selection list, and click one of the list entries (for example, the third) to select it. Open the *Lists 1* worksheet to check that the number 3 has been copied to the *cell link*, which is cell *rL1.PeriodSel* in this case. Repeat this test with at least one other selection.

> **Tip** In certain cases, it may be extremely difficult to spot an error caused by incorrect configuration of a control. Therefore, it's important not to just dismiss tests like these, even if they appear silly and unnecessary. This kind of nitpicking really does pay off in the end. Anyone who's ever thought "I'm sure it'll turn out just fine," only to end up losing several valuable hours of work knows exactly what I'm talking about here.

Below you'll find a summarized overview of the individual settings made for all of the controls in the *Focus 1* worksheet. A summary of all possible control properties is provided further below in Figure 7-11.

Controls for Selecting a Period   Two controls are used to select a time period in our example. Note the following with reference to Figure 7-8:

The configuration of the *combo box* with the (optional) name of *oF1_BoxPeriod* was described in detail earlier.

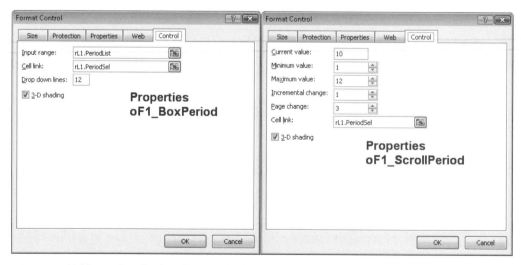

FIGURE 7-8 Making settings for the selection of a period

Since they both use the same *cell link*, the *scroll bar* with the name *oF1_ScrollPeriod* is also functionally linked with this *combo box*. Additional settings for this control:

- *Minimum value*: 1, *Maximum value*: 12, *Incremental change*: 1. This means that, each time the user clicks an arrow on the *scroll bar*, the *scroll box* (the "slider" on the control) selection will increase by an increment of 1. A value between 1 and 12 will also be displayed in the *cell link*.

- *Page change*: 3. Each click in the areas *between* the scroll box and either of the scroll arrows on the left or right of the horizontal *scroll bar* (or at the top and bottom of a vertical *scroll bar*) moves the *scroll box* forward or backward by an increment of three (or increases your selection by three).

Note If you draw an object with a width greater than its height, its direction is horizontal. If its height exceeds its width, its direction is vertical. Unfortunately, this does not also apply to *spin buttons*, which are very similar in terms of functionality.

If you use *ActiveX controls* instead, you can set a *Minimum value* that is greater than the *Maximum value* in order to reverse the direction of the control. This is well worth doing if it helps you meet specific logical and ergonomic requirements.

Control for Selecting an Indicator Category   The *combo box* with the (optional) name of *oF1_BoxIndicators01* must be configured so that an indicator category can be selected. If you've already created and configured the first *combo box* (for selecting a period) as described above, you can repeat the procedure very simply as follows thanks to the naming conventions of the rS1.Method:

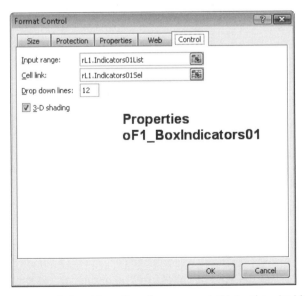

FIGURE 7-9 Apart from the references used, this is otherwise identical to the control for selecting a period.

1. Hold down the **Ctrl** key, and click the existing control object to select it.

2. Press and hold down **Ctrl** again, and use the mouse to drag a copy from the original object. If you hold down **Ctrl+Shift**, you can generate a copy that is aligned on the same axis (horizontal or vertical) as the original object.

3. The copy has the same properties as the original object. Because the number of list entries is the same in both objects in our example (12 periods and 12 indicators), you only need to change the references in the new *combo box*. To do this, simply replace the *Period* string with *Indicators01* in the *Input range* and *Cell link* boxes.

4. After a procedure like this, it's essential to test whether the new object works correctly and as desired.

Controls for Displaying Additional Data Series   The two *check boxes* allow you to enable and disable the display of additional data series in the chart. You'll find out how this works later on in our discussion of the relevant formulas in the *Basis 1* worksheet. These formulas process the output values of the two *check boxes*; that is, they respond to the value TRUE or FALSE, depending on which of these appears in the *cell links* of the controls after the user clicks to make a selection.

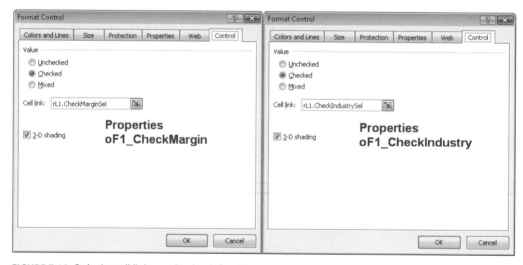

FIGURE 7-10 Only the *cell links* need to be defined here.

Proceed as described above in relation to the two *combo boxes*:

1. Start by creating the first *check box*. Select the default text (*Check box n*) in the object, and overwrite this with a text of your choice.

2. Copy the range name of the relevant cell link to the clipboard.

3. Right-click the object, and select the *Format Control* option in the context menu. Open the *Control* tab, and paste the contents of the clipboard into the *cell link*.

> **Note** As you can tell from the *Colors and Lines* tab in the dialog boxes shown in Figure 7-10, you can also define a fill color and a border for *check boxes* (as you can for *option buttons*).
>
> These or similar options are not available for other *form controls*. *ActiveX controls*, on the other hand, allow for complex formatting.

4. Test the control to verify that it works correctly.

5. Create a copy of the new control, change the description text displayed for users, and define the neighboring cell as the *cell link* for the copy. Finally, test it!

Properties of Selected Form Controls

	Form Control		Control Properties MUST (using rS1.Method)	Output Values
1	☑ Caption	Check Box	Cell Link	TRUE FALSE
2	⦿ Caption	Option Button	Cell Link	Number according to position in group
3	April / May / June / July / August / September	List Box	Input Range Cell Link	Number according to click on item
4	June ▾ / May / June / July / August / September	Combo Box	Input Range Cell Link	Number according to click on item
5	◀ ▶	Scroll Bar	Minimum Value Maximum Value Cell Link	Number according to click on arrows
6	▲▼	Spin Button	Minimum Value Maximum Value Cell Link	Number according to click on arrows

FIGURE 7-11 Properties used in the *Form Controls* in the rS1.Method

Figure 7-11 provides an overview of the control properties of the form controls used in the rS1.Method. The sequence selected there is no longer derived from the rather confusing menu provided on the *Developer* tab (see Figure 7-7). Instead, it is based on the functional "relatedness" of the various objects.

Common Properties of Controls

I used the title of this section to show that the information provided here applies equally to both types of controls.

A *Properties* tab is contained in the *Format Control* dialog box, which you can open from the context menu after you right-click the object, assuming it's a *form control*. If it's an *ActiveX control*, it can only be opened in *design mode* after you right-click the object.

FIGURE 7-12 These properties can be defined for *all* controls.

Here, you can make the same *object positioning* settings recommended for all graphics objects in Chapter 5, namely *Move but don't size with cells* or *Don't move or size with cells*. However, I would never recommend using the first option (*Move and size with cells*).

Deciding whether an object is to appear in the printed version of a solution will depend, first and foremost, on the aesthetic requirements.

- An argument for: it is useful to print controls together with a chart or table because, in most cases, they are of a similar character to a label or a legend.

- Argument against: printed controls don't generally look great.

Therefore, if you're concerned about the visual impact of the printed version, you should deactivate the printing option here in the dialog box shown, and use formulas to separately generate the important texts that are to be printed (for example, hidden *behind* the controls or elsewhere). If you can't figure out how this works based on the information in this chapter, the technique is illustrated in several examples later.

Note Unfortunately, a minor naming conflict in relation to these *properties* shows up when you use *ActiveX controls*. It has existed for years, and while it remains unresolved will continue to cause small but annoying user errors. The term *properties* is used here to describe what are in fact the complex *functional properties* of the objects. Later in the chapter, you will clearly see that this also applies (in fact, it applies first and foremost) to ActiveX controls.

Formulas

The formulas used in this model may be a little more sophisticated than what an inexperienced Excel user is used to, in particular in relation to the use of names. However, you'll soon become accustomed to such constructs and even learn to enjoy using them, in particular because they are easy to create and understand, despite their sometimes cumbersome appearances.

Note Refer to the section entitled "Entering Formulas" in Chapter 2 and, if necessary, repeat the exercises described there with the example provided in that chapter or with one of your own.

Wherever functions are used in the following text (and in later chapters) that have already been discussed earlier in the book, I'll only explain these briefly if at all (in the current example, the sources of information are Chapter 2 and the *rS1_Method_2007.pdf* file). In cases like this, you'll find the keyword index at the back of the book useful. As a rule, the first page number listed there for a function name directs you to a theoretical explanation of that function.

In a workbook structured according to the rS1.Method, calculations essentially follow the same general structure in which worksheets go from right to left or from the back to the front. The descriptions below follow this same sequence.

Whenever I mention a range containing several formulas of the same type (for example, K24:V24), I'll only explain the first formula in each case (here, the formula in cell K24). You can assume that the same explanation applies to the other formulas in the range, the only difference being the row and column references if these are used.

Formulas in the *Data 1* Worksheet

The yearly averages for the indicators are calculated here in row 24. The results of this calculation aren't required in the chart focus but are used for other purposes not specified here. However, it's worth explaining these formulas because they can also be used, in modified form, for many other purposes.

The first formula to discuss is in cell J24 (see Figure 7-13), and is also the most difficult formula in the entire workbook. It concatenates a character string with the result of three nested sub-formulas. The purpose of the exercise is as follows: we want to generate a row label for the yearly averages that always expresses the current status of the data (in the sense of complete to). The formula has 12 possible results, depending on the number of #N/A values in column K; i.e., *Cumulation Jan* through *Cumulation Dec* inclusive.

Let's examine the basic information about the functions used, before turning to the formula itself.

The =LEFT(reference,num_chars) function reads the number of characters (from left to right) in reference as determined by num_chars.

The =INDEX(array,row_num,column_num) function was described in detail in Chapter 2. It reads, within a specified cell range, a value whose position within the cell range is determined by the row and column specified.

The =COUNTIF(range,criteria) function counts the frequency with which a search term occurs in range. You usually enter the search term in a cell to which the formula refers, rather than in the formula itself (although this would be superfluous in this example). This naturally makes the formula much more flexible, because a new task can be assigned to the formula each time a new search term is entered.

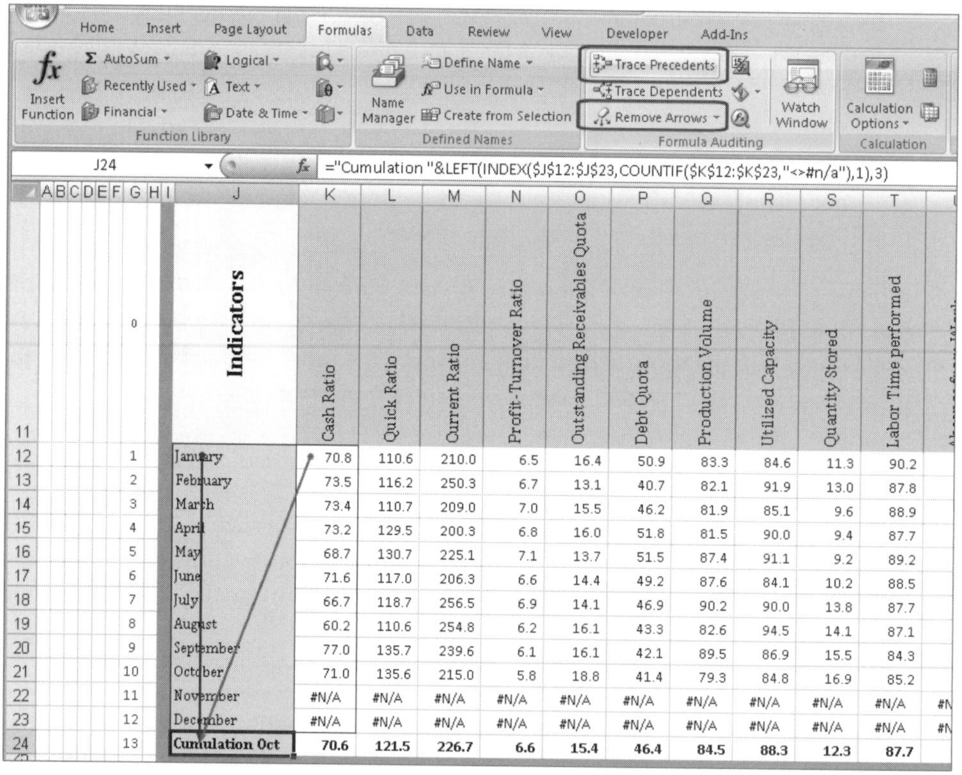

J24 ="Cumulation "&LEFT(INDEX($J$12:$J$23,COUNTIF($K$12:$K$23,"<>#n/a"),1),3)

	Indicators	Cash Ratio	Quick Ratio	Current Ratio	Profit-Turnover Ratio	Outstanding Receivables Quota	Debt Quota	Production Volume	Utilized Capacity	Quantity Stored	Labor Time performed
1	January	70.8	110.6	210.0	6.5	16.4	50.9	83.3	84.6	11.3	90.2
2	February	73.5	116.2	250.3	6.7	13.1	40.7	82.1	91.9	13.0	87.8
3	March	73.4	110.7	209.0	7.0	15.5	46.2	81.9	85.1	9.6	88.9
4	April	73.2	129.5	200.3	6.8	16.0	51.8	81.5	90.0	9.4	87.7
5	May	68.7	130.7	225.1	7.1	13.7	51.5	87.4	91.1	9.2	89.2
6	June	71.6	117.0	206.3	6.6	14.4	49.2	87.6	84.1	10.2	88.5
7	July	66.7	118.7	256.5	6.9	14.1	46.9	90.2	90.0	13.8	87.7
8	August	60.2	110.6	254.8	6.2	16.1	43.3	82.6	94.5	14.1	87.1
9	September	77.0	135.7	239.6	6.1	16.1	42.1	89.5	86.9	15.5	84.3
10	October	71.0	135.6	215.0	5.8	18.8	41.4	79.3	84.8	16.9	85.2
11	November	#N/A	#N/A	#N/A	#N/A	#N/A	#N/A	#N/A	#N/A	#N/A	#N/A
12	December	#N/A	#N/A	#N/A	#N/A	#N/A	#N/A	#N/A	#N/A	#N/A	#N/A
13	Cumulation Oct	70.6	121.5	226.7	6.6	15.4	46.4	84.5	88.3	12.3	87.7

FIGURE 7-13 A text is generated by the concatenation of a character string and three nested functions.

```
="Cumulation "&LEFT(INDEX($J$12:$J$23,COUNTIF($K$12:$K$23,"<>#N/A"),1),3)
```

The start of the formula is easy to grasp. It essentially issues the order to Excel to do the following: "Write the string *Cumulation*, followed by a blank space. Then add three text characters (this is indicated by the & text operator), which result from the remainder of the formula." This is where things become a little more difficult. The three text characters to be determined are the first three letters of the *last* month in the range J12:J23 to which *no* #N/A value is assigned in the K12:K23 range. In this example, the month in question is *October*. The correct result of the formula is therefore the text *Cumulation Oct*. Try out some alternatives in the sample file. For example, if you temporarily overwrite the data from the month of May onwards with #N/A, the formula should return *Cumulation Apr* as a result.

How does this work? It's easiest to understand if you take the nesting apart and examine its individual parts separately.

- In our example, the LEFT function should take the first three characters from the *October* string. In a very conservative and rigid form, the corresponding formula would be =LEFT("October",3).

- However, we want the formula to be a dynamic one. It should be possible to determine the first three characters in the name of *any* month in the J12:J23 range. The reference argument in the LEFT function must therefore be designed as variable.

  You can do this, for example, using the =INDEX(array,row_num,column_num) function and by making the row_num argument in this function flexible. The formula =INDEX($J$12:$J$23,10,1) would calculate the contents of row 10 and column 1 (the first and, in this case, only column) in the J12:J23 array, to give the string *October*. So there's nothing flexible there either.

  The formula =LEFT(INDEX($J$12:$J$23,10,1),3) would return the string *Oct*. That means that all we need to do now is make the row argument of the INDEX formula variable. Rather than a static *10*, we want this to be a number between *1* and *12*. But not just any number in this range. Rather, we want it to indicate the last month in the K12:K23 cell range to which no #N/A value is assigned.

- The number required for the row argument of the INDEX formula can be determined here with COUNTIF. In our example, =COUNTIF($K$12:$K$23,"<>#N/A") returns the value *10*. What it essentially instructs Excel to do is: "Count the number of entries that are not equal to #N/A in the K12:K23 range." If there were only four entries, the formula would return the number 4 instead. In this case, the row argument of the INDEX formula would be 4, and =LEFT(INDEX($J$12:$J$23,4,1),3) would return the value *Apr*.

I'll recap how these individual elements of the nesting are put together to give a complete formula, working from the inside out:

Element 3:

=COUNTIF($K$12:$K$23,"<>#N/A")

In our example, this returns the value *10*.

Element 2 with element 3 integrated:

=INDEX($J$12:$J$23,COUNTIF($K$12:$K$23,"<>#N/A"),1)

In our example, this returns the value *October*.

Element 1 with elements 2 and 3 integrated:

=LEFT(INDEX($J$12:$J$23,COUNTIF($K$12:$K$23,"<>#N/A"),1),3)

In our example, this returns the value *Oct*.

The complete formula is as follows:

="Cumulation "&LEFT(INDEX($J$12:$J$23,COUNTIF($K$12:$K$23,"<>#N/A"),1),3)

In our example, this returns the value *Cumulation Oct*.

The following three aspects are also important in building this formula:

- If you use names instead of the cell references $J$12:$J$23 and $K$12:$K$23, the formula becomes a little more unwieldy. We'll address this later in relation to variant 2.

- The formula requires that the complete K12:K23 range is filled with values from top to bottom, which are then followed by #N/A values for the months for which indicators are not yet available.

- In the company in our example, the first indicator (*Cash Ratio*) is the most important because it is the most sensitive and must be examined more than once a month. If any of the indicators are going to be ready when needed, it's this one. The K12:K23 range therefore serves as a reference range to indicate how up-to-date the data is. This is in principle a failing in the solution, but one that's acceptable without difficulty.

I should also point out that, as is almost always the case in Excel, there were several other ways in which we could have accomplished this same task. If you're an experienced user, you can take this as a hint to experiment on your own.

Let's turn now to the formulas in the K24:V24 range, which are used to calculate the average of the indicators to date. First, I'll briefly introduce another function that's needed here:

The =SUMIF(range,criteria,sum_range) function is the equivalent of COUNTIF and can be used in several different ways. It searches for criteria in range and, in the same or a parallel range (in sum_range, which may be any distance from the range), it adds together the contents of cells. The example shown in Figure 7-14 explains the principle much more effectively than a longer description that I could provide.

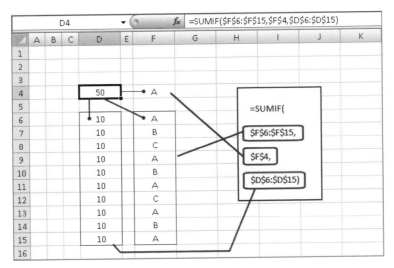

FIGURE 7-14 Syntax of the *SUMIF* function

What it essentially instructs Excel to do is as follows: "In the D6:D15 range, add up the values of the cells whose neighboring cells in column F (range F6:F15) contain the search term from cell F3 (i.e., *A*)."

The variant used in the following example doesn't require the third formula argument (sum_range) because it adds values in the same range in which the search criteria are found.

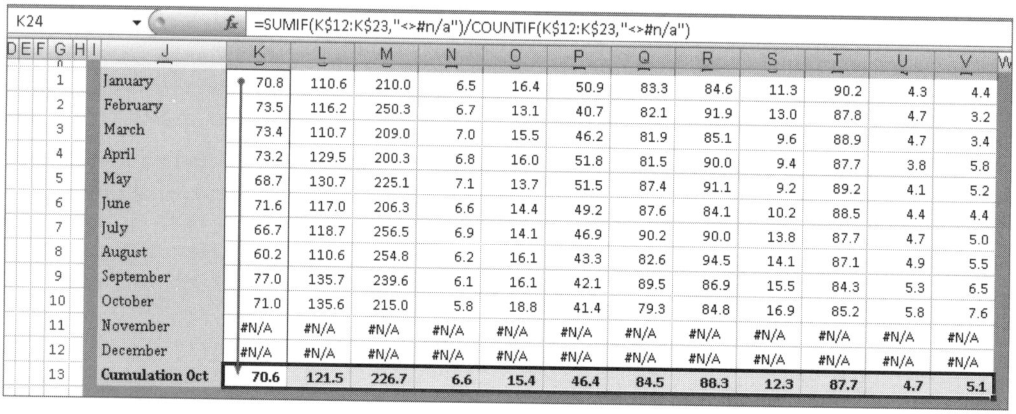

| K24 | | f_x | =SUMIF(K$12:K$23,"<>#n/a")/COUNTIF(K$12:K$23,"<>#n/a") | | | | | | | | | | |

	J	K	L	M	N	O	P	Q	R	S	T	U	V
1	January	70.8	110.6	210.0	6.5	16.4	50.9	83.3	84.6	11.3	90.2	4.3	4.4
2	February	73.5	116.2	250.3	6.7	13.1	40.7	82.1	91.9	13.0	87.8	4.7	3.2
3	March	73.4	110.7	209.0	7.0	15.5	46.2	81.9	85.1	9.6	88.9	4.7	3.4
4	April	73.2	129.5	200.3	6.8	16.0	51.8	81.5	90.0	9.4	87.7	3.8	5.8
5	May	68.7	130.7	225.1	7.1	13.7	51.5	87.4	91.1	9.2	89.2	4.1	5.2
6	June	71.6	117.0	206.3	6.6	14.4	49.2	87.6	84.1	10.2	88.5	4.4	4.4
7	July	66.7	118.7	256.5	6.9	14.1	46.9	90.2	90.0	13.8	87.7	4.7	5.0
8	August	60.2	110.6	254.8	6.2	16.1	43.3	82.6	94.5	14.1	87.1	4.9	5.5
9	September	77.0	135.7	239.6	6.1	16.1	42.1	89.5	86.9	15.5	84.3	5.3	6.5
10	October	71.0	135.6	215.0	5.8	18.8	41.4	79.3	84.8	16.9	85.2	5.8	7.6
11	November	#N/A	#N/A	#N/A	#N/A	#N/A	#N/A	#N/A	#N/A	#N/A	#N/A	#N/A	#N/A
12	December	#N/A	#N/A	#N/A	#N/A	#N/A	#N/A	#N/A	#N/A	#N/A	#N/A	#N/A	#N/A
13	Cumulation Oct	70.6	121.5	226.7	6.6	15.4	46.4	84.5	88.3	12.3	87.7	4.7	5.1

FIGURE 7-15 How to calculate averages within ranges containing numbers and #N/A Values

The AVERAGE Excel function calculates a value based on *total divided by count*. This wouldn't work in this case because the reference range of a corresponding formula (such as =AVERAGE(K12:K23)) contains #N/A values, and so the result of the formula would also be #N/A. What we need to do is keep the principle of *total divided by count*, but exclude the cells containing #N/A values from the calculation. One possible solution would be the following:

K24   =SUMIF(K$12:K$23,"<>#N/A")/COUNTIF(K$12:K$23,"<>#N/A")

This essentially instructs Excel to do the following: "Add up the cells in the range K12:K23 that contain values other than #N/A, and divide the result by the number of cells in the range K12:K23 that contain values other than #N/A."

Formulas in the *Basis 1* Worksheet

This worksheet provides the basis for the dynamic chart in the form of a table. The table is a variable collection of the data required to visualize the chart. It is based on formulas containing arguments that are partly determined by controls.

This worksheet largely consists of formulas, with the relevant cells highlighted in color. The bright orange border around the K11:023 cell range indicates the data basis of the chart.

Roughly speaking, the task of the formulas can be classified as follows: if specific conditions are met, a certain type of data is to be read (extracted) from the *Data 1* worksheet, and otherwise, not. Two functions are used to fulfill this task:

The =OFFSET(reference,rows,cols,height,width) function is explained in detail in Chapter 12, "More Than Numbers." It returns the value located in a cell that is a certain number of rows and cols away from the reference. The reference argument thus defines the starting point for accessing another cell or cell range. The optional height and width arguments are not of relevance in this example.

In its basic form, the much-used function =IF(logical_test,value_if_true,value_if_false) returns the logical value TRUE or FALSE as the result of logical_test. In the logical_test part of the formula, you almost make a "claim," and Excel then checks to see if this claim is true. If the result of logical_test = TRUE, Excel follows the instruction specified in the value_if_true part of the formula. If the result of logical_test = FALSE, Excel follows the instruction specified in the value_if_false part of the formula.

Note In some of the graphics below, "traces of precedent" cells are shown in relation to the display of formulas. These may explain why other cells (or their content) affect the result of the formula in the cell currently selected. The pertinent question becomes: Where are the values located that the formula in the selected cell requires in order to return a correct result? If these "supplier cells" are located in the same worksheet, the traces in question are indicated with arrows and, in some cases, with borders. If they are located in another worksheet, a small table icon appears at the end of a dotted arrow line. If you double-click this line, the *Go to* dialog box opens. There you can see the cross-sheet reference, and you can specify whether you want to go to that worksheet for the purpose of verification.

The "Trace Precedents" tool is located in the *Formula Auditing* group of the *Formulas* tab in the Ribbon. The *Trace Dependents* command in the same group allows you to locate the cells that are affected by (i.e., depend on) the value in the cell that is currently selected. The *Remove Arrows* command deletes the traces.

The formulas in cell L11 determine the label text of the indicator category configured by the user for use in the legend labels.

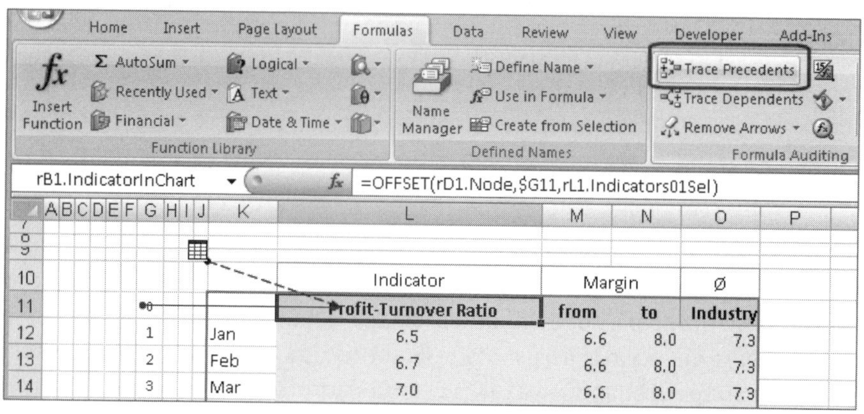

FIGURE 7-16 Formula for determining category labeling

L11   =OFFSET(rD1.Node,$G11,rL1.Indicators01Sel)

This essentially serves as an instruction to Excel to do the following: "Based on the cell with the name *rD1.Node*, read the value in another cell. Starting at *rD1.Node*, move down the number of rows specified by the number in cell G11, and move the number of columns to the right as is currently specified by the number in the *rL1.Indicators01Sel* cell."

The user thus varies the column argument of the formula based on the list selection made in the *oF1_BoxIndicators01* combo box, which is linked with the *rL1.Indicators01Sel* cell.

The formulas in the L12:L23 range calculate the month-specific values of the indicator category selected by the user, taking account of the visualization period configured by the user.

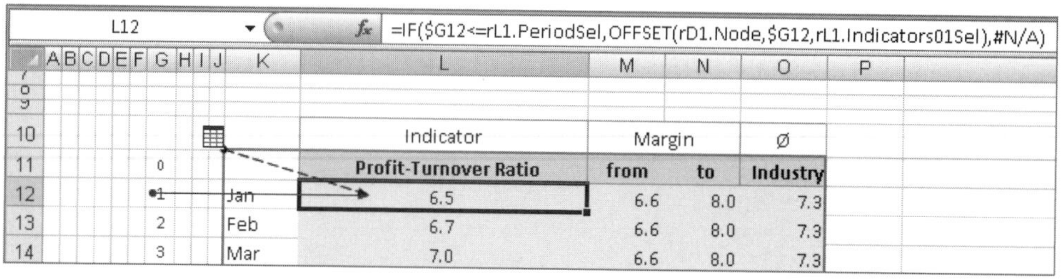

FIGURE 7-17 Formulas for calculating indicator values

L12   =IF($G12<=rL1.PeriodSel,
        OFFSET(rD1.Node,$G12,rL1.Indicators01Sel),
        #N/A)

What it essentially instructs Excel to do is as follows: "If the value in cell G12 is less than or equal to the value in the cell with the name *rL1.PeriodSel*, start at the *rD1.Node* cell and, from there, read the value in another cell. Starting at *rD1.Node*, move down the number of rows specified by the value in cell G12, and move across the number of columns to the right that are currently specified by the number in the *rL1.Indicators01Sel* cell. Otherwise (i.e., if the value in cell G12 is *not* less than or equal to the value in the cell with the name *rL1.PeriodSel*), write the error value #N/A."

The user therefore determines which indicator category is displayed and the period for which the corresponding data series is to be drawn. To be more precise:

- The list selection in the *oF1_BoxIndicators01* combo box, which is linked with the *rL1.Indicators01Sel* cell, determines the selection of the indicator category by generating the column argument of the OFFSET ... part of the formula.

- The user's list selection in the *oF1_BoxPeriod* combo box or a click in the *oF1_ScrollPeriod* scroll bar, both of which are linked with the *rL1.PeriodSel* cell, determines whether this part of the IF formula is used, or whether the #N/A value is written instead.

For example: The user selects the period *Jan – Jun*.

- The value in *rL1.PeriodSel* is 6. It is therefore less than or equal to the 6 that is shown in cell G17, and is therefore assigned to the "June row." The check result of the IF formula is TRUE, and it consequently accesses a cell in the *Data 1* worksheet.

- The value in *rL1.PeriodSel* is 6. Therefore, it is *not* less than or equal to the 7 that is shown in cell G18, and is therefore assigned to the "July row." The check result of the IF formula is therefore FALSE, and it consequently does *not* access a cell in the *Data 1* worksheet, but instead returns the error value #N/A. As a result, no more data points are drawn in the assigned data series of the chart as of this point.

The formulas in cells M11 and N11 determine whether column headers are shown or hidden (for use in the legend labels).

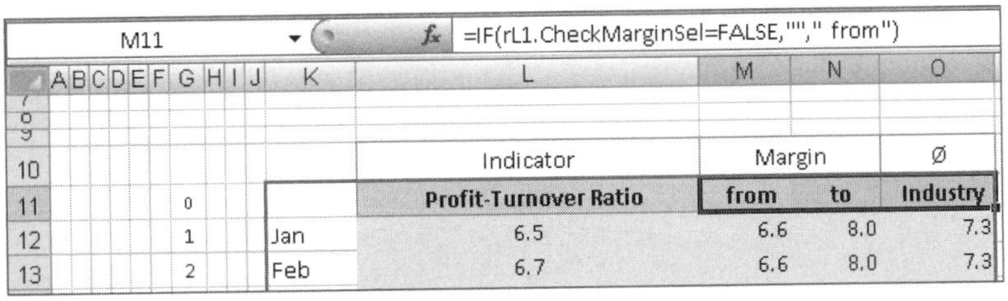

FIGURE 7-18 Additional formulas for determining legend labels

M11   =IF(rL1.CheckMarginSel=FALSE,""," from")

N11   =IF(rL1.CheckMarginSel=FALSE,""," to")

This essentially instructs Excel to do the following (formula in cell M11): "If the value in the *rL1.CheckMarginSel* cell is FALSE, write nothing. Otherwise, write the string *from* (or, in the case of cell N11, the string *to*)."

The user thus determines whether or not the column header is shown by clicking the *oF1_CheckMargin* checkbox, which is linked with the *rL1.CheckMarginSel* cell. This is important because this column header supplies the corresponding legend entry. Always remember: A legend text belonging to a line that is *not* currently visible in the chart should also be invisible.

> **Note** If you instruct Excel to write *nothing* (i.e., if you use the string "" (no characters between the quotation marks), an "empty text" is generated instead. A cell that contains an empty text appears to the user as though it actually contains *nothing* (no value). For Excel, however, this cell is *not* empty (empty text is considered a value in Excel). This is an important difference, which may cause errors after some copy operations and subsequent formula constructions that refer to a cell of this type (for example, if you use the COUNTA function). These errors are sometimes difficult to detect. Therefore, proceed with caution when you copy cells like this to another location or refer to such cells in formulas.

The formulas in cells M12:M23 and N12:N23 determine whether #N/A values or the margin values for the selected indicator category are to be read.

	M12			*fx*	=IF(rL1.CheckMarginSel=FALSE,#N/A,OFFSET(rD1.Node,M$5,rL1.Indicators01Sel))

	K	L	M	N	O	P	Q
			-4	-3	-5		Coloring: Cells cont
							Outlined Cells:
		Indicator	Margin		Ø		
0		Profit-Turnover Ratio	from	to	Industry		
1	Jan	6.5	6.6	8.0	7.3		
2	Feb	6.7	6.6	8.0	7.3		
3	Mar	7.0	6.6	8.0	7.3		
4	Apr	6.8	6.6	8.0	7.3		
5	May	7.1	6.6	8.0	7.3		
6	Jun	6.6	6.6	8.0	7.3		
7	Jul	6.9	6.6	8.0	7.3		
8	Aug	6.2	6.6	8.0	7.3		
9	Sep	6.1	6.6	8.0	7.3		
10	Oct	5.8	6.6	8.0	7.3		
11	Nov	#N/A	6.6	8.0	7.3		
12	Dec	#N/A	6.6	8.0	7.3		

FIGURE 7-19 Formulas for extracting margin values from *Data 1*

```
M12:M23    =IF(rL1.CheckMarginSel=FALSE,
           #N/A,
           OFFSET(rD1.Node,M$5,rL1.Indicators01Sel))
```

```
N12:N23    =IF(rL1.CheckMarginSel=FALSE,
           #N/A,
           OFFSET(rD1.Node,N$5,rL1.Indicators01Sel))
```

This essentially instructs Excel to do the following (according to the formula in cell M12): "If the value in the *rL1.CheckMargin* cell is FALSE, return the error value #N/A. Otherwise, read the value in a cell related to the *rD1.Node* cell. Starting at *rD1.Node*, move down the number of rows specified by the value in cell M5, and move across the number of columns to the right that is currently specified by the value in the *rL1.Indicators01Sel* cell."

The user therefore decides two things here:

- First, clicking the *oF1_CheckMargin* checkbox, which is linked with the *rL1.CheckMarginSel* cell, determines whether the cells are to be filled with #N/A values, If not:

- The list selection in the *oF1_BoxKategorie01* combo box, which is linked with the *rL1.Indicators01Sel* cell, determines the column argument of the OFFSET ... part of the formula.

The formula in cell O11 determines whether the column header is to be displayed or not.

The formulas in cells O12:O23 determine whether #N/A values are used, or whether the industry values for the selected indicator category are to be read.

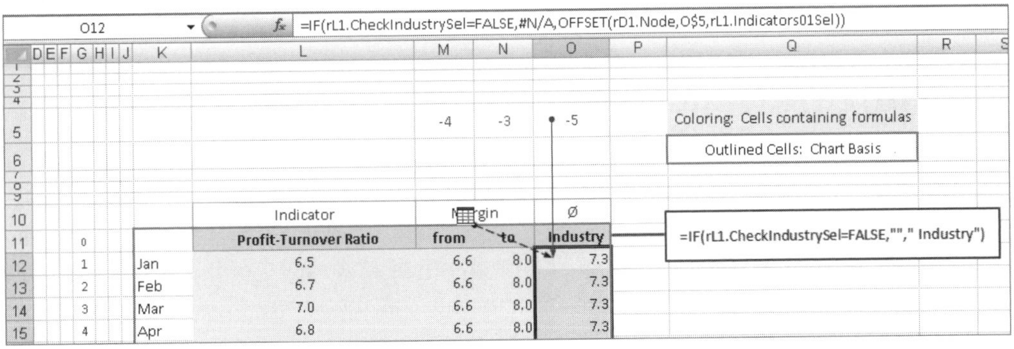

FIGURE 7-20 Formulas for determining the column header and industry values

These formulas work on the same principle as that described above in connection with Figure 7-18 and Figure 7-19. The only differences here are the values and references used.

```
O11    =IF(rL1.CheckIndustrySel=FALSE,""," Industry")
```

and

```
O12:O23    =IF(rL1.CheckIndustrySel=FALSE,
           #N/A,
           OFFSET(rD1.Node,O$5,rL1.Indicators01Sel))
```

> **Tip** Don't generate the chart until you've created and tested all of the formulas in the *Basis 1* worksheet. Start by generating the chart in its basic form with some cursory formatting in the *Basis 1* worksheet, and test how well it responds when you use the various controls. Only copy the chart, together with the controls, to the *Focus 1* worksheet when you're ready to add the finishing touches and formatting to it.

Formulas in the *Focus 1* Worksheet

You've already seen the only formula in this worksheet and its location in Figure 7-5.

```
V4      =rB1.IndicatorInChart&" / "&
        OFFSET(rL1.PeriodHeader,rL1.PeriodSel,0)
```

This formula instructs Excel to do the following: "Read the contents of the *rB1.IndicatorInChart* cell. Then add a character string consisting of a blank space, a forward slash, and another blank space. Then add a formula result to this. To get this result, go to the *rL1.PeriodHeader* cell, and move down the number of rows specified by the value in the *rL1.PeriodSel* cell, but do not move across any columns (0 columns) to the right or left."

The following formula would produce the same result (if you'd like to test it also):

```
P4      =rB1.IndicatorInChart&" / "&INDEX(rL1.PeriodList,rL1.PeriodSel,1)
```

Variant 2 (Advanced Model)

This section follows the same pattern as the last, and explains how to create the *0702_Indicators_02.xlsx* file. It focuses in particular on its dynamic elements, namely controls, formulas, and *conditional formatting*. Note that this section is limited to a discussion of the elements of this file that clearly differ from those of variant 1 of the model as discussed in the previous section (i.e., the basic version in the *0701_Indicators_01.xlsx* file). For the following discussion, I assume that you're already familiar with the information provided there.

> **On the Companion CD** Open the *\Samples\0702_Indicators_02.xlsx* file on the CD-ROM.

The advanced model is a little easier to use, and also implements the principles of the rS1.Method more consistently. The following paragraphs explain the main differences between it and the basic version in relation to the workbook structure.

How Is the Workbook Structured?

As usual, I'll answer this question by going from right to left in the workbook.

NamesIndex **Worksheet**

You can see that the number of range names listed here is calculated using the `=COUNTA(L:L)&" Names"` formula.

What this formula essentially instructs Excel to do is as follows: "Count the number of entries (of any type) in all of column L, and add a blank space, followed by the string *Names* to the result."

> The `=COUNTA(reference)` calculates the number of entries in reference. It counts entries of any kind, even the "empty text" ("") explained above.
>
> The `=COUNT(reference)` function only counts the numbers in reference.

Clearly, a couple of names have been added here to the list from the basic version (variant 1). I'll come back to these later when describing the formulas.

Parameters 1 **Worksheet**

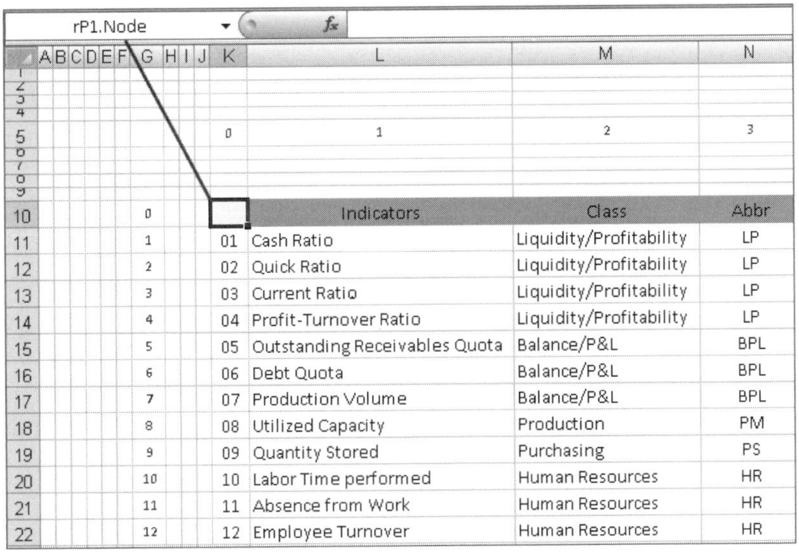

	0	1		2	3
0		Indicators		Class	Abbr
1	01	Cash Ratio		Liquidity/Profitability	LP
2	02	Quick Ratio		Liquidity/Profitability	LP
3	03	Current Ratio		Liquidity/Profitability	LP
4	04	Profit-Turnover Ratio		Liquidity/Profitability	LP
5	05	Outstanding Receivables Quota		Balance/P&L	BPL
6	06	Debt Quota		Balance/P&L	BPL
7	07	Production Volume		Balance/P&L	BPL
8	08	Utilized Capacity		Production	PM
9	09	Quantity Stored		Purchasing	PS
10	10	Labor Time performed		Human Resources	HR
11	11	Absence from Work		Human Resources	HR
12	12	Employee Turnover		Human Resources	HR

FIGURE 7-21 Master-data maintenance is used here.

Variant 1 doesn't have this worksheet. The main advantage of using it is that it allows you to manage and maintain your master data centrally. In this case, the master data consists of the names of the indicator categories. On the right next to the list of indicator categories is a list of the groups (in full text and abbreviated form) to which these belong. As you can see in Figure 7-21, this worksheet contains an *rP1.Node* (cell K10). This node is used to extract information with formulas and transfer this information to the *Data 1* and *Lists 1* worksheets (and thus also to the drop-down lists of the relevant controls). If changes need to be made to these texts, they only need to be made in the *Parameters 1* worksheet.

Lists 1 **Worksheet**

The appearance of this worksheet has also changed a little from the basic variant.

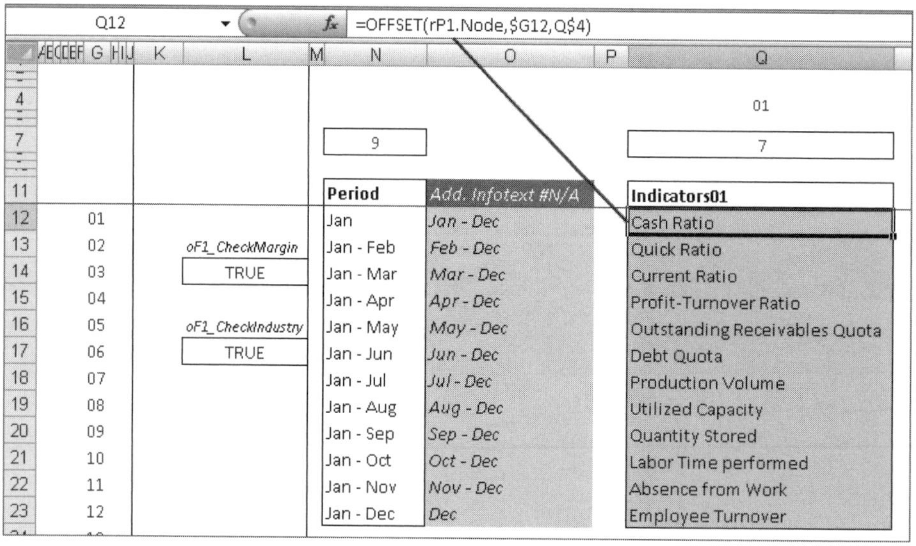

FIGURE 7-22 A reverse list in column *O* and a parameter copy in column *Q*

Column Q now contains formulas that can be used to read content from *Parameter 1*.

Users can configure 12 different time periods in the *Focus 1* worksheet. These include periods for which data is not yet available. This doesn't usually cause any problems or inconvenience, but it's worth adding a user-friendly tip all the same. You can do this in the form of an info-text. Assume, for example, that a user selects the period *Jan – Nov*. In this case, you want the following infotext to appear: *No Data for Period Nov - Dec 2008*. As you'll see later, this is easily done using the "reverse list" in column O, which contains the required text modules.

The reverse list is spatially assigned to the definition structures of the drop-down list for selecting the period, and therefore can simply be linked with this list. If the user clicks the eleventh entry in the drop-down list (*Jan – Nov*), the eleventh text module from the reverse list (*Nov – Dec*) is used.

It doesn't take long to manually enter a short list like this. However, if you'd prefer to avoid this tedious chore or need to enter larger and more complex lists, you can use formulas to do this job for you.

Using text formulas, it's often possible to generate a new list from an existing one (for example, to correct an incorrect list). As a prerequisite, a consistent default structure must usually exist in the data source; in other words, a structure that can be used when generating a new list.

> **Tip** Beware: The same structure may also mean the same errors! Complex and fast error correction in text lists is sometimes much easier in Excel than in Word because corrective text formulas can be used. A list of available text functions (and other function groups) is provided on the CD-ROM under *Materials\Functions.xlsx*.

In our example, the relevant range is N13:N22, which you can use as an identically structured data source. Enter the contents of cell O12 and O23 manually, and use formulas to generate the remaining entries in the range O13:O22. Two ways of doing this are shown in Figure 7-23.

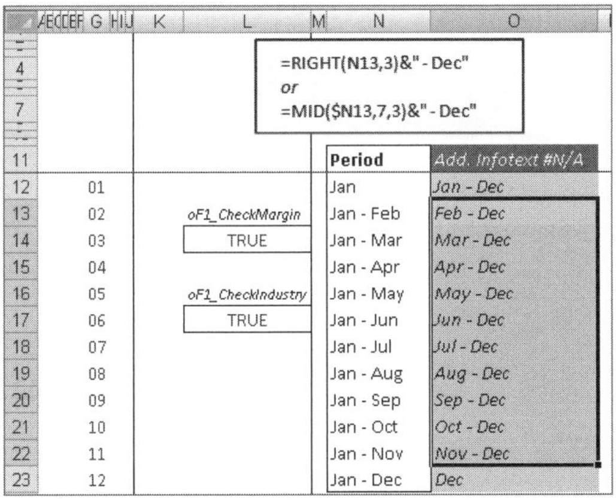

		K	L	M	N	O	
4					=RIGHT(N13,3)&" - Dec"		
					or		
7					=MID($N13,7,3)&" - Dec"		
11					**Period**	Add. Infotext #N/A	
12	01				Jan	Jan - Dec	
13	02	oF1_CheckMargin			Jan - Feb	Feb - Dec	
14	03	TRUE			Jan - Mar	Mar - Dec	
15	04				Jan - Apr	Apr - Dec	
16	05	oF1_CheckIndustry			Jan - May	May - Dec	
17	06	TRUE			Jan - Jun	Jun - Dec	
18	07				Jan - Jul	Jul - Dec	
19	08				Jan - Aug	Aug - Dec	
20	09				Jan - Sep	Sep - Dec	
21	10				Jan - Oct	Oct - Dec	
22	11				Jan - Nov	Nov - Dec	
23	12				Jan - Dec	Dec	

FIGURE 7-23 Faster than manual entry: most of the list can be generated using formulas.

The =RIGHT(reference,num_chars) function reads in reference the number of characters, starting from the right, that are specified in num_chars.

The =MID(reference,start_num,num_chars) function reads in reference the number of characters, starting at start_num (specifies a position as a number), that are specified in num_chars.

Once you've generated a list like this with formulas, the formulas themselves become superfluous and can be replaced by their results. Therefore, you can copy the range with the formulas and then overwrite this by selecting *Home/Paste/Paste Values*.

Data 1 Worksheet

In this worksheet, OFFSET formulas are used to read texts defined in the *Parameters 1* worksheet. These texts are the indicator names in the K11:V11 range and the group IDs in the K9:V9 range.

More important, however, is the fact that the K12:V24 range contains conditional formatting, which is used to indicate where the indicators move outside of the desired or anticipated margins. I'll explain how to generate this formatting in a separate section later. At this point, a few remarks about how these are designed and used will suffice.

This worksheet is used by the company's financial controllers, rather than by the Management team. Each month, all managers receive a protected version of the latest model, with all of the worksheets hidden except for *Focus 1*.

Once an indicator is entered or read, a color signal immediately appears if the values rise above or drop below the acceptable margins defined for that indicator (in rows 7 and 8). Try this out for yourself by temporarily changing some of the figures.

	K11				*fx*	=OFFSET(rP1.Node,K$2,$E11)									
				Cash Ratio	Quick Ratio	Current Ratio	Profit-Turnover Ratio	Outstanding Receivables Quota	Debt Quota	Production Volume	Utilized Capacity	Quantity Stored	Labor Time performed	Absence from Work	Employee Turnover
				1	2	3	4	5	6	7	8	9	10	11	12
2008		**Indicators 2008** (all values stated in %)													
	-5	Ø Industry	65.4	130.2	245.0	7.3	16.2	42.1	88.3	92.0	14.2	91.3	4.1	3.5
	-4	Target min	60.0	120.0	210.0	6.6	13.0	35.0	82.0	80.0	10.0	85.0	3.0	3.0
	-3	Target max	75.0	140.0	250.0	8.0	20.0	50.0	95.0	95.0	16.0	95.0	5.0	5.0
	-2	Class	LP	LP	LP	LP	BPL	BPL	BPL	PM	PS	HR	HR	HR
12	1	January	70.8	110.6	210.0	6.5	16.4	50.9	83.3	84.6	11.3	90.2	4.3	4.4
13	2	February	73.5	116.2	250.3	6.7	13.1	40.7	82.1	91.9	13.0	87.8	4.7	3.2
14	3	March	73.4	110.7	209.0	7.0	15.5	46.2	81.9	85.1	9.6	88.9	4.7	3.4
15	4	April	73.2	129.5	200.3	6.8	16.0	51.8	81.5	90.0	9.4	87.7	3.8	5.8
16	5	May	68.7	130.7	225.1	7.1	13.7	51.5	87.4	91.1	9.2	89.2	4.1	5.2
17	6	June	71.6	117.0	206.3	6.6	14.4	49.2	87.6	84.1	10.2	88.5	4.4	4.4
18	7	July	66.7	118.7	256.5	6.9	14.1	46.9	90.2	90.0	13.8	87.7	4.7	5.0
19	8	August	60.2	110.6	254.8	6.2	16.1	43.3	82.6	94.5	14.1	87.1	4.9	5.5
20	9	September	77.0	135.7	239.6	6.1	16.1	42.1	89.5	86.9	15.5	84.3	5.3	6.5
21	10	October	71.0	135.6	215.0	5.8	18.8	41.4	79.3	84.8	16.9	85.2	5.8	7.6
22	11	November	#N/A	#N/A	#N/A	#N/A	#N/A	#N/A	#N/A	#N/A	#N/A	#N/A	#N/A	#N/A
23	12	December	#N/A	#N/A	#N/A	#N/A	#N/A	#N/A	#N/A	#N/A	#N/A	#N/A	#N/A	#N/A
24	13	**Cumulation Oct**	**70.6**	**121.5**	**226.7**	**6.6**	**15.4**	**46.4**	**84.5**	**88.3**	**12.3**	**87.7**	**4.7**	**5.1**

FIGURE 7-24 Formulas and conditional formatting in the data sheet

If the value drops below the lower limit, it appears in a white font on a buff-colored background. If it rises above the upper limit, the background changes to light orange. Of course, neither color scheme is intended as a "real" warning signal. Here, the only purpose is to draw attention to the values. Given the type and composition of the indicators to be analyzed here, this solution is sufficient. In any case, no alternative is available. After all, exceeding or falling short of a company-specific threshold value may or may not be a problem, depending on the individual indicator and situation. In each case, the degree of fluctuation and the in-fluence of other factors must also be taken into account. Therefore, we have to leave it to the expertise and interpretative capabilities of the user to assess the significance of the fluctua-tions within or outside of the defined margins. The simple and overused traffic-light system (where green is good and red is bad) is not suitable here.

Basis 1 **Worksheet**

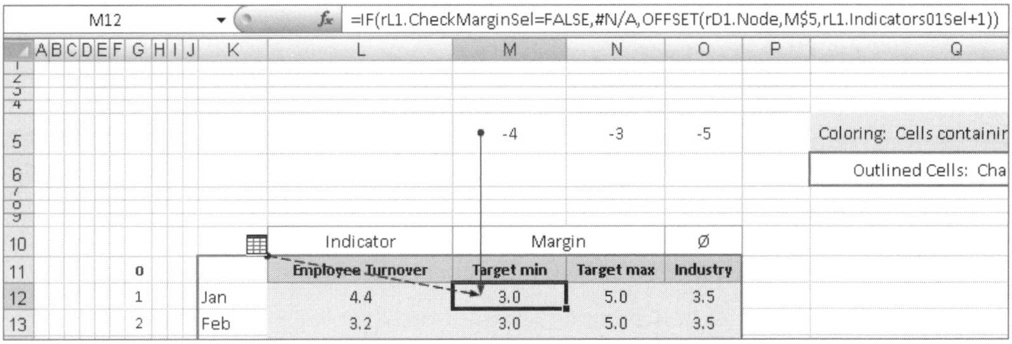

FIGURE 7-25 There are few changes here compared with variant 1.

This worksheet is almost identical to variant 1. The following minor adjustments have been made:

- The columns headers in cell N11 and M11 were changed. The texts *from* and *to* have been replaced with *Target min* and *Target max*.

- The formulas designed earlier for the *controls* need to be slightly modified because *ActiveX controls* are used in this variant. More about that later.

Focus 1 **Worksheet**

The revisions and modifications are most obvious in the *Focus 1* worksheet and not just be-cause the colors have changed.

- The chart legend is now positioned below the plot area. It now has a less obvious im-pact, and no longer interferes with the visual continuity between the data series and the control panel. In any case, the legend is only of minor importance in this solution and scenario. In fact, it could almost be dispensed with, because the necessary informa-tion is also well presented in the control area. However, this worksheet is also intended to be used as a color printout for external reports. The printout will only contain the chart itself and its header bar. Therefore, the legend must remain intact as it provides important additional information.

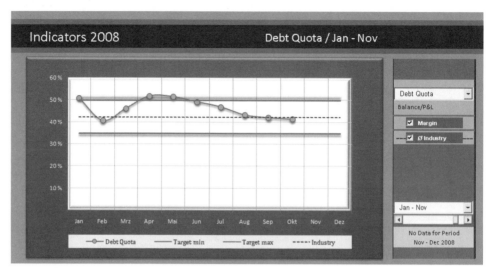

FIGURE 7-26 In many respects an improvement on variant 1

- The control panel has been redesigned in several ways:
    - The controls are now organized into thematic groups. The configuration options for the period (which are rarely needed or used) have found their rightful place at the bottom of this panel, and in proximity to the chart's horizontal primary axis, which indicates the months.
    - The *ActiveX controls* allow us to add a fill color here. The two most important selection elements (the drop-down lists for the indicator category and the period) have been visually highlighted.
    - When an indicator is selected, an infotext appears below this, indicating the indicator category to which it belongs.
    - With the two *checkboxes*, the relevant line colors from the chart are displayed as information in the legend.
    - An infotext (discussed earlier in relation to the *Lists 1* sheet) appears below the two controls for selecting the period if the user selects a period for which all of the relevant data is not yet available. It is highlighted against a color background, and it disappears (together with the color fill) as soon as a period is selected for which all of the relevant data is currently available. This is achieved by using a formula in conjunction with conditional formatting.

ActiveX Controls

ActiveX controls have the same function as the form controls described earlier in relation to variant 1 of our model, but they are much more complex and much more effective in many ways. The configuration options for these controls are extensive, which makes them ideal for use in flexible models with complex graphical features. This also applies incidentally, to programmed solutions. Much more is involved in creating these controls than is the case with form controls, and you need specific, detailed knowledge. All of the knowledge you require is provided below, as well as in later chapters.

Basics of ActiveX Controls

> **Note** When using the rS1.Method, you should first create a control in the *Basis 1* worksheet, test it there for both its functionality and its effects on the formula results in this worksheet, and then (and only then) copy it to its final destination in the *Focus 1* worksheet.

ActiveX controls are standard tools that can be used in various Microsoft applications. They were developed for use in programmed solutions and are still used predominantly for that purpose. It's rather unusual for them to be used to control solutions that are dynamic but not programmed, as described in this book. There's one consolation here: You don't need to be alarmed by the list of properties for this element, which is impressively long and hard to understand at first, because you're only going to need to use a tiny fraction of all the options available. All the rest are only relevant for programming.

Note the following essential points:

- *ActiveX controls* are not an integral component of Excel, and their behavior is similar but not identical to Excel or Office objects. Excel beginners need a little time to adjust to this fact, in particular when designing an rS1-model.

- *ActiveX controls* can be used in two different modes, but they don't function in *design* mode and can't be designed in functional mode. As a result, you need to constantly switch back and forth between the two modes. Or, to be more precise, you enable and disable *design mode* as required.

- *ActiveX controls* have complex, definable *properties*, which are only listed as programming terms.

- *ActiveX controls* have different types of *properties*:

  - Functional properties, which regulate the content and behavior of the object (what does the control show, and how does it respond?).

  - Formatting properties, which determine the appearance of the object and its contents (what does the control show, and how?).

- *ActiveX controls* have *properties* that can be changed in various ways in design mode:

    ❑ They can be changed indirectly when you manipulate a control or perform an action in relation to it, or when you use the control to manipulate or perform an action in relation to another object. Example: You use the mouse to change the width and height of the object. This determines the *Width* and *Height* properties. You can also explicitly define (or change) these properties in a dialog box.

    ❑ They can be changed directly when you explicitly define them in a dialog box. Example: You enter the range name of a cell in the *LinkedCell* text box.

    ❑ All controls (both *form controls* and *ActiveX controls*) are graphical objects. As such, they have the same properties shared by all graphical objects in Microsoft Office.

Recommended Method

To create a dynamic chart, you usually require several ActiveX controls, and, you often need to use more than one of the same type. For this reason, I recommend that you use the following sequence when creating these controls.

1. Plan and prepare your dynamic model.
2. Define and map out your workbook and worksheet structures (values, names, formulas, ranges, cells).
3. Create the first control belonging to a specific type.
4. Define the functional and formatting properties of this control.
5. Define the general properties of this control as a graphical object.
6. Test the functionality of the control.
7. Copy the control.
8. Modify the properties in the copies of the control.
9. Adjust and synchronize the general, graphical object properties of all controls.
10. Test the functionality of all controls in isolation and in combination with each other.

Creating ActiveX Controls

Before you create an *ActiveX control*, I want to make you aware of one hard-to-avoid issue with these objects, which you may encounter on your first attempt: the possibility of generating VBA program source code by mistake. This can be very annoying, but, as you'll soon see, doesn't pose a serious problem.

There are two reasons why it's almost impossible to avoid this mistake. At some point, when you're working in a standard Excel 2007 workbook (*xlsx* file type), with *design mode* enabled (more about that later) and a control selected, you're bound to do one of the following:

■ Accidentally click the *View Code* button in the *Controls* group of the *Developer* tab

■ Accidentally double-click a control

Excel interprets both these actions as instructions to create VBA procedures for the active controls, and you suddenly may find yourself in a completely unfamiliar window; i.e., the *Visual Basic* editor. The editor warmly welcomes you with a freshly generated procedure, and then waits patiently for you to write all manner of program code between *Private Sub* and *End Sub*, which would then be processed later when the user clicks the control. But that's not what you want to do. So, how do you escape?

In Excel 2007 (unlike earlier versions), you can simply close the *Visual Basic* editor and pretend this never happened. The next time you save your work, the program will issue the following message:

"The following features cannot be saved in macro-free workbooks

■ *VB project*

   ... (additional information)

   To continue saving as a macro-free workbook, click Yes"

This is exactly what you should do in this case. The VBA procedure you generated by mistake is then deleted from the workbook.

> **Note** If you want to save a workbook together with a VB project in Excel 2007, you must select the *macro-enabled file type* (*xlsm*) after the *Save As* command.
>
> If you want to open the *Visual Basic* editor again, the fastest way to do this is to press **Alt+F11**.

It doesn't matter where you create the control in the workbook or what size it is because, as a graphical object, it can be moved and resized as required. However, you may prefer to take a systematic approach from the start.

1. Plan the type of control you want to create and where you want it to be placed. If possible (and it isn't always), define the cell sizes of the "host" table so that a control can fit into a single cell.

2. Select the *Developer* tab in the Ribbon, and click the *Insert* button in the *Controls* group. Then click the icon of your choice in the bottom selection menu. Position your mouse in the worksheet (the mouse pointer becomes a crosshair), and—holding down the mouse button—drag the object horizontally until you're happy with its size.

330   Chapter 7   Elements of Dynamization

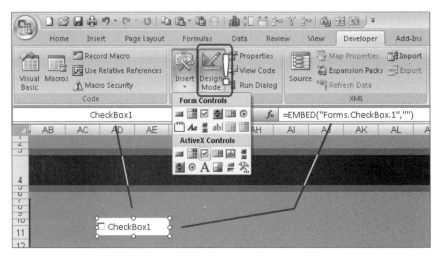

FIGURE 7-27 *Design mode* is automatically enabled when you create *ActiveX controls*.

3. *Design mode* is automatically enabled. A formula (such as =EMBED("Forms.
   CheckBox.1","")) appears in the formula bar, but can be ignored.

4. The control is selected as a graphics object. This means that you can scale it, use the
   Alt to adjust it to the fit into the cell(s), and use the arrow keys to move it around the
   screen.

5. Click the *Design mode* button in the Ribbon to exit this mode, or proceed immediately
   to define the *properties* of the control (see the next section).

> **Tip** It's important to bear in mind the following point from the start: Unlike *form controls*,
> *ActiveX controls* usually require a little more space (due to their height) than is normally
> available in a standard Excel table row. A row height of 18 is therefore a reasonable size to
> accommodate a control. Here, again, it will be easier to reduce the size later, if necessary,
> than to enlarge it.
>
> The next tip applies to all graphical objects. In this case, the prerequisite is that the cell
> that is to contain the object must be exactly the same size as the object to be generated:
>
> 1. Select the object in the Ribbon and point with the mouse (mouse pointer is a
>   crosshair) into the relevant cell.
>
> 2. Press and hold down the **Alt** key.
>
> 3. Next, hold down the mouse button and move the mouse pointer very slightly in any
>   direction, but do not move it outside of the relevant cell.
>
> 4. Release the mouse button, and then release the **Alt** key.
>
> The result is that the object virtually "drops" into the cell and adjusts to fit within the cell
> borders. In other words, it assumes the same size as its host.

Enabling/Disabling Design Mode

This isn't just important. It's *very* important, and it also takes some getting used to. While *design mode* is enabled, all you can do with your *ActiveX control* is edit it. This represents a clear difference between these objects and *form controls*, for which a mode of this kind doesn't exist.

I assume that you've already generated the object and configured the object. *Design mode* is enabled, and the object is selected. If you now click in any other location in the worksheet or press the **Esc** key, the object is deselected. In other words, the control is no longer active. However, it (and any other *ActiveX controls* you're using) is still in *design mode*. You can continue working on other parts of the worksheet, but if you click on the control, it doesn't function as a control. Instead, it can be edited and is therefore selected again as an object. The only way to access functional mode for the control is to disable the *Design Mode* option in the Ribbon.

However, if you want to edit the control again, you must switch on *design mode* again in order to select the object.

Note the following point in relation to Excel 2007 in particular: *Design mode* frequently is activated without the user knowing it because a tab other than the *Developer* tab is currently active in the Ribbon.

Note To help you check which mode you're in, remember that if you click a control with either mouse button and it appears within an object selection frame, then you know that:

❏ It's an *ActiveX control* (because this isn't possible with *form controls*), and

❏ Design mode is enabled

This note is particularly important because both types of control may be used in the same workbook in the dynamic models described in this book. Depending on their design and your own experience, you may not be able to distinguish between the two at first glance.

Modifying ActiveX Controls

Modifying or editing *ActiveX controls* involves two procedures, both of which require you to enable *design mode*:

■ Define the functional and formatting properties of the control

■ Define the general properties of the control as a graphics object (I've already explained how to define these in relation to Figure 7-12. The following discussion is therefore limited to the definition of functional and formatting properties).

You've defined an ActiveX control and want to configure its functions or define its formatting. The object is selected and *design mode* is enabled. Follow these steps with reference to

Figure 7-28: select the *Properties* command in the Ribbon, or right-click the object, and select the *Properties* command in the context menu. A dialog box opens, showing more or less extensive lists of properties.

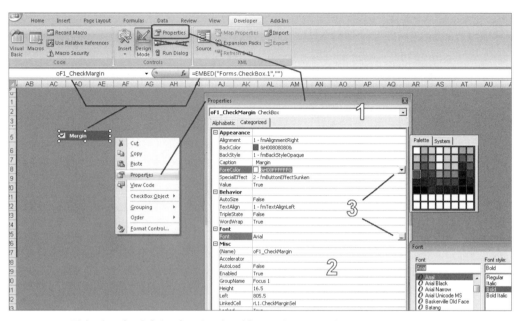

FIGURE 7-28 Dialog box for defining functional and formatting properties

1. All dialog boxes containing lists of *properties* of *ActiveX controls* have the same structure, but the options available depend on the type of control. The dialog box has two tabs with the same content, one arranged in *Alphabetic* order and the other organized into categories, or *Categorized*. For Excel beginners, I strongly recommend using the *Categorized* tab. It is much easier to understand because it divides the very extensive lists of properties into well-defined groups.

2. You can click the textual description of the property, click in the cell to the right of this description, and then select or enter the relevant value, or press **Ctrl+V** to paste the value from the clipboard.

3. When you click some of the rows, specific buttons appear that you can use to select predefined values. These values may appear as short lists (for example, in the case of *BackColor*) or small dialog boxes, or a standard Office dialog box may open (as with *Font*).

Properties When Using the rS1.Method

As I've promised, you only need to define a few control properties to lend dynamism to rS1 models. It's important to distinguish between properties that absolutely *must* be defined, those that *should* be defined, and those additional properties that *can* also be defined.

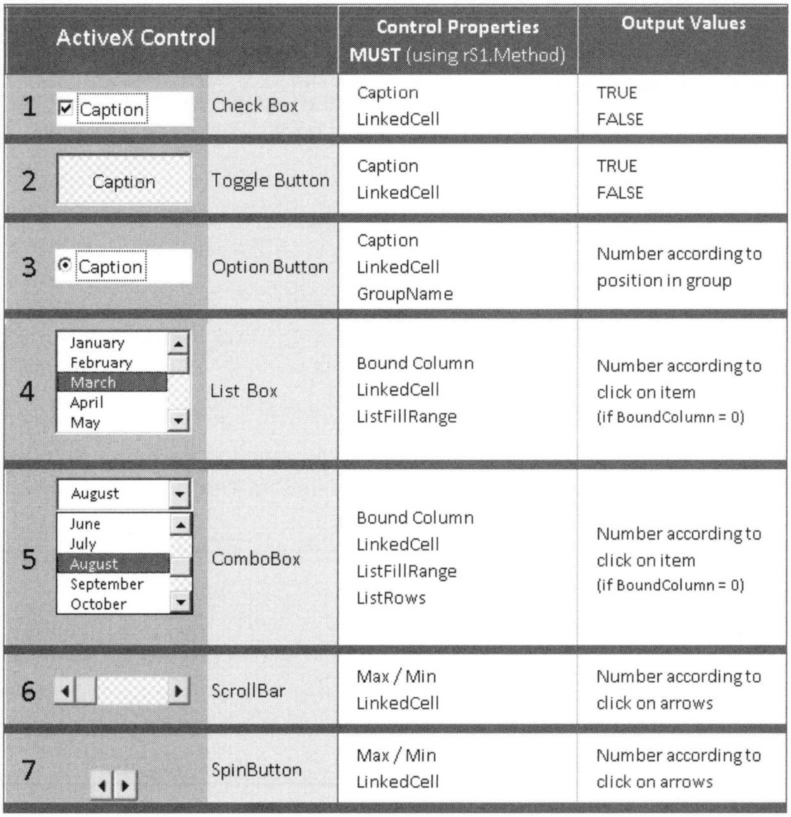

ActiveX Control		Control Properties **MUST** (using rS1.Method)	Output Values
1 ☑ Caption	Check Box	Caption LinkedCell	TRUE FALSE
2 Caption	Toggle Button	Caption LinkedCell	TRUE FALSE
3 ◉ Caption	Option Button	Caption LinkedCell GroupName	Number according to position in group
4 January February March April May	List Box	Bound Column LinkedCell ListFillRange	Number according to click on item (if BoundColumn = 0)
5 August June July August September October	ComboBox	Bound Column LinkedCell ListFillRange ListRows	Number according to click on item (if BoundColumn = 0)
6 ◄ ☐ ►	ScrollBar	Max / Min LinkedCell	Number according to click on arrows
7 ◄ ►	SpinButton	Max / Min LinkedCell	Number according to click on arrows

FIGURE 7-29 The mandatory ("MUST") properties of selected *ActiveX controls*

An overview of this topic is provided in Figure 7-29. I'll describe the most important aspects when using these properties in rS1 models, with reference to the *Control Properties* column in the figure that follows. I'll introduce you to other properties later with practical examples.

If you like, you can select the *Focus 1* worksheet in the *0702_Indicators_02.xlsx* file, unprotect the sheet, enable design mode, and then (as shown in Figure 7-28), access the dialog boxes of individual controls to compared their defined properties with the descriptions below. A more precise and specific explanation is provided in the next section.

- *Caption*: A control needs a label if you want to tell users what the control does or doesn't do when they click it. This applies to *Check Box, Option Button,* and *Toggle Button*. This isn't a *must* if the necessary information is conveyed in another way.

- *LinkedCell*: All controls require a cell link. The current output value of the element is directed to the linked cell. These are cells whose range names have the suffix *Sel*, and that are found in the *Lists 1* worksheet.

- *ListFillRange*: The table range from which the list is filled is naturally reserved for the *ListBox* and *ComboBox* controls.

- *ListRows*: Even though this property is not essential for functioning alone (and therefore isn't, strictly speaking, a *must*), you always define the number of list entries that are to appear in the drop-down list for a *ComboBox* control.

- *BoundColumn*: You'll discover later (by means of a practical example) why the "bound column" should usually be set to 0 (zero) for *ListBox* and *ComboBox*, even though the default value is *1*.

- *GroupName*: Several *OptionButtons* must share the same group name so that it is clear which of these are to be set to FALSE when one is set to TRUE.

- *Max* and *Min*: These are the maximum and minimum threshold values for the *SpinButton* and *ScrollBar* controls.

In addition to these essential properties, there are also properties which can be described as *Should* properties (i.e., properties that should ideally be defined), including the *(Name)* property, which is the object name of the element. Finally, many properties can be classed as *Can* (i.e., optional) properties. Most of the properties that fall into this last category are used to format the object and are discussed in some of the examples in later chapters.

Configuring ActiveX Controls

Let's move on now to the specific properties of the controls in the *Focus 1* worksheet of the *0702_Indicators_02.xlsx* sample file. The functions of these objects are identical to those described in relation to the form controls of variant 1. You may find it helpful to cast your eye over these again now (Figure 7-7 to Figure 7-12). When using *ActiveX controls*, you need to employ a completely different method to achieve the same end result.

Controls for Selecting Indicator Category and Period   As with the form controls, a drop-down list is used again here for the selection of the indicator type, in this case the *ComboBox* ActiveX control. The *period* shown in the chart is similarly selected using a *ComboBox*, which is linked with a *ScrollBar*.

Let's start with the *oF1_BoxPeriod ComboBox*. This control is identical to the *ComboBox* used to select the indicator category, the only difference being the use of range names.

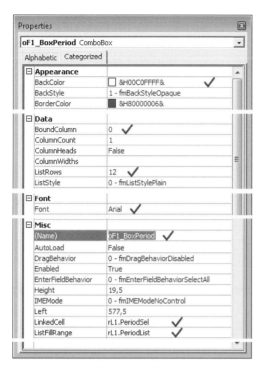

FIGURE 7-30 Only the rows with tickmarks are relevant.

The *Properties* dialog box of the *ComboBox* shown in Figure 7-30 has been truncated several times because it contained many entries that have no relevance here (in other words, only segments of the original list are shown). In this abbreviated list, we're only interested in the properties with tickmarks assigned.

The most important information (working from the top of the list down) is provided in the following table.

Property	Category	Importance	Value/Remark
BackColor	*Appearance*	Can	You can select the background color in a small dialog box.
BoundColumn	*Data*	Must	You must define the value *0 (zero)* for this property so that the object outputs a number (the index) that corresponds to the click position. Otherwise (if you use the default value *1*), the actual list contents of the click position (in this case, a text) would be output. This would be a good choice if you were using the VLOOKUP function for further processing, and wanted to use the output as a search criterion.

Property	Category	Importance	Value/Remark
ListRows	*Data*	Must/Should	This is the number of rows that users will see when they open the drop-down list. If the number is small (fewer than 20), all should be visible at once.
Font	*Font*	Can	You can define the font attributes in a dialog box. In these controls, the *Arial* font is clearer than most of the fonts delivered with Office 2007.
(Name)	*Misc*	Should	*oF1_BoxPeriod*—Enter the object name here (optional). Alternatively, enter it in the name box in the formula bar. It is then applied here.
LinkedCell	*Misc*	Must	*rL1.PeriodSel*—This cell contains the value that is output when a user clicks on a list entry.
ListFillRange	*Misc*	Must	*rL1.PeriodList*—The contents of the selection list are defined in this cell range.

There's not a lot left to say in relation to the *oF1_BoxIndicators01 ComboBox*. It is defined in almost an identical manner to the control described above. The only differences are:

- The *(Name)* property is, naturally different, i.e.: *oF1_BoxIndicators01*.

- *rL1. Indicators01Sel* was selected as the *LinkedCell*.

- The *rL1. Indicators01List* range is used as the *ListFillRange* .

> **Note** Here, once again, we can see just how cool the rS1.Method can be, and how much work it can save you. After you create, configure, and make a copy of the first control, all you need to do is change a couple of characters in the copy (which you can almost do "on autopilot," seeing as you're using conventions) to make it do what it needs to do.

The *Properties* dialog box of the *ScrollBar* that works together with *oF1_BoxPeriod* is shown in full in Figure 7-31. However, you only need concern yourself with those few properties that are highlighted here.

Before we start, note the following important point: The numbering of the index in a *ComboBox* or *ListBox* starts at *0* (zero), rather than at *1*, as is the case with form controls. This means that, when you click the first entry in a list, a *0* rather than a *1* appears in the *LinkedCell* and, when you click the tenth entry, a *9* is output in this cell, and so on. However, you can use certain constructs to intercept this problem. These are described later. If you link one of these controls with another, this second control must also have *zero* as its minimum value.

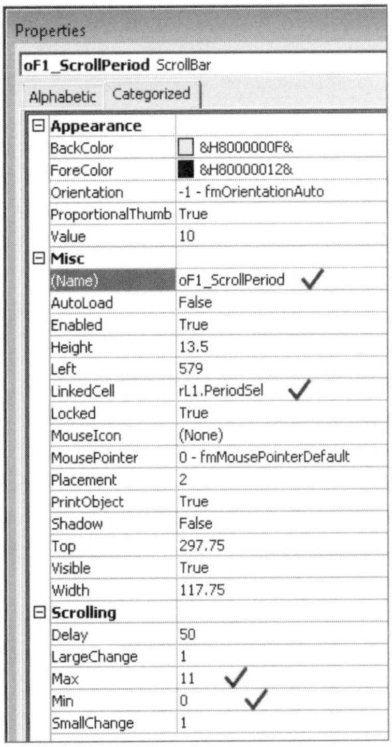

FIGURE 7-31 The complete *Properties* dialog box of the *oF1_ScrollPeriod* control

Property	Category	Importance	Value/Remark
Max	*Scrolling*	Must	The object is to output 12 values. However, the highest value must be *11* because the minimum value must be *0* (see the note above).
Min	*Scrolling*	Must	Here, the minimum value must be set to *0* instead of *1*.

As mentioned earlier, you can set the *Max* property of this control (or of a *SpinButton*) to a lower value than the *Min* property. For example, you could set the maximum to *0* and the minimum to *10*. The effect of this would be to reverse the object's "working direction." In this case, the scroll box would be at the extreme right of the horizontal *ScrollBar* rather than the extreme left if the value was zero (and clicking on the left arrow would be equivalent to counting backwards). On a vertical *ScrollBar*, the scroll box would be at the very bottom, rather than the very top, if the value were zero. This is an extremely useful feature for many constructs where the "logic" of direction comes into play.

LinkedCell	*Misc*	Must	*rL1.PeriodSel*, in order to functionally link the object with the *oF1_BoxPeriod* control.

Controls for Displaying Additional Data Series   You still need to know how to configure the two *CheckBoxes* to display the lines representing the margins of the defined range and the line representing the industry value. Once again, the two controls are largely identical. As a result, we only need to look at one of these in detail, i.e. the *oF1_CheckMargin* object. The complete dialog box for the properties of this control is shown in Figure 7-32.

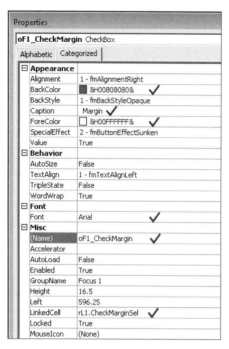

FIGURE 7-32 Properties of the *oF1_CheckMargin CheckBox*

Property	Category	Importance	Value/Remark
BackColor	*Appearance*	Can	The fill color, which is selected from a pallet.
Caption	*Appearance*	Must	The *Margin* text was defined here with a leading blank to create some space between it and the check box.
ForeColor	*Appearance*	Can	The foreground color, which refers to the *font color* in this element. Selection is the same as for *BackColor*.
Font	*Font*	Can	Once again, *Arial* was selected here as the clearest font.
(Name)	*Misc*	Should	*oF1_CheckMargin*
LinkedCell	*Misc*	Must	*rL1.CheckMarginSel*

The only differences in the second *CheckBox* are listed below:

- The (Name) property is as follows: *oF1_CheckIndustry*.

- Ø *Industry* is defined as the *Caption*.

- *rL1.CheckIndustrySel* is defined as the *LinkedCell*.

Formulas

In relation to the use of formulas, there are two differences between this workbook and the basic version in variant 1, namely:

- A couple of formulas have been added.
- The extracting formulas have been adjusted to suit the conditions of the *ActiveX controls.*

Formulas in the *Lists 1* Worksheet

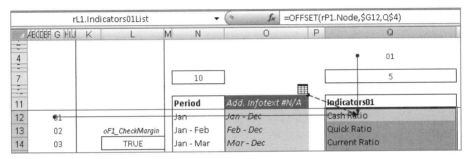

FIGURE 7-33 Reading data from the *Parameters 1* worksheet

Formulas of the now-familiar OFFSET type are used to read the names of the indicators.

Q12:Q23   =OFFSET(rP1.Node,$G12,Q$4)

Formulas in the *Data 1* Worksheet

In rows 9 and 11, master data is similarly extracted from the *Parameters 1* sheet using OFFSET. There's nothing to point out here that you don't already know.

K9:V9   =OFFSET(rP1.Node,K$2,3)

K11:V11   =OFFSET(rP1.Node,K$2,$E11)

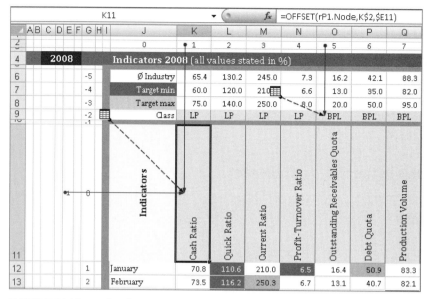

FIGURE 7-34 Master data from *Parameters 1* also appears in this worksheet.

Formulas in the *Basis 1* Worksheet

There are a few changes in relation to the table that represents the chart basis. It's rather marginal that the column headers in cells M11 and N11 are different. However, the formulas used for these are the same as those from variant 1 (see Figure 7-18).

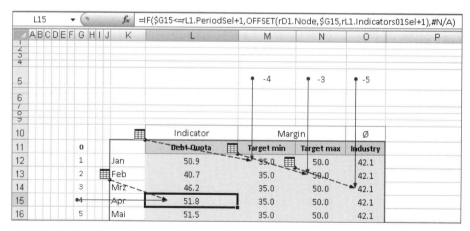

FIGURE 7-35 *Sel+1* is used in most of the formulas in this worksheet.

A more important change applies to all formulas that react to the output values of controls. The reason for this was explained earlier. The numbering of the index in a *ComboBox* or *ListBox* starts at *0* (zero), rather than at *1*. Clicking the first entry in one of these controls generates a *0* rather than a *1* in the corresponding *LinkedCell*. In all formulas that refer to these

LinkedCells, the value taken from that cell is increased by *1* (...Sel+1...). Take, for example, the formula in cell L15:

```
L15    =IF($G15<=rL1.PeriodSel+1,
        OFFSET(rD1.Node,$G15,rL1.Indicators01Sel+1),#N/A)
```

If you were to create this worksheet as a copy of the corresponding worksheet from variant 1 and adjust it as required, you could simply make a global change to all of the existing formulas using the *Replace* function: Find all instances of *Sel*, and replace these with *Sel+1*.

> **Important** This peculiarity (*0* rather than *1*) should make you particularly careful when testing the formulas. Does the formula return the value that you expect when you click the control? If you neglect to perform these tests, errors can soon creep in, and may not even be detected during a cursory check of the solution.
>
> One thing I always make sure to check is whether clicking the first list entry and last list entry returns the correct results.

Formulas in the *Focus 1* Worksheet

There are many new features here, most of which serves to make the worksheet more user friendly.

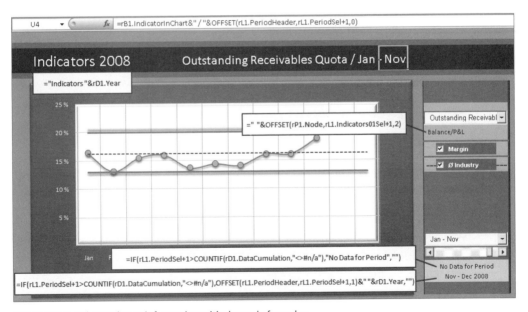

FIGURE 7-36 Enhanced user information with dynamic formulas

These are as follows, working top to bottom, and left to right:

D4   ="Indicators "&rD1.Year

This instructs Excel to do the following: "Write the string *Indicators* with a closing blank, and then insert the content from the *rD1.Year* cell." The year is specified in this cell.

U4   =rB1.IndicatorInChart&" / "
       &OFFSET(rL1.PeriodHeader,rL1.PeriodSel+1,0)

In U4, a header is composed in the usual manner. The only other difference here is that *Sel* is replaced with *Sel+1*.

X13   =" "&OFFSET(rP1.Node,rL1.Indicators01Sel+1,2)

The readout of the group ID for the selected indicator in cell X13 shouldn't be a mystery to you at this stage. Take note of the leading blanks generated by the formula.

The contents of cells X25 and X26 are a little more complicated. Here, two different formulas are used in two different cells to create a text that appears to the user as a single unit.

(Note also: The K12:K23 range in the *Data 1* worksheet has been assigned the name *rD1.DataCumulation*.)

X25   =IF(rL1.PeriodSel+1>COUNTIF(rD1.DataCumulation,"<>#n/a"),
       "No Data for Period","")

Translated into an instruction to Excel, this would read as follows: "If the value in the *rL1.PeriodSel* cell plus *1* is greater than the number of #N/A values in the *rD1.DataCumulation* range, write the string *No Data for Period*. Otherwise, write an empty text."

X26   =IF(rL1.PeriodSel+1>COUNTIF(rD1.DataCumulation,"<>#n/a"),
       OFFSET(rL1.PeriodHeader,rL1.PeriodSel+1,1)
       &" "&rD1.Year,"")

Translated into a an instruction to Excel, this would read as follows: "If the value in the *rL1.PeriodSel* cell plus *1* is greater than the number of #N/A values in the *rD1.DataCumulation* range, read the contents of a cell, which can be located as follows: Go to the *rL1.PeriodHeader* cell, and move down the number of rows specified in the *rL1.PeriodSel* cell plus *1*, and move across one column to the right (here we want to find entries in the "reverse list" explained above, see Figure 7-22). Insert a blank space, followed by the content from the *rD1.Year* cell. Otherwise, write an empty text."

Conditional Formatting

To conclude this chapter, we'll look at one more, very important element of dynamization. The appearance of a table should change whenever changes are made to its cell contents or to control values defined elsewhere. If you set up conditional formatting, Excel can generate a specific format in a cell depending on the content of that same cell (value-dependent) or of another cell (formula-dependent). You can either use predefined, integrated formats or customize your own.

The technique is very simple, and has a very similar effect to an IF formula:

- A condition defined by you is met (i.e., it is or becomes TRUE). Excel reacts by generating defined formatting for the relevant cells.

- A condition defined by you is not met (i.e., it is or becomes FALSE). Excel displays the basic formatting for the cells that have been assigned conditional formatting.

The conditional formatting feature is a little more complicated in Excel 2007. This feature has been significantly enhanced compared with earlier versions, with which you could only define three formatting variants for each cell (which was usually sufficient). Only time (and practice) will tell whether the variety of options now available will actually help improve the quality of information that can be conveyed. This most definitely won't be the case if the designer of a chart solution gets completely carried away and adopts the attitude *"If it can be done, why not do it?"* The result then will be psychedelic tables that confuse users rather than help them digest new information.

> **Important** Human perception is severely limited when it comes to interpreting small or non-pictorial symbols. If you plan to generate more than three different signals (of any kind) in one cell range in order to convey certain information to the user, you should have a very good reason for doing so.

Basics

Some general information about this feature is required before I explain the conditional formatting used in the *Data 1* and *Focus 1* worksheets. However, it wouldn't make sense to enter into too much detail in the context of this book, where conditional formats are relevant only as an enhancement of dynamic charts.

> **Tip** If you'd like to delve deeper into this multifaceted topic, and put the theory into practice by doing some exercises on your own, I recommend that you begin your experiments by creating a file similar to that shown in Figure 7-37:
>
> Fill several column areas (separated by color columns) with formulas that generate variable number series within a defined range (for example, with =RANDBETWEEN(100,999)). Define different conditional formatting in each column. When you press **F9**, new numbers appear, and the formatting you defined adjusts to suit the new values. Edit and change the conditional formatting based on the information provided in the following paragraphs.

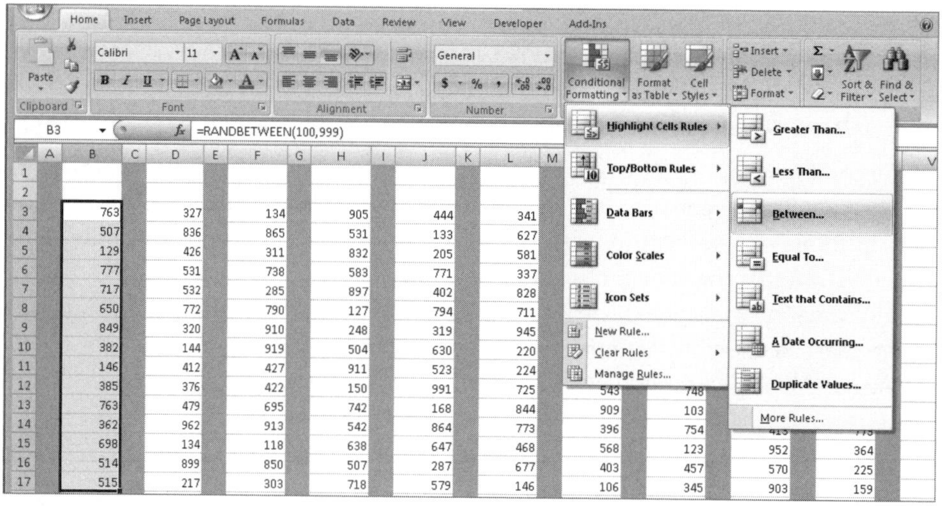

FIGURE 7-37 Accessing several conditional formatting variants

Let's examine a scenario based on Figure 7-37. Here you visually highlight cells that contain values within a certain range.

Select the *Home* tab in the Ribbon, and click the *Conditional Formatting* button in the *Styles* group. In the list that opens, select *Highlight Cells Rules*, and then select the type of rule you want to use (in this case, *Between*).

Then proceed as shown in Figure 7-38:

1. You define the limits of the value range (*BETWEEN ... and*) in a small dialog box.

2. Select one of the predefined styles listed, or click the *Custom Format* entry in the drop-down list.

3. If you select *Custom Format*, the *Format Cells* dialog box opens, with the tabs *Number, Font, Border,* and *Fill*.

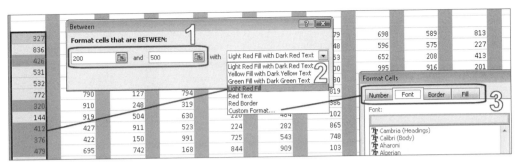

FIGURE 7-38 Simple options or complex design possibilities

Tip I must emphasize here that Excel 2007 now allows you to use number formats, including custom number-formats, in conditional formatting. This opens up a whole new range of possibilities, whereby number formats change automatically depending on specific values. And these values may be located in cells linked with controls. In other words, you could now simply click to control a number format.

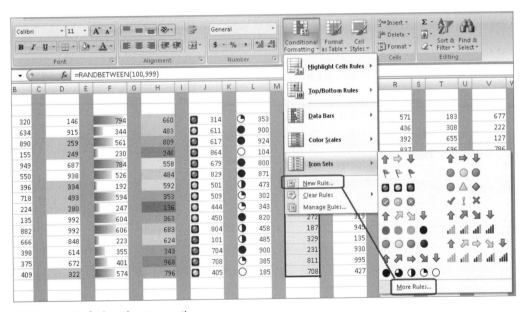

FIGURE 7-39 Default and custom options

Once you've found out all that you can do (and there's a lot!) with the predefined options available, you may want to explore the additional design possibilities, which I believe are more interesting. If you click *New Rule* or *More Rules* (framed in blue in Figure 7-39), the *New Formatting Rule* dialog box opens, which contains the options shown in Figure 7-40:

Note Note that the appearance of this dialog box changes considerably depending on the rule type selected (in step 1), and may differ from that shown here. The descriptions provided here serve as examples only, but they can be adapted to other variants.

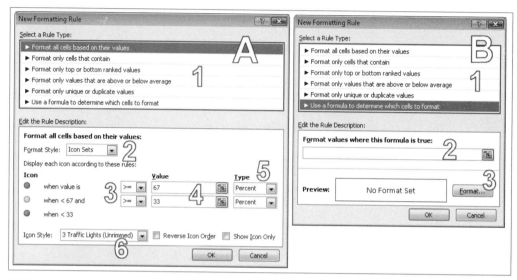

FIGURE 7-40 Dialog box for designing custom options

Example A:

1. Select a *Rule Type* from the list of descriptions.

2. Determine a formatting group to determine the *Format Style*.

3. Select logical operators.

4. Determine the value to be used in the *Value* box. You can define a value, a cell reference, or a formula here.

5. Under *Type*, select a data type for the *value* (which was selected in step 4).

6. Finally, choose a certain icon type within the *Format Style* group you selected (in step 2).

The method designated here as **Example B**, which involves using formulas to generate conditional formatting, is used much more frequently than the methods in *Example A* in rS1 models. Follow these steps:

1. Select the *Use a formula ...* rule type.

2. Enter a formula. This formula, like the `logical_test` argument in an IF formula, makes a certain claim, for example, =$K$5<=100 (the value in cell K5 is 100 or lower) or =rL1.CheckLightsSel=TRUE (the *rL1.CheckLightsSel* cell currently contains the value

TRUE). Each time this formula is calculated, Excel investigates whether this claim is TRUE. If it is, the conditional formatting generated in step 3 is assigned.

3. Click the *Format* button to define a format.

You manage conditional formatting in the *Conditional Formatting Rules Manager* dialog box. To open this dialog box, select the *Home* tab in the Ribbon, select the *Styles* group, and click the *Conditional Formatting* button. Finally, select the *Manage Rules* option.

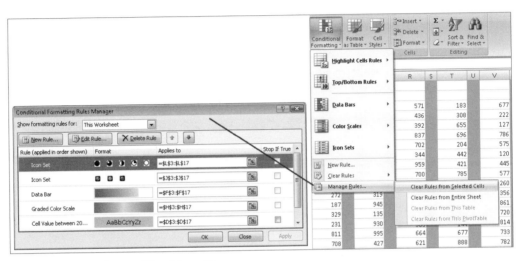

FIGURE 7-41 Managing conditional formatting

- At the top of this dialog box, you can choose to display rules, create a new rule, or edit (change) and delete existing rules. (You can also use other commands to clear rules; see Figure 7-41, right.)

- Each of the rows in the dialog box table provides essential information about the formats.

- You can change the reference in the *Applies to* column.

- If you double-click any part of a row entry, the *Edit Formatting Rule* dialog box opens, which is identical to the *New Formatting Rule* dialog box (see Figure 7-40).

> **Tip** The formatting rule manager dialog box is undoubtedly very useful. However, it may also be rather confusing and unclear, depending on the type, scope, and location of the conditional formatting used. It is essential that you remember to select the correct worksheet or table range in the *Show formatting rules for* box at the top of the dialog box. The only way to become accustomed to using this dialog box correctly is to deliberately practice using different formatting variants in various locations of your workbook.

Conditional Formatting: A Real-Life Example

Let's look now at the conditional formatting used in the \Samples\0702_Indicators_02.xlsx sample file:

Data 1 **Worksheet** Conditional formatting is used in the K12:V24 range.

> **Tip** If you want to select cells containing conditional formatting in the active worksheet, select the *Home* tab in the Ribbon, then select the *Editing* group, click the *Find & Select* button, and, finally, select the *Conditional Formatting* option.

These formats use formulas, and were created using the method described in Figure 7-40, example B.

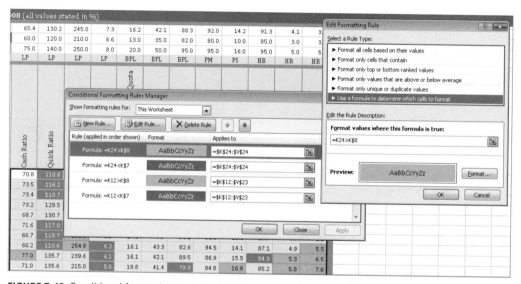

FIGURE 7-42 Conditional formatting in the *Data 1* worksheet

As shown in Figure 7-42, the formulas developed for the range of constants (K12:V23) were also assigned in the same way to the annual result line, in the K24:V24 range. This is yet another typical redundancy of the rS1 method. It's easy to imagine various ways in which the model might be modified in the future, for example:

- The conditional formatting in the result line should differ from that used for the constants.

- The conditional formatting applied to the constants should be removed, while the conditional formatting applied to the result line should be retained (or vice versa).

We've already made provisions for these eventualities, which didn't involve much additional effort at the time, but will save a fair amount of work and deliberation at a later stage.

Focus 1 **Worksheet**   The conditional formatting for the X25:Z26 range in the *Focus 1* work-sheet is similarly generated with a formula:

```
=rL1.PeriodSel+1>COUNTIF(rD1.DataCumulation,"<>#N/A")
```

> **Note** You can use formulas of any type or complexity for conditional formatting, including formulas much more complicated than those described here.

The basic formatting of the cells is the same as that of their neighboring cells, above and below. However, if Excel finds that the above "claim" is correct (TRUE), then the conditional formatting is applied, and these cells will be made to "stand out" from those around them. The intention here is to direct attention to the cell contents; i.e., the infotext, which—as explained earlier—was also generated using formulas.

Chapter 8
Chart Types—Conventional and Exceptional

You have studied the previous chapters and found the recommended practices interesting or important enough to implement the step-by-step instructions? Excellent: then you won't find it difficult to get the most out of the following, primarily practical, information.

Having laid the most critical theoretical foundations for designing attractive and dynamic charts, in this chapter I'll describe the technical development and editing of the most commonly used chart types. You will learn what is regarded as the default in Excel 2007 and how you can use some tricks to obtain rather exceptional results that aren't considered as "typical Excel."

Within the descriptions, you will find several charts that have already been presented to you in previous chapters (mainly in Chapters 3, "Perceiving, Interpreting, Understanding" and 4, "Colors, Areas, and Outlines") and that are available on the CD-ROM.

Because I assume that you've already received sufficient information on the use of Excel 2007 in the first seven chapters of this book, most of my explanations will be less detailed in the following sections.

Here are two examples:

- If you read the sentence "Select the command *Chart Tools/Layout/Axes/Primary Horizontal Axis*" (from Chapter 1, "Basic Information—Basic Techniques"), I assume you know that this is a command that you can access via the *Chart Tools/Layout* tab in the Ribbon which is only available if you activated a chart.

- The phrase "Set the custom number format #," k";; for the axis" presumes that you know the corresponding basic information from *Number Formatting in Charts*, in Chapter 6, "What, For Whom, How and With What?" You therefore know how to open the formatting dialog box for a chart axis and how you move there in an already open dialog box, that you then select the *Number* command in this dialog box, click *Custom* for the *Category*, enter the known code in the *Format Code* field, and subsequently click *Add*. In this context, I also assume that you are familiar with custom number formats which were described in Chapter 6.

Of course, nobody will expect you to know all of the numerous innovations of Excel 2007 by heart after you've reviewed the information for the first time. Refer to the index of procedures and the subject index at the end of this book to explore the sources of information you need.

Another important note: this is a very long chapter that includes numerous practical examples with detailed descriptions. You don't have to read it all at once.

Key Moves

To review some of the techniques already described in detail and to "warm up," I suggest that you create two relatively simple charts that are based on identical data and with different levels of complexity.

> **On the Companion CD** Open the file \Samples\0801_Stadium.xlsx on the CD-ROM.

You already know the scenario from Chapter 4; that's why I only provide brief information about the two variants:

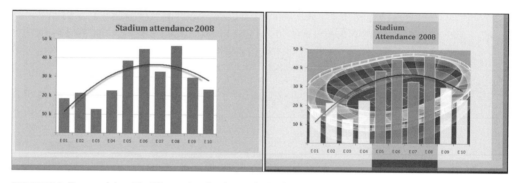

FIGURE 8-1 Two models with different levels of complexity for "copying"

You can see the attendance figures for 10 consecutive events that took place in a large stadium. The *Model 1 Final* worksheet (see Figure 8-1, left) shows a plain column chart that was created using simple defaults and also contains a trendline.

The version in the *Model 2 Final* worksheet (see Figure 8-1, right) is further developed on this basis and is designed with more detail for a presentation to be given potential new sponsors. The organization and design of such a chart is not particularly challenging in Excel 2007.

In the file, you can find the *Model 1 Practice* and *Model 2 Practice* worksheets right next to the finished models. To facilitate creation of the two models and simplify explanations, some preparations have already been made:

- The layout of the practice worksheets is already specified with regard to the background design (column width, row height, and coloring).

- For the plain Model 1, the data of the chart basis is in the same worksheet as the chart. If you use the rS1.Method, which plays only a minor role or no role in all examples of this chapter, this situation only occurs if there are good reasons that are based on the information value.

 Note You can find the figures for the individual dialog boxes mentioned in the following step-by-step instructions in the sections further below, where I describe individual chart types.

Model 1 (Standard Model)

Activate the *Model 1 Practice* worksheet and follow the step-by-step instructions. The sequence selected here does not claim to be a role model, only a recommendation. It rather follows the didactic requirements of this book and doesn't represent a "best practice." For my own work, I always consider that sequence best that suits me and that brings results within an acceptable time. Maybe some steps are more complex than necessary, but it surely won't do any harm, right?

1. Select the cell range B7:C16 as the data source of the chart.

2. Select *Insert/Charts/Column* and then *Clustered Column* under *2-D Column*. A chart is created and displayed with a selection frame.

3. Click one of the columns. Your screen should now look like Figure 8-2:

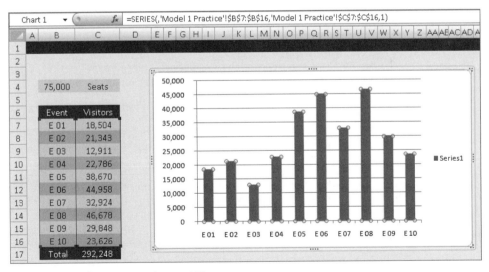

FIGURE 8-2 The first steps are done quickly.

❏ The chart and its only data series are selected.

❏ The *series formula* is displayed in the *formula bar*.

❏ The reference area of the data series (the tabular chart basis) is highlighted with two frames in different colors: one frame for the data source of the columns, the other frame for the data source for labeling the *primary horizontal axis* (previously referred to as *category axis*).

You could now change the existing references in two different ways (however, you shouldn't do so for the time being):

- Through manual change of the *series formula* in the *formula bar* (which is only recommended for experienced users)

- Or in an "administration window"—the *Select Data Source* dialog box—which you can open by clicking *Select Data* in the context menu of the chart. In this dialog box, you can make various edits:

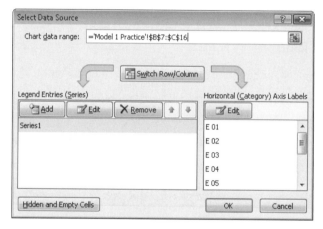

FIGURE 8-3 You can manage individual chart references here.

- ❏ Change the *chart data range*, (the reference to the cell range B7:C16).

- ❏ Change the orientation of the series content using *Switch Row/Column*; the column structure is based on rows or on columns. (Switching from *row* to *column* would be completely pointless in this example: the column orientation would result in a single category with 10 columns with different colors, and the labels *E 01* to *E 10* would then be found in the legend.)

- ❏ Change the series: add a new data series from another source, edit the reference and/or the name of an existing data series, or remove an existing data series.

- ❏ Specify and edit the *axis label range* (the source of the axis labels). The data for axis labels does not have to have a direct, spatial link with the series values. They can be assigned to the chart from any location, even from another worksheet, if necessary.

4. De-select the series selection (by pressing **Esc** or clicking on a free space in the chart). Only the *chart area* is now selected (the editing frame is displayed.) Resize the object using the *Chart Tools/Format/Size* command to dimensions of approximately 4 inches x 7 inches and move it to the top left corner so that it is placed near or in cell F2.

5. Select it in the legend and delete it by pressing the **Del** key.

6. Select the *plot area* and resize it to dimensions of approximately 3 inches x 5 inches using the mouse (unfortunately, you can't use the command listed in number 4). Use the specifications of the adjacent worksheet for the size and position of the *plot area*.

7. Select the columns again. Open the formatting dialog box (for example, using **Ctrl+1**), activate the *Series Options* tab, and set a *gap width* of 50 percent. This decreases the gaps between the columns and increases the columns' widths.

> **Tip** A *gap width* of 0 percent turns columns or bars into a step-like area, which can be a very useful effect. The effect of this area is even better, if you omit the color-fill effects, borders, and 3-D effects during formatting.

8. Select the *primary vertical axis* (previously referred to as *value axis*) and activate the *Axis Options* tab in the formatting dialog box. Assign a custom scale; that is, fixed values. For this purpose, click the respective *Fixed* option and enter numeric values in the corresponding field, if this is still necessary for the specifications provided by Excel: *Minimum: 0, Maximum: 50000, Major unit: 10000.* You can ignore the *Minor unit* option, because you only use *major gridlines* but no *minor gridlines* in the chart (you can find the commands for setting the vertical and horizontal chart gridlines under *Chart Tools/Layout/Gridlines*). Refer to the box at the end of these step-by-step instructions to find an explanation for the suggested specification of the axis values.

9. Set additional display types for the axis in the *Axis Options* tab: *Major tick mark type* (the axis' tiling with *major gridlines* orientation): *Outside, Minor tick mark type*: *None, Axis labels*: *Next to Axis*.

10. Change to the *Number* tab and set the custom number format #," k";; for this axis. The numbers are decreased to the thousands format and are supplemented by the character string *k* after a space. The display of the zero is suppressed.

11. Enable the *primary horizontal axis*. For the moment, you must only ensure for the *axis options* that the *major tick mark type, minor tick mark type*, and *axis labels* are set as described in step 9 and that the number *1* is set for the *Interval between tick marks* (at the very top of the tab). For each *major unit* of the gridlines a *major tick mark* is plotted in or on the axis. You are provided with more information on this topic later on.

12. Select the *Chart Tools/Layout/Analysis/Trendline/More Trendline Options* command, and choose the *Polynomial* option with the *Order: 2* setting in the dialog box that appears; a *linear trendline* has already been plotted and highlighted.

13. In the dialog box, go to the *Line Color* tab and choose dark red for the *trendline*.

14. Under *Line Style* define a *width* of approximately 2 pt.

15. Go to the *Shadow* tab and choose the following settings for the *trendline*.

- ❏ *Presets: Outer, Offset Bottom*

- ❏ *Color: Dark Blue*

- ❏ *Transparency: 60 %*

- ❏ *Size: 90 %*

- ❏ *Blur: 5 pt*

- ❏ *Angle: 80°*

- ❏ *Distance: 3 pt*

16. Now highlight the entire chart again (the *chart area*) and determine the following colorings in the formatting dialog box, going from the largest element to the smallest:

- ❏ *Chart area: Tan*

- ❏ *Plot area: White*

- ❏ *Columns: Blue*

- ❏ *Line color of axes and gridlines: Gray*

17. Select the axes and set the font color to dark red and specify other font attributes under *Home/Font.*

18. Click outside the chart to undo the selection. Use the command *Insert/Text Box/ Horizontal Text Box* to create an absolutely flexible chart title, which can also be used outside the chart. Click anywhere to activate the enter mode for the text box and enter the text *Stadium Attendance 2008.* Set *Cambria, 18, bold, dark red* as the font attributes. Make the text box fully transparent by setting the formatting properties to *No line* and *No fill,* and move it to the top right above the *plot area* using the mouse.

The default variant of the chart is now completed and can be used directly as the basis for the presentation variant. First, I still owe you the explanation for the custom specification of the axis values for the primary vertical axis (see step 8),

In the example provided here, there is a display problem for the presentation to the potential sponsors: the stadium with its 75,000 seats only had a poor attendance for the 10 events. This information is not supposed to be kept a secret, but should not appear at first glance either. For this reason, the maximum value for the axis is deliberately set to 50,000—just some 3,000 above the attendance of the most popular event—and the minimum value to zero. The "good" columns *E 05* to *E 08* almost reach the top of the chart—at least at first view—and are pretty long because they start at zero. The columns could also be shorter and only start at 10,000, because the smallest column is beyond that value.

It is irrelevant for evaluating this scenario that this classification is automatically suggested by Excel for the existing total number constellation. Don't rely on automated processes, and always pay careful attention to whether and how you can change the display and "rating" of your charts by means of axis scaling. The axes and their settings have an extremely high significance for the design of all charts. You will find from time to time that you can give your chart an entirely different effect with minor axis changes. This also applies to the *primary horizontal axis* (category axis), even though this is less significant.

A custom—i.e., fixed—scaling prevents Excel from creating an automatic axis classification based on the existing data. You may only set up the fixed scaling, however, if you know the limits of the data to be displayed. If you work with dynamic charts whose value ranges for display may vary considerably (for example, the key indicators charts of the previous chapter), or if you can't exclude future "outliers" to any direction, you may not suppress automatic scaling.

The automatic scaling of *major units* is set by Excel often with a higher density than would be necessary or good for an acceptable visualization. You must use a fixed, broader unit scaling than is automatically set by Excel if the precise visual differentiation of very similar values is not required (such visualization is only required in rare cases).

Simply try it out yourself: in the example chart, entering 10,000 as the minimum, 75,000 as the maximum, and 5,000 as the major unit. The axis label looks squeezed and the display of the attendance is not convincing at all. It gives a rather miserable impression, even though the displayed values haven't been changed. This way, you couldn't sell anything.

Model 2 (Presentation Variant)

When I create a presentation chart, I always start by generating a relatively plain basic variant and saving it. This serves as my starting point for implementing further design tasks, but also for my experiments (this procedure only makes sense, of course, if you implement any further work using copies of the basic version). This idea is now put into practice in the file *0801_Stadium.xlsx*: *Model 1,* which you created in the previous section and is now further developed to become *Model 2.* So, copy the chart that you created in the *Model 1 Practice* worksheet (or alternatively the basic model from the *Model 1 Final* worksheet) to the *Model 2 Practice* worksheet and position it so that the top left corner is located in cell E3.

The next steps are illustrated in Figure 8-4:

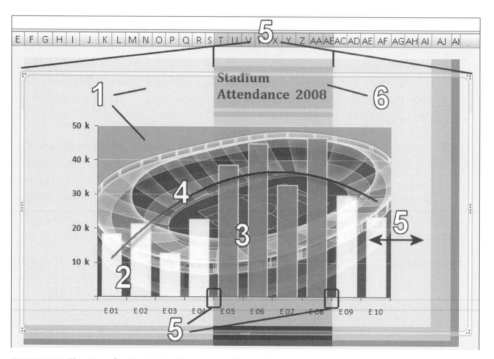

FIGURE 8-4 The steps for designing the presentation variant

1. Highlight the *chart area* and make it fully transparent by selecting the *No fill* option for the *Fill* in the formatting dialog box. Remove the display of the border with *Border Color/No line.* Next, select the *plot area,* and then choose the command *Picture or texture fill, Insert from/File* button in the formatting dialog box/*Fill* tab to insert the *\Materials\Pictures\Stadium.tif* picture file as the background of the data series.

2. Color the columns of the data series in white and set a transparency of 9 percent so that the outlines of the pictures are still slightly visible.

3. All columns are selected. Now click the selected column *E 05* to deselect all other columns. All subsequent commands only influence this single column and this specific *data point*, which is the term used in the Excel dialog boxes. Proceed as follows:

   ❏ Specify white as the *border color* and 2 pt as the *border style/width*.

   ❏ Use the **right arrow** key to go the next column and repeat the formatting. Repeat these steps until all relevant columns (*E 05* to *E 08*) have this format.

   ❏ Select the column *E 05* again and make the following settings: *Fill: Solid fill*, pale red, *Transparency* 9 %.

   ❏ Repeat these settings for the data points *E 06* to *E 08*.

4. Select the trendline that is to be provided with a gradient fill as well. If you assign a gradient to a line, you should imagine the object as a compact rectangle which you first color in a specific way and from which you then cut out a custom-shaped, thin strip, which is this line. Specify the following:

   ❏ *Line color: Gradient line*

   ❏ *Type: Linear*

   ❏ *Angle: 90°*

   ❏ *Gradient stop 1:* blue, *Stop position 0 %, Transparency 0 %*

   ❏ *Gradient stop 2:* green, *Stop position 58 %, Transparency 0 %*

5. Note that number 5 in Figure 8-4 includes three different positions: top, bottom, and right. This step is about the harmonization of the background (the colored table columns T to AB), with the columns *E 05* to *08*. The table structures become design elements of a chart:

   ❏ Press **Ctrl**+mouse click to select the chart as a drawing object (you can now see four selection corner points) and move it using the arrow keys **arrow right** or **arrow left** so that the *major tick mark* between the columns *E 04* and *E 05* is positioned on the left edge of the column T.

   ❏ Click an empty space in the *plot area* to activate the object as a chart again and to select the plot area at the same time. Position the mouse pointer on the handle on the right edge of the *plot area* and drag it slowly and carefully—if necessary, back and forth—until the *major tick line* between the columns *E 04* and *E 05* is on the left edge of column T. You may have to drag the left edge of the *plot area* again and then the right one as well to add the final touch or to move the entire plot area to obtain the desired match.

> **Note** As you can see, this whole thing is pretty tricky. For this reason, I want to present an alternative that is more convenient: you first create a transparent or—as in our case—partly transparent chart and not till then set the row and column colors as well as the row height and column width of the table background. Here, you don't adapt the chart to the table, but the table to the chart.

6. Create a text box just like in *Model 1*, or copy the text box from *Model 1*. Enter a line break after "Stadium" and then position the text box so that the character string *Stadium Attendance 2008* appears on the dark-colored background.

This concludes the two initial examples. The following sections provide you with further details on editing column charts and various other chart types. In this context, "editing" is used as the generic term for various designs and reorganizations that you can easily implement in Excel.

The explanations for column and bar charts will be a little more detailed than for the other chart types. This is because many of the moves described can be valid for various chart types, even if you obtain completely different results for those chart types.

Whether and how much you can use specific options in a chart mainly depend on the type of the existing or future data material and the general purpose of visualization. In other words, not every editing option that is available for a specific chart type can actually be used for every chart of this type. This naturally affects the following explanations. It will be useful if you go through the entire chapter (or other parts of this book) and, for example, experiment with applying the content described for use in column charts to area charts, or transfer line chart settings to scatter charts (XY) and the like.

Column Charts

> **On the Companion CD** Open the file *\Samples\0802_Columns.xlsx* on the CD-ROM.

First, I want to provide you with some examples based on the *Columns 1* worksheet in the file *0802_Columns.xlsx*. The chart shows those 13 countries/regions of the European Union whose number of inhabitants is greater than 10 million (see Figure 8-5).

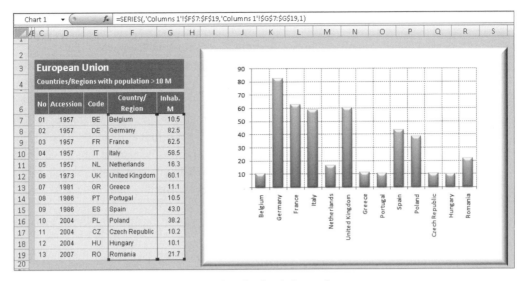

FIGURE 8-5 A simple column chart with a multitude of variation options

What needs to be considered for the basic design?

■ The data table is sorted according to two criteria (referred to as *levels* in Excel 2007): first, according to the accession years of the states, then alphabetically.

■ The contents of the data table are shown only in parts in the current version of the chart. The table range currently referenced by the chart is F7:G19. The columns C, D, and E don't play roles yet, but are retained for future use.

■ The primary vertical axis has a fixed—that is, custom—scaling (from 0 to 90 in increments of 10); and 0;; is set as the custom number format.

■ The evaluation of the columns requires a relatively detailed visualization of the actual number of inhabitants. For this reason, considerably tight gridlines (*vertical major gridlines* and *horizontal major gridlines*) are applied to the *plot area*. To keep the impression at a moderate level, the formatting is kept discreet by using gray dashed lines.

■ The label of the primary horizontal axis was done using the formatting dialog box and command *Alignment/Text direction/Rotate all text 270°*. Text with this alignment is not easy to read, but the formatting is much better than with any of the other rotation options. Note in particular that slanted texts can be read fairly well on a printout, but not in a video presentation. If you need to save space in the category labels—a horizontal text alignment would be hardly possible in this example—you must accept compromises in most cases.

Axis Options

Two texts, which appear in the two *Axis Options* tabs of the formatting dialog box (see Figure 8-6), give me reason to think about alternatives for the terms *primary vertical axis* (value axis) and *primary horizontal axis* (category axis), which are not ideal names in my opinion. For the formatting of the *primary vertical axis*, the dialog box uses the term *values* (this relates to the *reverse order,* which is described later in detail*)* and for the *primary horizontal axis* the term *categories*. It would seem obvious to use the terms *value axis* and *category axis*, primarily because these terms are neutral and prevent confusion. It is by all means possible that the values of a chart can also be found in a horizontal axis, in a diagonal axis, or in two axes with different alignments, and that no categories are classified.

Settings of the Primary Vertical Axis

First, take a look at the settings of the *primary vertical axis* (see Figure 8-6, part *A*). It measures the number of inhabitants of the 13 countries/regions. For the column chart variant, the most essential things have already been explained in the initial step-by-step instructions. But because you'll find some other column charts in the file's practices (some of them have already been presented in Chapter 3), I'll provide you with some basic remarks about the options in the dialog box.

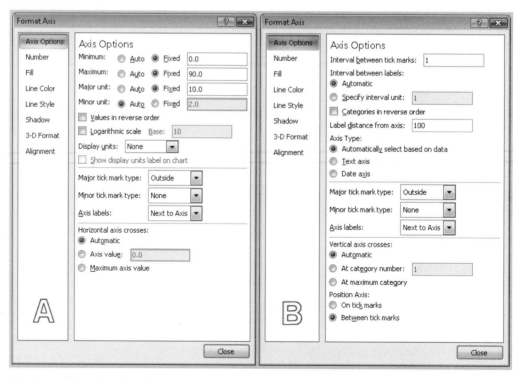

FIGURE 8-6 The axis options play an important role in virtually every chart.

- *Values in reverse order*: this would be impractical in this example; the category axis and all its labels would be set to the upper edge of the plot area, the values would be displayed in descending order, and the columns would hang from the axis, instead of standing on it.

- You can't use a *logarithmic scale* for these figures. It is required for very large value ranges whose scaling can't be displayed linearly. For example, you can display the value ranges in decimal powers; that is, in decades which differ from their adjacent decade by a factor of 10.

- I don't recommend the use of *display units* because they can be error-prone (cognitive rather than display errors). For this reason, I won't describe this option now, because it is only useful in very special cases. Always use number formats for displaying values. The options for custom number formats leave nothing to be desired.

- The tick mark types (*major tick mark type* and *minor tick mark type*) have already been discussed and are self-explanatory.

- The *axis labels* are positioning options. *Next to Axis* is the default, and occurs on the left of the vertical axis, irrespective of its location in the plot area. For this example, select the *High* setting [sic] to move the label to the right of the axis and thus to the other side of the *plot area* (caution: the axis itself, the axis *line*, remains on the left of the *plot area* and can only be selected there). By selecting the *Low* option (like *Next to Axis*) the label is returned to the left side of the axis. This becomes much more reasonable if the axis is not located at the edge of the *plot area* (which is usually the case), but *in the plot area*; further information on this is provided later.

- The *Horizontal axis crosses* option is described in the section on line charts.

Settings of the Primary Horizontal Axis

For the various uses of column charts, the setting options for the *primary horizontal axis* are much more interesting (dialog box in Figure 8-6, part *B*). In this context, compare the settings of the *Columns 2* worksheet with the following details. First of all, here is some basic information about the peculiarities of the example chart shown in Figure 8-7:

- This is a so-called "long sequence" of measurement values which have been determined every month over a period of three years; four values still need to be established. If you press **F9** you can generate new data.

- The data may also be negative.

- The gap between the columns has been set to 0 percent.

- For the column formatting, the *Invert if negative* option has been enabled in the *Fill* tab. This inverts the fill gradient of the negative columns pointing downwards.

- The scaling of the *primary vertical axis* is set to *Automatic*.

- The number format of the *primary vertical axis* is set as user-defined + `#,##0;` `[Red] - #,##0;0`.

- There are multiple columns that contain possible labels of the *primary horizontal axis*. The label actually used is generated in column F by means of formulas; a procedure that sometimes ensures useful flexibility.

- The *vertical major gridlines* are enabled. The lines are formatted more boldly than the horizontal major gridlines. Reason: the tiling according to quarters is to be clearly visible.

- In this chart as well, the columns are accompanied by a *trendline*, in this case as a "moving average."

The "moving average" is often used for examining and visualizing measurement values. Drawn as a line with varying bends, the moving average shows a value pattern or a trend. In the formatting dialog box you can determine how strongly the line reacts to differences of the underlying individual values, that is, how pronounced the coils or deflections are. Enter a number in *Moving Average/Period* that is between 2 and the total number of values to be included minus 1 (number of data points of the entire data series minus 1). This way, you determine how many of the series' values are used for calculating one of the data points of the respective trendline.

In this example, the period was set to *3*. The average of the first three measurement values is used as the first data point of the trendline (the line starts at the third measurement value). The average value of the second, third, and fourth measurement values becomes the second data point of the trendline, the average value of the third, fourth, and fifth measurement values become the third data point of the trendline, and so on. The longer the custom *period* for calculating the trendline, the more measurement values are considered for the individual data points of this trendline. In other words, the more period values you used for calculating a moving average, the more balanced and the "smoother" the trendline becomes.

I can't provide you with a general recommendation for the length of the *period* relating to the number of data in the series, because the requirements of the visualization of a moving average may vary considerably depending on the data type and display purpose.

- The *primary horizontal axis*—in this case, the term *zero line* would also be appropriate—is comparatively bold and formatted according to the trendline (width 1.5, dark red). The *major tick mark type* was set to *Cross*.

> **Tip** If you want to select the primary horizontal axis that is displayed within the *plot area*, it is still advisable to click below the *plot area*—that is, in the axis label—and not directly below the axis line (you would select the *plot area* for that) nor on the line itself (you would select the *plot area* or *data series*).

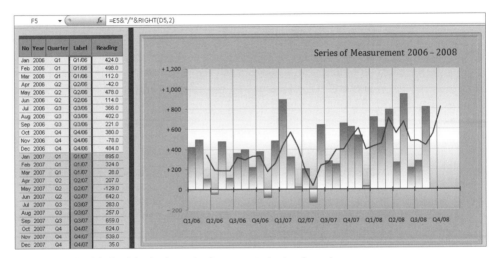

FIGURE 8-7 The labels of the horizontal axis are created using formulas.

The other formal peculiarities of this chart mainly depend on the axis formatting options, which are described below.

- *Interval between tick marks*: this value is set to *3*. Three categories (data points, monthly columns) are to be displayed between the lines of the *vertical major gridlines* or the axis's major tick lines. This setting splits the visualization of the three years into quite clear quarter segments.

- *Interval between labels*: the *interval unit* was also set to 3. As a result, only every third character string of the defined axis labels (from column F) is displayed.

- *Categories in reverse order*: activating this option would be unreasonable, because the *primary vertical axis* would move to the right and invert the data order; in other words, the time and data series would run backwards.

- *Label distance from axis*: here, you enter a number between *0* and *1,000* to determine the distance between the axis labels and the axis itself.

- *Axis Type*:

  - *Automatically select based on data*: this is the default. Excel checks the data existing in the axis label range and selects the appropriate axis type based on this check.

  - *Text axis*: the axis labels are displayed as text. The axis labels and data points are displayed in the chart with uniform spacing.

  - *Date axis*: the axis labels are displayed as calendar dates at automatic or custom intervals. The labels are shown with regular spacing, the data points with calendar-determined spacing; the period between two data points consequently defines their spacing in the chart. An example is provided in the section on line charts.

- *Major tick mark type* and *Minor tick mark type*: determine how the major and minor tick marks are to be displayed on the axis. The settings are self-explanatory.

- *Axis labels*: simply try out the three options available:

  - The *Next to Axis* option makes no sense for this chart. There can be negative values (press the **F9** key several times for simulation) and therefore columns can appear below the zero line; this would result in an optical conflict with the axis labels.

  - The *High* option positions the axis labels above the plot area, an acceptable variant for our example.

  - The preferred option for this example is called *Low,* which positions the axis label below the *plot area*. Your label is always in the same location no matter where the zero line is positioned within the plot area. The variant shown in the example usually presumes that vertical *gridlines* are displayed to ensure the optical relation between the axis line and their labels.

- *Vertical axis crosses*: you can specify the location where the *primary vertical axis* stands on or crosses the *primary horizontal axis*. When the *Automatic* option is set, the *primary vertical axis* usually stands on the left edge of the *plot area*. The example shown in Figure 8-9 indicates that the display can also be completely different.

- *Position Axis*: For two-dimensional area, column, and line charts, you can determine the alignment of the *data points* of the *data series* in relation to the *tick marks* (the vertical gridlines or the tiling of the axis):

  - *On tick marks* (variant *A* in Figure 8-8): the tick marks cross the data points.

  - *Between tick marks* (the—usually better—variant *B* in Figure 8-8): the data points are between the tick marks.

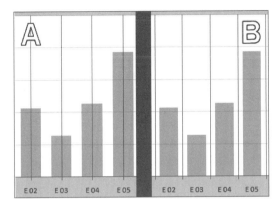

FIGURE 8-8 Different positioning of data points in relation to the axis tiling

To conclude the *Settings of the Primary Horizontal Axis* topic, open the *Columns 1* worksheet again and try to complete the task which is shown in Figure 8-9 and that is detailed as follows. This is primarily to recap the instructions given so far in this chapter.

- The table is sorted in descending order according to the population of the countries/regions.

- The chart shows the columns in ascending order from left to right.

- The label of the *primary horizontal axis* uses the data of the table's *Code* column with a regular alignment.

- The *vertical gridlines* appear more pronounced than the horizontal gridlines.

- The *horizontal gridlines* now have a gap of 20 (million) instead of 10.

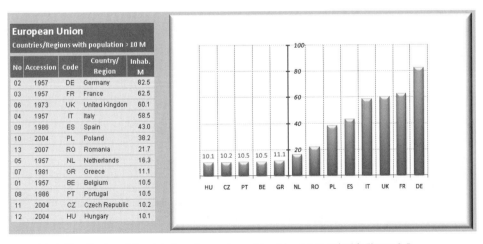

FIGURE 8-9 The display of the data has changed considerably compared with Figure 8-5.

- The *primary vertical axis* crosses at category 9 (in this case, you must count from right to left!).

- The label of the *primary vertical axis* is on the right side of this axis.

- The scaling of the *primary vertical axis* was reclassified and its number format was changed (the counting starts with 20—and would even start with 20 if the major unit of the axis had remained 10).

- The columns on the left side of the *primary vertical axis* are the five countries/regions with relatively low numbers of inhabitants, and their values are shown in blue for improved differentiability (in anticipation of the *Data Labels* topic further below).

Try to exactly reproduce this model.

If you don't feel like trying it yourself or if you want to compare your results, refer to the file *\Samples\0803_Europe_S13.xlsx*.

Multiline and Multicolumn Axis Labels

You create a category axis label:

- By including their tabular data range in the selection of the chart data range during chart creation, or

- By specifying or changing the reference of the *axis label range* in the *Select Data Source* dialog box following the creation of the chart using the *Select Data* command (context menu).

You've already come across several examples for multiline axis labels in this book. I use them quite frequently, because I can create clear and informative chart designs with relatively little effort. This doesn't necessarily apply to the live presentations, but particularly to the print versions of your charts.

You can find three examples in the file *\Samples\0804_AxisLabels.xlsx*. The labels presented there are categorizing; that is, they contain information to differentiate categories. Because we're still talking about column charts, the labels are located below the horizontal axis. For bar charts, whose category tiling is vertical, this is naturally different. You apply the same design techniques for bar charts, but you create multicolumn axis labels, not multiline axis labels.

 On the Companion CD Open the file *\Samples\0804_AxisLabels.xlsx* on the CD-ROM.

In principle, you should always ensure that a multiline label remains clearly presented. For this reason, the content should not exceed a limit of three lines.

For the font formatting, the following rules apply:

- If you assign font attributes using the commands of the Ribbon, these affect *all* lines of the label.

- If you assign a specific *alignment* via the formatting dialog box, this affects only the *first* line of the label.

There are multiple variation options for determining the content of multiline axis labels:

- Each line is completely filled with label data. As a result, the label looks like a table, which often appears unfavorably.

- One or more line(s) is/are not filled completely with label data. This results in an optical segmentation. The label receives the character of a ruler, which often appears favorably, particularly if the segments have a regular structure (see Figure 8-11). This way, you can often provide tiling information that is not available or insufficient in the chart image itself.

  An irregular segmentation (see Figure 8-10) only makes sense if the data material to be visualized requires such a tiling.

- Including or combining calculation results in multiline axis labels (see Figure 8-12) is a very interesting technique that can be helpful for the viewer.

Example 1, Two-Line, Irregular Segmentation   Open the *Columns 1* worksheet in the sample file. The chart probably looks familiar; however, it has a different data content than the previously discussed versions.

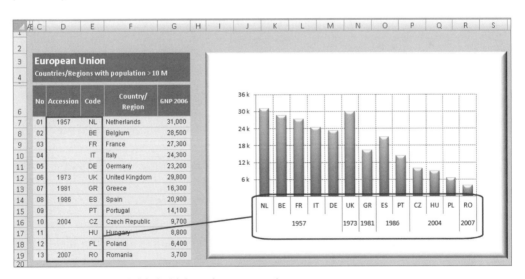

FIGURE 8-10 Two-line axis label with irregular segmentation

The chart shows the gross national product (in euros per inhabitant) of the selected 13 EU-countries/regions. Besides the label, you should also consider the following:

- The group-specific sorting of the data, first according to accession year, then according to value

- The scaling and number formatting of the value axis

Here is the most important technical information for multiline labels of the category axis:

- It references to the cell range D7:E19. The implementation of the existing column values in the chart label is carried out in columns from right to left and as rows from top to bottom.

- The segmentation and their display with line tilings is created automatically when you fill the first cell of a group in the data source that is, the table, and leave the remaining cells of this group empty. As a result, lines are set on the left and right side of the corresponding segment in the axis label of the chart and the content is aligned in the center of these two lines.

- The vertical tiling lines are extensions of *major tick lines* of the axis. Thus, the formatting of the major tick lines is used.

> **Tip** For one-line labels, the *major tick lines* of the axis are not extended. However, if you require this very useful display, you can simply define a two-line axis label and fill the cell range of the second label row with blank spaces (a procedure which I already mentioned in other examples).

Example 2, Three-Line, Regular Segmentation   The *Columns 2* worksheet shows the measurement chart that I already introduced earlier with a slightly different appearance and a different data structure.

I'll start with some general remarks, particularly with regard to the differences to the already known example:

- There are no negative values. You can create new data by pressing the **F9** key. The data range between 60 and 96 and indicate a slightly ascending trend in the overall view. The formulas in the range G5:G40 are responsible for this trend, which increases the upper value and consequently the random range. For example, the formula in cell G5 is: =RANDBETWEEN(60,60+$C5). The increase factor is the consecutive number in column C.

- Because the value range is limited, the same procedure applies for creating the value axis. It has fixed scale values between 50 and 100 at an interval of 10.

> **Note** This chart primarily focuses on the evaluation of a development and not on the "size." Therefore, you can (and should) adjust the presentable value range to its actually existing limits. If you had to convince an audience using increasing values that were "all above 60," you would select a scaling that started at zero.

- Based on my presentation experience, a "skyline" with trendline is very popular with audiences. The borderless columns, which have a gap width of 0 percent and a solid, pale blue fill, became a two-dimensional background figure that gives the optical priority to the trendline (which is to be in the spotlight anyway).

- The predominance of the trendline (moving average) is further enhanced by a shadow. Additionally, the line is supposed to give a "calm" impression. Therefore, its period was set to 6.

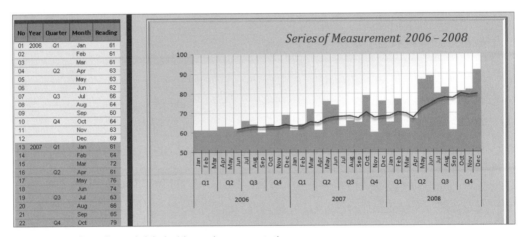

FIGURE 8-11 Three-line axis label with regular segmentation

There is hardly anything else to mention with regard to the technical aspects of the category axis label, because most aspects were already discussed in the previous example. The three-line regular structure uses a clear, readily identifiable visualization hierarchy according to years, quarters, and months. The entire chart is space-saving because the first row—that is, the months—was aligned with an angle of 270°.

Example 3, Three-Line, with Calculation Results in the Label　　The chart in the *Columns 3* worksheet is a variant of Example 2, in which the structure of the axis label has remained unchanged and the text contents have been supplemented by calculation results.

The moving average over the entire period, which is shown by means of the trendline, is the most essential factor here. The monthly values (appearing as "column area") and the averages of the years are of secondary importance. The latter are calculated in the data table and indicated in the bottommost label line together with the year.

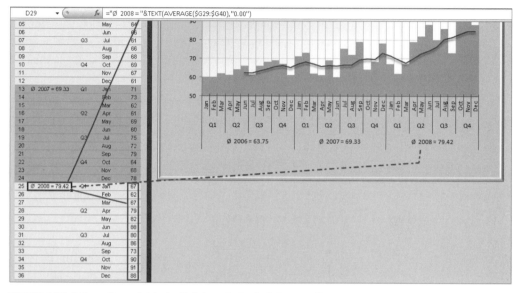

FIGURE 8-12 A three-line axis label with integrated calculation results

About the three corresponding formulas, based on the example in cell D29:

="Ø 2008 = "&TEXT(AVERAGE($G29:$G40),"0.00")

The verbalized instruction for Excel would be: "Create the character string Ø 2008 = and add the result of the average calculation of the range G29:G40 in the number format 0.00."

Note The Ø character is the ANSI character 216 of the standard fonts. Chapter 12, "More Than Numbers," provides information on how you can insert this and other characters which are not available directly on the keyboard.

The display of the average is to be limited to two decimals for aesthetic reasons and due to lack of space. Because AVERAGE($G29:$G40) is to become part of a text string, you must use the TEXT function to explicitly specify the number format, in which the number is to appear within the overall string, to avoid a display of up to 15 decimal places.

The =TEXT(value,format_text) function formats a number and converts it to text. You probably use the value argument only as a reference to a cell or cell range, so a better formulation would be =TEXT(reference,format_text). The format_text argument is any integrated or custom number formatting code (see Chapter 6) that must be put in quotes. The latter also applies if the custom code itself does contain its own quotes.

Data Labels

Another label element that is important for emphasizing and clarifying information has already been mentioned in connection with Figure 8-9.

Data labels are elements that must be assigned to *data points*. They can appear in all data points of a *data series* (for example, in each column of a column chart), or only in some or one single data point of a *data series*, which is an interesting option suitable for attracting attention.

 On the Companion CD Open the file \Samples\0805_DataLabels.xlsx on the CD-ROM.

The data label which is shown in the *Labels 1* worksheet and is introduced in Figure 8-13 can be created quickly. Note that the primary horizontal axis and its labels have been removed because the corresponding values are directly displayed at the data points.

Proceed as follows:

1. Right-click a *data point* to highlight the entire *data series* and to open the context menu at the same time.

2. Select the *Format Data Labels* command and specify your settings in the respective dialog box.

3. Specify the details to be contained in the data label. You can make your (combined) selection under *Series Name, Category Name*, and *Value*. In our example, the category names (which would normally appear in the category axis label) and the values of the data points are included in the label. The term *series name* will be detailed in the following example.

> **Note** From a practical point of view, the *data label* is to be considered as a *text box* to which Excel automatically adds specific content if the user requests it. Apart from that, you can freely design this object. You can format and move it like a text box, add custom supplementary contents, or correct already existing contents. This also means that you can apply different contents to the label strings than is provided in its sources in the chart basis. For these cases, you can use the *Reset Label Text* command button to undo custom changes and have the content of the data label displayed as it was set up by Excel based on your decisions in the formatting dialog box.

4. You can use the *Label Position* option to specify the position of the label in relation to the data point. The fastest way to find out the effects of your decisions is to simply experiment with the options yourself. For the column chart, the *Outside End* default is usually the most suitable one, at least if *all* data points have labels which to differentiate the category and the display of exact values (as in our example here).

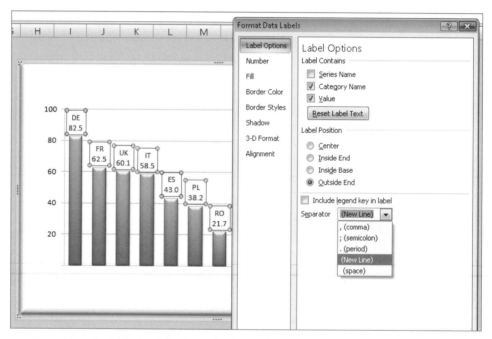

FIGURE 8-13 Standard data labels for the entire data series

5. In this example, the *(New Line)* default was selected as the separator, which I prefer if sufficient space is available because it usually provides the clearest overview. Here, you should particularly note that you can use a relatively free design in "text box style" as already mentioned in number 3. This also applies to the specification of wrapped texts, for example.

6. Specify the font attributes using the commands provided in the *Home* tab in the Ribbon.

> **Important**   You are provided with the entire range of number formats (including the custom formats) for formatting the data labels.

The data label shown in the *Labels 2* worksheet (see Figure 8-14) is a bit more sophisticated.

This example was intended to optically highlight the country/region with the highest gross national product. Much to the delight of the Dutch viewer (*"Oranje boven"*) this is done with an orange coloring of the column and a clearly visible individual label of this data point.

To implement this, first left-click the entire *data series*, then left-click the *data point*, and subsequently use the right mouse button to view the context menu where you can proceed as described in the step-by-step instructions stated above.

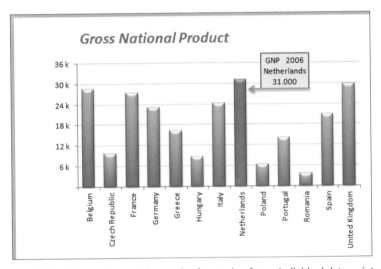

FIGURE 8-14 A data label with complex formatting for an individual data point

Some specifics of the data label design shown in Figure 8-14 are worth mentioning:

- The object has a colored area and a colored border (orange, of course) whose color and width is identical to the arrow. The arrow was inserted as a drawing object and formatted. Among other formatting, a shadow was added to the arrow. The arrow is along the entire bottom edge of the label box and was positioned exactly on this edge. As a result, the shadow as well as the arrow seems to be part of the box.

- The *data label* was moved—similar to working with a text box—from its originally selected position (*Outside End*) to the right and downward (the arrow was added subsequently).

- *Series Name, Category Name*, and *Value* were set as the three-line content. This gives me a reason to explain how a series name is created or changed.

The *series name* is a property of the data *series*. By default, the series name is created by Excel when a chart is generated. It is displayed in the legend provided that you selected this option. In many cases, this is all you need because you usually don't need any other information for identifying a *data series*—for example, in the series formula of the formula bar—or for navigating in the chart.

On the other hand, there are some scenarios in which the presence of a specific series name is also important in charts without a legend or enables interesting effects. Proceed as follows to specify and/or edit a series name in the context of Figure 8-15:

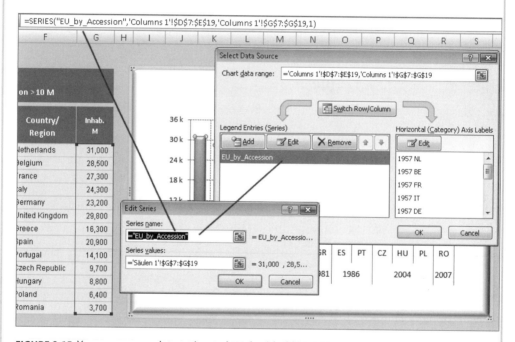

FIGURE 8-15 You can name a data series and work with this name.

1. Right-click the chart and choose the *Select Data* command in the context menu.

2. In the list, click the *series* you want to rename or edit.

3. Click the *Edit* button and enter the desired name (and/or a changed reference) in the small dialog box that now appears. You don't have to enter the name as a formula and in quotes as it is displayed in the figure. You can simply enter the required text. After clicking *OK*, Excel converts this text into a formula. Consequently, you can also enter the required name text in a cell and then refer to this cell in the dialog box.

From the latter, we can offer a tip for the ambitious readers:

❑   A series name can be included in a cell and therefore be the result of a formula.

❑   If the result of the formula is a number, it can be converted into text (for example, using the TEXT function).

❑   The series name taken from the cell can then be part of any data label and, if available, any legend.

From these ideas, you can derive many tricks for dynamic labels of data points and legends.

Series Overlaps

I'll use a less frequently required display option to conclude the general considerations for the "column charts." You can use the *data series overlaps* to vary the gaps between columns or column segments if multiple series exist and if multiple columns are provided in a category (as shown in Figure 8-16). Let's look at a practical example for this purpose.

On the Companion CD   Open the file *Samples\0802_Columns.xlsx* again and use the worksheet *Columns 6*, but also *Columns 4* and *Columns 5* for the practices.

With reference to Figure 8-16:

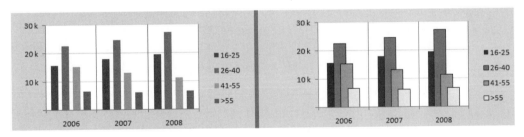

FIGURE 8-16 More Distance? Or the opposite?

The shown chart has four *data series*, whose *data points* are in three categories each and the *overlap* is set to 0 percent by default. As a result, they are displayed right next to each other.

In the example on the left side of the figure, one of the data series was selected and set to *-30 percent* under *Series Options* in the formatting dialog box; a negative value increases the distance between the *data points* (columns).

In the example on the right side of the figure, the *series overlap* was set to *50 percent*; the *data points* overlap by half. This is not only an occasionally aesthetically pleasing, but also a space-saving solution. Moreover, overlaps enable the setup of certain intersection displays in Excel 2007 (see Figure 8-17, right), because the column fills can be transparent and the area of overlap can be displayed in a mixed color.

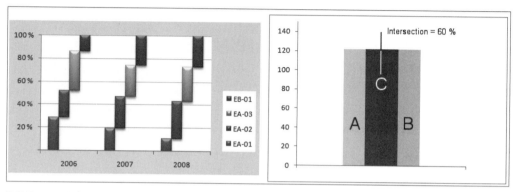

FIGURE 8-17 What you can use only occasionally and where it be can useful

If you use multiple data series that aren't displayed next to each other, but on top of each other in a stacked column chart (see Figure 8-17, left), you can move the individual segments using the *series overlap*. However, there are only a few professional situations where you can use this display.

Column Chart to Bar Chart

In case of insufficient planning or changes to the presentation targets, it is sometimes necessary to present the data in a bar chart (or an entirely different chart type) instead of column chart. This also applies to some of the models shown in this chapter. In the "Europe charts," for example, you could prefer to visualize the ranking orders instead of emphasizing the sizes. In this case, a bar chart clearly would be the best solution.

A global conversion doesn't constitute any problem at all provided that the chart types are structurally related to each other, which is the case for columns and bars. It's also not a problem if the template to be converted has already been completed.

> **On the Companion CD** Open the file \Samples\0802_Columns.xlsx again and use the *Columns 3* to *Columns 6* worksheets for basic practices.

1. Right-click an empty space in the column chart and choose the *Change Chart Type* command from the context menu. If you accidentally clicked a *data series*, the *Change Series Chart Type* would be displayed in the context menu. As you will learn later on in this chapter, this is a very useful option, but completely unwanted in this context.

Ensure that the command to be selected appears as *Change Chart Type* and thus relates to the entire chart.

2. In the dialog box, select the *Bar* group and the sub-type that matches your template
   or another sub-type if you want to make changes. After you've clicked *OK*, Excel implements the changes and tries to logically accept the properties of the template more or
   less successfully depending on the complexity and individuality of the template.

3. Carefully check what changes have been implemented in the newly created chart and
   make the necessary manual adaptations. It is particularly important to check the *axes*
   and their *labels* as well as the *gridlines*.

Bar Charts

Virtually everything that I've mentioned in the context of column charts also applies to bar
charts. From the technical point of view, the two types are very similar, and you'll hardly find
any differences in the relevant dialog boxes.

For this reason, I would like to refer you to the information already provided in the context
of column charts and consider the explanations for bar charts as a detailed recapitulation. If
you find new information that was not discussed for the column charts, the same rule applies
in reverse: working with a general rotation of 90°, characteristics and formatting variants of
column and bar charts can be interchangeable, with just few exceptions.

> **On the Companion CD** Open the file *\Samples\0806_Bars.xlsx* on the CD-ROM. The contents
> of the *Bars 1* to *Bars 4* worksheets will be discussed in the following sections. The models of the
> remaining worksheets will not be discussed and are intended for experiments at will.

The graphics contents of the previous chapters and the new formatting options of Excel have
now gotten their due. So, in addition to the details on the technical chart editing, you'll also
be provided with information on the formal design.

Charts to Evaluate Orders and Ranks

The bar chart sorted in descending order is one of the best means to display charts for rank
evaluations. You can find a corresponding example in the *Bars 1* worksheet of the file
\Samples\0806_Bars.xlsx, which is presented in Figure 8-18.

> **Note** In this chapter and in the following chapters of this book you will get more of these ready-made charts. The descriptions and annotations leave the general information behind and focus on to those aspects that are particularly important for creating these charts.
>
> So, examine all aspects of the example charts, but particularly those design properties that are mentioned in the texts. Try to create your own models in the same or a similar way. For example, save the files from the CD-ROM to your hard disk under a different name, remove the existing chart from the worksheet, and use the data table as the basis for your own creations.

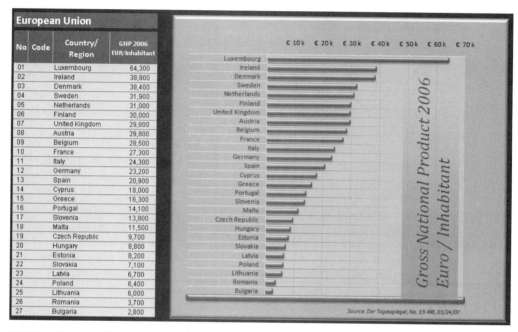

FIGURE 8-18 Interesting data—relatively high formatting effort

The chart provides information about the gross national product of 27 EU countries/regions (status 2006) sorted according to size. The "comb structure" of the data is rather balanced except for Luxembourg, whose bar juts out clearly. This gave the opportunity to position the chart label on right side of the *plot area*. It provides an optical balance to the bar comb.

The most important design aspects include:

- Reference: The chart takes its data
    - From the range F5:F31 for the *data series* (the bars)
    - From the range D5:E31 for the label of the two-column category axis. The range D5:D31 is filled with blank spaces, which results in the display of division marks in the category axis labels.

If you wanted to reverse the rankings or display the countries/regions in alphabetical order, you'd have to sort the data table differently.

> **Note** This example will be used in Chapter 10, "Presentation Solutions That Pack a Punch," to describe how you can set up these changed sorting of the chart display at the click of a mouse without any programming.

■ Formatting of the *primary vertical axis*: for this chart type, the *primary vertical axis* is the category axis. The most important *axis options* which can be found in the formatting dialog box include:

  ❑ *Interval between tick marks*: 1

  ❑ *Specify interval unit*: 1 (of course, all label texts are to be visible)

  ❑ *Categories in reverse order*: activated (the value axis is supposed to be on top)

  ❑ *Label distance from axis*: 100 (neither too close nor too far apart)

> **Tip** If you want to set a custom *label distance from axis,* you should do so at an early stage of the formatting work, because changing this measurement also influences other elements of the chart (for example, the plot area, legend, and inserted objects) and its absolute or relative positioning.

■ Formatting of the *primary horizontal axis*: For this chart type, the *primary horizontal axis* is the value axis. The numbers are fixed in the given example; a subsequent change is not expected. For this reason, the automatic scaling of Excel (*0, 70,000, 10,000*), which works very well in this case, can remain unchanged. The only special case of axis formatting which is worth mentioning is the already known number format € #," k";;

■ Formatting of the *chart area, plot area,* and *data series*:

  ❑ *The chart area,* the two-dimensional background of the chart, is the middle ground of the worksheet as is indicated by the color. Its *3-D bevel* accentuates it a little bit.

  ❑ The slightly brighter, solid *plot area* remains restrained and gives absolute priority to the staggered *data series,* as it should be.

  ❑ The bars have a bright color, whose dominant effect is further enhanced by the *3-D bevel* (*height 5 pt, width 2 pt*). Highlight the *data series* and then select the path *Chart Tools/Format/Shape Styles/Shape Fill* or—to obtain results more quickly—*Home/Font Color/Fill Color,* to find out whether you prefer another color for the bars taking into account the overall effect, of course.

- Formatting of the *gridlines*: The right part of the chart shows the result of an experiment with color gradients and transparencies. The *horizontal gridlines*, which have a clearly separating effect on the left side of the *plot area*, fade out the closer they get to the right. The vertical gridlines, however, remain unchanged, except for those two which cross the chart title rotated by 270 degrees. They are visible at the top and fade out the closer they get to the bottom. This may appear odd, when you become aware that you can only format the gridlines as a whole. For the horizontal gridlines, the solution is simple: they have a gradient filling that takes over the color of the plot area going from left to right (take a look at the settings provided on the **Line Color** tab in the formatting dialog box). The vertical gridlines are formatted uniformly as continuous solid lines. Their fading below the chart title is passive and is caused by the formatting of the *text box* that almost extends over the entire height of the plot area and contains the two-line chart title.

- Formatting of the *text box*: Click the chart title to select the *text box* and to identify its extent. Then, click the border of this *text box* to select it as an object in order to open its formatting dialog box. The object has no border (*Line Color/No line*) and a gradient linear color fill with two *gradient stops*, the second of which is 100 percent transparent. This makes the background increasingly visible at the upper part of the object and results in a (mainly vertically aligned) smooth transition between the *text box* and the *plot area*.

- Additional objects:

  - A rod-shaped drawing object/rectangle was positioned below the *plot area*. Its 3-D formatting accepts the shapes of the data points; its color, however, is adapted to the two-dimensional chart elements. The text box including the chart title touches this "rod" slightly as if it was connected to it or even looks like a flag being unwound.

  - The reference at the lower edge of the *chart area* is a borderless, fully transparent *text box*.

Mapping High-Lows

The visualization of high-lows is required quite often. "Floating bars" are a very good choice if these high-lows don't just define limits within which the data may range (for example, as bandwidths), but have their own "substance" such as a measured temperature range. A corresponding example is provided in the *Bars 2* worksheet.

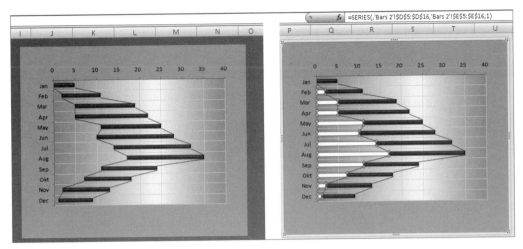

FIGURE 8-19 Floating bars—from cool to mild to warm and back again

You can see a chart that indicates the range of maximum day temperatures (in degrees Celsius) sorted by month. Note the following most important design aspects with reference to Figure 8-19:

- This is a stacked bar chart with two *data series*, of which you can only see one. Their references:

  - The range E5:E16 is the reference for the invisible data series. This data series forms the basis on which the second visible data series can be built. The same principle applies to the—less frequently used—"floating columns" where invisible segments function as supporting pillars for the visible column segments.

  - The range G5:G16 in which the differences of the data in columns F and E are shown as formula results is the reference for the visible data series.

- Formatting of the *primary vertical axis*: here again, the *categories are in reverse order* so that the value axis is in the upper part of the chart. I usually select this position for this kind of display because we normally view a chart from top to bottom.

- Formatting of the *primary horizontal axis*: the automatic scaling of Excel (*0, 40, 10*) was corrected to 5 for the major unit because some of the bars are quite short but should still touch some of the "measurement information."

- Formatting of the *plot area*: for a temperature chart, the gradient in the background is not a stagy accessory, but an important support of the information. The three colors used have a relatively even gradient within the overall spectrum (*Stop 1* at *0 percent*, *Stop 2* at *60 percent*, *Stop 3* at *100 percent*): from cool blue to mild yellow to warm orange.

- Formatting of the *data series*:

  - The bars of the visible series are supposed to dominate the color background with their strong color and be particular eye-catchers.

❑ The bars of the data series from column E (visible in Figure 8-19, right) were hidden with *Fill: No fill* and *Border Color: No line*.

- The thin *series lines* between the bars create an optical unit and lend a step-like appearance leading from top to bottom. Use the option *Chart Tools/Layout/Analysis/Lines/None* to find out how it would look like without these series lines.

Mapping Changes

Bar charts with centrally positioned category axes are ideal for visualizing deviations of any kind. The example shown in the *Bars 3* worksheet visualizes the changed expenses of 10 cost centers. An increase of the expenses is interpreted as unpleasant (which is not necessarily the case); therefore the color red is used for positive numbers, and blue for negative numbers.

The center axis of the chart is the base line and indicates the status of the year 2007, while the bars to the left and right of the center axis identify the corresponding deviations in 2008. The average of all these deviations is displayed at a central position at the top of the chart which is additionally indicated by a brace. Test the effect of the chart by pressing the **F9** key several times to simulate the readout of new data as though you would change your data source using controls (as has already been described for other models).

The data that changes for each recalculation is created in the range G13:G28 using formulas. The formula =RANDBETWEEN(-21,20)+ROUND(RAND(),2) serves as an instruction to Excel to do the following: "Create a random integer between -21 and 20, added up with a random number between 0 and 1 rounded to two decimals."

The =RANDBETWEEN(bottom,top) function creates a random integer within a range defined by bottom and top. Both values can also be negative, but top must always be greater than bottom.

The =RAND() function creates a random number between 0 and 1. This number has an accuracy of 15 or even 16 decimal places.

The =ROUND(number,num_digits) function rounds a number to the defined num_digits. If num_digits is 0 or positive, the argument applies to the decimal places. If num_digits is negative, the argument applies to the pre-decimal positions. For example:

- =ROUND(112.25,1) results in *112.3*
- =ROUND(112.25,-1) results in *110*

The base form of the threepart number formats used in the example has already been presented in the last main section of Chapter 6. The modification's applicable here:

- In the table and in cell K7: `[Red]  +* 0.0"  ";[Blue] –* 0.0"  ";0.0"  "`

  The signs remain in their position independent of the column width; the space up to the number is filled with blank spaces.

- For the data labels: `[Red] +  0.0"  ";[Blue]  –   0.0"  ";0.0"`

  There are always two blank spaces between the sign and the number.

The version presented in Figure 8-20 is designed as a presentation variant. The table on the left side of the screen is also part of the presentation, in contrast to some other examples shown so far. For this reason, the list of cost centers in the table was aligned with the cost centers in the chart (see the following text for further information).

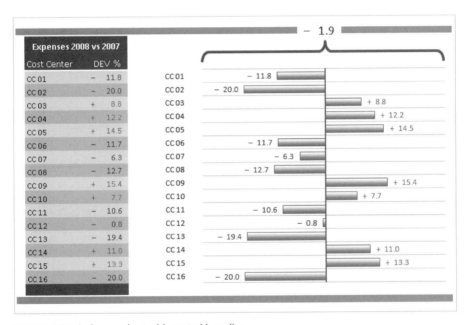

FIGURE 8-20 A change chart with central base line

The overall appearance has a character that is clearly different to the conventional charts. Basis structures such as chart area, plot area, and labeled axes are still existent; however, they are not visible or are designed in an unusual manner. Such deviations from the conventional designs are already appealing, simply because they are deviations. Make use of this fact!

What's special about it?

- Formatting of the *primary vertical axis*:

❑ *Categories in reverse order* so that the value axis, which will be invisible, is at the top of the chart.

❑ *Label distance from axis:* 500 (slightly larger than usual)

❑ *Major tick mark type:* None (the pronounced central axis is to appear completely smooth. A segmenting tiling is not required because this is created by the bars themselves and the gridlines enclosing them.)

❑ *Axis labels: Low* in order to not position these labels directly next to the central axis, where they would be inappropriate, but on the left side of the plot area.

■ Formatting of the *primary horizontal axis*: The scaling must be defined by the user and have the same values on both sides so that the base line remains in the center irrespective of the inserted figures. Moreover, the maximum value must be considerably higher than the maximum number to be expected—in our example this would be the maximum numbers -21 or +21—so that the data labels appearing next to the bars have enough space within the plot area. So, *Minimum:* -30, *Maximum:* 30, *Major unit* (not necessary here): 5.

When you create the chart, you first set up the axis to be visible and then hide it using the command, *Chart Tools/Layout/Axes/Primary Horizontal Axis/None.* The control attributes are still available; the axis still exists and is just not displayed. This option, which is also available for other chart elements, is preferable for hiding elements instead of removing the color from the axis components.

■ Formatting of the *chart area* and *plot area*: Fully transparent by specifying *None...* for the fill and border color.

■ The *data series* have a gradient that has no informational purpose but works to support the lightness of the overall appearance. For this reason, the horizontal gridlines are in a pale blue.

■ The brace above the *plot area* is a drawing object, an inserted *shape* taken from the repertoire of the *basic shapes.* The brace points to a cell (more precisely, a join of four cells), which includes a simple average formula with reference to the range G13:G28.

I'll now provide you with some information about the techniques for synchronizing the table range and the chart's *plot area*. First, you need to insert two thin horizontal guides ranging over the entire width (drawing objects, number 3 in Figure 8-21), which are then aligned with the respective positions in the table at the top and bottom. Subsequently, the top edge and the bottom edge of the *plot area* are aligned with the guides by moving or scaling the entire chart and/or moving or scaling the *plot area*. After you've completed this step, the guides can be removed again.

The object components concerned are summarized in Figure 8-21:

1. Selection frame of the entire chart

2. Marking points of the *plot area*

3. Marking points of the guides

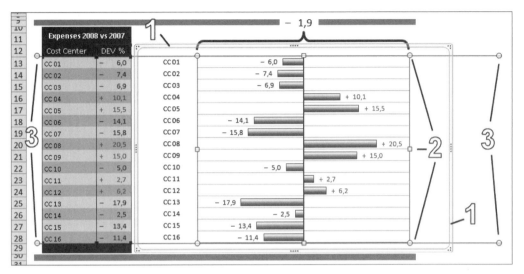

FIGURE 8-21 The plot area's height is adapted to the referenced table range.

Line Charts

The extremely versatilely useful line charts are very similar to column and bar charts when it comes to their basic structure and technical use. The chart type has already been presented with different models in previous chapters. The creation of a line chart as well as the development and formatting of its data series was explained in Chapter 2.

For this reason, the descriptions of the examples compiled in the file *0807_Lines.xlsx* can primarily focus on other aspects and present ideas whose implementation is also possible in other chart types, either directly or analogously.

On the Companion CD Open the file *\Samples\0807_Lines.xlsx* on the CD-ROM.

Mapping the Development of Values

The basic variant of a line chart, which can be created easily, is shown in the *Lines 1* worksheet. Some specific features are worth mentioning. A brief overview of the basic model is essential, because a modified and extended version is shown later on in the *Lines 4* worksheet.

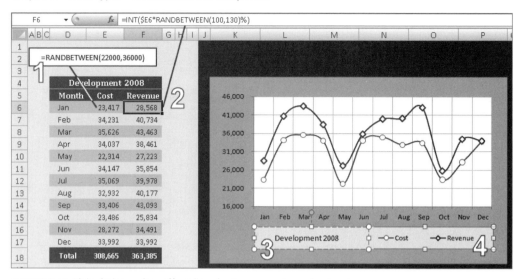

FIGURE 8-22 Plain design—clear effect: line charts are easy to understand.

The *chart data range* of the model is D5:F17. Here, the headings of the columns are also integrated and are therefore included in the *legend*. The specific features of the model in the context of Figure 8-22:

1. If you press **F9** you can simulate the reading of new data. The formulas in the range E6:E17—the cost side of the model—generate integers ranging between 22,000 and 36,000. Consequently, the scaling of the *primary vertical axis* can be limited to a minimum of 16,000.

2. The revenue in the adjacent cell range F6:F17 is provided with enterprise-friendly formulas; for example, the formula in cell F6. The formula =INT($E6*RANDBETWEEN(100,130)%) ensures that the revenues never fall below the costs, irrespective of how often you press **F9**.

> The =INT(number) function is a rounding function. It rounds a number down to the next smaller integer.

3. The left half of the label bar below the plot area is a *text box*.

4. The right half of the label bar is the chart's *legend*. Its height and color were adjusted to the text box.

If required, you can use this plain solution as a basis for various formatting practices.

Mapping Connections and Differences

The *Lines 2* worksheet shows two lines of the seasonal temperature profile of a travel destination that doesn't invite us with too pleasant temperatures, as you will find out soon. The visualization purpose of this chart is not to provide degrees and tenths of degrees but to show the data, which is not particularly appealing to tourists, in a half-decent light.

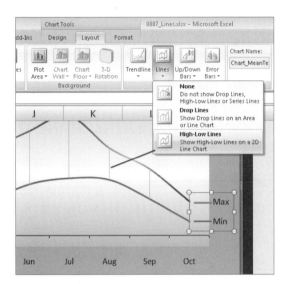

FIGURE 8-23 High-low lines and a legend as the data series continuation

"Light", that's also the keyword for the color scheme. A gradual filling with three pastel colors highlights the *plot area* against a dark background and the neutral middle ground.

The color specifications for the data series also aim to provide a positive touch. The line showing the minimum mean temperatures is not accentuated in color and therefore plays no significant role for the perception "at first glance." The line for the maximum mean temperatures was also improved thanks to the new design tools of Excel 2007. The gradual three-color fill ensures that the red peak of approximately 22° Celsius in July is perceived as quite hot.

With reference to Figure 8-23:

- The scaling of the value axis was set to a minimum of -2 to clearly visualize the horizontal category axis as a stable, supporting base line for the two temperature curves.

- The clearly visible differences of the temperature high-lows that become particularly tight in fall are interesting for climate observers, but not for potential tourists. This information is supported by the discreetly formatted high-low lines. Access via: *Chart Tools/Layout/Analysis/Lines/High-Low Lines*.

- The data as averages of the measuring results gathered over several years are historical; that is, static. This enables a rather interesting design of the legend, which constitutes a continuation of the data series in this case. The positioning of the freely movable, fully transparent, and borderless element is easy; its symbols can be aligned exactly with the series ends by manipulating the height of the entire *legend*. Note that great importance was attached to position the legend text outside the *plot area*.

User-Defined Positioning of the Category Axis

You were previously shown a chart in which the *primary vertical axis* was not in its default position—that is, the left border of the *plot area*—but within the *plot area* with some columns on the left side of the axis and some on the right side of the axis (see Figure 8-9). For this purpose, you can use the *Vertical axis crosses/At category number* option in the *Axis Options* of the *primary horizontal axis* and enter the number of the appropriate category.

An equivalent—the user-defined positioning of the *primary horizontal axis*—will be outlined in the *Lines 3* worksheet and with reference to Figure 8-24.

> **Note** It is quite logical but also a little bit confusing for the formatting of a chart that the positioning of the vertical axis is an option of the horizontal axis and the positioning of the horizontal axis an option of the vertical axis.

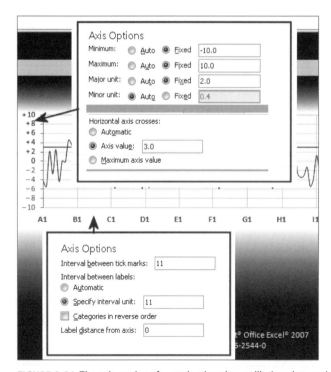

FIGURE 8-24 The axis settings for evaluating the oscillating data series

In this example, you must note that a fixed scaling (*-10, 10, 2*) was defined for the value axis that keeps the negative and positive range independent of the measurement values to be varied with **F9**. Excel would automatically set the category axis centrally; that is, to the position 0. If you want to change this, select the *Horizontal axis crosses/Axis value* option in the formatting dialog box of the *primary vertical axis* and enter the appropriate value. As you can see in the delivered version and in the figure, the value was set to 3.0 and thus uses a positioning for which no match exists in the axis labels. The setting must be made independent of the scaling of the value axis (or its *major gridlines*) and could also be set to -5.25 or 8.88. Simply try it out yourself.

Formatting of the *primary horizontal axis* had to take into account that the measurement data were collected at rather unusual increments of 11, which was also be indicated in the tiling of the axis and its label. This requirement was met with the axis options indicated in the figure: the values for *Interval between tick marks* and *Specify interval unit* were both set to 11.

Vertical gradients to the environment structures were set for the color of the chart. The plot area is not filled, and the chart area uses a gradual fill with four *color stops*, but only two different colors. Find out which variation options are available and how the overall impression can be changed, for example, by increasing the chart area at the lower edge.

Linear Data Series as a Category Alert

The *Lines 4* worksheet contains the chart that was already presented in the *Lines 1* worksheet. However, fate often decrees that an enterprise will encounter revenue or cost issues.

If you press the **F9** key several times, you may see that the costs are higher than the revenues from May to August. This either affects all of the four months mentioned or any other number of months. And sometimes this problem doesn't occur at all. This simulation of the ill-favored summer slump is caused by changing the formulas in the range F10:F13: The formula =INT($E6*RANDBETWEEN(80,130)%) allows that the revenues can be lower than the costs.

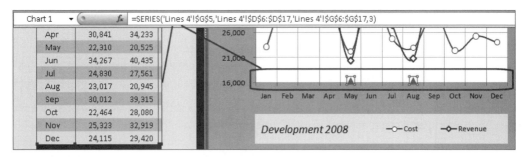

FIGURE 8-25 Red "warning triangles" appear if the costs are higher than the revenues.

It is much more interesting that the month in which the problem occurs is identified with a red "warning triangle" at the lower edge of the plot area. This is a very important additional visualization because the unfavorable crossing in the lines of the two data series is not particularly eye-catching at first. Nevertheless, the line chart, though not ideal in this version and for this particular purpose, was retained because its main focus is still on the periodic development of the data.

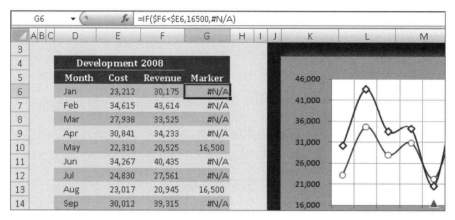

FIGURE 8-26 As in the majority of cases, the answer to the problem is quite simple.

But how can you explain the red symbols that appear and disappear automatically and depending on the value? The little secret is a hidden structure of the data table which will be given away in Figure 8-26:

- Another data series was added to the chart by changing its *data range* (now D5:G17). Its line is not displayed at all; the alert symbols are only shown if the described problem is to be visualized.

- The width of column G was decreased so that its content can't be seen. The formulas stored there ensure that the result in the respective cell is either the error value #N/A (*data point* is not displayed) or the value 16,500 (data point is displayed). For the displayed example =IF($F6<$E6,16500,#N/A), the message to Excel is: "If the value in cell F6 is less than the value of cell E6 (if the revenues are lower than the costs), then set the value 16,500, otherwise #N/A."

- Why 16,500? The scaling of the primary vertical axis still starts at 16,000. The line originating from column G is to be at the lower border of the *plot area* at all times. If some of its symbols become visible, they are to appear directly on the edge of the *plot area*.

For creating and formatting this additional line, you should use the chart provided in the *Lines 1* worksheet as the basis and proceed as follows:

1. Fill all cells of the range G5:G17 with constants—with the value 18,000 (the line is to be set a bit higher for editing purposes than is required later on)—and enter a heading in cell G5.

2. Change the reference of the *data range* to D5:G17 in the *Select Data Source* dialog box (see Figure 8-3).

3. Select the newly created line and set *No line* as the *line color*. Then specify the appearance of the marker symbols (in our example, these are triangles of size 10 with a white marker line and a red marker fill).

4. Now replace the constants in the range G5:G17 using the formulas presented above. Press the **F9** key to test the correct reaction of the formulas and the associated appearance of the new data series or the "warning triangles."

5. Select the newly added entry in the legend and delete it by pressing the **Del** key. Reset the legend to the original size and, if necessary, re-adjust its position in relation to the adjacent text box.

6. Decrease the width of column G so that its content can't be seen.

The Line as an Interval of Time

The *Lines 5* worksheet includes a data-collection line that appears above a time-scale axis. Every time you press the **F9** key, the values of the data source and—more importantly in this example—the intervals of the calendar days change; in other words, the simulation includes different measurement results *and* different measurement intervals.

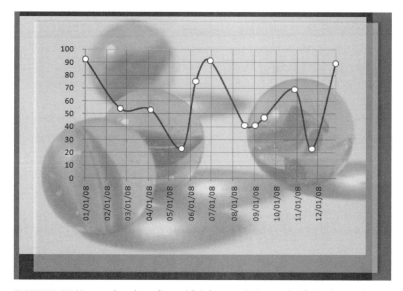

FIGURE 8-27 Harmonic axis scaling with inharmonic intervals of the data points

Copy the worksheet, remove the chart, and try the following:

1. Create a line chart from the range D4:E16 and format the elements to your specifications.

2. Select the primary horizontal axis and specify the following in the formatting dialog box:

   ❏ *Axis Type: Date axis*

   ❏ *Base Unit: Fixed, Days*

   ❏ *Minimum, Maximum,* and *Intervals* remain set to *Auto.* However, note the tiling options provided for the use of fixed scaling.

3. Press the **F9** key several times to test the result and particularly note how the category axis and the data series change:

   ❏ The category axis shows time intervals: it is subdivided by Excel into equal sections; the major tick lines don't indicate the calendar data existing in the data source, but dates at regular intervals.

   ❏ By contrast, the *data points* of the line are displayed at inharmonic intervals; that is, on those days on which the measurements were actually implemented. Each marker of the data series thus is displayed in the calendar-based "correct" positions of the time-scale axis.

4. Try out the following:

   ❏ Select the time-scale axis and change the *Base Unit* to *Months* in the formatting dialog box. Press the **F9** key several times and you will see that some months include multiple data points, while others remain empty. If you use years as the *base unit,* most of the randomly generated data combinations of all data points are displayed in one single category. Particularly the two settings mentioned last indicate that a line chart with time-scale axis is closely linked with the scatter chart (XY) and that you must decide for the individual cases whether it makes sense to display the line or whether you should limit the display to the markers of the line.

   ❏ In the formatting dialog box, define different combinations of various minimum and maximum values as well as fixed intervals of different types (days, months) and different sizes. Note the effects on the display of the category axis and the data series.

   ❏ In the source data range D5:E16, overwrite the formulas with their results *(Copy, Paste Special, Values)* and then sort the data at your discretion (both according to calendar dates and measurement results). Note that the display of the chart doesn't change. So, you can create a chart with a calendar-structured time-scale axis from a source data range that is not sorted chronologically.

The graphical presentation of the chart uses a background picture that is slightly offset to the *chart area*. The *plot area* has no fill; the *chart area* has a solid fill and is partly transparent. The different background colors and structures result in an interesting color mix and other effects that you may vary at your discretion. This is done by changing:

- The background picture,

- The table ranges that are positioned behind and next to the charts as well as their colors,

- The colors of the chart elements,

- The transparencies of the chart elements,

- The size and position of the flexible elements (background picture, chart area, plot area).

On the Companion CD The background picture can be found on the CD-ROM under
\Materials\Pictures\GlassMarbles.jpg,

Complex Solutions

Having obtained all basic information about the technical handling of column, bar, and line charts, the focus worksheets of the more complex solutions presented in previous chapters should no longer pose serious challenges.

On the Companion CD Open the following files on the CD-ROM again:

- ❏ *\Samples\0601_Indicators01.xlsx*
- ❏ *\Samples\0701_Indicators_01.xlsx* or *0702_Indicators_02.xlsx.*

With reference to Figure 8-28:

- The line chart on the left side of the figure uses a *primary vertical axis* with an automatic scaling. Only one of the four data series shows its data points by means of markers; the other three lines run horizontal (monthly data unchanged) and remain smooth (no marker symbols). The two horizontal lines for displaying the bandwidth are shaded (one line with the shadow on top and one line with the shadow below) to optically emphasize their meaning as user-defined limits.

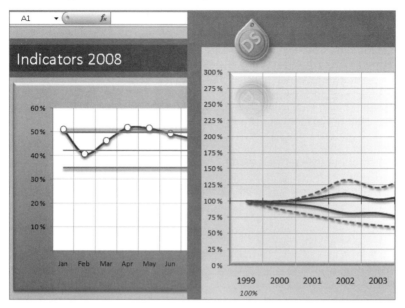

FIGURE 8-28 Line charts: plain design, strong effect

- In the line chart on the right side of the figure, the horizontal axis was positioned on the 100 percent line (*horizontal axis crosses* at *axis value* 100) for the formatting of the *primary vertical axis*, from where all data series originate starting with the year 1999. The axis scaling is fixed user-defined (*0, 300, 25*).

  The strong color formatting of the *primary horizontal axis* and the specification of the *major tick lines* as *Cross* indicate the central significance of this element. The *axis labels* were set to *Low* so that the year dates remain below the *plot area*.

Mixed Chart Types

If more than two series exist in a chart, you can specify a chart type for each data series individually. In many cases, this is an excellent opportunity to accentuate or differentiate various statements. From the vast collection of highly suitable variants, I want to present two small examples which are available in the file *0808_ColumnsLines.xlsx*.

Take this opportunity to let out your creativity and make as many experiments as possible. You will discover a lot more than can be described and detailed in this book.

On the Companion CD Open the file *\Samples\0808_ColumnsLines.xlsx* on the CD-ROM.

I've intentionally put the following information at this part of the chapter, because a smart combination of columns and lines is one of the most impressive visualizations and because it can meet many different requirements.

> **Note** I'll restrict my presentation to the combination of these two series types. Basically, you can combine virtually all types with one another, even though quite a few combinations make little sense (for example, a combination of columns and bars) and could only be used as tricky, dynamic decorative elements.

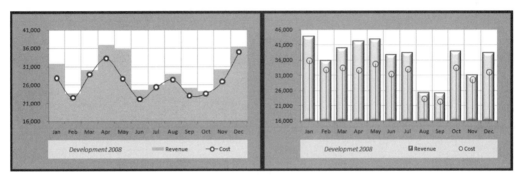

FIGURE8-29 Columns with line—two possible design variants

The *Lines 0* worksheet includes the chart that was already introduced in the last section. It is the basis for changes described below and the basis for your own practice.

The aim of the first example (variant in the *Mix 1* worksheet) is to emphasize that we have a periodically oscillating target of particular importance. For this, the chart must also indicate how the actual data met this target and how well it met the pattern of the target (in both oscillating directions). In the ideal case, all data points of the line were on the upper edge of the columns. Consider any deviation a potential problem.

> **Note** If you want to meet this display requirement with two lines, you can't ensure satisfactory results because there are overlaps of chart elements for the target and actual identities, and the two lines may be aligned more or less close to each other.

Here are step-by-step instructions (template in the *Lines 0* worksheet; the result can be viewed in Figure 8-29, left, or in the *Mix 1* worksheet):

1. Right-click the green data series of the actual data and choose the *Change Series Chart Type* command from the context menu.

2. Select standard columns as the chart type and format the newly created column series according to the "skyline" pattern; that is, without any gaps, no borders, and a re-strained solid area fill.

3. Format the remaining line of target data at your discretion, but note that the effect of this data is to be clearly the center of attention.

Press the **F9** key several times to test the results—both data series change and consequently simulate any possible data constellations—and change the formatting if the results don't meet your approval or requirements.

The second example (variant in the *Mix 2* worksheet) is similar to the base type, but focuses on other aspects and therefore uses different formatting. The target data is constant, while you can vary the actual data by pressing the **F9** key. Here, it is assumed that the target data (originating from vague revenue planning) is not of particular importance and not necessary as in the first example; it is more a wishful thinking than a target. It is good if the demand has been met every month; it is better if it has been exceeded, and it was bad luck or the weather if it was fallen below. The view particularly focuses on the actual data: what happened and, in addition, how does it meet our ideas.

The optical stress of the actual columns with their bold borders and 3-D bevel is clearly more distinguishable than the subtle target line. This is only a line from the technical point of view; in reality, it is perceived as points with a tiny stick or small circles that are in front of or directly in the columns. This effect was achieved:

■ By optical suppressing the links between the data points (*Line Color: No line*)

■ By omitting a marker fill

■ By setting *drop lines* (accessed via *Chart Tools/Layout/Analysis/Lines*

Charts with Secondary Axes

If we're constantly talking about primary axes, there must also be secondary axes. The charts of the types that have been discussed so far in this chapter can be equipped with second value axes and second category axes.

The prerequisites:

■ The chart consists of more than one data series.

■ If a second category axis is to be set up, a second value axis must already exist.

As a result, your chart can have three or even four axes instead of only two, and they can all be labeled. And it gets even a little more complex: as with the primary axis, your chart can also have secondary axes that remain invisible but still influence the design capability of the data series.

There are two main reasons for doing this:

- You want to or have to display different data series in one single chart, although their values to be displayed vary considerably in size. An example is revenue data relating to numbers of pieces or number of employees relating to personnel costs. In other words, you require two different, scaled value axes to present this data in one single *plot area*, yet with a clear design. This can only be done if the data series connected with different value axes have different types (for example, columns with line) or have a clearly different formatting. A very typical example is a specific climate chart in which temperatures and amount of precipitation are to be displayed at the same time. You can find a corresponding model in the file *\Samples\0809_3Axes.xlsx*. There you can see primary and secondary value axes with unequal scaling.

- You use two or more data series of the same type, but want to design the individual data series differently, which would not be possible under normal conditions. For example, you want to display a specific bar in a different color than the adjacent bars under data-driven—that is, dynamic—conditions, or narrow bars are to be displayed within wide bars. But let's go back to the variant which can be created more easily from the technical point of view: the climate chart example.

Two Value Axes with Unequal Scaling

> **On the Companion CD** Open the file *\Samples\0809_3Axes.xlsx* on the CD-ROM.

The *Climate 0* worksheet contains a table with mean temperatures and amounts of precipitation for the Spanish city of *Aranjuez,* two components of climate data and an already created, simple area chart (variant A in Figure 8-30). This chart is only used to emphasize the problem, but that's not the appropriate solution. The two different data types are both on the same value axis. As a result, the temperature appears optically compressed and the precipitation relatively high; at first glance, this city seems to have a rather humid and cool climate (what is not the case).

Apart from the effective, graphic accessories, the solution variant B in the *Climate Chart 1* worksheet is significantly better and particularly more realistic. In this case, realistic means that such a temperature curve shouldn't be displayed in a value axis that ranges up to 60 or easily exceeds a value of 100 as it would if designing charts for Irish or Scottish measurement points (see the *Climate Chart 2* worksheet). The highs and lows as well as the color of the chart show the climate that you can expect in this city: a rather dry summer with moderate temperatures (and in October, you can quote the German poet Schiller: *"The lovely days in Aranjuez are now at an end"*).

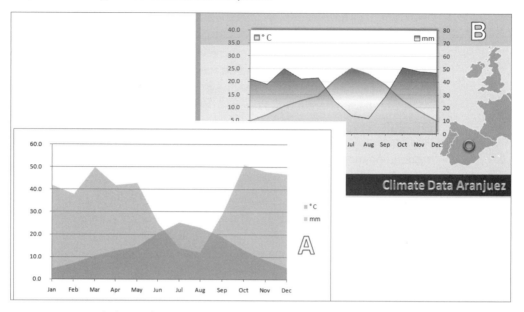

FIGURE 8-30 Instead of example *A*, stick to Example *B*

Select the *Climate 0* worksheet and restructure the chart:

1. Select the blue area of the amount of precipitation and choose *Plot Series On: Secondary Axis* under *Series Options* in the formatting dialog box. As a result, a second *value axis* is created that is positioned on the right side of the *plot area*.

2. Select this secondary axis and define a fixed scaling (*0, 80, 10*).

3. Select the primary axis on the left side of the plot area (which is now used only for temperatures) and also define a fixed scaling (*0, 40, 5*).

You've now created an appropriate and comprehensible relationship between the two data types, which the viewers will rapidly understand once they've figured out that the left side of the chart has different values than the right side of the chart. You must bear in mind, however, that you should use such mixed scaling with care and explain it in presentations. If you present such charts to the same audience again and again, you should also keep the same formatting. The reason is simple: the different scaling of the two value axes changes our perception of the relations between the values and consequently their meaning and significance. As a result, you could manipulate the audience; that is, you can use very simple means to create strongly varying impressions. Take a look at the *Climate Chart 2* worksheet which shows the climate data of *Malin Head*, the most northerly point of Ireland. The landscape is very exciting, but the climate is often very windy or even stormy, damp, and cool. By "adapting" the axis scaling—the primary axis with temperatures: *0, 20, 5* and the secondary axis with precipitation: *0, 160, 10*—the first impression suggests that it is a cozy place in June and July.

That's all the information you need in terms of the basic techniques; the rest primarily concerns design. For this purpose, select the *Climate Chart 1* worksheet and compare its formatting with the following list. I assume that I don't have to explain number formatting and other details already discussed. I want to zero in on the most interesting topics.

- The coloring, color gradients, and transparencies of the two series areas play particularly important and effective roles. In previous versions of Excel, this would not have been possible in this manner; for example, you would have had to use a combination of columns and lines or area and line. The improvement is possible because the forms are more easily differentiated and because we intuitively consider precipitation as a quantity (i.e., columns or areas) and temperatures as a height at a distance from zero (i.e., points or lines). Because you can use the effects of colors much better in Excel 2007 than ever before, these considerations could be pushed into the background, especially because you should have the opportunity to experiment with your own color and transparency designs. In the *Climate Chart 2* worksheet, the temperature area has been discolored and you can only see the border which conveys the impression of a line.

- The two legend entries are—at least indirectly—part of the different value axes; the program can therefore support the perceptual differentiation to display them in appropriate positions. But how can you position the two legend entries in the two top outer corners of the plot area? It's no problem in this case.

  The background of the chart is provided by the table structures. The *chart area* is transparent and, unlike the *plot area*, very wide (from column A to column R). As a result, the legend, which is based on the overall area of the chart, can also be very wide. By increasing the horizontal width, you also move apart the entries, in this case exactly as required.

> **Note** Make some experiments and decrease and increase the legends in both dimensions. You will discover wrap results that are particularly suitable for special effects, especially if you use longer texts as legend entries.
>
> If you select the entire legend and globally change the font size (*Home* tab/*Font*), you simultaneously influence the size of the displayed legend keys.
>
> If you select a single legend entry and change its font size, you also influence the size of all displayed legend keys; however, only the font of the selected character string.

- Decorative and supplementary elements:

    - ❑ A map of Europe was inserted (*\Materials\Pictures\Europe01.tif*). Then, the white color was removed (*Picture Tools/Customize/Recolor/Set Transparent Color*). Subsequently, the map was cropped a little and then positioned in the required relation to the *plot area*.

    - ❑ The marker ring in the middle of Spain is the inserted and formatted basic shape called *Donut*.

    - ❑ The title at the lower border of the chart picture is a borderless *WordArt* object with a transparent area.

Using Secondary Axes for Gridline Formatting

After you've created a secondary value axis, you can also define a second category axis for a chart. There are two primary reasons:

- The chart is either exceptionally high or exceptionally wide (for bar charts) and a second data label on the opposite side facilitates the perception and assessment of the categories.

- You use a secondary category axis and define its axis options (*intervals, interval units*) differently from those of the primary category axis. You then apply separate major gridlines (*Chart Tools/Layout/Gridlines*) for each axis; this results in two major gridlines that run in the same direction (and partly overlay) but can be formatted separately.

Figure 8-31 shows how you can use the latter scenario.

> **Note** In reference to Figure 8-31, I want to apologize for the fact that the linguistic chaos prevalent in Excel 2007 doesn't make it easier to use the program. Terms like *gridlines of the secondary category axis* or *gridlines of the second category axis* would be clear and you would be able to click the correct entry after a moment's consideration whether the lines are vertical (for example, in column charts) or horizontal (in bar charts).
>
> I would like to contrast this to the language actually used in Excel 2007 and shown in the figure:
>
> - ❑ *Secondary Horizontal (Category) Axis Major Gridlines*
>
>   means the same as
>
> - ❑ *gridlines of the second category axis*
>
> And *Horizontal (Category) Axis* means the same as the *Horizontal Primary Axis* command in the same tab of the Ribbon.
>
> But you can't ignore the confusing labels from the *Chart Tools/Layout/Chart Elements* menu completely, because you sometimes need to select elements that you can't see because of an overlay. Elements that can't be accessed or aren't visible using the mouse or keyboard can be opened via these menu commands.

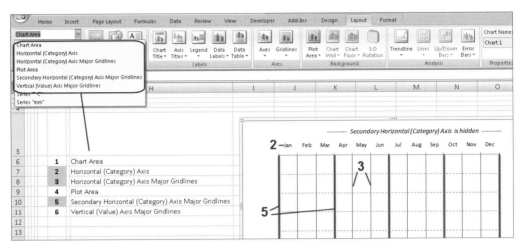

FIGURE 8-31 Differently scaled gridlines with two existing category axes

How was the result shown in Figure 8-31 defined? Would you like to try it out yourself? Then proceed as follows:

1. A chart with more than one data series and a horizontal category axis that is positioned at the bottom by default was created; for example, a column or line chart.

2. In this chart, a second value axis was defined (the *secondary vertical axis*).

3. The *major gridlines* of the *primary horizontal axis* and consequently the vertical *gridlines* of the *plot area* have been displayed.

4. The *primary horizontal axis* (i.e., the first category axis) was positioned above the upper edge of the *plot area* by setting the *Axis Labels: High* option.

5. Now, a *secondary horizontal axis* (a second category axis) was created under *Chart Tools/Axes*. The two category axes were positioned above the *plot area*: the first one directly on its edge and the second above the first.

6. The second category axis was set to *Interval between tick marks: 3* and *Specify interval unit: 3* and consequently has a scaling that is less detailed than the first category axis: the first one has a monthly tiling, the second one a quarter tiling.

7. *Major gridlines* were created for the second category axis (the one with the quarter tiling). Thus, there were two *major gridlines* with vertical, partly overlaying *gridlines*.

8. The first one of these major gridlines (monthly tiling) was selected via *Chart Tools/ Layout/Current Selection/Chart Elements* and formatted slightly. Then, the second major gridline (quarter tiling) was selected and formatted with bright lines.

9. Finally, the second category axis (the *secondary horizontal axis*) was hidden.

> **Tip** In the context of number 5, you read that the two axes can also be positioned directly on top of each other (either at the upper or the lower edge of the *plot area*). So if you have both category axes displayed and define the intervals and axis labels differently, you can create ruler or slide-rule effects which can be useful and effective in some cases. Give it a try!

Circular Charts

I refer to the pie charts and their "offset" (doughnut charts) as *circular charts* because both types are virtually the same from the technical point of view and are used in very similar ways.

This chart type is frequently used and well appreciated, which is not always appropriate because of its limited options. There are some basic deficits that should prompt you to carefully check whether the use of a pie chart is appropriate. You must consider the following:

- Such a chart doesn't have any axes, and consequently no axis labels. The provision of additional information is therefore limited to the legend, data point labels, and inserted text boxes.

- The number of clearly presentable segments is limited by two aspects: too many and too small slices:
  - Can't be differentiated sufficiently by our perception,
  - Can only be labeled in a sufficient display quality with a great deal of effort.

  One solution that compensates these weaknesses to some extent—"Bar of Pie"—will be presented further below.

- A pie chart can only display one single series in a self-contained image. This makes it difficult to display developments in pie charts or compare intervals.

> With reference to the last point, there are various visualizations (and, unfortunately, also some genuine software solutions) in which several pie charts are positioned next to each other to compare the data. This would still be acceptable for two or even three charts of this type under limited conditions (see Figure 8-32) where a few data points per chart are necessary. If you want to compare four or more pies, this is complete nonsense. I, for my part, can't see the advantage of four pie charts, which are positioned right next to each other and have five slices each, over a stacked column or bar chart with exactly the same content, particularly if the charts are supposed to be used for comparisons.

The frequent multiple use of tachometer charts in "management cockpits" (the name says it all!) is also closely linked with such critical assessments. Creating circular objects with pointers in Excel is rather easy if—for example—you use two partly transparent pie or doughnut charts that are on top of each other. It gets more complex and highly elaborate if you use the mathematic functions =COS(number), =SIN(number), and, if necessary, =RADIANS(angle), for designing the scale and pointers. However, I ask you to forgive me for not describing these two variants within this book. From my point of view, the effort would outweigh the result. Within the scope of this book, result means that a target group gets information that is as reliable as possible, quickly interpretable, plain, and "nicely" designed. Naturally, almost all of us can interpret the displays of circular gauges because we're used to them in everyday life. But if you're not trained as a professional pilot, you'll find it difficult to understand the optical and factual context of more than two of these instruments (as can be easily proven in tests). This is true especially if multiple interpretations are required for each individual project. For example, you can see a scale from x to y (what does it mean?), an associated pointer (is it good or bad or average, and to which extent?), two markers of a defined bandwidth (how do the pointers *relate* and what does the relationship mean?). On top of it all, there's then a benchmark symbol that must also be interpreted in its relation to the pointer, bandwidth, and main scale. In addition, everything is arranged in circles or semi-circles which—even if it looks "cool" and "sophisticated"—requires more concentration than interpreting the same information in plainly designed horizontal or vertical scales.

The information-processing capacity of the human brain is restricted, and it is an absurd myth that we are capable of multitasking like a modern PC processor. Nevertheless, this is exactly what is expected of the modern "homo mustbeonline." But what happens if someone requests an exciting multipartite "executive dashboard" in Porsche style? Well, the new Excel is equipped with excellent graphics options and provides absolutely everything. And if this dashboard is supplemented by a "dash of diligence"—that would be....

Select table data; create chart; format a little bit; done? That alone is usually not the solution for this type of chart, which is supposed to be created easily; at least not if you want to obtain convincing results. In the file *0810_Pies.xlsx*, I will detail what needs to be considered to achieve this goal and provide some tricks.

First, I'll point out that most information provided in this section for setting up a pie chart is only valid for static variants, but not for dynamic charts. This is due to the potential "sensitivity" of pie charts. Reading other data can change the overall impression considerably, even if this is not justified by the new value constellation. Even worse, it can move or change individual elements of the chart unfavorably beyond recognition. It is therefore necessary to check for every data update whether the formatting is correct.

> **On the Companion CD** Open the file \Samples\0810_Pies.xlsx on the CD-ROM.

Angles and Pie Explosion

The *angle of the first slice* and the *pie* or *point explosion* are among the most essential technical basics that should be considered in every design project. Both aspects are to be explained in the *Pie 1* worksheet, an example which has already been introduced in Chapter 3.

The three Benelux countries, occasionally considered as a unit, are rather different with regard to their populations and geographical sizes. This applies both absolutely and relatively. This can be displayed by different graphical means, among which is the pie chart, or preferably two pie charts side by side. It is only suitable, however, if comparable impressions can be created for the comparison display. In the current example (Figure 8-32, a typical publication chart) this is done by means of an optical "reference point": Luxembourg is emphasized in both charts and also kept at nearly the same position. Moreover, the small pie slice has been moved slightly from the chart to the foreground and is highlighted with another color as a contrast to its neighbors.

Some key steps for creating the basic design:

1. Select the data range D4:E6 in the table and create a pie chart of the *3-D Pie* type.

2. Select one of the 3-dimensional styles from the bottom row via *Chart Tools/Design/ Chart Styles*. Initially, the color is not important and can be changed later.

3. Optionally, adjust the *3-D Rotation* (direct access via the context menu after you've right-clicked the *plot area* or, indirect access via the formatting dialog box of the *plot area*).

4. Remove the *legend* and add *data labels*. Define *category names* and a *value* for the *data labels* and select the *(New Line)* option as the *separator*.

5. Specify the sizes and positions of the *chart area* and the *plot area*.

6. Determine the sizes and colors of the individual chart elements. You can select the *data points*—pie slices—individually and then conveniently color them via *Home/Font/Fill Color* without removing the 3-D color effects.

7. Copy the chart and insert the copy at another position. Right-click the copy and, following the *Select Data* command, change the *chart data range* in the *Select Data Source* dialog box. You now require a multiselection for the chart data range; that is, the range D4:D6,E4:E6. For this purpose, position the cursor in the input line, press and hold the **Ctrl** key to select the two mentioned areas in the background using the mouse.

8. Position the two charts side by side and create a title (in this example text boxes).

The initially described effects (position of the Luxembourg slice and moving it from the chart) are implemented at the end, because the final impression of these partly minimal effects can only be evaluated in the overall view.

For this purpose, you need to change the *angle of the first slice* and a moderate *point explosion*. In the context of Figure 8-32, you can see the measures used.

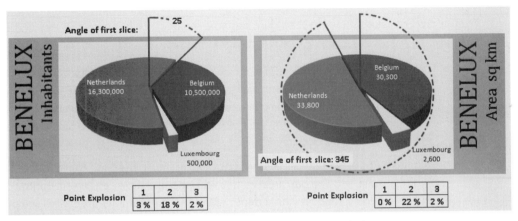

FIGURE 8-32 The angle is usually very important—and sometimes the explosions are too.

Angles

The first slice in this chart contains data about Belgium, the first row of the data source. Usually, the left edge of the first slice is positioned on the imaginary radius of the circle with an alignment exactly vertical to the top. If you now change the *angle of the first slice* (*Series, Series Options* formatting dialog box), you rotate this radius to the right; that is, clockwise. In the chart on the left side, the angle is 25°; the Belgium slice and all other slices are rotated to the right by this angle. In the chart on the right side, the angle is set to 345°. The chart was not rotated to the left, as you might assume, but also to the right; in this case almost completely. The effects:

- In both cases, a chart was created that appears less rigid than the standard version by avoiding vertical or horizontal lines.

- The desired "reference point" Luxembourg was moved to an exposed, "dominant" that is, optically attractive position that will be further enhanced in the following section.

- In particular, if you compare the two charts and begin with the Netherlands slice, you quickly notice the relations between number of inhabitants and areas; the Netherlands has a higher density of population than the other two countries.

Point Explosion

You can prepare the desired optical separation of the slices (a *pie* or *point explosion*) using the mouse (select and drag the segments individually) and subsequently refine it in the formatting dialog box of the series/series options. The effects to be obtained in the 3-D pie chart are both attractive and clear under Excel 2007. Although it's not one of my favorite features, I'll use a 3-D variant in this case because it really fits in this context.

The percent values shown in the figure describe the distance between the slice and the center of the pie. In this example, the results are as follows.

- Left chart: the Belgium slice (1) was moved slightly to the right, the Netherlands slice (3) slightly to the left. The gap that was created between those two slices (at the rear of the chart view) enables a sufficient three-dimensional effect. The Luxembourg slice (2) was clearly positioned at the front. As a result, the left side of the slice becomes visible; the element is "brought out."

- Right chart: the Belgium slice (1) was not moved at all, the Netherlands slice (3) only slightly to the left. The gap created between the two slices results—in contrast to variant 1—in a dark shadow with a depth effect that sufficiently emphasizes the plasticity. The Luxembourg slice (2) was moved to the front a bit further to enhance its optical presence once more.

Series Split and Second Plot Area

The example in the *Pie 2* worksheet includes a solution, or rather an auxiliary solution, to a basic problem of the pie chart. As you can see, the chart compares the annual revenue from 12 products. If this is to be implemented in a pie chart, the default variant would not be suitable in this case because there are four products with relatively high revenue and eight products with comparably low revenue. Depending on the data situation, you could barely differentiate the pie slices for the products 5 to 12, which would render the selected chart type useless. As an auxiliary solution, you can combine the smaller slices into one group slice and display the members of this group in an adjacent second *plot area*.

Note I use the restricting term "auxiliary solution" because this display makes great demands on the human perceptual and interpretation capability. Two different chart types (pie and stacked column) are positioned right next to each other which both want to provide common information. The desired interpretation is only possible if we first look at the pie and then at the stacked column and then transfer the received impression to the pie again. This may be used for a publication chart, if you want to assume that the viewer will pay careful attention, but I wouldn't use it for a presentation in front of an audience.

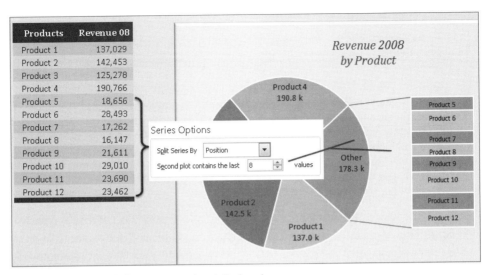

FIGURE 8-33 The small slices are treated and displayed as a group.

Here as well, you can press the **F9** key several times to simulate the reading of new data and evaluate the resulting impressions.

To create such a chart, complete the following steps:

1. Select the data range D3:E15 and create a chart of the *Bar of Pie* type. (Ignore the fact that you aren't creating *bars*, but a stacked column.)

2. Specify a basic formatting using the integrated styles.

3. Select the *data series* and open its formatting dialog box. Under *Series Options*, specify the following:

   ❑ *Split Series by: Position* (As you can see in the little drop-down list, you can also create other combinations. Just try it!)

   ❑ *Second plot contains the last 8 values.* You can change this summary by entering another number. The term *second plot area* refers to the stacked column. In the stacked column, you can see the values—indicated by two connecting lines—that are now segments of the pie chart's group slice.

4. Format the *data points,* or edit the automatically created formatting.

5. Create and format *data labels.* In the given example, the *data labels* required some fine-tuning; that is, individually selected labels had to be edited. The labels of the stacked column segments only contain the *category names*; the labels of the pie slices include the *category name* and the *value.* The category name *Other* is automatically created for the *data label* of the group slice, but you can also enter a custom name like for any other data label text.

Mapping Parts with Gaps and Transparencies

The example shown in the *Pie 3* worksheet effectively uses the new options of Excel 2007. Press the **F9** key to change the displayed return on sales.

> **Note** The display of the return on sales, like many other business measures, uses the normalization of any value to 100. This is a major benefit for chart designers both from the technical and the informational point of view: 100 points = 100 percent. That is a clear relation. I recommend you to try a normalization of the results to 100, particularly for each evaluation of research and surveys, irrespective of the size of the actually collected values and their range. The resulting charts are easy to understand for everyone, especially in fast-paced presentations.

The share in profit of the enterprise is presented as a light section of a euro coin. Its simplicity is convincing and informative. This type of chart could be used, for example, in an overview sheet for quick information for the CEO (the "management cockpit with executive dashboard" is not always necessary), and you could arrange several of these charts side by side without losing track.

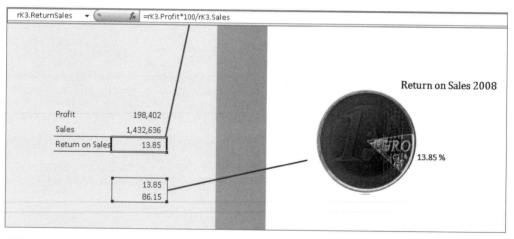

FIGURE 8-34 Return on sales as a section of a euro coin

The chart can be created easily and quickly. The most essential components are:

- The return on sales is calculated in cell C10 (as you can see, the rS1 range names are used again).

- The data source of the chart is derived in C13:C14 based on the before mentioned information. Both values always total 100, so the size of the pie slice concerned always corresponds to the percent—or cents—of sales on return.

- The chart background contains a picture that can be found on the CD-ROM under \Materials\Pictures\Euro.tif.

- A fully transparent pie chart created from C13:C14 is arranged in front of the picture. Its properties are:

  - The *chart area* and *plot area* have neither a border nor fill.

  - The *angle of the first slice* (the first slice is the return on sales) was rotated to 81°. As a result, in most cases the coin area with the character string *Euro* will be visible as the sales on return slice.

  - The first slice had neither a fill nor a border and is therefore fully transparent.

  - The *data label* of the first slice has the *Outside End* label position and the custom number format 0.00" %" (fortunately, a negative return on sales is not expected here and could not be displayed in a pie chart).

  - The second slice, the cover area, has no border and a dark solid fill with a transparency of 33 percent.

The only thing that could cause some problems in the creation of this chart is ensuring an exact match of the euro coin picture and the size and position of the two series segments; that is, the chart. For this purpose, you must use a combination of different work steps. Combination in this case means that you may have to execute the work steps several times in a row and if necessary in a changing order.

1. Scale the size of the euro coin picture proportionally as necessary or desired.

2. Scale the size of the *chart area* and the *plot area* in order to resize the chart view approximately to the size of the euro coin picture.

3. Use the mouse to drag the chart (the *chart area*) so that the two pictures overlap. Then position the two pictures in such a way that the edges of the two pictures cover each other at least at one point.

> **Note** Use the mouse for approximate movements and for scaling the *chart area*; hold down the **Ctrl** key and click the chart to select it as a drawing object, and move the chart in small steps using the **arrow left**, **arrow right**, **top arrow**, and **bottom arrow** keys.

4. Scale the *chart area* proportionately (reduce or increase it—and thus indirectly the chart image's *plot area*—using its corner points) and repeatedly move it in small steps until the euro-coin picture and the chart cover each other as desired.

> **Tip** For fine-tuning in connection with step 4, you can use exact specifications; i.e., minimal sizing, which you can specify in *Chart Tools/Format/Size*.

Rings and Inner Rings, Circles and Semicircles

By examining the chart in the *Pie 4* worksheet you can obtain an overview of the previous details of this main section. The last example of the "pie chart" topic is a variant of the pie chart: the doughnut chart. In Chapter 3, I already mentioned that its possible uses are even more restricted than those of the pie charts themselves. The use discussed in the following sections is primarily aimed to address some technical aspects and to explain the creation of a semicircle chart, which is requested occasionally.

The chart presented in Figure 8-35 forms a value ring around the euro coin. The portions of the upper slices change every time you press the **F9** key, while the lower slice with a portion of 50 percent remains unchanged. This structure (or rather the table range D6:D13) is the entry point for creating a semicircle or half-doughnut chart:

- If you total all data that is to be displayed in a semicircle, you obtain the data basis of a 200 percent chart; one half of this chart contains all data to be displayed, and the other half the quantity needed to fill up the full circle.

- Create a pie or doughnut chart on this 200 percent basis. Then set the angle of the first slice to 270° to specify a fixed position for the sum slice; that is, the lower half of the semicircle, independent of the respective quantity of the totalized individual values. Because you only want to see the upper half, it is sufficient to hide the lower semicircle by means of the corresponding formatting and to remove any existing labels (also from the legend, if present).

The *doughnut hole size* is one of the properties of the doughnut chart's *data series* that can be formatted. It specifies the size of the doughnut hole and indirectly the width of the doughnut. Here, the close relation to the pie chart becomes obvious: setting the value to 0 percent would turn the doughnut chart into a pie chart (but that is practically impossible because the range that can be set in Excel 2007 is between 10 percent and 90 percent). I won't detail the specifications for the selected doughnut-hole size, so you'll have to find it out yourself. Excel may accept a manually set *doughnut-hole size* but display a value that differs from the set value after you've closed the formatting dialog box and opened it again, even though the actual size hasn't been changed at all. If you then want to confirm the size displayed by Excel through manual update, this returns a wrong display result (the doughnut-hole size is either too small or too large).

In this chart, the size of the chart and the euro-coin picture was adapted as well. The techniques used correspond to the example shown in Figure 8-34, except for the specification of the *doughnut-hole size.*

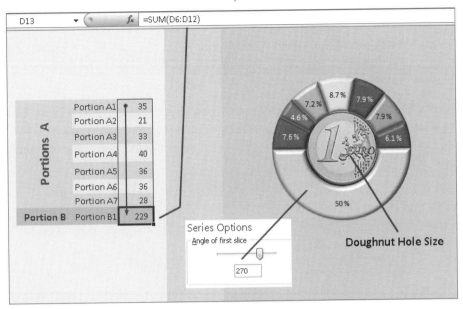

FIGURE 8-35 A full doughnut that can easily become a half doughnut.

Consider the size of the transparent *chart area* and the associated use of the table background for positioning the *legend*.

XY (Scatter) Charts

In this chapter, you've already been provided with a lot of technical basic information. Therefore, I will discuss the scatter charts only briefly. In technical terms, this type largely corresponds to the line chart. With only one exception: the *XY (Scatter) chart* uses no category axis, but two value axes (one vertical and one horizontal) in its standard version. As for the other types, there can also be secondary axes in addition to the primary axes; in some exceptional cases such a chart can also have four value axes.

The position of the data point of a scatter chart is determined by the coordinate of two values (X and Y) and can therefore be displayed in any position of the plot area. Any linear sequence of the points created in this way is possible, although it's in no case necessary. For the same reason, the data basis requires no specific sorting in most cases, at least as far as the drawing of the chart is concerned. In most of the common applications, a specific scatter pattern is displayed: an uneven, but (hopefully) meaningful distribution of data points, often referred to as *point cloud*. A corresponding example can be found in the *Height Weight* worksheet of the file *0811_Scatter.xlsx*.

On the Companion CD Open the file \Samples\0811_Scatter.xlsx on the CD-ROM.

Point Cloud in a Filter Chart

The chart presented in Figure 8-36 shows specific relationships of height and weight defined by age and sex based on the measurement values of 100 persons. A linear trendline is inserted in the chart to highlight the tendency of the data.

The model uses a "filter chart" as an extremely useful technique: the data series is based on the table range E7:F106 (two columns for one data series, each point requiring two values). You can filter this area as required to create user-defined subsets. These are then displayed in the chart.

Such a procedure enables a wide range of possible chart contents. This is interesting theoretically for the present small data pool, but for the evaluation of extensive primary tables in scientific settings it provides a major benefit: thousands of possible visualization requirements can be implemented in just a few seconds.

> **Note** The combination of a table range and the adjacent chart, which is provided in the present worksheet, is primarily aimed to provide a clear overview. In an actual solution, the chart shouldn't be positioned right next to the table to be filtered. If you use this layout nevertheless—this is rather common in some Excel instruments for initial analysis of scientific data—you should ensure that the chart is independent of the table rows. The visible number of rows decreases during filtering; that is, the table range becomes smaller. If the chart were not independent, its height would also decrease.
>
> Follow this path to exempt the chart: *Chart Tools/Format/Size* (click on the *Launcher* symbol)/ *Size and Properties* dialog box/*Properties* tab/*Don't move or size with cells* option.

To test the functions of this example you need to know the basics of filtering table ranges in Excel. If you know this feature from previous Excel versions (it used to be called AutoFilter), you surely won't have any problems with the new, clearly improved design, and you will feel a sense of achievement. If you don't know these procedures at all, I must refer you to the integrated Excel help or to other sources because a chart book can't cover *all* Excel topics. Apart from that, this chapter and Chapter 10 only provide brief information about this extremely useful analysis instrument.

In the context of Figure 8-36:

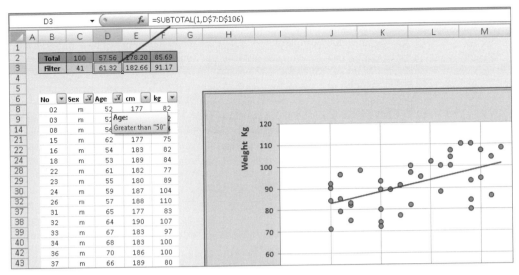

FIGURE 8-36 Scatter chart with filtered data

The design and formatting of this chart don't include any noteworthy special features, but the table range of the columns C to F sure does: rows 2 and 3 include formulas that relate to the table range C7:F106. The top row, *Total*, includes default formulas for determining the count and averages; the bottom row, *Filter*, contains formulas of the SUBTOTAL type to calculate which counts or averages are available in the currently visible rows of the list.

The function =SUBTOTAL(function_num,reference) executes a specific calculation in reference, whose type is specified by the argument function_num. Corresponding formulas are therefore multifunctional; they can execute different arithmetic operations, depending on your specifications. If you use them in filter tables, the formula results refer to the filter result; that is, only to the currently visible rows of the filtered list.

A number is required for the function_num argument. In the listing that follows, you can see the most essential specifications for determining the calculation type; that is, numbers that are used as the function_num argument.

1 = AVERAGE

2 = COUNT

3 = COUNTA

4 = MAX

5 = MIN

9 = SUM

> **Tip** Earlier, I used the term "multifunctional." Multifunctionality can be achieved even more elegantly: Of course, you can also use the function for table ranges not to be filtered. For example, =SUM(B2:B22) and =SUBTOTAL(9,B2:B22) have the same result if no filter is used. Here, the trick is to not enter the function_num argument in the formula, but in the cell to which you want to refer the formula; for example, =SUBTOTAL($C$3,B$2:B$22). You consequently obtain an adapted formula that can execute different arithmetic operations by changing the number specification in cell C3. Chapter 7, "Elements of Dynamization," already explained what that means: you are provided with controls; so if you use SUBTOTAL, different calculation types are available at a mouse click.

The data range C6:F106 is a filterable table with headings. Select a single cell (and only one single cell) *within* the list to be filtered (alternatively the entire list) and choose the *Filtering* command under *Home/Edit/Sort & Filter* to activate the filter and to display the filter arrows (including their drop-down lists) in the header row of the range. Click this command again to deactivate the filter and to hide the filter arrows. Equivalent commands can also be found in the *Data* tab in the *Sort & Filter* group.

Try some filter experiments and particularly notice the effects on the formula results in row 3 and the appearance of the chart:

1. Click the drop-down arrow of the *Sex* column to open the respective picklist and *deactivate* the entry *f* (female) to show the data of the males in the filter results. Click *OK* to implement the filter process.

2. Open the list of the filter specifications again and click *(Select All)* and *OK* to show all data again.

   Next, the filtered list and the connected chart should display only the data of all females older than 50.

3. Open the filter specifications in the *Sex* column and deactivate the entry *m* to select females only. Click *OK*. This filtering is additive, which means that you can further restrict your current selection.

4. Click the filter arrow of the *Age* column, and select the *Number Filters* command from the list of options displayed. Then choose the *Greater than* command and enter the number *50* in the *is greater than* field of the dialog box. Click *OK* to implement the filter process just defined.

Try some other filter options and use different combinations. The user guidance is very clear and most options are to infer from individual practice.

Note that a previous, very sensitive deficit of this feature has been partly solved in Excel 2007: if you set a filter in a column, the arrow symbol becomes a filter symbol to indicate that a filter exists in this column. If you place the mouse pointer on this symbol without clicking it, a little text information is displayed informing you about the filter criteria selected. Another (and badly missed) option that would be useful here: a text information for combined filtering that can also be used as a heading and that includes all implemented settings in a clear design. Up to now, this would have only been possible with programming.

> **Note** In case you were wondering:
> ❑ The table range B2:F3 and the SUBTOTAL function in row 3 are used for information purposes. For the chart, they have the meanings of an extended legend.
> ❑ The entire data range C6 : F106 forms the chart basis. Its content is reduced via filtering. There are no more tricks to offer in this context.

Grade Distribution in a Scatter Line Chart

The scatter chart looking like a line chart that is shown in the *Grades* worksheet has already been presented in Chapter 3. With this slightly updated variant, I would like to come back to one of the core topics of this book: the use of controls. Simultaneously, I want to present some unique features that will play a role in examples provided in the subsequent chapters. These involve the use of hidden structures.

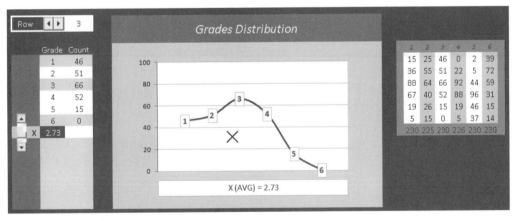

FIGURE 8-37 In this chart you can move a marker using a control.

What is possible?

■ In the top left corner of the worksheet you use an *ActiveX control*, a *SpinButton* ranging between 1 and 6 whose *LinkedCell* is F2. By clicking on this element, you read the data from the small table located on the right side of the worksheet. The respective grades, which could be results of quality checks or inspections, are displayed as a curve in the chart. The average of the results is indicated as a large blue X in the *plot area* and as text information below the *plot area*.

- On the left side of the worksheet you use another *ActiveX control*, a *ScrollBar* ranging between 1 and 100 whose *LinkedCell* is F11. You can use this control to move the blue X marker up and down within the plot area. (If you activated this control you can also use the arrow keys for this moving. This may look like a gimmick here, but it's a very useful tool in preparing for printing. Moreover, it plays a very decisive role in specific presentation models involving flexible, controllable visual alerts.)

> **Note** In Chapter 7, I detailed the ActiveX controls *SpinButton* and *ScrollBar* and remarked that their *Max* properties can have smaller values than the *Min* properties so that you can reverse the moving direction of the element. This was applied in our example here: *Max* is *1* and *Min* is *100*. This enables you to synchronize the movement of the *ScrollBar* and the connected object.

How does this work? As we're getting closer to the end of the chapter and I want to give the ambitious readers and advanced users the chance to experiment, I'll only provide a few key points.

In the context of Figure 8-38:

- The chart's data range is E5:F11 half of which consists of formulas. Consequently, the X marker is also an XY coordinate.

- Cell E11 contains a formula, cell F11 a variable that has been hidden via font formatting.

- Behind the chart, more formulas are stored that are used to calculate the average.

- The *legend* is not a real legend, but a *text box* that obtains its variable content by means of a cell link (linking cells and objects is described in Chapter 5, "Graphical Objects").

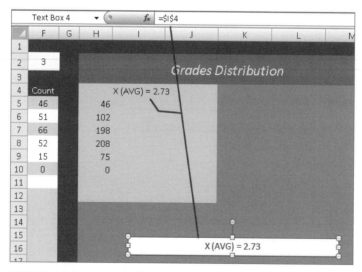

FIGURE 8-38 Calculating behind the scenes

About the chart:

- The *data points* are connected using lines. The data point markers are invisible and are replaced with *data labels*.

- As you can see, the blue X is also a data point of the chart (the seventh data point). This data point and its connection to the sixth data point are formatted slightly different.

> You can implement multiplications using the =PRODUCT(number1,number2,...) function.

Quality and Quantity in a Single-Point Chart

Many charts try to present a measured quality reflecting whatever the basis or goals may be. Most of these charts, however, don't indicate the actual informational value of this quality through a comprehensible specification of the quantity (the number of measurement results, for example). In some cases, you think hard about the reasons for omitting these values. The two charts of the *QQ 1* and *QQ 2* worksheets, however, clearly indentify the relations between quantity and quality. In other words, this single-point chart displays the quality and indicates how well the measured data supports the result.

Possible test results can be simulated here by using the *ScrollBars*. You can move the marker-point in all directions. In the "real version" of this model, the data was normalized in an evaluation system of 100 points. That means there were 100 quantity points and 100 quality points for each test result.

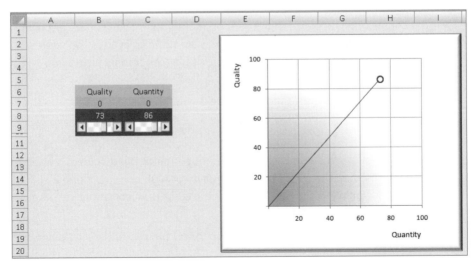

FIGURE 8-39 Data simulation with controls

The movable *data point* is permanently connected to the zero point of the two value axes. Its values are stored in the cells B7:C7, and its display is suppressed by its formatting. The visible and movable "QQ point" is connected with the zero point. A blue line is set between these two points that acts as a pointer and a "measuring tape." Measurement starts here: that's the distance; that's how good the result is. The more the shared marker moves to the right, the greater the quantity. The more it moves to the top, the better the quality. The possible optimum (the longest distance starting from zero) is X = 100 and Y = 100.

In the *QQ 2* worksheet, the same model has been edited with a considerably higher effort. Here are some tips (supported by Figure 8-40):

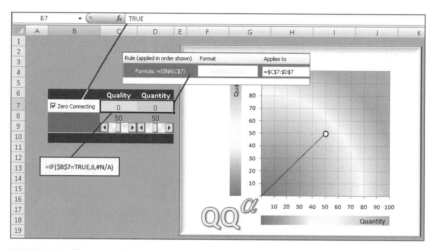

FIGURE 8-40 The somewhat more complex variant shows some special features.

- Both types of controls (*form controls* and *ActiveX controls*) are used in one worksheet.

- The connecting line between the zero point and the marker can be displayed and hidden. If it is hidden, the relevant zero values are not displayed in the table and the #N/A values that are available instead remain invisible (conditional formatting).

> The =ISNA(reference) function checks whether the value #N/A is in the reference and reacts with TRUE or FALSE.

- The greenest green belongs to the top right corner of the *plot area*. It was essential for the assignment of the colors that high quality or high quantity alone is not sufficient for the positioning in a green area. Note the color gradient of the yellow quarter ring between 80 and 80.

- The color formatting of the *plot area* is mirrored parallel to the axis labels in the text boxes.

- The bottom left corner of the chart contains two WordArt elements.

- When you've worked through this and all subsequent chapters, you'll soon be master of the greenest green.

Chapter 9
Dynamic Chart Formatting and Other Tricks

In Microsoft Excel, there are integrated formats, user-defined formats, and conditional formats. *Your* Excel may also include what I call "dynamic chart formats." In addition to reading changing content via controls, as already seen, you can also base the formal design of specific chart elements on changing content. This is mostly what I'll discuss in this chapter.

Minor examples were already introduced in Chapter 8, "Chart Types—Conventional and Exceptional:" There I introduced the "cheating" concept (legitimately and only in the interest of the target group): using hidden data and formulas with elements that are only sometimes visible is one of the most effective options in Excel's bag of tricks.

The files for this chapter that are available on the CD-ROM are mainly designed to be used for dynamic models; that is, for manually controllable data content of your charts. However, you can also easily implement most of the information provided here in static charts, adapted if required.

Once again, you can explore numerous formatting variants. I choose the term "explore" because this chapter doesn't describe design effects that have been used multiple times or only describes them with keywords. Therefore, you should select elements you're interested in and check their settings in the corresponding formatting dialog box.

Note If you note that an element formatting in the formatting dialog box is set to *Automatic*, either an integrated style has been defined or the formatting is the result of a conversion; that is, Excel 2007 has converted the file from an older file format.

Effects with Dynamic Chart Elements

In the examples in this section, some topics covered in the previous chapter are discussed again and reinforced. This section focuses on dynamic, value-dependent displays of visual alerts, variable axis labeling by means of formulas, and the use of scaling displays.

On the Companion CD Open the file \Samples\0901_DynamicIndicators.xlsx on the CD-ROM.

The file *0901_DynamicIndicators.xlsx* contains seven worksheets with sample charts. Except for *Example 1*, you can always change the values and displays using **F9**. This flexibility is based on the now familiar RANDBETWEEN function that you use to simulate the reading of data here and anywhere by use of controls.

Each worksheet contains a table area with data on the left side. In a "real" model, you would usually hide these areas or—far better—include them in an additional worksheet. However, this would be a little too complicated for our informational purpose here. Consequently, you should try to ignore the table area displayed on your screen if you want to assess the aesthetic value of the models.

> **Note** In most cases, the table areas with the yellow background contain the formulas that are the trick of the respective model.

Using a Spin Button to Change the Chart Type

In the *Example 1* worksheet, you can switch between the chart types of a data series using a control: the display switches between columns and lines. The blue range B7:C18 contains the data that is supposed to be displayed but is the chart's actual data source only with regard to the names of the months. The form control *spin button* is defined as a switch. It writes the values *1* or *2* in the respectively linked cell (E3). The IF formulas in the range E7:F18 respond to that. They transfer the values from column C either to column E or column F. Then, the other column range is completely filled with #N/A. Both columns are the source of the two data series of the chart; the columns are derived from column E and the lines from column F.

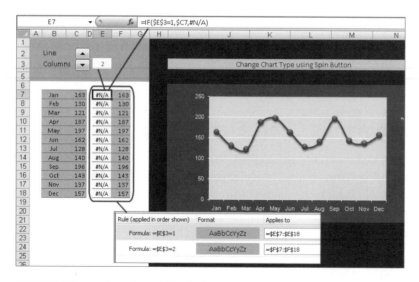

FIGURE 9-1 You prefer columns? They're just a mouse click away.

If you design such a model, after generating the table, you first generate the control and its cell link. The next steps are illustrated in the example shown:

1. Copy the original values from C to E and to F and create a column chart using these values. Assign the *Line* chart type to one of the two data series. Both data series are visible. Define B7:B18 as the *axis label range*.

2. Generate all formatting and additional settings in the chart.

3. Enter the following formulas:

   =IF($E$3=1,$C7,#N/A) etc. in column E

   =IF($E$3=2,$C7,#N/A) etc. in column F

The effect becomes visible: if you click on the control, you can see a series of either columns (E3=1) or lines (E3=2). The other data series is not displayed in Excel because it is completely based on #N/A values.

The entire range E7:F18 is yellow. However, the rules for conditional formatting illustrated in Figure 9-1 ensure that the range whose data is currently displayed in the chart is blue. This is not particularly essential in our example but can be very useful for developers in more complex models, during creation and also at a later stage.

Automatic Highlighting of Limits

Open the *Example 2* worksheet shown in Figure 9-2: each time **F9** is pressed, the column that displays the highest value is automatically capped by an orange dot. This is quite helpful for presentations when the values are close together; that is, they can't be immediately and clearly distinguished, and you want to highlight the maximum value.)

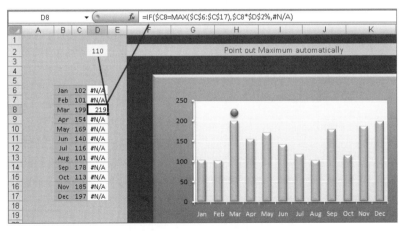

FIGURE 9-2 A cap of 110 percent for the maximum

The green range B6:C17 contains the source data of the column chart. In the yellow range D6:D17, the system uses the formulas of the type =IF($C6=MAX($C$6:$C$17),$C6*$D$2%, #N/A) to determine the appropriate maximum value, which is then increased or reduced by a percentage using a manually controllable variator from cell D2. You may enter there any number, normally between 80 and 120.

The formulas in column D ensure that only the maximum value that was modified in this way is displayed as a *data point* in a second data series (type: line chart). The marker can be displayed within the column (variator < 100), at the column's upper edge (variator = 100), or— preferably—above the column like the dot on the i (variator > 100).

That means that this chart is a combination of a column chart and a line chart. The line chart is drawn using the cells of the yellow range. It is formatted without a line, so only its marking points are shown. And in most cases, only one of these points is visible because all other values in the data series are set to #N/A.

Open the *Example 3* worksheet shown in Figure 9-3: each time you press **F9**, the *data point* with the maximum value of the line is highlighted, and the value itself is displayed with the appropriate marker.

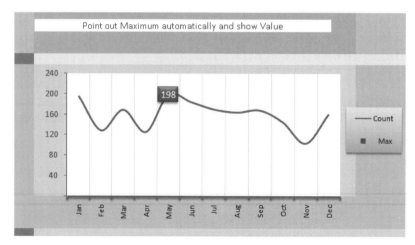

FIGURE 9-3 The maximum value displayed as a number

This works much like *Example 2*. It is a line chart with two data series, one of which is a line while the other consists only of small markers. Usually only one of these markers is used (for the maximum value), but it remains invisible because it is hidden behind its own 3-D-formatted *data label*. This *data label* contains the *value* of the *data point*, and its *label position* is set to *Center*; therefore, the marking point is covered.

Why should you set up a symbol when it is hidden anyway? It's time to bring back my key word "redundancy," which hasn't been mentioned for a long time. I also can imagine setting up a variant in no time at all where the marking point is visible because its label is positioned outside the chart. And because I had to format this data series anyway, it involves no additional work to proactively set up an element that I may need later on.

> **Note** In this and many other models with hidden or invisibly formatted elements, once you have completed your work you can no longer directly select specific elements with the mouse or keyboard to format them (in this case, for example, this applies to the data series *Max*). Select the *Current Selection* group in the *Layout* or *Format* tab of the *Chart Tools* menu item, and click the respective entry in the *Chart Elements* list. Open the formatting dialog box using the *Format Selection* command (same source) or the **Ctrl+1** shortcut.

Open the *Example 4* worksheet shown in Figure 9-4. This is an extension of *Example 3*. Each time you press **F9**, the *data points* with the maximum and the minimum values are highlighted and the values themselves are displayed with a *data label*.

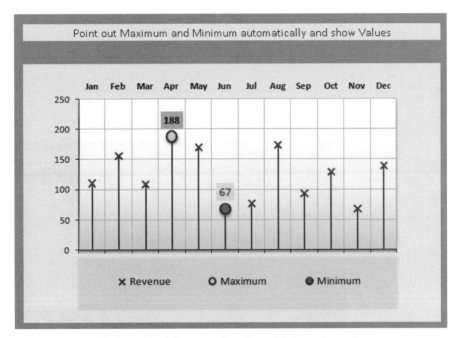

FIGURE 9-4 Even if it doesn't look like one: a line chart with three data series.

It is a line chart without lines with three *data series* that only displays the markers of the *data points*. The vertical lines that are standing on the category axis are *drop lines* (access: *Chart Tools/Layout/Analysis/Lines*). The data from column C is (or would be) completely visible as markers; however, for the *maximum* and *minimum*, they are covered by the markers of the other data series.

> **Note** Note that in this model the *primary horizontal axis* was moved to a position above the *plot area* using the *Axis labels: High* formatting option so that the space below the *plot area* can be entirely used by the generously dimensioned *legend*.

Open the *Example 5* worksheet shown in Figure 9-5. Each time you press **F9**, the two *data points* with the closest margin are highlighted and the difference value is displayed in the *legend*.

It is a line chart with four data series. The two visible markers are derived from the yellow ranges of columns F and G. Their values are again generated by means of the formulas whose structure has already been explained:

- Example from cell F6: `=IF($E6=MIN($E$6:$E$17),$C6,#N/A)`
- Example from cell G6: `=IF($E6=MIN($E$6:$E$17),$D6,#N/A)`

In column E to which the formulas refer, the difference values from *Revenue 01* and *Revenue 02* are calculated by simple subtraction formulas.

Their smallest values are processed in cell F5. This cell is the column heading and consequently supplies the content of the *legend*. That means the formula `=" Closest Margin = "&MIN($E$6:$E$17)` generates the desired legend text and specifies the minimum value.

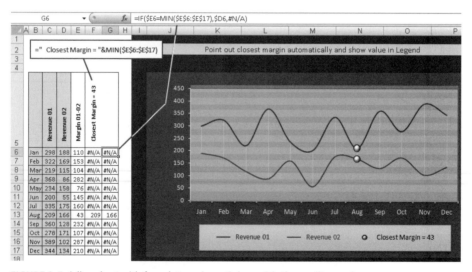

FIGURE 9-5 A line chart with four data series—Column E is the auxiliary column

Some notes on the formatting:

- The analysis elements *high-low lines* were set up to connect the *data series* with a vertical line.

- The boldly formatted *gridlines* of the horizontal major gridlines (*width: 10 pt*) are responsible for splitting the plot area into segments.

- The legend texts have individual colors that correspond to the appropriate lines.

Using Figure 9-5 as an example, you can find another exemplary instruction to create such charts:

1. Generate the master form with two data series from the range B5:D17, and format the basic design of the chart.

2. Generate and test the formulas (range E5:G17).

3. Transfer the additional data series with reference to the range F5:G17 to the chart. In the context menu of the chart, click *Select Data*, then click *Add* in the dialog box for *Legend Entries (Series)*, and define the reference.

4. Finally, format the two new data series so that only their markers are visible. Don't get confused, the two visible symbols have the same format but are markers of two different data lines.

Dynamic Multiline Axis Labels

Open the *Example 6* worksheet (shown in Figure 9-6) in the *0901_DynamicIndicators.xlsx* file. You've already come across several examples for multiline category axis labels in this book. This section takes up the topic again and deals with it in greater detail.

The category axis label is generated from the two-column range C6:D31. Column D contains the alphanumeric category labels. Column C contains formulas that generate the figures *1, 2,* or *3* using the LARGE function to display the first three ranks.

The function =LARGE(array,k) returnes the k-largest value of array. If the k argument, for example, has the value 3 (you want to determine the value with rank 3 from a list) the corresponding formula would return the third largest value of array.

The counterpart of this function is =SMALL(array,k).

If the values in the array are identical (for example, *100, 100, 100, 99, 99, 95*), this is no problem for Excel: in this case, the largest value is *100* and so are the second largest and third largest values. It becomes more difficult when we want to use this process for further calculations. Consequently, to continue the example, *99* is the fourth largest value after *100*. And the next *99* is the fifth largest. And *95* is the sixth largest. We might think this is funny, Excel doesn't.

This is rarely a problem, but that changes when we revert to the logic of LARGE with the beautiful function RANK, which plays a role in additional examples below (LARGE determines the number that corresponds to a rank. RANK determines the rank that corresponds to a number).

The function =RANK (number,ref,[order]) returns the rank that a number has within a list of numbers. If values in this list (for example, *100, 100, 100, 99, 99, 95*) are identical, problems occur for several presentations of results. This list then contains rank 1 three times, but not rank 2, not rank 3, rank 4 twice, not rank 5, and finally rank 6. This may be okay for mathematics but is not really helpful in a presentation (explain this to a sensitive audience; maybe even under pressure). This is also the reason why it is sometimes legitimate to manually change these values only by a few millionths, as described below in a different context. It is particularly legitimate if the following two aspects are essential:

- In a presentation, you need to present the ranking with descriptions that also include numbers (*Rank 1, Rank 2,* and so on). In this case, the presentation could also read *Rank 1 = 100, Rank 2 = 100,* and so on. Experience has shown that viewers don't have a problem with that. Obviously, it is more irritating when some ranks are missing in an overview.

- You must use the determined ranks in a continuing calculation. Here it might be possible that you require all of the rankings in a series without gaps.

Note The Excel help provides an additional variant with a different effect regarding the handling and presentation of rankings. It can be found in the explanations on the RANK function using the keyword *correcting factor*.

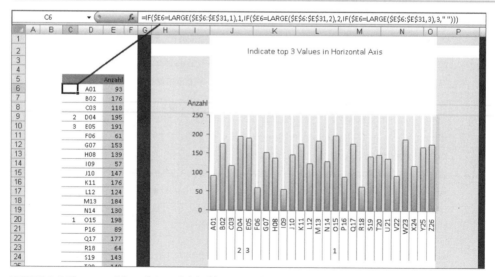

FIGURE 9-6 The second line of the axis label becomes dynamic thanks to the *LARGE* function.

The IF formulas in column C, which are nested three times, with their included LARGE formulas determine the value but write its ranking instead of the value itself into the cell based on a previous check and if the ranking is *1, 2,* or *3.*

```
C6    =IF($E6=LARGE($E$6:$E$31,1),1,
      IF($E6=LARGE($E$6:$E$31,2),2,
      IF($E6=LARGE($E$6:$E$31,3),3,
      " ")))
```

The verbalized instruction would be in short:

- If the number in cell E6 is the largest value in the range E6:E31, then write *1,*

- If the number in cell E6 is the second largest value in the range E6:E31, then write *2,*

- If the number in cell E6 is the third largest value in the range E6:E31, then write *3,*

- Otherwise, if none of these rules applies, write a blank space.

> **Note** Please be aware of the following:
>
> ❑ In this case, you must really generate a blank space for value_if_false of the IF formula and not empty text, which would be sufficient in other cases. Reason: these blank spaces are required to ensure exact, column-oriented scaling also in the second label line for the category axis label. Explore how it would look like if the blank spaces are not used: remove the blank space between the quotation marks at the end of the formula.
>
> ❑ The IF formula used here is nested three times. In Excel 2007, you can nest up to 64 IF checks (so far, there have been seven) with each other to implement highly complex conditional checks.
>
> ❑ In our example, you would achieve the same using the RANK function:
> `=IF(RANK($E6,$E$6:$E$31,0)=1,1,IF( … etc.)`

Open the *Example 7* worksheet shown in Figure 9-7. In this model, a category axis label with even five lines was set up based on the previously introduced concept. The first line indicates the name of the category, the second the corresponding value; the ranks 1 to 3 are displayed in a hierarchy with three lines in clear text, that is, "Rank 1" and so on. The previously introduced, three times nested IF formula was split and distributed across three different columns (C, D, E).

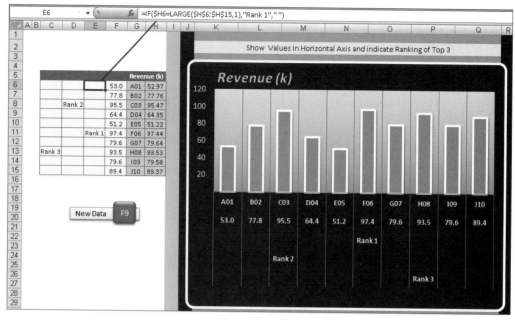

FIGURE 9-7 Axis labels with five lines as well as value and rank display

Note This chart looks rather dark in grayscales print. However, black or dark gray objects may be quite attractive as color prints or on the screen, particularly if you add some bright and vivid colors, as shown in this example.

You can round the corners of the *chart area* in the formatting dialog box under *Border Styles*.

Horizontal Scales

On the Companion CD Open the file \Samples\ 0902_Scale01.xlsx on the CD-ROM.

Open the *Scale 1* worksheet (excerpts are shown in Figure 9-8) in the *0902_Scale01.xlsx* file. Each time you press **F9**, the red scale pointers in the green bars move to a different position and indicate the percentage of a default value (which is not of interest here) that has been reached in the respective city. In a vertical examination of the figure, the relevant differences are immediately obvious.

Horizontal scales with fixed widths of 100 and a moving pointer are well suited for many presentation purposes, particularly if you want to represent a comparative visualization of approaches to a set value, as is the case in our example. However, there is hardly a better solution for result statistics on surveys (to which extent are the facts accepted?), measurements (how many of the planned tasks have been successfully completed?), and many other things.

This holds particularly true for comparisons across several categories, that is, for several similar scales.

> You can measure and test the following: a model that is designed like the example and also uses the same colors is probably initially automatically read from top to bottom, following the "red thread". When you take a second look, for example horizontally from left to right, following a specific interest—"where is our result"—the eye catches the line-specific red mark, measures its distance to the right—"how far are we from the maximum?"—and then explores the close proximity and the further vertical proximity— "are the others better or worse?" If you measure the reception speed of such processes and compare them with adjacent tachometer charts, for example, it becomes quickly obvious why the consequent effort for simplicity should always be held in high esteem.

Let's now take a closer look at the design details of the chart, with reference to Figure 9-8. In the adjacent worksheet, *RawVersion 1*, an "open" format is used for the same model. You can also follow the information there, as it provides a better overview.

Naturally, in a real-life report model of this kind, there are fixed value constellations. The dynamics of such solutions would be, for example, that you use controls to call different survey topics and their results. However, in this example, this option is simulated with **F9** for testing purposes. Additionally, you can customize the initial situation and the value constellations in the chart data source as you like.

You should note:

- It is a 100% Stacked Bar chart. A specific portion of a default value (specified in column G) is reached. This result is displayed with a red mark in percentages.
- The chart has three data series, each stacked bar consists of three segments:
    - The values from D9:D14 form the first bar segment; that is, the left part of the green bar.
    - The values from F9:F14 form the third bar segment; that is, the right part of the green bar. The format of both green segments is identical.
    - The values from E9:E14 form the second bar segment—that is, the middle part of the threepart stack (the red pointer). Its width or "thickness" can be defined by the user. The width is subtracted from the "remainder" (the third segment). Now compare the formula that is visible in the formula bar of Figure 9-8.

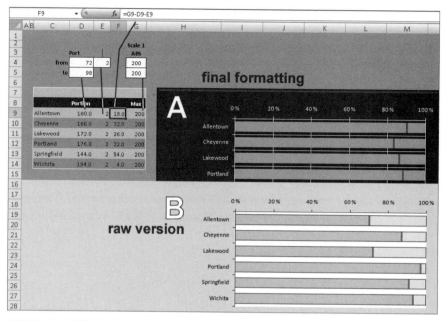

FIGURE 9-8 100% Stacked Bar chart as a scale

You can manipulate the value constellation of the data that is displayed in the chart by entering different values in the bright cells above the table.

- In cells G4:G5, you can either enter identical values (same set value for all) or define a range (lower value at the top). In the last case mentioned, you or the referencing RANDBETWEEN formulas create city-specific maximum specifications that are all indicated as 100 percent in the chart.

- In cell E4, you enter a value to define the width of the pointer. This value is transferred by formulas to E9:E14; that is, the same value is used in all rows.

> **Note** This method only provides completely correct optical results if the total of columns D and E is not more than 100 percent (not more than the set value from column G). Otherwise, because the value in column E would then be less than zero, the entire bar would be slightly indented to the left. In real life (where percentages of 100 would rarely be reached), this usually can be neglected but may have to be considered in some cases.
>
> If the individual, absolute set values in column G where each of the values represents 100 percent deviate considerably (which also rarely occurs in real life), the red pointers have different widths when this method is used. This would hurt the model's presentation value. You shouldn't use a standardized measurement in these cases but set up variable, line-specific widths of the pointers with a formula.

- In cells D4:D5, you specify a percentage range that determines in which range of this test model the red pointer is allowed to be displayed when **F9** is pressed.

This is very useful for your testing purposes, but may also be helpful in real life. I always use such constructions when I create an evaluation model for a survey or data collection and no actual data is available yet. Naturally, you can already define in the preparation phase how something is supposed to look, including all formal consequences.

Such activities include identifying deficiencies of a model and developing solutions. A general deficiency of the 100 percent chart is that it can't satisfy viewers' desire to see the underlying absolute values. However, there are many ways to compensate for this. An additional presentation of data in a table may be help, but that's not very creative and can be quite confusing.

Let's now take a closer look at the *Scale 2* worksheet, with reference to Figure 9-9. I've already mentioned a specific difficulty with presentation of the 100 percent solution described here: the absolute values of the set values in column G may be different. You can use labels to solve the problem:

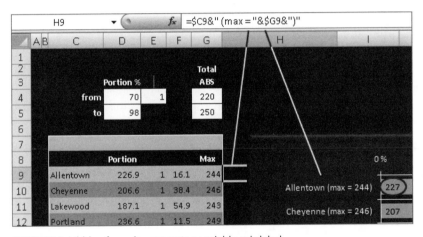

FIGURE 9-9 Hidden formulas generate a variable axis label.

What has changed?

- The category axis label is dynamic and is taken from column H instead of column C for this purpose. Column H contains invisible formatted formulas that concatenate the name of the city with a text that returns the maximum attainable value as an absolute number. The concatenating formula =$C9&" (max = "&$G9&")" implements this.

- Right next to this, a comparative value is displayed: on the left side of the green bar, the actual absolute value is shown by use of *data labels* of this bar segment using the position *Inside Base*.

We've solved one problem, but created another: the names of the cities are not directly next to the corresponding bars. If this disturbs you, you can use different settings as shown in the *Scale 3* worksheet and in Figure 9-10.

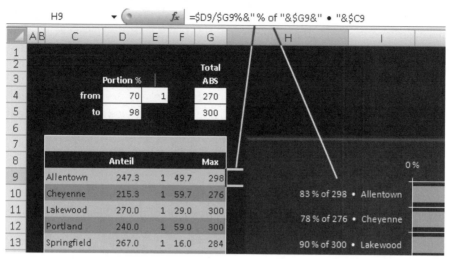

FIGURE 9-10 An acceptable result, but a formula with room for improvement.

The formula =$D9/$G9%&" % of "&$G9&" • "&$C9 is useful, but still has its deficiencies. It assumes (and justifiably so in this case) that the result of the calculation that is generated in the first part from D9/$G9% is always an absolute number. However, this is not realistic and needs improvement. But how? By means of the TEXT function introduced in Chapter 8. If you want to try this without taking a look, you don't need the information from cell H14 (formatting with one decimal).

We're not finished yet. There is a wide range of possible variations, not to mention color formatting. This holds true for using formulas (either for axis labels or the display or splitting of the bars), changes to axis scaling and gridlines, some elements that can be activated or deactivated via controls, and much more.

Pointer Elements in Column Charts

On the Companion CD Open the file \Samples\0903_Scale02.xlsx on the CD-ROM.

Our Italian moments are sometimes more creative than the monotony of our daily life. This feeling was implemented for the *Scale 1* worksheet in the file *0903_Scale02.xlsx* by means of a more elaborate design (see Figure 9-11).

When you press **F9**, the heights of the yellow columns that are derived from the default column E (*Dare*) and the related results from column F (*Esito*, displayed with orange, horizontal markers) change. These markers are narrower than the columns and can be displayed within the columns, at their upper edge or above the columns.

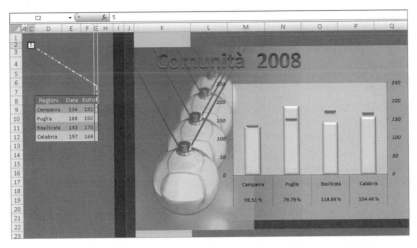

FIGURE 9-11 A success report as a Stacked Column chart with design embellishments

If you require a vertical scale with pointers as described in the sample bar chart of the previous section, you could use the same method; a similarly set up 100% Stacked Column chart provides the same functional results. Naturally, I don't want to bore you with that here; therefore, I chose a different presentation format, namely, the vertical variant.

The chart uses absolute values on a fixed scaled value axis (*0, 250, 50*). As you will quickly see, this is only half the truth. There are two identically scaled value axes. For this example, I also provided a *Raw Version* worksheet (see Figure 9-12) that enables you to quickly understand the basic design of this model.

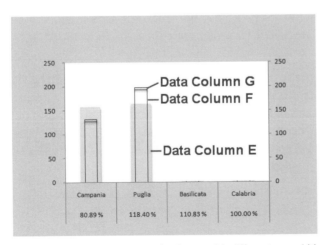

FIGURE 9-12 Two value axes and columns with different *gap widths*

■ The completely visible, yellow columns from data of column E are linked to the *primary vertical axis* (the first value axis).

- Column G contains results of formulas. These are hidden and inconspicuous due to the user-defined number format ; ; ; (three subsequent semicolons suppress the display of all numbers, irrespective of their value) and minor column width. These refer to and use an input value in cell C2 (see Figure 9-11). This way you control the height (thickness) of the markers.

- The invisible data from column G together with the visible data from column F (result data) form a Stacked Column chart that is linked to the *secondary vertical axis* (the second value axis).

- Because their gap width is larger, the stacked columns on the second value axis are narrower than the columns on the first value axis.

- The visible markers are the upper segments of the stacked columns; that is, they are "shouldered" from the hidden column segments of the actual values from column F.

- The category axis is labeled in two lines. Formulas generate the second line in range C9:C12, which was hidden via font formatting. The user-defined number format of the category axis is 0.00" %".

I could explain the embellishments in detail, but you will certainly find all these tricks by yourself. Just one hint: the image is stored on the CD-ROM under *Materials**Pictures*\\ *RowOfBalls.tif,* but it looks quite different in this chart. Chapter 5, "Graphical Objects," described how you handle such graphical objects.

Gauges in a Test Model

On the Companion CD Open the file *Samples**0904_Instruments.xlsx* on the CD-ROM.

The file *0904_Instruments.xlsx* also uses a model that is based on the rules of the rS1.Method. Although it was designed carefully, it is still an interim solution. The developer wants to introduce several chart variants to his or her customer and check which variant works best for the purpose of the visualization. Therefore and because the variants are supposed to be viewed together, the *Focus 1* worksheet contains a rather odd combination of charts. It is obvious that a final version certainly shouldn't look *like that.*

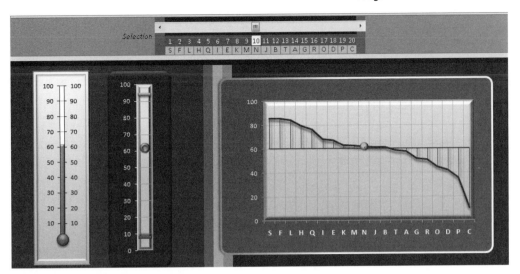

FIGURE 9-13 Focus on three test charts

The background: in a customer survey, 50 persons commented and—with a possible range from 0 to 100 scores—evaluated 20 topics. Such data, introduced without additional key figures and parameters here, provides many interesting evaluation options. However, I limit myself to presenting the average values; that is, evaluating the topic-specific average valuations.

Functionality and Structure

Some notes on the functionality: you use the *scroll bar* at the top of the screen to specify one of the 20 topics. In the version that will be handed over, the results are sorted by the reached score in descending order. However, you can easily change this setting. Below the scroll box of the control, the currently defined topic number is highlighted; check the conditional formatting settings.

Three charts visualize the data in different ways. From left to right:

- In a "thermometer chart," a column increases or decreases to the value that was reached for the defined topic.

- In a "measuring staff chart," a blue dot marker increases or decreases to the value that was reached for the defined topic. The relation to the topic-specific valid range between maximum and minimum is displayed with two boundary value markers. The *plot area* has a relatively strong valuating color formatting.

- In a line chart, the average values of all topics are displayed as a blue line that decreases from left to right. It is crossed by a dark red, horizontal line that displays the average value of all survey results. These two data series are connected by high-low lines. A marker moves along the blue, descending line in sync with the settings of the scroll bar. The marker changes its shape and color if it moves below the horizontal line; that is, if its value falls below the overall average value. The *plot area* has a slightly valuating color formatting.

Overall, these models have interesting and lively effects, particularly the last two objects. This is especially useful in live presentations when you want to summon the data alphabetically or in any way other than in its usual precedence.

Before I describe the construction and some pros and cons, I will provide information on contents and individual worksheets. From right to left:

■ As usual, the range names of the worksheet are defined in the *NamesIndex* worksheet.

■ The *Lists 1* worksheet contains only one selection cell, namely, the linked cell of the *scroll bar.*

■ The 1,000 results of the survey and the corresponding calculations are specified in the *Data 1* worksheet.

> **Note** Note that the name *rD1.SortRange* exists. You can use it to select the cell range K8:AD62 and sort it by columns, using the data in rows 8 to 12. This changes the alphabetical display in row 5 of the focus as well as the display of the line chart.
>
> Switching between line and column sorting: *Data/Sort & Filter/Sort,* and then click the *Options* button in the dialog box that appears.

■ The *Basis 1* worksheet contains the data sources of the three charts generated with formulas. This will be described in detail later.

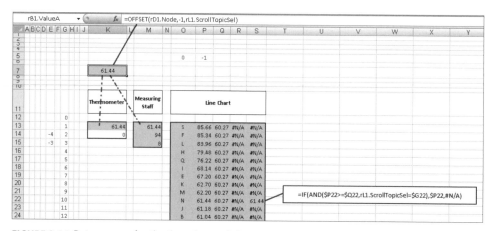

FIGURE 9-14 Data sources for the three focused charts

Let's now take a closer look at the constructions and formulas in the *Basis 1* worksheet, with reference to Figure 9-14. Open this worksheet, and make sure that you are absolutely clear about the structures and functions of the formulas that are not explicitly explained in the text below. You're expected to know them by now.

- All blue cells contain formulas.

- The formula in cell K7 with the name *rB1.ValueA* determines the average value of the currently set topic. This value is then used by cells K13 and M13.

- The data basis of the thermometer chart consists of only two numbers: a constant zero and the value from *rB1.ValueA*.

- The data basis of the measuring staff chart consists of three numbers: the value from *rB1.ValueA* and the corresponding maximum and minimum values that were readout with formulas.

- The data basis of the line chart is much more complex:

  - The values for the category axis labels in column O are also readout with formulas because the labels need to be flexible for different possible sort sequences of the source data.

  - This applies also to the topics' average values in column P (they are calculated in row 11 of the *Data 1* worksheet) that are used to draw the blue data series of the chart.

  - In column Q—again with deliberate redundancy—all cells are filled with the overall average value (from cell AE11 of the *Data 1* worksheet with the name *rD1. AvgTotal*). This data is used to draw the red, horizontal data series of the chart.

  - In columns R and S, only one cell may contain a value. All other cells are automatically set to #N/A with the respective formulas (one of them will be explained below).

So that's the trick for implementing the change of the markers: the values in column R are the basis for a data series. A number—a value that can be defined in the chart—is only created if the value in column P in the relevant row (that corresponds to the settings of the control) is less than the overall average value (that is specified in the adjacent cell, column Q). This data series uses the red marker. If all cells are set to #N/A, *no* symbol at all is created within this data series. The same construction rules apply to column S: a number that can be displayed in the chart is only created if the value in column P in the relevant row is greater than or equal to the overall average value (the one that is specified in the adjacent cell, column Q). This data series uses the green marker. Of course, it can only be displayed if all columns are set to #N/A.

In conclusion, that means that this is a line chart with four data series. Two of them are always completely visible, and either the third or the fourth data series displays just one marker. In other words, one marker is always visible: either the red below the average value line or the green above the average value line.

Here are the corresponding formulas, based on the example in cell S22 (see Figure 9-14):

The function =AND(logical1,logical2,…) returns the logical value TRUE if *all* of its up to 255 arguments are TRUE. That means you can define up to 255 arguments (so far: a maximum of 30) within one AND formula. Only if all of them are true the result of the formula will be TRUE. Consequently, this function is particularly well suited to implementing multiple conditional checks in IF formulas simultaneously.

The =OR(logical1,logical2,…) function is the logical equivalent; it returns the logical value, TRUE, if at least *one* of its up to 255 arguments is TRUE.

=IF(AND($P22>=$Q22,rL1.ScrollTopicSel=$G22),$P22,#N/A) as an instruction to Excel means the following: "If it is true that the value in cell P22 is greater than or equal to the value in cell Q22 **and** if it is also true that the value in cell rL1.ScrollTopicSel is equal to the value in cell G22, then use the value from P22. Otherwise write #N/A." Thus, the values are compared but the program also is checking whether its possible result is relevant for the display. Relevant in this context means that the possible result is only supposed to be displayed if its position corresponds to the selection that the user defined via the control.

Creation and Application

How are the three charts designed, and what is their presentation value for this data?

The Thermometer Chart

This column chart is created in a few steps. Create it in the *Basis 1* worksheet and then copy it to the *Focus 1* worksheet.

1. Enter any number to cell K14, except for zero (during the design phase, you need a visible second column). In the example described, I entered 20.

2. Select the range K13:K14, and use it to create a standard column chart.

3. Open the *Select Data Source* dialog box, and click *Switch Row/Column* to convert the chart with one data series to a chart with two data series.

4. Position the second data series (with the temporary value 20) on a secondary value axis. Now, the two columns overlap each other.

5. In cell K14, enter zero again to hide the second data series.

6. Define a fixed scaling of *0, 100, 10* for both value axes.

7. Assign a gap width of *0 percent* to the remaining column so that the width of the *plot area* is completely filled.

8. Remove the *legend*. Turn the *chart area* into a high rectangle and adapt it to the dimensions of the *plot area* (which at this point shouldn't be too small).

9. Format the column, the *plot area*, the *gridlines*, and the axis labels. Then, reduce the width of the *chart area* and *plot area* until they correspond to your idea of a conventional thermometer.

10. At the bottom of the column, add a circular shape, and format it according to the column. Carry out the required positioning and formatting steps.

This simple image displays only the selected *data point* of the corresponding average value. That's all it does and is supposed to do. (Make a habit of asking: "Do we mean an average value as a column?") Its presentation value is that it primarily looks like a known, common object. However, this is also its main deficiency. You must be careful when using realistic graphical thermometer charts. Their symbolism is strongly based on "learned daily temperatures" in degrees Fahrenheit. That means values of 32 or 176 "degrees"— even if you don't use degrees as a scale—may trigger associations that don't correspond to the display objective and bewilder readers more than they help them to quickly understand the chart. I wouldn't use this chart for the purpose of presentation in our example. However, in a different context and for a different purpose, it may be an attractive addition.

For comparative presentations, this chart type is also unsuitable. Multiple thermometers displayed next to each other look strange—"unnatural"—and don't have advantages over other types for conveying information.

The Measuring Staff Chart

This line chart can be easily created and contains vertically movable markers of three data series. Its design doesn't create unusual requirements:

1. In the *Basis 1* worksheet, create a *Line with Markers* chart from the range M13:M15.

2. Open the *Select Data Source* dialog box, and click *Switch Row/Column* to convert the chart with one data series to a chart with three data series. The points now are vertically aligned with each other.

3. All other work is formatting work identical or similar to the step-by-step instructions above for creating the thermometer chart, including the fixed axis scaling. I chose the bar symbol as a marker for the limits, defined a 3-D format, a size of 20, and a shadow (pay attention to details: upper bar, bottom shadow; lower bar, top shadow). The blue dot in the middle is the marker symbol circle with a size of 15 and 3-D format (one of the few cases where this is useful). The plot area has the 3-D format *Bevel/Convex*.

4. Then, reduce the width of the *plot area* so that the markers barely fit in.

In line with the specific purpose of presentation, this object has a very high presentation value. It clearly and dynamically shows the topic's essential aspects. The valuating relationships (high-lows, relative and absolute positions) are particularly clear. From an optical perspective, this chart is quite attractive, and you can easily imagine that two or more of these charts displayed next to each other still make a good impression.

But what's the use of "easily imagine"? Just try it.

The Line Chart

Of these three charts, the one that provides the highest benefit is also the chart that is created most easily—after the corresponding data basis has been established. Technically, the line chart shouldn't provide any surprises for you. Therefore, only a brief instruction with some keywords:

1. Position the *scroll box* of the *scroll bar* in the *Focus 1* worksheet centrally. Thus, the columns R and S of the *Basis 1* worksheet return a number as the result of the formula in only one cell. In this row, temporarily overwrite two formulas with constants: *90* in column R and *5* in column S. Highlight both cells with an eye-catching color so that you don't forget to overwrite these constants with the formulas again later on.

2. Create a *Line with Markers* chart from the data range 013:S32 (five columns). Two complete lines and—as a result of step 1—two markers are displayed at clearly visible and easily selectable positions.

3. Format the two complete lines and markers (considering the example) as you like.

4. Replace the constants manually entered in step 1 with the formulas again.

5. Perform the remaining formatting work, and define a fixed scaling of *0, 100, 20* for the value axis.

> **Important**   Note that the visualized values were based on a survey where the participants could choose among scores of 0 to 100. Therefore, you also need to define these limits as the minimum and maximum in the value axes of the charts in order to obtain a realistic visualization of the results.

If this appeals to your ambition or you just feel like making the result a little bit more attractive, you can use three markers instead of two, with the upper green and lower red markers the same as before. The marker of an additional series in the middle (placed within a certain range of fluctuation along the horizontal data series containing the average values) then has a third and more neutral format. However, in an example with such a small amount of data, this third marker is more about technique than necessity. Such solutions become interesting if you require a more detailed quick orientation for the user according to the criteria *positive—critical—rather uninteresting for the time being* for more complex models with strong value fluctuations.

This is a chart with a very high informational avail. It is particularly well suited for analyzing the results of the survey because it provides much critical information at the same time. In addition to giving results in detail and in general, this includes the evaluation of the data quality or the usefulness of the results of the survey. However, this object that is well suited for analyses can lead to problems in the presentation. The information provided in the chart is very complex by itself, so it needs to be explained when it is presented to an audience or introduced in publications.

As a first approach for discussions with the customer, I would suggest using this chart with some small modifications for general basic information (for presentations and publications) and using one or more measuring staff charts (in parallel) for a quick explanation of the details, including oral comments in front of an audience. Don't forget: if individual results need to be compared in more detail, you should use a bar scale of 100 percent described earlier (see Figure 9-8).

Additional Lines as Eye-Catcher

For dynamic models that are used for presentations in front of an audience, the control of attention is a very important component. Everything must be flexible here, the viewer's attention should be attracted by different things and—even more important—should be caught there for a while. A relatively eye-catching screen element changes its position and remains at the new position until you define another position for it. This effect is hard to achieve with strange-looking pointers but rather easy with a visual alert that is located anywhere in the object and whose position can be changed.

To the most effective elements of that kind belong moving lines—running either horizontal or vertical or both—with an eye-catching but not overpowering format and optional markers at both ends in order to more clearly differentiate them from "normal" lines of the value visualizations. In many cases, such lines also serve to display a value range with their length, width, or distance to each other, for example, providing bandwidth information.

Two relevant real-life examples are described below. First, I'll share basic technical information on this design variant.

Crossed Lines and Ladder Chart

The sample file, *0905_TestingLine.xlsx*, summarizes basic information on dynamic marking lines but also introduces or repeats some additional details that are useful for designing attractive Excel presentations.

 On the Companion CD Open the file \Samples\0905_TestingLine.xlsx on the CD-ROM.

As is usually the case for sample files, the worksheets are protected without password. To use the worksheet, you should keep the protection, but to check the different settings and formats, particularly in the *Line Crossing* worksheet, you must unprotect the sheet.

Working with the *Line Crossing* worksheet provides an overview of the main areas of use.

- A blue, horizontal line with three *data points* (of which only the point in the middle is a symbol) represents data that has been collected or measured. We'll call this *process data*.

- A red, vertical line crosses the blue line in the *data point* in the middle. It represents a visual alert ("attention, this point is important") and alternatively or also a value range (bandwidth) within which the crossed *data point* of the blue line can, may, should, or must lie.

- The blue line may have different shapes, and the red one can have different lengths and vertical positions. If you press **F9**, you can generate new data. Two variants are available:

  - You have selected (number 1 in Figure 9-15) the option *Automatic*: both the horizontal line and the vertical line change. This simulates the reading of new process data that also includes an individual, data-specific planned and actual bandwidth.

  - You have selected the option *Manual* and entered limits for the red line. If you press **F9**, only the blue line changes. This simulates the reading of new process data that you compare with a planned bandwidth that you have defined as universally valid.

Both valuation types are considerably significant when checking and presenting findings of a study (surveys, data collections) of all kinds.

Note For some data constellations generated with **F9**, the lines do not cross each other because the process data (blue) is outside the range (red), so the "crossing" image turns into a "confluence" image. This is particularly essential in real life, for example, if you want to exclude specific data as an "outlier" from an analysis, assign it to another class, or redefine the limit evaluation when checking measuring results.

Let's now take a closer look at the structure and use of the worksheet, with reference to Figure 9-15.

1. You use the *OptionButtons* to select the respective option. Both are linked with cell A1 named *rT1.BasisSel* (this shouldn't be on a *focus* worksheet, but this can be excused for this test model not complying with the rS1.Method). In A1, either *1* or *2* is chosen, which is then processed by formulas.

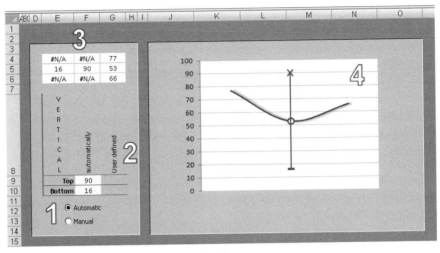

FIGURE 9-15 Crossing of data line and marker line

These are *form controls*, which you can easily create:

❏ Create the first form control, label, format, link, and test it. Its output value is automatically *1*.

❏ Create a copy of the first form control including its link. The output value is automatically *2*.

2. Depending on your setting configured in step 1, the formats in the cell range F9:G10 change. Of course, this is based on conditional formatting that reacts to *rT1.BasisSel* (cell A1). Column F contains two formulas that determine the length of the red line between *top* and *bottom* if you have selected the option *Automatic*.

   If you have selected the option *Manual*, the values in F9:F10 become invisible and the two input cells in column G become visible. Here, you can enter the limits for determining the red line, which become also valid now. You can also make entries when these cells are invisible; that is, flying blind. You can easily move to these cells in a protected worksheet using the **Tab** key.

   I have restricted the input options to integers in a defined value range (top *55 – 100*, bottom *0 – 45*). All other entries are rejected by Excel. If you want to check or change this validation check, select—after first unprotecting the sheet—the *Data Validation* command in the *Data Tools* group of the *Data* tab.

3. The data source of the chart includes #N/A values as constants and numbers as formula results. The two formulas in E5 and F5 directly react to the content of the cell named *rT1.BasisSel*; that is, indirectly to the user selection made with the *OptionButtons*.

4. The chart consists of three line data series. Based on the tabular data source, one of the data series contains three *data points* (the history data of the blue line; only the point in the middle of the three *data points* is displayed as a symbol). Meanwhile, the two other

data series only indicate one *data point*: an X at the top, a small bar at the bottom. The *data points* have a *high-low line* that is used to generate the vertical line; that is, the line crossing between blue and red, between horizontal and vertical.

This concludes this test object. Simply try it out yourself, and try to change it according to your needs.

The adjacent worksheet, *Ladder Chart*, (see Figure 9-16) contains a variant that is based on the basic system described above, but has more relevance in real life. The model is only supposed to introduce the purpose of such a chart, so it is quickly formatted.

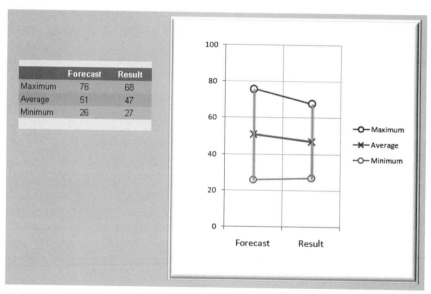

FIGURE 9-16 The ladder chart provides a quick overview when comparing forecasts and results.

I guess it is quite obvious why—for practical reasons—I call this object *ladder chart*. However, it requires a short comment why the rungs of the ladder are more or less tilted each time you press **F9**.

With every new chart, you visualize the data of a plan or forecast (for example, "That's what we've expected the evaluation of this survey topic to be") on the left compared with the actual result: "That's what came out." The more tilted the rungs (all or some of them; synchronously tilted or asynchronously tilted), the weaker or more inaccurate the plan or the forecast, the more worthy of consideration, and perhaps the more interesting the result. This is a simple presentation for comparisons that carry high informational value. Limits, average values, and high-lows; three data series with two data points each. Very simple, very useful, and freely extensible—leaving nothing to be desired.

> **Tip** For these charts, you should use coarsely meshed and clearly formatted gridlines (see Figure 9-16). Instead of clarifying numbers, its main purpose is to map symmetry with the aim to emphasize asymmetry.

Test this chart in detail. Its flexibility suits it particularly well for presentations of such figures. The main reason for this is that the shape of the graphically connected data series forms a symmetrical "ladder," that is a so-called "good figure" according to the laws of perception (see Chapter 3, "Perceiving, Interpreting, Understanding"). Each asymmetry that occurs is noticed—"This is tilted: why?"—and thus grabs attention, generates a need for interpretation, and ensures a quick understanding of differences.

A Shifting Eye-Catcher

> **On the Companion CD** Open the file \Samples\0906_Marker.xlsx on the CD-ROM.

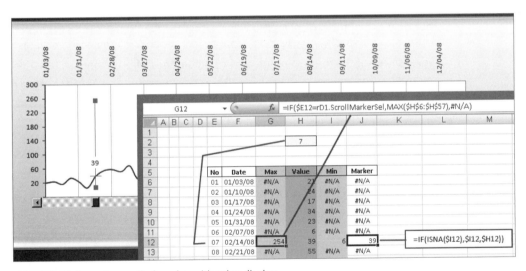

FIGURE 9-17 A moving vertical marker with value display

In the *Focus 1* worksheet, you can use a *ScrollBar* to move a vertical line as a shifting eye-catcher across the chart. This red marker line has an automatic "bandwidth length," it is stretched out from the maximum to the minimum of the blue data series, even if its data changes. When you move this focusing line, each of the 52 data points of the blue line is exactly crossed by a cross marker. The absolute value of the data point selected in this way is displayed in the red vertical marker line.

> **Tip** Explore the settings of the *primary horizontal axis*, which is defined as a time-scale axis.

The *Data and Basis 1* worksheet and Figure 9-17 illustrate how you can design this type of chart. It is a line chart with four data series. Only one of them displays the values that are supposed to be considered, while the three other data series provide information for the red marker line.

In detail:

- The output value of the *ScrollBar* is written to the yellow cell H2 named *rD1.ScrollMarkerSel.*

- Column H contains the data of the blue chart line.

- The formulas in columns G, I, and J generate data series of which only one data point has a value that can be displayed while all others are set to #N/A.

How do you determine the shape and position of the movable vertical line?

- All formulas in column G (*Max*) determine the maximum of column H in the same way, but only one of them displays the value. Using the Figure 9-17 as an example: if the value in cell *rD1. ScrollMarkerSel* is set to 7 by using the *ScrollBar,* the formula in the seventh cell of the formula range returns a number. Cell E12 contains the used row number 7. Consequently, =IF($E12=rD1.ScrollMarkerSel,MAX($H$6:$H$57),#N/A) returns a number, all other formulas in column G display #N/A.

- It works in the same way in column I (*Min*) using the minimum:

  =IF($E12=rD1.ScrollMarkerSel,MIN($H$6:$H$57),#N/A)

- In turn, the adjacent formula in column J (*Marker*) reacts to the value of column I:

  =IF(ISNA($I12),$I12,$H12) returns either the #N/A value from column I or the data point value from column H.

> The function =ISNA(value) returns the result, TRUE, if the value is #N/A, otherwise it returns FALSE.

Which formats does the red vertical line generate?

- The three already mentioned formula columns thus generate three data series of which only one *data point* is visible. The three *data points* are placed one above the other and connected with a red *high-low line*. The most essential element of the vertical marker line is thus a series line of *data points*.

- I defined a square as the marker for the bottom and top *data point* and formatted the point in the middle (read from column J and positioned at the crossing of the blue and the red line) as a bar, which generates the cross at this point.

- The data point in the middle of the vertical line forms the crossing. Its value is equal to the crossing point and is displayed as a *data label* with a *label position* set to *Above*.

Note The collaboration between Excel 2007 and *ActiveX controls* has still been in development at the time of the creation of the book. If you use a *ScrollBar*, the data that is controlled via the ScrollBar (in this case, the red marker line) may not be updated directly as it has been in earlier versions but with a considerable delay. Depending on your use of the data, it may be easier to use the *scroll bar* form control.

Unfortunately, you may also experience application crashes if you use the *ListBox* ActiveX control. Alternatively, use the *ComboBox* control or a form control.

A Practical Example

On the Companion CD Open the file \Samples\0907_Bloodpressure.xlsx on the CD-ROM. If an error message appears after the opening, you can ignore this by clicking OK.

The *Focus 1* worksheet contains a chart that I already introduced in Chapter 6, "What, For Whom, How and With What?," in the section "A Question of Ergonomics."

It is a model for a medical seminar where 36 pairs of values of a long-term blood pressure measurement are introduced in a line chart (this is one of the relatively rare cases where it is important to display a so-called "long sequence" as a whole). Each pair of values is connected with a high-low line that symbolizes the amplitude of the measurement. The *scroll bar* above the *plot area* enables the presenter to move a blue, vertical marker line across the chart in order to call attention to a specific measuring point. For the pair of values selected in this way, the measurement results are automatically shown as absolute values on the right side of the chart. Below, at category axis label level, are the relevant parameters of the time when the measurement was taken and the sleep-awake state of the patient.

Two peculiarities are particularly worth mentioning and should be explained in detail:

- The movable vertical line includes a variable gap that adapts precisely to the amplitude of the selected measurement value data points at each position, including some additional space. It seems to be tunneling through the two data series. An optical illusion? Of course, but a quite interesting one. Because this is not possible with the previously described usage of *high-low lines*. But how is it possible?

■ The *chart area* is not transparent. At the right side, it still displays tabular structures of changing content and changing colors. How does this work?

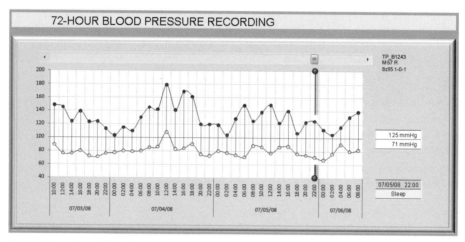

FIGURE 9-18 A so-called "long sequence"—including some special features

To explain the construct of this model and to clearly answer the questions just posed, two digressions are required:

Digression 1: Error Bars

The *errors bars* initially introduced in Chapter 1, "Basic Information—Basic Techniques," are best used in scientific charts. They indicate possible error amounts of individual or all data points of a data series. The following information solely includes technical aspects of these analysis elements. Please refer to other sources for information about explanations for the content and mathematical background of this topic.

The most essential characteristics are as follows (see also Figure 9-19):

■ Use is limited to two-dimensional bar, column, line, area, XY (Scatter), and bubble charts.

■ These are formattable lines that have a certain, variable length based on a *data point* that is supposed to be used to indicate the measurement of the error amount. The length is oriented towards the scaling of the *data point*'s value axis.

■ From the *data point*, the lines can point to plus, minus, or both directions.

■ The value axis of the *data point* defines the directions of the axes of the *error bars*. Since only the XY (Scatter) chart of the chart types listed above has horizontal *and* vertical value axes, it is the only chart where *error bars* can be simultaneously displayed in both directions of the axes.

- All or none: you can only create and format error bars for the complete data series, but not for individual data points. Consequently, you can't delete individual error bars.

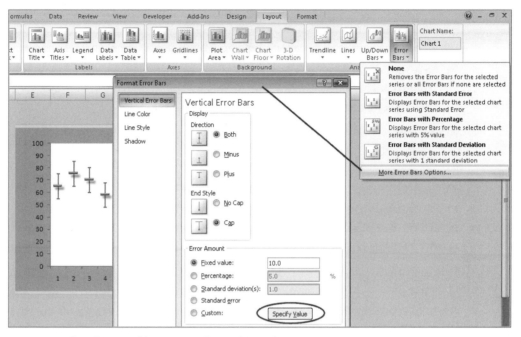

FIGURE 9-19 Error bars provide numerous formatting options.

To create an error bar, select a *data series*, and choose the *Error Bars* command in *Chart Tools/Layout/Analysis*. Then, in the picklist (see Figure 9-19), you specify a type or directly open—which is usually the better idea—the formatting dialog box by clicking on *More* .... Here, you define:

- *Direction* (already mentioned above),
- *End Style* (with attached end cross bar or without),
- *Error Amount* (select one of the options available and specify a value—in three cases).

The *Custom* option of the last bullet is of particular interest if you want to use the error bars for purposes other than the intended, as described below. It enables you to access the *Specify Value* option and thus enter a table range reference—every error bar can then have an individual length specified in the reference. Of course, you've already figured that out yourself: it is exactly this that generates the variable lengths of the vertical lines in the marker element of the blood pressure chart.

Digression 2: The Excel Camera

The Excel *camera* has the following three attributes:

- It is an excellent tool,

- It has been available for a long time now but is unfortunately hardly known.

- It is better hidden by the developers from version to version. I've no idea why they do that. There are many options that are much easier to find (including verbose and not very helpful descriptions) but considerably less useful.

FIGURE 9-20 The camera—best placed in the *Quick Access Toolbar*.

Since I use this tool (which has become desperately lonely in Excel 2007) quite often and because there are no commands that correspond to it, it is best to add its symbol to the *Quick Access Toolbar*. For this purpose, navigate to *Excel Options/Customize* (see Figure 1-13 in Chapter 1).

Then, take a picture of a selected table range and insert the created picture objects, including a link, elsewhere. The most welcome effect (that unravels our little mystery about the dynamic pseudolegend) is that—due to the link—all changes in the source (regarding content and format) are also displayed in the picture object at the other location.

> **Tip** Another interesting aspect: using the camera to take pictures of charts or, even better, parts of the charts. The tool can be generally used when table cells are selected. If this selection of the cells is behind a chart, the part of the chart that corresponds to the dimensions of this selection becomes the picture object.

Using the Camera is quite simple:

1. Fill the table range with content, format it (don't forget borders, if required), and select the range that is supposed to be pictured.

2. Click the *Camera* tool. The mouse pointer becomes a cross. It represents the upper left corner of the place where the picture will be inserted. Position the cross where you want to insert the picture (temporarily), and click the mouse.

3. The object is inserted. Key aspects:

❏ It has a number (visible in the *name box* of the *formula bar*); that is, it has attributes of a picture object (but not all).

❏ It is linked to the source range via a reference formula (visible in the *formula bar*) and consequently is dynamic (all changes in the source range are transferred to the picture, and all changes of the reference formula affect the content of the picture). If you delete the reference formula in the *formula bar*, the link is also deleted, and the picture becomes static. Not bad!

❏ You can move and scale the object just like any other graphical object (however, in most cases, you shouldn't scale it. Instead, you should define the dimensions in the source range *before* you take the picture). Of course, you can now also link and group the picture with other graphical objects. For example, to add brief notes or comments in the form of text fields.

Technical Background of the Model

After these two digressions, let's get back to the *Focus 1* worksheet of the file *0907_Bloodpressure.xlsx*. I assume that you've already explored this dynamic chart and thus describe its elements and structure in the *Data 1 and Basis* worksheet. Let's examine the content in Figure 9-18 and Figure 9-21.

The model consists of four data series. Instead of using the *error bars* for the intended purpose, it uses them as display objects for this presentation chart. Its variable values similar to a legend at the right of the *chart area* are linked picture objects that were created with the Excel *camera*.

■ The two horizontal lines of the measurement values indicate the blood pressure values in their high-lows between the upper value (systolic) and the lower value (diastolic) in a category axis with two lines that is structured by date and time. High-low lines to display the blood pressure amplitude run between the corresponding two data points. This is a broad field: nearly all of these values, value combinations, value constellations, and value sequences can be critical or indicate pathological statuses, depending on the initial situation and patient-specific parameters. Consequently, a comprehensive consideration and presentation of all data and its details is essential for this example.

■ The value axis has a fixed scaling of *40, 200, 20.*

■ The marker that you can move using the *ScrollBar* at the top of the *plot area* belongs to a further data series, which was provided with minus *error bars* (only one of them visible) whose length adapts to the upper blood pressure value with the same corresponding position but doesn't completely reach this data point.

■ The movable marker at the bottom of the *plot area* belongs to another data series with plus *error bars* whose length adapts to the lower blood pressure value with the same corresponding position.

That means the length of the *error bars* varies in sync with the currently selected values of the data series. In the *Data 1 and Basis* worksheet, you can explore how this works. First, you should take a look which range names are assigned and where the named ranges are located.

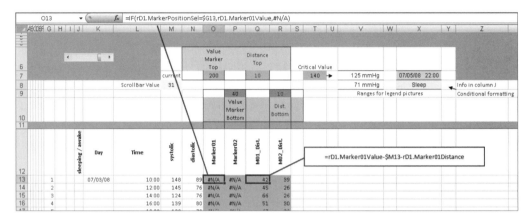

FIGURE 9-21 Unraveling the little mysteries

Please find the explanations on the structures and formulas below. From left to right in the worksheet:

- Column G: this is the often used auxiliary column with its number series for formula arguments.

- Column J: it indicates whether the person slept at the time when the blood pressure was measured. The specification *S* for sleep is used by the *conditional formatting* in cell X8.

- Columns K and L: this data is used to generate the category axis labels with two lines.

- Columns M and N: they indicate the measured blood pressure values. These values are then used to form the two data series, which are connected by high-low lines.

> **Note** In this context, I'll introduce a model with constant data. The time-consuming effort of creating it is only worthwhile if you further develop this or a similar model according to the rS1.Method, which then enables you to insert any number and type of measurement series with a mouse click. In these cases, the data in columns K to N wouldn't be constants but results of formulas, too.

- Column O: in this column, the data series for the display of the top marker is generated by formulas. Cell O7 (*rD1.Marker01Value*, default setting = 200) contains the value that controls the marker's height. To get even fancier, you can generally position the marker at a lower level by reducing the default value.

- Column P: in this column, the data series for the display of the bottom marker is generated by formulas. Cell P9 (*rD1.Marker02Value*, default setting = 40) contains the value that controls the marker's height.

- Column Q: in this column, formulas generate the values that define the length of the minus *error bar* pointing downward from the top marker. The default value in cell Q7 (*rD1.Marker01Distance*, default setting = 10) enables you to define the distance between the vertical line and the respective systolic blood pressure value.

- Column R: in this column, formulas generate the values that define the length of the plus *error bar* pointing from bottom to top. The default value in cell R9 (*rD1.Marker02Distance*, default setting = 10) enables you to define the distance between the vertical line and the respective diastolic blood pressure value.

- Cell M8 (*rD1.MarkerPositionSel*): this cell controls the output value of the *ScrollBar*.

- Cell T7 (*rD1.Critical*): here, you enter a value. Every time the currently selected systolic blood pressure value in cell X8 (and this in the chart legend) exceeds this value, a visual alert is generated. In a comprehensive presentation solution with numerous measurement series, I would provide either this value as a patient-specific parameter or different values in a drop-down list for a user-defined selection.

- Cells V7:V8: with reference to the current selection, the INDEX formulas determine the relevant values from columns M and N. An Excel picture was inserted into the chart. (*mmHg = millimeters of mercury* is the common measurement unit for blood pressure). The label is generated by means of a number format.

- Cells X7:X8: with reference to the current selection, the formulas determine the relevant values from columns J, K, and L. An Excel picture of these cells was inserted into the chart. Here, the time when the measurement was taken and the sleep-awake state, which is important for the valuation, are inserted with reference to the currently selected values. Cell X8 is in blue. Depending on the sleep-awake state, the color of the conditional formatting changes and additionally displays a visual alert, independent of the sleep-awake state, when the threshold value defined as critical in cell T7 is exceeded.

Pseudocharts and Window Charts

The next example is completely different from the blood-pressure chart. It is a simplified variant of a real-life example. In this case, we also had a "long sequence"; that is, a value chain with even 96 values of eight consecutive years. This data collection was not essential as a whole in this case, but to provide an excerpt of any 12 months. The data pane should always be a freely definable eighth of the entire period. In addition, a specific user requirement had to be fulfilled: the user wanted to freely decide via simple mouse activities—also back and forth—which calendar month of which calendar year would be the first month of the currently displayed 12-month period.

These requirements were fulfilled with a "window chart," which I will describe below together with the background situation. First of all, I explain a "pseudochart" that is based on the same information and uses one of the innovations in Excel 2007 in an unusual way.

On the Companion CD Open the file \Samples\0908_LongSequence.xlsx on the CD-ROM.

From right to left in the worksheet:

As usual for rS1 models, there is a *NamesIndex*, as usual you should take a look at it.

The *Lists 1* contains 85 *year-month* label combinations that can be selected via a control. As mentioned above: a mouse click is supposed to decide which calendar month of which calendar year is the first month of a 12-month period. This requires only 85 list entries for 96 months.

The *Data 1* worksheet contains the 96 values including their calendar label text. Next to these, in column M, a flexible data block with the height of 12 rows is determined with identical average values using formulas. This at first looks like a strange construct, but it reacts to the setting of the control (to the value in cell *rL1.StartSel*) and is required for a specific presentation in the *Focus 2* worksheet.

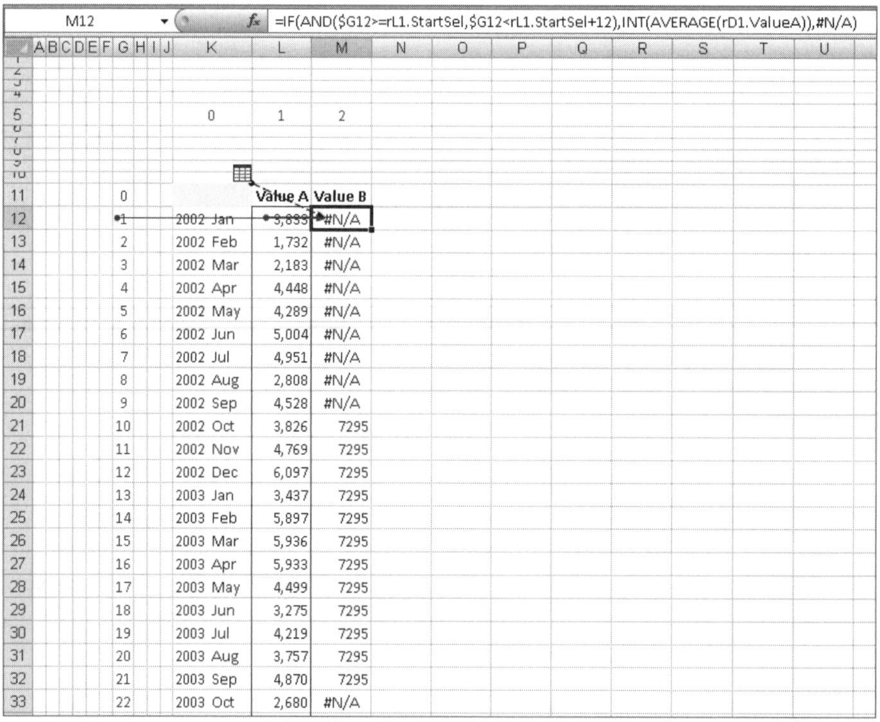

	M12		f_x	=IF(AND($G12>=rL1.StartSel,$G12<rL1.StartSel+12),INT(AVERAGE(rD1.ValueA)),#N/A)

		K	L	M
5		0	1	2
11	0		Value A	Value B
12	1	2002 Jan	3,833	#N/A
13	2	2002 Feb	1,732	#N/A
14	3	2002 Mar	2,183	#N/A
15	4	2002 Apr	4,448	#N/A
16	5	2002 May	4,289	#N/A
17	6	2002 Jun	5,004	#N/A
18	7	2002 Jul	4,951	#N/A
19	8	2002 Aug	2,808	#N/A
20	9	2002 Sep	4,528	#N/A
21	10	2002 Oct	3,826	7295
22	11	2002 Nov	4,769	7295
23	12	2002 Dec	6,097	7295
24	13	2003 Jan	3,437	7295
25	14	2003 Feb	5,897	7295
26	15	2003 Mar	5,936	7295
27	16	2003 Apr	5,933	7295
28	17	2003 May	4,499	7295
29	18	2003 Jun	3,275	7295
30	19	2003 Jul	4,219	7295
31	20	2003 Aug	3,757	7295
32	21	2003 Sep	4,870	7295
33	22	2003 Oct	2,680	#N/A

FIGURE 9-22 Shifting data blocks with 12 lines with calculated average values in column M.

```
M12    =IF(AND($G12>=rL1.StartSel,$G12<rL1.StartSel+12),
       INT(AVERAGE(rD1.ValueA)),#N/A)
```

The instruction to Excel is therefore as follows: "If the value in cell G12 is greater than or equal to the current value in cell *rL1.StartSel* and if this value is also less than the value in *rL1.StartSel* added to 12, then determine the integral average value from the range named *rD1.ValueA*. Otherwise, if the combined check returns FALSE, write #N/A."

The chart basis in the *Basis 1* worksheet isn't self-explanatory at first glance either.

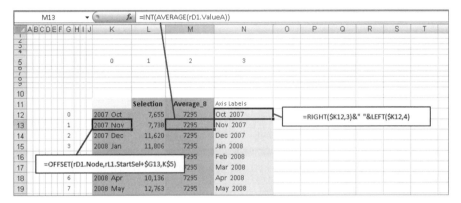

FIGURE 9-23 This chart basis is used for two different presentation variants.

With reference to Figure 9-23 a brief explanation below:

1. The OFFSET formulas in columns K and L extract, depending on the output value of the controls, the data from the *Data 1* worksheet for the display in *Focus 1*.

2. The results of the formulas in column M are required to draw a horizontal average value line in the chart of the *Focus 2* worksheet.

3. The formulas in column N turn the current strings in column K with a "quick right-left combination": *year month* becomes *month year*. You need this for the category axis labels in the *Focus 2* worksheet.

Before I turn to explaining the focus sheets:

■ The "pseudochart" in the *Focus 1* worksheet is based on the data in columns K and L.

■ The "window chart" in the *Focus 2* worksheet is based on the data in columns L, M, and N.

Pseudocharts Based on Conditional Formatting

I call the presentation in the *Focus 1* worksheet, shown in Figure 9-24, a "pseudochart" because it looks like a modified, extensively formatted, and dynamic Excel bar chart, but technically it is not a chart, but a table with conditional formatting.

Let's first take a closer look at its functionality: select one of the 85 possible start months using one of the two controls. The rows below directly change according to your setting:

- The data that corresponds to the settings is readout from the *Basis 1* worksheet.

- Next to it, bars are displayed, which are used to visualize the dimensions of the 12 numbers currently shown.

- Next to that, in turn, the current numerical values of the 12 visible data rows are expressed in ranks of which the first three are additionally highlighted in green.

If you use the *scroll bar*, you can very quickly switch between the 96 data records.

Before I describe the technical background, I should tell you that the informational value of such a presentation is rather low. This holds particularly true for the lengths of the bars that indicate how the 12 displayed months are related (this is the best of the currently visible months, this the second best, and so on) and are not subject to any scale. The same also applies for the display of the ranks. Along with the information provided here, such a solution has limited use here and is more useful for other evaluations. Still, I want to introduce the model because it uses some tricks, because you can try some interesting formats, and because it is well suited to demonstrate the differences between "pseudo" and "real" charts.

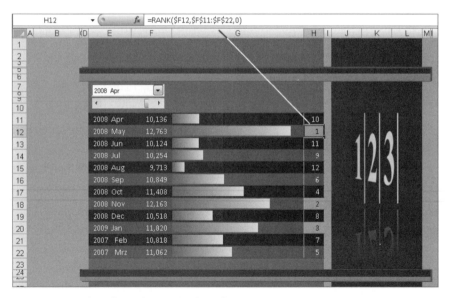

FIGURE 9-24 A chart that only seems to be a chart

The technical aspects can be explained rather quickly: the *conditional formatting* feature in Excel 2007 provides a wide range of variations. The so-called *data bar is* one of these integrated innovations. These bars are intended for a very different use than shown here. Usually, they are displayed in the same cell as the number whose value they symbolize. This may be practical and useful for brief analytical assessments, but often don't work well in presentations. Aesthetically sophisticated harmony can't always be implemented, depending on the formatting of cell, number, and bars. Therefore, I prefer to display these bars in the adjacent cells. This produces considerable scope for various formatting effects, as shown in the example.

This is achieved with a simple trick: the formulas in column G copy the values from column F on a one-to-one basis. Instead of in column F, the *conditional formatting* was implemented in column G using *data bars*. Then, you only need to hide the numbers in column G. This is achieved with the user-defined number format ; ; ; , which completely suppresses the display of values as explained earlier.

The ranking in column H is implemented using the RANK function, which has already been mentioned in conjunction with the LARGE function. Naturally, another conditional formatting rule ensures the variable green coloring of the ranks 1 to 3.

> **Note** Even if our brains resist this at first: instead of the higher ranks indicated by numbers, the *lower* ranks must be provided a visual alert when defining conditional formatting.

The used embellishment is stored on the CD-ROM under *Materials\Pictures\StartingRange.tif*. The image was turned, cut, and mirrored.

Window Chart

The "window chart" in the *Focus 2* worksheet provides much more information and is also better suited for the presentation that I'll describe in detail.

> **Note** The size and position of this chart are designed for use in the *full screen* view. If you frequently use this view—this applies to some examples of this book that are explained later on—you should place the respective symbol in the *Quick Access Toolbar*. The relevant procedure was described in conjunction with the Excel *camera* and explained in more detail in Chapter 1.
>
> (From the *full screen* view, you can return to the normal view by pressing **Esc.**)

When I first created such a variant—it can be used for nearly all types of charts—I was looking for the appropriate name to describe its concept of presentation. "Moving chart" seemed accurate, but I liked the image conveyed by the selected term better. Like an open window, the *plot area* is (apparently) placed in front of a data series, which, in total, is considerably longer than the window is wide. Using controls, the user moves this data series behind the window, and the viewer sees an excerpt of the entire information (that is, 12 of 96 data points in this example) through the window. It is particularly important that the user can freely define which of the possible excerpts he or she wants to view and valuate.

Such a procedure is appropriate if long-term changes are essential but you also require summaries of details. If summaries are important to the presentation, such a window chart is practically a must-have. Due to the high optical aggregation, displaying the entire value chain of 96 data points, for example, would prevent the viewer from recognizing essential details.

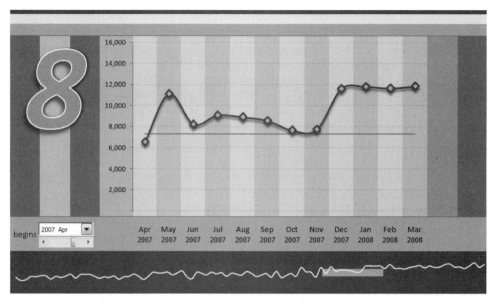

FIGURE 9-25 An eighth of the "long sequence" in the window, with the entire sequence below the window

A so-called "long sequence"—a statistical term used in this book—is in most cases designed for viewing information about the past. This example, which has been slightly changed to a lightweight version, has the following background: the chart, which had been created with quite a great deal of effort, was used only once, namely, in a presentation for the home bank of an enterprise. There had been difficulties and investment initiatives. The historically considered period of eight years was a critical and sometimes turbulent phase in the history of the enterprise. Now, trust had to be reestablished in the long-term, security-oriented corporate policy. This was attempted with different data and visualizations, of which this chart was a part (at least according to the type). You should obtain an overview yourself by using its controls, preferably the *scroll bar*.

The main window of the chart displays 12 data points as a segment of an overall development. These data points visually present the number of sold products. The line with widely oscillating sections is linked to a horizontal, pale red average value constant. This illustrates that there has been a continual increase in value despite all movements over the years: note when and how the oscillating data series exceeds the average value. The position of the excerpt visible in the window is shown with a yellow bar moving across a long line at the bottom of the model. This small chart contains all 96 data points. It shows the complete actual data and is thus particularly well suited for comparisons between the entire chart and the details of the excerpt. The excerpt of the chart shown in Figure 9-25 illustrates a particularly critical point in the talks with the bank: in the summer of 2005, some important personnel decisions were made and, since December 2005, things have improved. The overall development, which is particularly well demonstrated in the "mini chart," has become steadier and increased slowly but continuously. This description of the background should suffice for now. However, it is essential to mention that the high degree of flexibility of this presentation and its impressive design had a positive effect on the atmosphere and result of the talks. This is reason enough to consider the effort for creating such a model worthwhile. Another key aspect: if you can impress the partners who use Excel themselves (as was the case here) with an Excel solution that convinces them by mere technology and design ("You really did that with Excel?"—"Yes, and I did it without programming!"), you're almost halfway there.

Let's now take a look at the technical aspects of this solution. Unprotect the sheet and analyze the attributes or formats of the model's elements. Here are some key points with reference to the window chart:

- The value axis has a fixed scaling so that the long-term average value (the horizontal data series) always remains at the same position and is slowly but continuously exceeded when the chart is moved forward.

- Based on the font size and the limited space, the category axis label is automatically wrapped to the next line; that is, though it is created in one line, it is displayed in two lines. Therefore, the month is placed before the year, which fulfills an essential basic rule for axis labels: wherever possible, detailed labels must be closer to graphical data series than group labels.

- The position of the category axis label was optically synchronized with the position of the controls by defining a *label distance* of 300.

- The *plot area* of the chart is completely transparent. Table formatting is responsible for the colored separation of the columns as illustrated in the figure. When creating the chart—that is, in the final phase of the design work—you must ensure that the column limits of the table and the (later invisible) vertical *gridlines* of the chart correspond to each other. To achieve this easily, you must select *Don't move or size with cells* for the chart. Then, while the chart is fixed, you can reduce or increase the width of the table columns behind the chart.

The following applies to the mini chart at the bottom of the model:

- The two data series of this line chart are derived from *Data 1*, L12:M107.

- The moving bar is not a bar but a partly transparent average value line of the 12 data points that are currently not set to #N/A in their data source (*Data 1*, M12:M107).

- The weight of the moving bar is *10 pt*. Its *cap type* is defined as a *Square*; find out how it would look like using the *Round* option.

■ Except for its two lines, the chart has no other visible elements. They were removed or hidden via the formatting.

Automatic Sorting of Chart Content

In a lot of chart content, the graphic quality of the chart changes considerably when the data series elements are sorted in different ways in order to make the content easier to understand or to change the point of view (however we may interpret this term).

This can be done relatively easily for your own visual information by sorting the data source. Of course, you can't do that in a presentation, which means you need an efficient and safe way to sort your information without having to exit the chart. In most cases, you do *not* need programming, which shouldn't surprise you by now.

I'll introduce two procedures that you can use to automatically sort your tabular chart basis:

■ You deploy controls to use a sort sequence that was previously specified as a numerical series for a table with constant data.

■ You use formulas to repeatedly generate a sorted table from a variable table with unsorted data without further action.

Using Controls for Sorting

> **On the Companion CD** Open the file *\Samples\0909_AutoSort01.xlsx* on the CD-ROM.

Display the *Focus 1* worksheet of the file *0909_AutoSort01.xlsx* with the *full screen* view. There is a short list (a *form control* of the *list box* type; see Figure 9-26) in the lower right-hand corner that contains the entries of the sort sequences available in this example. If you click one of these entries, the chart changes accordingly. The current sort sequence is also displayed with more explicit text information in the second line of the chart heading.

The workbook is designed in accordance with the rS1.Method, so it contains the common working sheets. You should pay attention to the following specific features.

■ The *Lists 1* worksheet defines the content for the control. The text needed to label the second line of the chart heading is placed next to it.

■ Four green numerical sort sequences are defined in the *Data 1* worksheet. You see that a descending sorting by values is defined as the standard (column L).

■ The chart's data source in the *Basis 1* worksheet, the range L12:N38 may surprise you at first glance: it includes a column with the heading *Value 2* that contains only *#N/A values*—as constants.

- For better orientation, the chart in the *Focus 1* worksheet has two value axes but only one data series. In other words, only one *visible* data series. Of course, this has to do with column *Value 2*. More information is provided below.

- The category axis label of the chart has one column but always displays a number series in ascending order even when the countries are sorted in different ways. This is also due to the construct of the formulas in the *Basis 1* worksheet.

FIGURE 9-26 Four different sort sequences of this chart can be called at the click of a mouse.

First, some notes on the construct of the sort sequences specified in the *Data 1* worksheet:

1. The countries/regions and their values (the values that are now contained in columns P and Q) were contiguously listed in the default sort sequence, that is, by gross national product (descending), and by columns. The appropriate sort sequence 1 to 27, which is also the number sequence in the auxiliary column G, was generated and defined as the first of the green list columns.

2. The countries/regions and their values *including* the auxiliary column G were sorted alphabetically in ascending order. The resulting number sequence in column G was copied and placed as the second green sort sequence next to the first sort sequence.

3. The remaining sort sequences were generated in the same way in additional sorting processes.

4. The countries/regions and their values including the auxiliary column G were re-sorted to their initial state.

5. The four sort sequences generated in this way were positioned next to the names of the countries/regions in the order of the entries in the control. This has to do with the system of the rS1.Method and OFFSET: the names of the countries/regions are zero columns away from *rD1.Node*, the first sort sequence is one column away from *rD1.Node*, the second sort sequence...well you should know this by now.

All data values in the *Data 1* worksheet are and remain constants. Its variable presentation sequences in the chart are generated by formulas, which are described below.

With reference to Figure 9-27, let's now take a closer look to the results of such preparations in the *Basis 1* worksheet.

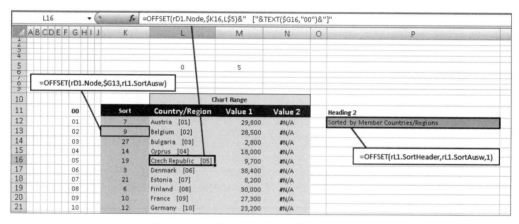

FIGURE 9-27 Data is automatically sorted and becomes the basis of the chart.

- The formulas in column L read the sort sequences that are defined in *Data 1*, depending on the output value of the control.

- The OFFSET formulas in columns L and M row-specifically access the relevant constants in the *Data 1* worksheet, using the changing data from column K.

- The formulas in column L add the name of the country/region, which changes for every sort sequence, with the numbers from column G, which never change.

- The formulas in cell P12 generate a text by accessing—caused by controls—the strings defined in *Lists 1*, column N. This text is linked to a text box that represents the second line of the chart's heading in *Focus 1*.

Charts can only have a second value axis if they contain more than one data series. It is not important whether, as in this case, the second data series does end up containing no data that can be displayed in the chart. It still exists as a data series. That is the purpose of the #N/A row in column N. During the design phase, it contained some numbers to make its bars in the chart visible and easy to select; finally all values were set to #N/A.

The image of the map of Europe used in the *Focus 1* worksheet is stored on the CD-ROM under *Materials\\Pictures\\Europe02.tif*. However, due to its close proximity to the upper value axis, Iceland (blue in the original image)—which isn't a member of the EU—would damage the visual impression. Therefore, my apologies to the Icelanders; I hid Iceland. How? You can easily explore this when you unprotect the sheet. However, it was more difficult to find the right color: *RGB 87, 107, 46*.

Using Formulas for Sorting

 On the Companion CD   Open the file *Samples\\0910_AutoSort02.xlsx* on the CD-ROM.

Display the *Focus 1* worksheet (protected without password) of the file *0910_AutoSort02.xlsx* with the *full screen* view. Each time you press **F9**, the ranking chart displays another combination of the top 10. This is just a gimmick related to objects, formats, and functions of Excel 2007. However, like every gimmick, it has an important background.

FIGURE 9-28 The best for our bests

This focus sheet is just padding. The main purpose of the model is to explain the automatic sorting using formulas. Before I describe this using the *Data 1 and Basis* worksheet, you need some basic information.

> This type of ranking, which often is very interesting in real life, and the following automatic sorting process via formulas can only be achieved without problems and gaps if the source that is supposed to be sorted only contains completely different values; that is, there are no duplicate values. However, for Excel, the difference may also be in the 10th or a higher decimal place. For example, *523.0000002571* and *523.0000007579* are identical for the viewer if the default number formatting with usually a maximum of two decimal places is used, but for Excel, they aren't.
>
> I won't discuss whether a numerically displayed ranking for apparently identical values is supposed to or may display different ranks (according to the pattern *1.503 = Rang 1* and *1.503 = Rang 2*). In real life where various variants are available, there are some equally good arguments for its advantages and disadvantages.
>
> In dynamic models, if I want to automatically sort data for which there probably are duplicate values, I modify every value that has been extracted from the data source using a minuscule adjustment factor. A sample formula would be G7+RAND()/1000000 when the value that is supposed to varied is in cell G7. That is, a tiny value (the millionth of a random number between *0* and *1* with up to 15 decimal places) was added. Now it is extremely unlikely that previously identical integers are still identical after such an adjustment factor has been used.
>
> Of course, there are values, value constellations, calculation methods, and display requirements where this or even a more careful manipulation of source data is not permitted. However, this is rarely the case for "normal" business data (quantities, currency data, key figures, and so on). Only after numerous calculations in extremely exceptional cases does it make an actually "countable" or even visible difference whether you use *523* or alternatively *523.0000007579* for further calculations.

Let's now take a closer look at the structures in the *Data 1 and Basis* worksheet, with reference to Figure 9-29. Our goal: the data that is alphabetically sorted by cities in ascending order in columns F and G is supposed to be automatically displayed in descending order by values in columns L:M.

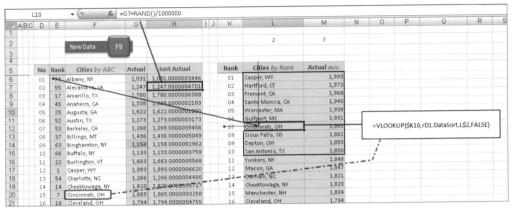

FIGURE 9-29 Formulas for fully automatic sorting in ascending order

- In column F, a list of 75 US cities is defined, sorted alphabetically in ascending order.

- The adjacent column G (*Actual*) once again simulates the dynamic reading of changing values. When you use the =RANDBETWEEN(1000,2000) function 75 times, the probability that some of the results are identical is rather high, as you can see when pressing **F9** several times: the values in the pale red colored cells of column G are returned more than once. In this case, this helps to emphasize the topic mentioned in the preceding sidebar.

> **Note** A pleasant innovation for many cases in real life under Excel 2007: *Conditional Formatting/Highlight Cells Rules/Duplicate Values*. This is also used in the sample file.
>
> An innovation which is almost more pleasant is that you can sort the cells by colors, especially when these colors were generated by means of conditional formatting. However, you shouldn't use this in the sample file because it doesn't harmonize with the numbers generated by chance here. Test this option in your own list with constants where you specify duplicate values.

- In column H (*Sort Actual*), the numbers from column G are read and varied with small supplementary values (refer to the sidebar on page 466 for more information) in order to avoid identical ranks that would prevent automatic sorting.

- The RANK formulas in column E now create a list of the ranks using the values in column H. Consequently, they are in the first column of the three-column range *rD1.DataSort* (E6:G80) because this range is always read with VLOOKUP formulas that always want to find their lookup_value in the first column of the table_array.

  (The function =VLOOKUP(lookup_value,table_array,col_index_num,range_lookup) was introduced in Chapter 2, "New Approaches—Getting Started," by means of the file \Samples\0201_Extract.xlsx in more detail.)

- The VLOOKUP formulas in columns L and M create the sorting we want by using the ranks listed in column E as search criteria. Now, the "original data" from column G is used again as relevant values that will be included in the chart (or in a continuing calculation). Therefore, duplicate values are once again displayed by means of conditional formatting. But—and this is important—these duplicate values still don't have identical ranks, due to the variation in column H.

- If you want the ranks to be sorted in descending order, the sequence of the numbers in the auxiliary column K had to be reverted. The example in the previous section showed that this—and much more—can also be achieved with a mouse click in the controls.

- The ten cities with the highest values (range L6:M15 with a pronounced border) are displayed in the bar chart of the *Focus 1* worksheet as "Our Top Ten." Each time you press **F9**, different cities are displayed.

As usual, you should explore further formatting attributes and characteristics of this worksheet on your own.

Chapter 10

Presentation Solutions That Pack a Punch

As the chapter heading suggests, this section shows how to create solutions that have a *powerful effect*. In this regard, the mouse has some work to do, and so have you. Some of the examples presented here are visually elegant and sophisticated. In the preceding nine chapters, however, you have acquired knowledge and experience that will make it easier for you to understand such constructs and their formats. Consequently, the descriptions and notes in this chapter are on the brief side, but an occasional glance at the index will certainly help you. I also remind you to take a very close look at the models available on the CD-ROM and to examine them thoroughly (a little like *CSI*, but without the *C*!).

Consider the solutions presented here as additional, consolidated information about everything already written in relation to the options provided in Excel 2007, or simply as a refresher. To employ these options, you need certain skills and some creativity. Sure, it can be a painstaking effort to acquire the necessary skills for such an extensive software, especially because Excel 2007 is an exciting but also a demanding beauty in this regard. However, if you're looking for ways to support and free your creative imagination, then Excel 2007 is a truly wonderful instrument that has found favor with many. So, let's get started and see what unfolds!

Sorting? You can do without

With our first example, I wish to show you that the rS1.Method can also be completed with conditions more difficult than those outlined previously.

The Task and the Problem

The task is to create a solution that successfully represents a product's quarterly sales figures, broken down into different years and cities. Monthly data is available for a total of 75 cities and we should be able to compare year with year and/or city with city.

The problem is that the necessary source data is delivered as monthly data that has been sorted in order of success. Therefore, the cities and their results are sorted in descending order, according to their sales figures. Consequently, the source data may display the cities in a different sequence each year. It is even more difficult to evaluate the data for the current year because the transferred data is sorted differently each month. However, this is necessary for other analyses and evaluations, and your orderer does not want this to change.

Incidentally, this all concerns the following question, which quite often must be answered: how can we obtain consistent information from inconsistent data? Naturally, numerous database solutions can provide an adequate answer to this question. Within Excel alone, there are many different sophisticated variants, some of which may or may not require programming. However, this also includes a model that is secure in any application and easy for anyone to create, namely the model of a dynamic, non-programmed presentation solution. I will describe how this can work below. However, first take a look at the result.

On the Companion CD Open the file \Samples\3Years.xlsx on the CD-ROM.

The *Focus 1* worksheet in the file *3Years.xlsx* is designed for the *Full screen* presentation view and is protected without a password.

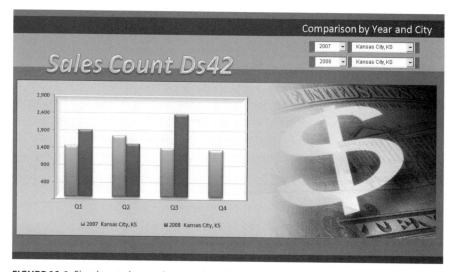

FIGURE 10-1 Simple yet elegant, in a number of ways

The upper right corner of the figure contains four *ActiveX controls* for making various different paired comparisons or cross-comparisons.

- For example, based on the information provided in Figure 10-1: what were the sales figures for Kansas City, KS in 2007 and how do they compare with 2008? (There is no column for Q4, 2008 because no data is currently available for this quarter.)

- However, what were the sales figures for Kansas City, KS in 2007, and how do they compare with the sales figures for Worcester, MA in 2007? Incidentally, in this *ActiveX control*, you do not have to move down 39 positions from Kansas City: it is enough to select the current entry (by double-clicking it) and then overwrite it with the two letters "*wo*" (lowercase is sufficient). It couldn't be easier. The chart is immediately updated to show the data from Worcester, MA.

- You can also determine the level of success achieved for product sales in Knoxville, TN in 2006 and how this compares with the result achieved in Oakland, CA in 2007. There are numerous scenarios that demand such comparisons, each of which seems somewhat strange at first glance. However, the text "Years AND Cities are unequal" below the chart draws your attention to a possible oversight in your query combination.

The above descriptions also clearly illustrate the following problem: a comparative query of 75 cities naturally makes it necessary to sort the city names in the control lists in alphabetical order. However, it is necessary here to extract data that is stored differently in three different data sheets; in other words, sorted according to values and on top of that sorted differently in each of the three sources.

Before we discuss how to solve such difficulties, let's consider the working objective again.

- It must be possible to address one of three possible worksheets as a data source by simply clicking a year in a control (as mentioned previously, and explained in greater detail below, this can be achieved using the INDIRECT function).

- It must be possible to extract the quarterly data for a city from each source data sheet without knowing which of the 75 possible row positions is occupied by this city (this does not work when you use OFFSET or INDEX, except in a very roundabout way, but it does work with VLOOKUP).

To make it easier to understand the formula constructions for the chart basis, let me first provide an overview of the data structure and the control designs. I doubt you will be surprised to learn that, once again, there are redundancies. The model is, in many ways, designed to satisfy changing requirements and therefore can be adjusted without much effort, even to meet needs other than those outlined here. For the purpose of this exercise, you may wish to use the material available to supplement this solution.

Organization of the Source Data

The most important information about the *Data 1 ...*, *Data 2 ...*, and *Data 3 ...* worksheets is provided below.

- All of the worksheets have the same structure, even if the data is sorted differently in each sheet. For fast and easy orientation, you will use different colors in the header area to differentiate between different types of data.

- The windows are fixed in both axes (*View/Window/Freeze Panes*) so that you can keep the labels in view even when the data range moves.

- Each data source has a *node* that corresponds to its sheet name: *rD1.Node*, *rD2.Node*, and *rD3.Node*. This is quite important. These range names differ in number only.

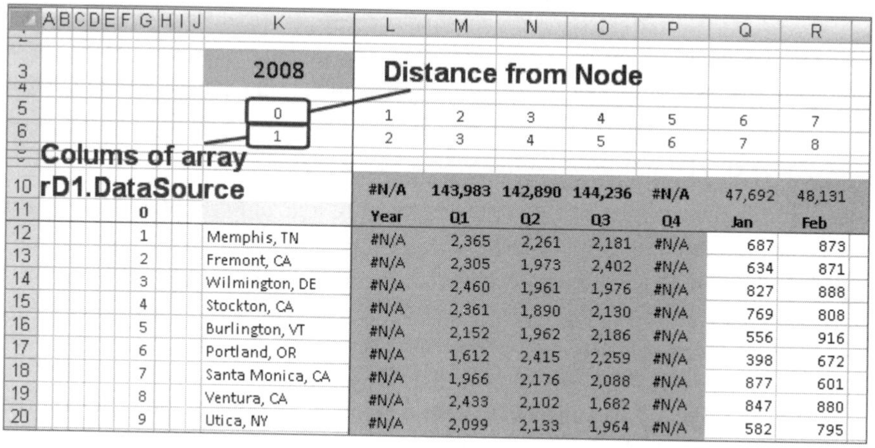

	2008		**Distance from Node**						
			1	2	3	4	5	6	7
	0		2	3	4	5	6	7	8
Colums of array	1								
rD1.DataSource			#N/A	143,983	142,890	144,236	#N/A	47,692	48,131
	0		Year	Q1	Q2	Q3	Q4	Jan	Feb
	1	Memphis, TN	#N/A	2,365	2,261	2,181	#N/A	687	873
	2	Fremont, CA	#N/A	2,305	1,973	2,402	#N/A	634	871
	3	Wilmington, DE	#N/A	2,460	1,961	1,976	#N/A	827	888
	4	Stockton, CA	#N/A	2,361	1,890	2,130	#N/A	769	808
	5	Burlington, VT	#N/A	2,152	1,962	2,186	#N/A	556	916
	6	Portland, OR	#N/A	1,612	2,415	2,259	#N/A	398	672
	7	Santa Monica, CA	#N/A	1,966	2,176	2,088	#N/A	877	601
	8	Ventura, CA	#N/A	2,433	2,102	1,682	#N/A	847	880
	9	Utica, NY	#N/A	2,099	2,133	1,964	#N/A	582	795

FIGURE 10-2 Two auxiliary rows with different number sequences

- The monthly data presented here in the form of constants is summarized in columns L to P with formulas for quarterly data and annual data (therefore, it would be easy to use month-specific analyses to enhance this analysis). The presentation chart requires only the values in the range M12:P91.

- There are two horizontal auxiliary rows with number sequences. The upper row describes the distance from the node. The lower row indicates the column numbers in an array used by VLOOKUP formulas. Each of the three arrays in these worksheets has, in addition to the aforementioned nodes, another range name that corresponds to the sheet name: rD1.DataSource, rD2.DataSource, and rD3.DataSource. Once again, these range names differ in number only. Depending on their actual use, the arrays span the entire values range and therefore also contain monthly data not visualized here.

- In the Data 1 ... worksheet, however, the cells that are retained for monthly data that does not yet exist but will in the future are filled with #N/A, which is usually the case with my models. Similarly, the relevant totals are also filled with #N/A and therefore invisible in the associated charts.

Controls with Text Output

The city names and years sorted in alphabetical order for use in the four model controls are defined in the Lists 1 worksheet.

Note the following in relation to the output values of the ActiveX controls: while the ComboBoxes for selecting the year output their index value in numbers from 0 to 2, as was previously determined and accepted (and can't be anything else for form controls), the ComboBoxes for selecting the city behave differently; they do not write a number. Instead, they write the text selected by the user to its LinkedCell. Excellent, but why? Because whoever has such text also has a search term that can be used in VLOOKUP (and in other functions).

How can this be set up? It's really quite easy: the *BoundColumn* property of the *ComboBox* must not be set to *0* (as was previously demanded), but to its default value of *1*.

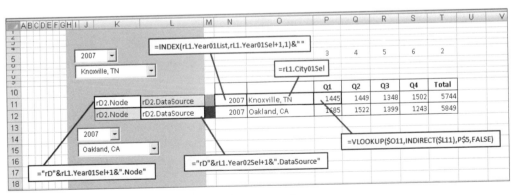

FIGURE 10-3 ActiveX controls can also output text

With regard to the *ComboBox* standards, the *MatchEntry* property makes it easy for users to control text entries within extensive lists, simply by entering the first letters. Selecting *fmMatchEntryComplete* triggers *extended matching*; that is, as soon as one or more letters are entered in the control (by selecting and overwriting existing entries), the object searches its *ListFillRange* for an entry that begins with the letter(s) entered and proposes it for selection.

Formulas of the Chart Basis

The chart data is compiled in the *Basis 1* worksheet. This sheet does not require copies of the four controls for the model to work. However, these copies provide you with a better overview when testing and checking the formulas.

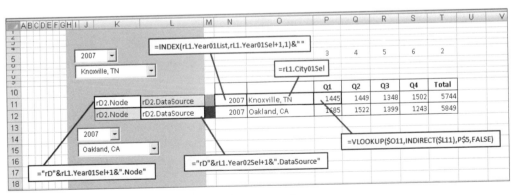

FIGURE 10-4 Just a few formulas, but still more than you need.

Note the following points with reference to Figure 10-4:

K11   ="rD"&rL1.Year01Sel+1&".Node"

When you use the output value of a control, this formula (and similarly the formula in K12) composes text, namely the name of the node that belongs to the selected year. If you click *2008*, that is, the first entry in the ComboBox, Excel generates the text *rD1.Node*. If you click 2006—the third entry—Excel generates the text *rD3.Node*. You now have a piece of information that you can use as a reference argument, in connection with INDIRECT, in many different formulas (for example, in OFFSET).

This describes an important key element of the rS1.Method that influenced my choice of naming conventions:

- Clicking a control generates a number.

- A formula uses this number to generate a specific range name (generally a node). The number alone is the variable element of the range name.

- The range name used as a variable in this way is the reference argument for other formulas.

In other words, you can click a control to determine the worksheet or cell range from which Excel should read the data that you're interested in.

While OFFSET occupies the "leading role" in the "presentation theater," the INDIRECT(reference,a1) function occupies the role of stage designer or "scene-shifter."

INDIRECT opens the third dimension of your presentation model, without any programming whatsoever. Until now, we spoke only of *one* array or *one* node. With INDIRECT, however, you determine simply and elegantly which of the numerous arrays or nodes you wish to address.

With INDIRECT, you can use text in a cell *outside* any formula as a reference argument *within* this formula. Here, I use the INDIRECT function to establish dynamic references and to define variable reference arguments in formulas. The examples below provide additional information.

In the syntax =INDIRECT(reference,a1), the optional argument A1 represents a logical value that specifies which type of reference is contained in the cell (TRUE for the A1 notation and FALSE for the Z1S1 notation). Because the latter does not play any role in the models provided in this book (nor generally anywhere else), this argument can continue to be ignored (which is then interpreted by Excel as TRUE).

Important   The INDIRECT function does not work if its reference argument references a cell in a closed file. Consequently, when you use this function you can work only with external cross-worksheet references if all of the files used are open at runtime.

This formation of variable node names is particularly useful in rS1 models, but is nevertheless not required here; both formulas potentially enhance the model's functions.

The formulas in L11:L12, on the other hand, will be used here immediately. The same principle provides the same benefits:

`L12   ="rD"&rL1.Year02Sel+1&".DataSource"`

Both cells therefore contain the optional text *rD1.DataSource, rD2.DataSource,* or *rD3.DataSource.* Make sure that cell L12 has *rL1.Year02Sel* instead of *rL1.Year01Sel* as in L11. However, both formulas are identical in every other regard. The same is true of the formulas in K11:K12.

`N11   =INDEX(rL1.Year01List,rL1.Year01Sel+1,1)&" "`

Similar cell: N12. These formulas determine the selected year, which is used as the first part of the relevant legend label in the chart. I used &" " to insert a space after the formula because I felt that the gap between the year and city name in the legend was insufficient.

`O11   =rL1.City01Sel`

Similar in cell O12: the second string for the relevant legend label in the chart and the search term for the VLOOKUP formulas. Because the relevant *ComboBox* outputs text (as shown above), this can be read directly from the control's *LinkedCell.*

P11:T12,
for example `P11=VLOOKUP($O11,INDIRECT($L11),P$5,FALSE)`

> **Note** In Chapter 2, "New Approaches—Getting Started," the file \Samples\0201_Extract.xlsx introduced the function =VLOOKUP(lookup_value,table_array,col_index_num,range_lookup) in detail.

Here is the gist of the matter: "determine a value that is to be localized as follows: use the search term provided in cell O11. Find this string in the first column of the array whose name is in cell L11 (and was created there as a variable for the use of INDIRECT). Once you find it, take the value in this row from the column in the array whose column number is provided in cell P5."

In our example, the notation =VLOOKUP("Knoxville, TN",rD2.DataSource,3,FALSE) would be a static equivalent of the dynamic formula. This is just one of 240 access options that can be controlled with two mouse clicks. This is the case for three source-data ranges. For other requests, however, there could be 10, 50, or more source-data ranges. That makes absolutely no difference when constructing such a chart basis.

> **Note** If, for the aforementioned formula, you were to use a control that also retained a variable column specification in cell P5, there would be 4,320 access options (rather than 240), each of which would require just three mouse clicks. You do not want this here, but you may find it useful some time in the future.

The two formulas in column T are "reserves" that are not required here.

The data range N10:S12 (colored pale red in the worksheet) is the data source for the chart that presents the collated custom data in the *Focus 1* sheet.

Specials in the *Focus* Worksheet

There are some special features here, but you can only explore these formatting considerations after you unprotect the sheet. Note the following three points:

- The "dollar sign" image is stored on the CD-ROM under *Materials\Pictures\Dollar.tif*

- It is interesting that there seems to be a smooth transition between the chart area and the image. Also, take a look at how the chart border has been formatted.

- The *plot area* is designed with the 3-D option *Soft Round*. This gives you a very slightly three-dimensional depth, like a framed picture. However, there is just one visually disappointing disadvantage associated with using column charts: the columns are generally too far "forward," practically on the "outer" edge of the mock border instead of being "set back" on the lower edge of the "picture area." In this case, a little trick rectified the problem. As is frequently the case, two very important components of chart design play a role here: axis scaling and number formatting.

It only remains for me to mention the formula that outputs the aforementioned alert:

```
J29  =IF(
     AND(rL1.Year01Sel<>rL1.Year02Sel,rL1.City01Sel<>rL1.City02Sel),
     "Years AND Cities are unequal","")
```

A Little Data; a Lot of Information

On the Companion CD Open the file *\Samples\1002_10Products.xlsx* on the CD-ROM.

The *Focus 1* worksheet in the file *1002_10Products.xlsx* is designed for the *Full screen* presentation view and is protected without a password.

The sales figures for 10 products and their regional distribution are displayed here. Select a product in the *ComboBox* at the top of the sheet. You may be surprised to see a two-column list that shows not only the product names but also their rankings. When a user selects a product, he or she can also become familiar with its ranking.

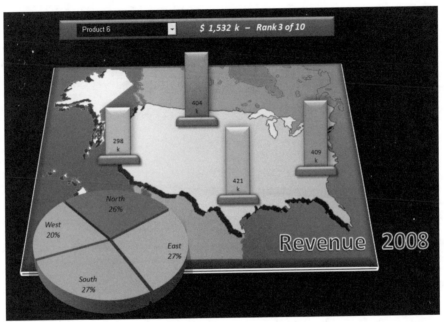

FIGURE 10-5 Copious information: absolute values, rank, regional success, percentage distribution

The results of your decision are shown in several different ways in this extensively designed presentation chart whose main purpose is to "look good":

- The header bar contains the product, its total sales in thousands of dollars, and its rank.

- The columns on the map represent the subtotals of the four regional sales values for the product selected.

- Each slice of the pie chart represents the percentages of the regional sales values for the product selected.

> **Note** When the control is activated (indicated by a blinking cursor in the object), you can also use the **Down Arrow** and **Up Arrow** buttons to move its contents; that is, to virtually "scroll" up and down the product list.

The source data and chart ranges are presented together in the *Data 1 and Basis* worksheet (see Figure 10-6). This is a simple structure with absolutely no surprises or special features to report. Therefore, I'll keep my comments brief.

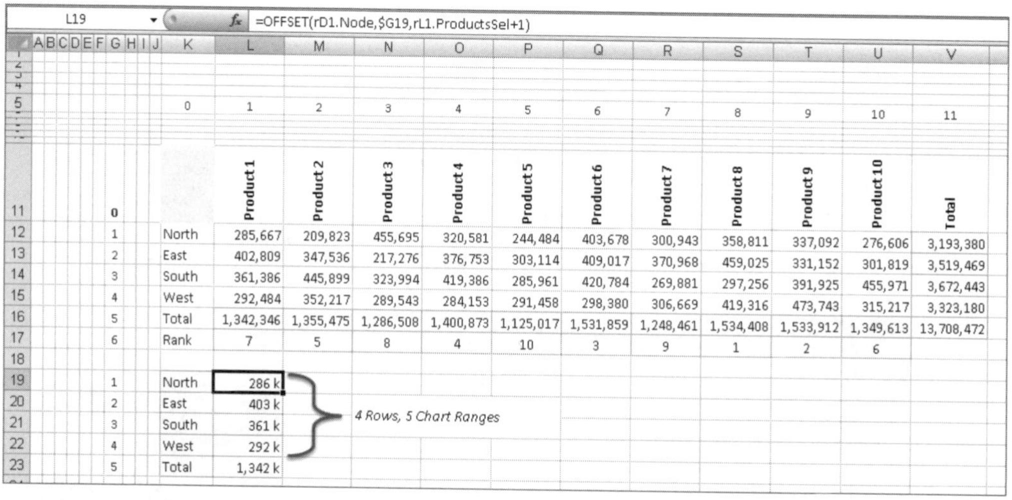

			Product 1	Product 2	Product 3	Product 4	Product 5	Product 6	Product 7	Product 8	Product 9	Product 10	Total
			0	1	2	3	4	5	6	7	8	9	10	11
11	0												
12	1	North	285,667	209,823	455,695	320,581	244,484	403,678	300,943	358,811	337,092	276,606	3,193,380
13	2	East	402,809	347,536	217,276	376,753	303,114	409,017	370,968	459,025	331,152	301,819	3,519,469
14	3	South	361,386	445,899	323,994	419,386	285,961	420,784	269,881	297,256	391,925	455,971	3,672,443
15	4	West	292,484	352,217	289,543	284,153	291,458	298,380	306,669	419,316	473,743	315,217	3,323,180
16	5	Total	1,342,346	1,355,475	1,286,508	1,400,873	1,125,017	1,531,859	1,248,461	1,534,408	1,533,912	1,349,613	13,708,472
17	6	Rank	7	5	8	4	10	3	9	1	2	6	
18													
19	1	North	286 k										
20	2	East	403 k										
21	3	South	361 k		*4 Rows, 5 Chart Ranges*								
22	4	West	292 k										
23	5	Total	1,342 k										

Cell reference: L19   =OFFSET(rD1.Node,$G19,rL1.ProductsSel+1)

FIGURE 10-6 Some source data and five small chart ranges, that's all you need here.

- Any cells that contain formulas are colored here.

- The ranks that are copied to the *ComboBox* and header row of the *Focus 1* sheet are calculated in row 17.

- The product-specific data from rows 12 to 16 is read in the rows 19 to 23. The values from the columns that correspond to the control setting are shown here. These values are decreased to the thousands format.

- The four-row range K19:L22 provides data for five charts; row by row for the column charts and as a block for the pie chart.

The structure in the *Lists 1* worksheet (see Figure 10-7) is even more interesting.

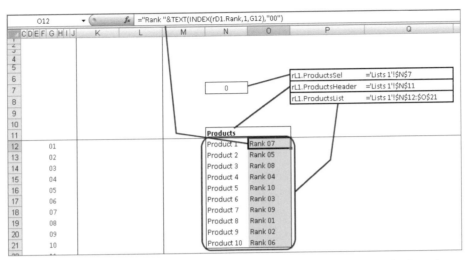

FIGURE 10-7 The list definition range for the *ComboBox* has two columns and contains formulas.

You have already seen that the opened control has two columns. The basis for this is a de-fined two-column *ListFillRange* with the name *rL1.ProductsList*.

Formulas of the type ="Rank "&TEXT(INDEX(rD1.Rank,1,G12),"00") generate a rank list by reading the relevant data from the aforementioned *Data 1 and Basis* sheet.

In this model, the *ActiveX control* in the *Focus 1* sheet is especially interesting. Here, numer-ous changes that warrant a more detailed description were made to the default settings.

Standard				Custom	
☐ Appearance					
BackColor	☐ &H80000005&		○	■ &H00800000&	
BackStyle	1 - fmBackStyleOpaque			1 - fmBackStyleOpaque	
BorderColor	■ &H80000006&		○	■ &H00800000&	
BorderStyle	0 - fmBorderStyleNone		○	1 - fmBorderStyleSingle	
DropButtonStyle	1 - fmDropButtonStyleArrow			1 - fmDropButtonStyleArrow	
ForeColor	■ &H80000008&		○	☐ &H00FFFFFF&	
ShowDropButtonWhen	2 - fmShowDropButtonWhenAlways			2 - fmShowDropButtonWhenAlways	
SpecialEffect	2 - fmSpecialEffectSunken		○	0 - fmSpecialEffectFlat	
Style	0 - fmStyleDropDownCombo			0 - fmStyleDropDownCombo	
Value					
☐ Data					
BoundColumn	1		○	0	
ColumnCount	1		○	2	
ColumnHeads	False			False	
ColumnWidths			○	60 pt;80 pt	
ListRows	8		○	10	
ListStyle	0 - fmListStylePlain			0 - fmListStylePlain	
ListWidth	0 pt		○	139.95 pt	
Text					
TextColumn	-1			-1	
TopIndex	-1			-1	
☐ Font					
Font	Calibri		○	Arial	

FIGURE 10-8 Numerous changes can be made using *ActiveX controls*.

On the left-hand side (A) of Figure 10-8, you see an extract of the default settings for a *ComboBox*, grouped into categories. On the right-hand side (B), you see a comparative list of properties applied to the object used here. The rows whose settings differ from the default settings have been marked with small circles.

In this case, the user has adjusted the following settings:

- Formats
  - ❑ *BackColor*: the object's background color
  - ❑ *BorderColor*: the border color
  - ❑ *BorderStyle*: the border property (*fmBorderStyleSingle:* the object has a border)
  - ❑ *ForeColor*: the font color
  - ❑ *SpecialEffect*: the object's appearance (*fmSpecialEffectFlat:* compared with the default setting, the object is not three-dimensional but flat and sets itself apart from its surroundings by nothing more than a border and/or color)
- Data-specific properties
  - ❑ *BoundColumn*: the setting *0* ensures that the control's index value is put out to the *LinkedCell*.
  - ❑ *ColumnCount*: the setting *2* assigns two columns to the drop-down list for this *ComboBox*. This requires a *ListFillRange* with two or more columns.
  - ❑ *ColumnWidths*: the setting *60 pt;80 pt* defines the width of both columns. A semi-colon separates the values. The font size should be defined before the final setting is made here. Generally, after some trial and error, you will be happy with the appearance that you achieve.
  - ❑ *ListWidth*: specifies the width of the expanded drop-down list. This value can also be a value other than the total value for *ColumnWidths*.
- Font: Here, the *Arial* font was determined as the *Font* property. Generally, this font is considerably easier to see in such objects than are most other fonts.

I won't describe the remaining properties here because, of these, only *LinkedCell* and *ListFillRange* are important developer settings. At this point, there is no need to say anything more about these settings.

I can therefore focus on providing some details about the design layout of the *Focus 1* worksheet.

On the Companion CD Several maps, including some for Europe, Ireland, and the United States, are stored on the CD_ROM under *Materials\Pictures*. The image used here is *USA_CA_Map.tif.*

- The chart columns appear to rest on a podium that comprises a rectangle and the aforementioned image, and they have been connected to a group. With regard to the elements in this group, which are tilted backwards, examine the values for *3-D rotation*, *3-D format* (including *material* and *lighting*), *line color* (this concerns the border, for example), *line style*, and *shadow*, among others.

> **Important**   The rectangle and image are turned 320° along the Y axis (that is, vertically) and assigned a perspective of 45°. However, as a grouped graphical object it continues to require as much room as if it had not been rotated (as you can see from its markers). Therefore, the object can't be moved up to its visible upper edge, which is the top of the screen, but only to its own hidden edge.

- The pie chart is adjusted to the location and perspective of the graphical podium. The *angle of the first slice* (North) was set to 320°, so that the distribution and positioning of all 10 possible slices essentially correspond to the cardinal points of the compass (North, South, East, and West).

- The pie chart has a slight *pie explosion* of 3 percent and the *data label* shows the *category name* and *percentage*. Of course, the colors here must correspond to the colors of the four column charts.

The column charts positioned in their regional locations are grouped objects that comprise a chart and a rectangle. In such images, objects of this type should never be used on their own to convey information. Because the columns are not standing directly next to each other, observers cannot clearly distinguish between the column heights. In this case, observers must rely on the *data labels* when making a comparison. The column heights must differ greatly if they are to be relied upon when making a comparison. Here, it is important to supplement the image with a pie chart, not only for visual reasons, but because it is a key design element that safeguards the information provided with the image.

When creating the column charts, I recommend the following:

1. Use the *North* data to create the first chart with a fixed scaling of the value axis.

2. Make all of the formatting settings and, when you are finished, make sure that you expand the *plot area* to the maximum *chart area*. Then, and only then, set the *chart area* size you require. When the *chart area* is the same size as the *plot area*, it is considerably easier to make any necessary exact adjustments to the width and height of the object at a later date. Of course, all four objects here must have the same dimensions, so that the same values result in the same column height.

3. Insert and format the *Round Same Side Corner Rectangle* which forms the base of the chart and position it carefully on the lower edge of the chart.

4. Connect both objects to a group and position these on the map.

5. Copy the object and place it elsewhere. Within the group object that you have copied, select the chart (to do this, you don't need to dissolve the group), and assign the *East* data as the *data source*.

6. Position the new object and then select its column to change its color. Naturally, you can also do this as a final step for all four charts, which is better if you have to choose your colors by appearance and comparison.

7. Repeat steps 5 and 6 for the two remaining tasks.

With regard to the overall page design: when using rotated objects, you should pay particular attention to the accuracy of the perspectives and the proportional correlation of the objects shown. In this case, this applies not only to the map and pie chart, but also to the relationship between the map and the header bars. To illustrate this, Figure 10-9 has two lines to highlight the central perspective.

FIGURE 10-9 Observe the perspective here

A Lot of Data—Compressed Information

This section presents two solutions (or three, depending on the how you count them). Each has a similar background (large amounts of data) and the same purpose (heavily compressed information), but can have a completely different appearance. This is hardly surprising, because the objective of a presentation or piece of work determines the layout of your model. Even just one body of data and one basic objective can give rise to hundreds of different solutions.

Chart of Key Data Over 10 Years

On the Companion CD   Open the file \Samples\1003_TenYears.xlsx on the CD-ROM.

The *Focus 1* worksheet in the file *1003_TenYears.xlsx* is designed for the *Full screen* presentation view and is protected without a password.

You already know this model from the later sections in Chapter 4, "Colors, Areas, and Outlines," which discussed the model's format. We will now discuss its overall structure.

The percentage line chart shows the development of eight operational key figures over a period of ten years. The chart basis here is the values from 1999, each of which has been equated with 100 percent. Therefore, the lines that trend upwards and downwards from the base line describe the direction and extent of any changes. Each line has an "on/off switch" to the right of the chart. Therefore, with a mouse click, a user can use a table that also acts as a legend to determine which lines should appear, how many of them, and in which combination. This produces a multifaceted, multivariable analysis: for example, how line A changes in terms of waveforms and intervals in relation to the 100 percent horizontal *and* in relation to line B, and at the same time to line C, or how B relates to C, or how does it look if—and so on. These simple figures can provide a wealth of information and conclusions. Let's just answer one of these questions in the context of Figure 10-10. (Since the different line colors can hardy be differentiated in the gray scale print of the book, you should use the file to follow along.) From 2001 to 2005, the company reduced its product range significantly. Around the same time—from 2002 and steadily after that—it witnessed a considerable rise in the number of high-revenue A customers and therefore (in a delayed yet pleasantly synchronous trend that did not seem to be coincidental) a significant jump in sales.

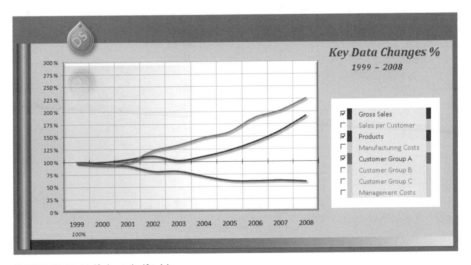

FIGURE 10-10 Half chart, half table

The data contained in the *Data 1* worksheet is divided into two blocks (see Figure 10-11):

- The upper block, *Data*, contains absolute values. Clearly, these numbers are already extremely compressed and are based on several thousand individual values.

- The lower block, *Chart Basis*, contains percentages. For 1999, the constant 100 was entered in all cells. Each of the subsequent years has formulas whose results (when you use each year's absolute values) express its relationship with the start year as a percentage (for more information, see the tip provided below). However, the results (and therefore the chart line) are only shown if the relevant switch for this line is "on."

The formula in cell G16 (in the context of Figure 10-11):

`=IF(rL1.GrossSalesSel=TRUE,INT(G6/$E6%),#N/A)` as a statement: "if the value in the cell *rL1.GrossSalesSel* is TRUE (if the corresponding *CheckBox* has been activated), the result is an integer that represents the percentage of the G6 value in relation to the E6 value. Otherwise (if the corresponding *CheckBox* has been deactivated), the result is #N/A."

> **Tip** In even easier-to-use models of this type, you can use controls to vary the start year for the calculation and therefore show other curve progressions that are flatter or steeper.

			G16			fx	=IF(rL1.GrossSalesSel=TRUE,INT(G6/$E6%),#N/A)						
	A B C		D	E	F	G	H	I	J	K	L	M	N
1													
2			0	1	2	3	4	5	6	7	8	9	10
3													
4													
5	0		**Data**	1999	2000	2001	2002	2003	2004	2005	2006	2007	2008
6	1		Gross Sales	14,513,330	14,590,320	15,359,350	16,339,820	15,032,630	16,235,240	17,858,760	20,358,980	23,616,410	27,867,360
7	2		Sales per Customer	3,972	3,978	4,477	5,347	4,848	5,556	5,957	7,133	9,703	11,535
8	3		Products	86	84	80	71						
9	4		Manufacturing Costs	1,284,530	1,502,970	1,713,380	1,679,110						
10	5		Customer Group A	256	244	255	316		rL1.GrossSalesSel		fx	TRUE	
11	6		Customer Group B	850	812	755	682		A B C D E F G H I J			K	L
12	7		Customer Group C	2,548	2,612	2,421	2,058	8					
13	8		Management Costs	1,306,199	1,162,517	1,034,640	910,483	9		01	rL1.GrossSalesSel	TRUE
14								10		02	rL1.SalesCustSel	FALSE
15	0		**Chart Basis**	1999	2000	2001	2002	11		03	rL1.ProductsSel	TRUE
16	1		Gross Sales	100	100	105	112	12		04	rL1.ManufactCostsSel	FALSE
17	2		Sales per Customer	100	#N/A	#N/A	#N/A	13		05	rL1.CustGroupASel	TRUE
18	3		Products	100	97	93	82	13		05		
19	4		Manufacturing Costs	100	#N/A	#N/A	#N/A	14		06	rL1.CustGroupBSel	FALSE
20	5		Customer Group A	100	95	99	123					
21	6		Customer Group B	100	#N/A	#N/A	#N/A	15		07	rL1.CustGroupCSel	FALSE
22	7		Customer Group C	100	#N/A	#N/A	#N/A	16		08	rL1.ManageCostsSel	FALSE
23	8		Management Costs	100	#N/A	#N/A	#N/A	17				

FIGURE 10-11 Each chart row has its own on/off switch.

The lower right insert in Figure 10-11 originated in the *Lists 1* worksheet where each *CheckBox* also has its own clearly discernible cell link.

The technical setup of the *Focus 1* presentation sheet provides only a handful of surprises for you, the most important being:

- The value axis has a fixed scaling and the category axis intersects it at the *axis value* 100.

- The *label position* of the category axis is set to *Low*.

- The *chart area* is completely transparent. Therefore, its background is the fill color of the table. This makes it easy to perceive the small table on the right as a "legend with switches."

- To reinforce this last impression: when you deactivate the entries, the color signals of the entries are deleted and the texts are hidden. Of course, this is based on *conditional formatting.* In this case, these only refer indirectly to the cell links to the CheckBoxes, namely to those values generated as hidden values in column Q. For example, Q8: `=IF(rL1.GrossSalesSel=TRUE,"x","")`. The reason for this detour is that it is much easier to construct the formula rules for *conditional formatting* if at the same time you can refer to a uniform cell range with the contents "x" or "" instead of having to use eight different range names.

- The CheckBoxes are not labeled and are transparent. However, their width spans the neighboring text in a table cell. As a result, the user can also (therefore indirectly) click the text whose line he wishes to see in the chart. This is both sensible and convenient.

- The logo is stored on the CD-ROM under \Materials*Pictures\LogoDS.tif.* Chapter 5, "Graphical Objects," provides information about how to delete its ambient color, scale the logo, rotate it, and create its reflection.

- What appears to be a column to the left of the chart is simply cell formatting. The same is true of the color gradient below the chart. Access via: *Home/Font/*click the Dialog Box *Launcher.* In the *Format Cells* dialog box, on the *Fill* tab, click *Fill Effects.*

Filtering with the Filter—and Filtering with Controls

This section shows how to present the findings of a study. You were introduced to some of this data and its presentation in Chapter 2, which was concerned with evaluating customer numbers as part of a "summer campaign." The following is a brief recap: a retail business with 100 branches launched a five-week promotional campaign to attract more customers into its branches and compensate for the expected seasonal dip in sales over the summer months. The chart's purpose can be summarized this way: "we launched a campaign and now want to see if it attracted more customers and, if so, when, and to which branches."

We will now take a look at the revenue findings from the same study, analyzing whether this summer campaign was successful in terms of revenue and, if necessary, how it succeeded.

This model brings us back to the subject of "filtering," which was mentioned briefly in Chapter 8, "Chart Types—Conventional and Exceptional." In this regard, the file *1004_ SummerCampaign.xlsx* contains two options that are based on different objectives or requirements:

- The Controlling department of the company, which has proficient Excel users, uses the *pivot* system (not part of the description here) and a slender filter model to analyze data. This gives rise to versatile analyses that have numerous selections and answer a multitude of questions. If, for example, one of the settings does not make any sense and produces strange results (or none at all), this is not a problem because the setting is quickly identified and corrected using the resources within Excel.

- Even though the management team of a company, which does not necessarily have to be proficient in Excel (that's why companies have specialists), has exactly the same data, it is housed in a much more "closely knitted" model that acts as a filtering report module rather than a filtering analysis instrument. It is not as slender as the Controlling module and it can't answer every question on the spur of the moment (that's why companies have financial controllers). However, it can answer most questions, especially the most important ones, without relying on any external assistance. Furthermore, it can do this in the easiest way possible: just a few mouse clicks in four selection lists containing clear text will retrieve the necessary information, without risk of error, and without any irritating program responses. That's exactly how it should be.

From a technical perspective, lots of things that have already been the subject of various discussions in this book converge here. However, Excel 2007 also introduces you to something completely new: formulas that virtually produce any differentiable filter result, without you having to filter!

 On the Companion CD Open the \Samples\1004_SummerCampaign.xlsx file on the CD-ROM.

The *Focus 1 Filter* and *Focus 2 Formulas* worksheets in the file *1004_SummerCampaign.xlsx* are designed for the *Full screen* presentation view and are protected without a password. To test the model, you should select these settings or leave them unchanged. Naturally, you should also unprotect the sheet if you wish to examine the structures.

Variant 1: The Complex Analysis Module

Activate the *Focus 1 Filter* worksheet, which is the analysis module for Controlling.

What is available and what is possible?

- Unlike many of the models introduced earlier, this module houses everything in just one sheet: the master data, chart basis, tabular results display, and chart.

- The sales figures for 100 branches and 10 calendar weeks are listed below a "frozen" sheet. The branches are classified into several columns; that is, assigned grouping characteristics. This is extremely important for variable filter analysis:

  ❏ Column *Type*: A, B, C—three different types of branches (divided according to type of business, foundation type, and localization at the business location)

  ❏ Column *RGN*: N, E, S, W—regionalization according to the cardinal points of the compass

  ❏ Column *CS*: 1, 2, 3—differentiation according to the number of inhabitants where the business is located

❏ Column *since*: years *1999* to *2006* (inclusive)—the year in which the branch was founded or acquired

❏ Column *User*: This stands for *user-defined* (custom) and is a very important column in filter models of this type. In practice, however, this kind of column is frequently missing, which is most unfortunate. Here, the user can specify his own classifications. In addition to existing and standardized characteristics, he can also define whatever he wants, wherever he wants. Therefore, he can also filter whatever he wants, however he wants.

Now let's take a look at the views that are currently possible. If you are working in a protected worksheet, take a look at the row numbers shown in Figure 10-12:

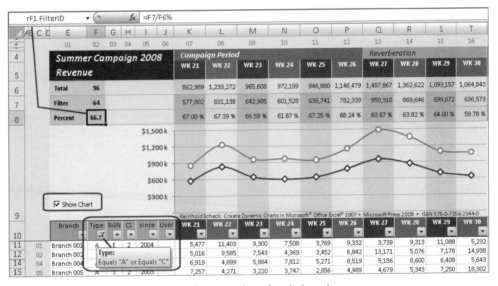

FIGURE 10-12 Such structures provide a large number of analysis options.

■ If the sheet does not have any filters, only the total results in row 6 are shown.

■ If you have set a filter, the absolute and relative filter results are also shown in rows 7 and 8.

■ If you have activated the *CheckBox* with the text *Show Chart*, all of the data (the "whole") is represented by an orange line. If a filter result also exists, it is represented by a blue line. Otherwise, the chart is hidden. (In many cases, the percentage results in row 8 are considerably more important than the trend waveform shown in the chart.)

Now let's take a look at the current settings made in Figure 10-12, where the user has set some filters. In the *Type* column, he has selected types *A* and *C* (respectively excluded type B). He has also activated the *CheckBox*. As a result, all of the aforementioned displays are shown.

In this sheet, cell F8 (*rF1.FilterID*) is particularly important. Its value expresses the percentage of branches contained in the filter. Therefore, if this number is 100, the sheet is not filtered. This specification is used by several formulas. For example:

```
K7    =IF(rF1.FilterID=100,"",SUBTOTAL(9,K$11:K$106))
K8    =IF(rF1.FilterID=100,"",K$7/K$6%)
```

> **Note** The =SUBTOTAL(function_num,reference) function, which you can use to calculate filter results, was described in the last main section in Chapter 8.

The chart basis (see Figure 10-13) is housed in the cell range X6:AG7 and made invisible through the font color chosen.

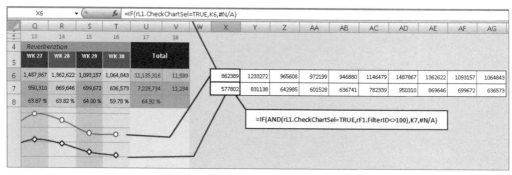

FIGURE 10-13 The chart basis is hidden here.

There are different formulas for creating these two data series. For example:

```
X6    =IF(rL1.CheckChartSel=TRUE,K6,#N/A)
```

If the *CheckBox* is activated, the value is read from cell K6. Otherwise, it remains as #N/A. Consequently, the line for the total data from row 6 is shown or hidden.

```
X7    =IF(AND(rL1.CheckChartSel=TRUE,rF1.FilterID<>100),K7,#N/A)
```

If the *CheckBox* is activated *and* if the value in cell *rF1.FilterID* is not 100, the value is read from cell K7. Otherwise, it remains as #N/A. The line for the filter data from row 7 is shown or hidden.

Experiment with different filters and take advantage of the clearly improved and more intuitively manageable options provided in Excel 2007. There are numerous analytical options. You will be spoiled by having so much choice, which is another reason why I highly recommend this type of data analysis.

Variant 2: The Easy-to-Use Report Module

Activate the *Focus 2 Formulas* worksheet, which is the report module for the Management team. This sheet in the file *1004_SummerCampaign.xlsx* is designed for the *Full screen* presentation view and is protected without a password. The filter options are suppressed, but can be activated without great difficulty. To keep this as a viable option in the future, the data structure as of row 24 corresponds to the filter model that I introduced above.

> **Note** Of course, in a real-life scenario, such a module would be protected with a password before it left a company's possession or its developer's hands, so that handling errors could be avoided.
>
> You can't set filters in a protected worksheet unless you explicitly permit the filter option (by activating the relevant *CheckBox*) in the *Protect Sheet* dialog box.

If you have not yet discovered all of the hidden new features of Excel, you will be very interested to learn that you can use simple *form controls* to group together a combination of criteria that Excel will immediately use to generate a corresponding results table and chart. It is worth noting that this does not involve any programming, has nothing to do with a *pivot* system, and is not the result of a filtering process.

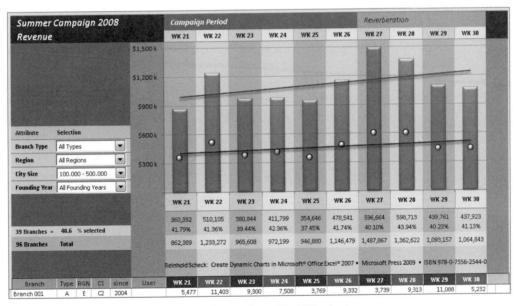

FIGURE 10-14 The Report module provides fast results and is child's play to use.

Behind the scenes lie new functions whose results once could be achieved only with pains-taking efforts and even then only in part (through the use of array formulas). I had longed for functions such as SUMIFS and COUNTIFS (note the *S* at the end; it's not a typing error) for such a long time and was overjoyed to find them. They make it considerably easier to per-form lots of calculation tasks and to create user-friendly models.

Before I explain these in greater detail, let me first provide a brief overview of what can be achieved with the model used here. Note the following points with reference to Figure 10-14:

- If you select *All* ... in each of the four controls, a chart that represents the whole is shown. Orange columns have white/blue dots on their upper edge, all of which are supplemented by a linear trend line (colored blue). These are relatively insignificant for the user, who needs to see them only once to know which purpose they serve. Furthermore, the line is a permanent fixture because its main purpose is to enable ob-servers to make comparisons.

- If you use the controls to select any other combination, the chart becomes a compara-tive presentation: a selected group in relation to the whole. The blue dots are now dropping down and show, as a data series within the *Total* columns, those values that correspond to the custom query. There are now two linear trend lines, a red trend line for the whole and a blue trend line for the combination selected. This data material, which assesses the success of a campaign, contains a particularly high and immediately intelligible informational value: the upper trend line shows the campaign's success in all branches. Therefore, if the lower trend line runs in parallel, the data selected es-sentially corresponds, in a qualitative manner, to the whole. If the lower trend line reflects an "inconsistency", the results of the selection were better or worse than the whole. Therefore, this is a method of fast, optional group analysis in relation to the overall success of the campaign. And if you wish to discuss the results in greater detail? Or if you wish to compare such groups with each other? This or similar Excel solutions could answer all your "if" questions. (Such a report module existed in this case, but deliberately not for the Management team, but for the working environment of the Controller.)

To be able to describe how this solution works, we'll need to take a detour via the *Lists 1* sheet.

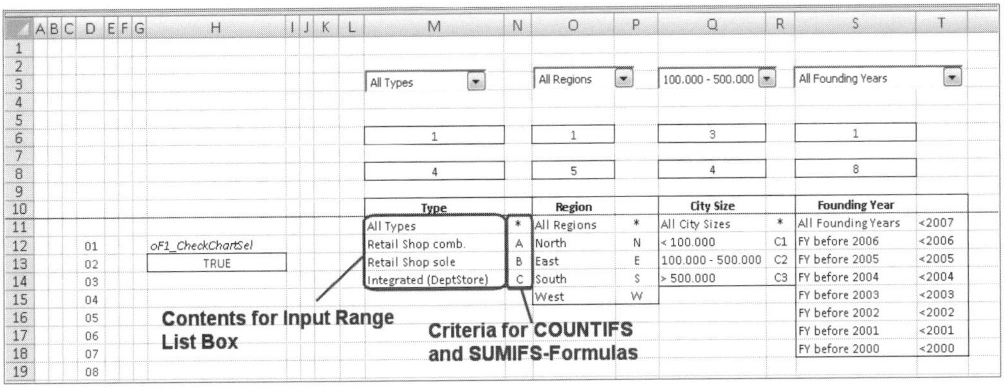

		Type		Region		City Size		Founding Year	
01	oF1_CheckChartSel	All Types	*	All Regions	*	All City Sizes	*	All Founding Years	<2007
02	TRUE	Retail Shop comb.	A	North	N	< 100.000	C1	FY before 2006	<2006
03		Retail Shop sole	B	East	E	100.000 - 500.000	C2	FY before 2005	<2005
04		Integrated (DeptStore)	C	South	S	> 500.000	C3	FY before 2004	<2004
05				West	W			FY before 2003	<2003
06	**Contents for Input Range**							FY before 2002	<2002
07	**List Box**		**Criteria for COUNTIFS**					FY before 2001	<2001
08			**and SUMIFS-Formulas**					FY before 2000	<2000

Controls shown: All Types, All Regions, 100.000 - 500.000, All Founding Years.
Values: 1, 1, 3, 1 and 4, 5, 4, 8.

FIGURE 10-15 The list selection in the control generates a search criterion for a formula.

Here, you see the list contents (in an arrangement that is now familiar to you) for the controls in the focus sheet (see Figure 10-15). For a better overview, copies of the controls are also provided in this sheet. Associated search terms are listed to the right of the clear text list contents. These are similar to those used in the filter analysis module to classify the branches. It is exactly those search terms that we require immediately. Whoever uses this module doesn't have to know which terms these are, where they are, and how they are used. From a functional perspective, the following happens:

1. The user selects a clear text entry (specific information) in a control and generates a number by doing so.

2. The number that is generated is used to determine the position of a search criterion (abstract information).

3. The search criterion found in this way is read in the focus sheet and used there by selective formulas.

4. These formulas write their results to a result line that is used to produce a chart line. Both the numeric values and the chart provide the information requested via the clear text query.

Therefore, the user only needs to know the importance of clear text information in a control, and he only needs to be able to use the mouse to click this clear text information. A structure that he does not have to be familiar with or even be aware of takes care of everything else. This paraphrases my approach to a useful management information system.

I will now describe the main formulas (the other few are not worth mentioning here). You were already familiar with the use of SUMIF and COUNTIF before reading this book or you were introduced to them in Chapter 7, "Elements of Dynamization," (if necessary, take another quick look at this chapter). You can understand and use the new functions SUMIFS and COUNTIFS as multiple variants of basic forms that are already very helpful.

But first, the theory.

The function

```
=SUMIFS(sum_range,
criteria_range1,criteria1,
criteria_range2,criteria2,
```
etc. to
```
criteria_range127,criteria127)
```

works as SUMIF, but can use not only one search criterion, but as many as 127 search criteria simultaneously! This enables you to perform extremely versatile calculations with multiple filters.

The argument sum_range describes the range (reference) to be totaled.

The arguments criteria_range1,criteria_range2, etc. are up to 127 ranges (references) in which the search criteria are to be found.

The arguments criteria1,criteria2, etc. are up to 127 search criteria (or, which is much better in reality, references to cells that contain search criteria.)

When simply expressed in relation to the current example, which is a row-by-row arrangement of the data to be calculated, the first part of the formula is:

```
=SUMIFS(sum_range,criteria_range,criteria1
```

- sum_range: you should use this column to create a total. What are the prerequisites? I will tell you now with a combination of criteria_range and criteria. However, I'll do it not with just one single combination, but with four or even 127!

- criteria_range: this column contains the search criterion. If the search criterion is contained in one row within this column, this is one of the rows that will be included in the total.

Stop right there, however: in our example comprising four combinations, this is only the case if the particular search criterion is contained in this row four times for four different columns; in other words, if this row contains the four different search criteria, column by column (and, in an extremely unlikely scenario, only if the particular search criterion is contained in this row 127 times for 127 columns, requiring a row that contains all 127 defined search criteria).

- criteria: this is the search criterion to be used or this is the cell that contains the search criterion to be used.

Similarly for COUNTIFS:

The function =COUNTIFS(`criteria_range1,criteria1,criteria_range2,criteria2,...`) works like COUNTIF, but it can evaluate not only one range with one search criterion, but as many as 127 ranges with 127 search criteria simultaneously.

- `criteria_range`: you should perform a search in this column
- `criteria`: you should search for this criterion

However, this does not involve just one of these combinations, but four or even 127, and this row is only counted if it contains all four or all 127.

When used for the first time, both functions (SUMIFS/COUNTIFS) definitely cause some confusion, not least because these functions can be used together to determine average values and because the syntax of SUMIFS does not correspond to the argument sequence for SUMIF. I recommend that you conduct your own experiments with these extremely useful functions. Therefore, I won't provide lengthy descriptions of the references used here in our example.

> **Tip** If you develop and test such formulas, you should also simultaneously set appropriate filters whose results you calculate with SUBTOTAL. Furthermore, you should check whether these results correspond with the SUMIFS and/or COUNTIFS results.

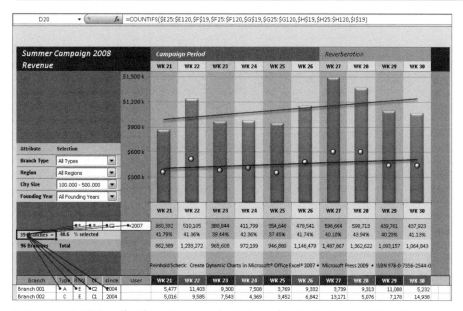

FIGURE 10-16 All this effort for just one number? It's an effort that will pay dividends!

The practical use of COUNTIFS is evident in our example in Figure 10-16. Structures that would otherwise be hidden by formatting are revealed:

- Cells F19:I19 contain the search criteria that result from clicking with the mouse in the control (see also Figure 10-15 and its accompanying text). They are read here through the use of OFFSET.

- The formula in cell D20 uses all four search criteria to find rows in which all four criteria exist or apply (columns E to H, column by column).

The custom number format 0" Branches = " is defined in cell D20 because: a) there was insufficient space outside the cell for this label, and b) text can't be generated in the cell itself because the number produced in each case is processed further in the neighboring cell for calculation.

> **Note** The wildcard character * (asterisk) is used here as a search criterion for finding *everything* (or to search for nothing in particular). Despite selective formulas, it is possible to determine a partial (column-specific) yet also a complete "whole." The search term *<2007* achieves the same result for the *Founding Year* column because this term includes every single year listed here.

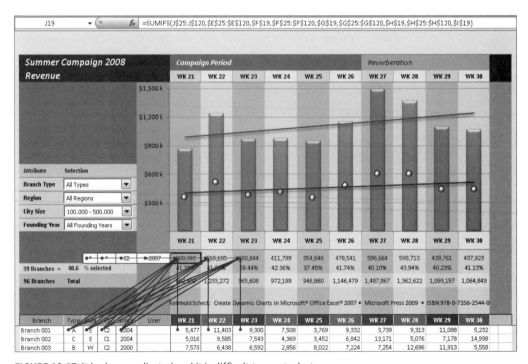

FIGURE 10-17 It looks complicated and it is difficult to create, but ... .

The structure of the SUMIFS formulas in row 19 are very similar in terms of how they are created, but they are a bit more complicated. In Figure 10-17, three of these formulas are shown with their reference lines. If the principle—sum there, find a search criterion there, use the criterion stored there—is clear, then a formula such as

```
=SUMIFS(J$25:J$120,
$E$25:$E$120,$F$19,
$F$25:$F$120,$G$19,
$G$25:$G$120,$H$19,
$H$25:$H$120,$I$19)
```

won't frighten you, especially if you know that these are just four of 127 possible segments.

The results of the SUMIFS formulas in row 19 are the data source for the blue chart elements. The results of the sum formulas in row 21 (ludicrous, aren't they?) are the data source for the orange chart elements.

Even though this concludes my discussion on the topic, it does not cover everything there is to know about analyzing the campaign. In Chapter 2, you analyzed the quantities, and you examined the revenue generated. You still need the following, for example:

- Single comparison of branches at revenue level,
- Group comparison
- Connections between customer numbers and business volumes as key figures: revenue per customer

You now have the campaign data, and this book provides numerous recommendations as well as instructions for displaying data. Therefore, you may want to use all of this material to develop your own model.

Not That It's Absolutely Essential

I'll change the subject now in order to discuss those finishing touches that make all the difference. Some seemingly minor things have become more important rather than less important in this age of so called globalization.

The scenario presented in the solution I'll describe is based on a real-life model: a German company has production facilities and sales offices in England, Ireland, the Netherlands, France, and Italy. The company's working language is English. Some employees take this completely for granted (the English and Irish, though perhaps with different attitudes), others see some benefit (the Germans), others are indifferent as long as the working language is not German (the Dutch), and the rest are not comfortable with this—and if it was only for historical reasons (the French and Italians).

Management considers itself to be European and uses this identity to pursue worldwide relationships. Those responsible at national level receive periodic business reports as Excel files. These reports are "multilingual," meaning that each recipient can display and print the report in his own national language, with a simple mouse click. However, he can also display and print the report in the other national languages. This is where the multilingual principle carries a powerful message: "We are one, but we should treat everyone equally, and with due respect. We respect your national pride as well as any national quirks (should there be some). Even though English is our working language, it does not have to be." Well done!

> **On the Companion CD** Open the file \Samples\1005_Multilingual.xlsx on the CD-ROM.

The *Focus 1* worksheet in the file *1005_Multilingual.xlsx* is designed for the *Full screen* presentation view and is protected without a password.

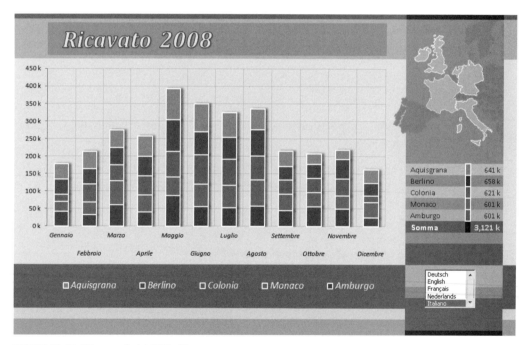

FIGURE 10-18 "Ma guarda te! Mitico!"

In Figure 10-18 you can see that something really "mitico" is happening here, something good and dynamic! You can use a *ListBox* to determine which of the five languages should be used to label the chart. The sales report shown here concerns sales data from German cities. It is highly commendable that the company also respects that these cities may have different names in other languages, even if they don't wish to use those names. Such hiccups are still going strong: "Mailand"—scherzi? "Lione"—fâcheux! "Londres?"—you must be kidding! Therefore, such labels are stored as variables here.

Never underestimate the entertainment value of presentation charts. Time and time again, I have witnessed the audience's acceptance of a solution whose information value may be boring or whose information content may even be problematic suddenly skyrocket when the presentation format shows something appealing.

A word of warning: do not introduce nonsensical gimmicks or special effects to paper over the cracks in the presentation. Out of courtesy, you could introduce something appealing that respects the needs of your target group; for example, the use of company colors and designs. Alternatively, you could introduce an additional unexpected feature, something that's "clever" and "looks good," something to be proud of.

Your solution will be accepted if it fulfills its brief. It will excel if it is also pleasing to the eye. If someone smiles, points to the screen, and says something along the lines of "look at that …" to his neighbor during your presentation, this is wonderful news for you. It means that you have accomplished something great; you have made someone happy.

In the example shown here, colleagues from France, Italy, and the Netherlands who were not particularly happy about English being the working language in a predominantly German company were "won over" by a setting that enabled them to view the report modules in their own national languages, with a mouse click. This was exactly the intention: the colleagues did not simply receive their own "national solution," but instead received an international solution that they had the option of localizing. The difference is small, but it counts. I'm sure you can think of some other similar scenarios.

Not that it is absolutely essential but it can still give great pleasure.

> **Note** The character sets and settings options available in Widows and Office set very few boundaries in terms of the languages you use. You can assign almost any language combination to models such as the one presented here. This also includes "foreign fonts;" in other words, non-Latin fonts from the Asian or Arabic-speaking world, for example. This is particularly important if globalization is truly your goal.

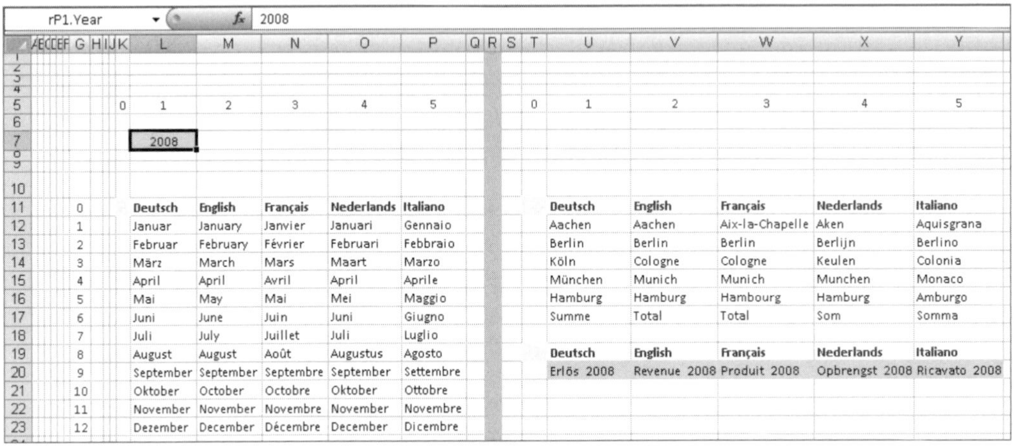

	rP1.Year		f_x	2008									

		L	M	N	O	P			U	V	W	X	Y
5	0	1	2	3	4	5		0	1	2	3	4	5
7		2008											
11	0	Deutsch	English	Français	Nederlands	Italiano			Deutsch	English	Français	Nederlands	Italiano
12	1	Januar	January	Janvier	Januari	Gennaio			Aachen	Aachen	Aix-la-Chapelle	Aken	Aquisgrana
13	2	Februar	February	Février	Februari	Febbraio			Berlin	Berlin	Berlin	Berlijn	Berlino
14	3	März	March	Mars	Maart	Marzo			Köln	Cologne	Cologne	Keulen	Colonia
15	4	April	April	Avril	April	Aprile			München	Munich	Munich	Munchen	Monaco
16	5	Mai	May	Mai	Mei	Maggio			Hamburg	Hamburg	Hambourg	Hamburg	Amburgo
17	6	Juni	June	Juin	Juni	Giugno			Summe	Total	Total	Som	Somma
18	7	Juli	July	Juillet	Juli	Luglio							
19	8	August	August	Août	Augustus	Agosto			Deutsch	English	Français	Nederlands	Italiano
20	9	September	September	Septembre	September	Settembre			Erlös 2008	Revenue 2008	Produit 2008	Opbrengst 2008	Ricavato 2008
21	10	Oktober	October	Octobre	Oktober	Ottobre							
22	11	November	November	Novembre	November	Novembre							
23	12	Dezember	December	Décembre	December	Dicembre							

FIGURE 10-19 Here you can define as many languages as you want.

It is quite easy to set up such a model:

- The *Parameters 1* worksheet, which is fully used here again, contains all of the label elements to be used in the relevant language versions (see Figure 10-19). Depending on the current control setting, they are transferred to the *Data 1 and Basis* sheet (see Figure 10-20) and shown in the chart.

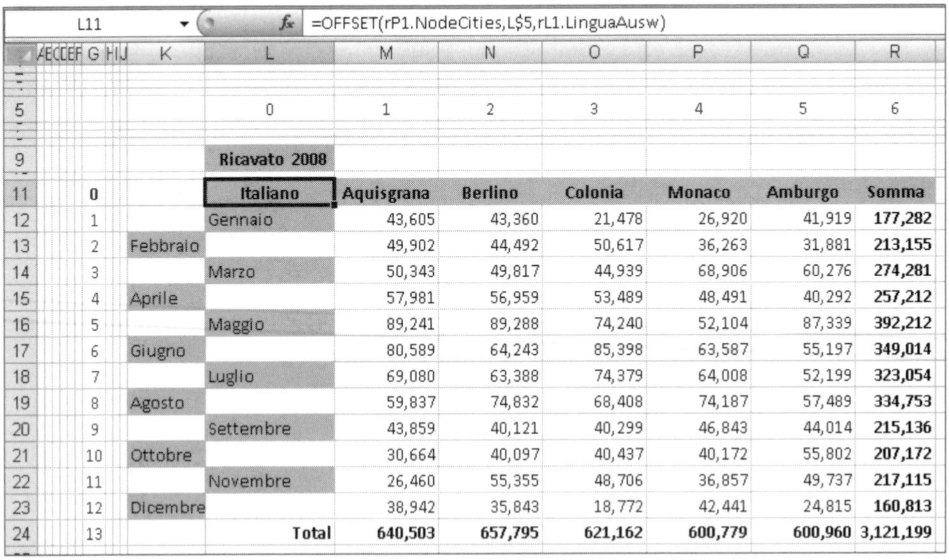

	L11		f_x	=OFFSET(rP1.NodeCities,L$5,rL1.LinguaAusw)						

		K	L	M	N	O	P	Q	R
5			0	1	2	3	4	5	6
9			Ricavato 2008						
11	0		Italiano	Aquisgrana	Berlino	Colonia	Monaco	Amburgo	Somma
12	1		Gennaio	43,605	43,360	21,478	26,920	41,919	177,282
13	2	Febbraio		49,902	44,492	50,617	36,263	31,881	213,155
14	3		Marzo	50,343	49,817	44,939	68,906	60,276	274,281
15	4	Aprile		57,981	56,959	53,489	48,491	40,292	257,212
16	5		Maggio	89,241	89,288	74,240	52,104	87,339	392,212
17	6	Giugno		80,589	64,243	85,398	63,587	55,197	349,014
18	7		Luglio	69,080	63,388	74,379	64,008	52,199	323,054
19	8	Agosto		59,837	74,832	68,408	74,187	57,489	334,753
20	9		Settembre	43,859	40,121	40,299	46,843	44,014	215,136
21	10	Ottobre		30,664	40,097	40,437	40,172	55,802	207,172
22	11		Novembre	26,460	55,355	48,706	36,857	49,737	217,115
23	12	Dicembre		38,942	35,843	18,772	42,441	24,815	160,813
24	13		Total	640,503	657,795	621,162	600,779	600,960	3,121,199

FIGURE 10-20 Something a little different: a two-row axis label from one text list.

- The data source for the chart is the range K11:Q23 in the *Data 1 and Basis* sheet. The unusual category axis label for the chart can be interpreted from Figure 10-20. It is easy to create this type of "offset" two-row structure, which is always an option if the text is longer than the width of the chart column, if it cannot or must not be wrapped, and if it should remain horizontal for the sake of legibility. The result is a little different—thus it is effective.

> **Note** The cells that appear to be empty in the range K12:L23 must contain blank characters. Otherwise, the entries in the second row will shift in the chart's axis label.

- The chart heading is a text field linked with the cell *rD1.Heading*.

- This map of Europe, in which the nations represented within the company have been highlighted, is available on the CD-ROM as the file *\Materials\Pictures\Europe03.tif*.

Profile Comparisons on the Radar Chart

The first time anyone sees a radar chart without its data series, they immediately think of a spider's web. So do these charts show what was the prey? Or do they plot the results of a managerial radar surveillance? Of course, they don't. The *data series* for this extremely helpful chart type appear as lines that have been closed to form shapes and/or molded areas. The term "profile chart" would be more appropriate because this is exactly what this chart produces best: easy-to-understand profiles and specific shapes that form a whole. "The chart clearly comprises comparatively similar shapes that differ in some regard," is an accurate description. You will immediately see why the radar chart is particularly good at any form of comparison and why it is my unrivaled favorite when it comes to comparative analyses for survey or measurement results.

> **On the Companion CD** Open the file *\Samples\1006_RadarComparison.xlsx* on the CD-ROM.

The *Focus 1* worksheet in the file *1006_RadarComparison* is designed for the *Full screen* presentation view and is protected without a password.

Allow me to set the scene: a beverages manufacturer has conducted sensory product testing several times and presented the results in a dynamic radar chart. This is part of a market analysis whose results will influence the company's new product range.

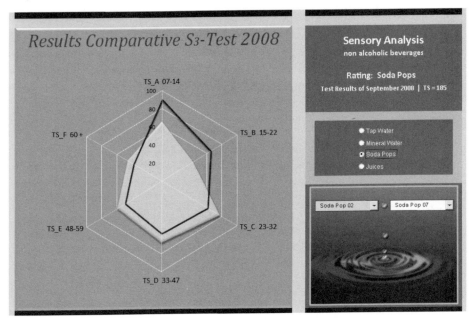

FIGURE 10-21 Whatever anyone tastes can be measured and compared using this chart.

First, you need to know how this model works. Note the following points with reference to Figure 10-21:

- You can use four *OptionButtons* to determine which test results you want to display: Tap Water, Mineral Water, Soda Pops, or Juices (the sensory rating of tap water is a benchmark for standardizing the testing modes).

- When you click an *OptionButton*, the selection lists for both underlying *ComboBoxes* are updated accordingly; in other words, their content changes. These lists, which are managed in parallel, enable you to make selections according to specific product groups and then compare, at product level, the data for each list entry against the data for another list entry. You can also remove either data series to display individual profiles.

- The double selection made in the *ComboBoxes* is combined to form comparison profiles within the chart. An area that belongs to the left ComboBox is compared against a shape with a blue outline. Each category in the radar chart has its own value axis. However, its scaling is shown only once and fixed in this example (*0, 100, 20*, which means that the testing subjects could award each drink a maximum of 100 points). The *data series* connect the six value axes. The closer a data series on a value axis approaches the outer edge of the radar chart, the better the product rating. The category abbreviations shown as *data labels* are age groups. For example, TS_C 23-32 stands for *Testing Subjects*, group C, aged between *23* and *32*. In short, the profiles show the popularity of each drink in each age group.

- The comparison shown in the figure, for example, clearly shows that Soda Pop 02 had half-decent to good results but it didn't prove to be very popular in the group *TS_B*. Soda Pop 07 received similar ratings in four groups (the same profile with slightly lower values), but was much more popular among children and young adults. In short: The profiles show which beverage is going down how well in which age group.

- The upper right corner of the sheet contains labels that were generated by formulas and indicate the product group currently being displayed, the number of participants, and the month in which the test took place.

Here's how to set up the worksheets:

The parameter sheet contains four editable lists that have alternating text. In other words, when you click an *OptionButton* in the focus sheet, the *ListFillRange* of the *ComboBoxes* is filled as required by the user.

The collated data, which has already been condensed and calculated according to the average and maximum values, is defined in the four *Data* ... worksheets.

The *Basis 1* sheet shows the entire chart basis (comprising formulas) whose structural components you already know from other rS1 models. Here, cell K7 contains the formula `="rD"&rL1.OptIndex&".Node"`. This allows you to correctly assume that the *Lists 1* sheet must contain an index entry that has something to do with the *OptionButtons*. Let's consider this in greater detail:

Unlike the *OptionButtons* for the form controls, the similar objects from the *ActiveX controls* group do not output any numbers here, but rather the values TRUE or FALSE, like the *CheckBox* and *ToggleButton*. However, formulas such as `="rD"&rL1.OptIndex&".Node"` require numbers. As already presented in another context, a text such as *rD1.Node, rD2.Node*, and so on, should be created dynamically. Therefore, you must first convert TRUE or FALSE into a number. The MATCH function converts the value in cell L7 (*rL1.OptIndex*) .

The `=MATCH(lookup_value,lookup_array,match_type)` function is equivalent to VLOOKUP. It does not provide cell content as results, but rather a position number. The position of `lookup_value` in `lookup_array` is determined here, whereby the latter is a one-column or one-row range. Consequently, you can use MATCH for providing number arguments required within other formulas.

Here, I use zero as the `match_type`. As a result, the function always returns the position of the first of possibly several values. This first value is the `lookup_value`, which ensures that the `lookup_array` elements do not have to be sorted alphanumerically.

Note the following points with reference to Figure 10-22:

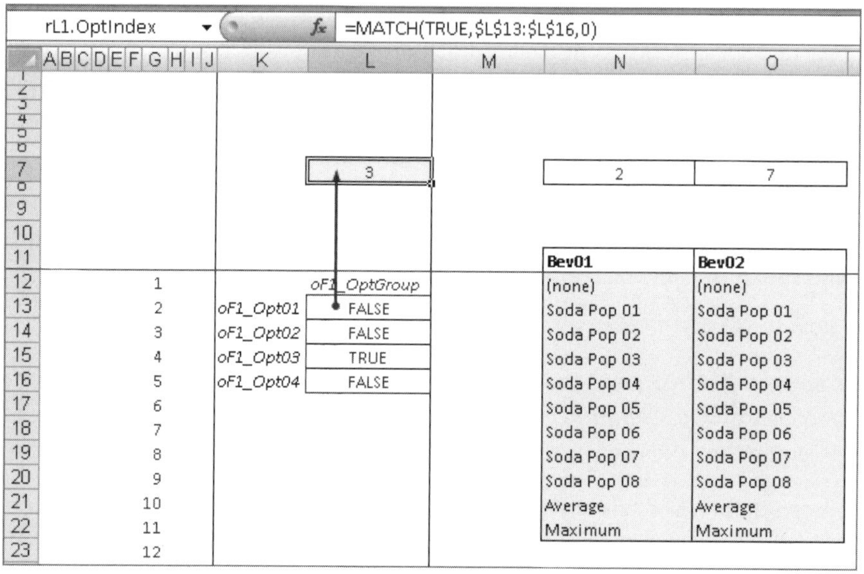

FIGURE 10-22 One number is determined from *TRUE* and *FALSE* in the *rL1.OptIndex* cell.

The formula =MATCH(TRUE,$L$13:$L$16,0) provides the position number for the cell that currently contains the value TRUE in the range L13:L16. It must be one of these cells. In a defined group of *OptionButtons* (additional information provided in the following paragraphs), only one cell returns the value TRUE and consequently all other cells return the value FALSE. Let's stick with our example: if you now click the *Soda Pops OptionButton* (the third button) in the *Focus 1* sheet, the following happens:

- The value in linked cell L15 (*rL1.Opt03Sel*) becomes TRUE and, at the same time, the values in cells L14, L13, and L12 become FALSE.

- As a result, the MATCH formula returns the value 3 in cell L7 (named *rL1.OptIndex*).

- Consequently, the *rD3.Node* reference text to be processed using INDIRECT is generated in cell K7 in the *Basis 1* sheet. As a result, the data from the *Data 3 ...* worksheet is now imported into the chart.

- Furthermore, the constants in the third list in the *Parameters 1* sheet become the *ListFillRanges* content for both *ComboBoxes*. This is ensured by the formulas in the ranges N12:N22 and O12:O22 in the *Lists 1* sheet. For example, the formula in cell N19:

    N19   =OFFSET(rP1.Node,$G19,rL1.OptIndex)

So when it comes to the dynamics of selection lists in *ComboBoxes*, there's nothing to it.

Let's return to the *Basis 1* sheet and the formula in cell L12, for example:

```
L12   =IF(rL1.Bev01Sel=0,"",
      OFFSET(INDIRECT($K$7),$G12,rL1.Bev01Sel))
```

If you clicked the first entry *(None)* in the *ComboBox*, the cell appears to be empty. Otherwise, the specific value is read from one of the data sheets. Instead of working with #N/A, I am using *empty text* here (as an exception) for such a function. However, I'm merely using it to show that in this case (not in all cases) it can also successfully suppress data series. However, this is neither systematic nor methodical.

In conclusion, I wish to briefly describe how to set up the controls in the *Focus 1* sheet.

If you have already worked with *CheckBoxes*, you will find it easy to set up *OptionButtons* because the options and properties are, for the most part, identical. However, note the following:

ActiveX controls of the OptionButtons category always occur in groups. To ensure that users can only ever select one of several similar elements, the group members must be "aware of each other" because only one of them can be assigned the value TRUE. This requirement is fulfilled by defining a group name that combines several *OptionButtons* to form one functional unit, irrespective of their formats or where and how they are positioned on the screen. The associated property is called *GroupName*. In our example, I used the group name *oF1_ OptGroup*. For informational purposes, this name is also shown in cell L11 in the *Lists 1* sheet. Here, it appears as a heading for those four cells used to process the user's selection.

The appearance of both *ComboBoxes* was approximated to match those of the data series in the chart, so that these controls have a similar "legend-like" appearance.

- The background color is determined using the *BackColor* property.

- You must use the *BorderColor* property to determine the border color of a *ComboBox*. This setting, in turn, only becomes effective if you also set the *BorderStyle* property to *fmBorderStyleSingle*.

On the Companion CD   The "water drop" image is stored on the CD-ROM under *\Materials\ Pictures\Drop.tif.*

Chapter 11
Fulfilling Special Requirements

The previous 10 chapters have shown you what the new version of Excel has to offer in terms of creating, designing, and improving the appearance of charts. Moreover, you have been introduced to many models and strategies that enable you to redefine the performance limitations of Excel spreadsheets without ever having to leave the program's "normal" working environment. As a result, you can perform common day-to-day tasks and solve problems in a dynamic, aesthetically sophisticated format that will win over its audience, without having to immerse yourself in complex calculation structures or acquire any programming knowledge. If you are successful with this format and more successful each time you use it, you will become a recidivist—sure enough. One aspect is particularly important here: the fact that it is *your* solution. *You* have done something clever, maybe even something extraordinary, and you didn't need any outside help!

In addition to the standard tasks associated with presenting numbers, which we have now discussed at adequate length, there are numerous special cases in which unusual questions need specific answers. This is exactly where Excel demonstrates its special strengths through its exceptional collection of solutions combined with useable options. In short—and this is by no means an exaggeration—"Excel can provide a solution for any problem that involves numbers." This has been the case for years and is by no means a special feature of Excel 2007. However, the software's new design options are especially well suited to presenting every product of your creativity in an attractive format.

In this chapter, I wish to discuss some "miscellaneous" cases that fulfill specific display requirements. Such cases represent hundreds of examples and variants (and even variants of variants). While they may seem like nothing special, remember that it is often something very trivial that complicates the simple and straightforward approach to a satisfying result. I'm sure this rings true for you. With Excel, finding another way or adopting another approach will often enable you to find the solution.

Cumulation with Controls

The OFFSET function I am so fond of achieves a little more than I've been able to show in this book so far.

The requirement: there is an array of 12 months and three related cost types (production costs are divided into material costs, personnel costs, and delivery/installation costs). Your task is to create a user-friendly solution that can create cumulative totals in this array, simultaneously in both axes. You need the following:

- Summaries of any contiguous chain of months; that is, not only the usual January to June and January to October, but also periods such as February to August or May to September, and so on.

- At the same time, a summary of costs in accordance with the following model:

  ☐ Material costs only

  ☐ Material costs plus personnel costs

  ☐ All three costs types together

You want to view and compare the results in a column chart; in other words, the total costs in relation to the costs portions selected by the user.

To cope with this basic requirement (custom, controllable, cumulative totaling), you need no more than three list controls and just one simple uncomplicated formula.

> **On the Companion CD** Open the file \Samples\1101_Cumulative.xlsx on the CD-ROM.

For this example, the organizational requirements of the rS1.Method are set aside once again. Here, we are solely concerned with the structure and contents of the solution components, which are compiled here in one worksheet. Note the following points with reference to Figure 11-1:

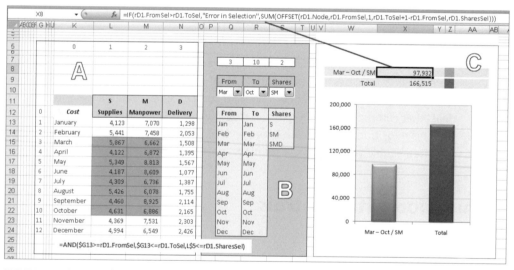

FIGURE 11-1 Any cumulations with *OFFSET*

- Range *A*: The four-column list contains the data to be calculated; its "neat and tidy" model would correspond to the *Data 1* worksheet.

- Range *B*: These structures and contents belong to the controls whose definition ranges usually would be part of the *Lists 1* worksheet.

- Range *C*: That's the focus of this solution, the result that is calculated and labeled in accordance with the user's specifications, and the associated column chart.

Essentially, you're already familiar with all of the above. The only thing that may require additional explanations are the two cells W8 and X8. Before we take a closer look at these cells, you should make sure that you are clear about the range names that have been assigned and the location of the cells concerned. The following cells are particularly important: *rD1.FromSel*, *rD1.ToSel*, and *rD1.SharesSel*. The click-results for the controls are put out to these cells.

> **Note** If you want to control and select cells W8 and X8, you have to use the arrow buttons on the keyboard; the cells are behind the transparent chart.

Let's take a closer look:

- You establish a selection combination in the three drop-down lists: month *from*, month *to*, summary of the share of costs. If the *from* month is after the *to* month, cell X8 displays the text *Error in Selection* in red. When you select a period correctly, even if it is a period of just one month, the total result is displayed in black. *Conditional formatting*, whose rule =ISTEXT($X$8) checks whether the cell contains text, changes the font color. If true the specified black font is colored red.

- The user selection is displayed in cell W8 as a piece of text that is also a category axis label in the chart.

- The chart is created and the range whose cells (indirectly) form the green chart column is selected in the data table and colored accordingly.

How is the numbers basis for the green chart columns created? Let's take a look at the calculation in cell X8 and therefore at the offset function that I regard so highly and frequently use, now in all its glory: =OFFSET(reference,rows,cols,height,width) can now use all five of its arguments here.

```
X8   =IF(rD1.FromSel>rD1.ToSel,"Error in Selection",
     SUM(OFFSET(rD1.Node,rD1.FromSel,1,
     rD1.ToSel+1-rD1.FromSel,
     rD1.SharesSel
```

The first part of this formula is used to generate an error message (optional). The value for the green chart column is calculated in the second part of the formula. The offset function, whose individual components will be described shortly, creates an array. This array contains all of the values in a cell range that is located in a particular place, is a certain number of rows high, and is a certain number of columns wide. The offset function is now also integrated into a sum formula that, for its part, adds the individual values of the array that we have just discussed.

> **Note** =SUM({5867,6662;4122,6872;5349,8813;4187,8609;and so on...})
>
> This part of the formula shows what Excel does in the background.

How does OFFSET create this array? Let's take a look at the following comparison. The relevant part of the formula is on the left and the syntax for comparison purposes is on the right:

```
OFFSET(                          =OFFSET(
rD1.Node,                        reference,
rD1.FromSel,                     rows,
1,                               cols,
rD1.ToSel+1-rD1.FromSel,         height,
rD1.SharesSel)                   width)
```

Let's start with a node in cell K12 whose row corresponds to the value *rD1.FromSel* (therefore determining the start month). Then move one column to the right. This is now the uppermost left cell in the cell range whose height and width are yet to be determined. Both steps are achieved with a mouse click. Using the values in our example:

- rD1.ToSel+1-rD1.FromSel, therefore 10+1-3. Therefore, the array range is eight rows high.

- rD1.SharesSel, therefore 2. The array range is therefore two columns wide.

The individual values in the cell range L15:M22 become array elements and therefore added by the formula. To clearly identify this range within the model, conditional formatting also applies a color to the range currently being totaled (see Figure 11-2):

		L13		f_x	4123								
	ÆCDEF G HIJ	K	L	M	N	O P	Q	R	S	T
5		0	1	2	3					
7							3	10	2	
8										
9			=AND($G13>=rD1.FromSel,$G13<=rD1.ToSel,L$5<=rD1.SharesSel)						
10							Mar ▼	Oct ▼	SM ▼	
11			**S**	**M**	**D**					
12	0	*Cost*	Supplies	Manpower	Delivery		From	To	Shares	
13	1	January	4,123	7,070	1,298		Jan	Jan	S	
14	2	February	5,441	7,458	2,053		Feb	Feb	SM	
15	3	March	5,867	6,662	1,508		Mar	Mar	SMD	
16	4	April	4,122	6,872	1,395		Apr	Apr		
17	5	May	5,349	8,813	1,567		May	May		
18	6	June	4,187	8,609	1,077		Jun	Jun		
19	7	July	4,309	6,736	1,387		Jul	Jul		
20	8	August	5,426	6,078	1,755		Aug	Aug		
21	9	September	4,460	8,925	2,114		Sep	Sep		
22	10	October	4,631	6,886	2,165		Oct	Oct		
23	11	November	4,369	7,531	2,303		Nov	Nov		
24	12	December	4,994	6,549	2,426		Dec	Dec		

FIGURE 11-2 Conditional formatting is based on a three-part *AND* rule.

```
Rule   =AND($G13>=rD1.FromSel,$G13<=rD1.ToSel,L$5<=rD1.SharesSel)
```

For each cell, the threepart AND formula in the formatting rule checks the match or non-match of row-specific and column-specific reference values from auxiliary column G and auxiliary row 5 with the output values of the three controls.

Now I just need to explain how Excel generates the label in cell W8. This is achieved by a concatenation of three INDEX formulas.

```
W8     =INDEX(rD1.FromList,rD1.FromSel,1)&" - "
       &INDEX(rD1.ToList,rD1.ToSel,1)&" / "
       &INDEX(rD1.SharesList,rD1.SharesSel,1)
```

Bubble Charts for Customer Analysis

At the end of Chapter 10, "Presentation Solutions That Pack a Punch," you may have longed for a task that would challenge advanced users and ambitious readers. Not to worry: this chapter contains two such tasks. The first is the bubble chart presented here. Its structure and formatting are only described in brief and are available for you to experiment with later.

However, immediately after learning about the structure requirements, you may wish to close this book for a while and experiment with a different model that fulfills the following specifications. If so, the CD-ROM contains the file \Samples\1102A_Data_Customers_ABC.xlsx, which contains only the model's source data.

The requirements for this special case are as follows:

- Using a bubble chart, create a user-friendly presentation solution that represents the interdependencies between grouped customer numbers, the absolute revenue, and the relative revenue (a certain number of customers in category X generates a certain amount of revenue in dollars and accounts for a certain percentage of the overall revenue).

- For this purpose, the customers are divided into categories that represent their lines of business. In other words, they are classified according to A, B, C, and D. This classification primarily complies with the "revenue-per-customer" characteristic. However, the source data does not comprise four, but rather six groups, which in turn are based on the responsibilities of management (M1 to M6, column L in the data source). Consequently, some groups have identical classifications. This problem is aggravated by an additional three different classification variants; therefore, an alternating assignment from groups to categories involves:

  ❑ The weakest differentiation between A and B (column Q in the data source). The resulting chart shows two bubbles.

❑   A medium differentiation between A, B, and C (column R in the data source). The chart shows three bubbles.

❑   The strongest differentiation between A, B, C, and D (column S in the data source). The chart shows four bubbles.

As a result, the data source cannot directly be the chart source. Instead, you need a summarized basis.

■   In the presentation chart, a control should be used to determine which of the three differentiation variants is to be displayed. However, this all has to take place in just one chart. Here, the equally feasible solution of using three charts in three worksheets and hyperlinks (see Chapter 12, "More Than Numbers") that enable you to toggle between each chart is not wanted.

Various different options are available to satisfy such requirements. This is almost always the case when you use Excel. I'll present some of these options in the following paragraphs.

On the Companion CD Open the file \Samples\1102_Customers_ABC.xlsx on the CD-ROM.

The *Focus 1* worksheet in the file *1102_Customers_ABC.xlsx* is designed for the *Full screen* presentation view and is protected without a password.

The bubble chart is an enhanced XY (Scatter) chart with the additional option of representing not only the X and Y values in each data point but also a third value. The model presented here is based on three data ranges:

■   The vertical position of a bubble is derived from the share of sales as a percentage. The higher, the better.

■   The horizontal position of a bubble is derived from the number of customers that it represents. The farther to the right the bubble is, the greater the number of customers. Moreover, the farther to the right the bubble is, the less favorable the situation may be, given that a large number of customers with a low "revenue per customer" means a greater effort and a low return.

■   The bubble's volume is derived from the absolute value for the revenue. The greater the volume, the higher this value.

In summary (and solely in relation to this chart): high, left, and large = positive; low, right, and small = negative.

The upper right section of the chart contains a partially transparent label field. You can use the *SpinButton* located there to switch, in three steps, between the differentiation variants that we have already described. This results in the following:

■   The bubbles change in terms of number, size, and position.

- The letters in the label field adapt to the user selection and remain centered at the diaphanous upper right corner of the chart's plot area. Therefore, this string is not centered in its container; the effect is achieved by other means.

- The bubbles show labels whose values change depending on the display variant.

 Note A classifying ABC bubble label is not required here. This is, first and foremost, a presentation solution. Therefore, it will be explained verbally. Second, in this case the positions, numerical values, and colorings are sufficiently clear to quickly identify which element is to be arranged into which category. Third, outside the chart, there is a rotated *ABC Analysis* label that contains the bubble colors (with the exception of D).

FIGURE 11-3 You can decide: *AB*, *ABC*, or *ABCD*.

In particular, note the scaling and positioning of the axes here (and in other bubble charts). Because of the revenue volume (bubble volume) when the number of customers is low (positioned to the left) in this example, the vertical axis cannot intersect at zero and the horizontal axis must have a minus range even though it is not possible to have a negative number of customers. Otherwise, however, the large bubble on the left would collide with the vertical axis or would only be partially visible. So why not simply place the vertical value axis on the right-hand side? This is out of the question here, especially because the "good" bubbles must remain visually close to the percentage scales in order to make their high proportionality obvious.

The horizontal axis ranges from *minus 5,000* to *plus 20,000*. In the axis label, however, you can only read *20 k* at the end of the axis (on the right). This results from a custom number format.

The following are some notes and illustrations in relation to the technical and structural aspects of the other sheets in this workbook. As usual, familiarize yourself with the range names and their locations before taking a closer look.

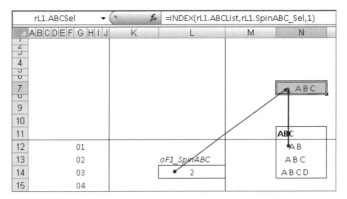

FIGURE 11-4 Something a little different: a *SpinButton* selects the heading.

The *Lists 1* sheet represents an atypical use of the sheet's structures (see Figure 11-4). The output value of the SpinButton is used in N7 to generate a string that, for its part, becomes the content of the linked label field in the *Focus 1* sheet.

	J12			fx	=INDEX(rD1.GroupParameters,$G12,rL1.SpinABC_Sel)							
	ABCDEF G HI J	K	L	M	N	O	P	Q	R	S		
5		0	1	2	3	4	5	6	7	8	9	

7 *Customers*

		0	Groups	Responsible	Revenue	Share of Sales	Customer Count	REV/Customer	ABC_1	ABC_2	ABC_3
11		0							ABC_1	ABC_2	ABC_3
12	•1	A	Group 1	M1	2,355,816	33.61 %	20	117,791	A	A	A
13		2	B	Group 2	M2	1,455,004	20.76 %	112	12,991	A	B	B
14		3	C	Group 3	M3	424,788	6.06 %	11,568	37	B	C	D
15		4	A	Group 4	M4	1,475,980	21.06 %	36	40,999	A	A	A
16		5	B	Group 5	M5	978,212	13.96 %	925	1,058	B	B	C
17		6	C	Group 6	M6	318,673	4.55 %	1,566	203	B	C	D
18		7			7,008,473	100	14,227				
19		8									

FIGURE 11-5 Three custom ABC classifications available for selection

The *Data 1* sheet (see Figure 11-5) contains the source data and parameters. Furthermore:

- In column J appear the classifications (stored in columns Q to S) that the user has selected via SpinButton.

- The range M11:017 is the indirect data source for this chart. (The direct source is in the *Basis 1* sheet).

- The sorting status of the data source is irrelevant. It is currently the responsibility of management (column L).

- The number of groups (column K) is also insignificant in such a model because the summary required in the chart basis automatically takes place at the higher *Category* (ABC) level. Therefore, it could also be 10 or 100 groups.

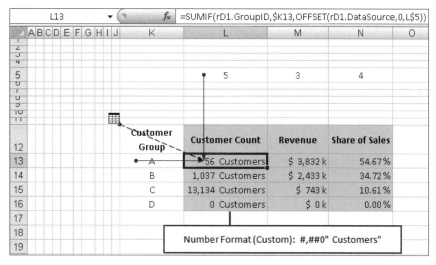

FIGURE 11-6 The chart basis compresses the source data.

In the *Basis 1* sheet (see Figure 11-6), the chart's data source is created by using compressing SUMIF formulas. This is unusual for two reasons: the formulas work in two different worksheets and use a variable totaling range.

=SUMIF(range,criteria,sum_range) is the syntax already known for this function. Let's compare this with the following formula:

```
L13    =SUMIF(rD1.GroupID,$K13,
         OFFSET(rD1.DataSource,0,L$5))
```

Here, the sum_range argument is generated by an OFFSET formula that works within the aforementioned *rD1.DataSource* range (J12:S17 in the *Data 1* sheet).

The number format used in column L, #,##0" Customers", is required because the cell content is used to create the data point (the bubble). It therefore must be a number and must deliver the *data label* for this bubble (a number with text).

XY (Scatter) Charts for Publication, Presentation, and Analysis

The *XY (Scatter) chart* is frequently used in scientific publications. However, it is a pity that it is rarely used there as a presentation variant when it could be used that way as well as all the other chart types that have played significant roles in this book.

> **On the Companion CD**   Open the file *\Samples\1103_ScatterXY.xlsx* on the CD-ROM.

If you already work with scatter charts (also known as scatter diagrams and scatter plots), you won't need any more information about how or why to create them. However, you may be interested to learn how you can design more appealing images and make them dynamic. I will use simple overviews from the medical field to discuss both chosen topics. Even if some readers possibly would not feel very comfortable with using such data, it can be transferred to hundreds of other themes in different fields. We are not merely concerned with the contents, but also with the techniques applied when working with such types of charts.

Formatting for Publication

The example in the *Publication 1* worksheet is designed for a print publication. Here, the aesthetically satisfying format is unfortunately secondary to its space-saving design. The sample object shown here represents an attempt to find a justifiable compromise in this conflict. Its components are as follows:

- A compact format without unduly "squashing" those elements that convey information
- Good, identifiable, properly separated data points and easy-to-read labels
- All of these are sufficiently identifiable in a small print layout, both in a color version and grayscale printed version of a similarly good display quality

The chart reports the sample sizes (number of diseases) among men and women, broken down into six age-dependent classes (A to F). Each class, in turn, comprises two age groups.

Note the following:

- The range E4:G16, which has a blue border, is the chart's data range.
- The values in column E are the average ages in each group. Formulas are used to produce these averages. This supports the aligment of the associated data points within the class divisions of the chart both evenly and clearly

- Experiment by entering the value *26* in cell G6 to produce equal values here for men and women. Now, the associated markers overlap each other. However, both are identifiable because the circle marker has a background color and the X marker does not.

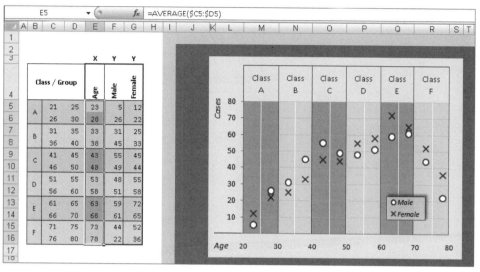

FIGURE 11-7 A compromise—but not out of "laziness"

- The horizontal value axis has a fixed scaling of *20, 80, 10, 5*. It is important to specify the minor unit 5, so that the white vertical lines (minor gridlines) are positioned where required. In this example, note that the major vertical gridlines in the chart are not colored (the table border divides the classes here) while the white minor gridlines subtly divide each of the six classes into two age groups.

- The data shown in columns F and G are constants. The chart is to be published with these values and the data point positions will no longer change. Therefore, as a space-saving measure, it is possible (and completely acceptable) for you to place the legend within the plot area. In Excel 2007, you can easily shadow the legend or make it partially transparent, so the legend is not particularly distracting where it is positioned but is nevertheless immediately discernible as a "detached" element.

Tip In this model, the table ranges in the background and the chart elements in the foreground also give the formal appearance of the overall image. It is easier to examine the model asking "What belongs where?" if you temporarily move the chart from its current position to somewhere else in the worksheet.

Variable Analysis with Scatterplots

The *Scatterplot 2* worksheet in the *1103_ScatterXY.xlsx* workbook contains a half-finished solution. As yet, no one has decided whether this chart will be printed only or also will be used
for presentation purposes.

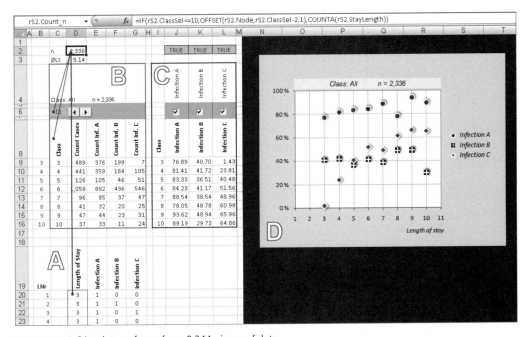

FIGURE 11-8 24 points or fewer from 9,344 pieces of data

With reference to Figure 11-8, let me provide an overview before explaining the composition
of the formulas used.

- Range *A*: The master data in the range D19:G2355 contains data collated from a total
  of 2,336 hospital patients. It concerns interdependencies between the length of stay
  (in days) and the detection of possible infections (three different types) attributable to
  long stays in hospital. In the survey conducted, patients spent three to 10 days in hospital. This length of stay is also the class division here. The master data is calculated at the
  top of the worksheet in two stages and then shown in the chart.

- Range *B*: The primary spreadsheet in the range C4:G16 (surrounded by a green border)
  summarizes the absolute values for the master data. A *SpinButton* makes this table dynamic. If the output value for the control is 11 in the cell *rS2.ClassSel* (C6), all of the class
  numbers are available in column C. Otherwise, only one is available while the others are
  set to zero. Additional calculation results are shown only in the row whose class number
  is not zero. As mentioned earlier, this is a half-finished solution. If this solution were to
  be used in a presentation, the *SpinButton* would not be a very effective control for this

purpose and would be replaced with a *ComboBox* (and the possibility of having a specific class selection).

A formula in C4 composes the text for the chart heading: the class that is set and the associated number of patients.

- Range *C*: The secondary spreadsheet (surrounded by a blue border) in the range I4:L16 converts the absolute values of the primary spreadsheet into a percentage distribution. At the same time, the formulas respond to the output values of the three column-specific *CheckBoxes*. The result is either a number, which is then shown in the chart as a data point, or the error value #N/A. This approach is preferable because it ensures that the chart contains only those values that the user wants to see there. The formulas in J8:L8 are created in such a way that they display or suppress the legend label for the chart and respond to the activation or deactivation of each *CheckBox*. The linked cells for the three controls are located in row 2.

- Range *D*: Depending on the number of points, differentiation levels, and chart dimensions, a XY (Scatter) chart can very quickly become confusing and unclear. While this might be acceptable for a printed publication sometimes (if the reader wants to or needs to, he or she will take the time to differentiate between the data points), it is unusable for a presentation. Therefore, the sample solution presented here facilitates an extremely versatile and dynamic presentation: from viewing just one data point (or no points at all) in several variations to viewing all of the data points. The controls determine the content of the chart, as follows:

  - You can use the *SpinButton* to decide which class is shown (one, a select few, or all).

  - You can use the *CheckBoxes* to select which of the three value groups (infection types) are drawn on the vertical value axis (Y).

  - Because you can use a combination of both, this ensures a clearly arranged presentation in every respect (and in different view orientations).

Let's now discuss the most important formulas in the model. Familiarize yourself with the range names and their positions before taking a closer look.

As always, let's look at the formula and then share a brief explanation. The formula:

```
D2    =IF(rS2.ClassSel<=10,
      OFFSET(rS2.Node,rS2.ClassSel-2,1),
      COUNTA(rS2.StayLength))
```

Either a number is read from the primary spreadsheet or the total number is calculated from the range *rS2.L_StayLength* (see also Figure 11-8) as follows:

```
C4    ="Class: "&IF(rS2.ClassSel<11,
      rS2.ClassSel&"              n = "&TEXT(rS2.Count_n,"#,##0"),
      "All             n = "&TEXT(rS2.Count_n,"#,##0"))
```

At first glance, the formula for putting together the chart heading appears to be rather confusing and unclear. However, this is merely due to the many spaces used to separate the two sections of text. The background for this structure is as follows: the chart heading is a text field linked with C4 whose link can reference to only one cell.

```
C9    =IF(OR(rS2.ClassSel=$B9,rS2.ClassSel=11),$B9,0)
```

Based on the setting for the SpinButton, either the reference value is read from the auxiliary column B or the value is zero. The value generated here is crucial for other formulas in the relevant row:

```
D9    =COUNTIF(rS2.StayLength,$C9)
E9    =SUMIF(rS2.StayLength,$C9,rS2.InfectionA)
F9    =SUMIF(rS2.StayLength,$C9,rS2.InfectionB)
G9    =SUMIF(rS2.StayLength,$C9,rS2.InfectionC)
```

If C9 has the value zero, which is not a class characteristic, the results are also zero.

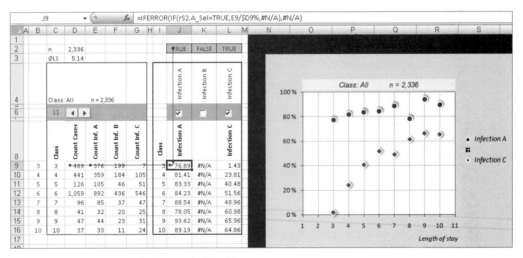

FIGURE 11-9 Points are switched on and off in this way.

The formulas in the range J9:L16 calculate the percentage values required in the chart.

Experienced users of earlier versions of Excel may find the formula introduced in Figure 11-9

```
J9    =IFERROR(IF(rS2.A_Sel=TRUE,E9/$D9%,#N/A),#N/A)
```

quite unusual and also "redundant." However, I have used it because it enables me to present a new and very useful feature in Excel 2007:

A formula that has been reduced to `=IF(rS2.A_Sel=TRUE,E9/$D9%,#N/A)` could deliver three results:

1. The result from `E9/$D9%`

2. The error value `#DIV/0!` if the value in E9 is zero (which can frequently be the case in this model)

3. The error value `#N/A` if the value in `rS2.A_Sel` is FALSE.

However, you want only two options: either 1) the division result as a number, or 3) #N/A. Furthermore, if a division by zero produces the error value #DIV/0!, you also want the formula result to be #N/A. Therefore, it is necessary to buffer the error here. For this purpose, we now have the new function `IFERROR`.

The function `=IFERROR(value,value_if_error)` uses `value_if_error` to produce a result that you have specified if the `value` argument (a formula used by you) produces an error. If your formula does not produce an error, the result of your formula is output.

In other words,

- The `value` argument represents a formula whose result is checked for an error. If there is no error, the formula result is shown. The following error types are evaluated: `#N/A`, `#VALUE!`, `#REF!`, `#DIV/0!`, `#NUM!`, `#NAME?` or `#NULL!`.

- `value_if_error` is a custom value that would be shown as the result if the `value` argument (the formula that has been checked) were to produce an error.

Let's take a look at a sample overview, with reference to Figure 11-10.

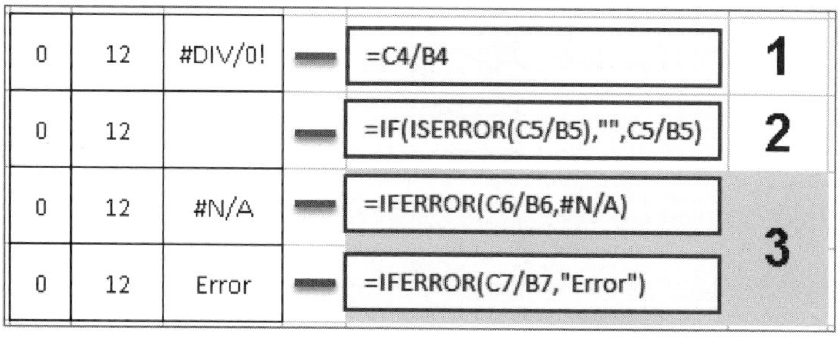

0	12	#DIV/0!	▬	=C4/B4	**1**
0	12		▬	=IF(ISERROR(C5/B5),"",C5/B5)	**2**
0	12	#N/A	▬	=IFERROR(C6/B6,#N/A)	**3**
0	12	Error	▬	=IFERROR(C7/B7,"Error")	

FIGURE 11-10 How it would be, how it was, and how it is now

1. The result of a division by zero is shown as the error #DIV/0!. This error frequently appears in many models. If, for example, the model is a presentation model, the error must be buffered to suppress it.

2. Previously, you could do this form of error buffering by executing the formula within an IF formula twice: if an error occurred during an initial check, it had to be buffered; if not, the formula was to execute. This may not seem to be a significant problem. However, if it had been necessary for you to use complex formulas, containing hundreds of characters, to buffer an error in this way, such formulas would have quickly become unclear and possibly rather tight. In such cases, the previous limit of 1,024 characters per formula was occasionally a very critical upper limit that forced you to find an alternative solution. It is good that you can now "go wild" and use up to 8,192 characters per formula, but you do not necessarily have to, at least not for error buffering.

3. The IFERROR function enables you to write the "checking" formula only once. In the second part, you define the value (or piece of information) that is to be displayed as the result if an error occurs.

Note In Excel 2007, you can use up to 8,192 characters per formula and up to 32,767 characters for other text content. This should be more than adequate when you consider that one page in this book (with no illustrations) contains approximately 2,500 characters.

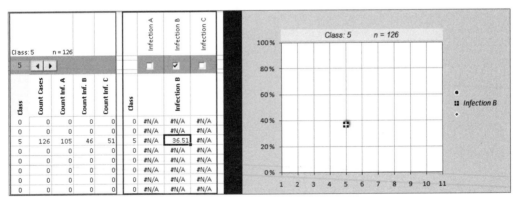

FIGURE 11-11 Only one data point is shown from a possible 24.

Figure 11-11 shows you what can remain from the possible 24 data points if you use the controls to make the maximum reduction (apart from displaying nothing at all). All kinds of variants can then be used to fully display the possible data points. Try it out yourself.

Box-and-Whisker Plot (Boxplot)

On the Companion CD Open the file \Samples\1104_Boxplot.xlsx on the CD-ROM.

Even though you may initially find the boxplot design strange, it is excellent for conveying lots of information about data quality at a glance. Please read the following descriptions with reference to Figure 11-12.

Note The box-and-whisker diagram or plot is generally known as a "boxplot" (*whisker* refers to a cat's whiskers).

In Excel, this chart type is a custom, modified line chart. It comprises five data series that display the following chart elements (from top to bottom and from bottom to top): *the marker for a data point, part of a high-low line, up/down bar with a marker inside, part of a high-low line, a marker.* This may sound complicated but it is created in no time at all.

However, before I provide an accurate description of the chart and its technical background, I must first explain some functions and terms.

You can use a box and whisker plot to indicate the distribution and quality of collated data. You therefore assess structures and/or portions of data that were collated as sample data or measured in test runs, for example. A variety of Excel functions or terms (optional, sometimes interchangeable, and used in different combinations) are used for such analyses.

The sample descriptions provided in the following paragraphs assume that a fictitious table range (in an array) $B$10:$B$209 contains 200 specific values for analysis.

- The *average*, determined using the formula =AVERAGE($B$10:$B$209), is the arithmetic mean of the array in accordance with the model *sum* divided by *number*.

- The *median*, determined using the formula =MEDIAN($B$10:$B$209), lies in the middle of the array. One half of the numbers has values lower than the median while the other half has values higher than the median.

- The *mode*, determined using the formula =MODE($B$10:$B$209), is the value that occurs most frequently in the array.

- The *percentile* (often also known as the *quantile*), as the function =PERCENTILE(array,k), delivers a value that is smaller than or equal to the k percentage in the array. An *80 % percentile*, for example, would be determined using the formula =PERCENTILE($B$10:$B$209,0.8).

- The *quartile*, which is determined using the function =QUARTILE(array,quart), is a special *"quarter percentile"*. In a frequency distribution, a distinction is made between three quartiles:

  ❑ *Quartile 1 = 25% percentile* or *lower quartile*,
    formula: =QUARTILE($B$10:$B$209,1).

  ❑ *Quartile 2 = 50% percentile* or *median quartile*,
    formula: =QUARTILE($B$10:$B$209,2). Quartile 2 is the *median*.

  ❑ *Quartile 3 = 75% percentile* or *upper quartile*,
    formula: =QUARTILE($B$10:$B$209,3).

  In such formulas, Excel also accepts 0, which corresponds to the MIN function, and 4, which corresponds to the MAX function, for the quart argument.

The following table below provides an overview. Here, the two or three formulas in each row produces identical results.

No.	Quartile	Percentile	Other
1	=QUARTILE ($B$10:$B$209,0)	=PERCENTILE ($B$10:$B$209,0)	=MIN($B$10:$B$209)
2	=QUARTILE ($B$10:$B$209,1)	=PERCENTILE ($B$10:$B$209,0.25)	
3	=QUARTILE ($B$10:$B$209,2)	=PERCENTILE ($B$10:$B$209,0.5)	=MEDIAN($B$10:$B$209)
4	=QUARTILE ($B$10:$B$209,3)	=PERCENTILE ($B$10:$B$209,0.75)	
5	=QUARTILE ($B$10:$B$209,4)	=PERCENTILE ($B$10:$B$209,1)	=MAX($B$10:$B$209)

Let's take a look at how boxplots are displayed in Excel. Note the following points with reference to Figure 11-12.

The entire image shows the scope of data for a value range from minimum to maximum. In between, there is a "box" that ranges from *quartile 1* to *quartile 3*, thus representing half of the entire value range. This range is also known as the interquartile range. The *median* lies within the box. The two *whiskers* are lines drawn downwards from *quartile 1* to the *minimum* and upwards from *quartile 3* to the *maximum*.

The size of the interquartile range (the box), the position of the median within the box, and the relative length of the *whiskers* (both relative to the box and relative to each other) clarify the shape of a value distribution. If you display the entire number series from 1 to 100 in the boxplot, its shape is completely symmetrical. (Depending on the material and purpose, this can be a quality characteristic of a figure, but does not have to be.) The image to the right of the illustration corresponds to such an equal distribution. Naturally, survey results or measurement series data almost always have an asymmetrical distribution. The boxplot indicates the type and scope of this asymmetry. This allows observers to make their own conclusions in relation to the usability of the data in a particular analysis, for example.

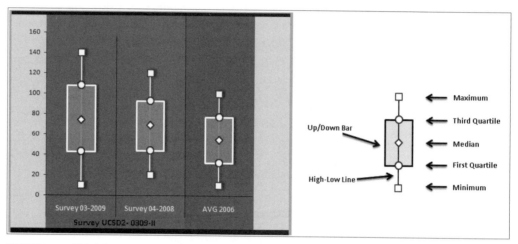

FIGURE 11-12 This is how to make symmetrical or asymmetrical value distributions visible.

In the sample file, you can press **F9** repeatedly to generate new data distributions and assess these in the *Focus 1* sheet, where a qualitative comparison of the survey data is simulated. The two presentations for March 2009 and April 2008 are dynamic and adjust to changes in their databases. The dynamic part of the chart is based, indirectly, on two arrays, each of which has 777 individual values in the *Data 1 and Basis* sheet. The third static element simulates the comparison with historical reference values.

Charts of this type are created quickly. Activate the *Data 1 and Basis* worksheet. Figure 11-13 also highlights everything you need to remember about the chart basis.

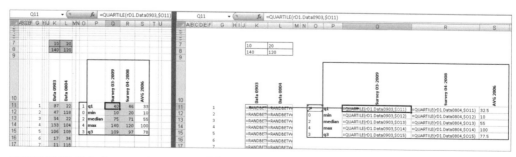

FIGURE 11-13 Note the correct sequence of the quartile formulas

■ Columns K and L each contain 777 pieces of data that have been generated with RANDBETWEEN and can be changed by pressing **F9**, and whose value range you can influence in cells K7:K8 or L7:L8 by entering threshold values.

■ The chart is drawn from the range P10:S15. The specifications defined in column O are read from the quartile formulas in columns Q and R. The constants in column S represent the strongly symmetrical results of a reference study. Tip: temporarily change certain values in these yellow-colored cells so that you can assess the effects of such changes on the associated boxplot.

■ Figure 11-13 contains a results view on the left and the corresponding formula view on the right. All of the data is determined using the QUARTILE function. Alternatively, I could have also used:

   ❏ The MIN function in row 12

   ❏ The MEDIAN function in row 13

   ❏ The MAX function in row 14

To enable you to create a boxplot from the line chart, you must not establish a logical row sequence; that is, according to a number sequence. Instead, you must do it in such a way as shown in the worksheet or illustration; that is, from top to bottom *quartile 1, quartile 0 (minimum), quartile 2 (median), quartile 4 (maximum)*, and *quartile 3*.

Once you have made these specifications, you are just a few steps away from creating the chart:

1. Select the range P10:S15 and create a *Line with Markers chart*.

2. Open the *Select Data Source* dialog box and click the *Switch Row/Column* button. Your line chart now has five data series, each with three data points. The legend contains the descriptions from column P.

3. Select the command *Chart Tools/Layout/Analysis* and insert a *high-low line* and an *up/down bar.*

4. Format one *data series* after another, removing the line view and assigning shapes and colors of your choice to the remaining data points.

5. Format the high-low lines (the *whiskers*) and the up/down bars (the box).

> **Note** With steps 4 and 5, as long as the data series and their markers are fully or partially behind the up/down bars and are formatted with visible lines, these markers are covered by the color fills of the up/down bars (unless you make these color fills transparent). However, as soon as you remove the line formatting (*Line Color/No line*), the markers appear in the foreground. Because Excel 2007 permits partially transparent colors, various different interesting design effects are now possible.
>
> With regard to the *Focus 1* worksheet: in this example, I once again worked with a transparent chart that uses table structures for both background and ambient formatting.

Costing Scenario

In terms of its structures, the last example for numbers-based charts in this book is another tricky exercise. With it, I renew my invitation—regrettably for the last time in this book—to ambitious readers and advanced users of Excel to conduct their own research.

Furthermore, this case concerns some very special requirements. It involves a model that is used to perform costing-based checks on a range of support activities and can be applied to other scenarios. The company's support activities continuously maintain very expensive and complex production machines used by customers. From time to time, the activity provider uses this Excel module to determine whether the activity quota and prices agreed on with each customer correspond to the number of activities actually needed or whether there is good reason to make other agreements.

In order to be able to clarify this special case, I must explain how the support activities in a customer-specific combined costing are classified and paid:

■ The support activities are recorded and billed, within a defined activity period, as activity units (*AU*). The prices for support activities are divided into basic units (*AU BASIC*) and additional units (*AU PLUS*). A fixed price of $8 or $12 is charged for each basic unit. The type and number of machines used by the customer are charged individually for each additional unit. These individual prices range from $7 to $14.

■ For each of 10 activity periods, the customer agrees to fixed activity quotas that are billed according to *AU BASIC*. Even if these quotas are not required during a period, the customer must still pay for them. If they are exceeded, this excess is billed according to *AU PLUS*.

■ The model is very complex, but gladly accepted by both parties. It provides a certain basic security for the activity provider as well as a sense of authority. After an activity period is over, the customer, together with the provider, can check the actual support activity profile as well as the costs incurred and determine whether changing the activity quotas to *AU BASIC* would make more financial sense and therefore should be agreed upon for the next activity period. The Excel model was created for checks of this type.

 On the Companion CD Open the file \Samples\1105_SupportCheck.xlsx on the CD-ROM.

The *Focus 1* sheet in the file *1105_SupportCheck.xlsx* is protected without a password. Here is some information about using this file:

■ In the upper right section of the worksheet, you set one of 30 possible customers. This customer's data appears in the 11 rows that form a detailed, informative spreadsheet, in a chart, and in the chart's status heading alongside the current system date.

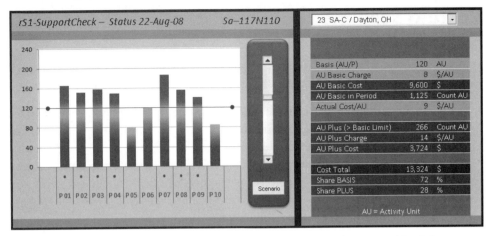

FIGURE 11-14 An agreement has been reached, but is it need-driven and customer-friendly?

■ The columns in the chart represent the activity quotas (sum of activity units) called in the individual activity periods.

■ A blue, horizontal line indicates the boundary between those activity units that have been billed according to *AU BASIC* and those billed according to *AU PLUS*. The column segments above this separator are red, and the ones below it are green. This is also the case if you move the separator up or down for the scenario described below.

■ The second row in the category axis label contains the names of the periods. In the first row, a red dot is used to indicate those periods that have exceeded the separator (or are considered in a scenario).

Please follow the descriptions provided below in the context of the specifications made in Figure 11-14 and Figure 11-15. Therefore, select the customer *23 SA-C / Dayton, OH* in the *ComboBox*. This customer's current total costs total $13,324. The main costing basis here (in addition to the prices agreed with this customer) is the guaranteed acceptance of 120 *AU BASIC* activity units per period (first row in the table). In the chart, you quickly realize that this specification was exceeded in seven of the periods concluded during this time. In this combined costing, however, the fact that the customer has exceeded the agreed activity quotas does not automatically mean that the customer is at a financial disadvantage. Often, the opposite is true. Therefore, in each case, a check must be performed to see whether the customer will benefit from increasing or lowering the basic activity units. The model is capable of "envisaging other scenarios" for this purpose. You can "raise the bar" or lower it. By doing so, you move the blue separator up or down, thus changing the relationship between the *AU BASIC* and *AU PLUS* activity quotas, and therefore changing each proportional cost and ultimately the total cost. You can then track the immediate effects of such actions directly in the table and chart.

If you click the *Scenario ToggleButton*, the presentation changes, and you can use a *ScrollBar* to move the blue separator. Let's take a closer look:

- The content and color of the header row change to emphasize that the current view is no longer the status quo, but rather a scenario.

- The color and content of the first table row also changes: you see the AUs currently valid for this customer (120 in this example) on the left-hand side of the row and the number generated as a result of moving the *ScrollBar* on the right-hand side.

- The word *Notional* precedes the row labels *Basic Cost/AU* and *Cost Total*.

- Now use the *ScrollBar* to slowly move the chart's blue separator up and down. In most cases, you will obtain a constellation for which the notional costs are lower than the costs actually calculated. If that is the case, the *Notional Cost Total* row will become bright yellow. Even within the "yellow range," there are still differences. You can identify these by slowly moving the *ScrollBar* up and down. You can then determine a particular point that represents the lowest possible costs. It is exactly this point that would become the basis for renegotiating new terms, for example, determining a new basic quota (see the first table row in Figure 11-15; it previously was 120 AU, but might become 150 AU in the future).

- If you click the *ToggleButton* again, the presentation resets itself to the status quo and the chart and table no longer responds when you use the *ScrollBar*.

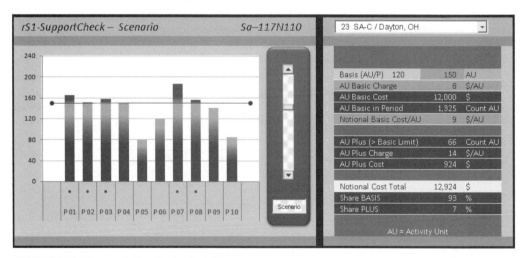

FIGURE 11-15 Whoever "raises the bar" might save some money.

If you check the costing levels of other customers in this model, which naturally works with fictitious figures, you will see that there were clearly incorrect specifications (some of which also concerned the negotiated prices), and that some customers were very pessimistic or cautious in their estimates and agreements while others were willing to take risks. Both groups experienced varying levels of success.

Experiment a little to see what works and, in particular, to see *how* it works. The next section contains some additional notes and illustrations.

rD1.Node   fx

	A B C D E F	G H	I	J	K	L	M	N	O	P	Q	R	S	T
2		0		1	2	3	4	5	6	7	8	9	10	11
4		-5	Code	Ba-18	Be-14	Br-16	Bu-1	Do-1	Du-1	Fr-17	Ga-1	Ge-1	Go-1	Gu-1
5		-4	Customer	BA-L / San Antonio, TX	BE-J / St. Paul, MN	BR-D / Portsmouth, VA	BU-J / Ventura, CA	DO-X / Gulfport, MS	DU-N / Warren, MI	FR-N / Manchester, NH	GA-X / Lancaster, PA	GE-E / Burlington, VT	GO-O / Wilmington, DE	GU-D / Buffalo, NY
6		-3	Basis Limit AU	60	70	70	140	180	180	160	180	80	60	60
7		-2	Cost AU <= Limit	8	12	8	12	8	8	12	12	8	12	8
8		-1	Cost AU > Limit	10	7	13	7	13	12	11	7	12	8	10
9		0												
10		1	P01	175	91	198	155	126	118	199	149	200	182	190
11		2	P02	186	181	108	80	200	161	186	172	197	95	182
12		3	P03	166	128	167	157	180	134	133	197	187	106	97
13		4	P04	116	98	88	177	128	133	108	175	100	115	108
14		5	P05	168	137	116	186	89	161	119	129	101	178	110
15		6	P06	142	196	160	127	115	175	103	94	148	99	81
16		7	P07	102	100	174	155	104	151	175	81	148	198	161
17		8	P08	99	192	194	135	114	129	102	132	189	179	100
18		9	P09	85	97	96	166	176	153	119	184	96	176	156
19		10	P10	193	84	156	138	199	83	141	200	168	171	140

FIGURE 11-16 Each customer has its own fundamental costing data.

Customer-specific data has been defined in the *Data 1* worksheet (see Figure 11-16). Above the node, you will find the basic quotas (*AU BASIC* activity units, with a limited number per period), followed by the prices for activities performed within and outside the quota.

Below the node, you will find the number of activity units provided for each period.

M13   fx =TEXT($G13,"00")&" "&INDEX(rD1.CustNames,1,$G13)

	A B C D E F G H I	J	K	L	M	N
8				22	
10				30	
12				Kunden	
13	01		oF1_ToggleScroll	01 BA-L / San Antonio, TX	
14	02	rL1.ToggleScrollSel	TRUE	02 BE-J / St. Paul, MN	
15	03			03 BR-D / Portsmouth, VA	
16	04		oF1_Scroll	04 BU-J / Ventura, CA	
17	05	rL1.ScrollSel	150	05 DO-X / Gulfport, MS	
18	06			06 DU-N / Warren, MI	
19	07			07 FR-N / Manchester, NH	
20	08			08 GA-X / Lancaster, PA	
21	09			09 GE-E / Burlington, VT	
22	10			10 GO-O / Wilmington, DE	

FIGURE 11-17 Structures in the *Lists 1* sheet

As is usually the case with the rS1.Method, the *Lists 1* worksheet (see Figure 11-17) contains the definition ranges for the controls. Note the formula structure in the *ListFillRange*.

Incidentally, the value range for the *ScrollBar* spans, for good reason, *Max = 50* to *Min = 200*.

| W9 | | f_x | =IF(rL1.ToggleScrollSel=TRUE,rL1.ScrollSel,OFFSET(rD1.Node,$M9,rL1.CustSel+1)) |

	-4	CUST: 23 SA-C / Dayton, OH			Scenario					Actual Agreement		
8	-4	CUST: 23 SA-C / Dayton, OH										
9	-3	Basic Limit AU	147						120			
10	-2	Cost AU <= Limit	8						8			
11	-1	Cost AU > Limit	14						14			
12	0		147	#N/A	###	#N/A			120	#N/A	#N/A	#N/A
13	1	P 01 •	#N/A	165	147	18		•	#N/A	165	120	45
14	2	P 02 •	#N/A	151	147	4		•	#N/A	151	120	31
15	3	P 03 •	#N/A	158	147	11		•	#N/A	158	120	38
16	4	P 04 •	#N/A	149	147	2		•	#N/A	149	120	29
17	5	P 05	#N/A	80	80	0			#N/A	80	80	0
18	6	P 06	#N/A	120	120	0			#N/A	120	120	0
19	7	P 07 •	#N/A	186	147	39		•	#N/A	186	120	66
20	8	P 08 •	#N/A	156	147	9		•	#N/A	156	120	36
21	9	P 09	#N/A	141	141	0		•	#N/A	141	120	21
22	10	P 10	#N/A	85	85	0			#N/A	85	85	0
23			147	#N/A	###	#N/A			120	#N/A	#N/A	#N/A
25	0		1	2	3							
26	1	Basis (AU/P)	147						120			
27	2	AU Basic Charge	8						8			
28	3	AU Basic Cost	11,760						9,600			
29	4	AU Basic in Period	1,308						1,125			
30	5	Notional Basic Cost/AU	8.99						8.53			
31	6											
32	7	AU Plus (> Basic Limit)	83						266			
33	8	AU Plus Charge	14.00						14.00			
34	9	AU Plus Cost	1,162						3,724			
35	10											
36	11	Notional Cost Total	12,922						13,324			

FIGURE 11-18 The combined costing data is compiled here.

Two costing ranges are evident in the *Basis 1* worksheet (see Figure 11-18). They are partially redundant, but nevertheless more informative than their shortened structures would be.

- If you work in a scenario, both sets of figures are different. Otherwise, they are identical.

- The cell ranges surrounded by a bold blue border are the basis for the chart. Here, it is particularly interesting to explore the following:

  - How the blue, horizontal line is created and how it can be moved,

  - How the green and red column segments are created,

  - How the points are added to the axis label.

Finally, the *Focus 1* sheet contains numerous formulas, the majority of which, however, only affect data taken directly from *Basis 1*. However, take a look at the formulas in F3 and M8. Here, you will also discover conditional formatting.

Chapter 12
More Than Numbers

Excel is a program that works with numbers in tables. But it can do so much more than that. The software can be used for a wide range of tasks. This is particularly true of the latest version of Excel, which offers more possibilities than ever before. The "Big Three"—Excel, Word, and PowerPoint—are gradually moving closer together under the Office umbrella. Unfortunately, they still don't work in perfect harmony, but they've now happily reached a greater level of consensus on many points, some of which are discussed in this final chapter. I'll also explain the preparatory steps and techniques that are identical, or at least very similar, in Excel's two "sister" programs.

Using Character Codes

If you've not used character codes or character set tables in the past, you may find the formulas in Figure 12-1 a little odd. Here, formulas convert letters into numbers and numbers into letters.

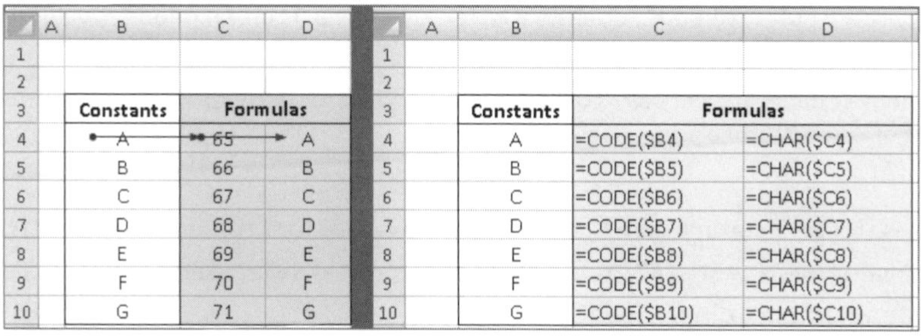

FIGURE 12-1 *A* becomes *65*, and *65* becomes *A*

The =CODE(text) function returns the character code of a text character. If you use a standard font like *Arial, Times Roman, Calibri,* or *Cambria* (to name just a few) and cell B4 contains the character "A," the formula =CODE(B4) returns the value "65."

This function's "counterpart," so to speak, is the =CHAR(number) function. It generates the character whose code number corresponds to the value of number in the character set table. The character actually displayed in the cell depends on the font configured for this cell. For example, if you use a standard font, the formula =CHAR(70) generates the character "F." In other character sets, however, code 70 may belong to an entirely different character.

To explain this a little better, I'll clarify a few basic concepts about the use of computer fonts.

- *ASCII*: This acronym stands for *American Standard Code for Information Interchange*, and refers to a method used to encode alphanumeric characters and control characters (for example, for print control). A numeric code is assigned to each character, which allows character strings to be exchanged between various computers and other technical systems. For example, the code number 65 is transferred instead of the letter A (in standard fonts). ASCII code is used to represent a total of 128 characters. This collection of characters is referred to as a "character set." A "character set table" contains the character set in numeric sequence. The first 32 characters in the ASCII character set table are control characters. Numbering starts at zero, and the first printable character in the table is the blank space, which has the code 32.

- *ANSI*: This acronym is short for *American National Standards Institute*. The *ANSI character set*, which has 256 characters, represents an extension of the *ASCII character set*. The original ASCII character set occupies numbers 32 through 127 of the ANSI character set, which also contains additional characters, such as the umlauts regularly used in German, diacritical marks, and special characters from Scandinavian and other languages.

> **Note** 1) Diacritical marks (also referred to as diacritical signs or points, or just diacritics), usually consist of small signs added to a letter to indicate a certain phonetic value, such as an accent or correct pronunciation.
>
> 2) Various systems are still based on the ASCII standard, and therefore do not permit the use of umlauts in email addresses, for example.

- *Unicode* is the proprietary name of a complex alphanumeric character set. It is an innovative development that seeks to unite all of the world's alphabets (Latin, Arabic, Asian, etc.) in standard encoding.

  But just to make things a little more complicated, the term UCS (*Universal Character Set*) is frequently used in relation to Unicode. UCS usually refers only to the UCS-2 character set, which contains 65,536 characters (this would lead you to assume—correctly—that there must also be other UCS character sets). But I'm not going to enter into any more detail on this less than delightful topic because, as always, we want to focus on the practical applications here.

In addition to the familiar characters on your keyboard and the "everyday fonts" you use on a regular basis, there are many more character sets, whose contents and possible applications can only be uncovered through painstaking searching and experimentation.

Almost all character sets (which represent all of the characters in a font) contain many more characters than are shown on your keyboard. These symbols or special characters—which can be classified in many different ways, all of which are irrelevant here—are often very useful and may help to complete many different design tasks.

There are several ways to insert characters in Windows and in the Office programs. Different fonts may have different character sets, so you should always select a font first, and then select a character from this font. The various options for doing this are described next.

Using the Character Map Program

You access this utility program at Windows level. It provides an independent resource that can be used in connection with Excel but is hardly ever required. I've included it here for the sake of completeness.

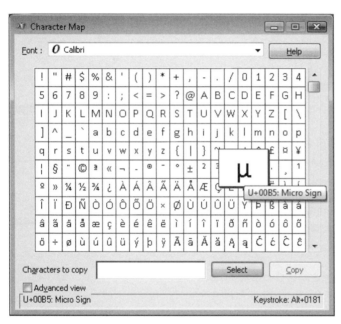

FIGURE 12-2 An extract from the character set of the *Calibri* font

1. To open the *Character Map*, which is a small utility program (see Figure 12-2), select *Start/Programs/Accessories/System Tools*.

2. Begin by selecting the *font*, and then choose the character. An infotext appears whenever you point to a character with the mouse. If you click a character, its display is enlarged.

   You can use the mouse to drag and drop an enlarged character into an Excel cell. However, this is an unnecessarily complicated procedure, as we'll see later.

3. Click the *Select* button to copy the character into the *Characters to copy* box. Then click the Copy button to copy the character to the clipboard.

4. Switch to Excel to insert the character at the cursor.

Direct Access in Excel

It's much easier to insert these characters in Excel (or Word or PowerPoint) directly. Follow the steps below with reference to Figure 12-3:

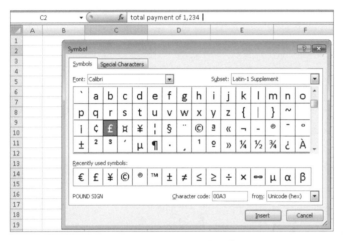

FIGURE 12-3 Accessing the character map directly

1. Type your text normally up to the point where you want to insert a character that isn't shown on your keyboard.

2. In the Ribbon, select *Insert/Symbol*. The relevant dialog box then opens.

3. Select the character, and click the *Insert* button.

Keyboard Input

If you need to insert a character quickly and often, it's particularly useful to know its numeric code. The *ANSI character set*, with its 256 characters (numbered 0 to 255) should suffice here. If you know the code of an *ANSI character*, or if you can look it up in a (printed) table, you can then enter the character directly with the keyboard.

In the case of characters 32 through 255, you can press and hold down the **Alt** key and then enter the code, preceded by a leading zero (don't forget this—it's important!) on the numeric keypad (the block of keys on the right of the main keypad). If you're using a laptop, you can use the **Fn** key in many cases to simulate the numeric keypad. Refer to the hardware documentation for more information.

Printed character-set tables of selected fonts are very useful if you use this method. You can create these easily yourself (for example, in Excel).

On the Companion CD You'll find the *Materials**CharacterSets.xlsx* file on the CD-ROM, which has three worksheets in which the CHAR function described above is used to generate the character set tables of various fonts.

Using these tables on-screen is not very helpful. Instead, you should print out these worksheets and keep them near your workstation. You'll find that such printed templates are often more helpful and faster to use than their on-screen equivalents. This is especially true once you've become accustomed to entering codes quickly with the **Alt** key, and you may even be able to memorize the codes you use most frequently. Some examples, based on standard fonts, are provided next:

- You can enter the *en dash* ("–") as a formatting character in Excel (see Figure 6.20 in Chapter 6, "What, For Whom, How, and With What?") using the **Alt**+0150 code.

- Enter the Ø character with **Alt**+0216.

- A bullet ("•"), which you can enter with code **Alt**+0149, inserted between two blank spaces, can be used as an effective separator if you don't want to use dashes or punctuation marks as separators in a single-line text.

- Left and right guillemets (also called angle quotes or «French» quotation marks), which can also look good in large-sized headings, are entered with **Alt**+0171 and **Alt**+0187 respectively.

If you also want to use the *CharacterSets.xlsx* Excel template for other fonts, create copies of the worksheets and simply format all cells containing formulas with the relevant font. Don't forget to indicate on the new worksheet the font to which the character set shown belongs.

Tip The quickest way to select all cells in an Excel worksheet that contain formulas is to press **F5**, click *Special* in the dialog box that opens, and select the *Formulas* option.

If you examine special character sets, such as *Wingdings*, *Wingdings 2*, or *Wingdings 3*, you'll discover many characters that are ideally suited to use in designs of many different types and can be used to dress up a presentation. Tip: Many characters look very different when enlarged extremely. The only way to learn which characters work best is to experiment and play around with them. You're sure to come across some new and surprising characters, and you may even find something that could be used to grab your audience's attention in your next presentation.

| | | | X21 | | ▼ | | f_x | =CHAR(W21) | | | | |

	H	I	J	K	L	M	N	O	P	Q	R	S	T	U	V	W	X	Y	Z	AA
9	94	♈		122	✲		150	☂		178	◇		206	☋		234	↓			
10	95	♉		123	✿		151	☃		179	✕		207	☌		235	↖			
11	96	♊		124	✱		152	☄		180	◆		208	♌		236	↗			
12	97	♋		125	"		153	☍		181	✪		209	♋		237	↙			
13	98	♌		126	"		154	☎		182	☆		210	♍		238	↘			
14	99	♍		127	☐		155	☏		183	☉		211	♎		239	⇐			
15	100	♎		128	①		156	☐		184	☉		212	♏		240	⇒			
16	101	♏		129	①		157	☑		185	☉		213	⌫		241	⇑			
17	102	♐		130	②		158	·		186	☉		214	⌦		242	⇓			
18	103	♑		131	③		159	●		187	☉		215	◀		243	⇔			
19	104	♒		132	④		160	·		188	☉		216	▶		244	☂			
20	105	♓		133	⑤		161	○		189	☉		217	▲		245	☂			
21	106	er		134	⑥		162	○		190	☉		218	▼		246	[↗]			
22	107	&		135	⑦		163	●		191	☉		219	C		247	☂			
23	108	●		136	⑧		164	◉		192	☉		220	⊃		248	☂			
24	109	○		137	⑨		165	◉		193	☉		221	∩		249	□			
25	110	■		138	⑩		166	○		194	☉		222	∪		250	□			
26	111	□		139	❶		167	▪		195	☂		223	←		251	✗			
27	112	□		140	❷		168	□		196	☂		224	→		252	✓			
28	113	□		141	❸		169	⅄		197	☂		225	↑		253	☒			
29	114	□		142	❸		170	+		198	☂		226	↓		254	☑			
30	115	•		143	❹		171	★		199	☂		227	↖		255	☂			
31	116	◆		144	❻		172	✳		200	☂		228	↗						

Enter:

Press [Alt] and keep pressed.

Then, with a leading zero, press listed code number from the number pad on your keyboard

as [Alt]+0236 for ↗

FIGURE 12-4 A character set table that can be adapted to any font in Excel

Note You can also use special characters and symbols in user-defined number formats. To do this, you need to use either the *Character Map* Windows utility described above and copy characters to the clipboard, or use **Alt** and enter the character code, which is faster and more practical. You can't access characters directly from the Ribbon (*Insert/Symbol*) when the *Format Cells* dialog box is open.

Navigation with Hyperlinks

Once you're able to exploit the versatile and dynamic options that Excel has to offer as a presentation program (without having to do any programming!), you'll ask yourself why you never did so before. Moreover, you'll convince and impress your audience with Excel's fast, responsive range of display options.

Can you really say all you need to say in a single Excel worksheet, when it would take you 10, 20, or even 100 PowerPoint slides to do the same? If you used well-structured data management, a carefully organized workbook, and combine the use of formulas with controls (in other words, if you use the rS1.Method), then the answer is "Yes; no problem." What if your workbook contains five, eight, or ten different worksheets for presentation? The ad-hoc opportunities for displaying various data at the touch of a button (or, rather, with a mouse click) will, in some cases, be limitless. All that's missing to give your presentation a touch of class is a navigational system that can also be controlled with your mouse. Before we look at how to put this in place, note the following capabilities:

- You usually go to the active worksheet in a workbook by clicking the sheet name shown at the bottom of the screen. However, you won't be able to do this in a well-designed presentation because the *sheet selector* will be hidden (to show them again, select *Office button/Excel Options/Advanced/Display options for this workbook/Show sheet tabs*).

- You can press **Ctrl+Page Down** and **Ctrl+Page Up** to scroll backward and forward through worksheets (even if their tabs are hidden). Although often useful, particularly when similar worksheets are located close to one another, this method can be clumsy when navigating your way around a presentation, and may also cause errors.

The solution to such problems is a very simple one. User-defined hyperlinks allow you to access range names and worksheets with your mouse.

Different approaches are used in the two examples described below.

Pictorial Graphics Objects for Scrolling in the Workbook

The model for presenting a report shown in Figure 12-5 and Figure 12-6 was developed for a large, multinational enterprise. Six focus sheets are used, so it's very important to create a system for scrolling quickly and smoothly backward and forward through these. For one thing, the settings made using a control in one focus sheet also affect the neighboring worksheet, but are shown there from a different perspective.

You can click a directional arrow to jump to the neighboring worksheet. The direction is quickly and easily configured. Follow these steps with reference to Figure 12-5:

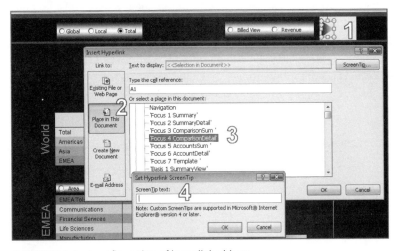

FIGURE 12-5 Fast configuration of hyperlink objects

1. Create and format the arrow drawing object, select it, and select the *Insert/Hyperlink* option to open the relevant dialog box (it's usually quicker to do this by selecting the context menu or using the **Ctrl+K** keyboard shortcut).

2. In the *Insert Hyperlink* dialog box, click *Place in This Document* to display the list of possible destinations within the folder.

3. You can select a worksheet or a range name in the list displayed. In the example shown here, the *Focus 4 ComparisonDetail* has been selected as a target destination. Unless you change the setting, the A1 cell of the target sheet is activated by default. A click on this hyperlink will therefore always bring you to a perfect page layout.

4. Click the *ScreenTip* button, and enter a blank space as the *ScreenTip text*. This prevents the unwanted display of long link descriptions, which otherwise appear in a text box when you point to a hyperlink. The only other way to suppress this display is to change system settings. You can also define your own tip text here, although this is of no benefit when it comes to presentation models.

5. Follow the same steps for other objects.

Setting Up Central Navigation

Figure 12-6 shows the central point of navigation for the solution, which is effectively its "cover sheet," where you can simply click one of the list entries to navigate directly to the corresponding worksheet.

The six worksheets, which contain many tables and charts that can be manipulated with controls, are positioned next to each other in a specific, meaningful sequence. The central point of navigation is placed at the front (on the left). Six texts are displayed here in the style of section titles. If you point to one of these texts, the mouse pointer changes to a hand. If you click the text, the corresponding worksheet opens. In this sheet again, you'll find an arrow pointing to the left, which brings you back to central navigation. Note that this arrow should be always located in the same position in all worksheets. Naturally, this kind of system can be enhanced as required. For example, you can set up links between specific sheets or create arrows or other objects (as described above) that allow you to scroll one sheet to the left or right.

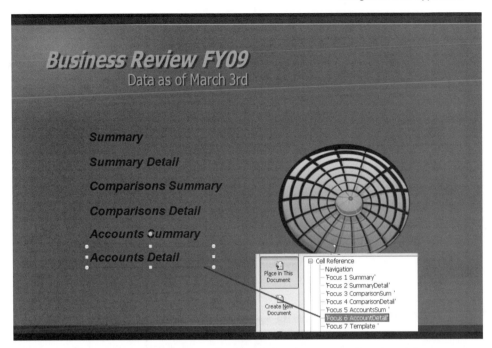

FIGURE 12-6 Central navigation allows you to navigate directly to any number of worksheets.

An overall navigational system based on these principles should only be set up when the structure of the model is complete, all of the presentation dynamics are working, all range names have been defined, and the names and positions of all worksheets are final. The process is then a quick and simple one, as described here:

1. Define the text list for accessing the various sheets in the *Navigation* worksheet. If you create the texts as objects (text boxes or WordArt), you can add hyperlinks to these directly. If you enter the text in cells, they are then covered over by invisible rectangles (drawing objects) adjusted to their size, and hyperlinks are added to these. The steps described below assume that you're using fully transparent drawing objects.

> **Note** A hyperlink can also be added to a cell directly. However, there are two drawbacks to using this approach in a presentation solution. First, you need to suppress the hyperlink text format (plus the *followed hyperlink* format). Second, you're also bound by the size of the cell containing the text in terms of the response of the mouse display. Both of these problems can be avoided by using transparent graphics objects. The main benefit of spatial adjustment (see step 4 below) is that the dimensions of the click option are adjusted to match the length of the text exactly. This represents a key component of usability in the case of texts with different lengths (as in Figure 12-6).

2. Create the first hyperlink as instructed in the last section, and test it.

3. Copy the object you've created and position it over the next text.

4. Adjust the size of the invisible object to suit the text. It should be no smaller, but not significantly larger, than the text over which it's positioned.

5. Right-click the object, and select the *Format Hyperlink* option in the context menu.

6. In the dialog box that opens, change the name of the linked worksheet.

7. Repeat steps 3 through 7 to finish setting up central navigation.

It's just as easy to create the links for the back arrows in the individual worksheets. Simply add to the first arrow formatted a reference to the *CentralNavigation* sheet, and then copy it to the other worksheets.

Printing and PDF Conversion

Each of the charts described and shown in this book can also be printed or used in PDF format.

Questions on Preparing Charts for Publication

If you don't intend to publish your presentation chart now, but might have to someday, there are some very important questions to be answered about its design and formatting:

- Is the chart suitable for use in a printed version without any changes or adjustments?

- Is it possible and sufficient to create a printed version based on the original?

- Is it necessary to create a separate printable version?

In other cases, such as when writing up the results of scientific research, the printed version is the only version. A different set of questions must be answered:

- Who is the potential target audience for the publication?

- What level of technical detail is expected? What can be assumed?

- Is the chart the main focus (is it to contain all of the essential information) or is it to be used to supplement and support an accompanying text?

- Do the content and design need to be tailored to the requirements of the audience?

- Do any third-party rights need to be considered?

- In what type of publication is the chart to appear?

- What kind of printing system or which reproductive medium is to be used (offset printing, digital printing, xerography)?

- Will the chart be printed in color, grayscale or black and white? In the case of grayscale printing, are color templates or grayscale templates to be provided?

- How large (in terms of physical proportions) and how detailed can/may/should/must the chart be?

Essentially, a whole range of information is required, and that's without even considering any technical problems. Do you feel that you know the ropes in this situation? Unfortunately, most readers won't, or at least not to the degree required. However, I'm afraid I can't provide a set list of requirements. This topic is vast, wide-ranging, and occasionally extremely complex. Any well-meaning advice offered may be wrong in a specific situation. This is because there are so many different permutations and rules, virtually none of which apply across the board.

So what can you do? The only really useful advice I can offer you is to ask! Use the right information sources, and ask the right people at the right time. But how will you know what, who, and when is right? Here are some clues:

- The right information sources are all sources that are directly (rather than just "in some way") related to your work, in particular those that are relevant for its practical implementation.

- The right people are the people at whom your presentation is directly aimed (customers, target audience etc.) and those directly responsible for executing its publication (print shop, copy shop, etc.).

- The right time is always before you even start your work and whenever ambiguities or uncertainties arise.

The amount of time and money lost through a general lack of communication is, sadly, outrageous from a cost perspective. And this large-scale trend is also true on a much smaller scale. Here's how it might show up in real life:

- An order is received (for example, for a complex written work including many charts) but insufficient definitions, specifications, and instructions are provided. These aren't requested (asking for better information isn't even considered). Instead, the attitude is "Let's just get started."

- So, a long time is spent merrily and diligently hammering away at the job ("It'll be just fine as it is") and the result is then sent for initial revision. The customer says: "Hmm... not bad. But we can't leave it like this." OK, why not? He explains. And all becomes clear.

- And so, even more time is spent hammering away at the job, making changes or even starting from scratch, only this time not so merrily or diligently. At some point, the result is then sent for final revision. This time, the customer says: "Great. But why couldn't it have been like this first time around?"

- Finally, the approved result is sent to the print or copy shop. The printing expert says: "Hmm...very nice. But we can't print it like this." At least, in this case, he didn't start with "Oh, no!" or end with "That'll cost you!"

Let's stop right there. Many similar tales of woe could be written; in particular, tales of great expense. You can avoid appearing in one of these stories yourself if you ensure that you're correctly informed from the very start. The only excuse for not taking care of this is if you already have clear written instructions or other specifications from a reliable source (your good friend who says "Just do it like this. That's how I've done it before" shouldn't be considered one of these).

If something's going to be printed (be it text containing charts or anything else), take particular care to obtain the correct information and find out about precise technical requirements. The most important basic questions are:

- What do I need to deliver and when so that my work can be printed without any problems and without incurring unnecessary costs?

- What kind of print templates are required? Are different templates required?

- Should the charts be implemented as Excel objects or as picture objects (bitmaps, etc.)? (For more information about this, refer to the section "Interaction with Other Programs").

- Are the charts/figures to be incorporated into a text document (for example, a Word file), and, if so, how? Are they to be delivered as separate templates?

- Which file formats and data storage options are to be used? For all of the print templates, and specifically for the figures?

- Is a PDF file expected (refer to the next section) and, if so, which settings are to be used?

- Is there a more cost-effective method that could produce results of a similar quality? Check with the customer whether you have approval to use such a method.

- Are the quality and colors of a test print guaranteed for all copies of the entire publication?

Of course, you can only ask this final question when you've received a test print. So insist on getting one. You can only afford to do without one if you don't mind risking extra costs and wasted time because you can't use a publication that was, for example, expensive to print but contained serious errors.

You may think that I've been too negative in relation to this topic. I hope that you'll instead see my comments as a positive recommendation and as motivation. Following this advice should also have a positive effect on your wallet and your stress levels!

Creating PDF Documents

To display PDF documents, you need *Adobe Reader*, which can be downloaded free-of-charge from thousands of different Internet sites and which you probably have installed already. What you may be missing is the option of converting Excel, Word, or PowerPoint files into universal PDF format. This is now a little easier with Office 2007.

Before we come to that, note that the reference program for creating PDF files is *Adobe Acrobat*, which allows you to create PDF files from any printable file on any platform. This program is, in every respect, the ideal solution but is relatively expensive for the occasional personal use.

There are also various other products from many different manufacturers, some of a lower quality and limited functionality, which you can also find online at lower prices or even free of charge. Most of these programs are free of application problems in terms of basic functions. However, if you need to use specialized functions (*Adobe Acrobat* offers a very wide range of these), you need to educate yourself before buying and installing a conversion program. However, if you're working in a professional publishing environment, the reference program will be your first choice.

> **Note** I use the term *reference program* to indicate software that, regardless of its price, sets the benchmark in a specific segment, meets the most rigorous requirements, and serves as a standard against which other products of the same type and for the same purpose are measured.
>
> For example, Microsoft Excel is the reference program for spreadsheet applications.

You can now also create PDF files with Office 2007. To do this, you need the free *Microsoft Save as PDF or XPS Add-in for 2007 Microsoft Office Programs*, which you need to install after you set up your Office programs.

You can access this if you enter *PDF* as a search term in the Excel application Help, and select the *Save a file in PDF format* or *Save as PDF or XPS* topic. A link is provided in both topics to a Web page where you can download the add-in.

After you install the add-in, you can choose to convert your Excel file to PDF format when you choose *Save As*. Note the additional settings you can make in the dialog box and the *Options* available.

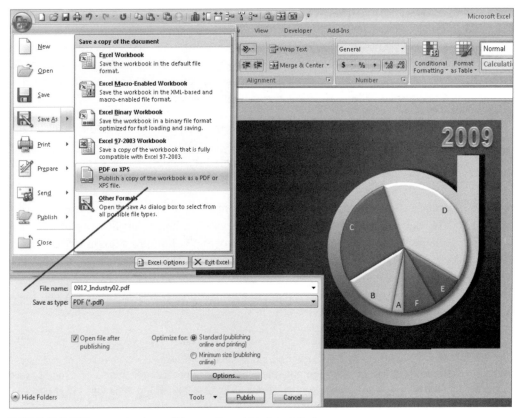

FIGURE 12-7 PDF conversion is possible once the add-in is installed.

SmartArt

In Office 2007, SmartArt allows you to format text to create illustrations. Text elements are added to containers of various shapes (arrows, boxes, pyramids, block cycles, hierarchical stacks, and many more) to provide a clearer illustration of content and connections. SmartArt encompasses a vast number of possibilities. In this book, I can naturally only provide a short and primarily technical overview.

You'll find the examples below in the *1201_SmartArt.xlsx* file.

On the Companion CD Open the *\Samples\1201_SmartArt.xlsx* file on the CD-ROM.

If you've learned to use the tools in the *Drawing* toolbar in earlier versions of Excel, Word, and PowerPoint, you'll already be able to create very pleasing pictures, with or without text. However, the problem with these tools is that they required various amounts of skill, experience, and time to produce results. If some or all of these ingredients were missing, then the result was: no graphic. But was this really a disadvantage? In the new version, less time is required, and you can produce a result with SmartArt in just a few minutes. But is this really an advantage? I'm not convinced that it is.

Before we examine this question, let's look again at concept of *SmartArt*. The *Char* worksheet of the sample file contains two graphics objects, which are shown in Figure 12-8. They aren't SmartArt products, but they do represent examples of text formatted for the purposes of illustration.

FIGURE 12-8 An example of text formatting for illustration—but is it smart and is it art?

Both objects can be classified as nonsense. In the case of the object on the left, the text and graphic contradict one another. Meanwhile, no text is discernible in the object on the right. However, both could still be classified as "smart," a term that can mean many things, including clever and cool. But could they be described as art(istic)? Of course, who could really argue against that? But could they be called SmartArt? Of course not. My only intention in providing this example was to illustrate the difficulties involved in discussing this concept and the general subject.

Note If you really enjoy tinkering with the program, what *you* could try to do here is to find out how the picture on the right was created and which formatting options were used. I'll just give you the following hint regarding the character found in the container: 0200.

This topic causes me difficulty because it's yet another new feature to appear in a standard program, and I regard it with a mixture of approval (for the technical component) and skepticism (for commitment to quality). I approve the fact that tools are provided that allow you to produce good or even professional designs with relative ease. I'm skeptical because it takes more than just hip, effective tools to create good or even professional design results. Also essential—and I don't mind repeating myself here—are knowledge, experience, and time.

Am I being too negative again? Perhaps. However, I do feel (and I know that I'm far from being alone in this sentiment) that I've suffered for years at the hands of countless unspeakable awful PowerPoint presentations that obviously have been put together without any theory (or without any thought), and which bombard their helpless audiences with every weapon in the program's arsenal. They are mercilessly versatile, mercilessly colorful, and mercilessly animated; in other words "effective", sometimes brimming over with effects. Whey would anyone create such a thing? Simply because they *can*. If something can be done, you can be certain that it will be done. And if lots of different things can be done at once, so much the better. It's exactly this problem that I foresee when I look at the impressive range of tools that can now be put to use with SmartArt.

Now it's time to look at the techniques involved.

Inserting SmartArt Graphics

You should view the creation of a SmartArt graphic as essentially the same as the preparation of a numbers-based presentation chart or chart for publication. You have a basic idea of what you want to convey and how you want to convey it, and you know the objectives of your work and the needs of your target audience. You know that you can change the shape and formatting selected in any stage in almost any way. In spite of this, you should have a relatively clear picture of the possible outcome before you even start working on the design.

The next steps are illustrated in Figure 12-9:

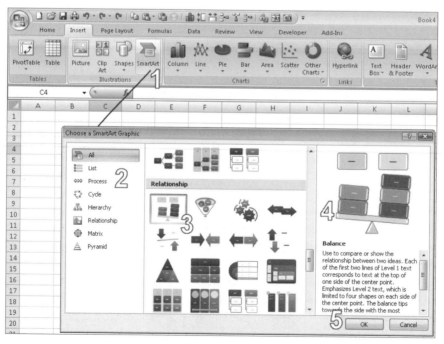

FIGURE 12-9 How to make your initial settings

1. In the Ribbon, select *Insert/Illustrations/SmartArt.*

2. In the *Choose a SmartArt Graphic* dialog box, select a thematic group of objects. If you're not yet sure which you want to use (which would put you at a serious disadvantage here if you need to fulfill a specific task), select *All*.

3. Take a look at the basic shapes, and decide which best suits your ideas or requirements.

4. For more information about any object, you can click its icon and read the sometimes very useful text that appears on the right of the dialog box. Note that important technical information is also provided here (for example, in relation to object-specific restrictions).

5. Click *OK* to add the object to your worksheet. Now let the designing begin!

Basics and Formatting Options

SmartArt graphics comprise a structured collection of shapes (drawing objects), which are predominantly configured as text containers. Default mechanisms allow you to edit an image in its entirety or the individual shapes it contains.

A SmartArt graphic is a close relative of the chart, and in may respects behaves like a chart. For example, it can be scaled in its entirety, regardless of how many individual objects it contains.

On the other hand, you can also design each of the individual elements the same way as when using drawing objects (see Chapter 5, "Graphical Objects"), which is especially helpful when it comes to personalizing your design.

If you already know how to format charts and graphical objects, SmartArt won't present a problem, in particular because the general techniques for using this feature corresponds to the technical design of Excel 2007, with which you're by now familiar (use of *SmartArt Tools*). You'll also find relatively comprehensive and condensed information about this new feature if you search for *SmartArt* in the Excel Help.

The object shown in Figure 12-10 is defined in the *Scales 1* worksheet of the sample file, and is included here to provide some basic information.

Note the following with reference to Figure 12-10:

1. Just like a numbers-based chart, the selected object is shown within a border with handles for scaling. If an individual element isn't selected, the entire object is shown within a border and can be scaled as a whole.

2. A small bar on the left side of the border shows two arrows. You can click these to open and close the *Text Pane*, which is the editor for SmartArt graphics (more about this in the next section). The Text Pane normally appears on the left of an object. If there isn't sufficient space there, it appears on the right instead.

3. Within a SmartArt graphic, you can select and format each element individually.

Once you activate a SmartArt graphic, you can access the *SmartArt Tools*, with the two tabs entitled *Design* and *Format*. A few details about these are provided in the following paragraphs.

> **Note** The surest way to achieve professional results is naturally to make sufficient effort. This involves acquiring both knowledge and experience, which are closely bound together. Both succeed (at least in the case of complex structures) not by acquiring knowledge second-hand, but by experiencing things first-hand: failures and errors included. When it comes to using the *SmartArt Tools*, experimentation and practice are therefore the most effective way to learn. You can use the templates provided in the sample file for this purpose or, better still, create your own objects.

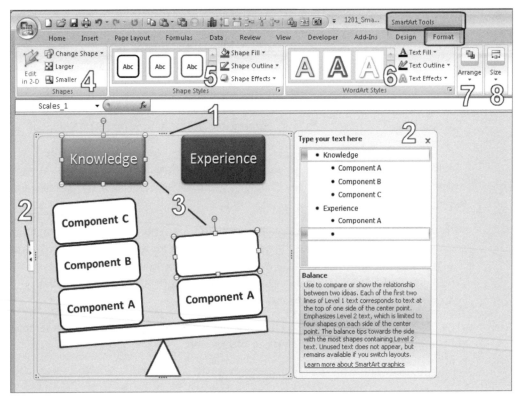

FIGURE 12-10 A balance hasn't been struck between knowledge and experience in this case. But this is possible!

A brief overview of the Format tab is provided below.

4. Commands in the *Shapes* group:

❏ You can edit a 3D graphic in a 2D view, which makes editing easier.

- ❏ You can transform a selected shape into any other shape, without losing the selected formatting.

- ❏ You can enlarge or reduce a selected shape in small, defined stages (one step per click).

5. You're already familiar with the commands in the *Shape Styles* group from other contexts. Here you can design the overall appearance of a shape down to the last detail.

6. The commands in the *WortArt Styles* group are used to design text characters.

7. You can use the commands in the *Arrange* group to help you position an object (which I find a rather superfluous option).

8. You use the commands in the *Size* group to determine the exact proportions of the SmartArt graphic as a whole.

> **Important** You can also begin detailed formatting of an element of a SmartArt graphic by selecting it and then opening its formatting dialog box from the context menu or using the **Ctrl+1** shortcut.

Changing SmartArt Graphics and Their Elements

You use the *Text Pane* and the commands on the *Design* tab to make important settings for a SmartArt graphic. Here you make decisions that essentially determine the quality and information value of your product. You should therefore pay close attention to the options on offer here when practicing on your own initiative.

1. Using the Text Pane is largely subject to the same rules as those for using a text editor, but also has surprises and peculiarities in store. The following descriptions are provided by way of example, and are based on the example in the *Scales 1* worksheet, which is shown in Figure 12-11. You may come across different effects when working with other graphics.

- ❏ When you activate a line of text, the corresponding shape is selected.

- ❏ If you delete a line of text, the corresponding shape is removed. If you press **Del** to delete the shape, the corresponding text line is also deleted.

- ❏ If you press **Enter** to create a new text line, a new form is generated in the corresponding position in the graphic. Therefore, use **Alt+Enter** to create line breaks *within* the shape. Existing formatting is copied or adjusted.

- ❏ If you position a third shape on the right of the weighing scales in the example shown, the scales will be balanced. If you create a fourth shape there, the balance will tip to the right. If you create a fifth shape, you will exceed the upper border of this structure, and a warning message will appear, accompanied by a red "X."

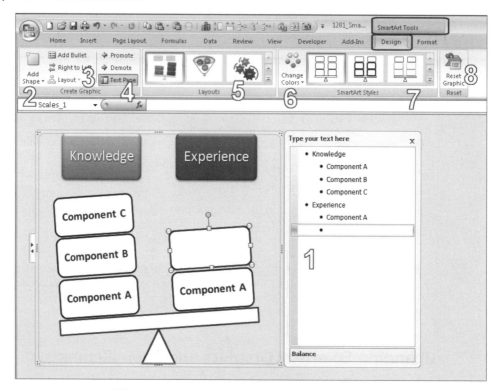

FIGURE 12-11 Many different modification options are available

We can now continue our discussion of Figure 12-11 with the commands of the *Design* tab.

2. The *Add Shape* option allows you to insert additional shapes, based on the position of the form that's currently selected.

3. The other commands in the *Create Graphic* group (see Figure 12-11) let you edit specific SmartArt graphics if these offer the relevant options or settings (for example, the option to add several text levels). Note the tips that appear when you point the mouse at one of these commands. The *Promote* and *Demote* options, which you can apply to a text (and the shape belonging to that text), produce very different results depending of the type of graphic in which they're used.

4. The *Text Pane* option opens and closes the relevant editing area. In other words, it has the same function as the small bar on the left of the border around the object.

5. The default types pictured in the *Layouts* allow you to check at any stage whether a structure other than the structure you've selected would achieve the same or a better visual effect. Simply point to one of these default structures to view a preview of the effect. Click this preview to assign it to your graphic.

This method is only useful if you haven't yet made any user-defined changes to the individual elements of your SmartArt graphic, or have made very few. It's therefore best to use this option, if necessary, early in development and then stick with your selection.

6. The *Change Colors* option allows you to assign a predefined color scheme to the entire SmartArt graphic; in other words, to all of its elements simultaneously.

7. This option allows you to assign complex formatting to the entire SmartArt graphic; in other words, all of its elements simultaneously (global application of a predefined style).

8. You can use the *Reset Graphic* command to undo all of the formatting you've applied so far. Note, however, that this doesn't affect layout changes (see step 5), and it restores a program-internal default rather than the last status saved. It's therefore preferable to use the *Undo* option and saved versions.

In spite of all of this automation, it's important to remember that almost all formatting options that you're familiar with from working with individual graphics objects can also be applied to SmartArt elements.

Variations

If you take account of all of the resources available and all the various combinations in which they can be used, the options for personalizing your SmartArt graphics are virtually infinite. I'll now illustrate some of the approaches you can use, based on the *Scales 2*, *Chevron 1*, *Chevron 2*, and *Gearwheel* worksheets, which are shown in Figure 12-12 and Figure 12-13.

Tip I strongly urge you to personalize your SmartArt objects. We can expect a huge wave of these graphics to be unleashed on a more or less enthusiastic public over the coming years. Most of these will be created using Excel's default formats (yawn!). In other words, you can expect your work to grab more attention and to be met with greater acceptance if you do things just a little differently and stand out from the crowd.

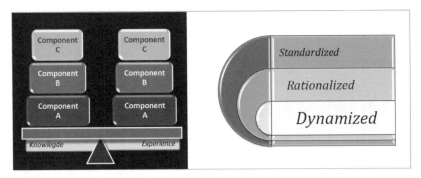

FIGURE 12-12 Two examples of personalized designs

- *Scales 2* worksheet (shown in the left of Figure 12-12): In this case, almost all of the default formatting was changed. This includes positioning, dimensions, proportions, colors, and detailed formatting of the individual elements. Particularly important, in my view, is the option of assigning a different "weighting" to each of the components *A*, *B*, and *C*, and the fact that the title has now been moved below the balance beam so that dominant titles have become explanatory labels.

- *Chevron 1* worksheet (not shown) and *Chevron 2* worksheet (shown on the right of Figure 12-12): Both of these examples remain relatively close to the standard format, the only difference being that different color formatting, font sizes, and text positioning are used.

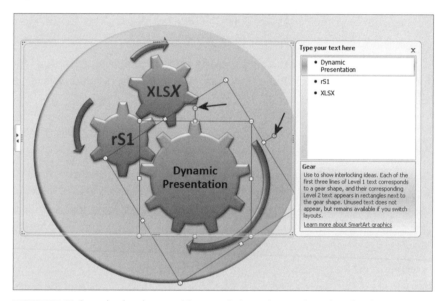

FIGURE 12-13 Gearwheel and arrow objects are independent and can therefore be rotated individually.

- *Gearwheel* worksheet (Figure 12-13): In this case, the SmartArt graphic is positioned on another drawing object to enhance the "revolving" effect of the image. In the figure shown, you can see that the gearwheels and curved arrows are objects that are independent of one another. This means that you can rotate the gearwheels in opposite directions (which is often useful or essential to ensure that their teeth clearly interlock), and also give the directional arrows individual positions.

Interaction with Other Programs

Which program should you use for which purpose? At first glance, this appears to be a very easy question to answer. Word is used for text processing, Excel for spreadsheets, and PowerPoint for presentation. You'd imagine, then, that it would be a very straightforward matter to decide which program to use and that the three programs would interact well with one another almost automatically. However, if you investigate this matter a little further, you'll find that it's a little more complex and problematic. For example:

- Word can also be used as a very effective, high-quality design program. Here I'm thinking in particular of the variable options available with Word tables.

- Excel is also in a class of its own when it comes to presentation. This is true in particular of the dynamic, multi-variable presentations that don't use any programming, which have been discussed in detail in this book.

- The latest versions of PowerPoint can also be used in some respects as a graphics program. This is possible because you can save objects and even entire slides in various graphics file formats in the presentation program.

For these reasons, it's not always easy to select which program to use for a certain project, or to decide whether to combine the strengths of the individual Office components in an optimized product. Despite significant advances made, this last option remains something of a pipe dream in Office 2007 because the programs have unfortunately not yet reached a point where you can simply jump between them, or choose among them at random without noticing a difference.

However, I do have some good news to report. If you already know how to create attractive and informative charts in Excel 2007, you won't have a problem doing the same in Word 2007 or PowerPoint 2007 because both these Office programs now use Excel, including all of its resources, as a chart editor. This means, for example, that everything you've learned in this book about the formal design of charts in Excel 2007 can equally be applied in its two sister programs.

Now for the not-so-good news. It's a shame that the strengths of Excel can't be perfectly combined with the strengths of PowerPoint because such a capability is badly needed. Instead, if you want to present figures, you can either used a non-programmed yet extremely dynamic, clearly laid out Excel solution and employ a few tricks to lend it some additional features of a PowerPoint presentation. Or, you can use the same data to produce a largely static and—because of the number of slides required—very complicated PowerPoint solution, which you can only make as dynamic as its Excel equivalent by spending a lot of time (and therefore money) on programming. Sadly, you still can't use an ideal combination of the best resources in each program or fully synchronize these with a minimum of effort.

In terms of the strategic and technical aspects of the interaction between Excel, PowerPoint, and Word, there are no differences significant enough to warrant a detailed discussion of any of these programs in their roles as source or target programs. It's sufficient to look at just one example of this, which I've provided here in relation to the transfer of charts from Excel to PowerPoint. The rules are essentially the same for any other program combinations and directions of transfer.

Creating Charts in PowerPoint 2007

It seems that PowerPoint has now fallen in love with Excel. One practical example of this is shown in Figure 12-14 and discussed in the following paragraphs:

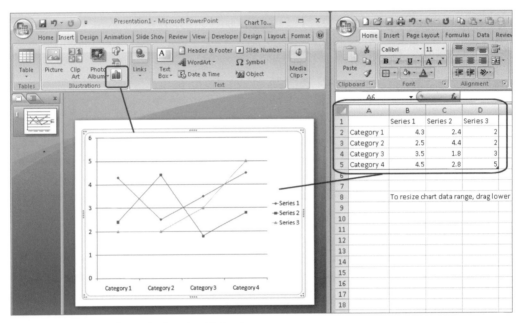

FIGURE 12-14 PowerPoint works directly with Excel.

You're using PowerPoint and want to create a chart. To do this, you choose *Insert/ Illustrations/Chart*. Once you select a chart type, the screen is split in two. One half continues to display the chart in PowerPoint, while Excel opens in the other half, showing a chart basis in a table. You can now change this chart basis as required in order to add the relevant content to your PowerPoint/Excel chart. The chart is fully integrated into PowerPoint, where it can be manipulated without any restrictions using the same chart tools and techniques available in Excel (note, however, that this is limited to formal design and doesn't include the use of dynamic components like controls).

The chart you created remains embedded in PowerPoint, while its source data is saved in an Excel worksheet that is integrated into PowerPoint.

To change this source data, right-click in the chart to open the context menu, and choose the *Edit Data* option to open the integrated Excel worksheet.

Exporting Excel Charts to PowerPoint

If you're able to create and format Excel charts in PowerPoint as described in the last section, it's very simple and often more efficient to do all of the work in Excel directly and then transfer the chart to PowerPoint. You can do this using a simple copying process, though one that is subject to certain restrictions on the quality of the results it produces. Try this out for yourself using two different and differentiated examples. Note, however, that you must first open Excel and PowerPoint 2007 and activate the slide in which you want to insert a chart.

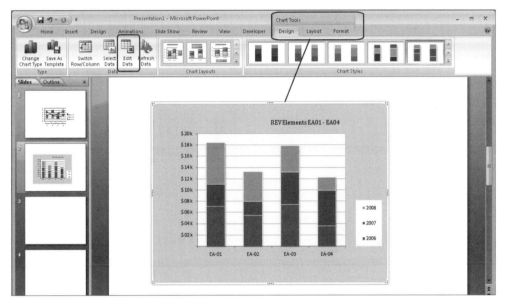

FIGURE 12-15 The chart is edited in the usual way.

1. Open the \Samples\0101_BasicSamples.xlsx file on the CD-ROM and activate the Chart 1 worksheet.

2. Select the chart it contains, and copy it to the clipboard.

3. Now switch to PowerPoint, and copy the chart from the clipboard (note that formatting in the source location that has the setting *Automatic* usually changes when copied to the target location). As long as the chart is selected, you can use the now familiar *Chart Tools* in the Ribbon, with the three tabs *Design*, *Layout*, and *Format*.

4. Choose *Chart Tools/Design/Edit Data*. This brings you to the Excel data source, where you can press **F9** in the example to generate new data, which is also immediately visible in the chart in PowerPoint. Unfortunately, you face the general restriction that a dynamic chart in Excel loses its dynamic features when copied to PowerPoint. This is because it's not possible to manipulate charts of any kind using controls in PowerPoint. The data content of the chart can only be changed in the data source, as least if programming isn't used.

The next example involves a more complex source structure.

1. Open the \Samples\0907_Bloodpressure.xlsx file on the CD-ROM and activate the *Focus 1* worksheet.

2. Select the chart it contains and copy it to the clipboard.

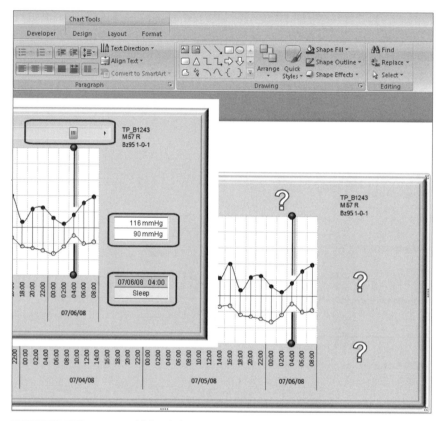

FIGURE 12-16 Important additional elements are missing in the copy.

3. Now switch to PowerPoint and copy the chart from the clipboard. You'll be disappointed by the result. Some elements from the source have disappeared. This isn't a big deal with respect to the scroll bar, which wouldn't work as you want it to in PowerPoint in any case. However, it's annoying that the two "photos" that function as legends on the right of the chart have been lost in transit.

If you copy the table range in which the chart is located, rather than the chart itself, the missing elements appear in the target PowerPoint file but their positions change and they are useless because they have no functionality (scroll bar) or cannot be changed (changes to the "photos" in the source are not shown in the target). Copying the chart by selecting *Paste Special/Microsoft Office Excel Workbook Object*—with or without a link—isn't a solution either because the bottom line is that the main problem already described still remains; i.e., the chart can't be controlled directly from PowerPoint. As a result, the Excel dynamism that is so effective and that can be achieved without any programming is sadly lost when you use PowerPoint. This rules out this type of collaboration between the two programs, at least when it comes to presentations (where you simply can't switch between various programs). What a pity!

The only option left is to transfer the chart as an image.

Exporting Excel Charts as Bitmap Files

I suggest transferring charts as bitmap files, and I'll explain this process as an example of one of the ways in which charts can be copied as images.

1. In Excel, copy the table range you want to transfer to PowerPoint. Important: Copy the table range containing the chart, *not* the chart itself. Otherwise, some details may be lost. You can choose the *Crop* option in the target file later to eliminate any unwanted borders.

2. In PowerPoint, choose *Paste Special*.

3. In the dialog box that appears, select the *bitmap* option, even though this has some minor disadvantages.

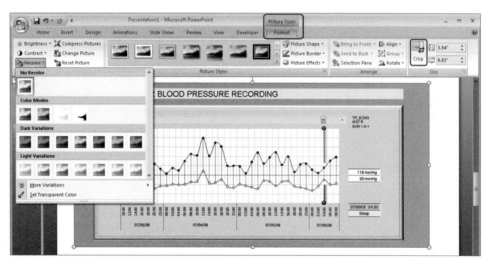

FIGURE 12-17 You can adjust the bitmap in PowerPoint using the *Picture Tools*.

The benefits of this method are as follows:

- The image is an exact replica of the image in the source range, down to the last detail. This makes the method a sound one for static transfer to PowerPoint, albeit one which relies on optimal screen display.

- The image transferred is of high quality. The scaling options are infinitely variable, and the image can also be reduced to almost any size without any impact on quality, a feature which is primarily of interest if the chart is to be printed (used in Word). However, this reduction often appears rather fuzzy on screen (though not on the printout). When transferring charts to PowerPoint, the source and target objects should therefore be the same size if possible.

  Enlarging a bitmap usually has a negative impact on quality.

- The image can be changed in many different ways using the *Picture Tools* (see Figure 12-17).

- This also allows you to view the results of the excellent formatting capabilities of Excel 2007 in older PowerPoint versions. After all, a bitmap is a map of bits—in other words, a screen image—and it doesn't matter how the chart was originally created or which technical options were used in the process.

The relative drawbacks of this method are as follows:

- A bitmap image occupies a very large amount of memory and therefore puts a strain on your RAM and—if the file is saved—on your hard drive, even if both only play a subordinate role in today's systems.

- A bitmap is static. If the source contains an error or if it changes, the copy process must be repeated after the source file is revised.

Before I Forget

> **On the Companion CD** Open the *1202_Knowledge.xlsx* file on the CD-ROM.

Nobody can know everything, and not even everything there is to know about Excel, apparently. But you don't need to; at least not all the time. The ability to forget is a powerful and useful one. I freely admit that I often have to refer to my own books when dealing with many Excel problems and questions. By the way, one of the reasons for writing them.

I really hope that you've managed to retain at least those ideas you found most relevant to you as you worked your way through this book. Or, if not, that you now know where to find the relevant information. To close, I'd like to wish my readers all the best, and to sum up with the following quotation and typical Excel 2007 file (it contains a formula after all!). It speaks volumes about knowledge, experience, and the ability and desire to get things done:

"Knowing things is overrated"

FIGURE 12-18 What more needs to be said?

Appendix A
List of Sample Files

No.	Filename	169 Charts	100 dynamized by using F9 (simulates the reading of new data)	22 dynamized by using controls	8 contain conditional formatting
01	0101_BasicSamples.xlsx	3	3		
02	0102_PracticeData01.xlsx	1			
03	0201_Extract.xlsx	3			
04	0202_Analysis_00.xlsx	0			
05	0203_Analysis_01.xlsx	1		1	
06	0301_MallCupola.xlsx	1	1		
07	0302_Limits.xlsx	7	7		
08	0303_Perception.xlsx	23	22		
09	0304_Columns.xlsx	5	3		
10	0305_Bars.xlsx	3	1		
11	0306_Lines.xlsx	6	5		
12	0307_Pie.xlsx	5	3		
13	0308_Scatter.xlsx	4	1		
14	0309_VariousTypes.xlsx	6	1		
15	0401_ColorMix.xlsx	0	2		2
16	0402_PracticeTemplates.xlsx	7	7		
17	0403_Ireland.xlsx	4	4		
18	0404_Stadium.xlsx	2			
19	0501_Graphics01.xlsx	0			
20	0502_Graphics02.xlsx	1	1		
21	0601_Indicators01.xlsx	1		1	
22	0602_BigAndSmall.xlsx	2	2		
23	0603_BordersLines.xlsx	2			
24	0604_DateFormats.xlsx	0			
25	0701_Indicators_01.xlsx	1	1	1	
26	0702_Indicators_02.xlsx	1	1	1	1

No.	Filename	169 Charts	100 dynamized by using F9 (simulates the reading of new data)	22 dynamized by using controls	8 contain conditional formatting
27	0703_Indicators_00.xlsx	0			
28	0801_Stadium.xlsx	2			
29	0802_Columns.xlsx	7	4		
30	0803_Europe_S13.xlsx	1			
31	0804_AxisLabels.xlsx	3	2		
32	0805_DataLabels.xlsx	2			
33	0806_Bars.xlsx	8	4		
34	0807_Lines.xlsx	5	4		
35	0808_ColumnsLines.xlsx	3	3		
36	0809_3Axes.xlsx	3			
37	0810_Pies.xlsx	5	3		
38	0811_Scatter.xlsx	4		3	
39	0901_DynamicIndicators.xlsx	7	6	1	
40	0902_Scale01.xlsx	4	4		
41	0903_Scale02.xlsx	2	1		
42	0904_Instruments.xlsx	3	1	3	
43	0905_TestingLine.xlsx	2	1	1	
44	0906_Marker.xlsx	1		1	
45	0907_Bloodpressure.xlsx	1		1	1
46	0908_LongSequence.xlsx	2		2	1
47	0909_AutoSort01.xlsx	1		1	
48	0910_AutoSort02.xlsx	1	1		
49	1001_3Years.xlsx	1		1	
50	1002_10Products.xlsx	1		1	
51	1003_10Years.xlsx	1		1	1
52	1004_SummerCampaign.xlsx	2		1	2
53	1005_Multilingual.xlsx	1		1	
54	1006_RadarComparison.xlsx	1		1	
55	1101_Cumulative.xlsx	1		1	1
56	1102_Customers_ABC.xlsx	1		1	

No.	Filename	169 Charts	100 dynamized by using F9 (simulates the reading of new data)	22 dynamized by using controls	8 contain conditional formatting
57	1102A_Data_Customers_ABC.xlsx	0			
58	1103_ScatterXY.xlsx	2		1	
59	1104_Boxplot.xlsx	1	1		
60	1105_SupportCheck.xlsx	1		1	1
61	1201_SmartArt.xlsx	0			
62	1202_Knowledge.xlsx	0			

Index of Procedures

The Index of Procedures contains page references to descriptions for specific procedures or step-by-step instructions.

Index

Symbols and Numbers

(digit placeholder), 281
#N/A, 392, 439, 488, 517
  as a placeholder, 297
& (ampersand), 84
? (digit placeholder)), 281
0 (digit placeholder), 281
1024 x 768 pixels, 2, 258
15 decimal places, 281
3-D bevel, 381
3-D charts, 126
3-D format, 224, 441, 481
3-D pie chart, 126, 408
3-D rotation, 222, 225, 481
32-bit color depth, 3

A

accent colors, 66
access to objects, 40
ActiveX controls, 91, 295, 334, 420,
    470, 479
  basics, 327
  creating, 328
  design mode, 331
  formatting properties, 327
  functional properties, 327
  general information, 327
  MatchEntry, 473
  modifying, 331
  moving direction, 418
  properties, 327, 332
add-in, 543
add shape, SmartArt, 550
adjustment factor, 466
Adobe Acrobat, 543
Adobe Reader, 543
affective objectives, 242
Alt+F1, 24
ampersand character (&), 84
analytical lines, 188
AND, 440, 509
angles, 406, 407
angle of the first slice, 406, 411, 481
ANSI, 532
ANSI character, 286, 372, 534
  set, 532

B

apparent columns, 120
approach, basic, 33
area chart, 149
area design, 266
area relationships, 266
array, 507
arrow, 537
  settings, 189
ASCII, 532
  set, 532
automatically select based on data,
    366
automatic scaling of major units, 357
automatic sorting, 462
auxiliary columns, 69
auxiliary rows, 69
auxiliary structures, 295
AVERAGE, 415, 521
axis, 188
  custom scale, 355
  labels, 25, 272, 363, 365, 368, 386
    high, 366
    low, 366
    multiline, 368, 427
    range, 354, 368
  options, 100, 355, 362
    examples, 362
  scaling in the bubble chart, 511
  secondary axes, 398
  settings, 362, 363
  type, 366

BackColor, 480, 503
background, 115, 208, 269
bar chart, 133
  stacked, 383
bar, moving, 461
bar of pie, 409
base unit, time-scale axis, 394
basic concepts and structures, 21
basic formats, 194
basis worksheet, 94
begin size, 228
begin type, 228
between tick marks, 366
bevel, 222, 224, 441
biological evolution, 110

bitmap, 557
blur, 192
borders, 188, 270
  color, 359, 480, 503
  style, 359, 480
BoundColumn, 334, 473, 480
box-and-whisker plot, 521
boxplot, 521
brackets, 217
  square, 284
brightness, 236, 269
brightness levels of an area, 269
bubble chart, 153, 509
bubble label, 511

C

calculating this workbook, 281
calculation options, 7
calibrating your screen, 159
calibration, 159
Calibri, 531
Cambria, 356, 531
camera, 452
caption, 333
cap type, 189, 461
categories in reverse order, 365,
    381
category axis, 129, 362
  positioning, 390
category name, 373
category number, 390
cell references, examples, 75
central data maintenance, 299
central navigation, 538
central perspective, 482
change chart type, 101, 378
change picture, 236
CHAR, 531
character codes, 531
character map, 533
character set tables, 535
characters in cell, number of, 3
characters in formula, number of, 3
chart
  3-D pie, 144
  area, 26, 98, 149
    specifically selecting elements, 38
  axis options, 362

About the Author

Reinhold Scheck (born in 1945) lives in Berlin, Germany. His freelance work is backed by 25 years of management experience in education, medicine, and software application development. His longtime business activity as entrepreneur—mainly in cooperation with KPMG—addressed the use of Microsoft Excel for operational and strategic controlling.

For several years now, he works freelance in a broad spectrum of activities: consulting, developing data-processing solutions based on standard software, designing training, learning and presentation concepts, and lecturing at professional seminars. His books have been published by Microsoft Press and have received excellent reviews. He also works for some periodicals and for the Berlin daily newspaper "Der Tagesspiegel" where he answers readers' questions about Microsoft Windows and Microsoft Office.

All this work is based on the following attitude:
Before customers spend a lot of money on expensive custom applications or external services, they should try to exploit their standard software, which can provide much more than most users are aware of.

Contact:
www.reinhold-scheck.de
info@reinhold-scheck.de

The graphics and photos provided in this book and its related materials have been made available by Nina Schiller. She is a freelance communication designer and lives in Berlin, Germany. Her services include skillfull designs for the printing industry, high-class illustrative visualizations for scientific presentations and marketing, as well as the development of corporate designs and design concepts for Web sites.

Contact:
www.ninaschiller-design.de
info@ninaschiller-design.de

What do you think of this book?

We want to hear from you!

Do you have a few minutes to participate in a brief online survey?

Microsoft is interested in hearing your feedback so we can continually improve our books and learning resources for you.

To participate in our survey, please visit:

www.microsoft.com/learning/booksurvey/

...and enter this book's ISBN-10 or ISBN-13 number (located above barcode on back cover*). As a thank-you to survey participants in the United States and Canada, each month we'll randomly select five respondents to win one of five $100 gift certificates from a leading online merchant. At the conclusion of the survey, you can enter the drawing by providing your e-mail address, which will be used for prize notification only.

Thanks in advance for your input. Your opinion counts!

* Where to find the ISBN on back cover

ISBN-13: 000-0-0000-0000-0
ISBN-10: 0-0000-0000-0

Example only. Each book has unique ISBN.